FAISAL I OF IRAQ

FAISAL I
OF IRAQ

ALI A. ALLAWI

YALE UNIVERSITY PRESS
NEW HAVEN AND LONDON

For information about this and other Yale University Press publications, please contact:

US office: sales.press@yale.edu   www.yalebooks.com
Europe Office: sales@yaleup.co.uk   www.yalebooks.co.uk

Set in Minion Pro by IDSUK (DataConnection) Ltd
Printed in Great Britain by TJ International Ltd, Padstow, Cornwall

Library of Congress Cataloging-in-publication Data

Allawi, Ali A., 1947–
   Faisal I of Iraq / Ali A. Allawi.
      pages cm
   ISBN 978-0-300-12732-4 (hardback)
1. Faysal I, King of Iraq, 1885–1933. 2. Iraq—Kings and rulers—Biography.
3. Iraq—Politics and government—1921–1958. I. Title.
DS79.5.A45 2014
956.704 1092—dc23'
[B]
                                                                    2013021873

A catalogue record for this book is available from the British Library.

10 9 8 7 6 5 4 3 2 1

The old order changeth, yielding place to new,
And God fulfils himself in many ways,
Lest one good custom should corrupt the world.
Comfort thyself: what comfort is in me?
I have lived my life, and that which I have done
May He within himself make pure!

Alfred, Lord Tennyson,
Idylls of the King – The Passing of Arthur

CONTENTS

························

ACKNOWLEDGEMENTS

T HE IDEA of writing a biography of Faisal of Iraq had been germinating in
my mind since 1998. In that year my father passed away in London and I
was responsible for editing his papers, which later formed the basis of a book
of memoirs. My father was the first of his generation of our family to attend a
school with a modern curriculum, and later to graduate in the first cohorts of
the newly established Baghdad medical college. His youth and university
education in the 1920s were spent in the period when Faisal reigned in Iraq.
His recollections of that period were replete with the sense of unbounded
possibilities and optimism about the future of Iraq that he and his generation
felt. He and many others like him enthusiastically took to the challenges of
building a modern country which, in those days, were inextricably linked to
the leadership that Faisal brought to this task. Their career paths often led to
the pinnacles of their professions and to high public office, and would have
been inconceivable without the modern institutions that Faisal so assiduously
championed. My father's respect and admiration for Faisal was mirrored by
nearly all who shared with him their formative experiences in Iraq of the 1920s.
My first debt of gratitude therefore goes to my late father, Dr 'Abd al-Amir
Allawi, who first kindled my interest in Faisal.

Closely following are two of my father's colleagues and friends. They, in
their London exile, formed the band who, together with my father, were affec-
tionately known as 'The Three Musketeers', elder statesmen of the Iraqi exile
community who brought caution, foresight and wisdom to the business of
opposing the regime of Saddam Hussein. They were also products of the
Faisalian era: patriotic, proficient and dedicated men. 'Abd al-Ghani al-Dalli
was a former Iraqi minister of agriculture and ambassador; 'Abd al-Karim
al-Uzri was monarchical Iraq's last minister of finance and an authority on
modern Iraq's history. Both were driven into exile after the 1958 revolution
that did away with Iraq's monarchy and the kingdom that Faisal had

established. 'Abd al-Ghani al-Dalli had always spoken of the debt that Iraq owed to Faisal, and repeatedly mentioned that Faisal had not yet found his biographer. I promised al-Dalli that I would write a biography of Faisal, not quite appreciating the scale of the task that I had set for myself. In numerous discussions with 'Abd al-Karim al-Uzri I came to realise that Faisal occupied a position of signal importance in the formation of Iraq. He also asked for a comprehensive biography of the king.

Last of this group to whom I owe a debt of gratitude is Muhammed Fadhel al-Jamali, the internationally known pedagogue and past prime minister of Iraq. His first cabinet in 1953 included a number of talented Iraqis who had grown into manhood under Faisal. Though later based in Tunis, al-Jamali's frequent visits to London were the occasion when I had the chance to hear him reminisce about the Faisalian era. His son, and my good friend, Usameh, kept reminding me of the need for a biography of Faisal, and when I had started on the work he often asked about it, keeping me alert to the task at hand. I hope that with this book I have fulfilled my promise to all these people and to their memory.

This book would not have been possible without the support of various academic institutions and scholars of Iraq and the Middle East who welcomed such a biography. In Britain, I would like to extend my thanks and appreciation to the Middle East Centre at St Antony's College, Oxford University, and to its director, Eugene Rogan; at the School of Oriental and African Studies, London University, I would like to thank Professor Charles Tripp for his insights and for reading the manuscript of the book. In the United States my appreciation and thanks go to Professor Roger Owen of Harvard University. His support and advice have been invaluable.

Professor Peter Sluglett of the University of Utah, and now Research Professor at the Middle East Institute of the National University of Singapore, has been unstinting in his advice and comments. He is deservedly one of the leading academic authorities on Iraq and especially on the period covered in this biography. I would like to thank him profusely for his detailed remarks and his careful reading of the manuscript. At Williams College, Massachusetts, I would like to express my gratitude to Professor Magnus Bernhardsson. He graciously agreed to read and comment on the manuscript of the book, and provided invaluable comments on the socio-cultural setting of the Faisalian era.

I would like to thank the Carr Center at the Kennedy School of Government, Harvard University, for offering me a fellowship for the 2008–2009 academic year. It allowed me time to reflect and ponder on the biography, and to use the incredible facilities of Widener Library at Harvard. This extraordinary library should be classified as one of the national treasures of the United States. My thanks also go to Rory Stewart, MP, the then director of the Carr Center, and to Charlie Clement, the Carr Center's executive director.

In Iraq, I extend my deepest appreciation to Dr Saad Eskander, the head of the National Library of Iraq. He allowed me full access to the library and archives of the country, and to the National Library's collection of early Iraqi newspapers.

Several people have helped me in researching the book. Ibrahim al-Marashi was my first research assistant and helped to trawl the National Archives of Britain. Alper Bahadir was my assistant in Harvard and helped to uncover Ottoman-era documents at both Harvard and from the Ottoman archives in Istanbul. Lamia al-Gailani provided me with rare photos of the period, recovered from the former Royal Palace in Baghdad. Tamara al-Daghestani provided me with photos as well as detailed information about the extended Hashemite family. Russell Harris provided me with remarkable photos of Faisal, and I would like to thank him for his support.

Ann and Henry Wilks were extremely generous in sharing with me the recently discovered diaries and letters of Sir Henry Dobbs. I reserve special thanks for them, and for Patrick Cockburn, who was kind enough to introduce me to the Wilks family.

Lastly, I offer my appreciation and thanks to Sharif Muhammed ibn al-Hussain, grandson of King Ali of the Hijaz. Sharif Muhammed has been an indefatigable reader of the biography in its various drafts, and his comments and observations have always been constructive and apt. He has proven to be the true mirror and reliable commentator that any writer needs.

✦✦✦✦✦✦❖❖❖✦✦✦✦✦✦

ILLUSTRATIONS

MAPS

✦✦✦✦✦ ✿✠✿ ✦✦✦✦✦

KEY PERSONALITIES

Sharifian family

Faisal ibn al-Hussein – king of Syria, king of Iraq, third son of Hussein ibn Ali.
Hussein ibn Ali – amir of Mecca and instigator of the Arab Revolt.
Ali ibn al-Hussein – eldest son of Hussein ibn Ali, later king of the Hijaz. Acted as Faisal's confidant and regent.
Abdullah ibn al-Hussein – second son of Hussein ibn Ali, later amir of Transjordan.
Zaid ibn al-Hussein – youngest son of Hussein ibn Ali. Half-brother to Faisal. Assisted Faisal in Arab Revolt, and in Arab government in Syria.

Iraqis

Ja'far al-'Askari – former Ottoman officer; resisted the British in Cyrenaica; senior commander of regular units of Arab Revolt. Many times minister, prime minister and ambassador under Faisal.
Rashid 'Ali al-Gailani – from a branch of the al-Naqib family. Ambitious and inveterate intriguer. Last of Faisal's prime ministers.
Yasin al-Hashimi – rose to become an Ottoman general and stayed loyal to the Ottoman cause. Joined the Arab government of Faisal in Damascus. Minister and prime minister in Iraq under Faisal. Enigmatic and ambitious.
Grand Ayatollah Abul Hassan al-Isfahani – most senior ayatollah in Iraq. Issued fatwa that forbad participation in elections for constituent assembly. Chose self-exile to Iran in solidarity with al-Khalisi, but returned in 1924 eschewing formal politics.
Ali Jawdat – former Ottoman officer; early recruit to Arab Revolt. Commanded Syrian forces in the Beqa'a Valley; later provincial governor and minister under Faisal.
Shaikh Mahdi al-Khalisi – powerful ayatollah from Kadhimain. Anti-British and often hostile to Faisal. Deported to Iran in 1923 by al-'Sa'adoun, which triggered self-exile of senior Shi'a clerics.
'Abd al-Muhsin al-Sa'adoun – Istanbul-trained lawyer from powerful southern Iraq tribe. Prime minister, but stayed aloof from Faisal. Instigated confrontation with Shi'a religious hierarchy. Favoured by the British. Committed suicide in 1929.
'Abd al-Rahman al-Naqib – head of a powerful religious order and a senior Baghdad notable. First prime minister of Iraq. Opposed and then reconciled to Faisal as king.

Nuri al-Sa'id – statesman. Former Ottoman officer; saw action in the First Balkan War, member of the secret society al-'Ahd; joined Arab Revolt. A founder of the Iraq army and later minister and prime minister under Faisal.

Naji al-Suwaidi – from a prominent Baghdad family. Minister and prime minister under Faisal.

Ja'far Abu al-Timmen – from a prominent Baghdad mercantile family. Strongly nationalist and anti-British. Had ambivalent relations with Faisal.

Ottomans

Sultan 'Abd al-Hamid – sultan/caliph of the Ottoman Empire; deposed in 1909.

Enver Pasha – one of the triumvirate that ruled the Ottoman Empire in its final years.

Jamal Pasha – supreme commander of Ottoman forces in Syria for most of the First World War.

Mustafa Kemal – commander of Ottoman forces in Syria in the last stages of the war. Founder of the modern republic of Turkey.

Syrian/Palestinian/Lebanese

'Awni 'Abd al-Hadi – secretary to the Arab delegation in Paris. Part of Faisal's entourage and adviser; later an important figure in the Palestine national movement.

Rustum Haidar – Faisal's friend and confidant; later minister in Iraq.

Ahmad Qadri – Tahsin's brother. Early member of the Arab secret society al-Fatat. Adviser to Faisal.

Tahsin Qadri – Faisal's aide-de-camp and companion.

Ali Ridha al-Rikabi – military governor of Syria under Faisal.

British

Edmund Allenby – commander of Egyptian Expeditionary Force and allied forces in Syria and Palestine.

Gertrude Bell – oriental secretary to Percy Cox, later founded the Iraq Museum. Championed Faisal for king of Iraq.

Winston Churchill – secretary of state for the colonies, presided over the Cairo conference of 1921, which set Britain's Middle East policy.

Gilbert Clayton – intelligence officer, later high commissioner in Iraq.

Kinahan Cornwallis – director of Arab Bureau in Cairo. A friend of Faisal and later ambassador to Iraq.

Percy Cox – senior political officer in Iraq during the war in Mesopotamia and first high commissioner in Iraq.

George, Lord Curzon – foreign secretary; resisted independence for Syria.

Henry Dobbs – longest-serving high commissioner in Iraq. Had troubled relations with Faisal.

Francis Humphrys – last high commissioner in Iraq until independence.

David Lloyd George – prime minister in the First World War; one of the Big Four at the Paris Peace Conference.

T. E. Lawrence – Faisal's adviser and organiser of guerrilla forces in Arab Revolt; championed Faisal at the Paris Peace Conference and Cairo conference of 1921.

Chaim Weizmann – scientist and Zionist leader.

French

Robert de Caix – influenced French policy in the Levant.

Georges Clemenceau – prime minister. Entered into an abortive deal on Syria with Faisal.

Qaddour ibn Ghabrit – Moroccan translator and interlocutor with the Faisal-led Arab delegation in Paris.

Henri Gouraud – high commissioner in Syria and Lebanon; implacable foe of Syrian independence.

••••••◆ː◦••••••

CHRONOLOGY OF EVENTS

1517 Ottoman Empire assumes suzerainty over the Hijaz; confirms office of the sharif/amir of Mecca.

1876 Promulgation of Ottoman constitution. Accession of Sultan 'Abd al-Hamid.

1878 'Abd al-Hamid prorogues Ottoman parliament, suspends constitution and establishes autocracy.

1883 Birth of Faisal, third son of Hussein ibn Ali, in Ta'if.

1883–1890 Faisal raised by the Bedouin tribe of Bani Abadila.

1893 Faisal joins his family in exile in Istanbul.

1900 Construction of the Hijaz railroad begins, linking the province to the rest of the Ottoman Empire.

1904 Faisal marries his cousin, Huzaima, daughter of Sharif Nasir ibn Ali. She bears him four daughters and one son, Ghazi, later king of Iraq.

1908 Young Turk revolution restores constitutional rule in Ottoman Empire.

1908 Faisal's father, Hussein ibn Ali, installed as sharif of Mecca by order of Sultan 'Abd al-Hamid. Faisal returns to the Hijaz.

1909 Sultan 'Abd al-Hamid deposed after the failure of a counter-coup.

1911–1912 Faisal commands Sharifian and Ottoman forces battling the Idrisi in 'Asir province.

1912 Faisal elected to Ottoman chamber of deputies as member for Jeddah.

1912 Outbreak of First Balkan War. Ottoman Empire loses most of its Balkan territories.

1914 Ottoman Empire enters First World War on side of the Central Powers.

1914 Anglo-Indian forces land in southern Iraq, capturing the city of Basra.

1915 Faisal visits Damascus and is inducted into the Arab secret society al-Fatat.

1915 Sharif Hussein enters into correspondence with Sir Henry McMahon, high commissioner in Egypt, regarding an Arab revolt against the Turks.

1916 Faisal slips from Damascus to Medina, in time for the outbreak of the revolt in June. He leads tribal forces in the vicinity of Medina.

1917 Faisal commands the field forces of the Arab Revolt. Capture of Wejh; Fall of Aqaba to Faisal's army.

1917 Baghdad captured by Anglo-Indian forces under Sir Stanley Maude in March.

1917–1918 Intensification of the revolt; fighting throughout Transjordan; attacks on the Hijaz railroad.

1918 Faisal's forces enter Damascus on 1 October amidst scenes of jubilation.

1918 Ottoman Empire accepts armistice on 30 October; Arab government led by Faisal established in Damascus.

1918 Faisal leaves Syria in November for the Paris Peace Conference.

1919 Faisal presents the Arab case for independence to the Council of Ten in February.

1919 Faisal returns to Syria in April.

1919 Convening of the Syrian Congress in June.

1919 King–Crane Commission arrives in Damascus in July.

1919 British decision to evacuate forces from Syria by November.

1919 Faisal returns to Britain and France in September.

1920 Faisal returns to Syria in January, with an outline agreement with Clemenceau.

1920 Syrian Congress reconvenes in March, declares independence of Greater Syria and proclaims Faisal king of Syria.

1920 Allies declare Iraq, Syria, Lebanon and Palestine as mandates of France and Britain at San Remo Conference in April.

1920 Henri Gouraud, French high commissioner for Lebanon and Syria, issues ultimatum to Faisal and Arab government.

1920 French forces under Gouraud rout the army of Faisal's Arab government at the Battle of Maysaloun on 24 July; Faisal driven into exile.

1920 Major tribal uprising challenges British rule in Iraq from July to October; put down at great cost.

1920 Faisal arrives in London in December, after several months in northern Italy.

1921 British officials broach subject of the throne of Iraq with Faisal.

1921 Cairo conference in March, under Colonial Secretary Winston Churchill, formalises Britain's policies in Iraq and the Middle East.

1921 Faisal lands in Basra in June.

1921 Faisal enthroned as king of Iraq after a plebiscite.

1922 Faisal falls seriously ill in August. Anglo-Iraqi Treaty signed in October, formalising Britain's role in Iraq.

1922 'Abd al-Muhsin al-Sa'adoun appointed prime minister in November.

1923 Deportation of Ayatollah al-Khalisi in June; self-exile of leading Iraq-based ayatollahs to Iran.

1924 Constituent Assembly convened in March, ratifies Anglo-Iraqi Treaty and promulgates Iraq's constitution.

1925 League of Nations awards the Ottoman province of Mosul to Iraq in December.

1925 Collapse of the kingdom of the Hijaz; Faisal's family joins him in Baghdad.

1926 Death of Gertrude Bell in July.

1926 Outbreak of sectarian tensions in Iraq, partly defused by Faisal.

1927 Faisal makes first bid for outright independence for Iraq, rebuffed by Britain.

1929 Suicide of 'Abd al-Muhsin al-Sa'adoun.

1930 Nuri al-Sa'id appointed prime minister; New Anglo-Iraqi Treaty signed in November, paving the way to independence.

1931 General strike targeting the Nuri government.

1931 Faisal composes wide-ranging memorandum on the condition of Iraq.

1932 Iraq achieves independence and is granted admission to the League of Nations in October.

1933 Rashid 'Ali appointed prime minister in March.

1933 Faisal travels to Britain in June on official state visit.

1933 Assyrian crisis breaks out in July.

1933 Faisal leaves Switzerland for Iraq in late July to handle Assyrian crisis.

1933 Faisal returns to Switzerland in early September to continue medical treatment.

1933 Faisal dies in Berne, Switzerland on 8 September 1933, aged fifty.

PROLOGUE

✦✦✦✦✦◁✤▷✦✦✦✦✦

SEPTEMBER, 1933: DEATH OF A KING

B Y THE time Faisal I, King of Iraq, had returned to his interrupted holiday in Switzerland in early September 1933, he was in a dangerously exhausted state. Less than a year before, on 3 October 1932, Iraq had finally gained formal independence by being admitted to the League of Nations as a fully fledged member country. The hated mandate system, which the victorious Allies had decreed for the territories of the Ottoman Empire in the 1920 Treaty of San Remo, was finally terminated. It was a goal for which Faisal had tirelessly worked, ever since he had been crowned the first king of modern Iraq, and throughout the tumultuous intervening period, during the turbulent vicissitudes of domestic Iraqi and regional politics and his often strained relationships with Britain, the mandated power over Iraq, he had never wavered from this end. Iraq's independence would go a long way in ameliorating the bitter disappointments and even betrayals that most Arabs had felt had been meted out to them, in unjust recompense for their part in helping the Allies secure their victory in the Middle East.

Earlier that year, Faisal had been to Britain on an official state visit, the first time as the king of an independent Iraq. Arriving at London's Victoria Station on 20 June 1933, Faisal had been received with great fanfare. King George V himself headed the reception committee that welcomed Faisal and his entourage. He had stayed at Buckingham Palace and had then visited Scotland for a relaxing few days that included a round of golf at the Gleneagles Hotel and tea with the royal family at Balmoral Castle. Queen Mary, George V's consort, was aware that Faisal intended to spend a period of rest and recuperation in Switzerland after his official tour of Britain had ended. His punishing pace of work and its toll on his often indifferent health was a matter of common knowledge. She suggested to Faisal that while in Switzerland, he should consult Albert Kocher, a well-known Bernese doctor. Kocher had developed a number of 'remedies' for his celebrity patients that included subcutaneous injections and other unorthodox treatments.¹ Faisal had followed Queen Mary's advice and put himself in Kocher's care. The forty-strong Iraqi delegation that accompanied Faisal checked with him into the grand Bellevue Palace Hotel in Berne.² The hotel was ideally situated between the Swiss Federal buildings and the River Aar. The quiet Swiss capital with its historic medieval quarter was decked out in lights to celebrate 'Electricity Week'.

Faisal's entourage included several ministers as well as his elder brother, the forlorn Ali, ex-king of the Hijaz, who had lost his kingdom in 1925 after only a few months on the throne to the forces of the dynamic Nejdi ruler, 'Abd al-Aziz ibn Saud. Faisal's stay in Berne, however, was quickly interrupted by events in Iraq. An uprising by segments of the minority Assyrian Christian community in Iraq, abetted by their patriarch, the Mar Shimun, had shaken the nascent government to its foundations. Cursing the regnant politicians in Baghdad for letting the situation get out of hand, Faisal returned to Iraq to tackle the evolving crisis.

On the day before his departure, Faisal confided to his friend, the noted writer and anti-colonialist figure the Lebanese Druze Prince Shakib Arslan, who was then in exile in Switzerland, ' "I have to return to Baghdad because I fear that the Iraqi people might attack the Assyrians, whom they accuse of being ingrates. The Assyrians might start murdering Iraqi military personnel and mutilating their bodies. The Kurds might also take matters into their own hand and slaughter the Assyrians in their villages. This will only confirm to ill-wishers that we Iraqis are not worthy of independence. The British government has already warned me that the crisis could threaten my rule. I simply have to return to Baghdad." Arslan said, "Well why don't you take the boat from Brindisi to Egypt rather than an aeroplane? This will be far easier on you." Faisal replied by saying, "I will take the plane instead, it will save me a number of days of travel." Arslan retorted, "You are acting more like a general than a king"; to which Faisal replied, "Yes, I am not a king; only a soldier in the service of his nation." '³

Faisal took the train from Geneva to the port of Brindisi in Italy. There he embarked on a plane that started him on his gruelling journey to Baghdad, a journey that passed through Athens, then Cairo, followed by a train trip to Gaza, where he spent the night, and then on to Baghdad by another plane.⁴ He arrived in Baghdad on 2 August 1933, and spent a month there in the boiling summer heat managing the consequences of the Assyrians' insurrection and the heavy-handed way in which it was suppressed by the Iraqi army in Faisal's absence. This threatened to poison Iraq's relations with the League of Nations, which was under the influence of the European colonial powers. The League had been concerned that independent Iraq, shorn of the oversight that the mandate power had previously exercised on its government, might mistreat its minorities. However, the suppression of the Assyrians was broadly popular in Iraq, and Faisal had felt sufficiently confident of the country's internal stability to return to his interrupted rest in Berne on Thursday, 31 August.

Soon after his return to his quarters at the Bellevue Palace Hotel, Faisal began to receive a stream of visitors, mostly Arabs from Palestine, Syria and Lebanon, such as the Arslan brothers, 'Adil and Shakib, and the Syrian politician Ihsan al-Jabiri who had all known Faisal during the First World War and his short-lived rule in Syria, when the idea of an independent Arab kingdom that covered most of the Arab Middle East, under the rule of Faisal and his Hashemite family, was not a preposterous notion. Faisal continued to exude the authority of one who had championed the broader Arab cause and successfully manoeuvred against the great powers to achieve a degree of independence for his country. He still held out the promise, no matter how remote, of being the leader who could deliver them and other Arabs from servitude to the mandate powers. But there were other visitors who were only distantly connected to Iraq or to the struggle for Arab emancipation. Faisal was never an active proponent of pan-Islam – the worldwide confederation of Muslims under the authority of a caliph – but a delegation of Muslim clerics from Bosnia and Herzegovina sought him out in the Swiss capital, no doubt to proclaim their discontent about the conditions of Muslims in their country and around the world. Faisal, renowned for his forbearance and toleration, had time for all of them.

Faisal's days in Berne were spent in receiving guests, and the evenings in watching his entourage and friends engage in games of bridge or chess, or playing ping-pong.[5] There was little female companionship as none of the wives or female relatives had accompanied the entourage. At that time it was simply not done for Middle Eastern men, or other men for that matter, to travel with their womenfolk. Whatever female company there was, was provided either by the secretary of the Iraqi legation in Geneva, a tall, winsome English blonde named Miss Reed, or by a Miss Nelson, reputedly the descendant of Horatio, Lord Nelson, who was accompanying her ailing father at the hotel.[6] An Indian Parsee lady, Bapsy Pavry, a daughter of the head of the Parsee community in Bombay, was also staying at the Bellevue Palace with her brother, Dr Jal Pavry and were inducted into Faisal's entourage. They were not total strangers as they had visited Baghdad earlier in the year and had met the king.

Shakib Arslan visited the king briefly on Wednesday, 6 September 1933, where he reported that the signs of the king's earlier fatigue were still clearly visible on his face. Faisal had subsisted on an unchanging diet of oranges, eggs, coffee and limitless cigarettes during his month in Iraq. Arslan visited Faisal at the Bellevue once again on Thursday, 7 September, where he found him in a cheerful, even ebullient, mood, despite his continuing frail appearance. Faisal announced his intention to take a drive to Interlaken, a beauty spot in the mountains of the Bernese Oberland nestled between two lakes, where he was to have lunch at the Victoria Jungfrau Hotel.[7] Accompanied by Bapsy, her brother Jal, and Ali, Faisal rode in one of the two cars on the drive to Interlaken. The other car carried Faisal's Chief of Protocol Tahsin Qadri, Iraq's foreign minister, Nuri Pasha al-Sa'id, and Faisal's long-standing friend, the Lebanese-born Rustum Haidar who had served (and would again serve) as Iraq's finance and economy minister.[8] Returning to Berne in the afternoon, Faisal headed for Kocher's clinic where another of Kocher's patients, Lady Paget, a former nurse on the Serbian front during the First World War, saw him. She later reported that Faisal appeared to be looking particularly well. Faisal returned to the Bellevue Palace Hotel, and at about 6 p.m. was seen by Lady Paget having a late afternoon tea. According to Lady Paget's testimony, Faisal was suddenly taken ill at around 7 p.m. and sent for Kocher, who apparently administered one of his injections and gave him something to drink. Faisal retched violently, but appeared to settle down. Neverthless he continued to vomit and finally succumbed to a heart attack later that evening. On the basis of her nursing training, Lady Paget surmised that the king's violent vomiting might very well have been caused by poison.[9]

However, the testimony of Faisal's chief of protocol, Tahsin Qadri, was considerably at odds with Lady Paget's as well as with Bapsy Pavry's recollections given to the *Daily Express*, which would give rise to a host of lurid speculations as to the circumstances of the king's death.[10] According to Qadri, the king was worn out by the trip to Interlaken, saying that he was suffering from palpitations, and retired to his room in the hotel immediately upon returning from his trip. Qadri called in Kocher who checked Faisal's pulse, gave him an injection and pronounced that he was all right. But Qadri thought otherwise and insisted that a nurse be posted to watch over the king. He persuaded the king to rest and to avoid coming down for dinner. Qadri had serious reservations about Kocher and his competence, and later believed that Kocher's treatment may very well have worsened the king's condition and hastened his death. He had reported that during a reception for Faisal given by the president of the Swiss Republic, the president had warned the king about Kocher, whom he believed to be a quack. He said he had known at least three people who had recently died after having received treatment from Kocher, and Qadri had little doubt that Kocher's treatments were directly responsible for the deterioration in the king's condition.[11] Just before midnight on 8 September 1933, the nurse sent for Qadri. The king had just died of an apparent heart attack. He was only fifty years old.

Whether Faisal died of natural causes, was poisoned, or died as a result of Kocher's dangerous treatments, the fact remained that he had lived a most tumultuous life. He had passed through extraordinary and epochal times, fraught with terrible dangers, bitter setbacks, disasters and trials, but also with some successes. What he had undergone would have taxed the most formidable of constitutions and he had always been of indifferent health. But now he was laid out on his bed with an awful yellow-green pallor, his eyes open, his mouth gaping and a curious bandage wrapped around his chin. Or so the scene was described by Musa al-Shabandar, a young official at Iraq's legation in Geneva and part of Faisal's Berne entourage, who was at the hotel that night. (Al-Shabandar would go on to become a foreign minister of Iraq.) Shabandar was awoken in his room by violent banging on the door by Miss Reed, who shouted at him that the king was dying and that he was needed immediately. Hurriedly dressing, al-Shabandar rushed to the king's room where he saw that the king had already died. Faisal's brother, Ali, was inconsolable in his grief, striking his head continuously with the palm of his hand. Others were pacing in the hallways muttering, 'What a disaster for the Arabs . . . What a disaster for Iraq . . .'[12]

On 9 September 1933 Faisal's body was taken to the hospital of the University of Berne for a cursory post-mortem, which determined that the cause of death was due to a ruptured artery caused by advanced arteriosclerosis. Nevertheless, even though three doctors had presided over the post-mortem investigations, this did not put to rest the unease about the circumstances of Faisal's death. It gave rise to rumours and wild conspiracies that subsequently abounded and swept Iraq, the Arab world and Europe. The body was washed, placed in a coffin that was then sealed, and brought back to the Bellevue Hotel. The coffin, covered with the Iraqi flag, was placed in one of the hotel's salons, with a guard of honour comprising Iraqi and Arab students in Switzerland.[13] A stream of visitors came to pay their respects, including leading figures of the Arab and Muslim world who were in Switzerland at the time. Faisal's coffin was then carried by train to Brindisi, where on 11 September it was conveyed, with full military honours, on board a British warship, HMS *Despatch*, for the journey to Haifa in Palestine. It was accompanied by eight of Faisal's entourage, including his brother Ali, Nuri Pasha al-Sa'id, Rustum Haidar and Faisal's acolyte, the then Iraqi envoy to Britain, Ja'far Pasha al-'Askari. On 14 September, HMS *Despatch* docked at Haifa harbour.[14]

After a short reception ceremony at the harbour, attended by a number of Arab dignitaries as well as the British high commissioner for Palestine, the cortege was supposed to wend its way through the main streets of Haifa to a designated location, where a religious ceremony was to be held in remembrance of Faisal. The cortege would then move to the nearby aerodrome, from which Faisal's coffin was to be flown to Baghdad. The harbour ceremony had a very restricted audience, by invitation only, but the route that the cortege was to take was open to all. The mass of people lining the route was estimated at nearly 30,000, and included hundreds of mourners who drove down the coast to Haifa from Lebanon and Syria.[15] This was the first indication as to the depth of feeling in the Arab Middle East that accompanied the news of the king's death. Many thousands of mourners had already pressed against the Haifa Customs House enclosure before the cortege moved out of the restricted zone on to the streets of Haifa. The emotional crowds surged around the hearse, but the cortege's progress continued apace until it reached the site of the religious ceremony. The crowds rushed to the hearse, hoping to touch the coffin or to carry it on their shoulders, but the police intervened to stop the bier being overrun and possibly overturned by the crowd. It was with the greatest difficulty that Ali and other dignitaries could be escorted away from the scenes of pandemonium. The eulogies read by the Palestinian Muslim leader, Ali al-Tamimi, and by the Greek Orthodox Bishop of Haifa, Mattar, could barely be heard over the din and wailing of the crowd. All the formal preparations, including the religious ceremony, had to be abandoned and the cortege broke up. The coffin was carried to the waiting aeroplane, where, on the evening of 14 September it was flown to Rutba in the Western Desert of Iraq, and then on to Baghdad. The crowds in their thousands watched the plane depart and then marched silently back towards Haifa.[16] The scenes of grief and turmoil that gripped the Palestinians of Haifa were an indication of what was to follow in Baghdad.

At around 7.30 on the morning of Friday, 15 September 1933, a Vickers 'Victoria' biplane freighter flown by the RAF landed in Baghdad's western aerodrome, carrying Faisal's coffin.[17] Another plane landed at the aerodrome shortly thereafter, with Ali and six senior members of Faisal's entourage on board. The planes were guarded by a squadron of nine Iraqi airforce planes as soon as the two aircraft entered Iraqi airspace at Rutba. Ever since the news of Faisal's death had reached Baghdad, preparations were being made for a huge outpouring of mourners, but the size of the crowds that had assembled in Baghdad from the city itself and from all of Iraq's provinces, as well as from nearby Arab lands, was far in excess of what officials had been expecting. The numbers were certainly in the hundreds of thousands, with a frequently repeated figure of 400,000 people. Something like a fifth of the male population of Iraq had turned out to receive Faisal's coffin and to witness its passage through Baghdad to its final resting place. It was by far the biggest popular manifestation experienced in Iraq for hundreds of years, and one of the largest to occur anywhere in the 1930s. In present terms it would translate into a figure of about four million Iraqis emerging on the streets of Baghdad. It was on a par with other expressions of mass grief that have more recently gripped the Middle East, such as the crowds that attended the funeral procession of

President Nasser of Egypt in Cairo in 1971, or that of Ayatollah Khomeini in Teheran in 1988. It was extraordinary by any standard.

The walnut-wood coffin was taken down from the plane by a group of Iraqi officers and then received by the new king of Iraq, Faisal's only son, Ghazi. He saluted his father's coffin and turned to embrace his uncle Ali, as the crowds at the aerodrome let out huge wails and cries. The coffin was placed on a gun carriage drawn by twelve horses, but before the procession to the Royal Palace, a good four miles distant, started, the customary Muslim funeral prayer was recited. The procession of the gun carriage, followed by the new king and dignitaries, had to pass through vast throngs crowding the route as they crossed Maude Bridge, linking the west and east banks of the Tigris. (The bridge had been named after Sir Stanley Maude, the commander of the British army who had expelled the Turks and occupied Baghdad in 1917.) The procession then passed through Baghdad's main thoroughfare, Rashid Street, on the way to the Royal Palace, with scenes of great sorrow and grief. Black banners, the Muslim signs of grieving, covered the streets and women gathered on roof tops crying uncontrollably and letting out screams of mourning. At the Royal Palace five hundred dignitaries had gathered for nearly three hours awaiting the arrival of the cortege. When it finally arrived, King Faisal's favourite steed, draped in black, was brought out to add further poignancy to the procession. It was a remarkably sad scene for the huge crowds which broke out in ever louder expressions of grief at the loss of their leader.[18]

During the last leg in Faisal's cortege, from the Royal Palace to the royal cemetery, an even more extraordinary event was enacted. All of Baghdad's guilds and crafts, together with delegations from the provinces, had organised themselves into marching groups behind huge black banners, reminiscent of the annual processions of mourners commemorating the martyrdom of Imam Hussein, the Prophet Muhammad's grandson. The symbolism was not lost as Faisal could trace his lineage directly to the Prophet of Islam's family. That he died as a martyr in the manner of his ancestor was, of course, yet another powerful source for grieving imagery for the crowd. As the head of the American legation in Baghdad at the time wrote in a note to the State Department, describing the events of the day, 'The scenes en route to the grave were probably unprecedented at the funeral of any other Moslem monarch.'[19] He might as well have stopped at the word 'unprecedented' in his despatch.

Near the burial site the artillery began to fire 101 rounds at regular intervals, adding further solemnity and poignancy to the occasion. Amidst dense crowds, the coffin was removed from the gun carriage to a bier. The final Muslim prayer for the dead was performed, for which nearly ten thousand people had lined up. The coffin was then carried by six Iraqi officers to the gravesite and lowered gently into the grave. Three volleys were fired into the air, and a lone trumpet sounded out the funerary notes. Wreaths were laid out by the new king, members of the royal family, government ministers and senior officials and members of the diplomatic corps. The new king received a stream of visitors offering their condolences. With the formal aspects of the funeral over without serious incident, the vast crowd broke up peaceably.[20] Faisal, prince of the Hijaz, ex-king of Syria, king of Iraq, the man in whom countless Arabs had at one or time or another during the past quarter-century invested their hopes and aspirations, was finally laid to rest.

Faisal's life intersected with so many of the formative events of the period that his imprint had spread far and wide. Commemorations were held around the world but, apart from Iraq, none were accompanied by a greater sense of loss than in the lands of the Arab Middle East – Syria, Lebanon, Transjordan and Palestine – which were still under the rule of Britain and France.[21] It was more than merely the memory of earlier, more hopeful, times that drove people to pour out their sympathies, when Arabs thought that they had come tantalisingly close to achieving their independence. It also expressed the residual hopes of many Arabs for some form of eventual resolution of their predicament under the leadership of Faisal. The form of independence that Iraq had achieved under Faisal was a constant reminder of the stifling rule of Britain and France that still bestrode the former Arab territories of the Ottoman Empire. The idea of Iraq under Faisal acting as the catalyst for a revived Arab nation had been a very real prospect. That form of realistic, purposeful and constructive patriotism also died with Faisal, to be replaced with the far more strident, volatile and angry nationalism that swept the Arab world after the end of the Second World War.

Throughout the cities of the region, from Damascus, to Aleppo, Latakia, Beirut, Jerusalem and Amman, black flags of mourning were everywhere to be seen. Markets, cafés and restaurants were closed to signify respect; official and trade bodies met to register their anguish; and memorial services and prayers were held. Editorials in all the leading Arab newspapers were replete with fulsome accounts of Faisal's life, struggles and achievements, and expressed the general sense that his untimely death was a body blow to the greater cause of the times, be it independence or countering the gathering strength of the Zionist movement in Palestine.[22] Even those who had opposed Faisal, like dynastic rivals such as ibn Saud, or the domestic opposition in Iraq, sensed that a historic leader had passed from the scene and responded accordingly. In Iraq, opposition leaders and newspapers used the seemingly murky circumstances of Faisal's death to blame the British for their perfidious actions and darkly hinted that Faisal had been poisoned by them; this was the same Faisal who had earlier featured prominently in their accusations as a British stooge!

The imperial power with the greatest influence and interests in Iraq, Great Britain, marked the passing of Faisal with banner headlines, and several columns were devoted to his life in the main dailies, notably *The Times*, the establishment paper with the greatest range of readers and impact. In its obituary of 9 September 1933 the 'Thunderer' pronounced in rather florid, but nevertheless insightful, language that 'King Feisal . . . had many great qualities and some of their defects. To the dignity of his race and to a high-strung courage he added an intense patriotism and a conscientious industry. He was far more than the fortunate cavalier of popular imagination and his failures were due rather to the immense and insuperable difficulties of his position. He could not always restrain the impetuous nationalism of his followers; he was too civilised, too constitutional a ruler to deal with opposition on the crudely vigorous lines adopted by the dictatorships of our day . . . Arab nationalism owes much to his powers of military and political leadership; the Kingdom of Iraq owes even more to his moderation and self-sacrificing industry.' Memorial services were held in Faisal's honour, and Field Marshal Lord Allenby, the commander of the Allied forces in the Syrian and Palestinian theatres of war and under whom Faisal's Northern Arab Army had nominally served, laconically observed. 'He was a good soldier, an able politician and – what many politicians are not – honest with it. His sense of duty was great, and I presume he sacrificed himself to his country. A King has to do that sort of thing.'[23]

France's relationship with Faisal had veered between strained and suspicious, to the downright hostile. It began to improve only in the late 1920s when the country's policies in the governing of Syria under its mandate openly failed. There, the response to Faisal's death was more muted, reflecting the still ambivalent position of the mandate power to this former challenger to their rule in the Middle East. This showed in the range of opinions that were expressed, from the barely concealed hostility of the colonialist mouthpiece *L'Intransigeant*, to the more measured tones of the authoritative *Le Temps*. But there was no getting away from the significance of Faisal. One of the newspapers, *Le Journal*, went so far as to call him 'The Greatest Personality known to the East.'[24] In the United States, caught in the throes of the Great Depression and still wedded to its isolationist policy, the echo of events in the Middle East was fainter. Its memory of Faisal was slight, mainly connected to his dramatic presence at the Paris Peace Conference and Woodrow Wilson's ill-fated fourteen points promising self-determination to emerging nations and peoples. (The Arabs of the Middle East, as well as other nationalities of the region such as the Kurds and Armenians, thought it should be applied particularly to them.) The official response was therefore more muted, but President Roosevelt nevertheless sent a personal message to the organisers of a memorial service in New York on 22 October 1933 in the auditorium of the Roerich Museum. Recitation from the Quran was followed by poems in tribute to Faisal, and a specially commissioned violin solo was dedicated to him.

Faisal had a large and devoted following among Arab immigrants in North and South America, especially among the large community of Arab Christians (notably those of a Greek Orthodox background) who had emigrated from Syria and Lebanon. They saw themselves as custodians of the secular Arab nationalist ideal, of which their expatriate Arabic language newspapers and publishing houses, mainly based in New York, were important mouthpieces. Faisal was considered sympathetic to this ideal and was raised to an elevated status among large sections of this community. The extent of this hero worship in the Arab diasporas is best illustrated by the example of a Christian Arab playwright, Khalil Ibrahim al-Nabout, who lived in Argentina. Shortly after Faisal's death, Nabout wrote a four-act play about Faisal, first performed in Buenos Aires in 1934. It was called *The Leap of the Arabs* and set in Damascus during the First World War in the immediate post-war period when Syria was ruled by Faisal's Arab government. The play presented Faisal as a courageous champion of Arabism, beyond any considerations of sect, religion or ethnicity. It was dedicated to the memory of Faisal and, tellingly, 'to all those who believe in brotherhood as a creed, in equality as a code and in liberty as a religion.'[25]

An American writer, Grace Dickinson Sperling, wrote a sixty-five page epic poem *Feisal, the Arabian* in 1933, celebrating Faisal's victories in the desert campaign and in Syria. The poet must have been influenced by the immensely popular travelling show on T. E. Lawrence and the Arab Revolt produced by the writer and broadcaster Lowell Thomas, as well as by early Hollywood films on the romantic desert warrior. It was written before Faisal's death but had an addendum following news of his demise simply entitled '*Khallas* – It is finished!'[26]

Faisal's legacy continued to reverberate in Iraq and the Arab world until the advent of the Second World War. At that point the tumultuous events that engulfed the Middle East, not least the partition of Palestine and the creation of the State of Israel, cast a pall over the type of policies that Faisal had propounded and the moderate and subtle form of politics that was his hall-mark. It also grievously compromised the regimes that seemed to owe their existence only to western support, and catered to small but privileged economic and social elites. Sects, tribes, ethnicities and regional loyalties – in fact any recognition of the diversity of populations and complexity of loyalties in the Arab Middle East – would be swept away by a stultifying and hollow radicalism. It was an age of angry revolutionaries denouncing the past in all its forms, and a new rendering of history became the stock-in-trade of the new generation of Arab nationalists and other ideologues who dominated the post-war era.

These nationalists of the post-Second World War era held the previous rulers to be hopelessly entangled in western schemes to perpetuate the ance of colonial and post-colonial regimes, and thwart the rise of a Arab nation. The Hashemite family, from which Faisal sprang and in ....ular Faisal's brother 'Abdullah who became king of Jordan, was considered complicit with the Zionists in the partition of Palestine.[27] They were held directly responsible, through their subservience to the west, for the catastrophe that befell the Palestinians, the *Nakba*, as hundreds of thousands of Palestinians left or were driven out of their ancestral homes in 1947 and 1948. Communists, nationalists, socialists and assorted leftists in Iraq, who held sway for decades after the 1958 revolution that overthrew the monarchy in Iraq, considered the monarchical regime to be a tool of class interests, of large feudal landlords, tribal chieftains and mercantile oligarchs. Islamically minded ideologues were never partial to Faisal. The Shi'a religious hierarchy could never forgive Faisal for the summary way in which he handled their threat to his rule when they called for the boycott of the institutions of the nascent Iraqi state. At the same time, Sunni pan-Islamic opinion could not reconcile itself to a revolt that had helped to dismember the only state that claimed to be built on the principle of Muslim unity, the Ottoman Empire. Worse still in their view, the revolt was instigated, financed and then betrayed by the forces of the Christian west waging war against a legitimate Muslim power. Some leaders of Iraq's liberal or social democratic opposition surfaced as short-lived participants in power with the officers who fomented the 1958 revolution. Their implicit verdict on Faisal was acquiescence in the destruction of the monarchy that he established and the murder of his grandson, the young King Faisal II. And by that time those who could still recall the days of Faisal and objectively assess it had aged or died. A new paradigm was established, and the history of the 'Faisalian' era in Iraq and the Middle East became clouded by the prejudices, interests, embitterment and hatred of those who presided over the new dispensation.

Even so, Faisal personally escaped the obloquy and contempt that was heaped on other leaders of the pre-war generation, but memory of his rule and achievements began to fade as a result of official and sometimes hostile indifference. It was difficult to square the violent attacks on the monarchical period in Iraq, which was popularly known as the *'Ahd al-Bai'd* or the 'Expunged Era', while maintaining a favourable attitude to Faisal that exempted him from the real or imagined transgressions of that era. After the revolution of 1958, Faisal's equestrian statue that graced one of Baghdad's main squares was removed. It was designed and executed by a well-known Italian sculptor of the Mussolini era, Pietro Canonica. Faisal's exhibits, which had been housed in a special room in the Iraqi Museum, were removed to the basement, safely away from public view, and his image – on stamps, coins, banknotes – disappeared over time. Few Iraqis of the period bothered to delve into their past to establish the course of events and the role that Faisal played in the emergence of their country. In Syria, the loss of historical memory was even more complete, with little knowledge of, or interest in, the Faisalian period there. It was seen as a short and mostly obscure interlude between the end of the Ottoman Empire and the imposition of the hated French mandate. In Jordan, where the Hashemites continued to rule, it was the memory of King 'Abdullah that was kept alive.

The remembrance of Faisal in the west also underwent a significant change from the effusive obituaries at the time of his death. Faisal, of course, features prominently in one of the great classics of modern literature, T. E. Lawrence's *Seven Pillars of Wisdom*. He was the hero for whom Lawrence was searching, and the book revolves in considerable measure around the king and his qualities as a political and military leader in the Arab Revolt. Faisal was also memorably portrayed in 1962 in a major film, *Lawrence of Arabia*, by Sir Alec Guinness. A leading British artist, Augustus John, painted two portraits of Faisal in 1919 during the Paris Peace Conference, one of which now hangs in the Ashmolean Museum at Oxford. But western historians, as well as Arabs trained in the methods of western historiography, had developed their own interpretation of the significance of Faisal, the Arab Revolt and the Arab nationalist idea generally.

Many dismissed the 'Great Men' school of history, and saw leaders and heroes as merely instruments of impersonal forces that played themselves out over long spans of time. They claimed that biography may make for interesting reading, but that it plays little part in determining the course of events. To such people, there was a certain inevitability to the flow of events, and it was claimed that individual leaders, no matter how dashing, can only play an auxiliary part in the making of history. When extrapolated to the canvas of the Middle East in the early twentieth century, brilliant leaders such as Faisal had to concede their role to the greater forces of history, operating in long cycles as meta-historical forces of economic or ideational change, or as their opposite, as micro-history, part of the history of elites and groups, institutions and cultures. Another school, that of the anti-colonialist dependency theory, saw the regimes of the post-First World War settlement in the Middle East simply as colonial tools that could not change by one iota the unequal and dependent relationship on the metropolitan power. Iraq under Faisal was just such a state, condemned to being little more than an appendage to the schemes of its colonial over-master. The virtues of a ruler become irrelevant in practice and then subsumed by the all-encompassing nature of the model.

It took a peculiar turn of events to change the perspective on Faisal, which emerged in, of all places, Saddam Hussein's Iraq. As Iraq was coming out of the debilitating eight-year war with Iran in 1988, a clutch of books by 'revisionist' Iraqi historians appeared in Baghdad.[28] The fact that these were subsequently published by the rigidly controlled state-owned press meant that approval for their publication had to come from the highest sources, in other words from Saddam himself. To some extent, they benefited from the opening in the 1960s of the restricted archives of Britain that covered this period. Arab and Iraqi scholars could now access these vital archives to refashion their understanding of the events of the period. But in reality they signalled a more objective assessment of Iraq's early monarchical history and a re-examination of the role of Faisal himself, in state building as well as in the regional and international context in which he operated. The events were sufficiently distant so that a reassessment need not have threatened the hold of the Ba'ath Party on the country. In some ways it resembled the 'rediscovery' of Russia's Tsarist past through figures such as Ivan the Terrible and Peter the Great at the outbreak of the war between Germany and Russia to buttress Stalin's claims as a patriotic leader. Taking on the mantle of Faisal may have helped Saddam in burnishing his patriotic claims and linking him to a figure of great historical import. As part of this process of rehabilitating Faisal's position and significance, Canonica's equestrian statue of Faisal was displayed once more at a different, though equally prominent, site in Baghdad. The Royal Mausoleum was also refurbished, after a long period of official neglect, partly at the prodding of King Hussein of Jordan, who was a staunch ally of Saddam during the Iran–Iraq War.

Alongside this re-evaluation of Iraq's early monarchical heritage, important memoirs that cast a favourable light on the Faisalian era were reissued and several new biographies provided a more balanced analysis of the leading politicians of the monarchy, such as Nuri al-Sa'id. Labels such as 'traitors', 'stooges' and 'agents' that had been liberally attached to these figures were discarded in favour of a more nuanced and often positive interpretation of their policies and personalities.

The era that preceded Faisal's final move into Iraq also came under a new spotlight, mainly prompted by a more liberal access policy for scholars to the Ottoman archives in Istanbul. A number of studies seriously questioned some of the main assumptions that underlay the conventional narrative of the Middle East on the eve of the First World War, in particular the state of Turkish–Arab relations in the final decades of the Ottoman Empire, the extent and significance of the Arab nationalist movement in the early years of the twentieth century, and the factors that undermined Faisal in achieving his goals at the Paris Peace Conference in 1919 and in his short-lived Kingdom of Syria.[29]

All these elements have played a part in establishing the need for a comprehensive reappraisal of the period. General accounts of the times are now seriously out of date and some are patently inadequate. One of the standard accounts of the end of the Ottoman Empire made no use of any Arabic language sources.[30] The problems and crises that have bedevilled the Middle East in the past century have their roots mainly in the post-Ottoman settlement. The difficulties that the nation states of the area have encountered in establishing security, stability and responsible and accountable government can be traced to the nature of the systems that were installed in the wake of the dismemberment of the Ottoman Empire. The transition was neither an easy nor a happy one, and left massive unresolved issues that continue to define the landscape of the Middle East. The list is almost endless, from the most subtle that deal with people's basic loyalties (whether to religion or to state, and the meaning of citizenship), to the nature of legitimate government, the permanence of the state boundaries that were defined in the peace settlement, the treatment of minorities, the divisions between a once dominant Sunni orthodoxy and the large Shi'a and other heterodox populations, and, of course, the resistance and violence that accompanied the waves of Jewish immigration into Palestine as the Balfour Declaration's support for a Jewish National Home in that Country became realised.

The life of Faisal, more than any other figure of his time, is emblematic of the huge adjustments that people had to undergo to move from one type of world, governed by its own rules and standards, to an entirely different one. Faisal had to contend on an almost daily basis with the massive problems that arose as a result of the dismantling of the Ottoman Empire and the conflicting claims on the successor states – by nationalists, imperial powers and domestic groups that felt left out of power. Three conflicting and ultimately irreconcilable principles defined the Middle East after the First World War: the Sykes–Picot Agreement, which enshrined the division of the Ottoman Empire into spheres of influence awarded to European powers, that is, mainly, Britain and France; the Balfour Declaration that lent British support to the idea of a Jewish National Homeland in Palestine, and which subsequently became the driver towards a Jewish state; and the various exchanges between Sharif Hussein of Mecca, Faisal's father, and the British authorities that seemed to promise an independent state or states after the war for most of the territory covered by the Arab provinces of the Ottoman Empire.

The fact that these agreements and declarations were made during wartime when the consequences of what they proposed had not been properly thought through did not stop their proponents – whether Arab nationalists demanding full independence, Zionists demanding unrestricted Jewish immigration into Palestine, or the governments of Britain and France imposing mandates on their assigned territories – from seeking strict implementation of their terms, to their particular advantage, after the war. Iraq was another matter, and another theatre of war, and in addition the dynamics of the post-war settlement in Iraq owed as much to the revolt of 1920 as it did to any pre-war deal.

Faisal, having been plunged into this maelstrom, endeavoured to steer a course through these mighty and turbulent currents, a course that seemed to promise at least a reasonably good outcome for his people. In his lifetime, the often tortuous twists and turns that had to accompany such a course were misread: dissimulation was confused with deceit, cooperation with capitulation, realism with abandonment of principle. Only later would Faisal's intentions and goals become far clearer.

The apparently cyclical nature of events in the Middle East, topped by the inept and incoherent US and UK invasion and occupation of Iraq in 2003, demonstrates parallels with an earlier age, when Britain rather than the US was the dominant power. It is the differences in approach and outcomes that stand out, made more marked by the obvious disparity in the quality of leadership between those earlier times and now. In many ways, therefore, this biography is an attempt to understand the interplay between leadership and events, and how the elusive quality of leadership can often make the difference between success and failure. It is also about ideals, means and ends; about coming to terms with the poor hand that is often dealt peoples and nations by history; about dealing with manifest injustices and making do with what is available. It is to do with how transitions are managed; how to keep to the median path when you are always being pulled to the extremes; how to push for the common good in fractious and disputatious settings. It is to do with disparities in power and influence while slowly, methodically, deliberately building capabilities and expanding horizons. These and more were the challenges that met Faisal during the First World War and its immediate aftermath, during his brief rule in Syria, and finally in Iraq, where, in just over twelve years, he presided over the building of an entirely new state.

PART I

AN EMPIRE DISINTEGRATES
The Ottoman Era (1883–1914)

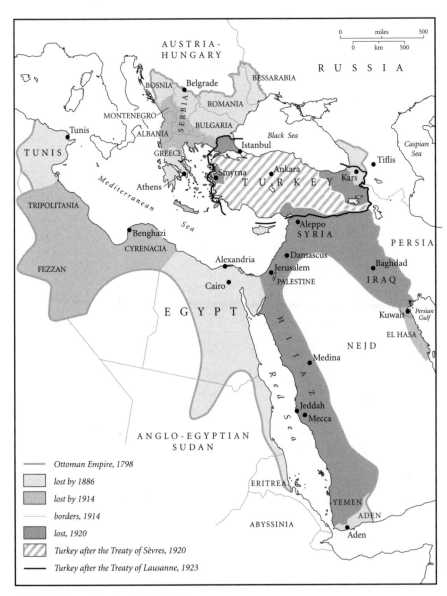

1. The Ottoman Empire, 1798–1923

CHAPTER 1

++++++❖❖++++++

FROM THE DESERT TO
THE METROPOLIS

THE LATE nineteenth century into which Faisal was born was a world of empires, and none marked it more for him and all Arabs than the Ottoman Empire. By 1883, the year of Faisal's birth, the empire had shrunk considerably from its peak centuries, when it bestrode three continents. The empire had once included large parts of Eastern Europe, the Balkans, Turkey, Crimea and the Caucasus, the Near East (the Arab territories of the Ottoman Empire and Egypt) and nearly all of North Africa, but it had retreated under the pressure of stronger, more determined and dynamic adversaries: expansionist European empires and the new forces of ethnic nationalism. A series of constitutional, legal and economic reforms were enacted in the mid-nineteenth century to check the slide of the empire and begin its modernisation. These reforms, collectively known as the *Tanzimat*, effectively transformed the Ottoman state from a dynasty ruled by an eclectic mix of sharia law for Muslims, religious law for non Muslims, customary laws and privileges and autocratic decrees, into something approximating the idea of a modern European state.

This period of reform culminated in 1876 with the promulgation of a constitution, written mainly by western-educated intellectuals and bureaucrats known as the 'Young Ottomans'. They were fired by the ideals of liberal democracy and bent on establishing a new identity and focus for the empire's hugely mixed population: the idea of Ottomanism. The Young Ottomans engineered a coup that eventually led to the enthronement of a scion of the ruling Ottoman family, 'Abd al-Hamid, who was proclaimed sultan. 'Abd al-Hamid agreed to rule as a constitutional monarch and the first elected parliament of the Ottoman era was called into being. It met twice, in 1877 and 1878, coinciding with the disastrous Russo-Turkish war. At its second session in 1878, 'Abd al-Hamid initially suspended, and then entirely prorogued, it. He subsequently ruled as an autocrat for three decades. His long reign had a profound effect on the course of the Ottoman Empire and its Arab provinces, and loomed over the life of the young Faisal.[1] Nearing the end of the nineteenth century, the Ottoman Empire had reached a quasi equilibrium, balancing its diverse ethnic and religious groups and managing to fend off the continuing dismemberment of its non-European territories. But this was to be short-lived.

The sharifs of the Hijaz

The Arab provinces of the Ottoman Empire had languished in the centuries that proceeded the era of reforms. The exercise of Ottoman central authority was minimal and a variety of local dynasties or powerful governors ruled, under the nominal authority of the sultan. This provision applied to the Hijaz, the province in which Faisal was born. The Hijaz is the name given to the western parts of the Arabian Peninsula, stretching from the Gulf of Aqaba in the north to the Yemen foothills in the south, and from the Nejd plateau in the east to the Red Sea in the west. The word 'Hijaz' derives from the word meaning 'barrier' in Arabic, and refers to the string of mountains that stretch along the spine of this land. West of these mountains lie the lowlands of the Tihama, in which are the two holy cities of Mecca and Medina. Torrid heat, scant rainfall and an inhospitable terrain had made the Hijaz a place of sparse settlement. Agriculture was only possible in a few oasis towns, and a large part of the population was composed of Bedouin tribes, ever on the move for pasture for their livestock.[2]

The population of the Hijaz in the mid-nineteenth century probably did not exceed one million, with the city of Mecca accounting for about 100,000 people, followed by Medina, 60,000, and the port of Jeddah with about 50,000. A significant number of the residents of the cities were foreign born, drawn to the Hijaz by the pilgrimage trade and the presence of the two holy cities. In fact, the life, culture and history of the towns of the Hijaz are inexorably linked to the course of Islam and its origins in the towns, oases, valleys and deserts of the region – the places where the Prophet Muhammad received his revelations, delivered his message, and lived his life. It was in Mecca that Islam's holiest shrine, the Ka'aba, was to be found, towards which Muslims around the world direct their daily prayers. Once in their lifetime, believing Muslims are obligated, if able, to conduct a pilgrimage to Mecca. And it is in Medina that the Prophet Muhammad established his first community of Muslims and where he is buried.

The pilgrimage traffic was the main economic activity of the area well into the twentieth century, and the control, management and safeguarding of pilgrims became the main concern of all the authorities that governed the Hijaz. Supplying the pilgrims with food, accommodation, transport and guides was the foundation of the Hijazi economy, and there were generous subsidies provided by the empires and dynasties that controlled the destiny of the Hijaz, for the upkeep of holy places and in support of the pilgrimage traffic. Foreign-born traders and merchants were also attracted to the area by the large throngs of pilgrims, and many stayed on as permanent residents of the towns of the region. Control over the area was a matter of honour and prestige, providing a profound source of legitimacy for the Ottoman Empire, probably more important for it than for its predecessors, given its non-Arab provenance. But before such control could be established, the Ottomans had to contend with the presence of a powerful local dynasty, the sharifs of Mecca, whose authority over Mecca and the surrounding tribes had been established for centuries.[3]

The sharifs of Mecca were direct lineal descendants of the Prophet Muhammad through his daughter Fatima, her husband Ali (the Prophet's cousin as well as son-in-law) and her eldest son Hassan. The title, *sharif* (singular, *ashraf* plural) means 'noble' or 'honourable', in recognition of the holder's connection to the household of the Prophet. The Islamic empire that grew after the death of the Prophet Muhammad in 632 CE covered vast stretches of the known world. It was first centred on Damascus, but under the Abbasid dynasty the capital moved to Baghdad. Inevitably, central authority over this huge territory weakened, thus allowing local dynasties and warlords to emerge. In the Hijaz, Qatada, a sharif from the Yanbu' area seized power in Mecca in 1200. He established the line of the Banu Qatada who continued to rule Mecca and its dependencies until the twentieth century. Their authority was consolidated by the long reign of one of Qatada's descendants, his great grandson, the energetic and stern Abu Numayy (1254–1301). Until the Ottoman ascendancy in the sixteenth century, the Hijaz was often the centre of complex manoeuvrings between the reigning powers of the time. The one constant was the Mamluk dynasty in Egypt (1250–1517) which frequently intervened in the internal affairs of Mecca, not only in support of one faction of sharifs over another, but also to ensure that their regional rivals did not obtain a permanent foothold in the Hijaz. When the Ottomans destroyed Mamluk power in Egypt in 1517, and assumed the latter's role as suzerains over Mecca and the Hijaz, the ruling amir in Mecca, Barakat ibn Muhammad (1497–1525), acknowledged the Ottoman suzerainty over the Hijaz.[4]

The Ottomans confirmed the sharifs as the rulers of Mecca and afforded them wide latitude in the conduct of their internal affairs. Their two main requirements were that the name of the Ottoman sultan be mentioned in the Friday congregational prayers, and that the annual pilgrimage traffic be adequately protected from brigands and marauding tribes. The Ottomans even assisted the sharifs in extending the range of their authority to cover nearly all the Hijaz. Even so, the Ottomans did appoint a mufti (religious official) to Mecca, as well as a governor for the district of Jeddah. Apart from these overt symbols of Ottoman presence, however, the sharifs were virtually autonomous in their rule, to the extent that the Bedouins and townsmen of the Hijaz recognised no other authority. The sharifian family nevertheless often splintered into warring factions as one or other sought supremacy, and three different clans emerged that contested for power. These were known as the *dhawi* (clan of) Zaid, the *dhawi* (clan of) Barakat and the 'Abadilla, vying between and within themselves for power, while still maintaining a degree of reciprocal protection so that the amirate did not slip away from the overall control of the descendants of Qatada.

By the late eighteenth century, sharifian power was stable and extended along most of the Arabian littoral of the Red Sea as far south as Yemen. They were a force to be reckoned with, but were still not yet in a position to sever their ties to the Sublime Porte – the seat of Ottoman government in Istanbul – completely. One of the enduring characteristics of the sharifs was that their life was simple, and their rule was largely in harmony with their surroundings. They did not live lives of lavish opulence, as did other eastern rulers, and kept close to the tribes and townsmen of their territories. They maintained a personal guard of slaves, servants and freedmen, and a contingent of mercenaries to keep the peace and enforce their writ in Mecca, while relying more on the adroitness of their dealings with the tribes to maintain countrywide order.

However, the mid-eighteenth century saw the rise of the Wahhabis, followers of a literal and puritanical version of Islam. They emerged out of Nejd, the desert plateau that covered most of central Arabia and directly threatened the rule of the sharifs of Mecca. In the early parts of the nineteenth century, the Wahhabis turned their attention to the Hijaz. In 1803 they occupied Mecca and in 1805 Medina. In 1807 they ordered all the remaining representatives of the Ottomans to quit the Hijaz and effectively took over the entire province. The Wahhabi state that was established in the Hijaz was built on a creed that was considered heretical by most Muslims. It stretched right to the frontiers of Syria, and was a serious embarrassment and potential threat to the Ottomans. But the empire did not have the means to undertake the difficult and expensive operation required to dislodge the Wahhabis from the holy cities and destroy their power in their Nejd stronghold. In 1809, the Ottoman sultan turned to his nominal client the governor of Egypt, Muhammad Ali, to undertake the task on behalf of the Ottoman state.[5] Muhammad Ali landed his troops in the port of Yanbu' on the Red Sea, and in 1818 his son Ibrahim captured the Wahhabi stronghold at Dar'iya. Muhammad Ali's control over the Hijaz was now complete and the Amirate of Mecca was in his power to bestow. In 1827 Muhammad Ali appointed Muhammad ibn 'Awn, of the *dhawi* 'Awn to the sharifate. This was the beginning of the sharifate of the clan to which Faisal belonged.[6]

Muhammad Ali's tenure as lord over the Hijaz ended in 1840 when the Egyptian army that buttressed his power was withdrawn to meet other, altogether more serious, duties. An Anglo-Austrian fleet had assembled to threaten Muhammad Ali and his ambitions to become a power independent of the Ottoman Empire. The Hijaz once again came under Ottoman dominion, but this time the Ottomans were determined to curtail the powers of the sharifs and exert their own authority through their appointed governors. The restoration of Ottoman power and formal authority over the Hijaz coincided with the period of the *Tanzimat*. The Ottomans were bent on introducing the new patterns of administration into all their provinces and to draw the provinces more tightly into a centralised state. The sharifs, however, could counterbalance the new supremacy of the Ottoman state in the Hijaz by recourse to the sultan-caliph in Istanbul, to whom they owed their primary loyalty. The ensuing struggle between sharifs and governors see-sawed over the latter half of the nineteenth century and became a permanent feature of the politics of the Hijaz until the outbreak of the Arab Revolt in 1916.

Arabs in the empire

The accession of 'Abd al-Hamid to the sultanate in 1876 coincided with the end of a disastrous war in the Balkans in which the Ottoman Empire lost huge tracts of territory to the newly established states in Romania, Serbia and Montenegro. Bulgaria also achieved quasi-independent status. These Slavic states were backed by the military power of a belligerent and expansionist Russia, determined to extract the maximum advantage from a weakening Ottoman empire. At the Congress of Berlin in 1878, the independence of the three Balkan states was confirmed. The loss of the mostly Christian Balkan territories shifted the population balance of the Ottoman Empire further towards the Muslims, and a determined effort was made by the new sultan to build on the continuing loyalty of his Muslim subjects to the Islamic identity of the empire. Nationalist sentiments amongst the Muslim population of the empire in that period hardly existed, and were only exhibited by a very small band of intellectuals and literary figures. There were still large Muslim populations remaining in the Balkan areas under the control of the Porte, in Albania, Macedonia and Bosnia, but the bulk of the empire's Muslim populations resided in Turkey proper or in the Arab lands of the empire. It was towards these groups that Sultan 'Abd al-Hamid directed his new policies. They were the best internal defences against the creeping ambitions of the great powers.

'Abd al-Hamid built his new policies on three essential pillars. The first was a strong authoritarian and centralised state under his immediate supervision, enhancing the empire's identity as an Islamic power. The second was the protection of Muslim interests, which would be achieved by building on the religious symbolism of the functions of the sultan as caliph, and by propounding the idea of pan-Islam, or Islamic unity, as a counterweight to nationalism.[7] His third aim was to promote economic and technological modernisation and the development of a key transport and communications infrastructure that would bind the empire's core provinces together. The remaining Arab provinces of the empire therefore became crucial to the plans of 'Abd al-Hamid. In North Africa, the territories of Algeria and Tunisia had already been lost to the French – the former in 1832, the latter in 1881 when France forcibly imposed a protectorate – leaving the vast desert lands of Libya, lying between Egypt and the French dominion in North Africa, as the only remaining Ottoman province in that region. Egypt had already slipped out of the Porte's control with the rise of Muhammad Ali, and with the establishment of the British presence there in 1882 it became a colony in all but name. It was only remotely and nominally connected to the empire. The Arab provinces of the Near East, especially those of the Fertile Crescent – Syria, Lebanon, Palestine and Iraq – consequently became the centrepiece of the empire's newly found interest in Arab territories. Governors sent to these provinces were graded higher on the Ottoman bureaucratic register with commensurately higher salaries. Larger military units were posted to the Arab territories and garrisons were strengthened with new fortifications. The Arab role in the propagation of Islam was stressed, and 'Abd al-Hamid appropriated this legacy to strengthen the Ottomans' claim to the caliphate.[8]

There were only very faint stirrings of separatist consciousness amongst the Arab Muslims of the empire. These were, if anything, aimed at improving the circumstances of Arabs within the empire, and linked to achieving greater opportunities for Arabs in the bureaucracy and military institutions of the Ottoman state. The greater power and wealth of notable families in the Arab provincial cities at the beginning of the Hamidian era were partly owing to land laws, which made some of them exceedingly wealthy. This class was more inclined to assimilate within the structures of the empire, and many sent their sons to the burgeoning modern schools in Istanbul and to its military and civil administration training academies.

It was during this time of imperialist expansion, desperate Ottoman consolidation, the beginnings of nationalism, pan-Islam and religious reform, as well as radical economic and social change, that Sharif Faisal ibn Hussein ibn Ali ibn Muhammad ibn 'Abd al-Mo'in ibn 'Awn was born.

Sharif Hussein and the birth of Faisal

There is some confusion as to the exact date and place of Faisal's birth. This is not unusual for the time as neither were records of birthdates common in the period nor was the occasion of a person's birth of much note. The lives of prominent men and women were marked by the anniversaries of their deaths, not by their date of birth. The confusion is compounded by the fact that three different calendars were operative in the Ottoman Empire towards the end of the nineteenth century: the Gregorian calendar; the lunar Islamic Hijri calendar, which starts with the year of the migration (*Hijra*) of the Prophet Muhammad to Medina (CE 622); and a solar calendar used by the Ottoman state, the so-called Rumi calendar, dating from the era of the *Tanzimat* reforms. It came into official usage in 1840. In the Rumi calendar the years were counted from the date of the *Hijra*, but thereafter according to the solar Julian calendar. Faisal himself did not clarify the matter in interviews and conversations, prob-ably because of a general indifference about birthdates amongst the Arabs of the period. Birth anniversaries were remembered in terms of specific events of consequence or under which ruler they occurred. One was born in the Year of the Big Earthquake, or the year in which a particular sultan died.

There are three possible combinations of places and dates that have been advanced for Faisal's birth. The first is that he was born in the mountain town of Ta'if, seventy miles from Mecca, on 20 May 1883; the second that he was born in Mecca itself on the same date; and the third that that he was born in Ta'if on 20 May 1885. However, the sources also use the Hijri date of 1300 to mark the year of Faisal's birth, which makes the date of 1883 more plausible, as 1300 AH is mostly equivalent to 1883. The use of 20 May as the exact day and month of his birth is common to all the sources. On this basis, however, a birth date of 20 May 1885 would have placed Faisal's birth in the year 1302 AH, which no sources corroborate. It is therefore most likely that Faisal's birth occurred on the twelfth day of the month of Rajab in the year 1300 AH. This would mark his date of birth as 19 May or 20 May 1883. At the same time, Ta'if is more likely as his birth place as the sharifian family would have likely decamped to Ta'if with its more clement weather before the advent of the scorching summers of Mecca. An expectant sharifian mother would have probably been sent to this resort well before the onset of the summer and the birth of her child.[9]

The walled town of Ta'if lies on a high table southeast of Mecca, on the ancient caravan routes that linked Mecca with the highlands of 'Asir and Yemen. The town itself is nondescript, but the surrounding area provides a unique microclimate within the harsh desert environment of Arabia. It takes in the edge of the monsoon, which, together with the winter rains, provides for a reasonable degree of fertility. The countryside supports considerable agricul-tural activity, with wheat fields, fruit orchards and flower cultivation, especially roses. The latter forms the basis of the Hijaz's renowned essential oils and perfumery trade. For centuries, the wealthy of Mecca and the Hijaz have main-tained second homes in Ta'if to which they move their entire families during the summer months. The sharifs of Mecca maintained their summer palace on the outskirts of the town, and Ta'if became their capital during this torrid season. It was in this palace that Faisal was most probably born. He was given the name Faisal, which in Arabic means 'the one that separates', another word for a sword and in particular the downward stroke of a sword. The name Faisal, though common enough amongst the Bedouin tribes, was actually quite rare in a sharifian family, whose names were mainly derived from names of the Prophet's descendants or names that glorify the Almighty. Faisal's father was Sharif Hussein ibn Ali; his mother, 'Abdiya, was Hussein's first cousin, the daughter of Sharif 'Abdullah, who became amir of Mecca in 1858. Faisal could therefore claim direct patrilineal and matrilineal descent from the Prophet Muhammad. He was the third son born to Sharif Hussein and Sharifa 'Abdiya, preceded by his elder brothers Ali, born in 1879, and 'Abdullah, born in 1882.

At the time of Faisal's birth, Sharif Hussein was about thirty years old. Very little is known of his early life. His father, Ali, was one of Sharif Muhammad ibn 'Awn's five sons, and the only one who did not become amir of Mecca. He died prematurely in 1861 when Hussein was seven or eight years old. Hussein had been born in Istanbul, and his mother was a widow of Yemeni origin.[10] His father had moved to Istanbul to escape the rivalries of the Zaid clan, whose leader 'Abd al-Mutallib was in power in Mecca. However, Hussein returned to Mecca in 1861, after the death of his father, and lived there under the guardianship of Hussein's uncle, 'Abdullah, who had now become amir of Mecca.[11] For the next twenty years, Hussein stayed in Mecca, learning the ways of the tribes, and developing the courtly skills needed to survive in an environment of intrigue and rumour. He also roamed the countryside, observing and learning about the flora and fauna of the Arabian Desert, which would later make him an authority on the subject.[12]

In 1880 Hussein once more returned to live in Istanbul, accompanied by his uncles. In Istanbul, Hussein seems to have fallen foul of Sultan 'Abd al-Hamid. The ubiquitous palace intelligence services linked Hussein to rumoured meetings between his uncles and foreign legations in the capital. His uncles were reported to be conspiring with European powers for the restoration of the sharifate to their clan under European protection.[13] The veracity of these reports was immaterial to 'Abd al-Hamid, who issued a thinly veiled warning to the sharifs in Istanbul to desist from these contacts. This was sufficient to prompt Hussein to risk returning to a Mecca under the rule of the rival Zaid clan, rather than incur the wrath of the sultan. Hussein then remained in Mecca until February 1892, when he was ordered to return to Istanbul.[14]

Hussein was a man of slight stature, a little under average height, with a fairish complexion and full beard. He had delicate hands and his eyes were large and piercing. He always wore traditional Arab clothes consisting of a *jubba* (outer cloak) over a white, ankle-length shirt. He covered his head with a Meccan turban, which he preferred to the Arab tribal headgear of a cotton cloth fastened down by an *agal*, an accessory made of cord. He had a powerful personality and was frequently described as obstinate and unbending in argument, with an iron will. Deeply religious, he was often consulted on religious and theological issues. He was also imbued with exquisite manners, derived from both his sharifian lineage and his exposure to the formalities and ritual of the Ottoman court. Although indifferent to worldly pleasures and personal material aggrandisement, he was also a very ambitious man, ever concerned about his rightful claim to the sharifate, and this frequently drove him to intrigue and political manoeuvre. His views were essentially shaped by a pre-modern, even medieval, conception of politics and social order, and he could not relate the tumultuous events that accompanied the last decades of the Ottoman Empire to the birth of a fundamentally new world order. It was this deeply traditional perspective on life that prompted him to entrust the raising of his third son Faisal to the tribe of the Bani 'Abadila of the 'Utaiba confederation. Only eight days old, Faisal was sent off to the village of Rahab in the region of Ta'if to spend the traditional seven years with the tribes.[15]

A desert childhood

The Arab custom of sending newborn infants of town dwellers to the nomadic tribes to be raised through early childhood is an ancient one. The hosting tribe is usually related by blood to the parents, or is closely connected in some other way such as by a formal alliance or trade. The Prophet Muhammad himself had been sent to the desert encampments of the Bani Sa'ad tribe, to which his wet nurse, Halimah bint Abi Dhu'ayb, belonged. The hosting tribe accepts to raise the child as its ward, and considers it a great honour to be asked to undertake the task. There are no payments expected, although the biological parents do send gifts at their discretion to cover the cost of the child's upkeep. The parents also maintain regular access to the child, and the child often returns to his town for months at a time.[16]

The condition of the desert tribes of Arabia at the time of Faisal's birth was the same as it had been for centuries. The faint traces of the modern world – telegraph lines, a few manufactured goods – were immaterial to their living patterns. They continued to roam the land in search of pasture for their camels, horses and sheep, and pitched their tents wherever the grazing was good. When the pastures gave out they packed their meagre possessions on the back of their beasts of burden and moved on, unconstrained by authority or by attachments, their lives marked only by the turn of the seasons. Each tribe had its own territorial patch and an elaborate ritual governed the interaction of the tribes themselves. Cooperation and collaboration might quickly give way to rivalry, conflict and blood feuds – or the reverse. It was a harsh, primitive life but not without a certain nobility, and it was in just such an environment that Faisal was raised in the crucial early years of his life. It was an exhilarating, challenging and sometimes dangerous life for a child: living in tents, moving with the caravans across the desert, running bare-headed and half-naked under the beating sun or through the bitterly cold nights. Any small ailment or untreated wound might easily end in a premature death, but it could also toughen and strengthen a child's temperament and instil virtues of character that would serve a lifetime.

It was a matter of course that the children of the encampment would compete against each other in games and mock battles, in jumping and running, in horsemanship and archery. In later years, Faisal did not dwell much on his childhood, saying in one instance to a British writer, 'What can I say about my childhood? Very little. I was brought up in a Bedouin tent in the desert. As I grew older I played with my foster brothers and other boys. I remember breaking my arm while climbing some rocks and I still have a scar on my head where a stone hit me during a mock battle . . . but I never think of those things now.'[17] His reticence may have been due to an assumption that the details of a desert childhood would not be of any interest to a modern audience. However, when speaking to Amin Rihani, a Lebanese writer of the 1920s, he was more forthcoming. He did recall one particular incident that seems to have affected him considerably. The children of the tribe had divided into two teams to enact a mock battle. Faisal managed to seize the headgear and belt of his foster brother, which led to boasting, then a verbal altercation and near blows. The tribal chief emerged from his tent with a cane in his hand to adjudicate the dispute. Turning to Faisal, he said, 'Listen, Faisal. You are our foster son and this is your foster brother, and there should be no boasting on your part. If you are good to him, he will be good to you; if you do ill to him, he will do ill to you.'[18]

A crucial benefit that Faisal gained from his desert upbringing was his ease with the form of Arabic spoken by the desert tribes. Those who came across him in later life would marvel at his command of the spoken language and the trove of old poems and songs that he knew by heart. These could only have come about from his long immersion in the culture of the desert tribesmen and in listening to their recitations over the camp fires. Another great asset that Faisal earned from these desert years was a deep knowledge of tribal ways and thinking, a familiarity with tribal problems and concerns, and an abiding respect for tribal customs and traditions. Knowing how to gain and retain the respect and confidence of the tribes was a vital ingredient in Faisal's subsequent military and political career.[19]

After his seven-year period with the desert tribes, Faisal returned to Mecca where his formal learning began. His father was now widowed, as Faisal's mother, 'Abdiya, had died in 1886. This period has been described by Faisal's brother 'Abdullah, later King of Jordan, in his memoirs. The early education of youth meant above all reading and memorising the Quran, mastering the basics of the Arabic language, and learning the art of calligraphy. Apart from being the central text of Islam, the inimitable style and beauty of the Quran's Arabic was traditionally viewed as the best introduction to the correct forms and usage of the language. The three brothers, Ali, 'Abdullah and Faisal, were assigned the same teachers at the palace. Teachers were expected to instil in their charges a healthy respect for discipline, and resorted to free use of the cane to achieve their disciplinary and pedagogical goals. One of their quranic teachers was an aged shaikh, Ali al-Mansouri from Egypt, who had also taught their father the Quran. He terrorised his pupils, for he liberally employed the dreaded *fallaqa* or *bastinado*, striking the gathered soles of the feet with a cane. A more easy-going and altogether more effective teacher of the Quran was the mild-mannered Shaikh Yassin al-Bassiouni of Ta'if. Nearing his tenth year, Faisal had memorised nearly a quarter of the Quran; later, he would commit the entire Quran to memory.[20]

Three different teachers taught the boys the art of writing, each specialising in one or other form of calligraphy, including the way to write Ottoman Turkish. Faisal also picked up some Turkish from the numerous Turkish speakers in the palace and amongst officials. 'Abdullah, known as a cunning prankster, recalled a prank on one of their calligraphy teachers in which Faisal was unfairly implicated. The teacher in question used to set a very punishing pace, demanding that his charges write a hundred lines of calligraphic script. The teacher unfortunately suffered from bleeding gums, and had the unpleasant habit of licking the point of his pen before dipping it into the inkwell. 'Abdullah decided to play a practical joke on the teacher. He took some extremely hot chilli powder from the palace's eunuch quarters, and filled Faisal's inkwell with it. The following day, Faisal presented his homework to the teacher. The teacher dipped his pen into Faisal's inkwell in preparation for marking it, but, after licking the tip in his customary manner, he then felt the full effect of the chilli powder on his mouth and lips. The teacher naturally claimed Faisal was the culprit and prepared him for the *bastinado*. The undeserved punishment was only avoided when 'Abdullah confessed to his father, and Faisal was spared a most painful chastisement.[21]

Youth in exile

The short Meccan interlude in Faisal's early life came to an abrupt end when Sharif Hussein was called to Istanbul by Sultan 'Abd al-Hamid. The circumstances behind Hussein's summons to Istanbul are unclear. Hussein had lived a largely uneventful life in Mecca, but suspicions continued to be harboured against him by the sultan that he was intriguing against his uncle Amir 'Awn-al-Rafiq, and that he maintained a back channel to the British agency in Jeddah. The sultan's intelligence services had earlier written in connection with Hussein that he was 'a wilful and recalcitrant person whose views, on the rare occasions when he consented to express them, revealed a dangerous capacity for original and independent thinking.'[22]

Whether the dispute between the relatives amounted to actual intrigue by Hussein against his uncle is uncertain. Nevertheless, the Porte sent a mission headed by Ratib Pasha, the sultan's aide-de-camp, to investigate the cause of the dispute. The mission recommended that Hussein be removed from the Hijaz to defuse the tensions between the two camps. But Hussein's summons to Istanbul also served the long-standing Ottoman policy of keeping a possible contender for the sharifate under close watch in Istanbul.[23] It was a useful pressure point against an incumbent amir and kept, as it were, a 'replacement' amir in reserve. In February 1892 Hussein left by steamer for Istanbul, and a year later his family joined him.

So in early March 1893, Faisal, accompanied by his brothers Ali and 'Abdullah, embarked in Jeddah on the paddle steamer *Izzeddine*, bound for Istanbul. On board were their paternal grandmother, Basmahjehan, the wife of their great uncle 'Abd al-Illah, and the attendant entourage of thirty-two ladies and retainers. The seas were moderately rough and the entire party suffered from seasickness until the steamer reached Suez. Passing through the Suez Canal, the sons saw for the first time the astounding sight of women unveiled. The seas became much rougher after leaving Port Said and the steamer was forced to head for Limassol in Cyprus to await calmer conditions. They faced more rough seas before the *Izzeddine* finally reached Istanbul on 30 March, docking at a berth in front of the Royal Palace.[24] It was the beginning of a long exile for Faisal and his brothers, which only ended in 1908.

They settled with their father in a comfortable mansion on the Bosporus provided by the sultan, but had to live within a very tight budget. Sharif Hussein's allowance from the Porte was limited and he had no access to further financial resources. Faisal later remarked that they lived very poorly, with meat available only once a week. 'Perhaps it was a good discipline', he added ruefully.[25] Although their father was appointed to the Council of State, an advisory office composed of high personages of the empire, in effect he was in involuntary residence in the capital, his every move reported on by the ubiquitous secret police of the sultan. After Hussein's arrival in Istanbul the sultan remarked that Hussein had been summoned to the capital so that he, the sultan, and the state would be benefit from his services, but this did not alter the reality of the situation.[26] Sharif Hussein and his family were entirely hostage to the policies of

Sultan 'Abd al-Hamid and to events in the Hijaz. But the Istanbul to which they had been exiled was not some decaying, backward city of a crumbling empire. Rather, it was in the throes of modernisation and expansion, and its traditional buildings and streets were augmented by new quarters, thoroughfares and boulevards. These would only add to the magnificent older mosques, schools, palaces, state offices and bazaars that defined the metropolis. Appealing new buildings, both official and private, sprang up, designed in an eclectic style, a successful mélange of traditional Ottoman designs and the architecture of the European Mediterranean. This style spread throughout the main cities of the empire, especially the Levant countries, and its elegance continues to reverberate to this day.

For Faisal and his brothers, Istanbul and its environs must have been a totally different experience to the deserts and heat of the Hijaz, and life in the closed and pre-modern world of Mecca. For one, the weather was markedly seasonal, with winters that could be bitterly cold and snowbound. In fact the brothers had stocked up on winter clothing during their voyage to Istanbul when the *Izzeddine* had docked at a number of ports en route. Istanbul's location straddles two continents, and the magnificent waterway of the Bosporus was unsurpassed for its natural beauty. Its hills were wooded and islands dotted the surrounding seas. Istanbul was the capital of a multinational empire, and all manner of people crowded its streets: Turks and Greeks, Armenians and Bulgars, Bosnians and Jews, Europeans, Kurds and Arabs. Men in uniform or in the dress of the many nationalities of the empire; women wearing their distinctive yashmaks or face veils; gypsies and beggars – all considered the city to be their home. Its waterways and harbours were filled with many types of vessels: ferries that criss-crossed from the European to the Asiatic side of the city and back, private launches carrying passengers to various points on the waterway, boats laden with provisions for sale, merchant ships passing between the Mediterranean and Black Seas. When the sun set, the minarets and domes came into their own and dominated the skyline of the city. It was truly a glorious spectacle, and must have made Faisal's exile far more bearable than it would have been otherwise.

Fifteen days after the group's arrival in Istanbul, Second Lieutenant Safwat al-'Awa, a Syrian from Damascus who was an assistant lecturer at the Military Academy, was appointed by imperial decree to be the tutor for Faisal and his brothers. Safwat was about thirty years old, and his first concern was that they learnt the Turkish language. He forbad them to use Arabic in his presence. He taught them Turkish, Ottoman grammar and syntax, geography, arithmetic, and Ottoman and Islamic history. To improve their proficiency in Turkish the lads had to read out continuously in a loud voice. Faisal became very fluent in that language, which he would later use as a form of code when addressing other

Turkish-speaking Arabs in the presence of non-Turkish speakers. Faisal also developed a working knowledge of French and picked up the rudiments of English. However, it appears that he was not as conscientious as his brothers in his preparation for Safwat's classes and was often careless in his homework. Safwat complained to Hussein that Faisal was always late for classes and was lazy, saying that he had even threatened him with a beating if he did not persevere like his brother 'Abdullah. 'Beat him and don't be afraid!' Hussein replied. He then called Faisal and took him to task. 'O Faisal, if you do not persevere today in your work you will regret it tomorrow. Don't just take for granted that you are a sharif, and that that alone is sufficient for you [in life]. A sharif, my son, is one because of his knowledge and works, and on account of his manners and conduct.' This seems to have put Faisal back on track in his studies with Safwat.[27]

Their father took upon himself personally the duty of teaching them the Quran. A Syrian from Aleppo, Shaikh Muhammad Qadhib Alban, a graduate of al-Azhar, Islam's pre-eminent religious academy in Cairo, taught them Arabic. Another cleric, Muhammad Tawfiq Effendi, taught them calligraphy. A noted Turkish litterateur, Muhammad 'Arif Pasha, was also employed as their tutor somewhat later. 'Arif Pasha's mother shared Sharif Hussein's wet nurse, so, according to Arab custom, she was the boys' foster aunt and 'Arif Pasha was a type of cousin.[28]

The social life in the conservative household of Sharif Hussein was limited. There were a number of sharifian families in Istanbul, including those from the Zaid clan, who were kept in an enforced stay in the capital by the sultan. However, the rivalry between the clans did not stop friendships being formed by the younger generation of distant cousins. Faisal and his brothers were frequent visitors with their father to the estate of Sharif Ali Haider, the patriarch of the Zaid clan in Istanbul. Ali Haider, who became the deputy head of the Ottoman upper chamber of parliament, was an open and generous man. Unusually for a sharif of the period, he had married a European, the daughter of an Irish colonel serving the Ottoman Empire, Isobel Dunn. His estate was about an hour's carriage drive on the Asiatic side of Istanbul. There the brothers would beat a path to the stables where a number of magnificent Arab horses were kept, and Faisal, an expert horseman, would indulge his love for riding. But most of the time the brothers kept to their own company. The three brothers developed close bonds, but at the same time there were hints of sibling rivalry, especially between 'Abdullah and Faisal. 'Abdullah would later exhibit intense jealousy with regard to his brother's prominence. 'Abdullah saw himself as his father's favourite and his political heir. Ali was growing into the mild-mannered, bookish man that he would become, scrupulously observant in religious matters and something of a scholar. He was physically weak and probably suffered from tuberculosis. 'Abdullah already showed formidable political skills and ambition, even opportunism, and never lost his mischievous character. He was shrewd and calculating, but also very charming.

Faisal, the youngest of the three, grew up taller than average, and his frame emphasised the angularity of his body and made him seem taller than he really was. He was slim and slightly narrow-shouldered. His vigour and apparent robustness hid a somewhat delicate constitution. Although not an intellectual, he was curious, eager to learn, and had a powerful retentive memory. He had developed a good capacity for observation and was self-controlled, serious and hard-working. He also had a streak of impulsiveness that was kept in check by a sense of realism. He had a magnetism that marked him out as a natural leader of men. Their father had remarried into the Turkish elite after the death of their mother, 'Abdiya. His second wife was Adila Hanim, a granddaughter of the mid-nineteenth-century Ottoman reformer Rashid Pasha.[29] She bore him a son, Zaid, in 1900, and three daughters. Zaid, being nearly a generation younger than his half-brothers, was not raised with them, but would later serve Faisal in an auxiliary capacity, providing him with important support during the Arab Revolt and in Syria and Iraq.

Sultan 'Abd al-Hamid

Faisal's years in Istanbul coincided with the last period of the long rule of Sultan 'Abd al-Hamid. The sultan had consolidated his power and ruled as an unchallenged autocrat, but he was not a typical tyrant. Terrible epithets have been attached to his name: the 'Red Sultan'; 'Abd al-Hamid the Damned'; 'The Recluse of Yildiz', and his rule was caricatured in the western press as the epitome of the decadent and violent oriental despotism that was the Ottoman Empire. In French and British opinion, the Ottoman regime had moved from being valued allies in the Crimean war of 1853–56, and a bulwark against Russian expansionism, to a parodied, widely despised, tottering empire that was hostile to the national aspirations of its ethnic groups. Such increased hostility to the Ottomans became focused on the person of the Sultan 'Abd al-Hamid, whose peculiar personal characteristics, stature and demeanour did not help to reduce the opprobrium that was heaped on the Ottomans in Europe by the press and sometimes even by chanceries. His supposed villainy and tyranny became a recurrent theme in Arab nationalist lore. But many Arabs also saw 'Abd al-Hamid's policies, especially his pan-Islam, as the last, best chance for the Ottoman Empire to weld its Muslim populations into an abiding loyalty to a universal Islamic state.

'Abd al-Hamid was installed as sultan as a supposed liberal, but it did not take him long to cede from the constitutionalists and isolate their main protagonists, in particular the reforming statesman Midhat Pasha, one of the architects of the 1876 constitution. But he was not simply a reactionary despot, determined to cling to the old ways at all cost. He was genuinely concerned with the fate of the empire if it were not to find a new organising principle that would allow it to buy time to reform and strengthen itself, and meet the profound internal and external challenges that threatened its integrity and existence. His chosen ideological tool was pan-Islam and a willingness to expand the traditionally Turkish governing elite to include other Muslim nationalities of the empire, especially Arabs. He was personally pious and disliked signs of outward opulence. His years in power were marked by a great acknowledgement of the centrality of Islam in the identity and affairs of the state.

However, 'Abd al-Hamid had a suspicious personality that bordered on the paranoid. He has been described as a 'strange complex and psychologically unsettled man' who was also 'wilful, industrious and methodical'.[30] He never smoked or drank. He personally supervised the preparation of his meals from a special kitchen to ensure that he would not be poisoned. He stayed as a near recluse at the Yildiz Palace, minutely involved in the details of governing his empire. He concentrated power in his own hands and developed the scope and powers of the palace secretariat to act almost as a parallel government that side-stepped the official state. The secret police provided a daily diet of raw intelligence reports called *jurnals* (journals), which 'Abd al-Hamid spent hours sifting and reading.[31]

By the turn of the century, 'Abd al-Hamid had prematurely aged, a small, hunched man with a henna-dyed beard and a huge fez pulled down to cover his ears. He rarely ventured outside the palace walls, and built a special mosque nearby to which he would proceed for Friday prayers rather than undertake the drive to the large congregational mosques of Istanbul. He was a passionate admirer of photography and assembled a huge collection of photographs of the places, peoples and buildings of his empire. All Ottoman sultans were expected to master a craft, a commentary on the ephemeral nature of power, and not to take their exalted status for granted: 'Abd al-Hamid had also become an expert carpenter. Palace visitors could see for themselves the quality of his handiwork. In addition, he was a devotee of detective stories. Above all he was a true workaholic, ferociously toiling in all hours for what he thought was the salvation of his realm. The head of the *Mabeyn*, 'Abd al-Hamid's personal secretariat, was the veteran statesman Kucuk Sa'id Pasha, and the second in command was an Arab from Damascus, Izzat Pasha al-'Abid. The other prominent Arab in the sultan's entourage was a Syrian from Aleppo, Shaikh Abul Huda al-Sayadi, 'Abd al-Hamid's main religious adviser.

The paradox of 'Abd al-Hamid's rule is that it mixed apparently contradictory policies: a neo-traditionalism marked by a focus on the Islamic identity of the empire, an illiberal and centralised state, press censorship and a pervasive secret police network, with thoroughgoing, even radical, reforms that affected major aspects of the empire's administration, economy and finances, education and military preparedness. A number of the reforms that altered the character of the empire can be attributed directly to Kucuk Sa'id Pasha.[32]

A new vigour had entered the life of the Ottoman Empire, and by the turn of the century the 'Sick Man of Europe' appeared to be recovering. Thousands of kilometres of roads were constructed. Elementary and secondary schools proliferated in all the provinces, and the main professional schools in Istanbul, of medicine, law, commerce, engineering, public administration and military sciences, were expanded. The empire's first public university, Dar-al-Funun, opened its doors in 1900. Istanbul was the centre and focus for all this activity, which attracted ever increasing numbers of students and visitors from the provinces. The Mulkiye boarding school was opened to cater for just such students. Arabs formed a large component of those provincial students who were attracted to the capital by the prospect of earning the necessary qualifications for a career in the empire's administration, judiciary and especially the military. They were mainly sons of provincial notables, landlords and clergy, or from modest families where the father was a nondescript bureaucrat or official.[33] But Faisal and his brothers shared little with such Arabs. They came from an entirely different background, a princely family with real claims on power in the most religiously significant province of the empire. Their education was not going to take place in the new Ottoman schools but rather at home with private tutors. However, unbeknown to Faisal at the time, his life would indeed intertwine later with a number of Arabs who were in Istanbul at the same time as he was.

Marriage and children

The first years of the twentieth century were profoundly significant for Faisal's private life. Barely aged twenty-one, Faisal was married to his cousin, Huzaima, the daughter of Sharif Nasir ibn Ali. Huzaima was born in Mecca in 1884. Huzaima's twin sister, Misbah, had earlier married Faisal's brother, 'Abdullah. Ali was already married to another cousin, the daughter of his great uncle, 'Abd al-Illah. The marriages were all arranged in the traditional manner of the Meccan sharifs, where marriages between cousins were actively sought and encouraged. Very little is known regarding Faisal's wife in her earlier years, and while Faisal became a major actor on the international stage, Huzaima stayed well away from the public arena as befits a lady of the Meccan nobility. It was only after she had joined Faisal in Iraq that a little became known about her. The marriage was no love match. It was urged upon Faisal by his father and there was no question of Faisal hesitating or refusing his father's instructions. Huzaima was neither particularly attractive nor much of a homemaker, failing to entice Faisal into domesticity. Later, the two seemed to have reached a degree of intimacy and mutual respect, with Faisal compensating for his earlier indifference to his wife with presents and gifts.

Huzaima bore Faisal four children: a son, Ghazi, future king of Iraq; and three daughters, Izzat, Rajiha and Rafi'a. Rafi'a was severely disabled as the result of an accident at a very young age, and was never able to speak or move. A nurse had accidently dropped her charge from a height when she was only a few months old. Faisal became particularly attached to his disabled daughter and she to him, recognising him whenever he approached and caressed her. She died only a few months after Faisal's death in 1933, perhaps sensing that her father had passed away and that she would not see him again. Faisal took little part in the raising of his other children, leaving the task to their mother and to the other women of the household. The results were not altogether salutary. Two of the children grew up headstrong and spoilt. Ghazi could never quite escape from the shadow of his renowned father, and Izzat was troubled.[34] Faisal's third daughter, Rajiha, married an Iraqi air force officer and lived a modest, unassuming life.[35]

++++++◊❖◊++++++

CHAPTER 2

RETURN TO MECCA

B Y THE beginning of the summer of 1908 Faisal, alongside his family, had settled for an exile of indeterminate length. There were no signs that conditions in the Hijaz would change to their advantage, or that the sultan would relax his control and supervision of their activities. However, in the space of a few weeks in mid-summer of that year, cataclysmic changes would occur in the Ottoman Empire that would pave the way for a return to their homeland. It would also set in train a chain of events that would ultimately end in the break-up and demise of the millennium-old state, events that would catapult Faisal on his extraordinary course towards war and kingship.

The Young Turk revolution

The thirty-year-old autocracy of Sultan 'Abd al-Hamid was resisted by those who sought to limit the powers of the sultan and return the empire to constitutional rule.[1] 'Abd al-Hamid's assertion of his personal power in 1878 and his suspension of the constitution and proroguing of parliament had left the constitutionalists in complete disarray. Many fled to Europe where they continued in ineffectual opposition to the sultan, and pockets of dissent could be found in cities such as Paris and Geneva. There, many of these oppositionists became imbued with European ideas that were then in vogue, such as positivism and Social Darwinism.[2] New publications that reflected the views of these groups sprang up, printed in European cities and distributed in the Ottoman Empire. They evaded the empire's press censorship laws and controls over the post by relying on foreign couriers and diplomatic pouches. In 1889, a group of students and junior instructors at the Military Medical School in Istanbul organised themselves as a secret society, the Ottoman Union, modelled after the Italian Carbonari. It was the first of many such societies that would later coalesce into an empire-wide movement conspiring to end the autocracy of the sultan. Many members of these underground groups, either evading arrest or choosing exile, also found themselves in Europe where they joined the earlier cadres of exiles.

This loosely knit group of writers and intellectuals, dissident officers and civil servants – and even members of the Imperial family – were collectively known as *Les Jeunes Turcs*, the Young Turks.[3] By no means were their adherents all of Turkish ethnic descent as the name would imply. All the empire's varied nationalities were represented in the opposition to the sultan's autocracy. However, the participation of Arabs was far more qualified and circumspect. 'Abd al-Hamid's pan-Islamic policies and his reliance on Arabs in his private camarilla played some part in diffusing resentment to his personal rule.[4] But a more likely explanation is the sultan's cooption of local elites and notables in the administration of the Arab provinces, and the very weak sense of ethnic Arab nationalism that existed at the turn of the century. Even reform-minded Arabs saw their future in the bosom of the Ottoman Empire, perhaps in a more decentralised state with devolved powers.[5]

Some organisational unity was imposed on these groups through the founding of what became later known as the Committee of Union and Progress (CUP), under the leadership of Ahmed Riza, a former director of education in the city of Bursa. Riza, a keen follower of the positivist philosopher Auguste Comte,[6] believed in a strong, centralised state, albeit subject to constitutional limits and controls. Another current, led by the sultan's dissident nephew, Prince Sabah al-Din, placed far more emphasis on administrative decentralisation and a liberal economic and social order.[7] These two groups came together and met in two separate congresses in Europe, in 1902 and 1907, to iron out their differences and to agree a common plan of action against the rule of Sultan 'Abd al-Hamid. By 1908, the existence of a widespread organisation dedicated to the reintroduction of constitutional rule to the empire was widely known. The CUP had spawned a number of cells throughout the empire, and the secret police could barely keep up with the rapidly evolving situation. Conditions were now ripe for a dramatic development, which started in Macedonia, still an Ottoman province. In early July 1908 a rebellion by units of the Ottoman Third Army Corps, with headquarters in Salonika, calling for the restoration of the constitution, quickly spread throughout the province.[8] On 24 July the government in Istanbul capitulated and 'Abd al-Hamid issued a decree restoring constitutional rule.

However, the Young Turk revolution was not met with the same scenes of jubilation in all the cities and provinces of the empire, in particular not in the Arab provinces. Many Arabs who had held high positions in the palace were dismissed or arrested.[9] It is no wonder that for many Arabs of the empire, a government beholden to unknown coup plotters from Macedonia, promising to dilute the Islamic foundations of the empire with reckless promises of equality and ill-defined freedoms, was not a welcome alternative to the traditional and venerated rule of a sultan-caliph, no matter how autocratic and idiosyncratic.

The reaction to the coup in most of the traditional cities of the Arab provinces was either guarded or hostile.[10] The events of July disturbed the social and political equilibrium in the Arab provinces and exposed the growing cleavages and divisions within society. They were deeply disturbing to a mainly conservative and traditional society, only a small fraction of which had been exposed to modern ideas of political freedoms. Most of the population outside the coastal cities of the Levant that had had a long exposure to Europeans and European ways had little knowledge of the meaning of constitutional rule. In the Hijaz, Sharif Ali, the amir of Mecca, was openly antagonistic.[11] He refused to proclaim the news that constitutional rule had been restored in the empire, and even ordered the public flogging of some unfortunates who were caught talking about the constitution and freedoms. These acts, of course, did not endear him to the new powers in Istanbul, and in September 1908 Sharif Ali was dismissed.

The new amir of Mecca

The disturbed conditions of the Hijaz and the fear that the Bedouins would take advantage of the revolutionary turmoil to attack the newly opened Hijaz railroad made it imperative that a new sharif be appointed to the province.[12] The Hijaz railroad was the lynchpin of 'Abd al-Hamid's plans to draw the Arab provinces of the empire closer to the central government. Later, it would feature prominently in Faisal's desert campaigns during the First World War.[13] Construction of the railroad was started in 1900 and would not be completed until 1908, when the line finally reached Medina, linking it and a string of way stations to Damascus. It began to carry pilgrims soon after its opening, but was also used extensively by the Ottoman military to strengthen its control over the territories through which it passed. Troops could be moved farther and faster, and supplied quickly and efficiently. Trade also expanded in the areas along the railroad's route and improved the lot of the Bedouins who roamed in the vicinity of its tracks. What the Bedouins seemed to have lost in abandoning brigandage and despoiling of unprotected pilgrims and travellers, they gained by more secure methods of earning their livelihood. The sharifs of Mecca, however, saw another aspect of the opening of the railroad. There was real fear that the strengthening of the empire's military capabilities in the Hijaz would undermine the autonomy of the sharifs and reduce their status to mere powerless local dignitaries holding a traditional religious office.

Following the dismissal of Sharif Ali, and the unexpected death of his replacement, Sharif 'Abd al-Illah, two candidates emerged for the Amirate of Mecca: Faisal's father, Sharif Hussein and his distant relative of the Zaid clan, Sharif Ali Haider.[14] The latter's candidature was weak from the start. Although apparently the candidate of the CUP, he lacked the necessary base of support in the palace, which was still the most significant factor in the appointment of the sharifs. Also, he did not have the necessary drive, determination or political skills, to secure the amirate for himself.[15] Sharif Hussein was therefore summoned to the palace and, on 24 November 1908, Sultan 'Abd al-Hamid signed the necessary decree formally to invest Sharif Hussein with the office of the amirate of Mecca.

The 1908 CUP-led revolution had cast a pall of uncertainty on all the empire's relationships with traditional groups: the religious classes, provincial notables and tribal leaders. An office such as that of the sharif of Mecca, built on custom and owing a great deal of its power to the qualities of the relationship between the ruling amir and the sultan, could not adjust easily to the structures of a modernising state. Should the sultan's powers be reduced, if not quite eliminated, how could this bond, with its strong religious overtones, be replicated in terms of loyalty to a fractious group of officers and civilian conspirators – often secular if not completely irreligious – who were claiming legitimacy for the new order in Istanbul? Hussein was assuming the amirate at a time when the powers of the sultan were coming under serious threat. 'Abd al-Hamid's championing of a botched counter-coup against the CUP in July 1909 finally led to his deposition and exile.[16] He died in obscurity on 10 February 1918, a few months before the final defeat and dissolution of the empire over which he had presided for thirty years. The powers of the sultan were greatly curtailed, leaving Hussein to face the CUP without the full countervailing power of the sultan on his side.

Faisal, the Idrisi and the 'Asir campaigns

Sharif Hussein's return to Mecca coincided with the beginning of the Haj season and he was soon to be tested on his ability to manage one of the key functions of his office. He succeeded in safeguarding the returning caravan of pilgrims from Mecca to the railroad terminus in Medina, against the rampant lawlessness of the Bedouin tribes.[17] Hussein's other main task was to secure the land from rebellious tribes and also to secure his frontiers eastwards towards Nejd with the growing power of 'Abd al-Aziz ibn Saud and the Wahhabis, and southwards towards 'Asir, where a charismatic spiritual leader, the Idrisi, entrenched himself as an independent ruler. Faisal, at the head of forces gathered by the amir of Mecca, comprising mainly loyal tribesmen and the amir's own private army, led fifteen of these expeditions and raids to quell tribal recalcitrance and assert his father's authority.[18] These forces were at times stiffened by regular Ottoman detachments drawn from the Ottoman garrisons in the Hijaz. It is clear that even in his late twenties Faisal's leadership and combat skills were recognised and acknowledged by his father. He was appointed to head the Bedouin and tribal affairs unit of his father's administration.[19] Faisal was involved in the campaigns against ibn Saud, but it was against the Idrisi that he would earn his spurs as a battlefield commander and tactician.

Sayyid Muhammad ibn Ali ibn Ahmad ibn Idris, known in Arabic sources as al-Yamani (the Yemeni) or al-Idrisi, and in European sources as simply 'the Idrisi', was a leader of a Sufi order founded by his ancestor, Ahmad ibn Idris, a native of Fez in Morocco.[20] Sayyid Muhammad himself was born in Sabia in the 'Asir in 1876, of an Indian mother.[21] He studied with his father, made the pilgrimage to Mecca, and around 1896 spent some time in al-Azhar religious academy in Cairo. There he seems to have made some contact with the Italian embassy. In 1905–6, the Idrisi returned to 'Asir, a year before the death of his father. Appalled by the neglect and desolation of the country under Ottoman rule, the Idrisi launched a rebellion against the Turks, calling for the establishment of a just state ruled by Sharia, and, tellingly, a state that would be part of the Arab community (*Ummah 'Arabiya*). Reports began to spread about the rise of the *Mahdi* (Redeemer), who had supernatural powers and who was establishing Sharia rule amongst the tribes and in the towns of the 'Asir. The rise of the Idrisi threatened not only Ottoman rule but also the hold of Sharif Hussein on the tribes of the area, some of which had accepted Hussein's lordship and were part of his bailiwick. It also complicated the rivalries between the European powers in the Red Sea area, mainly between Britain and Italy, with the latter seeking ways to extend its influence into Eritrea and Yemen.

The Idrisi's rebellion in 'Asir had effectively driven the Turks from most of the country by the end of 1910. Abha, however, held out and the governor and an Ottoman garrison were bottled up. Attempts by Ottoman forces coming up from the Yemeni coastal town of Hodaida to relieve Abha were unsuccessful, and there was a real chance that the besieged town would fall into rebel hands, with the Ottomans unable to mount a relief expedition or to convince the Idrisi to accept some form of autonomy under Ottoman suzerainty. There was no alternative for the Istanbul government but to ask Sharif Hussein to lead an expedition against the Idrisi and to re-establish Ottoman authority.[22] The Porte sent two battalions of regular Ottoman troops with artillery to join Hussein's force of five thousand armed Bedouins and militia. On 15 April 1911 Hussein, together with his two sons 'Abdullah and Faisal, marched out of Mecca to relieve Abha.[23]

One of the columns, about three thousand strong and led by 'Abdullah, with Faisal in charge of the cavalry and the sharifian units, had reached the town of

Qunfudha on the way to Abha. The weather was scorching hot and the land-scape bleak and desolate. The column was ambushed by the Idrisi forces in a place called Quz Aba al'Ir. In the ensuing battle that lasted six hours, both sides suffered heavy losses, but the Idrisi had the better of 'Abdullah, who was obliged to retreat to Qunfudha with a greatly reduced force.[24] Regrouping, the force, now stiffened with about 1,200 regular Ottoman troops, once more left Qunfudha fifteen days later. They met the Idrisi near the site of the earlier battle. Intense fighting ensued, in which Faisal led his cavalry against one of the Idrisi columns trying to break the relief force's formations, and routed them.[25] The second battle was decided in favour of the combined Ottoman and sharifian forces, but another enemy laid them waste: cholera. A third of the relief force came down with the dreaded disease, which disproportionately affected Turkish troops with their reduced immunity. Faisal later related the extent of the disease's devastation. He ordered one of his sentries to shout out that the enemy was near. The call was carried into the tents, but out of a force of nearly seven thousand only five hundred were able to get up and prepare themselves for battle. Faisal could only thank God that in fact there was no enemy in the vicinity.[26]

The two battles of Quz showed both the courage and cruelty of the regular Ottoman troops. Their reprisals against innocent villagers whom they suspected of supporting the Idrisi were fearsome, and the burning of people alive, the impaling, mutilations and beheadings all profoundly disturbed Faisal. It was an early exposure to the horrors of war. Such dreadful scenes would multiply during the Arab Revolt.

Hussein's forces finally entered Abha on 16 and 17 July 1911. The Idrisi forces fled to the mountains, but the 'Asir campaign did not end the rebellion. The Idrisi's influence on the tribes did not diminish and he continued to rule from his headquarters in Sabia, biding his time for another uprising. Nevertheless, Sharif Hussein could claim victory as he did lift the siege of Abha. His forces had done their fair share of fighting and the Istanbul government acknowledged his help in containing the threat of the Idrisi's secession in 'Asir by awarding him medals. Sharif Hussein, 'Abdullah and Faisal returned to Ta'if in triumph in August 1911. Faisal, however, was carried on a litter. He had contracted malaria towards the end of the campaign, which debilitated him for a long time afterwards.[27]

The confrontation with the Idrisi took another turn when the Italians declared war on the Ottoman Empire on 29 September 1911. Italy had coveted the Ottoman provinces of Libya ever since they had dreamed of an Italian overseas empire to rival that of Rome and put Italy on the same footing as other western imperial powers. On the pretext of the Ottomans' 'mistreatment' of the Italian colony in Tripoli, the Italians invaded and occupied the coastal areas. The interior, however, continued to resist.[28] The Idrisi took immediate advantage of this Italian declaration of war. The Italians promised him financial, military and logistical support. The Italian navy controlled the Red Sea and freely attacked Ottoman coastal installations. The port of Luhayya was besieged by the Italian navy from the sea and by the Idrisi's forces on land. Elsewhere the Idrisi took over the important town of Jizan, which the Ottomans had evacuated. He then concentrated on cutting the Ottoman lines of communication between the 'Asir and the Hijaz, and with the sea route blocked the Ottomans had little means of confronting the renewed challenge from the Idrisi. For the second time, they called on Sharif Hussein to help them in their predicament. Hussein agreed and this time put Faisal in charge of the campaign.

Faisal rode out at the head of a force of 1,500 Bedouins and 400 irregular troops of the sharif's own private army (the *bisha*) and a Turkish-financed mercenary force of tribal Arabs from the Qasim area (the *'uqail*).[29] The *'uqail* fighters only rode female camels on their expeditions, while the *bisha* mainly comprised people of African origin, that is, freed slaves. They were paid from the sharif's own resources and were entirely loyal to him. They were frequently used for escorting pilgrim caravans. Faisal's force reached Qunfudha and joined up with two Ottoman battalions that were already in the town. The Idrisi was also assembling his army in the area of Qunfudha in preparation for the expected battle. The Italian navy had sent its warships to support the Idrisi with their guns and to land Italian troops into Qunfudha. A fierce battle ensued between Faisal and the Turks and the Idrisi's army supported by the Italian naval guns. The Italians abandoned the landing of their troops when the Idrisi was defeated on land, and fled the battlefield with the remnants of his troops.[30] In spite of Faisal's military victory, the Qunfudha encounter did not eliminate the threat from the Idrisi. Faisal returned to Mecca, and the Idrisi continued in his activities against the Ottomans. The peace treaty that ended the Italian war in October 1912 left the Idrisi in his position and later Ottoman attempts to come to terms with him led nowhere. The situation in 'Asir at the outbreak of the First World War had not fundamentally changed since 1912. But the Italians gained Tripoli, which the Ottomans had to concede to face a far bigger threat that broke out in September 1912: the First Balkan War.

In early 1913, Faisal made a field inspection of the military conditions in the 'Asir and to reconnoitre the movements of the Idrisi. He wrote to his father about the dire circumstances of the troops stationed there. The Hijaz units had 'no intention of staying here for one more minute. Their condition is embarrassing due to their undignified abasement and their ardent desire to return to Mecca . . . They will flee if any one of their columns is attacked by ten riflemen. The garrison in Abha are ill-disciplined . . . If no measures are taken the consequences will be terrible . . . And what I am most concerned about is Abha and its artillery and weapons cache [if it falls to the Idrisi].' Faisal went on to report that his recurrent malaria attacks kept him in bed for half the month. Faisal was anticipating that the Idrisi would take advantage of the terrible weaknesses of the Ottoman situation in 'Asir, and attack Abha. If this were the case, Faisal wrote that he would lead the Hijazi units back into the Hijaz proper to defend the coastal plains, implying that the Idrisi could well march into the country.[31] It was fortunate for Sharif Hussein (and the Ottomans) that the Idrisi did not – or could not – mount an attack on Abha and seize 'Asir in such a moment of weakness and thereby change the strategic circumstances in the Arabian Peninsula.

The character of the young Faisal

In the early days of his rule in Mecca, Sharif Hussein would keep his own counsel. His sons had not yet matured politically. They aided and supported him, and did his bidding. They may have proffered advice if asked, but it is not at all certain that he would have listened to them. The sons were in awe of their father. They had neither the experience nor the independent base of support to allow them to challenge their father on essential differences of opinion. They also had to reimmerse themselves in the life of the Hijaz after spending a good part of their formative years in Istanbul. As Faisal admitted to Lawrence during the desert campaign, 'I am not a Hijazi by upbringing; and yet, by God, I am jealous for it.' Faisal's confidence and assuredness of touch, however, would grow, and by the outbreak of the Great War he would fully come into his own.

When Faisal first returned to Mecca from Istanbul – the exact date is not known but it was probably in late February or early March of 1909 – he had been very much influenced by his years in Istanbul. However, Sharif Hussein made sure that Faisal would shed his European clothes, to which Faisal had taken a liking, and abandon any Turkish mannerisms. Until well into the Arab Revolt, Faisal would wear only Arab dress. Faisal's spoken and written Arabic was impeccable, but his father assigned him Meccan companions to ease his reintroduction into Hijazi and tribal society. He also ordered Faisal and his brothers into the Camel Corps, and Faisal recalled the occasions to Lawrence when he went out with the Camel Corps on extended missions into the wilds of the country to patrol the pilgrim routes. These could go on for months at a time in all seasons and weather. Faisal was afforded no special treatment. He and his brothers had the same food, bedding and hard saddles as the rest of the corps. They met and handled all kinds of men, and learnt new methods of riding and fighting. It was a life designed to toughen them and make them self-reliant, and to instil in them knowledge and respect for the people and the land over which they were to help their father rule.

The childhood years with the Bedouin in the desert, youth in the metropolis of Istanbul and young adulthood travelling in the lands of the Hijaz all played their part in the moulding of Faisal's character. He was now a grown man, over twenty-five years old when he returned to Mecca from Istanbul, but he looked older. He stood resplendent in his long white robes, with a gold cord marking his sharifian lineage fastening his head-cloth. A slender, erect, tallish man, certainly taller than most of his kinsmen, with a pale face, slightly sloping eyes and a trimmed black beard, by all reckoning a very handsome and imposing figure. He was 'pillar-like . . . graceful and vigorous, with the most beautiful gait and a royal dignity of head and shoulders', as Lawrence described him. He habitually crossed his hand over his dagger as he stood receiving guests and visitors, and spoke with a rich, musical tone. With the tribes he would use the dialects of the desert; with the townsmen, a more refined and courtly language; and with other Arabs – of Syria, Iraq or the Levant – a classical but precise Arabic delivered in the pleasing Hijazi intonation. He had a curiously halting way of speaking, carefully choosing his words and phrases, which added to their authority and earnestness. The impression was always effective, and drove even the most hard-boiled tribal warriors and chiefs, traditional leaders and urban notables, as well as modern-minded Arabs, instinctively to trust him and accept his leadership. He was a past-master at wit and banter, which he used effectively to defuse tensions and anger, and he was loved, even idolised, by his followers.

But Faisal was also impetuous, often hot-tempered and constantly driven to action. The latter trait could easily end in setbacks, even disaster, if not checked by careful prior thinking and planning which he was not often prone to do. There is no doubt that he was courageous; it would have been well nigh impossible to lead Bedouins into battles and raids if he had not displayed the requisite degree of courage and bravery. But his courage and drive to action was often checked by his physical weakness, compounded by excessive cigarette smoking. There was many a time when his men would carry him off a battlefield, after an encounter had ended with victory, unconscious from the physical exertion of leading his men into battle, encouraging them to fight, or directly charging the enemy.

He was a good judge of men and often had to deal with tribal chiefs whose pride had to be assuaged, devious and grasping politicians whose ambitions had to be addressed, and trouble-makers of all kinds whose mischief had to be contained. He was not naturally suspicious, but was careful in trusting or accepting people at face value. Later, as he became more embroiled in the turbulent and treacherous world of international diplomacy and politics, he would exhibit the characteristics of ambiguity, dissimulation and indirectness, which others confused with deviousness. These characteristics, however, were more to do with finding a way out of often impossible situations and choices. His knowledge of the affairs of men and the world were gained at breakneck speed, for a huge number of events and experiences were crammed into his life over a very short period. The wisdom and foresight of his later days came from bitter experience rather than from reflection and consideration.

CHAPTER 3

•••••❖❖❖•••••

PRELUDE TO WAR

IN THE few years between the 1908 revolution and the outbreak of the First World War in 1914, the empire was buffeted by enormously powerful currents that would have shaken the resilience and integrity of any state. Historical forces of a profound nature were playing out on the tableau of a shrunken empire, one which had moreover embarked on an untested system of governance. The pressures building up on and within the empire in its last years may not have led to its dissolution without the catalyst of a world war, but they were relentless nevertheless. The loss of most of the empire's remaining Balkan territories and the provinces of Libya had concentrated the attentions of the CUP on the Arab provinces. The empire had become increasingly defined by its two largest ethnic groups: the Anatolian Turks and the Arabs of the Near East and Arabia.

Although the CUP's leaders were mainly secular, they were obliged to accept the fact that the most powerful glue that would hold the empire together after the loss of the mainly Christian provinces of the Balkans had to be Islam. There was simply no other unifying identity that would keep the empire's Muslim populations loyal to the empire, now that the sultan-caliph had been reduced to an almost symbolic figure with little effective power. The constitutional principles that the CUP had thought would placate the empire's restive minorities and reaffirm their commitment to Ottomanism were clearly inadequate. The controversial pan-Islamic policy of Sultan 'Abd al-Hamid was partly resurrected and given a new impetus as the CUP and its sympathisers sought to keep the loyalty of the empire by a now decidedly Muslim majority. This was indeed ironic, as the leadership of the CUP was uniformly composed of members of Masonic lodges, with a scepticism exhibited towards all forms of religion.[1] New elements had therefore entered into the delicate and complex balance between the sharifs of Mecca and the new order in Istanbul.

Ottomanism, Arabism and secret societies

Unlike most of the ethnic nationalisms that had gripped Europe in the nineteenth century, Arab nationalism did not evolve in a determinist fashion towards the ideal of a state in which a homogeneous, linguistic, ethnic and cultural group would find their apotheosis and realisation. In spite of the best efforts of Arab nationalist ideologues of the post-First World War era, the grand narrative of Arab nationalism as a progressive process of challenge, rebellion and finally liberation from the 'Turkish yoke' is not borne out by the facts.[2] The emergence of an Arab consciousness was actually a hesitant and uncertain affair. It was only towards the end of the Ottoman Empire that the idea of an Arab destiny that was in any important way separate from the loyalty to the centuries-old empire was entertained by a small but significant number of Arabs.[3]

These disparate strands of intellectual and cultural ferment would not by themselves have created the bases for an Arab consciousness. They had to meld into a receptive political and social setting that would accommodate and amplify these ideas into something that would be recognisably nationalist. That 'something' was the tensions and struggles in the Arab provinces for power, status, resources and authority within local groups, and between them and the imperial centre in Istanbul, nowhere more so than in Greater Syria, the most advanced region of the Arab provinces. To a large extent, therefore, early Arab nationalism was linked to its proponents (or opponents) in Greater Syria, and to the cadres of student administrators and cadet and junior officers who had come from the Arab provinces to attend the specialist imperial academies in Istanbul.

The Young Turk era allowed these tendencies to emerge to a much greater extent than they had done during the long rule of Sultan 'Abd Al-Hamid. The huge territorial losses of the empire in the aftermath of the 1908 revolution, especially the loss of the overwhelmingly Muslim province of Libya to the Italians, raised the issue of the vulnerability of the Syrian lands to foreign conquest. This was further exacerbated by the continuing rumblings from French colonial circles about the importance of asserting France's 'historical' rights of protection over the Christians in Syria in the event of the further disintegration of the Ottoman Empire. There was genuine concern that the Ottoman Empire might not be able to protect the Arabs of Syria from falling under the control of foreign powers, and this prompted speculation as to whether the people of Syria would not be better served by devolution of power to the province so that it could organise its own defence. The idea of administrative decentralisation and greater devolution of powers to the provinces was thus partly a by-product of the concern regarding the ability of the central authorities to safeguard the interests of the provinces adequately.[4]

The perceived slant of the CUP, towards centralisation, 'Turkification', and the gradual ascendancy of the Turkish ethnic component inside the Ottoman Empire, drove a number of Arab activists to consider counter measures that would at least safeguard their community's interests in the empire. In August 1909, a law was passed that banned the formation of any political grouping based on ethnic nationalism, thereby effectively blocking any overtly Arab political party. But this did not stop the founding of Arab secret societies, two of which, al-Fatat (Youth) and al-'Ahd (the Covenant), would have the greatest impact on the course of the early Arab national movement. Leaders and ordinary members of the two movements would later join the Arab revolt and provide a significant part of Faisal's political and military advisory staff. Al-Fatat was formed in Paris in November 1911 by a group of Arab students who were pursuing their higher education in the French capital. From its onset the society was bound by strict protocols of secrecy. The founders were quickly able to assemble a wide network of members throughout the Ottoman Empire. Most were drawn from the notable families of Greater Syria, with very few individual members from the less developed Arab provinces of Iraq, Hijaz and the Yemen.

The political programme of al-Fatat in its early days was to call for Arab autonomy within the Ottoman Empire, with the goal of turning the empire into a dual monarchy like that of Austro-Hungary, an Arab-Turkish empire with an Ottoman monarch. Al-Fatat affirmed that such an outcome should in no way prejudice the unity and integrity of the Ottoman Empire. One of the founders of al-Fatat, Tawfiq al-Natur, later reminisced about the founding years of the society. 'The idea of Arab nationalism, or Arabism, had not yet evolved or strengthened [when al-Fatat was founded]. All we Arabs wanted was to enjoy the same rights and duties as the Turks within the Ottoman Empire, and that the Empire would be built on two powerful pillars – the Arab people and the Turkish people.'[5] Al-Fatat's head offices moved with its leadership, first from Paris to Beirut, and then to Damascus at the outbreak of the First World War.

The other major secret society, al-'Ahd,[6] was built around the Arab officers of the Ottoman army. It was founded in 1913 by an Egyptian officer, 'Aziz Ali al-Misri, the only Egyptian of note in the early Arab national movement.[7] Misri was involved in the Arab societies that sprang up after the July 1908 revolution, principally the Qahtaniya, a secret society that also advocated a greater Arab role in the empire. He was a controversial hero of the Libyan war of 1911, when he was charged with organising the defence of Cyrenaica. His abrupt departure with his troops from Cyrenaica was used against him by the Ottoman authorities, who accused him of treason and sentenced him to death. Misri's case became a cause célèbre amongst Arab nationalists of the period and a great hue and cry followed his trial and imprisonment. He was released after many representations were made on his behalf by the Anglo-Egyptian authorities. He returned to Egypt in triumph just before the outbreak of the First World War.[8] Misri's path would cross with that of Faisal in 1916, during the early stages of the Arab Revolt.

The al-'Ahd society followed a similar programme to al-Fatat, that of Arab self-rule within the empire. The majority of al-'Ahd's adherents were Iraqi officers, a number of whom would go on to have distinguished careers with Faisal in the Arab Revolt, in Syria, and later in independent Iraq. Following the arrest of Misri, al-'Ahd's leadership devolved for a period on to Nuri al-Sa'id, a young Iraqi officer of exceptional political and military skills.[9] It was only when al-Fatat's main leadership had moved to Damascus that the two secret societies began to establish contact with each other and coordinate their responses to developing events.

Other reform movements calling for decentralisation and local autonomy sprang up in the Arab provinces in the wake of the Balkan war, when the empire was in imminent danger of collapse.[10] In Paris, a group of Syrians, both Muslims and Christians, called for a general Arab Congress to be held in Paris in June 1913, to consider the rights and prospects for Arabs of the Ottoman Empire. The congress convened in the hall of the French Geographical Society in Paris, with three hundred people in attendance. The congress was presided over by 'Abd al-Hamid al-Zahrawi, a member of parliament from Homs in Syria and a founder of the Entente Liberale party.[11] In the Ottoman chamber, al-Zahrawi was an indefatigable champion of Arab causes but had still not broken with Ottomanism. The CUP had tried to block the congress from being organised, but after its successful opening it decided to open negotiations with the leadership and to consider the implementation of some of their demands.[12]

Faisal in the Ottoman parliament

In the years between the July 1908 revolution and the outbreak of the First World War, three elections were held in the empire for the Ottoman parliament, the Majlis al-Mab'uthan, in 1908, 1912 and 1914. All the elections were based on an indirect electoral system, and with the franchise restricted to males.[13] The first followed soon after the revolution itself, and although the CUP had begun to organise itself formally and openly throughout the empire, it was unable to establish an electoral lock on the new parliament. There were too many independent deputies to allow the CUP an unfettered majority. In the Hijaz, the 1908 elections preceded the arrival of Amir Sharif Hussein. The Hijazi elections were highly irregular, with little public interest either in the process or the outcome. Two Hijazi deputies from Jeddah and Medina took their seats in the new parliament, but the two from Mecca did not even arrive in Istanbul. (One refused to leave Mecca, and the other turned back, homesick, having reached Egypt en route to Istanbul). In a special election held in February 1910, Hussein arranged for the notables and electors of Mecca to vote for his son 'Abdullah and Shaikh Hassan al-Shayba, from a prominent local religious family, as deputies. The CUP, who were shut out from the Hijaz special election, manoeuvred to block the appointments but failed.[14]

The 1908 parliament raised issues of great concern to the Arabs of the empire, and was the venue to which can be traced the beginnings of an expressly Arab set of priorities. The liberal opposition, who fared badly in the 1908 elections, had reorganised themselves as the Entente Liberale and were beginning to appeal to specifically Arab concerns. There were other such parties, such as the Moderate Liberal Party which had a large number of Arab deputies and stood in opposition to the CUP. There were several areas of concern that deeply engaged the Arab deputies. They included the empire's unpreparedness in countering western imperial commercial and political designs, which many believed were targeting the Arab provinces. The Hijaz delegates, though not specifically noticeable in the resulting debates, were nevertheless influenced by the tenor of the often acrimonious exchanges on the chamber's floors.

One of the issues that caused great anxiety to many of the Arab deputies in the Ottoman parliament was that of Zionism.[15] The immigration of Jews from the Russian and Austro-Hungarian empires into Ottoman Palestine began in earnest after the Second Zionist Congress of 1898, when the financial and organisational wherewithal to encourage and support such migration was put into place.

The sultan had insisted that any Jews immigrating to Palestine from Europe had to take Ottoman citizenship and be part of the Ottoman millet system.[16] There was real fear that Jews emigrating from Europe would seek the protection of foreign powers, under the 'Capitulation' concessions, rather than seek Ottoman citizenship. The Ottoman government set up a series of control measures to track and restrict the immigration of European Jews to Palestine, and tried to prevent the sale of land in Palestine to Zionists. Nevertheless, by 1908, there were nearly 60,000 Jews in Palestine, three times the level of 1882 when restrictions on Jewish immigration were first put into place.

The elections of 1912 were hastily organised by the CUP after their public support had precipitously dropped. The campaign between the CUP and its opponents, principally the Entente Liberale, was very heated, with both parties vying for the Arab vote. All the competing parties claimed to respect the tenets and role of Islam in society, to recognise ethnic and minority grievances, and to recognise the need to devolve power to the provinces. The CUP employed both fair and unfair methods to secure its advantage. In the end, the CUP's

superior organising methods and its control over the government machinery
proved decisive. The results were reflected in a parliament with lopsided
CUP support. No wonder the 1912 elections were known as the 'Big Stick'
elections.[17]

As in previous elections, the Hijaz proved an exception to the rest of the
empire. Sharif Hussein ensured that 'Abdullah was returned as member for
Mecca but this time with his brother as member for Jeddah. The British Consul
James Henry Monahan wrote from Jeddah: 'About a fortnight ago two telegrams, signed each by the Grand Shereef's agent in Jeddah and thirty traders
and pilgrim guides of the town, were sent to Mecca, one to the Grand Shereef
proposing his second son Faisal as member of parliament, and the other to
Faisal offering him membership, and favourable replies have been received.
The popular impression seems to be that the election is now over, but there is a
small party of Jeddah notables who insist on a regular election according to
law, and put forward three candidates none of whom is supposed to have any
chance.'[18] Faisal was duly elected to the Ottoman Chamber of Deputies in the
elections of 1912 as member for Jeddah. He was nearly thirty years old.

Hussein needed to have both 'Abdullah and Faisal in the Ottoman Chamber
of Deputies. There would always be one or both of them in the capital to keep
a watchful eye on the plans and machinations of the government and to maintain the sharifian family's network of allies and supporters in Istanbul. In any
case, the regular sessions of parliament were not that lengthy and allowed the
two brothers to be available to assist their father in the Hijaz when the need
arose. Hussein was shrewd enough to know that the forms of Ottoman public
life were changing and the significance of the new parliamentary institutions
would only grow in the future. It would have been inconceivable to allow deputies influenced by the CUP to sit in parliament representing the Hijaz. The
Hijaz deputies had to reflect the views and interests of the paramount power in
the Hijaz, the amir of Mecca, and to lobby the government and parliament
effectively to ensure the continuing privileges and special status of the province. Hussein was deeply concerned about the determination of the CUP to
extend the government's authority in the Hijaz, partly through schemes such as
the extension of the railroad to Mecca and the implementation of the provisions of law of the provinces. The presence of his two sons in the chamber
would visibly and amply demonstrate the special status of the Hijaz and the
established power of the amir of Mecca. Their fluency in Turkish, their knowledge of the capital from the years that they spent in residence there, and their
contacts with the Turkish and Arab provincial elites were all factors that made
them most suitable as deputies for the Hijaz.

Faisal's arrival in Istanbul to attend the opening of the new parliament in
mid-May 1912 coincided with radical shifts in the power equation in the

capital. The Libyan war was still raging and new threats to the empire were emerging from a revolt in Albania and the looming clouds that presaged the First Balkan War. This war, which broke out in October 1912, was a disaster for the Ottomans who had insufficiently prepared for the conflict. On 23 February 1913, Edirne, formerly Adrianople and the Ottoman capital, was starved into submission by the besieging Balkan army. Amidst terrible scenes of carnage and devastation, Turkish peasants were driven out of their lands into Asiatic Turkey. Edirne was the last Ottoman city fully inside Europe. The road to Istanbul was open. The First Balkan War ended with the Treaty of London signed on 9 June. With the city of Edirne in enemy hands, the Ottoman Empire had now lost all its Balkan territories, Crete and the bulk of the Aegean Islands.[19]

The capital itself witnessed a desperate struggle for control over the government between the CUP and its enemies. In June 1913 a botched coup by the Entente Liberale led to the assassination of the war minister. This gave the CUP the pretext to seize control over the state and inaugurated the CUP dictatorship that led the empire so disastrously during the next five years – into the First World War and ultimately to its destruction. However, the CUP's seizure of power was very quickly rewarded when it took advantage of the collapsing alliance between the victorious Balkan countries as they scrambled to devour the spoils of the war. In the Second Balkan War the Ottoman army moved to retake Edirne and all of eastern Thrace. A series of treaties followed that set the boundaries between the independent Balkan states and the Ottoman Empire. The western boundaries of the empire, with minor exceptions, were to form the boundaries of present-day Turkey. The recovery of Edirne was met with immense popular relief in the empire and launched the CUP's second chapter in power with mass support and even adulation. Thus emerged the triumvirate that would rule the empire and with which Faisal and the Arabs had to contend: Talat Pasha, the party leader and strategist; Jamal Pasha, the skilled soldier, utterly ruthless with enemies; and the most flamboyant and popular Enver Pasha, patriotic, energetic and courageous. It was mainly Enver who would chart the empire's close collaboration with Imperial Germany.

Many young Arab officers who would later join Faisal in the Arab Revolt, or who formed the core of Faisal's government in Iraq, had cut their teeth as field officers in the First and Second Balkan Wars. The most prominent of these was Nuri Pasha al-Sa'id, who would become a key figure in the desert campaigns of the war and would later go on to have a long and eventful career as Iraq's leading politician until his death in the revolution of July 1958. Ja'far Pasha al-'Askari, Nuri's future brother-in-law and a dedicated fighter and commander in the Arab Revolt, was wounded in battle in the retreat from the Edirne front. Another young officer who distinguished himself in the Balkan Wars was Yasin al-Hashimi, a future minister and prime minister of Iraq.

The 1912 parliament faced significantly different problems to those of the 1908 parliament. To some extent, the issues that dominated the agenda for some Arab deputies had now been defused or sidelined by the growing recognition that the empire's death knell might sound if further dissension continued and the state was dangerously weakened and allowed to drift. Arabs now accounted for an even larger percentage of parliamentarians, and a sense of shared responsibility for the fate of the empire began to seep into the speeches and actions of the Arab deputies. The crises of the Balkan wars and the return of the CUP to power had effectively sidelined the Chamber of Deputies, which passively watched the unfolding power struggles in the capital. The CUP itself, in its second manifestation in power, had chosen to accommodate Arab concerns for better representation in state and government. It was not openly challenged in parliament, and the main figures in Arab provincial life adjusted to its pre-eminence. The CUP went so far as to encourage the election of some of its Arab opponents from the broken Entente Liberale party in the 1914 elections. These were called to ensure that the Chamber of Deputies better reflected the changing demographics and ethnic composition of the empire. Arab representation in parliament was dramatically increased and two Arab ministers were included in the Ottoman cabinet. The CUP conceded that appointees to posts in the Arab provinces had to have a proficiency in the Arabic language.

Faisal maintained a regular presence in Istanbul during the crises that affected the empire in the 1912–1914 period, although he is not known to have participated in the infrequent debates of the chamber in the short parliamentary sessions that were held during this time. His passage to and from Istanbul and the Hijaz was mostly through Egypt, where during his stops he developed a number of relationships with leading Egyptian and Arab families resident in Cairo.[20] Faisal's first visit to Syria took place after the 1913 Haj season. The Ottoman government had feared that marauding Bedouins would attack the Haj caravan returning to Syria via the Medina railhead and requested that Faisal should accompany the pilgrims with a detachment of armed troops. The caravan returned safely to Damascus and Faisal used the opportunity to acquaint himself with the leading notables and figures of Syrian social and political life. He stayed with the Bakri family, the same Damascene notables who had hosted his brother 'Abdullah during his earlier visit to Damascus.[21] The Bakri family became closely connected with the sharifian family of Hussein, and it was through their offices that Faisal had his first contacts with Arab secret societies.

Faisal's preoccupations in Istanbul were mostly connected with the affairs of the Hijaz and ensuring that his father's interests were well represented during the tumultuous periods that the empire was passing through. He was also open to receiving all kinds of visitors and office-seekers from the Arab provinces. A well-known Arab nationalist figure of later years, the writer As'ad Daghir, described his first experience with Faisal in his memoirs of the times: 'I did not know Sharif Faisal personally in Istanbul. I used to see him with the other representatives from the Hijaz in the Majlis al-Mab'uthan [the Ottoman Chamber of Deputies]. But an event happened that changed my impressions of this great man. A Shaikh of the 'Asir region happened to be staying in Istanbul for several weeks during the early part of 1913. No one paid him any attention or attributed to him any particular significance.' Daghir then relates how Enver had thought the shaikh might be useful to him and provided him with a car and an escort. The shaikh started to develop airs, wearing unbecoming western clothes and contacting foreign embassies to offer privileges in his native region. The Italian ambassador fobbed the shaikh off by asking him to have his offer to 'sell' the 'Asir region corroborated by Faisal. Daghir picks up the story. 'On the following day, the Shaikh went to the Ottoman Chamber of Deputies wearing a formal frock coat and asked to meet Sharif Faisal. Faisal who had already seen from his window the Shaikh approaching, wearing the frock coat, told his secretary, "Tell him that I am busy." But the Shaikh insisted on a meeting to discuss an important matter and asked the secretary to pass on a note to Faisal with the details of his proposal to 'sell' the 'Asir. Faisal returned the note to the Shaikh but wrote on it saying, "Brother . . . Isn't the attire of our ancestors more becoming and dignified for us and causes people to respect us? By God, please take off these clothes that do not suit you."' Faisal was too considerate of the shaikh's pride to tell him that his scheme was absurd and was content to deflect the shaikh's attention to his inappropriate clothes instead of the sale of his province to a foreign power. Daghir concludes his story by saying, 'From that time my regard for Faisal increased immensely. Before that I used to prefer others to him.'[22]

PART II

BREAKING THE BONDS
THE FIRST WORLD WAR AND THE ARAB REVOLT
(1914–1918)

2. The Ottoman Empire, 1914

CHAPTER 4

THE ROAD TO THE RISING

F ROM HIS perch in the Ottoman parliament and his frequent travels to and from the Hijaz, Faisal experienced at first hand the intense and dramatic changes affecting the empire.[1] The lands that he traversed and the people he encountered impressed upon him the changes the empire had undergone since the deposition of 'Abd al-Hamid. The territories of the empire had been drastically reduced by foreign occupation and losses in warfare; its government was now effectively in the hands of a military junta, albeit with a constitutional camouflage. This came about as a result of bewildering shifts in power in the capital: revolutions, counter-revolutions, elections, assassinations and disastrous military defeats. The triumvirate in power at the onset of the First World War – of Talat, Enver and Jamal – had by now consolidated their control. They were intent on centralising the state, while paying lip service to regional and provincial demands for local autonomy. The pattern of government was a mixture of bureaucratic inertia, attempts at administrative and military modernisation, and the increasing authoritarianism of the CUP leadership.

In the few years before the outbreak of the First World War, the empire was in a constant state of crisis. No one was quite sure how it would all play out. Certainly, no Arab figure of any consequence, at least before the outbreak of the war, was actively prepared to seek the empire's dismemberment as a necessary condition for redressing the growing mood of Arab disquietude. The empire was simply too old and established as the legitimate state for Arabs to open up the possibility that its dissolution could serve the interests of the Arab provinces. When the internal challenge finally came – from the Arab Revolt centred at first on the Hijaz – it was from the province least affected by the currents of Arab national consciousness. Faisal himself would move in this period from a parochial and dynastic concern with the fate of the Hijaz, to a greater identification with broader Arab demands. The fortunes of Faisal and the sharifian family became intertwined in ways that would have been inconceivable before the war, towards a goal that had been barely articulated previously. The story of the modern Middle East had its unlikely beginnings in these crucial years between 1908 and 1916, and Faisal, from the outbreak of the war, was in the midst of these momentous changes.

Crisis in the Hijaz

The parade of governors of the Hijaz who were either outmanoeuvred, recalled, or who simply became exhausted came to an abrupt end with the appointment of a senior general, Wahib Pasha, in early 1914. He was charged with establishing the state's authority over all the Hijaz, curtailing the powers of the amir of Mecca, and removing the political obstacles to the expansion of the Hijaz railroad to Mecca. He combined in his person the twin posts of governor and commander of the Ottoman forces in the province. It was an ominous development, coming at a time when the CUP was ever more apprehensive of foreign designs on the Arab territories of the empire. The entanglements of the foreign powers with the affairs of the Arab provinces of the empire also reached new heights. The Germans were intent on building on their privileged relationship with the CUP's leadership to extend the Berlin–Baghdad railroad; the French on exploiting their historic links with elements of the Christian communities in Syria; and the British, who were busy making commercial inroads into Iraq, as well as formalising their protectorates over the chieftaincies of the Persian Gulf. The CUP was also aware that a number of Cairo-based Arab intellectuals, under the leadership of the religious scholar Rashid Ridha, were mooting the possibility of a union of the Arab provinces of the empire to form a new caliphate. In fact, a secret society, al-Jami'a al-'Arabiya (the Arab League) was organised by Rashid Ridha to this end, and contacts were established with Sharif Hussein to discuss the proposal.[2]

The fact that these disclosures came at the same time as news that direct talks had taken place between the British authorities in Egypt and Sharif 'Abdullah increased the CUP's determination to exert its undivided authority over the Hijaz. The Istanbul government, however, was aware that it had to tread carefully with Sharif Hussein, and in spite of Wahib's confrontational tactics, they urged on him a conciliatory policy with Hussein. Wahib went so far in one of his despatches to Istanbul as to urge the government to prevent 'Abdullah and Faisal from leaving the capital, essentially to be held as hostages against their father's behaviour.[3]

The escalation of the conflict between Hussein and Wahib Pasha divided official opinion in Istanbul as to how to handle Hussein's intransigence. The Bedouins, partly under the quiet instigation of Hussein, had risen in revolt against Wahib's feared measures. The situation quickly deteriorated and got out of control. The roads between the Hijaz's main towns were cut and provisions in the cities fell precipitously, threatening famine. Panic set in throughout the towns of the area and in Jeddah conditions became chaotic. Sharif Hussein sent Faisal at the head of a detachment of troops to the town to quell the disorders and repel the Bedouin raiders.[4] Both parties now backed away from escalating the crisis, but Hussein had decided that serious problems might arise if he allied himself with the CUP. Behind the scenes, Hussein and 'Abdullah had started to make contact with the British in Egypt, seeking allies where they could find them in case another confrontation erupted with the CUP.

'Abdullah had first met with Lord Herbert Kitchener, the British agent in Egypt in the spring of 1912, but this had been more in the line of a courtesy call. However, the second set of meetings between 'Abdullah and Kitchener were held under entirely different circumstances. These took place on 5 and 6 February 1914 while 'Abdullah was travelling back to Istanbul through Cairo. 'Abdullah was instructed by his father to sound out Kitchener regarding the position of the British if the CUP moved to depose Hussein. Kitchener reported on the talks and gave a non-committal answer.[5] The significance of these early discussions with the British was hotly debated in later years, between supporters and opponents of the Arab Revolt. The former saw these contacts as justifiable, precautionary measures to safeguard the historic privileges of the amirs of Mecca. The latter saw them as harbingers of treasonable actions that helped to destroy a centuries-old Muslim state.

'Abdullah arrived in Istanbul after his eventful stay in Egypt and was taken to see the various high officials of the state: the grand vizier, and Talat and Enver, respectively, then the ministers of interior and war. The meetings, which had started amicably enough, markedly changed, and he was sent back to the Hijaz with a non-negotiable position to relay to his father. Essentially, the sharif was offered a third of the revenues of the extended Hijaz railroad, and an assurance that the sharifian office would remain in his family after his death. Otherwise, Talat said in a veiled threat, the Porte would do what it had to do.[6] 'Abdullah returned to the Hijaz in April of 1914 to relay the message to his father. As usual, he passed through Egypt where he met with Ronald Storrs, Kitchener's oriental secretary. Storrs stressed the official British position of non-interference in the affairs of a friendly power, and an unwillingness to aid the Arabs of the Hijaz in case of a revolt.

Sharif Hussein angrily turned down the proposal made by the Porte. The family – Hussein and his sons, Ali, Faisal and 'Abdullah – held a number of conclaves to evaluate the situation and to determine the options and likely course of action. 'Abdullah was the most forceful, and pushed for an uprising against the Turks, with backing from Arab units of the Ottoman army in Syria and Iraq. The goal would be the formation of a large, independent Arab state.

'Abdullah's working plan was a bit fanciful, as it called for the seizure of pilgrims during the feast after the Haj. This would oblige the foreign powers to put pressure on the Porte to release the pilgrims, and when this failed the foreign powers would be forced to negotiate directly with Hussein for their release.[7] Faisal and Ali, however, vehemently opposed 'Abdullah's plan on the grounds that the Turks were too strong, and convinced their father to consider it only as a matter of last resort. Faisal later commented on this episode, saying, 'The Arab intellectuals were divided into two camps. One party considered that the complete separation of the Arab countries from the Ottoman Empire, or a revolutionary movement against the Sultan, would cause the breakup of the whole empire, including the Arab countries themselves. This party advocated a gradual and progressive solution. My eldest brother Ali and I belonged to this group. In the other camp were extremists like my brother 'Abdulla who wished to start a revolution without any preparation and without counting the heavy sacrifices that it would entail. The Amir Hussein, finding himself confronted by two different schools of policy, tried to gain time in order to act for the best.'[8] 'Abdullah's plans were shelved pending the outcome of further negotiations with the Porte. Hussein cabled the Porte that he was sending 'Abdullah back to Istanbul again to continue discussions. Faisal had already left for Istanbul to attend the sessions of the Ottoman parliament.

'Abdullah's arrival in Istanbul coincided with the assassination of Archduke Ferdinand and his wife in Sarajevo. Faisal was already in Istanbul to attend the sessions of parliament, and received 'Abdullah at the pier upon his arrival. Faisal expressed his concerns to his brother about the deteriorating relations between his father and the Porte, and suggested that 'Abdullah's delayed return to Istanbul had angered the Porte. However, the outbreak of the First World War on 1 August 1914 changed every party's plans and calculations. Even though the Ottoman Empire was not yet a belligerent, the issues of the Hijaz paled before the demands of the global conflagration. The Hijaz delegation to the Ottoman parliament, including Faisal, prepared to depart home on the first available steamer. On 7 August, Faisal embarked on the khedival vessel the *Ismailia*, heading for Egypt. As the vessel reached the Dardanelles, they were escorted by an Ottoman destroyer through minefields until they reached the open sea and then directed to the port of Izmir. There the *Ismailia* remained for a day until the British consul instructed them to sail to Piraeus in Greece, then a neutral country. The ship was kept in Piraeus harbour so as not to hamper the pursuit of two German warships, *Breslau* and *Goeben*, which were then in the Eastern Mediterranean. Eventually, the passengers on board the *Ismailia* were instructed to disembark, ostensibly because the ship had missed its scheduled voyage to Alexandria and had to return to Istanbul. 'Abdullah and Faisal arranged with the other passengers, mostly vacationing Egyptians, to charter another vessel for the voyage to Alexandria. They were befuddled when they found out that the *Ismailia* had already sailed for Alexandria.[9]

The Ottoman Empire enters the war

Hussein's quarrels with the local governor Wahib Pasha, and his ill-concealed suspiciousness and even hostility to the CUP and its policies, did not necessarily endear him to the Arab nationalists of Syria. There was general wariness with regard to Hussein's conservative and traditional sympathies, and few Arab nationalists were prepared to cede to him the leadership of their cause. Hussein's participation in the campaigns against the Idrisi was held against him in nationalist circles.[10] Early approaches made by nationalists to the Arab amirs of the empire – the Idrisi, ibn Saud, and the amirs of Kuwait and Muhammara – did not include Hussein, by far the most prominent member of the Arab princely families. However, Hussein and his sons maintained excellent relations with a number of prominent families of Syria and Lebanon that harboured individuals who were active in Arabist circles. The most significant of these belonged to the Bakri family of Damascus. Hussein used his influence to ensure that a scion of the family, Fawzi al-Bakri, would serve his period of conscription attached to the office of the sharif in Mecca, rather than join the regular formations of the Ottoman army.[11] Fawzi's younger brother Nasib was already a member of al-Fatat, and it was this connection that allowed the Arab nationalists in Syria to approach Sharif Hussein to seek his leadership for their movement at the onset of the Great War.

The Ottoman Empire's entry into the war on the side of the Central Powers became a foregone conclusion after two German warships, *Breslau* and *Goeben*, made a surprise attack on the Russian Black Sea coast on 29 October 1914. These ships had been rebranded as Ottoman warships, and their German commander given a high rank in the Ottoman navy. Four days later, Russia, followed by the other Entente powers, declared war on the empire. The Ottoman government was already under strong pressure from Germany to enter the war on the basis of the secret alliance of 2 August, drawn up by Germany and the Ottoman Empire.[12] The latter had become ever more dependent on German logistical support, materiel supplies and financial subventions. There were a large number of German officers already attached to the Ottoman army and navy. A German general, Liman von Sanders, the head of the German military mission, became the Ottoman army's inspector general and head of an entire Ottoman army corps, the First Army. Faisal was well acquainted with the scale of German support for the Ottoman army and in fact had developed a friendship with von Sanders. In his memoirs the latter wrote of Faisal, 'I knew Sharif Feisal well from the summer of 1914. He was the type of an Arabian grand seignior. He had a European education and spoke English. Mutual interest in sport had brought us together in various places, and we had visited each other at our homes. The harsh Arabian policy of the Turkish government made him its bitter enemy.'[13]

Faisal and 'Abdullah returned to the Hijaz in late August, and their reports on the conditions in the capital made Hussein very apprehensive about the momentum gathering for war and its implications for the empire, the Arab provinces, and especially the Hijaz. He wrote a letter of advice and warning to Sultan Muhammad Rashad, but his entreaties not to join the war fell on deaf ears, as did his demands to reinforce and properly provision the Ottoman forces in the Hijaz, 'Asir and Yemen.[14] The Ottoman declaration of war was accompanied by a call for jihad by the sultan-caliph. The declaration of a jihad, however, had a limited effect. There was considerable scepticism about the religious sincerity of the CUP and there remained the inconvenient fact that the Ottoman Empire had allied itself with two major Christian powers: Germany and Austro-Hungary.[15] Nevertheless, Sharif Hussein was put in a quandary with incessant demands from the Porte that he also join in the call for a jihad. Coming from a religiously impeccable source, and one that did not conceal its differences from the CUP, such a move on Hussein's part would have added to the authority of the declaration of a jihad.

The Ottoman Empire launched the land war with a disastrous campaign against the Russians in the Caucasus in the winter of 1914–15. The Ottoman Third Army, led by Enver, was effectively destroyed at the Battle of Sarikamish. The campaign on the Caucasus front was part of a two-pronged effort to launch surprise attacks against the Entente. The second front, under the command of Jamal Pasha, was to be opened by an assault on the Suez Canal. Jamal had been appointed commander of the Ottoman Fourth Army based in Syria, and was given vice-regal powers over the province. The Ottoman forces in the Hijaz were also placed under his control. Jamal set about preparing his attack on the Suez Canal, expecting the mere presence of Ottoman troops in the canal area to be a catalyst for Egyptian nationalists to rise against the British. The Ottoman forces that were being assembled included the division from the Hijaz, under the command of the Ottoman governor Wahib Pasha. Jamal had asked for support for the campaign from the amirs of Arabia. Ibn Saud and the amir of Hail, ibn Rashid, sent a large number of camels for the campaign.[16] Hussein was asked to provide volunteers to accompany the Hijaz division under Wahib and agreed to supply volunteers to accompany the Ottoman forces, putting them under the command of his son, Sharif Ali. The force, however, did not get beyond Medina, thus angering Jamal. He complained bitterly of the behaviour of Ali in Medina, whom he accused of interfering with the work of the Ottoman officials.[17] The Suez offensive ended in failure, when the Ottoman forces came under heavy fire from Anglo-Indian forces and could not cross the canal. The expected Egyptian uprising did not take place and the Ottoman divisions withdrew to their bases in Beersheba in Palestine. The whole campaign had been ill prepared and badly conceived, and the attacking force too small to achieve anything of consequence.[18]

Hussein's motives in keeping the volunteers in Medina were many. He might have wanted to prevent the Hijazi volunteers from actually participating in the fighting, using them instead to strengthen his son's authority in Medina against the Ottoman garrison commander. But another factor might have been equally, if not more, important. A trove of documents fell into the hands of Sharif Ali on the march towards Medina.[19] These revealed a series of secret correspondence between Wahib Pasha and the CUP leadership, which discussed the assassination of Sharif Hussein and his sons, and the suppression of the Hijaz's special status in the empire. The outbreak of the war seemed to have put a stop to this correspondence. Sharif Ali halted his march to Medina and refused to join the Ottoman detachments leaving for the Suez front. He returned to Mecca with the incriminating documents, which had their expected effect on Hussein. Sharif Hussein then used his knowledge of the contents of the documents to demand the removal of Wahib as governor of the Hijaz. He also decided to send Faisal to the capital to demand an explanation for Wahib's actions and to elicit a formal apology and a redress. Faisal was selected for the mission partly because of his still pro-Turkish sentiments.[20] Later, Faisal recalled in an interview that 'in spite of the gravity of the offence, the Amir [his father], who still wished to remain faithful to the Empire, only took the step of handing over the documents to me and desiring me to present them to the Grand Vizier in Constantinople.'[21] Faisal visited Istanbul in due course, and in meetings with the grand vizier, Talat and Enver he set out the sharifian family's case against Wahib and their dismay regarding his dangerous conduct. Talat and Enver acceded to Faisal's request and replaced Wahib with the much more acceptable figure of Ghalib Pasha, a kindly disposed general. Ghalib was instructed to draw close to Sharif Hussein and to be accommodating and conciliatory in his dealings with him.[22]

However, Faisal had another and more dangerous mission. He was also to use the occasion of his visit to Istanbul to pass through Damascus, where he was charged with establishing direct contact with the Arab nationalist movement and secret societies.

Faisal's allegiance to the Ottoman Empire

In September 1914, with the war already ablaze in Europe and the Ottoman Empire apparently bent on entering the war on the side of Germany, Kitchener instructed the British Residency in Cairo to sound out the opinions of Sharif Hussein in the event of outbreak of hostilities between the Entente and the Ottoman Empire.[23] Hussein was friendly to the overtures but non-committal. He was still not ready to break with the Ottoman Empire. Throughout the latter part of 1914 and the early part of 1915, the exchange of messages between London and Cairo, and between Cairo and Mecca, continued apace, with the British keen to draw the amir of Mecca into a break with the Ottoman Empire. However, there was widespread fear that breaking with the Ottoman Empire would only lead to the Arabs falling under European tutelage, and the British did their best to show their disinterestedness in Arab lands.[24] These exchanges, which preceded the opening of a formal channel of correspondence between Sharif Hussein and the British government, are critical for understanding the evolution of the sharifian mindset and position in the period between the outbreak of war with the Ottoman Empire and the fateful summer of 1915.

Faisal was privy to all the exchanges, and was also aware of the deteriorating conditions in Syria and the rapid alienation of an important element of the Arab intelligentsia and notable classes from the Ottoman cause. This percep-tible shift can be mirrored from what we know of his public and private state-ments regarding the Ottoman Empire, the war and the future of the Arabs inside the empire. By all accounts Faisal was a supporter of the empire – a loyal but critical Ottomanist – at least until the formal entry of the Ottomans into the war. He acted as a counterweight to his brother 'Abdullah's more impetuous positions, and was conscious of the uneven balance of power between the amir of Mecca and the central Ottoman authorities. Any attempt to challenge the Ottoman Empire without great cause was not only politically dangerous but also guaranteed to fail given the great disparity of power between the two. In any event, the idea of a specifically Arab identity that needed to find full expression in an Arab state was far from his mind. The position of the Arabs, for historical, religious and political reasons, had to be within the bosom of the Ottoman Empire.

Faisal's ideal of empire was a collection of ethnically and religiously diverse bodies held together by loyalty to a legitimate sultanate. The nation state for Arabs as the focus of his attentions and aspirations was too remote, too theo-retical, to allow it to be substituted for the still living body of the Ottoman Empire, with its mighty religious and historical authority. In fact Faisal consid-ered those who advocated a serious Arab challenge to the empire as 'extremists' and kept a fair distance from them. It was 'Abdullah who, until the outbreak of war, had kept tabs on the Arab nationalist movement and was inducted into their ranks, though only tangentially and formally. Referring to his brother 'Abdullah's relations with Arab nationalists before the war, Faisal said some-what disapprovingly in an interview: 'The Amir 'Abdallah represented Mecca in the Turkish parliament and he often came into contact with the chiefs of the Arab revolutionary movements in Constantinople. He ['Abdullah] himself disapproved strongly of the Turkish administration and when returning from his journeys between Mecca and Constantinople would impart not only his own views to his father, but also those of the Arabs who begged him to persuade the Amir to put himself at the head of the movement.'[25] But Faisal was also aware that for dynastic reasons, he had to be firmly on the side of his father in asserting the rights and privileges of the Hijaz against the encroachments of the central state under the CUP.

A combination of factors that converged in a very short period of time caused Faisal to change his previously adamant support for the empire. These factors undermined the foundations of his previous position and caused him to reassess his views radically on the desirability – even permissibility – of continuing to support the Ottoman Empire when it had fallen under the charge of the reckless triumvirate of Talat, Enver and Jamal. In addition to the clear determination of the unionists to destroy the Hijaz's autonomy when conditions were ripe was added the discovery of the Wahib documents. Faisal now had to fear for his father's and his brothers' lives, and the continuation of the sharifian dynasty. The argument that it was only the empire that could defend Arab lands was greatly weakened with the failure of the Suez campaign and the British landings in Basra in southern Mesopotamia. Arab lands might now well fall under the control of foreign powers as the Ottoman army's defensive capabilities were weakened by the draining of troops towards the Russian and Dardanelles fronts. Although the British were making reassuring comments about their lack of interest in controlling Arab lands, these had not yet been grounded in official agreements to allay Faisal's natural suspicion of British intentions. But what actually proved decisive in pushing Faisal firmly into the camp that pressed for an insurrection against the Turks was something else entirely. According to Faisal's own testimony, it was the brutal treatment meted out to the Arabs of Syria and the harsh measures of Jamal Pasha against Arab dissenters that tipped him into an open breach with the Ottoman Empire.

Faisal and the Syrian Arab nationalists

Sharif Hussein's choice of Faisal to spearhead the relationship with the Arab nationalists of Syria would at first appear unusual. It was 'Abdullah who had cultivated these contacts and had greater experience in dealing with their leadership. He was also temperamentally more inclined towards their aims and goals than Faisal. However, Hussein carefully matched specific tasks to the particular capabilities of his sons, and as 'Abdullah was the focal point for the exchanges with the British in Cairo, Faisal became the more appropriate choice for developing the connection with the Syrians. At the same time, he was a far better military commander than 'Abdullah, and could assess the capabilities of both the Ottoman forces in Syria as well as those of the dissident Arab movements. Although often hot-headed and impulsive in action, Faisal was also deliberative and calculating. His advice would be based on his cautious predisposition and a realistic assessment of the options available. Furthermore, Faisal's known partiality to the Ottoman cause would stand him in good stead in his dealings with the Porte, and might allay the suspicions of the CUP leadership about Hussein's intentions.[26]

Following the discovery of the Wahib documents, Sharif Hussein cabled the grand vizier and offered to send Faisal to Istanbul to discuss outstanding issues, including, of course, the case of the incriminating letters. The reply from the grand vizier was encouraging and Faisal set out for Istanbul, via Damascus. He arrived in Damascus on 26 March 1915 and stayed there for four weeks before proceeding to Istanbul.[27] The Bakri family, under their patriarch 'Ata Pasha al-Bakri, were his hosts throughout the period. Earlier in the year, Fawzi al-Bakri, Ata Pasha's eldest son, had arrived in Mecca to serve out his period in the Ottoman army, on secondment to Sharif Hussein's personal guard. Fawzi had been briefed by the secret societies, as he had recently joined al-Fatat, about their plans for an Arab state in the event of the Ottoman Empire's incapacity or defeat, and to sound out Sharif Hussein's position if he were to lead this movement. The message that Fawzi carried was that senior figures in Syria and Iraq, including Arab officers in the Ottoman army, were planning for Arab independence in the event that 'the Ottoman state was not able to effectively reform itself in a manner that would prevent foreigners from seizing the opportunity to occupy and colonise these [Arab] lands'.[28] Hussein was asked either to receive a delegation from the secret societies, or to send a trusted representative to meet with them in Damascus.

Prior to Faisal's arrival in Damascus, the two main secret societies had expanded their membership considerably. Al-Fatat had extended beyond its base amongst the Arab intelligentsia and government officials, and managed to attract leading tribal figures to its ranks. These included Shaikh Nuri al-Sha'lan, head of the powerful Ruwala tribe that effectively controlled the deserts between Syria and Arabia, and the Druze leader Nasib al-Atrash. Another recruit was General Ali Ridha Al-Rikabi, a prominent Arab officer in the Ottoman army who had fallen foul of the CUP. Meanwhile, al-Fatat and al-'Ahd, had established contact with each other, acting through a liaison, Yasin al-Hashimi, a Baghdadi officer who was the commander of a mainly Iraqi division of the Ottoman Fourth Army based in Syria.[29] Yasin was a long-standing member of the al-'Ahd society.

Faisal made a courtesy visit on Jamal Pasha who received him coolly. However, he was feted by all the leading notables of Damascus, and in these social settings he became well acquainted with the main protagonists of the Arab secret societies, especially al-Fatat. At first, the leaders of al-Fatat were hesitant about confiding their inner secrets to Faisal, especially as his pro-Turkish leanings were well known. In time, however, mutual trust began to grow as Faisal explained to them that his pro-Turkish position was more to do with his fear that European powers would come to dominate the Arab lands if the Ottoman Empire was further weakened or fell. They briefed him in detail about their organisation and plans, especially after Faisal had indicated that he would accept membership of al-Fatat. Faisal was administered the oath of the society, and in turn he informed them of the contents of Kitchener's letters to his father. Most of Faisal's meetings with the secret societies took place after midnight at the Bakri house, after the departure of the ordinary visitors who had come to greet him.[30] Faisal's induction into al-Fatat opened the door for him to meet the Arab officers who made up most of the membership of al-'Ahd society. Faisal in a 1933 interview recalled the period in the following terms:

In April 1915[31] I arrived in Damascus en route to Constantinople where I was going in order to fulfil the mission of which I had spoken [presenting the Wahib documents to the Porte]. At Damascus I met a great number of intellectuals, amongst whom were Bedawin [tribal leaders], notables of Damascus, Syrian *ulema*, and officers of an Arab division belonging to the Syrian Army Corps [the Ottoman Fourth Army]; one of the Chiefs of Staff was Yasin Pasha [al-Hashimi], the present Minister of Finance of Iraq. They all assured me that they were prepared to start the revolution and begged me to raise the standard of revolt.

I replied that I was only charged by my father to study the situation in Syria and the general aspect of affairs in Constantinople and that without the support of some powerful organisation or of one of the Great Powers, I could not accept the responsibility of a revolution (I was a moderate in those days!) and also that I must go to Constantinople and return by Syria to Mecca to report progress to my father.[32]

Faisal left Damascus for Istanbul in late April 1915. He was met with great fanfare and cordiality by all the leading figures of the empire, and was received by the sultan, allowing him to reiterate his family's loyalty to the Ottoman state and the person of the sultan.[33] He held several meetings with the grand vizier and with Talat and Enver. He relayed his father's deep concerns about the plots that were being hatched against him and set out the incriminating documents that were discovered in Wahib's baggage. Faisal was reassured by the responses he received from the leadership in Istanbul. However, the government was anxious to extract a call for a jihad from Sharif Hussein, and for his active support and participation in the war effort. Faisal carried letters to his father from the grand vizier, Talat and Enver, urging him to take this course of action.

Faisal also experienced the increasing pressures on the Ottoman Empire and the disquietude that had gripped senior figures in the capital. They had become alarmed by the dangerous direction towards which the empire was veering under the policies of the ruling triumvirate. A combined British, French and ANZAC landing had just taken place on 25 April 1915, in the Gallipoli peninsula. The ultimate objective of the assault was to seize Istanbul itself. Although the Ottoman armies put up a brilliant defence, which ulti-mately led to a great victory for the empire, the outcome of the battle in April and May of 1915 was still uncertain. In a later interview, Faisal said of his time in the capital:

> When I arrived in Constantinople, I found the situation very confused following the attack on the Dardanelles. My mission, which was to present my father's documents to the Sublime Porte was accomplished. The Porte disapproved of the conspiracy against the Amir and an inquiry was started. Meanwhile, I met several Ministers and Turkish notabilities, amongst them two generals who were considered the most experienced and far-seeing commanding officers in the Turkish army. Everyone advised me to return immediately to Arabia and to warn my father of this adventure of the Young Turks who, according to the two generals, were dragging the Empire to ruin. They even told me frankly that my father's duty was to save the Arab countries by joining the Allies, as the tragic end of the Ottoman Empire was fast approaching. The Turks were at that moment carrying their archives and their treasures into Anatolia. I decided then to join the extremists [proponents of Arabist demands] and to return at once to Mecca to help my father to save Arabia.[34]

The atmosphere of foreboding and gloom in the capital did not detract from the overall success of Faisal's visit. Not only had the offending Wahib been replaced by the more obliging Ghalib, but the Porte seemed more accepting of his father's authority and status.[35] However, Faisal had become finally convinced of the recklessness of the triumvirate's policies. It was very difficult to remain loyal to a CUP-dominated regime when the collapse of the empire and the occupation of Arab lands had become a real possibility. It was in Istanbul that he seriously reassessed his previously pro-Ottoman position.[36]

Faisal arrived in Damascus in late May 1915, and this time was received with great fanfare at the railroad station by Jamal Pasha himself. It was in marked contrast to his earlier visit to Damascus, when Faisal had registered a noted coolness towards himself. In fact Jamal had received messages from both Talat and Enver asking him to be particularly courteous and accommodating to Faisal. Enver encouraged Jamal to seek Faisal's advice on Arabian matters, while Talat urged Jamal to drop his reservations regarding Faisal and seek his friendship and support.[37] Faisal soon departed with Jamal for Jerusalem, the forward headquarters of the Ottoman Fourth Army, and visited the Sinai front. He gave a fervently patriotic speech at the banquet organised in his honour there, addressing the senior officers of the army corps. He could still publicly proclaim his support for the Ottoman cause. In his memoirs, Jamal Pasha makes Faisal swear to the audience, on the soul of the Prophet, his loyalty and fealty to the Ottoman cause.[38]

Upon his return to Damascus from the visit to the Sinai front and Jerusalem, Faisal once again stayed at the Bakri house. Visitors and emissaries from the secret societies continued to pour in. During his absence in Istanbul, al-'Ahd and al-Fatat leaders had drafted a protocol, setting out the terms and conditions for their cooperation with Britain in the war against the Ottoman Empire. Faisal was asked to carry the statement to his father in Mecca, and establish whether the protocol could form the basis of a concerted plan of action with the British. This was the first clear statement regarding the conditions set out by the secret societies for entering the war on the side of the Allies. It explicitly defined the meaning of an Arab state, which was roughly equivalent to all the Arabic-speaking lands of west Asia and areas where there were Arabic-speaking majorities such as Alexandretta and Cilicia. The statement also demanded the abolition of the exceptional privileges to foreigners under the Capitulations system.[39] The new Arab state was to have a defensive treaty with Britain and was to award it a preferential economic status.[40] The protocol that was discussed with Faisal (later known as the Damascus Protocol) was to serve as Sharif Hussein's key document in his negotiations with the British for his possible entry into the war.

Faisal's arrival in Damascus on the return leg of his journey back to Mecca came at a troubled time in Syria. Jamal Pasha's rule had turned repressive and bloody. A number of prominent figures in the Arab movement had been arrested in April 1915 for treason and were awaiting trial. As Faisal recalled later, 'In Syria [after his return from Istanbul], I found that the situation was extremely critical; all those whom I met begged me to enter into an agreement with the heads of the movement in order to discuss what was the best way to start freeing the country. I left for Mecca after having promised the members of the Secret Committees to persuade my father to conclude a treaty with the Allies and to return to Syria, where the revolution was to be proclaimed.'[41]

Faisal recognised that the plans and demands of the Arab nationalists were fraught with danger, and he was very concerned that the movement's leadership had seriously underestimated the risks of a revolt. Their capabilities and resources – military, political and financial – might be inadequate for the great task of launching a revolt in the midst of a global war. The bevy of visitors that came to the Bakri house to meet with Faisal included: Dr Ahmad Qadri, the secretary of al-Fatat branch in Damascus and one of the founders of the society; Dr 'Abd al-Rahman al-Shabandar, later a prominent member of Faisal's Arab government in Syria; General Ali Ridha Pasha al-Rikabi; and General Yasin Pasha al-Hashimi. It was Yasin's assurances about the vigour and resolve of the national movement that had the greatest effect on Faisal.[42] Yasin had a forceful personality that inspired trust and confidence. In addition, his voice carried weight as he was the chief of staff of the mainly Arab divisions of the Ottoman army in Syria. Any successful rebellion in Syria had to carry these divisions. After a long period of deliberations, Faisal asked Yasin what they expected from the Hijaz in terms of support. 'We ask for nothing and need nothing. We have all what we need. All we ask of you is to lead us and be in the vanguard,' said Yasin. Faisal offered to send Hijaz tribal detachments in support of the revolt in Syria, saying, 'We are in agreement with the tribal leaders of the Hijaz. They are loyal to us and are prepared to work with us.'

'We have no need of them,' came Yasin's confident reply.[43]

Faisal also met with other notables and prominent tribal and Druze leaders during his second visit to Damascus. Nearly all of them pressed upon him the need for action and expressed their support for Sharif Hussein as their leader in the event of revolt. As a token of their commitment, both Shaikh Badr al-Din al-Hassani, the leading 'alim (religious authority) of Damascus, and General Ali Ridha Pasha al-Rikabi, at that time head of the Damascus municipality, gave Faisal their signet rings. The latter two added their signatures to a manifesto that called upon Sharif Hussein to lead them as their king.[44]

Faisal's second visit to Damascus was not incidental to the evolution of the Arab Revolt, as some have claimed, but rather instrumental. The range of personalities who expressed near unanimity for action was unprecedented. There was also general agreement that the sharifian family members should act as the emblems and natural leaders of such a revolt. But equally importantly, a consensus was established that the guiding principles and justification for the revolt, and for seeking the support of Great Britain, was the document prepared by the al-Fatat leadership. The sharifian family's parochial and dynastic concerns were now intertwined with broader purposes. The fact that these two issues were linked in the minds of the nationalists and Faisal at this early stage is of signal importance in the road to the revolt. It undoubtedly was a major factor behind Sharif Hussein's re-engagement with the British after the hiatus of the early exchanges between Kitchener Storrs and 'Abdullah.

Before Faisal finally left Damascus, he had promised Jamal Pasha to raise a contingent of 1,500 Hijazi tribesmen under his leadership to join the Ottoman army on the Sinai front. The CUP leadership, and especially Jamal, saw this as a confirmation of Sharif Hussein's support for the Ottoman cause, and a way of entangling him in the war effort to keep him away from possible mischief-making.[45] Faisal returned to Mecca in mid-June 1915, and in his own words, 'explained all these circumstances to my father and told him of the desires of the Arabs; I also told him that, after having belonged to the moderate party, the changed situation and the prayers of the Arabs had influenced me to join them in begging him to take the lead in the revolutionary party.'[46] For the next six months Faisal remained in Mecca, witnessing the unfolding of momentous developments, both in Syria and in his father's relationships with the British. The deterioration of the nationalist position in Syria in this period fed directly into Hussein's negotiations with the British on a rising against the Turks.

Jamal and Arab dissent in Syria

Jamal was one of the few CUP leaders who was a dedicated pan-Islamist and was not known for any Turkish supremacist tendencies. His arrival in Syria was met with celebrations and festivities in all the main cities that he passed through. In his memoirs he wrote of the people of Syria: 'All the people of the land that I passed through were highly patriotic and loyal to the Ottoman cause. I was filled with joy when I saw and felt that the majority of the Arabs will not stint in sacrificing their all in this Great War to liberate the Islamic Caliphate [from foreign control].'[47] As soon as he was ensconced in his new position, Jamal drew into his advisory councils a number of personalities known for their Arabist tendencies. In a public speech in Damascus in January 1915, he encouraged the assertion of Arab rights within the Ottoman Empire and in the context of Arab–Turkish solidarity. 'Work for the elevation of the Arabs and Arabism. Renew your civilization . . . Nothing will repel evil more than the continuing unity of Arabs and Turks under one Caliph [and nothing worse] than their separation into two different entities.'[48] Jamal's conciliatory and accommodating policies were met positively by all the leading sections of Syrian society and augured an excellent start for his governorship. However, this honeymoon period was short-lived.

Soon after his arrival in Damascus, Jamal was given a dossier seized from the French consulate in Beirut containing documents that appeared to impli- cate a number of politicians and dignitaries in collusion with the French, in preparation for a possible French landing on the Syrian coast. But the docu- ments were obsolete and many of those accused had made their peace with the government and were loyally serving the Ottoman cause.[49] At first Jamal did not act against those whose names appeared in the incriminating documents, and adopted an attitude of wait and see. But in April 1915 he decided to act. He ordered the arrest of a number of political figures and young people, all known for their Arabist positions but not necessarily named in the offending documents. The detainees were then brought in front of a specially convened military court in Aley, in the foothills of the mountains east of Beirut. Thirteen of the defendants were found guilty of treason; a further seventy were sentenced to death in absentia. On 21 August 1915, eleven of the defendants were hanged in Burj (later Martyrs) Square in Beirut. They included scions of leading families of Lebanon and Syria (such as Saleh Haider of Baalbek), lawyers (Muhammad Mahmassani) and newspaper editors (Ali al-Armanazi). 'Abd al-Karim al-Khalil, the head of the Arab Literary Club and a supposed intimate of Jamal Pasha, was also one of those executed.

The Turkish novelist and feminist Halidé Edib, who was visiting Syria and Lebanon to inspect schools at the invitation of Jamal Pasha, wrote of the profoundly disturbing effects of the executions, not only on the Arabs but also on Turkish officers. Colonel Fuad Bey, who regularly called on Edib and her companions, told her about the executions. 'I came to Beirut on the day of the executions. It was before the government house. There were a series of gallows and some had already been executed. There was one among them who marched among the condemned. He had been a reserve officer and wore a *calpak* [a type of hat]. He was quiet and entirely above the fear of death. He sat on one of the benches and smoked until his turn came. He chose his own particular gallows, and he passed the knot around his neck and said, "Born an Arab, I have served the Arabs, and I am dying for the Arabs." I was so much hurt at the idea of killing this great Arab that I did not even ask his name. But the Syrians would know him.'[50] Jamal followed these executions with a widespread purge of the Arab officers of the Fourth Army and their reassignment to the various fronts, away from the Arab heartland.

A second wave of arrests of leading figures in Syria and Lebanon took place in the autumn of 1915. This dragnet was more sweeping than the April arrests and was aimed at those who symbolised the nationalist movement, rather than those specifically mentioned in the dossiers of the French consulate. In fact there were only three people who were arrested in this batch and whose names had been quoted in the dossiers. The military court found most of the defendants guilty but avoided handing out death sentences.[51] However, Jamal did impose death sentences on twenty-one of the defendants. They were publicly executed on 6 May in Beirut and Damascus. The executed included: 'Abd al-Hamid al-Zahrawi, a member of the Ottoman upper chamber; Shafiq al-Mouayyad; Shukri al-Asali; Amir Omar al-Jaza'iri (the latter three were members of the Ottoman chamber of deputies); and a number of political and literary figures such as 'Abd al-Ghani al-'Uraisi, editor of al-Fatat newspaper *al-Mufid*. Zahrawi was in fact executed without a trial.

What were the reasons that prompted Jamal to such draconian action when his rule had begun on a note of concord and harmony? Jamal himself has attributed his actions to plans to organise a revolt in Syria that would lead to the establishment of an Arab caliphate under British protection and to install an Arab prince to rule Syria and the Levant. Although he had tried to work with the nationalists (or 'reformers' as he called them), they had been insincere and were constantly conspiring with the enemy. A number of incidents had heightened his suspiciousness, not least the attack by Bedouins on sailors who had survived the sinking of a German warship in the Red Sea. Jamal believed that it was Sharif Hussein who was responsible for instigating the attack. According to Jamal, Hussein was obviously trying to send a signal to the British, indicating that he would not tolerate any German presence in the Hijaz. The defeat of the Suez Canal offensive and the entry of the Italians on the side of the Entente – which effectively bottled up the Syrian coast from access to the rest of the world – were additional factors that made Jamal feel besieged. But Jamal was a rigid person, who assumed that all Muslims, especially Arabs, should share in his pan-Islamic sentiments.[52] Lukewarm support for the Ottoman war effort, or any signs of hesitancy or criticism, would be greatly magnified by such a personality, and conflated with betrayal and treason. Jamal also pointedly notes in his memoirs that meting out drastic punishment for the elites and notables was to send a powerful signal that no one should feel safe from his fury if found guilty of disloyalty.[53] Jamal's insistence on ordering executions when his own staff, as well as the government in Istanbul and its German military advisers,[54] were urging him to caution and moderation, is indicative more of an unbending and stubborn will, rather than cold calculation.

Jamal's reign of terror had its desired effect. The nationalist movement in Syria was effectively smashed, its leaders killed or in exile and the Arab officers in Syria, who would have been crucial to any successful rising in Syria, scattered to distant fronts. The consequences for Faisal, including a potential uprising, were very disturbing. Faisal saw that many of his friends and associates had been arrested, cowed into silence, or reassigned away from Syria. Remembering those times, Faisal said, 'During these three months [since his departure from Damascus], the Turkish authorities had dispersed a great number of Syrian and Iraqi nationalists; some had been hanged; others imprisoned or expatriated far away in Anatolia. The twenty-fifth Division, composed of Arab officers and men, which was to have been the kernel of the Revolutionary Army, and also the officers of the reserve, all young nationalists, had been sent to Romania and Galicia. The psychological moment for a rising had passed.'[55]

The Hussein–McMahon letters

Faisal's return from Damascus and Istanbul and his report on the conditions in empire and in the Syrian provinces provided vital new information and assessments, and prompted the reopening by his father of the channels with the British. Although Faisal was by now a convert to the idea of revolt if all other options failed, he was still not prepared to counsel an immediate uprising. He recommended to his father that any uprising should be delayed until conditions were more propitious, when the Turks had either been mauled in battle or the Allies had landed on the Syrian coast. During the family's retreat to their summer residence in Ta'if, away from the prying eyes of informers, the brothers debated with their father about the plans and timing for a revolt. Faisal's cautionary approach was finally set aside in favour of 'Abdullah's forceful call for a commitment to a revolt against the Turks. It was in the Ta'if meetings of July 1915 that the date of a possible revolt was set for June 1916.[56] The decision to launch a revolt was made at a time when the extent of Jamal's crackdown on the nationalists in Syria was not yet clear. The Hijaz and Syria were to anchor the revolt. At this stage the provinces of Iraq did not feature in the planning for the uprising, nor did other Arab provinces and districts of the Ottoman Empire under local rulers and amirs such as ibn Saud in Nejd, the Idrisi in 'Asir, or Imam Yahya in Yemen.

Hussein reopened the formal contacts with the British in Egypt, after a gap of several months. At first, the contents of Hussein's notes were not taken too seriously by the British authorities in Cairo. Storrs in his memoirs makes scathing comments about the pretensions of Sharif Hussein to lead the Arabs, raising familiar objections about Arab disarray and the expected rejection of other Arab rulers of Hussein's claims.[57] Sir Henry McMahon's answer to Sharif Hussein, dated 30 August 1915,[58] was non-committal regarding the borders of an independent Arab state, and simply welcomed Hussein's offers of friendship between the Arabs and Britain. Hussein was very upset with regard to McMahon's letter. It seemed to him to be evasive and cold in tone, and he said as much in his response, which was received in Cairo on 17 October. Hussein reiterated to McMahon the significance of an agreement regarding the new Arab state's borders, irrespective of the conflicts and disputes that existed inside Arab lands.[59] An impasse was building, with Hussein insisting on the demarcation of borders of the new Arab state as an essential precondition to a rising, and McMahon continuing to display Britain's non-committal and ambiguous position on the meaning, size and powers of an Arab state or states.

However, concurrent with these first exchanges, a development of prime importance occurred that profoundly affected British policy towards the issue of an Arab revolt. A young Arab Ottoman officer, Lieutenant Muhammad Sharif al-Faruqi, from a well-known Mosul family, had crossed the lines on the

Gallipoli front to the British forces.[60] Faruqi, a member of the secret al'Ahd society, insisted to the British that he was not a deserter but a bearer of important information regarding conditions in the Arab provinces. In Cairo, Faruqi held several meetings with Colonel Gilbert Clayton, head of British military intelligence. Faruqi spoke of the existence of a wide network of support for the secret societies in the Arab lands and that they were determined to achieve independence for the Arabs, preferably through cooperation with the British, but if that was not forthcoming, with the Germans if necessary. Faruqi appeared knowledgeable about the exchanges between Sharif Hussein and the British in Cairo, and was aware of the contents of the Damascus Protocol. Clayton's interviews with Faruqi convinced him that the British authorities had to respond more encouragingly to Sharif Hussein's calls for a territorially demarked Arab state, otherwise the opportunity to instigate an Arab rising, spearheaded by the secret societies, would be missed. Clayton's assessments of the urgency of the situation were strongly supported by General Sir John Maxwell, the head of the British military in Egypt, as well as by McMahon. All called for a re-examination of Britain's previously reserved policy towards an independent Arab state and a more positive engagement with Hussein's demands.[61] Edward Grey, the British foreign secretary, allowed McMahon to draft a letter to Sharif Hussein that embodied the new policy assessments, prompted by Faruqi's interviews and disclosures.[62] Reginald Wingate even suggested that the message to Sharif Hussein should commit the British government to 'recognise and support . . . the principle of Arabian independence within the boundaries defined on behalf of the Arab people by the Sharif Mecca'.[63] But McMahon chose to amplify as well as obfuscate the latitude given to him by Grey and produced his note to Sharif Hussein of 24 October 1915. This is the most decisive document in the entire exchanges between McMahon and Sharif Hussein, as it set out the British commitments regarding the boundaries of an independent Arab state.

> The districts of Mersin and Alexandretta, and portions of Syria lying to the west of the districts of Damascus, Homs, Hama and Aleppo, cannot be said to be purely Arab, and must on that account be excepted from the proposed delimitation. Subject to that modification, and without prejudice to the treaties concluded between us and certain Arab Chiefs, we accept that delimitation. As for the regions lying within the proposed frontiers, in which Great Britain is free to act without detriment to interests of her ally France, I am authorized to give you the following pledges on behalf of the Government of Great Britain, and to reply as follows to your note: That subject to the modifications stated above, Great Britain is prepared to recognize and uphold the independence of the Arabs in all the regions lying within the frontiers proposed by the Sharif of Mecca.[64]

Hussein's response was quick. In a letter of 5 November 1915, Hussein accepted removing Alexandretta and Mersin from the proposed Arab state, but rejected any concessions (to France) regarding the Syrian coast and the Christian parts of Mount Lebanon. Hussein also conceded that parts of Iraq under British occupation could be excluded from the Arab state, but only for a short while, presumably until the end of hostilities. The correspondence between McMahon and Hussein regarding strictly territorial issues continued until the middle of January 1916, and there were sufficient grounds for Sharif Hussein to believe that his demands for an Arab state – broadly within his understanding of McMahon's sometimes encouraging, sometimes ambiguous statements – would be honoured if he launched a revolt. Throughout the first period of exchanging notes with McMahon, Hussein kept 'Abdullah by his side as his main adviser. Faisal and Ali went to Medina, both to allay any Turkish suspicions regarding the contacts with the British and to prepare the volunteer force that Faisal had agreed to lead to join the Ottoman forces on the Suez front.

Faisal returns to Damascus

Jamal Pasha had held Faisal to his promise to bring a detachment of 1,500 Hijazi volunteers to the Suez front and sent several reminders regarding their despatch. Faisal felt that he could not hold out for much longer in Medina without arousing serious mistrust on the part of Jamal. 'I was daily receiving the most alarming news from Syria concerning people who were suspected of having been in touch with me and urgent telegrams arrived daily from Jamal Pasha insisting on my return to Syria with the contingent promised by my father as reinforcement for the army in Sinai,' Faisal said.[65] In early January 1916, Faisal arrived in Damascus at the head of a forty-strong detachment of his personal cavalry that included a number of his relatives. This was to be the advance guard of the promised Hijazi volunteer force. It could also act as his personal bodyguard in case Jamal took action against him. As usual Faisal stayed at the house of the Bakris and Jamal provided him with an office at his military headquarters. Faisal's cavalry detachment was quartered at a farm owned by the Bakris on the outskirts of Damascus.

It wasn't long before Faisal found out that the situation in Syria had changed beyond recognition from his stay there several months earlier. Jamal's severe measures, directed against all those who could have formed the backbone of an uprising, had proved effective. Executions, arrests, deportations and reassignments had effectively drained the vitality of the nationalist camp. According to a contemporary account, nearly five thousand Syrian families, many of them notables, were deported to Anatolia.[66] Syria was totally quiescent and the nationalist movement, where it still lingered, had been driven underground.

Furthermore, the economic conditions in Syria and Lebanon were appalling, and the countries were about to experience a terrible famine.[67] These factors all conspired to eliminate the chances of a successful uprising.[68] Faisal's arrival in Damascus also coincided with news of the withdrawal of the Anglo-French forces from Gallipoli in January 1916, which provided a major boost to the confidence of the leadership in Istanbul.

Faisal's assessments of the deteriorating position in Syria played a part in modifying Hussein's position in his later correspondence with McMahon. No revolt that was based mainly on the Hijaz could be launched without British support. In an undated letter to his father, probably in March 1916, he wrote: 'The people of Damascus are in great hardship and despair as a result of present circumstances.' Erzurum and Bitlis in eastern Anatolia had just fallen into Russian hands, with great losses for the Ottoman armies. Faisal feared that the Russians would advance to Diyarbakir, close to the Arab heartlands of Syria and Iraq. Arab areas might then be severed from Turkish ones with no military capability for defence. Without an Arab force able to withstand a Russian attack, Arab lands would be wide open to the invaders. He urged his father to organise an Arab army as a matter 'of utmost necessity', to 'defend the Arab heartlands and the gates to the two Holy Shrines [Mecca and Medina]'.[69] Faisal was clearly driven by a real fear that the Ottoman war effort, under the misguided policies and poor leadership of the CUP, was leading the empire – and the Arabs – into a disaster. Even at this late a stage, the desirability, let alone the certainty, of an uprising against the Turks was not a foregone conclusion. Faisal still hoped that a revolt could be side-stepped if the Turks drastically modified their war policies and treatment of Arabs, and allowed for genuine power-sharing in the empire. This option, however, was rapidly becoming untenable.

In February 1916, the war minister Enver Pasha arrived in Syria to investigate the deployment and formations of the Fourth Army, and on Jamal's suggestion agreed to visit Medina accompanied by Jamal Pasha and Faisal. There were other dignitaries in the party, including religious leaders from a number of Arab towns. An invitation was extended to Sharif Hussein to join the visiting group, but Hussein declined, perhaps fearing the worst, and remained in Mecca. However, Faisal, on behalf of his father, presented Enver and Jamal with two inlaid swords as gifts and as tokens of his loyalty.[70] The visit, which was designed to show the extent of Arab support for the Ottoman war effort and to exhibit the religious credentials of the CUP leadership, was widely reported on and hailed as a success. Enver, apparently overwhelmed with emotion, broke down in tears at the Prophet's tomb. But the underlying tensions were still there. Faisal, Enver and Jamal also inspected the Arab volunteers of the Hijazi force. 'Are all these volunteers for the Holy War?' asked

Enver. 'Yes,' replied Faisal. 'Willing to fight to the death against the enemies of the faithful?' continued Enver. 'Yes,' replied Faisal, leaving the definition of 'the faithful' out of his reply. During the parade one of Faisal's men whispered in his ear, seeking his permission to shoot Enver and Jamal as a prelude to taking over Medina. But Faisal would have none of it. He dismissed the suggestion by saying that the two men were guests and that it was degrading for Arabs to betray a guest, no matter the extent of the enmity between them. In fact Faisal kept close watch over the two Ottoman generals to make sure that no harm befell them, and returned with them to Damascus.[71]

While he was still negotiating with the British in Cairo, Hussein had not quite closed the door on the Turks. He had procrastinated with their demands to declare a jihad against the Entente, and had held back sending his volunteers to the Suez front. After his Medina visit, however, Enver had become more insistent on a clear demonstration of Hussein's support for the Ottoman war effort. On his return to Istanbul Enver cabled the sharif demanding that he declare a jihad and immediately send volunteers to the front. Weapons for the Hijazi volunteers were already being stockpiled in Medina. Hussein was now put on the spot and could not temporise much longer without arousing grave suspicions.

On 16 March Hussein cabled the grand vizier, for the first time linking his support for the war to a series of measures that he expected the government to take to regain Arab trust and confidence. The demands were bold and landed as a thunderbolt on the Istanbul authorities and on Jamal, who was made privy to them: a declaration of amnesty for all political prisoners; Syria and Iraq to be granted a decentralised political system; confirmation of the amirate of Mecca to the dynasty of his family through his sons, and respecting its traditional rights that were granted it since the time of Sultan Salim. If these demands were met, Hussein wrote, 'the Arab nation would perform its duties out of loyalty [to the Ottoman state], and I will commit to mobilise the Arab tribes for jihad, under the command of my sons, for the fields of battle in Iraq and Palestine . . . And if these demands are not met, then I ask you not to expect me to participate in a war that I advised should not be started . . . and it will suffice me to pray for the state's victory and glory.'[72]

The response of the grand vizier and Enver was summarily dismissive of Hussein's demands – or pretensions as they saw them – and included a thinly veiled warning to keep Faisal with the Fourth Army until the end of the war.[73] Hussein immediately cabled the grand vizier and Enver rejecting these warnings and defiantly added, regarding Faisal, 'As for my son Faisal, I have not sent him to you and I do believe that I shall see him again. Do what you will then.'[74] The grand vizier responded with a more conciliatory cable and offered that Jamal Pasha would discuss the issue of the political prisoners directly with

Faisal. In his response Hussein insisted that the Hijazi volunteers would not leave for the front without Faisal at their head. The grand vizier agreed that Faisal would be allowed to return to Medina to accompany the volunteers to Damascus, but also asked that Ali be recalled back to Mecca because of his disagreements with the governor. Hussein then cabled, 'Upon the return of Sharif Faisal Bey, Sharif Ali Bey will leave Medina.'[75]

Jamal Pasha had been given a précis of the exchanges between Hussein and the Porte. In Jamal's memoirs, Hussein's messages appeared to be far more inflammatory and challenging to Ottoman authority that what actually transpired.[76] Jamal called Faisal to a meeting to discuss the contents of these cables and asked General Ali Fouad, chief of staff of the Fourth Army, to be in attendance to witness the discussions. Faisal had been pleading with Jamal to show clemency towards the political prisoners. Jamal started by complaining to Faisal about the conduct of his brother Ali in Medina, and his appropriation of powers that were legitimately the governor's. He stated that he had always respected the rights and privileges of the amir of Mecca, and stood by his side against the intrigues against him, not least from his own clan (presumably the *dhawi* Zaids in Istanbul). He then handed Faisal the cable from Enver, which supposedly summarised the exchanges between Sharif Hussein and the Porte. According to Jamal Pasha, Faisal became agitated and his colour changed. Faisal exclaimed his deep regrets at the cable and assured him of his father's loyalty and good intentions.[77] Following these discussions with Faisal, Jamal, on his own initiative, sent a cable to Hussein refusing to pardon traitors and holding Hussein to task for bringing up the matter of a hereditary amirate in the Hijaz at a time when the empire was at war and all resources had to be mobilised in its defence. He ended with a thinly veiled warning that even if Hussein was granted his demands, in the event of victory, what would 'stop the government from dealing with you in the harshest terms after the end of the war?'[78]

Faisal continued to visit Jamal Pasha on an almost daily basis to seek pardons for the accused. The Aley military court had already passed its verdict on them. The exchanges with Jamal now revolved almost exclusively around this matter. Faisal carried the added burden of having to represent the pleas of the numerous dignitaries who called on him and sought his intercession with Jamal on behalf of the accused.[79] Although Jamal had accepted Faisal's lunch invitation at the al-Bakri estate in al-Qabun on the outskirts of Damascus, where Faisal persisted in his pleadings, Jamal was unyielding in his determination to see the accused executed. A few days later, on 6 May 1916, the accused were hanged.

Faisal received the news of the executions while he was staying at the Bakri farmhouse at Qabun. A special edition of *al-Sharq* newspaper, a mouthpiece for Jamal Pasha's policies, had carried the details of the trial and the executions, and was being distributed free on the day of the executions. A runner had brought the paper to Faisal while he was breakfasting with his hosts. One of the Bakris read out the terrible news and a hush descended on the assemblage, punctuated by quiet invocations for the dead. 'Then like one suddenly demented, Faisal leapt to his feet and tearing his *kufiya* [headgear] from his head, flung it down and trampled on it savagely with a cry of: "*Tab al-maut ya 'Arab*" (Death has become sweet O Arabs!).'[80] It was time to take up arms. But first Faisal had to get out of Damascus.

Earlier in April, Jamal had received Hussein's response to his cable. Hussein reiterated his request that the government grant a pardon to all political prisoners. This response had infuriated Jamal. He called in Faisal and warned him in no uncertain terms about the actions of his father and his brother Ali in Medina. Jamal complained that in spite of the goodwill shown his family, Ali had grossly interfered in the affairs of Medina. While the Ottomans were equipping the Hijazi volunteers for action on the Suez front, Faisal's father had shown separatist tendencies. Jamal addressed Faisal: 'If you want to maintain our friendship then you have to obey the laws of friendship. However, if you have other intentions then you had better resort to arms and revolt, putting an end to this masquerade and each would then be the other's open enemy, and the affair would be left to God [to decide]. If you hold no evil indentions then write to your brother Ali to come to Damascus at once and to slop abrogating the governor's powers.'[81] According to Jamal, Faisal then said to him, with his hand on his heart, 'My apologies Excellency! How can you attribute to us these accusations? How can we be traitors when we are descendants of the Prophet and we are the most loyal subjects of the Caliphate? My father, brother and I are not traitors to the people or the government. We are servants to those who are loyal and faithful to our honoured Sultan, who has showered us with his blessings. Be assured that I will mediate in the dispute between Basri Pasha [the governor of Medina] and my brother, and I will instruct my brother to come [to Damascus] to kiss your hands [pledge his allegiance].'[82] Jamal's warnings were backed by more forceful action. A contingent of 3,500 Turkish troops had arrived in Medina, ostensibly heading for Yemen, but with the potential to be deployed to enforce whatever measures the Turks might take against Sharif Hussein and his family.[83]

Jamal's strategy was to secure both Faisal and Ali as hostages in Damascus, but Faisal suspected as much and prepared for his escape from Syria. His presence in Syria was too dangerous now, especially as he had given up hope that any Syrian military support for a revolt would be forthcoming. Faisal had been awaiting the results of an Ottoman conscription drive, which was to raise nearly a hundred thousand additional troops, most of whom would undoubtedly be Arab. But the newly raised Arab formations were quickly dispersed to other fronts and Syria was effectively under the control of mainly Turkish units.[84] Faisal went to see Jamal Pasha in mid-May 1916 to inform him that his father had ordered Ali to march with the Hijazi volunteers to the Suez front, and that he, Faisal, sought Jamal's permission to join his brother in Medina, after which both would march to Jerusalem with the volunteers. His presence with the volunteers would greatly boost their morale and fighting spirit. Jamal agreed, surprisingly given his deep suspicions about Hussein's intentions. However, he must have felt reassured that the presence of large numbers of Turkish troops, as well as the despatch of Fakhri Pasha, an experienced Ottoman general, to Medina would give him the wherewithal to crush a revolt, march on to Mecca, and arrest the sharif and all his sons if the worst came to the worst.

Faisal left Damascus for Medina by rail on 16 May 1916, accompanied by his close friend Nasib al-Bakri and three other dignitaries delegated by Jamal, leaving his bodyguards at al-Qabun as guests of the Bakris. The guards were to await further instructions on when to leave for the Hijaz. Faisal was elated at finally escaping Jamal's clutches. He was met in Medina by large crowds, and went to stay at his brother's house. In the afternoon, Faisal visited the Mosque of the Prophet in Medina. Asif Bey, one of the notables who had accompanied him on the journey to Medina and the legal adviser to the Fourth Army, approached Faisal in the mosque. With tears streaming he warned Faisal, 'If you can escape do so, and don't return to Damascus, for they [Jamal and the CUP leadership] wish you ill. I am telling you this in deference to your ancestor [the Prophet] who is buried in this shrine.'[85]

Hussein was rapidly reaching a decision. His negotiations with the British led him to believe that they had by and large accepted his understanding of the boundaries of a future Arab state. Exceptions, such as the degree of French influence on the northern Syrian coast, were only to be temporarily entertained because of the exigencies of war. In his letter to McMahon of 18 February 1916, Hussein expressed delight at McMahon's support for a strong alliance between Britain and a future Arab state. He had assumed, or perhaps wanted to assume, that all the vital matters that might have impeded an Arab revolt backed by the British had now been resolved, leaving only the details to be sorted out later. By mid-May 1916, communications with the British were mainly to do with supplies, logistics, and financial support for a possible revolt. At the same time, the tone of messages emanating from Jamal's headquarters, as well as from Istanbul, was becoming increasingly menacing.[86]

Hussein was acutely sensitive to the dangers that faced his sons, Faisal and Ali. The Turks had assembled enough forces in the Hijaz to oust him if necessary. The flows of exchanges with the Porte and with Jamal, and the disposition of Turkish forces, were all indicating imminent action against him. But for a conservative and deeply religious man, a definitive rupture with the Ottoman

Empire was not a task that could be lightly entered. Nevertheless, Hussein believed that he had exhausted all the options with the CUP-led state, and that for his family's sake, for the sake of the dynasty, for the sake of the Hijaz, and for the sake of the cause that he had recently embraced – that of the Arab nation – he had to act. He informed Faisal by secret cipher of his decision to launch the revolt in early June 1916. Faisal pleaded with his father in a long letter to delay the revolt until at least August of 1916. The harvest would be in by then and the tribes would be well provisioned for the coming period of confrontation and fighting. Hussein said in his reply that Faisal had to hasten in preparing for the revolt since time was of the essence. There was no room left for delay.

Faisal called in Jamal's delegates who had travelled with him to Medina and informed them that he intended to stay behind in Medina with his brother to attend to some urgent business. The departure of the volunteers was being held up since their mode of transport had not been settled, whether by train to Damascus or directly to the front. Once this matter was resolved, Faisal would leave for Damascus. Meanwhile, there was no need for them to stay in Medina and he instructed the volunteers to return to Damascus. Amongst those whom Faisal asked to leave was his friend Nasib, possibly to allay any suspicions of conspiracy. Faisal had agreed with Nasib that once he received a telegram reading, 'Send the brown horses', that would be the signal that the revolt was imminent. As soon as Nasib reached Damascus he arranged for his family to depart immediately for Mecca, and three days later, towards the end of May, the coded cable arrived. Nasib went to his family's estates at Qabun where Faisal's bodyguard detachments were still awaiting him, and together they left at night for the Hijaz by way of the Iraqi desert. Jamal, who was in Beirut when these events were happening, sent a detachment in pursuit of the group, but it was too late. Their whereabouts were lost in the trackless wilderness.[87]

On 30 May Faisal and Ali went to see the newly arrived Fakhri Pasha, now commander of the Ottoman forces in Medina. Fakhri was an intensely religious man and firmly believed in the sanctity of the Ottoman cause, but was also conciliatory in his attitude to Arabs.[88] Faisal and Ali showed him the contents of Enver's 12 May cable to their father and asserted that they could no longer continue to cooperate with the Ottoman authorities under such threats. Accordingly, Ali was to leave Medina and return to Mecca. Faisal would continue to remain in Medina, however, to prepare for the departure of the volunteers to the Suez front. Fakhri apologised to the brothers asserting that the cable was drafted in a hurry and expressing his wish that all the outstanding issues between the Porte and Sharif Hussein be resolved. The tensions appeared to be defused. At about the same time, the brothers had entertained Fakhri Pasha at the volunteers' camp at Sayidunna Hamza,[89] a dozen miles outside of

Mecca. Fakhri Pasha saw for himself the preparations for the volunteers' departure and their high fighting spirit.[90]

On 1 June, Ali left Medina. He gave his farewell greetings to Basri Pasha, the governor, and Fakhri Pasha, explaining that he intended to stay the night at the Sayidunna Hamza camp, after which he would depart for Mecca. Faisal accompanied Ali to the camp, supposedly to bid him farewell before Ali's departure to Mecca. On the morning of 2 June, Faisal and Ali sent a number of letters to Fakhri Pasha, carried by a Turkish officer who was acting as Faisal's aide-de-camp. The first letter addressed to Fakhri Pasha was from Faisal and read, 'As those in the government had thought the worse of us and since this [attitude] has affected our ability to work with the government, we have returned to Mecca according to our father's instructions as we cannot continue to stay here.'[91] The other two letters were coded, from Sharif Hussein to Jamal Pasha and to the grand vizier. In these, Hussein informed the government that he would not participate in the second Suez campaign until his conditions, which had been set out in his cables to Enver Pasha two months earlier, were met.[92] Jamal later received a coded letter from Faisal, which read, 'I have received an order to stop the transport of the volunteers to Syria for reasons I hope to explain to you in person later when we meet. I have been greatly distressed by the new circumstances; and I am pained that I will not be able to see you again until the issues [between us] are resolved satisfactorily. I am honoured to inform you that I am leaving for Mecca to spend some time there.'[93] The message was hedged and ambiguous, and did not carry any imputations that hostilities were imminent.

Faisal and Ali quickly abandoned the camp and departed from Sayidduna Hamza on the evening of 1 June, with their personal guards and two hundred warriors. They left for a point on the Mecca–Medina route, but doubled back to Abyar Ali near Medina on 2 June. There they sent out calls to the tribes and within a week nearly six thousand fighters had assembled at their new base. For a week the brothers awaited the response to their father's messages to the Turks. None was forthcoming. On 9 June the Arab forces under their command cut the railroad near Medina. A force from the Medina garrison led personally by Fakhri Pasha came out to repel the attackers at the Muhit railroad point near Medina. The battle raged for over a day with the Arabs finally withdrawing to Bi'r al-Mashi. They had run out of ammunition. A second retreat was ordered and the Arab forces withdrew to al-Ghadir, where the two brothers separated. Faisal pulled back with his forces to the small Red Sea port of Yanbu'. Ali stayed in al-Ghadir, preparing for battle and awaiting the formal launch of the revolt.

On 10 June, Arab forces attacked the Turks in towns across the Hijaz. In Mecca on the same day Sharif Hussein formally proclaimed the beginning of the Arab Revolt.

✦✦✦✦✦ ✖ ✦✦✦✦✦

CHAPTER 5

THE ARAB REVOLT I:
CONSOLIDATING THE REVOLT

T HE DECISION to launch the revolt against the Ottoman Empire was taken by one man: Sharif Hussein. Faisal, pushed and pulled in different directions by conflicting sentiments and calculations, had no choice but to agree to his father's verdict. Unlike 'Abdullah, who was at times recklessly eager in his enthusiasm to challenge the Ottomans, Faisal had been more deliberative and more aware of the fateful consequences that might accompany such a venture. But events were happening so fast that reflection was almost impossible. The margins for delay and procrastination were rapidly reduced by conflicting pressures from all sides for commitment and action: from the British, from the Ottomans, from the Arab nationalists, as well as from military exigencies and the outcome of battles and campaigns. Inaction, even while awaiting clarification from, and improvement of terms with, the British, was no longer a viable option. The risk of the discovery of the secret correspondence and contacts with Cairo grew daily, while the Ottomans were laying on the pressure for a clear demonstration of the sharif's enthusiasm for the war effort. The parallel exchanges between Mecca and the Porte were not merely subterfuges meant to deflect attention from the sharif's increasing entanglements with the British; they had their own realities, and not only as a fallback position in the event that the negotiations with the British had to be abandoned. If Enver had acceded, or at least acknowledged, the seriousness of the sharif's demands, and the anxieties and fears that underlay them, Sharif Hussein might well have concluded that a revolt would no longer be necessary to meet his objectives. It would have been far preferable at that time to remain within the bounds of a centuries-old relationship than to leap into the unknown in an untested alliance with the British, who, moreover, were locked into their own pact with the less palatable French. But other questions also loomed in the minds of Sharif Hussein and his sons. What would be the fate of the Hijaz and the Arab provinces if they continued in their loyalty to the empire and the war ended in an Entente victory? Would they not surely fall under foreign control, occupation and division as enemy territory? And how would a triumphant triumvirate of Enver, Talat and Jamal deal with the obdurate amir of Mecca if the Ottomans prevailed or were spared the division of their lands?

At the age of thirty-three, Faisal was thrust into a path that for sheer drama and eventfulness would have few parallels in modern times. But preparation for the trials and tests ahead were incomplete at best. He had never fought a modern army before; his previous encounters with recalcitrant Bedouin tribes and the Idrisi forces were quite unlike confronting a better equipped modern army. His political skills were honed at an early age – amongst the tribes of Arabia, with parliamentarians in the Ottoman assembly, with crafty and suspicious Ottoman officials, with hot-headed nationalists and dignified notables – but they were all within the confines of a world that he understood. His exposure to the west and to western ways and people had been sparse at best, limited to the few foreign diplomats and German officers he had encountered in Istanbul. His knowledge of international affairs was seen through the prism of the late Ottoman Empire, its disastrous retreats and its vulnerabilities, and his newfound concern with Arabs and Arab issues had to be integrated into an equally pervasive concern with the dangers of leaving the Ottoman fold only to fall into the tight grasp of foreign powers. His fear, exaggerated though it may have been, that Russian victories against the Ottomans would open the pathway to the conquest of Arab lands, was symptomatic of this abiding concern. This would seep out, and even erupt, to colour his actions in the future, whenever the issue of Arab national rights and freedoms would appear threatened or constrained by imperial powers. Faisal was acutely aware of the limitations of the power of the amir of Mecca and the imbalance that existed between the Hijaz and the Ottoman state, and later between the Arab states and Britain and France. This engendered a healthy caution, but never paralysed him when he felt that there was room for action. In those days of early June 1916, however, Faisal was not swept along by the euphoria of the rebel embarking on a fateful adventure; he was compelled more by the inevitability of action when all other alternative avenues were closing. The hints that some final compromise would obviate the need to declare war on the Ottomans was the clear undertone of his final exchanges with Fakhri Pasha and Jamal Pasha. It was not a position that a defiant rebel would take when throwing the gauntlet down to his oppressors; rather, it was the recognition that a long-enduring partnership was in its last throes, but with a faint, lingering hope that the relationship could still be salvaged.

Raising the standard of revolt

The revolt that was prematurely launched in Medina had started with barely any military preparations, and with ill-trained tribal detachments, poor equipment and little financial resources. The element of surprise was barely sufficient to keep the momentum of the revolt going, and in Medina the revolt came perilously close to being throttled at its inception. The early battles with the Turks showed the deplorable condition of organisation, logistics and supplies of the insurrectionists, and no amount of bravery and leadership skills on the part of Faisal could overcome these inherent weaknesses. His contingents were drawn from the tribes of the Medina area, most of whom were loyal to the cause of the sharifians. They had been worked on for months by Sharif Ali, and this incessant parleying with the tribal chiefs drew the ire of the Turkish commanders, both in Medina and further up the chain in Damascus and Istanbul.[1] The tribes, however, had complex motivating factors that made them fickle allies. Money, plunder and loot, resentment of other tribes, blood feuds and personal aggrandisement were all mixed up with a fear of the Ottomans and their retribution, as well as loss of their stipends and privileges. A deep realism, bordering on amoral cynicism, and a healthy respect for power prevailed in their dealings with all established authority and those who sought to challenge it. The tribal chiefs of the Medina region – the Harb, Juhayna, Billi, Banu Salem, Masrouh, and the branches of the great tribal confederations of Anizah and Utaiba – were all drawn into Ali and Faisal's plans when the hour came.

However, the first encounters with the well-equipped and numerous Ottoman forces in Medina proved dispiriting. The tribal Arabs were subjected to artillery barrages to which they were not accustomed, and they became terrified of the exploding shells. Faisal and Ali rode out in the open in front of the men to rally them and to show their disdain for the shells, but to no avail. The weapons that they had, mainly antiquated rifles, were no match for the Ottoman arms. Some of the tribal detachments left the battlefield to seek shelter, but others, such as the Bani Ali, approached Fakhri Pasha with an offer to surrender if their villages were not despoiled. While the two sides were discussing the surrender, the Turks attacked the Bani Ali villages in the Awali area near Medina and killed dozens of innocents.[2] The brothers had to retreat away from Medina to the hills midway between the town and the Red Sea. They were running out of ammunition and supplies and had no money to offer the tribes. Faisal had to resort to a ruse to convince the tribesmen that he had large sums under his command. He filled a chest with stones, and 'had it locked and corded carefully, guarded on each daily march by his own slaves, and introduced meticulously into his tent each night. By such theatricals, the brothers tried to hold a melting force,' as T. E. Lawrence would later write.[3]

Messengers were sent to Rabegh, the Arab supply base on the Red Sea, to inquire about their provisioning and munitions, but here the local shaikh, Hussein ibn Mubarak, had already decided that the Turks were going to prevail. He appropriated the supplies and arms that had been unloaded by the British to support the revolt and stashed them away in the villages under his control. Ali left for Rabegh in late June or early July of 1916, to confront the machinations of ibn Mubarak, leaving Faisal alone in the hills with a dwindling band of tribesmen and with next to no resources to sustain either the fighters or the revolt. It was an inauspicious start. If the Turks in Medina had been aware of the parlous condition of Faisal's army, the revolt would have come to an inglorious end almost before it had begun.

Elsewhere in the Hijaz, the situation evolved somewhat more successfully than the haphazard way in which the revolt in Medina had been launched. On 23 May 1916, 'Abdullah had sent a message to his friend Ronald Storrs in Cairo, asking him to journey forthwith to the Hijaz as the revolt was imminent. Storrs, accompanied by the director of the recently formed Arab Bureau in Cairo, David George Hogarth, and with a bureau officer, Kinahan Cornwallis, embarked for the Hijaz and arrived in Jeddah on 5 June, with fighting already having begun in Medina.[4] Hussein was pushing for a new front to be launched in Syria by a landing of the British on the Syrian coast to cut the Ottoman supply routes to the Hijaz, but Storrs was in no position to endorse this request. All he could promise was a regular supply of weapons, food and funds, but only for the narrowly circumscribed limits of the Hijaz. No weapons or money were available for any broader objective of the revolt.[5]

By June 1916, Ottoman forces in the Hijaz numbered about 12,000 men. The force was distributed along a line of garrisons from Medina to Yanbu', Mecca, Ta'if, and Jeddah, as well as in cantonments on the Hijaz railroad. These were the forces of the 22nd Hijaz Division, divided into three regiments (128, 129 and 130), and augmented by three battalions that were temporarily in Medina, en route to Yemen under the command of Fakhri Pasha. The Hijaz force also included two companies of the Asir division, technically a part of the Ottoman detachments in the Yemen, which were stationed in Qunfudha and in al-Laith in the southern reaches of the Hijaz. The force was well equipped with modern rifles, machine guns and good artillery, and was generally well commanded and officered. The Ottoman forces could also draw on tribal contingents, if and when the occasion demanded. The greatest concentration of forces was in Medina, where Fakhri Pasha commanded nearly four thousand men. In Ta'if the Ottoman forces numbered about 3,500, with ten artillery pieces, under the command of Ghalib Pasha, the governor. He and his staff had moved to Ta'if for the summer season to escape Mecca's sweltering heat. In Mecca the Ottoman garrison comprised about 1,200 men with twenty guns, under the command of Darwish Bey. The Jeddah garrison numbered about 2,600 men with twenty guns and fifteen heavy machine guns. Other troops were stationed in garrisons on the coast in Yanbu' and Wejh. With the sea routes dominated by the British with their unchallenged command over the Red Sea, the Ottoman forces had to rely on the lifeline of the Hijaz railroad, linking them to supplies and reinforcements from Syria and from further afield.

The revolt was launched officially at dawn on 10 June 1916, when Sharif Hussein leaned out of a window from his palace in Mecca and fired a single shot in the air in the general direction of the Ottoman army headquarters. This was the agreed signal for his men, who had massed the previous night at various concentration points in Mecca, to rise against the main Ottoman strongholds in the town.[6] Communications between Mecca, Jeddah and Ta'if had already been severed the night before when the telegraph wire had been cut. The Ottoman response was quick and fierce, with artillery barrages levelled against the attackers and the palace of the amir. Sharif Hussein exhibited remarkable sang-froid as his palace came under bombardment. He did not change his daily routine and insisted on remaining in his office throughout the working day, even as the bombs were raining down on his home.[7] The situation was salvaged when Muhammad Sharif al-Faruqi arrived from Jeddah, where the rebels had secured the town and seized two artillery pieces from the surrendering Ottoman troops.[8] Faruqi had convinced six Arab gunners from the surrendering Ottoman forces to march with him to Mecca to deploy the guns. The final Ottoman outpost in Mecca, the Jarwal fortress, fell on the ninth day of the uprising, where nearly 1,200 were taken prisoner.[9]

Jeddah was the first town to fall to the rebels. Nearly four thousand Harb tribesmen surrounded the Ottoman garrisons in the town and cut off their access to water. The Ottomans were unable to break the siege and their attempts to leave Jeddah and concentrate their forces in Mecca were thwarted by Bedouins who controlled the road. On 13 June, three British warships (the *Dufferin*, *Hardinge* and *Fox*) sailed along the Jeddah coast and began firing at the Ottoman fortifications. Three days later the Ottoman forces in Jeddah surrendered.

In Ta'if the situation was more uncertain. 'Abdullah was in charge of the preparations for the revolt in the town, which had the largest Ottoman garrison outside of Medina and where the governor, Ghalib Pasha, had retired for the summer months. The town was well fortified and a sequence of attacks by mainly ill-disciplined tribesmen from various points failed to penetrate its defences. Ottoman artillery dominated the battleground and the attackers were reduced to putting the town under a desultory siege. 'Abdullah was far more concerned about preserving lives than taking the town by a frontal assault.[10] The arrival of an Egyptian artillery detachment with its four mountain guns, sent by British-commanded forces in the Sudan, hardly changed the balance of power between the besiegers and the besieged. But the besiegers had access to the plentiful provisions of the villages in the area, and as the supply situation in the town became critical, 'Abdullah allowed the residents to leave the town. On 23 September the Ottoman garrison of nearly two thousand men and a few dozen officials, including the governor of the Hijaz, surrendered to 'Abdullah. All were treated with scrupulous respect and honour.[11] The main towns of the Hijaz, with the notable and very troubling exception of Medina, were now under the control of Sharif Hussein.[12]

An early setback

Faisal, however, was left dangerously exposed, even marooned, in the hills between Rabegh and Yanbu'. In August 1916 he met Colonel Cyril Wilson at Yanbu'. Wilson had served as the administrator of the Port Sudan district, which served as the main supply conduit to the Hijaz. He was sent by authorities in Cairo, with the strong recommendation of the sirdar of the Sudan, Sir Reginald Wingate, to advise on the military and civil preparations in the Hijaz and to act as liaison with Sharif Hussein. He carried with him the innocuous title of 'pilgrimage officer', ostensibly to help in the preparations for the pilgrimage season, which that year fell in early October. The British generally, and the India viceroyalty in particular, were concerned that the rising in the Hijaz should not affect the pilgrimage and thus shield the British (and Sharif Hussein) from Ottoman accusations that they had interfered with a key Islamic rite. Wilson was also concerned that the Ottoman forces in Medina might be reinforced by units coming in from Syria via the Hijaz railroad. Ominous signs were already apparent that the Ottoman garrison in Medina was preparing to break out in a march towards Mecca to put an end to the rebellion. German and Austrian officers were sighted in Medina, supposedly directing operations, which gave substance to these fears. One report mentioned a thousand Germans and Austrians.[13] A battle between Ottoman forces and Faisal and Ali's tribesmen under Faisal's command had already occurred at Ghadir Rabegh. The encounter, in which two Turkish battalions were destroyed, was a significant victory for Faisal and temporarily checked the Ottoman advance out of Medina. Faisal told Wilson that the Ottoman garrison in Medina now numbered 24,000, and that these could be reinforced by the arrival of the Smyrna Division from Syria with a further 15,000 troops. Faisal greatly impressed Wilson, who readily acceded to relaying his demands for more and better guns, and field artillery. However, when these did finally arrive, they were only four vintage guns with a limited range, operated by a detachment of Egyptian gunners.[14]

Nevertheless, the guns did give Faisal's tribesmen a positive fillip and encouraged them to go on the offensive against the Ottoman outposts in the vicinity of Medina. Fakhri Pasha quickly strengthened the exposed forts, especially the one at Bir Abbas that was expecting an imminent attack from Faisal's tribesmen. The Ottoman guns, which had nearly treble the range of the outdated guns of Faisal's forces, quickly mastered the battlefield. One shell landed precariously close to Faisal's tent as he was meeting with his chief lieutenants. The pathetic response of the Egyptian gunners compounded the sense of despondency. Faisal could not confront the enemy given the unequal weaponry. He had already lost a great many men, and his remaining fighters were tired and longed to return to their families. His only winning tactic against the Ottoman troops was to harry them by camel charges against the rear of Ottoman columns. He seemed to be carrying the entire burden of the war on himself. 'Abdullah was in Mecca involved in high politics and administration, while Ali and Zaid were holed up in Rabegh. In October 1916, Faisal, with the rump of his forces, withdrew to the vicinity of Al-Hamra, midway between Medina and Rabegh. He left the sub-tribes of the Harb in the Bir Abbas region to harass the Ottoman forces with raids against their supply columns and lines of communication.

T. E. Lawrence first met Faisal in the village of Al-Hamra, after Faisal had withdrawn from the Bir Abbas area.[15] Lawrence had personally requested a visit to Faisal's encampment, but it was only through the intercession of Storrs that Sharif Hussein reluctantly allowed this strange English officer to proceed to Rabegh and thence to Al-Hamra. Lawrence had joined the military intelligence staff of Gilbert Clayton in Cairo and was later responsible for launching the *Arab Bulletin*, the regular secret weekly compendium of intelligence reports and analyses on Arab affairs.[16] His involvement with the affairs of the Hijaz had been incidental. He had in fact been sent to the Mesopotamian front after the Anglo-Indian forces in Kut, under the command of General Charles Townsend, had been surrounded. It was a quixotic mission, designed to raise the tribes of southern Iraq to surround the besieging Ottoman forces; failing that, Lawrence was to bribe the Turkish commanding officer into lifting the siege of Kut. By October 1916, with the Arab Revolt apparently stalled and heading for defeat (according to the gossip of staff officers in Cairo), Lawrence, by now a captain, obtained permission to visit the Hijaz in the company of Storrs. He was overwhelmed by his first encounter with Faisal. He described the circumstances as follows:

He [a household slave] led me to an inner court, on whose further side, framed between the uprights of a black doorway, stood a white figure waiting tensely for me. I felt at first glance that this was the man I had come to Arabia to seek – the leader who would bring the Arab revolt to full glory . . . I greeted him. He made way for me into the room, and sat down on his carpet near the door. As my eyes grew accustomed to the shade, they saw that the little room held many silent figures, looking at me or Feisal steadily. He remained staring down at his hands, which were twisting slowly about his dagger. At last he inquired softly how I had found the journey. I spoke of the heat and he asked me how long from Rabegh, commenting that I had ridden fast for the season. 'And do you like our place here in Wadi Safra?' 'Well; But it is far from Damascus.' The word had fallen like a sword in their midst . . . Feisal at length lifted his eyes, smiling at me and said, Praise be to God, there are Turks nearer us than that.[17]

Faisal appeared apprehensive about Fakhri Pasha's intentions, especially now that the Ottomans had the wherewithal to march towards Mecca via a number of routes that passed through Rabegh. His tribesmen were not used to passive defence and the Ottomans had kept them in a state of constant imbalance and alarm. He described to Lawrence his operational plan of action to counter the growing Turkish threat. Faisal was now preparing to retire even further, towards Yanbu', where he hoped to raise fresh levies that he would then deploy to block the Hijaz railroad north of Medina. With Ali marching simultaneously from Rabegh and Zaid keeping the large Turkish detachment in Bir Abbas off balance, Medina could be invested, or at least the Turkish push southwards would be warded off.

Lawrence stayed about a week with Faisal at Al-Hamra, reconnoitring the area of Wadi Safra. In these few days he had formed a vivid impression of the revolt and the tribesmen that formed its core combatants, and the qualities of Faisal as their leader. Already Faisal looked much older than his thirty-three years: eyes bloodshot, hollow cheeks deeply lined and 'puckered with reflection'. Lawrence offered the portrait of an impetuous, courageous and proud man, adored by his followers. Faisal used his dignified bearing to great effect and effortlessly commanded the respect and attention of the tribesmen. He 'seemed to govern his men unconsciously: hardly to know how he stamped his mind on them, hardly to care whether they obeyed. It was a great art . . . and it concealed itself, for Feisal was born to it.'[18]

Daily life in Faisal's camp followed a routine of sorts. The arrival of dawn was announced by the call to prayer by the army's imam. An hour later Faisal would open his tent to callers from his household and any privileged visitors to the camp. Breakfast was a staple of dates and sweetened tea and coffee. Faisal's manservant, Hejris, presided over the breakfast rituals. Faisal would then attend to his correspondence, assisted mainly by Faiz al-Ghusain, a Syrian from the Hawran region who had joined the revolt at the beginning.[19] At around 8 a.m., Faisal would proceed to his reception tent where, seated on the carpeted ground and facing the tent's entrance, he would receive callers. His personal bodyguard, composed mainly of freed slaves, would maintain order at the tent's entrance, where the callers would line up, seated or squatting on the ground. Faisal would normally rise from the reception tent by noon, moving to the living tent where lunch would be served on large trays holding several dishes. Faisal ate sparingly, and when he had judged that his household and guests were satiated he would wave for the trays to be carried away. He would use the early afternoon to read, talk with his guests, or take a short nap. He would then remove to the reception tent where the parade of visitors and callers would continue until the business of the day was finished. 'I never saw an Arab leave him dissatisfied or hurt,' Lawrence wrote.[20] The sunset prayer was an occasion when Faisal would often join the group and perform its rituals in public. He was not an overtly religious man, but he was scrupulous in his personal observances and respected the times and obligations of prayer. The evening was used to go over the military events of the day and plan for the coming days' field work. The evening meal was served between six and seven. Faisal went to bed late and the late evening and night were for relaxation and amiable discussions. He would often call in tribal elders to regale him with stories about their tribes and genealogies, or listen to some tribal poet reciting poems of war, or events and incidents in his tribe's history. He often adjudicated poetry competitions and handed out prizes to the winners. He was a great connoisseur of Arabic poetry.

Lawrence could discern in Faisal puzzlement, even the germ of suspiciousness, about the real intentions of the Allies, especially the British, in their dealings with the Arabs. 'And though I know the British do not want it [the Hijaz], yet what can I say, when they took the Sudan, also not wanting it? They hunger for desolate lands, to build them up; and so perhaps, one day, Arabia will seem to them precious. Your good and my good, perhaps they are different, and either forced good or forced evil will make a people cry with pain. Does the ore admire the flame which transforms it? There is no reason for offence, but a people too weak are clamant over their little own. Our race will have a cripple's temper till it has found its feet.'[21]

What spurred the tribesmen to revolt was not their primitive sense of 'Arabness'. The tribal notion of being an Arab was more a straightforward awareness of their tribal and racial lineages and had nothing to do with the elaborate nationalist ideologies and sentiments of the urban intelligentsia. Religion could not have been a factor, for the Turks were also Muslims with the same rites. Neither did they harbour a special hatred of the Germans; if anything, the kaiser had earned considerable good will amongst the empire's Muslims for his laudatory comments about Islam. It was more a dislike of the

Turks as symbols and carriers of a central authority that curbed their freedoms and undermined their livelihood, and a promise that sharifian rule would be more legitimate and accommodating. The *ashraf* were not a separate ruling class; in fact, nearly every tribe had its share of those who claimed descent from the Prophet. The Arab Revolt enlisted nearly a thousand of the *ashraf* who acted as its vanguard and missionaries. Faisal, according to Lawrence, fulfilled this promise. He was the 'prophet who, if veiled, would give cogent form to the idea behind the activity of the Arab revolt. It was all and more that we [the British] had hoped for, much more than our halting course deserved.'[22]

Lawrence, to his credit, understood the inherent limitations that faced the leader of an essentially tribal force confronting a modern, disciplined army. Recruits to the Arab Revolt did not flood in as a result of nationalist fervour or the enforcement powers of the sovereign state cajoling or conscripting the citizenry into its military machine. Negotiating with, and obtaining the allegiance of, tribes was something that had to be painstakingly gained. Faisal, though a past master at this, nevertheless had to spend an inordinate amount of time with tribal shaikhs and elders to ensure that they committed to the fighting, even though such commitments were often conditional and limited. In fact, several of the northern tribes of Arabia remained neutral in the conflict, and a few even took the Turkish side. The tribes were also impressed by success, and Faisal and Ali's initial attempts to secure Medina had ended in failure. This was bound to leave a poor impression on wavering tribes, and Faisal had to militate against a consequent draining of support. To a person trained in modern warfare and the way of modern armies, the skirmishes and battles against the Ottomans in the early days moved in odd fits and starts. It wasn't so much lassitude or risk aversion that kept Faisal's fighting force inactive for long periods of time, as some of the cables reaching Cairo from English field officers in the Hijaz suggested; rather, it was the necessity of ensuring that tribal support remained firm at each stage of the encounter with the Turks before battle was joined.[23] And this was not always forthcoming.

A tribesman in Faisal's early army might be anyone aged from twelve to sixty: in fact, anyone old enough to shoot. Tough, wiry and hardy, they could ride for immense distances and across the most inhospitable terrain. Faisal offered them £2 a month, double that for a camel. But he kept the men – and their families – fed. Faisal also offered a reward of a pound a head for each captured prisoner, a considerable encouragement to take prisoners rather than simply slit their throats. The numbers in his army fluctuated wildly, from a few hundred to over ten thousand. Men came and went, obeying the call of family, tribe or simply because they had become bored or needed a rest. There was no such thing as a chain of command to which they felt bound. They served only under their tribal shaikhs, but often accepted the loose authority of the *ashraf.*

The vast majority of the fighters were hill-men, firing at the enemy from under crags and behind rocks, and slipping away into caves and redoubts whenever danger threatened. Perhaps only a tenth were camel riders who could be used to harry the enemy in mobile raids against its rear or flanks. The tribesmen were poorly equipped with ancient, and often faulty, guns, but it was the lack of artillery that was most telling. Ottoman artillery had a devastating psychological effect on the tribesmen, and the mere possession of field guns was a great boon, a totem in effect. Faisal clearly understood this, and his demands on the British for artillery pieces were as much determined by their effect on morale as by their military potency.

The tribal forces exhibited maddeningly contradictory qualities. Incredible feats of individual bravery were mixed with slovenly, even cowardly, behaviour. Looting and the never-ending quest for booty in a society that lacked nearly all material possessions were never far from the surface. To ill discipline, wild firing and inexplicable disappearances was added the bane of the tribes: blood feuds and vendettas. Faisal tried to keep these rivalries and feuds in check but they never completely left the camp or battleplace. The baffling behaviour of the tribes could lead to disastrous consequences. In one notorious case, the Juhayna tribe withdrew from the battlefield at a critical juncture . . . to have coffee! Faisal, thinking they had been routed, called a retreat.[24] The Juhayna's coffee break took place in the area of Nakhl Mubarak, as Faisal was preparing to retire to the port of Yanbu'. A Turkish force composed of three battalions, a cavalry company and artillery had marched from Medina towards Faisal's forces and encountered them on 15 October 1916.[25] The battle was going Faisal's way and success was very near, when the left flank, held by the Juhayna, wavered and withdrew. Faisal, with nearly two thousand of his men, retreated to Yanbu'. He regrouped his tribesmen, and having accepted the outrageous explanation of the Juhayna chiefs, sent them back to harass the Turkish lines of communication.[26] Yanbu' was well defended, and had the added protection of five British warships off its shores, as well as two seaplanes that could be used for aerial bombardment of the enemy positions. The Turks were only three miles out of town, but chose to withdraw. Faisal reoccupied a number of the outposts that had been ceded to the Turks and prepared for the next stage of the war. It was a touch-and-go affair, and the revolt could have been crushed there and then. As Lawrence wrote regarding the Turkish withdrawal from the gates of Yanbu', 'So they turned back: and that night I believe, the Turks lost their war.'[27]

This was not a force that could take the enemy head on, at least not in this shape. It could be used as a guerrilla army, but only in support of a more disciplined and trained fighting force composed of regular troops. It could hold the hills and ravines of the Hijaz, but could not be expected to drive the

Turks out of Medina. However the obverse was also true. The Turks could only control those territories that they physically occupied. Their lines of communication and supplies were always at risk from attacks by these guerrilla warriors. Faisal was well aware of the limitations of his tribesmen – as well as their qualities.

When Lawrence first met Faisal in October 1916, he also saw Mawlud Mukhlis, a gruff and recklessly courageous Iraqi from Tikrit, and the first formerly regular Ottoman army officer to join the revolt. Mawlud had been reprimanded for his nationalist activities by the Ottoman authorities and had spent two years as an exile in Nejd in the service of the pro-Ottoman ruler of Hail, ibn Rashid. At the outbreak of war he was recalled to the lines, but had been taken prisoner by the British at the Battle of Shu'ayba in 1915 in the early days of the Mesopotamian campaign, while leading the Ottoman cavalry force. When the Arab Revolt broke out, he volunteered for the sharifian cause and joined Faisal as his de facto aide-de-camp. Faisal wanted more such Arabs who had been regular officers in the Ottoman army, and the British had a number of them in their prisoner-of-war camps.

Consolidating the revolt

The dependence of the revolt on the actions of 'irregular' tribal forces was always a matter for considerable concern. The Arab Bureau wrote to Wingate that the revolt suffered from 'lack of regulars, shortage of artillery, lack of a common plan and danger of melting away.'[28] Despite the widespread success of the revolt in the first two months, the strategic position by September 1916 had begun to deteriorate. The offensive capabilities of the Ottoman troops in Medina were still formidable and had nearly dealt a death blow to the nascent rebellion when they reached the outskirts of Yanbu'. There remained the real risk that the Turks would march to Mecca via the Rabegh route, and in the absence of an organised and capable defensive force, would overwhelm the tribal forces arrayed against them. The recalcitrant and well-armed ibn Mubarak with his followers remained in the area of Rabegh as an ever-present threat to the revolt. The tribes themselves might switch sides if the Turkish advance became imminent. Faisal knew this and informed Colonel Wilson, by now the British consul in Jeddah and the chief liaison with Sharif Hussein and his government, that a trained force of at least three thousand men needed to be sent to Yanbu' to consolidate the position.[29]

A month earlier in September 1916, Aziz Ali al-Misri, the hero of the Tripolitania War, left Egypt, with British acquiescence, to join the sharif's revolt in the Hijaz. Sharif Hussein appointed him his chief of staff and despatched him to Rabegh to organise a regular Arab force capable of facing the Turkish troops. Awaiting him there was his former aide, Nuri al-Sa'id, who had earlier arrived in the Hijaz in the company of nearly seven hundred Iraqi soldiers and officers, who had been released from a prisoner-of-war camp with the expectation that they would agree to join the Arab Revolt. They had been kept in a holding camp in Suez, but only a few of the prisoners of war were prepared to join the revolt against the Ottoman Empire. Those who agreed to do so were herded on board a ship that was to take them to the Hijaz. Nuri himself had been kept under loose house arrest in India before he was allowed to leave for Egypt in December 1915 to join his former commanding officer, Misri.[30] These early Arab volunteers to the revolt were later augmented by somewhat more successful recruiting drives in the prisoner-of-war camps of India, Iraq and Egypt, but the overall numbers of Arab recruits from Syria and Iraq remained small. The regular fighting units of the Arab Revolt could not rely on their manpower needs from the ranks of non-Hijazi Arabs.[31] Nevertheless, these few Arab officers and men were the nucleus of the force that would come into its own as the revolt moved northwards into Syria in 1917,[32] and the significance of the Arab officers in Faisal's army became even more notable later. Iraqi officers, and to a lesser extent Syrian officers, were deeply involved in Faisal's short-lived government in Syria, and later on a more durable and sustained basis in the affairs of the future Iraqi state. Most of Faisal's lieutenants and advisers in Iraq were drawn from this cadre.

Misri himself always had to keep one eye cocked on his master, Sharif Hussein. Never content to delegate his powers, Hussein was a suspicious and difficult person, and this trait bedevilled his relationship with all those who had to deal with him, from the British in Cairo to his own sons. Misri was a respected nationalist figure with considerable military experience, and a formidable character in his own right; it was only a matter of time before the two would clash. In the six months that Misri spent in the Hijaz, he put into place the organisational framework of the Arab force that was to fight alongside the tribal irregulars. But he was unable to wrest operational command over the force or allowed to strike out with the force in an independent manner.[33] He was kept on a tight leash by Hussein, who refused Wilson's request to provide Misri's force with a separate budget. Misri's own attempt to convince Cairo to provide him with a direct budget also came to nought. The British were unwilling to treat his force as a separate unit from the revolt under Hussein's leadership.

The nascent Arab force fell under the nominal command of Sharif Ali, whose base was in Rabegh. Soon after its formation the latent tensions between an officer class hailing from more advanced Arab regions and with modern perspectives, and a tribally based, essentially Hijazi revolt, bubbled to the surface. The Arab officers were there mainly for genuinely nationalist reasons, although quite a few saw significant career opportunities open up for them in the newly formed military. Most deeply distrusted the Allies, especially the French with their intentions and post-war plans for the Arab lands, and harboured pro-German sympathies. Some, such as Misri, had earlier ascribed to the theory that the ideal outcome for the Arabs was a reconfiguration of the Ottoman Empire as a dual Arab–Turkish state, and Sharif Ali might actually have believed that Misri continued to hold such views and would use the Arab force to advance this very end. In a planned march on to Medina, Ali recalled the Arab force because of false rumours reaching him that Misri was planning to contact Fakhri Pasha and perhaps switch sides.[34] This atmosphere of suspicion and the extended periods of inactivity drove a number of the Arab officers to leave the force and slip away to join Faisal's army. Faisal was more open to the Arab officers and their nationalist aspirations than his very traditionally minded elder brother, and for those seeking action, his army was the only force that was in constant engagement with the Turks.

The faltering pace of the revolt raised alarm bells in Cairo and London, but opinion was divided and confused as to the proper course of action required to prevent the revolt from collapsing. The idea of landing a large regular detachment of British troops in Rabegh, at least a brigade-size unit, was seriously mooted, but its deployment would have clashed with the mobilisation requirements of the expected Sinai offensive by the British expeditionary force. There were additional objections of a political nature. A foreign force of a 'Christian' power in the Hijaz might prove a public relations disaster with Muslim opinion, especially in India, and also might seriously undermine the religious credibility of Sharif Hussein. It would also irretrievably commit Britain to the revolt as a principal combatant, with all the attendant political consequences of such an act. But supporters of a British landing in Rabegh, such as High Commissioner Henry McMahon, were even more concerned about the collapse of the sharif's revolt and its effect on the credibility of the Allies' promises and commitments.[35] The War Cabinet in London contemplated the Rabegh crisis, but dithered and could not formulate a specific plan of action. Hussein himself was of two minds, first agreeing to support a landing in Rabegh and then reversing, his decision.[36] He was conscious that the presence of foreign troops in his supposedly sovereign and wholly Muslim territory would prove humiliating. At the same time he was acutely aware of the risks to the revolt if a Turkish advance to Rabegh was confronted only by tribal detachments. Hussein's clan rival, Sharif Ali Haider, was brought down by the Ottomans from Istanbul to Medina in October 1916, where he was set up as a counter-sharif. His propaganda shrilly proclaimed that Hussein was in league with the enemies of Islam.

'Abdullah was very much a supporter of the landing of a British brigade, and so was Faisal at first. However, in spite of the tribes' apparently divided loyalities, the withdrawal of the Turkish force from the gates of Yanbu' made Faisal change his mind about the need for foreign troops and adopt another course of action to break out of the Rabegh trap. He constantly met with the tribes of the area, especially the Juhayna and the Harb,[37] and arranged for a reconciliation between two major clans of the Harb who had taken different sides in the revolt. In one instance, Faisal rode alone to a conclave of the Juhayna tribe to convince them to continue on a march.[38] Faisal was the major instrument of mediation between the tribes, working 'every day and all day at this internal pacification'.[39] The unusual sight of having a high-ranking personage such as Faisal devote so much time to binding the tribes together in a higher cause was to have a long-lasting effect, partly shifting their loyalties towards something beyond their narrow interests.

Lawrence later wrote of Faisal's tireless endeavours with the tribes: 'In all Arab minds [Faisal] now stands above the tribes, the tribal shaikhs and tribal jealousies. His is the dignity of the peacemaker and the prestige of the super-imposed authority. He does not take sides or declare in their disputes: he mediates and ensues a settlement.'[40] To his mother, Lawrence wrote on 16 January 1917, 'He has a tremendous reputation in the Arab World as a leader of men, and a diplomat. His strongpoint is handling tribes: he has the manner that gets on perfectly with tribesmen and they all love him.'[41] Faisal exhibited none of the partiality to one or other of the tribes that affected his brother 'Abdullah. This made him a leader of tribes rather than simply a tribal leader or leader of a faction. In one of the intelligence reports, the observation was made that Faisal 'never cuts short a petitioner. He hears every case, and if he does not settle it himself, calls one of his staff to settle it for him. His patience is extreme and his self-control rather wonderful.'[42]

Fakhri Pasha had withdrawn from Yanbu' only to regroup, and a large Turkish force of nearly five thousand moved along the Sultani road towards Rabegh. The tribes in the pathway of the Turkish advance were wavering, awaiting the outcome of the fight to throw their weight behind one party or the other. Faisal had to rush between the tribes to ensure their steadfastness and prepare for a counter-attack, hoping to trap the Turkish column between his forces and those of Sharif Ali's forces marching from Rabegh. But Ali's tribesmen, acting on a false rumour that some of the tribes had withdrawn from the expected battle, had fallen in disorder back to Rabegh. The situation at Rabegh had become critical.

At this juncture, Faisal committed to a bold plan to strike out at Wejh, a small settlement about two hundred miles north of Yanbu'. It was an ideal base from which the Hijaz railroad could be attacked and Turkish communications between Medina and Syria disrupted. If successful, this move would force the Turks to recall their mobile columns and concentrate their forces only in

Medina. The threat to Rabegh would be removed and the revolt would be secure from its capital in Mecca. Faisal had won over one of the main clans of the Billi tribe in the Wejh area, and they had already cut the lines of communication between Wejh and the railroad point at al-'Ula. A British intelligence field report had confirmed that if Faisal took Wejh, the tribes of the area, mainly the Billi and the northern Juhayna, would join the revolt.[43] Another added effect would possibly be to win over the support of Nuri al-Sha'lan, one of the main tribal leaders of southern Syria with whom Faisal had been in contact during his stay in Damascus in 1915. At a meeting on board the British warship *Dufferin* docked outside of Yanbu', in which Faisal met with Wilson and Lawrence, agreement was reached that Faisal would march on to Wejh, while the British would ferry five hundred of his tribesmen and regulars there. Agreement to the plan was then sought from Sharif Hussein. Lawrence wrote of the Wejh expedition: 'It was their [the Arabs'] last chance not so much of securing a convincing siege of Medina, as of preventing the Turkish capture of Mecca.'[44] On New Year's Day 1917, Faisal prepared his army to march to Wejh.

The departure of Faisal's army was a spectacular event. Nearly ten thousand tribesmen with had gathered their camels at a rendezvous point in a valley outside Yanbu'. When Faisal arrived, they all quietly saluted him and awaited the drummers' signal to mount their camels and for the march to begin. Faisal, dressed in white robes with his bodyguards packed tightly behind him, rode in front. The army, arrayed behind Faisal and with banners flying and drummers beating, began the march to Wejh.[45] It was a deeply symbolic moment. This was the first time in recent history the tribes had gathered together in a common cause. It was also the first time that tribesmen had ventured outside of their lands, not in search of booty, vengeance or raiding but as members of an Arab army united behind a single leader. For the moment, 'Faisal had Billi, Juhayna and Harb, blood enemies, fighting and living side by side in his army'.[46] There was another reason for this splendid display. It was a proclamation of the growing power of the Arab Revolt and the sharifian claim to supremacy over the tribes. Wavering tribes would now have to contend with the apparently unstoppable march of the revolt, backed by gold, weaponry and the manifest support of a world power.

The march to Wejh lasted over three weeks, during which Faisal received the support of the tribes in the Wejh area. However, his army saw no fighting. Wejh had already been seized by the five hundred tribesmen and regular soldiery of Faisal's army, which had been transported by the warship *Hardinge* to Wejh. A landing party attacked the town, which was held by a small Turkish detachment of about two hundred troops. Backed by the guns of the *Hardinge* and other warships, the attackers assaulted the town and the defenders quickly surrendered. Wejh fell on 24 January 1917, and Faisal's army arrived the following day. The fear that lightly defended Yanbu' might fall to a determined Turkish advance did not materialise. Faisal had developed a plan to dissuade the Turks from any advance from Medina to Yanbu' by having 'Abdullah seize a point on the Hijaz railroad north of Medina at Wadi 'Ais. With the Turks blocked off from the north and with Wejh under his control, an advance to Yanbu' from Medina would have been far too risky.[47] Faisal had earlier written to his father about the expected Wejh campaign and his plans to seize the initiative: 'Once we consolidate our position in Wejh we will have gained a sanctuary that will be our forward base [for operations] . . . You might believe that all these opinions and views are in the manner of fantasies and dreams. But in reality everything is difficult when you start, but action is the key to success.'[48]

The occupation of Wejh completely changed the strategic map of the war in the Hijaz. An important supply base in the northern reaches of the Hijaz coast had been established in addition to Rabegh and Yanbu', and following the seizure of a number of small coastal settlements to the north of Wejh, the entire Hijaz coastline was now in the hands of the sharifian forces. Regular and effective attacks could now be launched against the Hijaz railroad and Turkish outposts in the northern Hijaz. The threat to Yanbu', Rabegh and Mecca had been removed, and Turkish forces remained bottled up in Medina, in spite of German pleas to abandon the town. It was a waste of Ottoman resources and manpower that could have more effectively been deployed on other fronts. For the Turks to continue to control one of the two holy cities of Islam, thus maintaining their level of prestige in world Muslim opinion, meant the deployment of nearly 25,000 troops – 14,000 in Medina itself and a further 11,000 guarding the key railroad points in southern Syria and northern Hijaz. The occupation of Wejh also paved the way for even greater inter-tribal cooperation under Faisal's leadership by bringing in important tribes from southern Syria into the folds of the revolt, which now moved into its second phase.

CHAPTER 6

THE ARAB REVOLT II:
BREAKING OUT

THE CAPTURE of Wejh effectively positioned Faisal and his army at the gates of southern Syria. Faisal's forces of combined tribal and regular troops were now designated the Northern Army, to distinguish them from the tribal forces under Ali and 'Abdullah. These were mainly deployed to continue the loose investment of Medina and to harass the Turkish garrison from time to time. But any move northwards would now push the revolt into an altogether different military, political and diplomatic terrain. It would no longer be confined to the limits of the Hijaz, a territory that did not much feature in the deliberations then underway in London and Paris about the post-war make-up of the Arab lands of the Ottoman Empire. However, a march by Faisal into Syria would raise a thicket of very thorny issues indeed: the revolt's relations with the Egyptian Expeditionary Force's plans for the campaign in Palestine and Syria; the political reach of Sharif Hussein of Mecca into Syria and beyond; and the secret protocols of the Sykes–Picot Agreement, which divided the Arab lands of the Ottoman Empire into spheres of influence. It is no wonder that the command in Cairo at first sought to limit the range of military activities of Faisal and the Northern Army to operations against the Hijaz railroad and not to extend their campaign into the control of territory outside of the Hijaz proper. In this Cairo was actively supported by the French, who had, a few weeks after the outbreak of the revolt, despatched a French military advisory body to the Hijaz, under Colonel Edouard Brémond. Bremond's brief was both to extend conditional support to the revolt and to monitor its activities, reporting on, and if necessary thwarting, the plans of the sharif and his sons, especially Faisal. France's interests in Syria were recognised and delineated in the Sykes–Picot Agreement, and any march of Faisal into southern Syria had always to be seen by the French in light of their ambitions and future dispositions in the area.

Faisal in Wejh

The capture of Wejh was accompanied by widespread looting and destruction by the occupying force. Faisal had in fact warned the townsmen of the impending attack, and had urged them either to revolt against the two-hundred-strong Turkish garrison or to leave the town. But they did neither, most being Egyptians from across the Red Sea rather than Hijazis proper, and unsympathetic to the cause of the revolt. Order in the town was quickly re-established, however, when Faisal appointed Mawlud Mukhlis as town governor.[1] His ruthless measures cowed the looters (and the townsmen), and Wejh soon served as the new headquarters of Faisal's Northern Army.

Soon after the fall of Wejh, the revolt was greatly strengthened by the arrival of Ja'far al-'Askari, an Iraqi officer of Kurdish extraction who had graduated from the Istanbul military academy and had received advanced officer training in imperial Germany before the outbreak of war. 'Askari was a loyal Ottoman officer who had seen action in the Libyan Desert as part of the Ottoman contingent that supported the Sanussi tribesmen against the British. In fact 'Askari had commanded the forces of the Sanussi, based in Burqa, in several encounters with the British forces coming from Egypt. In one such battle, which had turned into desperate hand-to-hand combat, he had been wounded by a sword blow and fallen prisoner to the British. He was transported to Egypt at the beginning of 1916 to a hospital in Cairo for prisoners of war, from which he tried to escape in a misadventure that ended with him hospitalised once again with a broken leg.[2] In his second confinement in hospital, 'Askari was approached by several nationalists, including his future brother-in-law, Nuri al-Sa'id, and the Syrian Dr 'Abd al-Rahman al-Shabandar, later a foreign minister in Faisal's government in Damascus, and encouraged to reassess his position of support for the Ottoman cause. Both these people fed 'Askari with detailed information about Arab secret societies and the deprivations of the CUP against the nationalists in Syria. During 'Askari's absence in Libya, little information had percolated through to him as to what was transpiring in Syria, particularly with regard to the extent of Jamal Pasha's repressive measures. Dr al-Shabandar was in regular contact with the Arab Bureau's key personnel in Cairo, such as Clayton, Hogarth and Lawrence, and arranged for 'Askari to meet them and to gauge for himself the prospects for the revolt.

'Askari's offer to join the forces of Sharif Hussein did not initially elicit any response, probably because Hussein's emissary in Cairo, al-Faruqi, fearful of 'Askari's prestige, had deliberately blocked 'Askari's communication with Sharif Hussein.[3] However, as the need for a regular Arab force to stiffen the revolt became increasingly apparent, 'Askari became the obvious choice to lead this detachment in the field, in spite of Sharif Hussein's suspicions regarding regular army officers and his general dislike of urbanised Syrians and Iraqis.[4] In the end it was Faisal who prevailed over his father's reservations. He addressed a letter directly to 'Askari, inviting him to join the Arab Revolt, and offering him command of the regular forces of the Northern Army.[5] In early 1917, 'Askari set sail on the *Hardinge* heading for Wejh.

'Askari described his first meeting with Faisal upon landing in Wejh in the following terms: 'I saw a lean youthful prince with delicate features, who drew me to his chest in an embrace saying, "I had wanted this meeting for a long time, and thank God for it [being achieved] . . . We have not, unfortunately, been able to organise a regular force because of the difficulties we have encountered from all directions, but now I hope that we will be able to exert all our efforts to form an organised army that could undertake all of its military missions under all circumstances."'[6]

'Askari found Faisal immersed in administrative and political issues and understood that he could not devote the necessary time to the detailed management of military affairs. Faisal willingly delegated this responsibility to 'Askari and agreed to his request to centralise all military decision-making on operations and deployment in a formal command structure reporting to 'Askari and ultimately to Faisal. The tribal contingents of the Northern Army, by far the most significant numerically, would be brought under some form of military command discipline. After the fall of Wejh, the British had also seconded a number of officers, apart from Lawrence, to strengthen the Northern Army's capabilities in demolition and the use of explosives and to advise on operations. They included the explosives experts Colonel Stewart Francis Newcombe and Captain Herbert Garland, and the operations officer Major Pierce Charles Joyce. It was these skilled advisers who bore the brunt of the British effort to support Faisal's Northern Army, but it was Lawrence who garnered the fame. By his own admission, Lawrence saw himself primarily as an intelligence officer and liaison with Faisal.[7] However, because of his function as the essential node through which weapons, supplies, information and money flowed between the Allies and the revolt, Lawrence built a commanding position for himself with Faisal. All these advisers congregated in Faisal's camp at Wejh as preparations were made for the next stage of the war.

Faisal knew that the progress of the revolt depended as much on the tribes through whose territory his army planned to march as on the preparedness of his regular troops and tribal contingents. However, a strategic direction for the revolt had to be established in light of the conflicting perspectives held by the protagonists. Faisal and his father were determined that the revolt move into its Syrian phase as the spearhead and catalyst for the establishment of an independent Arab state. Hussein's determination, however, was tempered by his anxieties regarding his possible loss of control and influence over Faisal and his army, the more they became distant from, and independent of, Mecca. Faisal, on the other hand, was eager to move into southern Syria as soon as his alliances with the tribes of the area became firm, but he in turn was held back by the priority given by the British to targeting the Hijaz railroad and maintaining the siege over Medina. The British total control over supplies, money and weaponry were most potent levers that they held over Faisal and the revolt in general. Their concerns and priorities could not be dismissed except at great peril. In February 1917, the War Cabinet assigned a political officer to the Egyptian Expeditionary Force to advise on the political situation east of the Egyptian frontier and to ensure that there was constant coordination with the French. The British were well aware of the constraints on their actions and the support they could give to the Arab Revolt if these conflicted in any way with their commitments to the French.[8]

The French, represented in the field by the military mission of Colonel Edouard Brémond, were pushing for the involvement of formal Allied troops in the campaign in the Hijaz and to bring the revolt clearly within the fold of a strategy that gave the Allies mastery over the campaign. In this, Brémond was ever vigilant in pursuing the goals of French policy in the area, which included the preservation of France's interests in Syria under the Sykes–Picot Agreement, as well as ensuring that no independent Arab state emerged out of the campaign that would threaten France's expected hold over the Levant. In fact, Brémond had strongly urged that regular Anglo-French troops, made up mainly of Muslims from their respective empires (presumably, India and North Africa) but under European officers, mount a landing in Rabegh and engage the Ottomans directly in warfare in the Hijaz.[9] Brémond had now arrived in Wejh to offer his congratulations on the capture of the town and to push for an Allied landing in Aqaba.[10] The French were determined to hinder the advance of Faisal's forces into Syria by pre-empting him and seizing, thorough an Anglo-French force, as much territory as possible in his expected line of march.

Faisal's camp in Wejh, a mile from the sea, was an elaborate affair, with tents pitched in clusters for guests, staff, servants, reception areas and living quarters. Regular troops and tribesmen, English advisers and the British-led Egyptian detachment surrounded Faisal's camp with their own tents, often widely apart.[11] Faisal was under constant pressure from the British to launch raids against the Hijaz railroad and to harry the Ottoman positions around Medina. These pressures became more acute when faulty intelligence was received that the Turks were about to abandon Medina and withdraw their troops to reinforce their positions against the expected British action in southern Palestine. 'We told Feisal the frank position, and that Allied interests in this case demanded the sacrifice, or at least the postponement of immediate advantage to the Arabs. He [Faisal] rose, as ever, to a proposition of honour, and agreed instantly to do his best,' wrote Lawrence.[12] The march northwards had to be postponed. All available resources had to be focused on disrupting communications and supplies to the Turkish garrison in Medina by intensifying the attacks on the Hijaz railroad.

Apart from Faisal's army in Wejh, the other main forces of the revolt were under Sharif Ali at Bir Darwish near Medina, with a much weaker force under 'Abdullah, at Wadi 'Ais north of Medina. In late March 1917 Faisal rode to Wadi 'Ais in the company of Ja'far al-'Askari, now commander of the Northern Army, and his assistant Mawlud Mukhlis, to meet his brother and discuss the future plans of action for the combined forces of the revolt. The journey to Wadi 'Ais, a dry, barren gulch, took two days and passed through desolate land, strewn with twisted, thorny, leafless trees. The beating sun was fearsome, driving the camels to seek whatever shelter they could, only to have their riders' clothes and sides torn by the sharp thorns.[13] The conditions in Wadi 'Ais were terrible. For three days a raging sandstorm pelted the area, but Faisal and his entourage endured it. The former Captain, now Major Joyce and Kinahan Cornwallis, the Arab Bureau's political officer who had been sent to Wejh on a field mission, also accompanied Faisal, as did Captain Rahu, a French officer of Algerian origin attached to Brémond's Hijaz advisory group.[14] A proposal to unify the three field commands under 'Askari could not be effected, mainly because of the difficulty of communications with Ali's armies. Faisal and 'Abdullah, however, agreed on an operational plan which did not involve either party being obliged to come to the assistance of the other, given the inherent difficulties in communications and speedy movements for reinforcements and supplies.[15]

Faisal's other preoccupation in Wejh was securing the support of the main tribes of the area and those along the planned route of march into southern Syria. The Billi tribes around Wejh had all declared their support for Faisal, as had the majority of the Juhayna. The support of the Bani Attiya, masters of the deserts immediately to the north-east of Wejh, was secured when their chief, Asi ibn Attiya, swore his allegiance to Faisal soon after the fall of Wejh. However, the main tribal confederations of the southern Syrian Desert, the Ruwala, Anizah, Bani Sakhar and above all the Howeitat, had to be won over before any serious operations could commence in their territory.[16] The chief of the Ruwala, Nuri al-Sha'lan, had already made contact with Faisal during the latter's days in Damascus in 1915 as the unwilling guest of Jamal Pasha. Al-Sha'lan's tribe dominated the eastern boundaries of the Syrian Desert, ranging from al-Jawf (in the north-western part of the Arabian Peninsula) right up to Jebel Druze, south-east of Damascus. Faisal had been cultivating Sha'lan for some time, and regularly exchanged gifts with him. Faisal's secretary, Faiz al-Ghusain, was sent to Sha'lan's base in al-Jawf to seek his support. Sha'lan, by then an old man, was much feared but respected, having risen to his position as uncontested leader by the murder of his two brothers. The other main tribe that bestraddled the planned march northwards was the Howeitat of the Tawaiyha branch, whose leader was the most venerated and celebrated warrior in Arabia at that time, Auda Abu Tayeh. The Howeitat were dominant in the area between Ma'an, a key point on the Hijaz railroad, and the small port of Aqaba.

In early February 1917, an emissary from Nuri al-Sha'lan arrived at Faisal's camp at Wejh, bearing a mare as a gift. It was an expression of implicit support, but Nuri al-Sha'lan would not publicly break with the Ottomans until serious fighting had commenced. On the same day a delegation came from the Howeitat, carrying Auda's greetings and expressions of support. Faisal welcomed the visitors with open arms, but he wanted Auda to be physically present, not only so as to gauge the extent of his commitment but also to learn detailed plans should the revolt extend into his territory.[17] The presence of these two emissaries representing the great tribes to the north of Wejh added further impetus to the droves of tribesmen and shaikhs rushing to express their support for Faisal and the revolt. In a letter to his father of 23 March 1917, Faisal talked of the arrival at his camp of 'two thousand riders from the Ruwala, Shararat, Howeitat, Bani Sakhar and Amirat [tribes], with 242 shaikhs, ninety of whom brought with them 140 horses and weapons. Faisal recruited them into his ranks by administering an oath of allegiance sworn on the Quran. The oath obliged the person to: 'Wait while he [Faisal] waited, march when he marched, to yield obedience to no Turk, to deal kindly with all who spoke Arabic (whether Baghdadi, Aleppine, Syrian or pure-blooded) and to put independence above life, family and goods.'[18]

On 5 April 1917, a delegation of tribesmen arrived at Faisal's camp in Wejh, amongst whom was Auda Abu Tayeh.[19] Auda stayed nearly a month at Faisal's camp, planning for the forthcoming operations against the Turks in the Ma'an area. Lawrence describes in detail the first encounter between Faisal and Auda: 'Auda caught his [Faisal's] hand and kissed it, and they drew aside a pace or two and looked at each other – a splendidly unlike pair, typical of much that was best in Arabia, Feisal the prophet, and Auda the warrior, each filling his part to perfection, and immediately understanding and liking the other.'[20] The tribes of the area were now all on board thanks to Faisal's indefatigable patience and perseverance in settling tribal disputes and smoothing over sensitivities. In this he was helped in no small measure by the copious material and financial support that was offered him by the British. On 21 February 1917 the War Office approved the despatch of a further 30,000 rifles and 15 million rounds of ammunition to Faisal's forces in Wejh. Earlier in January Faisal had requested £50,000 from Wingate in Cairo to gain influence with the various tribes of northern Hijaz. Wingate recommended that the request be granted, but limited the total tribal subvention to £100,000.[21]

The fall of Aqaba

The daring capture of Aqaba has been etched into the public consciousness by its association with Thomas Edward Lawrence, and this incident, probably more than any other of his many real and imagined exploits, secured for him the sobriquet Lawrence of Arabia. Lawrence's war memoir, *Seven Pillars of Wisdom*, in immensely evocative passages, provides a detailed description of the events leading up to the fall of Aqaba. Lawrence provided himself a central role, not only in planning and directing the operations that culminated in the capture of Aqaba but also in their conception. Few of his biographers have previously examined or refuted his claims. This is most likely due to their inability or unwillingness to access sources in Arabic, including the recollections and memoirs of the main protagonists of the Arab Revolt. These, however, without necessarily denigrating or diminishing Lawrence's important role in the Aqaba campaign, offer an altogether different emphasis to the actions of the various players.

In all Arabic accounts, Faisal emerges as one of the earliest and keenest proponents of the strategy to capture Aqaba. In a letter sent to his father in mid-December 1916 (dated 21 Rabi' al-Awal 1335 AH), Faisal wrote that 'after [the fall of] Wejh, we are left with only Dhiba and Mullaiha [on the northern Hijaz coast] and both are weak [ill-defended] now. After that, we have only to take Aqaba and join up with the English forces [marching from Sinai]'[22] In a note of 1 March 1917, Major Vickery, a gunnery officer in the Sudan service who was sent to Wejh, wrote to the Arab Bureau that Faisal was very concerned about capturing Aqaba *with his own forces*, given the immense impact this would have on Syrians, and that Faisal had requested that British warships should carry his troops by sea to assault the port. Clayton wrote back that Faisal should be dissuaded from moving on to Aqaba at present as this would distract him from his primary task of attacking the Hijaz railroad. In any case, no warships were presently available for his task.[23]

The significance of Aqaba to the war aims of Faisal and his father cannot be underestimated. Aqaba was not only an important extension to the territory held by the revolt into Syria proper; it was also a base from which the revolt could rapidly spread out into Syria and establish the Arabs' claims to independence. Sharif Hussein's war aims were in fact spelt out by Faruqi after his meeting with the sharif in June 1916. The gist of the conversation was carried in a note from the Arab Bureau in Cairo to Clayton, who was then in London.[24] First, Sharif Hussein wanted to be acknowledged politically by the Allies as the sovereign head of an Arab kingdom. Second, he wanted to assemble a military force and march on Syria as soon as was practicable. The occupation of Syria by his own forces would give him a very strong position from which to assert his authority and the priority of other claimants, namely France. Hussein was dependent on the material and financial support of the British, who could exert enormous pressures on him to suit their demands and needs, but he could still pursue his aims whenever circumstances allowed him to do so. Aqaba was central to his ambitions. Moreover, Faisal had other reasons to push into Syria. He had many friends and followers in that country, who looked on him as the leader and symbol of a nationalist revolt. His army had to be seen to be moving towards control over specific territory rather than just attacking the transport and supply routes of the Turks.

Another factor that might have prompted Faisal to focus on the advance into Syria relates to the existence of the Sykes–Picot Agreement, which may have been suggested to Faisal by Lawrence in February 1917.[25] This may explain Joyce's frustrations in getting Faisal to concentrate on the Hijaz railroad and Medina, rather than look northwards towards Syria. 'It appears to me he [Faisal] is too inclined to concentrate his ideas on the North and Syria whereas so far as my information goes Medina should be the first objective of all the Sharif's forces and I have endeavoured to explain this clearly to him,' wrote Joyce to Wilson.[26] In April 1917, Faisal was alarmed by rumours that the French were planning to land 60,000 troops in Syria, a development that could have destroyed the possibilities of an independent Arab state that included most, if not all, of Syria.[27] The occupation of Aqaba by forces clearly associated with the Arab Revolt, and under Faisal's overall command and direction, would be an immensely significant event, strengthening Arab claims to an independent state and forestalling French attempts to thwart such an eventuality. In fact, the composition of the advance guard that Faisal approved to spearhead the mobilisation of the southern Syrian tribes against Aqaba clearly demonstrates this intent. In a letter to his father of 14 April 1917, Faisal wrote: As for your servant's [Faisal's] efforts in Syria, matters are proceeding in the best way. In the next two days, Auda Abu Tayih will be marching northwards, basing himself in al-Jafr, three hours ride from Ma'an. He will be accompanied by Sharif Nasir ibn Ali, and perhaps also your servant Nasib [al-Bakri, the Damascene] who will be heading for the direction of Jebel Druze [south of Damascus] to undertake the necessary arrangements for a general rising.[28]

There was no mention of Lawrence. Faisal selected Sharif Nasir to head the expedition and to act as his representative with the northern tribes.[29] The other two members of Faisal's command that joined the expedition were Nasib al-Bakri, who was Faisal's close friend and a member of the al-Fatat secret society, and Zaki al-Duroubi, a regular officer formerly with the Ottoman army. The presence of the two Syrians was mainly for the purposes of establishing contacts with dissident Syrians to assist in the battle for Syria. Lawrence joined the expedition as an explosives expert after he pleaded with Faisal to allow him to join the group.[30] Although he neither originated the plans for the expedition nor led it, his presence was vital in the subsequent conquest of Aqaba.

The expedition left Wejh on 9 May in the company of thirty-five trained Bedouin volunteers, with rifles, explosives and £20,000 in gold. The party crossed the desert eastwards, then diverted northwards, crossing the railroad line until reaching Wadi Sirhan in twenty days. Within two weeks, Sharif Nasir and Auda were able to recruit five hundred fighters from the Ruwala and Howeitat tribes and marched with them westwards, but the force was too weak to attack and hold Ma'an. On 2 July 1917, they met a Turkish battalion near Ma'an at Abu al-Lissan, and a fierce battle ensued. Nearly 300 Turks and conscript Arabs were killed, and 160 prisoners fell into the hands of the expeditionary force. It was a significant victory, the credit of which must go to the valour of Auda and his tribesmen. The victory encouraged many wavering tribes to join the force, and opened the road to Aqaba. Several Turkish garrisons in the vicinity surrendered or withdrew to fortified positions around the town. The Turkish defences there were mainly aimed at blocking an attack from the sea and could not withstand the Arabs' frontal assaults. On 6 July the Aqaba garrison surrendered and Sharif Nasir and his force entered Aqaba. Forty-two Ottoman army officers and seven hundred soldiers surrendered. Their killed and wounded numbered nearly six hundred.[31]

Sharif Nasir wrote Faisal a detailed letter from Aqaba in the common dialect of the Bedouins, dated 6 July 1917 (15 Ramadhan, 1335 AH), describing the events.[32] In Sharif Nasir's account of the expedition and the fall of Aqaba, Lawrence's name was mentioned once, and then only as a member of a party that reconnoitred the Zarqa area. There was no mention of Lawrence's role in the planning and organisation for the attack. Nasir gives credit only to the tribesmen and their courageous action, and since Nasir was known for his veracity, the letter is strong evidence that Lawrence greatly exaggerated his role in the campaign. Immediately afterwards, Lawrence and eight volunteers set out to cross the Sinai desert, aiming for the Suez Canal, to bring the British the news of the Arab victory. Lawrence's report of the capture of Aqaba to the British army in Egypt, now under the overall command of General Edmund Allenby, who had recently replaced Archibald Murray, took most of the credit for the victory for himself. The reality, however, was greatly at variance with Lawrence's claims. It was the beginning of the legend of Lawrence of Arabia, the artful embellishment of a mainly true narrative of heroism and derring-do, and rendered in stirring prose, in the full knowledge that the other actors, overwhelmingly Arab, were in no position to contradict or correct the story.

While the expeditionary force under Sharif Nasir was engaging, and then prevailing over, the Turks in Aqaba, Faisal himself led a sizable contingent out of Wejh to attack Turkish positions on the Hijaz railroad. The force comprised the recently formed 'Qibla Battalion' of regular troops under Ja'far al-'Askari, a cavalry detachment of two hundred riders and a further two hundred Bedouins on horses and camels. They marched towards Wadi Jaida, where Faisal encamped and called on the Juhayna tribe of the area to join his force in an attack on the railroad stations. A series of raids were then launched against vital railroad positions at Zumurud, but the campaign was cut short when Faisal ordered the attacking forces to return to Wadi Jaida and thence to Wejh, to prepare to be transported to Aqaba. News of Aqaba's fall had just reached him.[33]

The news of the fall of Aqaba to the forces of the Northern Army was generally well received by Allenby. The spread of the revolt to the eastern and southern reaches of Syria would greatly assist the planned campaign into Palestine by the Egyptian Expeditionary Force.[34] A decision was made by the High Command to place Faisal's army under the overall leadership of General Allenby and to fit its operations within his strategy and plans for the Syrian campaign. The Northern Army would henceforth function within the framework of Allenby's command structure rather than under the independent authority of King Hussein. The latter had recently assumed the title of 'king', to the consternation of the Allies. They reluctantly acceded to calling him king of the Hijaz rather than king of the Arab Lands, the title he had given himself.[35] Hussein was upset by this and complained that the British had earlier offered to recognise him as caliph, a far more exalted title than king. The issue greatly affected Hussein's perceptions regarding the sincerity of Britain's commitments to him and to the broader cause of the revolt, and contributed to souring the relationship between the Arabs and the British for a number of years.

Lawrence was chosen by the High Command to obtain Hussein's agreement for the transport of Faisal's army to Aqaba and to bring it under the strategic command of Allenby. He met Hussein in late July 1917, midway between Mecca and Jeddah, in the company of Colonel Cyril Wilson, the principal British liaison with Hussein. Hussein agreed to the proposed changes regarding the attachment of Faisal's army to the Egyptian Expeditionary Force. But in a letter that he sent to Faisal regarding the latter's future relationship with the British he was more equivocal, giving Faisal a free hand in dealing with Allenby 'to facilitate the cooperation between my army and that of Great Britain.'[36] Hussein continued to view himself as the ultimate commander of Faisal's

Northern Army. In the first week of August 1917, most of the Northern Army under the command of al-'Askari was transported by sea and land to Aqaba. On 23 August, Faisal himself arrived in Aqaba, to be joined later in the year by his younger half-brother Zaid, with 1,500 fighters and a number of his *ashraf* relatives, including Sharif Nasir and Sharif Shakir. The entire Northern Army had been reassembled in Aqaba. The army spread out to occupy the hills between Aqaba and Ma'an, and strengthened its defences against a possible Turkish counter-attack. It was reinforced by the arrival of mainly Iraqi volunteers from the prisoner-of-war camps in India, who were now languishing in Ismailia. Al-'Askari organised them into a new battalion, the Ismailia Battalion.[37]

Faisal's Northern Army was now a collection of three separate formations. The first comprised the regular troops under Ja'far Pasha al-'Askari, composed of two brigades of infantry, a Camel Corps battalion, a battalion of mule-mounted infantry under Mawlud Mukhlis, and eight field guns under the command of the Iraqi Jamil al-Madfa'i. Nuri Pasha al-Sa'id, who had recently joined the Aqaba army from his attachment to Ali's forces near Medina, was the chief of staff. The second formation consisted of the Egyptian and British section commanded by the former Captain, now Colonel Pierce Joyce, with an armoured car battery, a detachment of machine gunners from an Indian cavalry regiment, a transport platoon and a wireless station in Aqaba. The third formation was a French–Algerian pack battery of four mountain guns and machine guns commanded by a Frenchman, Captain Rosario Pisani. To these regular formations were added far larger groups of tribesmen that converged on specific areas and locales to engage the enemy in battle. By the end of the war, the Northern Army would nearly double in size.

Faisal's finances improved after the capture of Aqaba. The British subvention to Hussein to sustain the revolt and his administration was increased to £200,000 per month in the summer of 1917. Of this sum, the amount allocated to Faisal was fixed at £50,000 per month, on a par with the allowance of 'Abdullah. But in a letter to King Hussein dated 12 September 1917, Wilson urged Hussein to increase Faisal's financial subsidy to £75,000 per month, given his expanded field of activity and the need to sustain his new tribal supporters. 'There is no doubt,' Wilson wrote, 'that Amir Faisal's operations now are of the greatest importance to the outcome in the Hijaz and . . . Syria, and it is necessary that to ensure continuing success all the possible financial support be given to Amir Faisal. For it is the very success of the northern operations that has justified the [British] increase of the subsidy [to Hussein].'[38] The increase in Faisal's resources, though, did not necessarily imply that he had ready access to them. His British advisers, through whom the money was passed on to him, played with the disbursements of these subsidies in ways that would have undoubtedly increased Faisal's anxieties and uncertainties regarding the funds actually at his diposal. Joyce reported to his superiors on one such occasion when he withheld funds from Faisal, 'Lawrence and I did a dreadful thing and only gave him [Faisal] £10,000 instead of £50,000. The other £40,000 remains on the *Humber* to be given him as occasion arises.'[39]

Throughout autumn 1917, the Northern Army was engaged in fierce battles with the Ottoman army, which was seeking to recapture lost ground in the Ma'an–Aqaba theatre. At Wadi Musa a day-long battle ended with the Turks in retreat, leaving over four hundred killed, wounded or captured. Other battles were fought in Dalagha, Wahida and Quwaira; all settled in favour of the Arabs. These battles coincided with Allenby's major push in southern Palestine in November 1917, when he captured Gaza, Beersheba and Jaffa and prepared for the battle of Jerusalem. The contribution of the Northern Army to Allenby's successful campaign was recognised by Wingate in a note to the Foreign Office in November 1917. Wingate stated that the Arabs had successfully blocked 20,000 Ottoman troops between Ma'an and Medina from participating in the battles of southern Palestine.[40] At the same time the British drew on Faisal's credibility and influence with the peoples of the area to gain their support for Allied operations. After the fall of Gaza and Beersheba, Faisal was asked to send one of the *ashraf* to help to promote the British offensive and secure the assistance of the tribes in the pathway of the advance. Faisal despatched Sharif 'Abdullah ibn Hamza to the tribes of the area and to ensure their support and cooperation with the British army in Palestine. The British also used planes to drop leaflets carrying the original message of revolt from Sharif Hussein, as well as one that called on Arab officers and soldiers in the Ottoman army to desert their ranks and join the British army in Palestine, 'which will include representatives of the King of the Hijaz. They will welcome you and you will help them in liberating the Arabs.'[41] These drops had their effect and a stream of Arab deserters joined the British advance and then the forces of the Northern Army. Little did they know that the promises about Arab liberation were at odds with secret agreements already entered into by Britain and France regarding the post-war division of the Ottoman Empire's Arab territories, to which was soon to be added a declaration by the British government that would drastically alter the composition of the overwhelmingly Arab population of Palestine.

Secret agreements and public declarations

Soon after their seizure of power in Russia in the October Revolution of 1917, the Bolsheviks published the details of a secret agreement, to which the Tsarist Empire was signatory, that effectively partitioned the Middle East between the Allied powers into spheres of influence and occupation. This agreement, known as the Sykes–Picot Agreement, became formal Allied policy after Sir Edward Grey sent a note to the French ambassador in London on 16 May 1916, setting out the terms of the agreement and the final approval of the British government for its stipulations. A detailed analysis of the circumstances that led to the agreement is beyond the scope of this biography, but it is central to understanding the actions and motivations of the main players in the unfolding drama in the Middle East at the end of the First World War and in its immediate aftermath.[42]

It was Tsarist Russia that initiated the process which culminated in the Sykes–Picot Agreement. The Gallipoli campaign launched by Britain and France, partly to relieve pressure on Russia and bring about the quick defeat of the Ottoman Empire, opened up the thorny issue as to what would happen to the lands and peoples over which it ruled. On 4 March 1915, Russia put in a claim that the Straits of Constantinople should come under the control of Russia, a historic goal of its foreign policy. Although accepted grudgingly by the British and French, Russia's demands prompted the French, in a note of 14 March 1915, to open detailed negotiations with the British as to the disposition of Ottoman territories in the Middle East after an Allied victory. France's opening gambit that the entire Syrian littoral, defined by them as Syria proper (including Palestine) and Cilicia, should fall under French control was unacceptable to the British. Palestine in particular was regarded by Britain as a separate entity, and this, together with the holy sites of Islam in the Middle East, was thought to deserve a special regime.

The future political order in the Middle East remained a subject of toing and froing between London and Paris until the approaches made to Sharif Hussein to launch his revolt, and his demands for a clear commitment to the territorial boundaries of an independent Arab state, brought the matter to a head again. On 21 November 1915, Grey addressed a note to the French ambassador in London asking that France nominate a representative for discussions to evolve a joint Allied position on the political order in the Middle East after the war. The French nominated François Georges-Picot, formerly France's consul in Beirut, to head their delegation. The British settled on Sir Mark Sykes. It was a fateful decision, as Sykes was neither a conventionally cautious diplomat nor an academically trained expert on the society and cultures of the Middle East. Born into a wealthy Yorkshire family and heir to a baronetcy, Sykes had enjoyed an eclectic upbringing. Armed with a degree from Cambridge, and widely travelled in the Ottoman lands, Sykes became something of a Middle East specialist. He often spoke in parliament on matters affecting the Ottoman Empire in his function as member of parliament for the Conservative Party. He was known for his strong support of the Ottoman Empire in the face of Russian expansionism, but his views underwent a great change after the Young Turk revolution, which he deplored. He subsequently became more sympathetic to the national aspirations of the non-Turkish populations of the empire.[43] A veteran of the Boer War, Sykes came to Kitchener's attention during his assignment to the War Office, and Kitchener appointed him to the De Bunsen Committee on Middle East policy, where Sykes stood out.

The agreement that was worked out by Sykes and Picot, guided and aided by the Foreign Office and the Quai d'Orsay, appeared to reconcile the imperial objectives of these rival powers in the soon-to-be-dismembered territories of the Ottoman Empire. It designated spheres of influence and control for each power, which the others accepted. The territorial divisions were colour coded for ease of the reader! Russia's ambitions did not include the Arab territories of the empire. Moscow was satisfied with Constantinople, and the four eastern wilayats of Anatolia with their substantial Armenian population. France's domains, however, included the greater part of the Syria coast, southern Anatolia, and the northern parts of the Mosul wilayat. These were coded blue on the map. Britain awarded herself most of Iraq (coded red), including the cities of Basra and Baghdad, down to the western shores of the Gulf. Britain also expected to annex the ports of Haifa and Acre and their hinterlands. Other Arab parts of the Ottoman territories were designated 'A' and 'B' areas. The 'A' territories, which included the Syrian hinterland and the cities of Damascus, Aleppo, Homs and Hama, were allocated to an 'independent' Arab ruler, where France would maintain her supremacy by providing advisers and administrators with executive powers, and having priority over projects. A similar arrangement involved British primacy over the 'B' area, which awkwardly connected most of Transjordan to the Anbar desert and Kirkuk. This was primarily motivated by Britain's desire to dominate the oil fields of Kirkuk and to link them by pipeline to the port of Haifa. The view that Britain should hold territory that would facilitate imperial communications between Suez and the East, first formulated by Kitchener, also played an important part in the negotiations. Palestine, designated brown on the map, would have an international government formed in consultation with Russia, the rest of the Allies and the sharif of Mecca.

The Sykes–Picot Agreement's vision of the post-Ottoman order was never realised exactly; it was supplanted in the peace treaty by the mandate system. Nevertheless, it is a 'shocking document' or a simple 'fraud', as Lawrence called it.[44] The subsequent Middle Eastern order in the Arab territories did not stray too far from its broad intent. The agreement mixed the implausible and unsustainable together with the downright stupid. Relatively advanced populations on the Syrian coastlands, and to a lesser extent in Baghdad and Basra, were placed under direct rule, while desert lands with nomadic populations were given a semi-independent status. There were undoubted divisions in these territories between the various population centres, cultural, social and religious; nevertheless, there was a commonality of language and the first stirrings of a national identity. The division of these territories into spheres of influence by rival powers with their different colonial administrative systems simply pushed back whatever small chance there might have been to organise a common, perhaps loose, political entity for the Arab populations of the area.

The agreement was negotiated without the knowledge of Sharif Hussein. The tortuous negotiations between Hussein and McMahon in prelude to the revolt carried no hint of the secret deal that was being concocted by the Allies, except for a vague phrase that spoke of 'the interests of our ally, France', as McMahon put it. There is no doubt that Hussein would have scuppered the possibility of a revolt if the details of the Allies' post-war plans had been made known to him. At the very least it was a serious breach of trust, an issue that became increasingly obvious and uncomfortable for Britain as the country's promises to the French collided with the spirit of its commitments to Hussein, no matter how vaguely or equivocally worded. Sykes himself later became aware of the obvious contradictions in British policies and commitments, to which he had made no small contribution, but these scruples were none too apparent when he embarked for Wejh to meet Faisal and then proceed to Jeddah to meet King Hussein. Sykes had already visited Cairo, where he had met with a delegation of prominent Syrian Muslims and given them a loose description of the post-war plans for the Arab territories of the Ottoman Empire. Rumours circulating in Cairo about the existence of a Franco-British deal might have reached the ears of King Hussein, but there is no evidence that Hussein was aware of any specifics. Clayton, in a note to the Foreign Office of 10 March 1917, stated emphatically that Hussein had no knowledge of the details of the Sykes–Picot Agreement.[45]

Sykes's visit to Cairo was a prelude to his meeting with Faisal on 2 May in Wejh. Sykes gave no details of his discussions with Faisal, merely reporting that he had given Faisal 'the principle of the Anglo-French Agreement in regard to Arab Confederation.'[46] It is unlikely that Sykes volunteered any specifics that implied a form of French annexation for the Syrian coast and an international status for Palestine. Following his discussions with Faisal, Sykes left for Jeddah where he met with King Hussein and gave him a message of greetings from King George V, as well as the welcome news that the British government had increased its subsidy to him to £200,000 per month. Sykes was under clear instructions not to divulge the contents of the agreement but rather try to calm Hussein's anxieties regarding French objectives in Syria.[47] During the talks Hussein impressed on Sykes that there must be no compromise on Arab independence, and that France could not be allowed to annex Syria. It would have been a betrayal on his part if he had encouraged the Syrians to revolt against the Ottomans only for them to be handed over to a foreign power.

Hussein was clearly apprehensive about French designs on Syria, and his apprehension was no doubt exacerbated by the presence of Picot in Cairo with a large French delegation in attendance. In Cairo, Picot had made a number of speeches and remarks that clearly pointed to France's desire for having a permanent say in the running of Syria, especially regarding its coastal areas. Hussein was now keen to meet directly with him. Sykes returned to Egypt, reported on his mission, and once more embarked for Wejh, this time in the company of Picot. On 17 May, Faisal met with Sykes and Picot again, and, together with Stewart Francis Newcombe, the Northern Army's military adviser, left for Jeddah to meet with King Hussein. A few weeks earlier, on 11 March 1917, the British army in Iraq, under General Stanley Maude, took Baghdad in a major victory for British arms in the Middle East theatre of war. The type of occupying administration that the British intended to establish in Iraq was very much in the minds of the parties assembling in Jeddah.

On 19 May 1917, Hussein met for three hours with Sykes and Picot; with Faisal and Fouad al-Khatib, Hussein's Lebanese foreign affairs adviser, in attendance. The meetings continued the following day with the same people, but this time also with Colonel Wilson, the British representative in Jeddah. These meetings have given rise to a great deal of controversy as to whether Hussein was informed of the details of the Sykes–Picot Agreement. Sykes himself wrote a very brief report on the meetings, which throws no light on this matter. Others, however, including Wilson himself, Picot, Fouad al-Khatib and Newcombe, who met with Faisal immediately after the second meeting, also wrote in some detail on the meetings. What emerges is that neither Sykes nor Picot gave a detailed account of the agreement to Hussein. Hussein did not guess its scope and extent, and interpreted French ambitions in Syria more in terms of a desire for influence and advantage that could be worked around or even partly accommodated, rather than a hard and fast plan, already agreed with the British, to annex the greater part of Syria. Hussein, partly out of conviction and partly out of necessity, sought to believe in British representations and, under sustained pressure from Sykes in the meetings, agreed to accept a role for the French in Syria akin to that of the British in Baghdad. Sykes, of course, did not tell Hussein what the British plans for Baghdad and Basra really were. Hussein believed that the British sought to create an independent Arab state in Iraq after the war's end, and that their present administration of the country was purely due to the exigencies of the moment.

Both Wilson and Newcombe were greatly concerned that Sykes did not clarify the ambiguities of the British position and left matters hanging in a most unsatisfactory way. Newcombe wrote that a number of key issues were completely ignored and not raised with Hussein, and went so far as to say that if the British continued in this evasive manner with the king, failing to tell him of the contents of the agreement, they would be playing a most duplicitous game.[48] Wilson, in turn, wrote a twelve-page letter to Clayton in which he raised the issue that Hussein had no knowledge of the true British policy in Iraq. If he was aware of it, Wilson wrote, Hussein would surely not accept it. Hussein continued to be, or chose to be, under the impression that the occupation of Iraq was a temporary affair and that the British subventions to him were in the manner of rent paid in compensation for British administration of Iraq.[49] Wilson ended his letter by urging his government to take immediate steps to disclose the true facts lest the sharif and the Arab peoples had good cause to accuse Britain of deception.

The other profound development that affected the course of events in the Middle East was the the Balfour Declaration, which committed Britain to supporting the establishment of a 'Jewish National Home' in Palestine. The statement was in the form of a letter sent to Lord Walter Rothschild by Arthur Balfour, Britain's Foreign Secretary, on 2 November 1917. It detailed the cabinet's policy position in support of political Zionism, albeit hedged with a qualification regarding some of the rights of the existing Arab inhabitants, accounting at that time for 93 per cent of the population of Palestine. 'His Majesty's government view with favour the establishment in Palestine of a national home for the Jewish people and will use their best endeavours to facilitate the achievement of this object, it being clearly understood that nothing shall be done which may prejudice the civil and religious rights of existing non-Jewish communities in Palestine, or the rights and political status enjoyed by Jews in any other country.'[50] Probably no other declaration in modern times has had such an impact on entire peoples, has been so mired in controversy and has had such astounding consequences.

The genesis of the Balfour Declaration is beyond the scope of this book; nevertheless, it is important to emphasise that it affected the Arab Revolt directly in a number of ways. First, it presupposed that the British government would have a free hand in Palestine as a territory directly under its control in order to give the declaration an effect. Second, it presupposed that the Arabs of Palestine, in whatever guise – nationalists, supporters of the Arab Revolt, or simply dwellers in Palestine – had no right to determine their political future, only that their 'civil and religious rights' would need to be respected by some foreign or international body. Both of these clashed with Hussein's interpretation of his correspondence with McMahon and his view that Palestine constituted an integral part of Syria, which was to form the heart of an independent Arab state. Hussein was sympathetic to the plight of Jews in Europe, as was Faisal, and welcomed Jews' presence in, as well as their migration to Palestine.

He even exhorted the people of Palestine to welcome Jews as brethren and to cooperate with them for the common good.[51] But this was a far cry from acknowledging and accepting the Zionist claim to the right to form a state for Jews in Palestine, and relinquishing the Arab claim to sovereignty over all of Palestine. Faisal himself thought of Arabic-speaking Jews in no different terms than other Arabs, and hoped that they would be inspired by the goals of the Arab Revolt. In a letter to Sykes, Lawrence wrote regarding Faisal's views on Palestinian Jews and those of European origins,

> You know of course the root differences between the Palestine Jew and the colonist Jew: to Feisal the important point is that the former speak Arabic, and the latter German Yiddish. He is in touch with the Arab Jews (their HQ at Safed and Tiberias is in his sphere) and they are ready to help him, on conditions. They [Arabic-speaking Jews] show a strong antipathy to the colonist Jews, and have even suggested repressive measures against them. Feisal has ignored this point hitherto, and will continue to do so. His attempts to get in touch with the colonial Jews have not been very fortunate. They say they have made arrangements with the Great Powers, and wish no contact with the Arab Party . . . Now Feisal wants to know . . . what is the arrangement standing between the colonist Jews (called Zionists sometimes) and the Allies . . . What have you promised the Zionists and what is their programme?[52]

In order to allay Hussein's concerns, the British sent David George Hogarth, of the Arab Bureau in Cairo, to meet with Hussein between 8 January and 14 January 1918. In the course of his meetings, Hogarth delivered a solemn message from the British government that assured Hussein that 'Jewish settlement in Palestine would only be allowed in so far as would be consistent with the political and economic freedom of the Arab population.'[53] This unequivocal statement was finally sufficient to dispel Hussein's apprehensions about the ultimate intentions of the British government in Palestine. Messages went out to Faisal in Aqaba that he should not be too concerned with the implications of the Balfour Declaration, now that he, Hussein, had received satisfactory clarifications from the British government that safeguarded Arab rights in that country.

By the end of 1917 both Faisal and Hussein became aware that the political landscape had changed dramatically from what it was when the revolt was first mooted. Lack of detailed knowledge regarding the Sykes–Picot Agreement did not stop them from recognising that the French expected to extract major concessions from the British in the Middle East and that they were determined to carve out for themselves an empire in the Levant. The ambiguities and evasions of British policy also caused them no end of anxieties, and both in their own way sought to achieve their personal, dynastic and national goals by constant manoeuvring and dissimulating in the midst of this complex play of war and the ambitions of imperial powers. In Faisal's case, the deck could be stacked to his advantage by the march northwards, by creating facts on the ground, and by proving his army and tribesmen's worth to the main Allied military force in the field – the Egyptian Expeditionary Force under Allenby. Only then could the Arabs amass enough weight and credibility to challenge seriously the machinations of France (and even those of Britain, which ultimately sustained the revolt), and hope to keep and safeguard their prime goal of creating an independent state from the Arab territories of the Ottoman Empire.

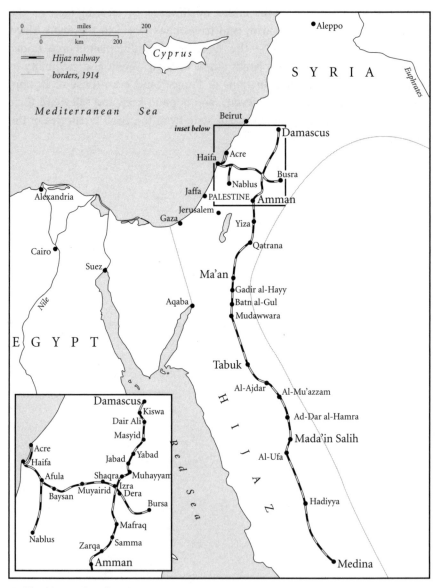

3. The Hijaz railroad, 1914

CHAPTER 7

++++++◆⊰⊱◆++++++

THE ARAB REVOLT III: RAILROAD WAR

THE NORTHERN Army's base in Aqaba had expanded considerably by the end of 1917. The position around Aqaba had been consolidated and an advanced outpost on the Guweira Plain, several miles inland, had been established. The British navy maintained regular supply convoys, and ferried not only troops but also the heavier armoured vehicles that had been previously been at Wejh. The armoured cars were used successfully by Joyce in a number of raids out of Aqaba targeting the Hijaz railroad. The regular formations were also receiving an increasing flow of Arab officers – deserters from the Ottoman army and those recruited from prisoner-of-war camps – all eager to prove their worth in the developing campaigns. Other Arab civilians – doctors, administrators, and ambitious politicians – also began to gravitate to this new nucleus of the Arab Revolt, to serve as well as to position them for advantage in a possibly new order. A small group of Armenian volunteers, refugees from the massacres in Anatolia, had also joined the Arab Revolt in Aqaba. They were later withdrawn to Egypt where they formed the nucleus of a larger force of Armenians attached to the Egyptian Expeditionary Force (EEF).

The Aqaba camp itself was built around Faisal's main tent complex, which included the tents of his *ashraf* relatives, his personal guards and the reception and dining areas for his entourage and visitors. In another part of the camp were the tents of the officers and infantry of the regular formations. The British had also built a canteen for use by the officers and the advisers attached to the Northern Army, as well as a small airport. In time, the Northern Army would have its small 'air force' of light reconnaissance and transport aircraft that doubled up as bombers and was used to strafe the enemy. The camp had its share of tradesmen, mainly Hijazi merchants who followed the army as it moved north.[1] The apparent hustle and bustle of the camp covered up periods of extreme boredom and inaction, punctuated with endless drilling for the infantry. Nascent divisions between this variegated army had already begun to be felt. The gaping differences between the whisky-sipping officer class from the Arab cities and the tribesmen of the interior were the most obvious,[2] but others, more pernicious and lethal, were the regional, religious and sectarian prejudices that often put the lie to passionately expressed nationalist sentiments. A contemporary witness describes how Syrian officers bitterly complained about the monopolisation by Iraqis of all the senior positions in the army, and how Iraqis, Syrians and Hijazis congregated into cliques. This fragile and often conflicting coalition, behind which loomed the domineering presence of British (and French) imperial power and ambitions, had to be carefully managed by Faisal as, together with his advisers, he prepared the next phase of the campaign. But Faisal first had to navigate through the bombshell that fell in the midst of the Arab Revolt by the publication of the Sykes–Picot Agreement and the advantage that the Turks hoped to extract from its revelations.

Peace overtures to Faisal

The existence of secret agreements relating to the partition of the Ottoman territories into zones of influence and occupation were first announced to the world in November 1917, following the success of the Bolshevik Revolution in Russia. Trotsky, a leader of the Bolsheviks and the regime's first foreign minister, ordered the publication of all secret agreements and pacts that were in the archives of the Russian Foreign Ministry.[3] The newspapers *Pravda* and *Izvetsia* published the details of the Sykes–Picot Agreement in their editions of 23 November 1917. The *Manchester Guardian*, drawing on a despatch from its Petrograd correspondent, published the Sykes–Picot Agreement in its editions of 26 and 28 November 1917. Questions were raised in parliament about the agreement, but Arthur Balfour, the British foreign secretary, glossed over its significance and refused to countenance extensive debate on the matter. It was left to Jamal Pasha, in a speech delivered in Beirut on 6 December 1917, to inform the citizens of the Ottoman Empire and the broader Muslim world about the details of the agreement and its implications for Arab dreams of independence. Jamal himself knew that the fall of Jerusalem to Allenby's army was imminent and that his own position as the Ottoman supreme commander in the Syrian–Palestine theatre of war was under threat. But he was also speaking from a relative improvement in the Ottoman Empire's military fortunes by the withdrawal of Russia from the war and the redeployment of Ottoman divisions from the Russian front to the Near East.

Jamal denounced the agreement, describing it correctly as calling for the creation of Arab states carved out of Ottoman territories, only to be 'placed under the tutelage and protectorate of [foreign] powers'. The Arab Revolt, Jamal went on to say, was no more than a revolt 'to suit the designs of the

British who, needing tools and catspaws to serve their own ends, encouraged certain Arabs to rebel by giving them mendacious promises and hoodwinking them with false hopes.' After depicting Sharif Hussein as an unwitting but delusional agent of imperial powers, who succeeded only in bartering the dignity of the caliphate for 'a state of enslavement to the British', Jamal let on that he had addressed a letter to Sharif Hussein, calling on him to 'turn against the British and return to the fold of the Caliph and Islam.'[4] The speech was delivered in Turkish, but a careful translation was read out in Arabic by a religious dignitary. Newspapers in Syria were encouraged to publish the text and copies were sent to Medina from whence they were smuggled into Mecca and elsewhere in the Arab east outside Ottoman control.

The letter that Jamal alluded to in his speech was not in fact sent to Sharif Hussein, but rather to Amir Faisal in Aqaba. Another, shorter communication was also sent to Ja'far Pasha, the commander of the regular formations of the Northern Army.[5] Jamal's letter to Faisal, dated in the Ottoman Rumi calendar and equivalent to 26 November 1917, was carried by a secret emissary to Aqaba. It was carefully worded and appealed to Faisal's Muslim sensibilities and sense of solidarity, as well as to the occasions in the past when he, Faisal, had concurred with Jamal's policies. Jamal justified the Ottoman Empire's entry in the war purely in terms of its commitment to the defence of Islam: '[so as to improve] the disgraceful condition of the Muslim world to a more independent and stronger existence; or to die in honour and dignity towards this end.' And he reminded Faisal that he too shared these aims. 'In the many meetings that we had, you also generally agreed with my own positions, and I heard you on several occasions concurring with me.' Jamal went on to say that the Arab Revolt could only be justified on one ground: to gain complete independence for the Muslim world and to provide it with strength and prosperity in perpetuity. But then he posed to Faisal a most troubling question: 'But how can you visualise an Arab state tasked with managing the affairs of the Muslim world in an independent and honourable manner when the Allies have announced that Palestine will fall under an international administration, while Syria will be ruled by France and Iraq by Great Britain?' Jamal then opened the door for negotiations and possible reconciliation between the Ottoman Empire and the forces of the Arab Revolt. 'It is possible that at the beginning [of the Revolt] you did not expect such an outcome, but the British army that has gradually annexed Palestine, has proven to you these realities and made them clear for your sight ... But irrespective of these matters, the point is that the opportunity to rectify the situation and remove past misapprehensions has not completely slipped away. If you agree with what I have said, let us examine the issue and try to reach a better understanding, and renew our old friendship. I believe that by writing this letter I have met my religious obligations [to act truthfully]:'⁶ Jamal also appended the terms on which the Turks were prepared to negotiate with the Arabs. He offered Faisal the widest possible forms of autonomy for the Arab provinces of the empire. To add further credibility to his offer, Jamal said that any such deal would also carry the sultan's imprimatur as well as a collateral guarantee from the German government.⁷

It is unclear when Faisal actually received the letter, for it was not until three weeks later, in a brief cable of 14 December 1917, that he told his father of its contents and said that he would forward it to him post-haste. It is improbable, though, that Faisal would have sought to reopen channels with Jamal Pasha without the knowledge and support of his father. His relationship with Sharif Hussein had not yet exhibited the tensions that emerged later between father and son. None of the memoirs of those in Faisal's entourage of the time mentioned that Faisal might have discussed Jamal's overtures with them, and there is no record that Faisal discussed the letter with any of his British advisers before passing it on to his father. Neither at that time did Faisal contact the intermediary that Jamal had nominated for him to relay the views of the Ottoman government, Shaikh Badr al-Din al-Hassani, the well-known religious dignitary from Damascus. Faisal knew the shaikh well from his earlier sojourns in Syria. Badr al-Din al-Hassani had in fact given Faisal his unequivocal support for a rising in Syria in 1915. The only other party in Faisal's camp that might have been aware of the Ottoman feelers was Ja'far Pasha, to whom Jamal also addressed a message, probably despatched at the the same time as Faisal's letter. Jamal's letter to Ja'far Pasha referred to the latter's loyal service to the Ottoman Empire, and reminded him that he now served alongside Allenby's army, which had taken the very Palestine that Saladin had fought to keep for Muslims. Jamal appealed to Ja'far's sense of duty to nation and suggested to him that whatever grievances he might have had could no longer justify the continuation of the revolt in the face of the Allied advance into Palestine.⁸ Faisal and Ja'far Pasha would surely have exchanged their views on Jamal's letters, but there is no contemporary record as to what transpired between the two, and whether they sought to formulate a common position on the matter.

Faisal did not respond to Jamal's letter and awaited his father's reaction. Sharif Hussein instructed Faisal to send Jamal a rejection of his offer. In a letter of 17 December 1917, Hussein wrote to Faisal: 'Your response to the [Turkish] offer is that its time has passed . . . and may Mercy descend on those remaining [Arabs] whom [the Turks] had crushed and oppressed because of [the Turks'] caprices'.⁹ Faisal was to continue with his military operations and also to await the responses to Hussein's communications with the British regarding Jamal's overtures. Jamal's letter did not specifically refer to the details of the Sykes–Picot Agreement, so Hussein's exchanges with the British on this issue may have occurred without him knowing the full details of the agreement.

Nevertheless it is improbable that Hussein viewed the Turkish approach as a disconnected offer of peace.[10] Hussein was clearly concerned about the implications of secret agreements, the details of which he was only partly aware, and wanted reassurances regarding the intentions of the Allies for the future of the Arab east. Hussein forwarded the correspondence with Jamal to High Commissioner Wingate in Egypt and asked him to explain Jamal's references to the partition of the Arab territories of the empire. At the same time, Hussein affirmed his loyalty to the alliance with the British by saying that he suggested that Faisal should respond to the effect that it would not be possible for the Arabs to discuss conditions for peace without the agreement of, and prior discussions with, the Allies.[11]

Wingate, alarmed at the turn of events and fearful of the effect of the Ottoman disclosures on Arab opinion, referred the matter to the Foreign Office. He called for a clear statement denying Jamal's assertions that Britain would keep Palestine and Iraq while France was to take over Syria. Britain's formal response to Hussein regarding the Turkish allegations was developed by the recently established Eastern Committee, a high-level body of cabinet ministers chaired by Lord George Curzon, and charged with formulating policies on all Middle Eastern matters. The resulting message from Foreign Secretary Balfour, delivered through the acting British agent in Jeddah, J. R. Bassett, to Hussein, and dated 8 February 1918, was a 'dishonest communication' and unclear[12]. The message did not deny or verify the authenticity of the Bolsheviks' disclosures, but disparaged Jamal's intentions. The note's concluding sentences were couched in terms that could only be understood as a clear commitment to the cause of Arab independence.[13] It was no wonder that Hussein thought that this statement held a profound British commitment to the cause of full Arab independence.

Hussein's perceptions of what he thought was an unambiguous reaffirmation of Britain's support for a united Arab state, were further reinforced by a cable from Wingate. The Sykes–Picot Agreement was rendered as an innocuous exchange that amounted to no more than explorations into possible policy options for the disposition of Ottoman territories after the war.[14] Hussein should have no fears regarding British plans for the Arab lands.[15] The disingenuous and convoluted elaborations on the true nature of Allied policies for the Arab territories were accepted by Hussein, partly because he had primed himself to accept these assurances without undue probing. It was far better to plough ahead with a false sense of comfort than to find out that he had been ensnared by conflicting policies that would have seriously undermined the bases for his revolt against the Ottomans. Word went out to Faisal that the assurances received from the British were strong and that the representations from Jamal regarding the division of Arab territories after the war were baseless and could therefore be safely ignored. Faisal was instructed to cut off communications with Jamal.

However, the Turks, and behind them their German allies, persisted in trying to peel off the Arabs from the Allies. In late February 1918, Jamal Pasha the Younger,[16] another Ottoman general on the Syrian front, delegated a chieftain of the Bani Hassan tribe to approach Faisal and repeat the Turkish offer to open discussions between the two sides, so that Muslim lands did not fall under the control of foreign powers. Faisal responded by demanding that the Turks demonstrate their true intentions by withdrawing from Medina, Ma'an and all railroad points up to Amman, prior to any negotiations. If this were to happen, he would use his best offices with his father to open peace talks. Hussein, however, preferred to rely on his understanding of the Allies' commitment to Arab independence and closed all doors to the Turks unless their armies withdrew beyond the 'borders' of Hussein's presupposed new state.[17]

Faisal, however, was not completely willing to abandon the possibility of a separate peace deal with the Turks. There is no doubt that Faisal's behaviour following Jamal's peace overtures masked a deep anxiety about Allied intentions regarding the Arabs. He certainly did not share his father's ostrich-like attitude to the gathering evidence that the Allies were hiding their true intentions and the implications for the Arab Revolt of both the Sykes–Picot Agreement and the Balfour Declaration. But Faisal was caught in a very tight vice. His army was a belligerent on the Syrian–Palestine front, acting as the effective right flank of Allenby's forces. The momentum of war necessarily created conditions on the ground that impacted on any peace talks. Faisal was totally dependent on the British for his supplies and armaments, and a bevy of British advisers was attached to his forces. They kept close tabs on his operations and political dealings, especially Lawrence who provided copious intelligence and analysis to his superiors in Cairo. Lawrence also had a number of intelligence sources within Faisal's own camp, which provided him with the means to assess Faisal's dealings, and perhaps counter any tendencies that might go against the British position. Faisal was, of course, aware that his British advisers had dual roles and that there was a limit to which he could take them in his confidence. He was also aware that his father was quite capable of making life very difficult for him if he discovered that Faisal was holding secret talks with the Turks.

Faisal's contacts with Jamal Pasha the Younger continued at least into June 1918. Lawrence had caught a whiff of these secret talks, writing later that 'Djamal was willing to give independence to the Arabs, and autonomy to Syria, and half the riches of Turkey to Feisal, if the Arab Army would rejoin the Turks against the British'.[18] Lawrence had earlier claimed that he encouraged Faisal in his correspondence with the Turks, mainly to sow dissension within Turkish ranks between the militarists/nationalists and the Islamically minded officers, foremost of whom was Jamal Pasha the Elder.[19] But as Lawrence later confided to the British military historian Basil Liddell Hart, these talks with Jamal the Younger were getting out of hand and far more serious than he, Lawrence, would let on. Liddell Hart's jottings on these conversations were as follows: 'Feisal never told [Lawrence] about his negotiations in the summer of 1918 – Feisal was definitely 'selling us'. He thought the British were cracking ... [Lawrence] heard through agents in camp.'[20] Lawrence apparently succeeded, through his agents, in purloining a copy of a letter that Faisal had sent to Jamal Pasha the Younger, dated 10 June 1918. The details of the letter were passed on to Hogarth in Cairo. It made for remarkable reading. Faisal set out his conditions for a separate deal with the Turks:

a. that all Turkish troops south of Amman should be withdrawn from there;
b. that all Arab officers and men serving in the Turkish army in other provinces should be returned to Syria where they would join the Arab army;
c. that if the Arab and Turkish armies fought side by side, the Arab army should be under its own commander;
d. that Syria's future relationships with Turkey should be modelled on the relationship between Prussia, Austria and Hungary;
e. that all supplies and foodstuffs in Syria should be handed over to the Arab army.

The fact that Faisal was prepared in principle to reach a separate peace deal with the Turks if they acknowledged Arab independence did not go unnoticed by the British. The British felt that Faisal understood that there were impossible contradictions between the declared Allied position and the terms of the secret protocols with the French, and that in Faisal's view these could only undermine the possibility of Arab independence. These concerns were reflected in the stream of messages between Cairo and London regarding the manner in which Faisal could be assuaged and dissuaded from pursuing further talks with the Turks outside the purview of the British.[21] Faisal was offered an acknowledgement of his authority in the territories east of the Jordan River, as well as a meeting with Allenby to reinforce his status. However, these gestures did not completely dispel Faisal's misgivings. A number of clear inferences regarding Faisal's true feelings can be gleaned from the 10 June 1918 letter to Jamal Pasha, and in particular a willingness to conceive of the empire as a confederation of states inside which Arab aspirations could be met.

Reverberations from two declarations

News of the Balfour Declaration reached Faisal's camp in Aqaba by the beginning of 1918, arousing profound feelings of disquiet amongst the officers and men of the Northern Army. Grumbling and even rebelliousness prevailed for a while, with the officers refusing to fight alongside the British unless they received assurances that Britain would in fact meet its pledges to the Arabs. Faisal cabled his father regarding the misgivings of his officers and men, seeking some form of confirmation from Hussein that he could share with his men and allay their fears. In the event, Hussein cabled Faisal on 11 January 1918, confidently stating that 'the Allies are greater and more honourable than that they would stray from even a single letter from their agreement with us, and they are the most scrupulous in their attention to such details.'[22] This was yet another example of Hussein's wilfully trusting nature when it came to Allied – and especially British – promises; even so, it had the desired effect of temporarily quieting the unrest in Faisal's camp. But the issue would not go away, and neither would the rumbling restlessness related to the Sykes–Picot Agreement. The unease in the ranks of Britain's Arab allies was beginning to affect the officers of the Arab Bureau in Cairo, as well as the real policy-makers in the Eastern Committee in London. Turkish claims about Allied perfidy were beginning to ring true. Something had to be done publicly to stop the slide in Britain's credibility with the Arabs, even though Hussein clung to his unshakeable belief in Britain's ultimately honourable intentions.

An opportunity to 'clarify' Britain's position on these matters for the Arabs presented itself when seven Syrians resident in Cairo presented the high commissioner with a memorandum dated 26 April 1918, addressed to the foreign secretary. The group, whose name was kept secret at the time, included prominent Syrians, some of whom had been, or were still, members of Arab secret societies.[23] The British focus on the sharifian family as the effective representatives of the Arab 'movement' left the more urbane Syrian notables and intellectuals isolated from British policy-makers until the Arab Bureau in Cairo assigned an intelligence officer, Osmond Walrond, to establish contacts with these groups. Walrond succeeded to the point where he got himself inducted as the only European member of one of the secret societies, al-Qahtaniyya. Walrond detailed the extent of anti-sharifian feeling amongst the urban Syrians, and posed the difficult question of whether the Syrians would accept Hashemite rule after the war.[24] Although Faisal appeared to be acceptable to this group, there were strong reservations about the more traditional Hussein, no doubt fostered by the disdain that the urbanites had for the Bedouins of the desert.[25]

On 16 June 1918, the Foreign Office responded to the Syrians in the form of a statement known later as the 'Declaration to the Seven', which was read out by Walrond to some of the authors of the original memorandum in a formal ceremony at army headquarters in Egypt. A copy of the statement was also sent to Hussein. The declaration affirmed that the British government would recognise the complete and sovereign independence of territories that were already independent before the war, as well as those liberated by Arab arms (essentially the lands under the control of Faisal's Northern Army). Regarding territories liberated by the Allied powers (Iraq and parts of Palestine), the British government would act on the basis that their future government would be based upon the principle of the consent of the governed. For territories still under Turkish control, it was 'the desire of His Majesty's Government that the oppressed people in those territories should obtain their freedom and independence.'[26]

The Declaration to the Seven was a straightforward confirmation of Britain's support for Arab independence with none of the caveats or hedging that accompanied the Hussein–McMahon correspondence and subsequent prevarications and ambiguities of British officials. It also established the boundaries of the Arab region clearly in a way that was no different from Hussein's understanding of it. Furthermore, the declaration established the principle that Britain sought the freedom and independence of the Arabs and would not establish any government in their lands that did not have the consent of the people. It was received with jubilation in Faisal's camp and dispelled the gloom that had descended on it on account of rumours of secret deals and plots. President Woodrow Wilson's speech a few weeks later,[27] enunciating the principle of self-determination for subject peoples as an Allied objective for any post-war settlement, reaffirmed the main points of the declaration and added further lustre to its import. It was a significant factor in motivating and energising Faisal's campaigns in the last few months of the war, and pushing him to liberate as much territory as he possibly could. After all, such territory would clearly be part of an independent and sovereign Arab state.

British damage control regarding the revelations of the Sykes–Picot Agreement also had to be extended to the matter of the Balfour Declaration. Clayton in Cairo wrote to Sir Mark Sykes on 28 November 1917, that 'Christians and Moslems view with little short of dismay the prospect of seeing Palestine and even eventually Syria in the hands of the Jews, whose superior intelligence and commercial abilities are feared.'[28] In the spring of 1918, a delegation of leading British Zionists, headed by Dr Chaim Weizmann, leader of the British Zionist Federation, arrived in Palestine. The visit of the Zionist commission had been approved by the Eastern Committee. Its primary mission was to prepare the basis for putting the terms of the Balfour Declaration into effect, but it was also charged with allaying the fears of the Arab community regarding Zionist intentions.[29] One of the main Arab figures that the Arab Bureau in Cairo wanted Weizmann to meet was Faisal.[30] Lawrence had earlier written to Clayton that he would prevail on Faisal to take an accommodating attitude towards the Zionists, at least for the duration of the war.[31] But Faisal had already seen the effects of the Balfour Declaration on his own officers of the Northern Army, and it is quite likely that he shared their general apprehensions and misgivings. In fact, Lawrence himself admitted that 'The real imminence of the Palestine problem is patent only to Feisal of the Sharifians. He believes that we intend to keep it ourselves, under the excuse of holding the balance between conflicting religions, and regards it as a cheap price to pay for the British help he has had and hopes still to have.'[32]

In late May 1918, arrangements were made for a meeting between Faisal and Weizmann in Aqaba.[33] Lawrence was not available to attend the meeting – he had joined Sharif Nasir on a raiding expedition – and his place was taken by Joyce. The meeting between Faisal and Weizmann took place in Aqaba on 4 June 1918. The meeting lasted for forty-five minutes, and Joyce kept the minutes. 'Sharif Feisal expressed his opinion of the necessity for cooperation between Jews and Arabs . . . As regards definite political arrangements, [Faisal] was unwilling to express an opinion, pointing out that in question of politics he was acting merely as his father's agent and was not in a position to discuss them . . . Dr. Weizmann pointed out that the Jews do not propose setting up a Jewish government, but would like to work under British protection with a view to colonizing and developing the country without in any way encroaching on anybody's legitimate interest . . . Feisal declared that as an Arab he could not discuss the future of Palestine, either as a Jewish colony or a country under British Protection . . . Later on when Arab affairs were more consolidated these questions could be brought up.'[34] Weizmann, of course, was being disingenuous when he said that the Zionist movement was uninterested in a Jewish government for Palestine. As Lawrence wrote later, after a meeting with Weizmann in mid-June 1918, 'Dr Weizmann hopes for a completely Jewish Palestine in fifty years and a Jewish Palestine, under a British facade, for the moment.'[35]

There are no Arab records relating to Faisal's first meeting with Weizmann, so Joyce's notes remain the only source of information on the event. Faisal appears to have accepted Weizmann's assurances regarding Zionist intentions in Palestine, even to the point of recognising that these might entail territorial claims. But, once again, this is a far cry from acknowledging, let alone tolerating, the idea that Arab territory would be irredeemably signed over to Jewish colonists from Europe. Faisal appeared to be aware, perhaps vaguely, that the Balfour Declaration hid some other, more portentous, outcomes for the Arab peoples of Palestine, but he had neither the information nor the means, at that stage, to discuss the political implications of the Zionist project. At the same time, Faisal was aware that British Jewry might play a part in maintaining the British government's support for the Arab Revolt, and perhaps even deflect the more ominous implications of the much speculated upon secret agreements. An idealised affinity between the Arab and Jewish peoples, with each benefiting from the other's nationalist aspirations, frequently cropped up in the despatches and notes of British officials, and Faisal was not unaware of them. An acknowledgement of the role that Zionism might play in the development of the hoped-for Arab state was often affirmed by Faisal. This was perhaps a genuine expectation, or simply a pose to strike the right note with those British officials who were hoping that the Zionist project would be seen by Arabs as helpful to their own nationalist aspirations. But there is no doubt that Faisal, and certainly his father, held a kindly disposition to the Jews of the empire and the Arab world. His father's feelings regarding Arab Jews were those of the traditionally minded; Faisal's position was affected by such views, but further buttressed by the sense that the Jews – and the Christians – of the Arab world were first and foremost Arabs and were to be treated as equal citizens in the new Arab state.

Joyce's notes on the first Faisal–Weizmann meeting must be understood in the light of the unequal status of the protagonists. There was a huge discrepancy between the worldly Weizmann with his intimate knowledge of, and dealings at the highest levels of state in, Britain, France and the United States, and the limited awareness that Faisal had of the true workings of the governments and societies of the Allies. Faisal's early reliance on his British advisers, especially Lawrence, to provide him with accurate renderings of Allied decisions, plans and intentions, might also have coloured his understanding of the issues. However, he would soon learn to test the representations and opinions of the British advisers attached to his camp with those of his more worldly Arab advisers. These were not always disinterested parties, often having their own predispositions and interests. Nevertheless, they did provide a useful counterpoint to the opinion of his British advisers. Faisal was developing his own knowledge of the Allies, and would increasingly would keep his own counsel. But in June 1918 Faisal was still at an early stage in his education as a statesman, and he exhibited an uncertain grasp of complex international issues by sticking to a cautious and non-committal position. It would have been too much to expect that a person with only tangential understanding of the ways of great powers could have held out on his own against such an experienced lobbyist and advocate as Weizmann, but Faisal acquitted himself well. He gave very little away, in spite of later attempts by Zionist historians to portray him as indifferent to, or even a benign supporter of, the Zionist project in Palestine. These narratives simply take Faisal's comments out of context to make their

points. Extreme Arab nationalists have also latched on to the vague pronouncements of the first Faisal–Weizmann meeting and have condemned Faisal for
being insufficiently aggressive in rejecting outright any aspects of the Zionist
plan as then expounded by Weizmann.

The campaigns of the Dead Sea

Allenby's capture of Jerusalem was a brilliant feint that caught the Turks off
guard. They had been expecting the brunt of the attack to fall on the
coastal plain, but instead the EEF swung inland to capture the city. Allenby's
entry into Jerusalem on foot on 11 December 1917 and the moving victory
ceremonies in the newly seized city – conceived by the fertile mind of Mark
Sykes – captured the imagination of the public. The victory was effected with
remarkably small cost in lives and materiel. It also opened up a new phase in
the war in the east. As the possibility of a final victory over the Turks became
that much more real, the political implications of an Allied victory began to
become evident. The French, whose part in the Palestine campaign had been
close to nil, were eager to assert their rights under their agreement with the
British. Allenby chose to pause and recalibrate his strategy for the next, and
possibly decisive, phase of the war. Supplies also had to be replenished and new
troop transfers, mainly from the Mesopotamian theatre, had to be integrated
into the EEF. The burden of fighting the Turks in this period was to fall on
Faisal's army.

In December 1917 Faisal and Joyce had planned for a campaign in the
area south of the Dead Sea with the aim of taking the town of Tafila, nearly
150 miles to the north of Aqaba and 30 miles to the south-east of the Dead Sea.
This area was relatively fertile and produced useful quantities of grain and
timber that were used for the Hijaz railroad. Faisal also wanted to gain support
from the string of villages between his new forward base in Guweira and the
Dead Sea.[36] These villages were not particularly connected to any tribe and
would be the movement's first encounter with non-tribal settlements. They
were a good standard by which to gauge the support of ordinary Arab villagers
and farmers for the revolt. Faisal put his half-brother Zaid in charge of the
force that was to move to capture Tafila. Zaid, though young and still relatively
inexperienced, was nevertheless a brave man and had won the respect of the
tribal forces under his command. Faisal and Joyce developed a plan whereby
Sharif Nasir, with a force of 1,000 tribesmen and 150 regulars under Nuri
al-Sa'id, would cut the railroad line between Ma'an and Dera'a, and two
columns, one marching from the south out of the village of Shobek and the
other from the west, would take the town of Tafila. On 10 January 1918 Tafila
was in the hands of Faisal's army, and Zaid prepared to march northwards to

Kerak. The Turks, however, were planning a counter-attack to retake Tafila, and the stage was set for the largest battle between the Ottoman army and the forces of the Arab Revolt. On 23 January 1918, a large Turkish force under General Hamid Fakhri was sent out to recapture Tafila.[37]

The Northern Army detachment in Tafila was under the command of Ja'far Pasha al-'Askari, and the battle was a major victory for Faisal's army. The Turkish attacking force numbered no less than 1,500 infantry, together with nearly 750 cavalry, transport, and other support soldiers. It was the better part of the Ottoman 48th Division. Of this force of nearly 2,000 soldiers, 250 were captured, 420 retreated back to Kerak and nearly 1,330 were killed.[38] General Hamid Fakhri was amongst the dead, having fought valiantly to the end. A month later, the Turks, learning from their disastrous encounter in the first battle of Tafila, retook the town, with the Northern Army's detachment retreating south to Shobek. But the Turks withdrew from Tafila in late March 1918 to reinforce their positions in expectation of a British attack on the Turkish lines north of the Dead Sea. Tafila was then reoccupied by Zaid.

The Battle of Tafila was described in considerable detail by Lawrence, who gave himself pride of place in rallying and directing the defence.[39] His version of events, however, has been vigorously contested by Arab officers who also participated in the battle. Their meticulous description of the battle, corroborated subsequently by evidence from officers who had fought with the Turkish army, attributed the victory to the heroism of the officers from Faisal's Northern Army (especially the Iraqis), the rallying of the Bedouin forces by a primitive communication system and the resistance of the armed peasantry of the area. Lawrence was generally disliked by the regular officers of Faisal's army, and memoirs of Arab officers who served in the revolt often described Lawrence in less than flattering terms. A young officer at the battle of Tafila, Subhi al-'Umari, describes a scene where Lawrence pops up with his aide, camera in tow, who proceeds to snap a photo of Lawrence with 'Umari, in the middle of a mound of captured Turkish machine guns. 'Umari had supervised the collection and safeguarding of this booty. 'Umari then relates his astonishment on seeing the very same photo reproduced in an English-language magazine with a caption implying that Lawrence had been responsible for securing the victory, with the captured machine guns as evidence.

While the Battle of Tafila was raging, Faisal had personally led a detachment to attack the railroad station at Mudawara, about seventy miles to the east of Aqaba. He was accompanied by Nuri al-Sa'id, the chief of staff for the Northern Army. The detachment comprised Bedouins (mainly Howeitat, Bani Attiya and Imran), together with regular troops backed up with artillery, and armoured cars under British command. On 23 January 1918, Faisal gave the order to attack. In spite of initial successes, the raid on Mudawara was a disappointment. The raiding party was unable to silence the Turkish guns, even with aerial support, or to seize the station. Faisal was bitterly disappointed. In a letter to Zaid of 24 January 1918, he wrote,

> As for us we failed in our raid on Mudawara. And there is no explanation for our retreat except the will of God. We reached Mudawara with large numbers [of troops] . . . and we found in front of us about 200 [of the enemy]. There was a slight skirmish involving artillery and planes. The detachment did not attack on the first day. No one knows the reason except God: laziness, hesitancy, and spinelessness. I couldn't hold out for the second day because of the lack of water and other supplies, and we had to withdraw for no good reason. And it is proof that a person who does not rely on God but only on his own devices is bound to fail . . . We have now returned to the Truth [belief in God's supremacy]. By God, my brother, I thought we would prevail over them in less than five minutes . . . and all others thought the same. As our Lord 'Umar ['Umar ibn-al-Khattab, second Caliph of the Muslims after the death of the Prophet] said at the battle of Hunain [which the early Muslims decisively won]: This is God's Decree.

With the growth of the regular formations of the Northern Army and its increasing significance in the campaign for Palestine and Syria, Allenby appointed a liaison officer to coordinate between the Egyptian Expeditionary Force and Faisal's army. Colonel Alan Dawnay became the principal strategist for the Northern Army as he sought to integrate its campaign plans within the overall strategy of the EEF. Dawnay took up his appointment in February 1918, and succeeded brilliantly, both in representing the needs and requirements of Faisal's army to Allenby, and in integrating the various campaign plans of Faisal, Lawrence and Joyce into workable and achievable goals within the broader framework of the EEF's strategy. But this increased integration of the movements of the Northern Army with the EEF had its negative side. The Arab officers in Faisal's army began to feel that their autonomy was now seriously compromised and they could no longer think of the revolt as the vanguard of a larger Arab movement for independence. To some, the Northern Army had become an adjunct to the EEF.

Matters came to a head in early April 1918, when a large group of officers presented Faisal with a memorandum detailing their concerns about the direction of events and the subordination of the Northern Army's battle plans to the needs of the EEF. The person charged with delivering the note to Faisal was Mawlud Mukhlis, by now the commander of the Northern Army's First Division. Mukhlis had just been ordered to lead a force to attack the Fassoua'a railroad station, a commission that he strongly objected to. Faisal relieved him of his command and ordered him detained until his transfer to Mecca. Ja'far Pasha took over the task of attacking the Fassoua'a station, but the expedition ended in disarray. The bitter cold of that year, the breakdown in the supply convoys and the terrible marching conditions led to a near sedition and the troops forced Ja'far Pasha to withdraw. The bedraggled force beat a disorganised retreat, with many perishing from cold, hunger and thirst. Faisal got wind of the disaster and personally marched to meet the retreating column with food and medical supplies. He pardoned Mukhlis, having witnessed the results of the expedition that confirmed Mukhlis's objections. He then proceeded to convince the recalcitrant officers that the British advisers were not there as provocateurs but rather to help the Northern Army in arranging its supplies and to play a supporting role in combat. The near-mutinous conditions in the Northern Army subsided, but the suspicions and hostility of some of the officers towards the British persisted.[40]

March 1918 saw a lull in the fighting, partly due to the very poor weather that hampered operations, but plans were being set by Faisal and his advisers for an assault on Ma'an, an important and well-defended rail junction. The capture of Ma'an would also seal the fate of the large Turkish garrison in Medina. The Arab plan of attack was to coincide with Allenby's preparations for the seizure of Salt across the Jordan River, to protect his flank as he marched northwards. The capture of Salt would also allow for disruptions in the lines of supply and reinforcement for the Ma'an garrison. Faisal's attacking force was divided into three columns; the first, led by Ja'far Pasha was to attack north of Ma'an at Jerdun. The second column, led by Nuri al-Sa'id, was to attack the railroad station at Ghadir al-Haj, south of Ma'an; and the third column, led by Mawlud Mukhlis, was to attack the heights of Semna, immediately to the west of the Ma'an station.[41] However, Allenby's raid on Salt and Amman had been a failure, and Dawnay was called upon to convince Faisal to delay the attack on Ma'an. At a testy meeting at Faisal's new advanced quarters at Abu al-Lissan on 7 and 8 April, Dawnay sought to delay the attack against strong resistance by Faisal's senior commanders. Too much had already gone into preparing for the attack, and the grounds for holding off so as to accommodate Allenby's timetable were unacceptable to Faisal and his commanders. Eventually Dawnay relented, and a modification of the original attack plan was adopted.

On 11 April, Mawlud, supported by Howeitat tribesmen, succeeded in capturing the heights of Semna. He showed formidable courage in directing the battle with a splintered hip bone. Ja'far Pasha captured the railroad station at Jerdun, taking 150 prisoners, and Nuri also succeeded in seizing the railroad station at Ghadir al-Haj. By 14 April the three columns had established contact with each other in readiness for an assault on Ma'an. Aircraft then dropped proclamations under Faisal's signature, calling on the Ma'an garrison to surrender and promising to treat all prisoners honourably. On 15 April, Faisal, at his advanced post in Wahida, ten miles to the west of Ma'an, gave the order for a general attack on Ma'an. The attack advanced to within a few hundred yards of the town's fortifications, but Turkish resistance was fierce. Faisal was reluctant to call for another assault but was finally prevailed upon by his commanders to do so.[42] The final assault on Ma'an took place on 17 April, culminating in a frontal charge by Nuri al-Sa'id against the railroad station. The assault failed, mainly because the attackers had run out of artillery shells and ammunition.[43] In spite of the outcome, the battle for Ma'an provided a powerful boost to the confidence of the regular formations of the Northern Army. They were able to plan and master the complexities of a modern battle without the leavening of their western Allies. After Ma'an, Faisal was even more determined to march northwards.[44]

The arrival of Faisal's forces in the Ma'an area coincided with the great German offensive on the western front. Resources destined for the Palestine–Syria theatre of war were being diverted to stem the offensive on the western front, and Allenby's advance ground to a halt. Although Jerusalem and Jericho were captured, Allenby had to bide his time, to make his own grand offensive when circumstances were more propitious. It was at this juncture that Faisal's army came into its own. Throughout May and June Faisal kept up a relentless campaign in attacking the railroad north of Ma'an, and several raids were conducted against Turkish concentrations in Jerdun, Hesa and Faraifra. The Turkish garrison in Ma'an, with about four thousand soldiers, was still strong enough to withstand a direct assault, and could be relieved by a force coming in from Amman, where the Turks had nearly three divisions. The Northern Army therefore had to take the initiative against the Turks, and had to be equipped and supplied by Allenby to this end. The first sign that this was indeed happening was Allenby's agreement to provide the Northern Army with two thousand camels from the recently disbanded Imperial Camel Corps. These would be vitally needed to ferry supplies and men along a much wider arc, and allow the Northern Army to launch raids far from Faisal's forward base at Abu al-Lissan.[45] Dera'a, the important railroad junction and the main choke point for communications between the Turkish armies in the field, came within reach of the Northern Army. It was merely seventy miles south of the great prize, Damascus.

By the summer of 1918, Faisal and his army had needed to pass through grave trials and challenges, all played out within a tight geographical space. The political and military dimensions of the campaign were now closely inter-twined, and would become more so as the Northern Army pushed its way northwards, paralleling the Hijaz railroad. Faisal had to balance a variety of

factors without losing track of the vital objective of the revolt: the establishment of an independent Arab state on as large a piece of Arab territory as
possible. In addition to facing the military challenge from the Turks, Faisal had
to contend with myriad other issues that were not the standard concerns of a
field commander. He had to balance the tensions between his British advisers
and his senior Arab commanders, between the Iraqis and Syrians in his officer
corps, between tribesmen and the regular troops, between the tribes themselves that formed an uneasy coalition inside the revolt, and between the
demands of Allenby and the EEF on one side and the Northern Army on the
other. The political issues raised by the revelations of the Sykes–Picot
Agreement, the Balfour Declaration, the peace feelers from Jamal Pasha and
the cracks that were opening up with some of the urban Arab nationalists, who
were alarmed at the prospect of being ruled by Hijazis, needed to be addressed
and carefully managed. Any one of these issues held the potential for derailing
the entire political basis of the revolt. On a personal level, Faisal's relations with
his father had reached an alarming impasse. Hussein had for months refused to
receive Faisal in Mecca, inventing one excuse after another. A damaging rivalry
between father and son as Faisal's profile rose was now a serious prospect.
Hussein was also deeply apprehensive about the presence of so many Iraqi
and Syrian officers in Faisal's camp, as they were mainly opposed to his wider
political ambitions.

Faisal was now the cutting edge of the Arab Revolt, and the decisions that
he took – or avoided – would have major consequences for the cause of Arab
independence. It was probably in this period that Faisal begun to see himself as
an upholder and defender of a cause that was greater than the narrow dynastic
interests of his family or his own personal ambitions. Lawrence's characterisation of Faisal was adulatory in his despatches and in his writings, but Lawrence
later hinted privately to Basil Liddell Hart about other aspects of Faisal's
personality and character that he found problematic. Lawrence was nevertheless consistent in recognising Faisal's commitment to the Arab cause. '[Faisal]
would do anything for Arab freedom – his one passion, purely unselfish . . . it
made him face things and risks he hated,' Lawrence confided to Liddell Hart.[46]
Equally importantly, nearly all the Arab officers and civilians attached to
Faisal's army saw him in this light: as the one most committed to the overall
cause of Arab independence as its best figurehead. He was implicitly trusted,
by tribesmen as well as by the regular officers, to make the right judgement in
relation to the greater goal, and to lead the revolt into battle as well as through
the political and diplomatic minefields that were accumulating inexorably.

CHAPTER 8

✦✦✦✦✦❈❈✦✦✦✦✦

TO DAMASCUS!

THE TWO years that spanned the period between the launch of the Arab Revolt and the preparations for the march on Damascus profoundly affected Faisal's character and altered his understanding of the world. At the onset of the First World War, Faisal saw the world through the constricted perspectives of an Arab amir from a deeply traditional society, tempered by some exposure to the changes sweeping the world from his perch in the Ottoman parliament and from his contacts with the partly modernised elites of the empire. His relations with Europeans were tangential and could not form the basis for a proper understanding of westerners. He was certainly aware of and respected the authority and reach of the imperial powers, but these had not yet impressed themselves directly on the heartlands of the Arab provinces so as to be a factor in his daily life. After the revolt, however, not only did Faisal have to deal with the imperial powers through the parade of foreign officers and officials with whom he had to convene on an almost daily basis, but he also had to develop the rudiments of statesmanship and diplomacy as he came face to face with the political and colonial ambitions of Britain and France. His dependency on the British for money and supplies, as well as on military and political advice and support, were greatly complicating factors and had a direct affect on his behaviour, forcing him to balance conflicting and even contradictory objectives while maintaining a focus on the ultimate prize of political independence for the Arabs.

Faisal at thirty-five

The swirl of events and personalities, intermixed with a brutal military campaign, forced themselves on Faisal and contributed to the evolution of a persona that would mean different things to different people. To the Arab nationalist officers and effendis of Syria and Iraq, Faisal was the visible embodiment of Arab aspirations for independence, now made even more insistent by an uprising that had sundered the historic connections between Arabs and the Ottoman Empire. To the rank and file of Bedouins forming the bulk of his fighting forces, and for their chieftains, Faisal was the scion of what was probably Arabia's most noble family. He was a sharif, whose illustrious status put him above tribes and ethnicities and demanded respect in person and obedience in war. He was also the source of the gold the Bedouins were receiving in unaccustomed abundance for their contribution to the Arab Revolt. To the British officers attached to his camp, and especially to Lawrence, Faisal was the essential Arab face of the revolt, to be advised and nudged in the 'right' direction, one whose qualities had to be nurtured – and exaggerated, if necessary – to keep the forward momentum of the revolt continuing. To them, he was a person who had authentic qualities but was not quite capable of standing on his own against the weight of military officialdom and the complexities of international affairs. The French saw him almost in the opposite light. Faisal was the person most likely to thwart their ambitions in Syria and the Levant, and derail their carefully laid and agreed plans with the British for the political division of the Middle East. Faisal was also developing an international profile, greatly assisted by the publicity being generated for Lawrence in Europe and America by the American journalist Lowell Thomas.[1] Another aspect of Faisal's character was defined by his relationship with his father and brothers. The cause of the Arab Revolt could not be totally separated from the dynastic ambitions of the sharifian family, and Faisal had to also contend with the vicissitudes in his father's attitude towards him, which fluctuated from generous praise for Faisal's achievements to outright petulance. Hussein was loath to lose control over the activities of the Northern Army and often became suspicious of Faisal's motives and angry about Faisal's positions and relationships.

The way that others saw Faisal and sought to deal with him was determined by a personality that itself was undergoing a profound transformation and maturation process. The move from the relative certainties of an Ottoman-dominated world and the traditional social and political milieu of the Hijaz to the tumult of war and an alliance with European powers must of itself have been unsettling. Faisal had to develop in quick step a knowledge of the developing new order at a time when he had also to cope with the breakdown of the old verities. There were inherent difficulties and challenges in the process of transition from one set of rules and constants to another still undefined in their final contours. A measure of caution and hesitancy necessarily developed in Faisal as he had to come to terms with these new realities and variables, without possessing the tools of familiarity and experience. An unnatural hesitancy was thus born out of prudence, and ran counter to his innate impulsiveness and orientation towards action. The core of Faisal's character was a deep sense of duty – to his family, to the Arab cause and to the tribes that supported the revolt. Bonds of trust naturally evolved out of a sense of duty towards others, but this trust might easily be compromised by an imprudent course of action, one that would shatter a fragile alliance whose pathways to success were already fraught with risks and dangers. However, this caution might also be misinterpreted as timidity, as it was later by Lawrence when he alleged this in a post-war conversation with the military historian Basil Liddell Hart.[2]

At the age of thirty-five, Faisal was thus forced to develop a new set of perspectives and behavioural characteristics that overlay his personal predispositions. Until the arrival at his camp in August 1918 of a group of nationalist followers, one of whom would later become his closest external confidant, Faisal's most trusted counsellors were his own family members. In his letters to his father during the war years, Faisal emerges as a person marked by a deep sense of filial piety and concern for his brothers. This would be normal in the exchange of letters between fathers and sons raised in a traditional framework, but the terms of respect and endearment employed by Faisal were beyond the formulaic. As the revolt progressed, however, Faisal's letters became increasingly confident in tone, especially when relating and assessing military and political issues, and, though still couched in respectful terms, they indicated his growing self-assuredness. Although his family were the main repositories of Faisal's trust in the war years, his two brothers, Ali and 'Abdullah, were mostly involved in besieging the Turks at Medina, and were not able to provide the type of timely advice that he needed. His father was physically distant in Mecca, and Faisal's journeys to the Hijaz became less frequent with the progress of the campaign. His half-brother Zaid, though much younger, did fulfil the role of trusted aide, but he was too immature politically to play the part of an adviser. Faisal, however, did rely a great deal on the help and assistance of his *ashraf* relatives, some of whom were particularly close to him, such as Sharif Nasir. But none had the breadth of experience and openness to the outside world to be able to provide Faisal with the type of advice he needed to navigate the dangerous diplomatic and political waters. The tribal chiefs who were closest to him may have been brave, shrewd and cunning, but these were insufficient grounds for them to act as trusted advisers. The Arab officers in the Northern Army might have played this role. Amongst them, the closest person to Faisal was Ja'far Pasha, and to a considerably lesser extent Nuri al-Sa'id. The Arab officers, however, formed a clique of their own, given their shared experiences in the Ottoman military and their highly charged views on western powers and Arab independence. The few civilian Syrians in Faisal's camp, such as his personal secretary Faiz al-Ghusain, were, until the summer of 1918, insufficiently close to Faisal to act as advisers and confidants. Although the various Arabs around Faisal collectively provided a counterweight of sorts to the British military and political advisers in Faisal's camp, initially Faisal had little choice except to pay close attention to what the latter told him.

The role of the British advisers around Faisal and their influence on him – especially Lawrence's – have been exaggerated as well as underestimated. Contemporary accounts of the Arab Revolt were overwhelmingly the product of British officials writing their memoirs or histories of the campaigns against the Ottoman Empire in the east.[3] Towering above them all was Lawrence's own gripping war memoir, the *Seven Pillars of Wisdom*, and its abridged version, the *Revolt in the Desert*. Try as he might, Lawrence could not deflect the focus from himself: 'Retreating into the limelight,' as Churchill so deftly put it. Even though he credited Faisal with many initiatives and successes, the underlying tone of Lawrence's book was one of a sensitive and considerate, even self-effacing master dealing with an initiate.[4] The Arabs were not so much extras on Lawrence's stage as people who had to be guided, cajoled, bribed and spurred into action – with the British providing the discrete leavening and stiffening that made this all possible. Assembling the tribes, supplying, arming and transporting the Northern Army, advising on targets and tactics: these were all done by serving British officers reporting in a chain of command back to Allenby. Faisal was simply transported on the back of the herculean efforts of these selfless officers, foremost of whom was the charismatic and brilliant Lawrence. This narrative maintained its force until the opening of the British archives in the late 1960s, which had the effect of modifying without eliminating the thrust of the argument. The counter-narrative of Arab historians has been much weaker, both because of the paucity of war memoirs from the Arab side, the absence of any significant archival material from Arab sources, and the intrusion of ideological and hagiographical biases into the methodologies of historians and biographies. Essentially, Arab narratives either ignore or skip over the role of the British in the success of the Arab Revolt, or dismiss the entire Arab Revolt as a conspiracy to undermine Arab aspirations in which the Hashemites were induced, either wittingly or otherwise, to play the role of cat's paw for the imperialist powers.

There is no doubt that Faisal was greatly influenced by his British advisers. There was no getting round the fact that the insurrection against the might of the Ottoman Empire could only be sustained by an alliance with a foreign power, and with it came the advisers. Initially, the sense that the British Empire was an all-encompassing global affair with immense resources at its disposal, whose counsel and advice could not be ignored, coloured all of Faisal's dealings with the British. This was particularly true in relation to matters where Faisal felt he had little or no information or competence, or when he did not have the means to undertake an independent path of action using his own resources.

When he did, such as in his dealings with the tribes, Faisal acted at his own discretion and his advisers deferred to his judgement. But everything else in the early days of the revolt required extensive British support and assistance: training in explosives; tactics to be employed against mechanised enemy units; transport of troops; aerial support – the list is almost endless. A poorly equipped, often rabble-like force had to be melded into a fighting wing in support of an imperial power's military campaign, and this could not have been effected without the extensive involvement of a British advisory group.

However, it was at the boundary where military necessity rubbed against political plans and ambition that the issue of Faisal's reliance on, or independence from, his British advisers became most problematic. Faisal was a quick learner with respect to the conduct of great powers, and his initial hesitancy regarding the revolt reveals his guardedness of the ambitions of foreign powers in Arab lands. This underlying wariness formed the bedrock of his dealings with the British, but it was overlaid by the realities of dependency on them for military, financial, political and diplomatic support. Faisal was acutely conscious of Arab weaknesses and divisiveness, and the inherent fragility of the Arab Revolt. This generated a sense of anxiety in his character that was at times highly strung and impulsive. It fed into his sparse eating habits and his constant smoking, and had deleterious effects on his general well-being. Faisal's health was not always robust, but he carefully managed to hide his disposition behind his effusive and charming public manners.

Faisal was prone to mood swings when it came to assessing and responding to setbacks. The chance that the revolt might buckle under the blows of Turkish counter-attacks was lurking just below the surface. For example, the failure of Allenby's raids to take Salt and Amman in March 1918 badly affected Faisal, who believed that this would threaten the position of the Northern Army.[5] Faisal was keenly aware of the constant condition of vulnerability of the Arab Revolt, and this played an important part in his dealings with his advisers. He had to accept the advice proffered despite the fact that it might conflict with his broader goals and ambitions, or was less than what he had expected or demanded. His style, which later became famous as the 'u'ukudh thumma utlub' ('take and then demand more') strategy, created a great deal of misunderstandings and misgivings, and generated a number of erroneous ideas about his character. It gave rise to contradictory accusations of both duplicity and capitulation to foreign pressure. By accepting less than what was expected, nationalists would charge Faisal with caving in to foreign demands; by claiming more after appearing to settle for what was agreed, others would charge Faisal with double-dealing. In essence, these contradictory traits were obverse signs of a single strategy for someone whose position was precariously balanced between opposing currents. The accumulating pressures that forced Faisal to adopt this character trait first began to bubble to the surface in the spring and summer of 1918, but they would appear time and again the future. Above all, it was the shifting of the landscape for the Arab Revolt from the raids and battles of the Hijaz War to the increasingly politicised environment of 1918.

The enormity of the issues forcing themselves on Faisal began with the unease that was generated by both the Anglo-French agreements and the Balfour Declaration regarding the shape of the post-war Near East. While Hussein first chose to sweep their implications under the carpet, Faisal had to confront them on an almost daily basis in his camp. The Arab officers and his Syrian civilian followers were there to make sure of that. This necessarily generated issues regarding the trustworthiness of his British advisers, and the extent to which they were working with a dual agenda. However, Faisal's choices in this respect were severely curtailed. He had no choice but to trust his British advisers outwardly unless and until circumstances and events proved the contrary. Even then, he could not make a clean break with them as long as the dependency issue remained. Lawrence mistook this outward sign of acceptance of the advice that was offered by him and others as a measure of Faisal's impressionability. It often led to an easy, even condescending attitude that at times took Faisal for granted.[6] Faisal must have taken umbrage at these posturings, as his later comments would confirm, but he was also a realist who acknowledged and appreciated the often correct and constructive advice that he did receive. In the final analysis, Faisal accepted the influence of his British advisers, but only as the direct result of a clear calculation on his part to accept such advice where it did not conflict with, or contradict, his larger plan, or where he simply did not have the wherewithal to evolve his own position.

Until the launch of Allenby's major offensive against the Turkish lines in Palestine and Syria in September 1918, Faisal's military posture was driven by urgency to extend the territory effectively under his control, as well as by the demands of his British advisers that focused naturally on removing the Turkish threats to Allenby's right flank. Faisal's task from the British perspective was to counter the Turkish threat to Allenby by the destruction of as much of the Hijaz railroad as possible and the elimination of Turkish garrisons and military formations alongside its route. On the other hand, extending the reach of the Northern Army was connected in a fundamental way with establishing precedents that would help in the founding of an independent Arab state. Faisal recognised that Arab claims to independence would be greatly enhanced if the quality and range of his nascent staff would match the requirements of building a new state. This pushed him into reaching out to the educated elites of Syria and Iraq to attach themselves to his movement, a situation that also raised the possibility of increasing conflict not only with the tribal backbone of his army but also with his British advisers, some of whom, including Lawrence, were

very antipathetic to this class. Lawrence much preferred the company of
Bedouins and tribesmen, repositories of the virtues (and vices) that Lawrence
considered defined the authentic Arab character. Lawrence liberally applied
the epithets of deceitful, cowardly and craven to the urban effendis who began
to congregate around Faisal as the revolt took hold. 'With the noisy facility of
the Syrian – an ape-like people having much of the Japanese quickness, but
shallow – they [the Arab members of the secret societies] speedily built up a
formidable organisation. . . . They expected freedom to come by entreaty, not
by sacrifice.'[7] Faisal's camp abounded in such contradictions, and the thankless
task of managing highly strung people with egos to match fell on him. Faisal
had to put on many faces and masks to cater to each of these varied constituen-
cies, and most sought to identify him with their own particular cause or
perspective. To be able to carry this through over a prolonged period – even up
to his death – would have taken its toll on any lesser man.

An additional strain on Faisal, more personal and thus more wounding,
were the beginnings of an estrangement between his father and himself.
Hussein was not necessarily jealous of Faisal, his achievements or his growing
international stature. What concerned him most was that Faisal was slipping
outside of his control, and both physical distance, as well as the intensity of
Faisal's contacts with the main British protagonists in the field, created an alternative node of power. Hussein had a controlling character and frequently
resorted to inexplicable and counter-productive measures to assert his
authority. One of the most egregious cases in which Hussein showed his petulance and his disregard for consequences was an incident in August 1918
involving Ja'far Pasha al-'Askari. Earlier that month, Ja'far Pasha had received
from Allenby the CMG order, a high decoration honouring him in his capacity
as commander-in-chief of the Northern Army. Ja'far was greeted by a guard of
honour from the Dorset Yeomanry, the very same regiment he had encountered in the Libyan Desert when he was fighting alongside the Sanussi
tribesmen![8] On the following day, 17 August 1918, a proclamation in the official *Qibla* newspaper in Mecca, obviously published with Hussein's knowledge,
announced that Ja'far Pasha was merely in charge of one of the formations of
the Northern Army, and had never been appointed to the post of commander-
in-chief. Given that Faisal had made Ja'far commander-in-chief in 1917, admittedly without this appointment being formally approved by Hussein, the
assertion by Hussein regarding Ja'far's status was a direct affront not only to
Ja'far but also to Faisal.[9] Ja'far submitted his resignation immediately, and all the
senior officers of the Northern Army followed suit. In a telegram of 29 August
to his father, Faisal himself resigned from his post. Rumours of Faisal's resignation reached the irregular forces, and they in turn became sullen and mutinous. The whole imbroglio led to the suspension of military operations and

could have spelt the end of the revolt, at least in its old form. Wingate, Allenby and Wilson in Jeddah all scrambled to get the king to retract his statements, but to no avail. In fact Hussein went one step further and, in a cable to Zaid, called Faisal a traitor and put Zaid in charge.[10] The crisis was defused when Lawrence engineered an artful interception of the most poisonous messages from father to son and changed their content into less offensive passages.[11] Hussein was then encouraged by the British to wire a half-hearted apology, which Faisal accepted, announcing to all the assembled officers and staff after he had read Hussein's doctored cable: 'The telegraph has saved all our honour'.[12] This incident, grave though it could have been, ended well. However, as a reflection of the ends to which Hussein was prepared to go to assert his power over Faisal, it contributed to the growing alienation between father and son. In time, this alienation would extend to Hussein's other sons, as his obstinacy, suspiciousness and demanding nature grew to intolerable levels.

Faisal's last month at the camp at Wahida also coincided with the last of the Turkish peace overtures. Amir Sa'id al-Jaza'iri, a descendant of the great nineteenth-century Algerian rebel Amir 'Abd al-Qadir who spent his last years in Damascus, had been exiled by the Ottoman authorities to Anatolia. Amir Sa'id was allowed to return to Damascus in the summer of 1918, partly to act as an intermediary with Faisal. Jamal Pasha the Younger met with Amir Sa'id at the former's camp at Salt, where he asked him to deliver a letter to Faisal that called for a peace settlement between the warring parties.[13] On 12 August 1918, Faisal met with Amir Sa'id at the camp of Wahida in the presence of Faiz al-Ghusain (his personal secretary), Zaid and Nuri al-Sa'id. Jamal's letter carried no specific peace proposals, so Faisal was obliged to reply in general terms. Faisal warned Jamal that his forces were in imminent danger of destruction. All the Arabs wanted 'was to live free and in peace and harmony with the Turks. . . . [The Arabs'] relationship with you should be no different from that between Bavaria and Prussia.'[14] To his father, Faisal wrote: 'I was visited yesterday by Amir Sa'id al-Jaza'iri as an emissary from Jamal, with a letter from the latter. Jamal asked that there should be no more bloodshed between us, saying that he agreed to all our demands. I gave [Amir] Sa'id a stern response, and repeated to him that this was no more than a [Turkish] ruse and deception.' But both Faiz al-Ghusain and Amir Sa'id al-Jaza'iri later wrote that Faisal had asked Jamal to pull back Turkish forces from Arab lands and concede independence to the Arabs. According to Amir Sa'id, Jamal cabled Istanbul to accept Faisal's demands and claimed that Sultan Muhammad Rashad had acceded to them and ordered his cabinet to concur. But Enver, Talat and other CUP leaders ignored the sultan's instructions.[15] Thus ended the last attempt at reconciliation between the Turks and the Arab Revolt.

The advance on Azraq

On 30 August 1918 a band of tired and bedraggled men appeared at Faisal's forward camp at Wahida, near the besieged town of Ma'an. They were part of a caravan that had undertaken a dangerous and tortuous twenty-day journey from Damascus through Turkish lines to join Faisal's revolt. The group included senior members of al-Fatat secret society, one of whom, Rustum Haidar, would become Faisal's close friend and confidant, and one of his main advisers. Another, Tahsin Qadri, would serve as Faisal's personal aide.

Muhammad Rustum Haidar was born in Baalbek, Lebanon in 1899, the son of an Ottoman provincial administrator from a well-established Lebanese Shi'a Muslim family.[16] After graduating from a secondary school in Damascus, he attended the elite Imperial Academy in Istanbul to study political science and public administration, graduating in 1910. In Istanbul Haidar fell in with the nascent Arab movement and befriended its leading lights there, two of whom at the time were the Syrian Dr Ahmad Qadri and the Palestinian 'Awni 'Abd al-Hadi. They were to become Haidar's lifelong friends and would later serve under Faisal. Haidar then left for Paris to complete his studies at the Sorbonne, where he continued in his nationalist activities, organising an important Arab cultural club. Haidar was also involved in secret political activities and was one of the three founding fathers of al-Fatat society, whose structure was first conceived in Paris 1911.[17] Returning to Syria he became a history lecturer and teacher at a number of academies, finally heading the Salahiya College in Jerusalem, an institution promoted by Jamal Pasha to propagate a modernised version of an Islamic education. As Allenby's armies reached Jerusalem in December 1917, Haidar left for Damascus, where he would contact his old comrades from al-Fatat society in preparation for the move to join Faisal.

The group, which was the core of al-Fatat, still active in Damascus, had been in contact with Faisal throughout the revolt, mainly through the channel of one of its leaders, Dr Ahmad Qadri, Tahsin's brother.[18] Ahmad Qadri was providing useful intelligence to Faisal regarding the disposition and plans of the Ottoman forces through a sympathiser on the general staff of the Fourth Army.[19] Conditions in Damascus were becoming more precarious for the group, and Qadri contacted Faisal to see if he would allow them to leave Damascus and join his camp. Upon receiving Faisal's permission, Qadri organised the main party of al-Fatat leaders and sympathisers, who were then joined by a much larger group consisting of those who wanted to reach their families in Egypt and other areas occupied by the EEF. The caravan included dozens of Armenian families who had taken refuge from Turkish repression in the Druze Mountains, and whom Faisal had specifically taken under his protection. One of the al-Fatat members was Khalil Sakakini, a writer and poet who composed a famous ode in praise of Faisal that was set to music and became a rallying song of the revolt and the early Arab nationalists.

The arrival of the group coincided with the final preparations for the advance of a major force of the Northern Army on to Dera'a through the oasis town of Azraq, well east of the Hijaz railroad and the main Turkish concentrations. The major German offensive on the western front had been stopped, and Allenby's army, reinforced by units from Australia and New Zealand, Mesopotamia and India, was now poised for the decisive coastal offensive against the Ottoman forces in Palestine and Syria. The risk of a Turkish attack on Faisal's weaker forces in the Ma'an area, however, remained. If successful, this could have threatened the entire offensive, as well as disrupting Faisal's own plans to march northwards towards Dera'a and Damascus. A plan was laid out by Lawrence and Dawnay, with Allenby's approval and Faisal's concurrence, to mount a major raid on Dera'a from a base at Azraq, to take place on 16 September 1918. This raid was to coincide with Allenby's main push along the coastal plain, and was to confuse the Turks as to the direction of the major offensive as well as to disrupt their lines of communication and supplies. With the end of the crisis engendered by Hussein's peevishness, Faisal prepared to leave his camp at Abu al-Lissan for Azraq. On 9 September 1918, Faisal departed at the head of his force, accompanied by Joyce.

The march to Azraq was hazardous, with German planes on the prowl. The marches were often done at night to avoid the column being spotted. The heat of the day was intolerable. At one point in the desert before Azraq, the column had halted midday to rest. Colonel Walter Francis Sterling, who had only recently joined the Northern Army as a staff officer to the regulars, recounted a revealing story: 'Only a small tent shaded Feisal from the sun, his companions sitting around on camel saddles or sprawled on their sheepskins on the ground. Suddenly, in the distance, Bedouin horsemen were seen galloping towards them. Reining up by Feisal's party they dismounted and were drawn into the circle around the tent . . . Nuri [Pasha Sa'id] with a shake of his head indicated that he had no idea who they might be. In the long silence that followed Feisal remained calm. Finally, after coffee had been served, their visitors addressed Feisal. They were leaders of the great Ruwala tribe they said. They came on behalf of their chief, the Amir Nuri ibn al-Sha'lan. They were prepared to pledge their support, but at a price. Whatever the price, they represented an enormous grazing area and the greatest power in Southern Syria.'[20] Faisal's long cultivation of Nuri al-Sha'lan had finally paid off. On 12 September 1918, Faisal, together with the main body of the Arab regulars, arrived at Azraq.

The Arab force that assembled at Azraq was not only bent on securing Allenby's flank and cutting off Turkish forces in the east of the Jordan by severing Turkish lines of communication along the Hijaz railroad but was also preparing for the major breakthrough that would lead to Damascus, the symbolic objective of the military campaign. The regular formations included 450 in the camel corps and machine gun and artillery detachments, including the French battery under Pisani, as well as three British armoured cars. They were to be augmented by much larger tribal forces now that the Ruwala, led by Nuri al-Sha'lan, had finally joined the rebellion. The presence of the large force at Azraq was designed to deceive the Turks into thinking that the real direction of the attack was the much closer town of Amman rather than Dera'a itself. The disposition of the Arab force would also be seen as part of an Allenby strategy to attack eastwards once again, and deflect Turkish attentions from the true direction of the thrust, along the coastal plain. Dawnay wrote in a report: 'Measures have been taken to spread among the local Arabs rumours of an impending attack by Amir Feisal on Amman from the east.'[21] The true targets were Turkish communication lines around the town of Dera'a, especially the northern, western and southern railroads that converged there. Raiding parties left Azraq on 13 September. Nuri al-Sa'id was in charge of the larger northern operations, while Frederick Peake, a British officer commanding a mixed party of Egyptians and Gurkhas, moved against the railroad line south of Dera'a. The raids were successful and effectively cut off Dera'a from the north and the south. The attack on the branch line to Palestine west of Dera'a was also successfully carried out on 18 September, when Lawrence and Nuri al-Sa'id, leading the Arab regulars, attacked and destroyed the station at Muzeirib and demolished large sections of the rail lines. By 19 September, the raiding expeditions returned to their new camp at Umtaiye in Jebel Druze, successful beyond all expectations and with very few human and material losses. The Northern Army had completed its main mission regarding Allenby's upcoming offensive. Dera'a was effectively isolated, and elements of the Turkish Fourth Army east of the Jordan that was based in Amman were now cut off.

On 19 September 1918, Allenby launched his major and decisive attack. At the Battle of Megiddo (the biblical Armageddon), the Ottoman Seventh Army, part of the Yildirim Army Group commanded by Liman von Sanders and the only functioning Ottoman unit west of the Jordan, was effectively destroyed. Its retreating columns from the town of Nablus were mercilessly bombed by the RAF, leaving a six-mile trail of abandoned or destroyed transport, artillery and military equipment. For three days, however, no news of Allenby's victory reached the Arab army, who were anxiously holding their position and fearful of a major counter-attack from Turkish units based in Amman and Dera'a. Lawrence had returned to Azraq where Faisal had remained during the raids, hoping to catch an RAF plane that was scheduled to be in Azraq on 21 September with news of the outcome of the offensive. Lawrence was seeking to convince Allenby's headquarters to provide air cover for the Arab army in the event of Turkish counter-attacks. When the plane landed it brought news of the extraordinary victories of the EEF. It also brought a message from Allenby to Faisal: 'I send your Highness my greetings and my most cordial congratulations upon the great achievement of your gallant troops about Deraa, the effect of which has, by throwing the enemy's communications into confusion, had an important bearing on the success of my own operations. Thanks to our combined efforts, the Turkish Army is defeated and is every-where in full retreat . . . Prisoners already counted number eight thousand and we have taken over a hundred guns as a well as a great mass of war material of every description, the extent of which it is not at present possible to estimate. Already the Turkish Army in Syria has suffered a defeat from which it can scarcely recover. It rests upon us now, by the redoubled energy of our attacks, to turn defeat into destruction.'[22]

Dawnay sent another message to Joyce, delivered by the same plane, which carried Allenby's new instructions for the Arab Army. The railroad line south of Dera'a was to be completely smashed to eliminate once and for all the threat to the EEF's flank, and the tribes were to be mobilised to block any paths of retreat for the remnants of the Ottoman armies seeking to cross east of the Jordan. But there was also another part of the message that dealt specifically with Faisal and the march to Damascus: 'Above all he [Allenby] does NOT wish Feisal to dash off, on his own, to Damascus or elsewhere – we shall soon be able to put him there as part of our own operations, and if he darts off prematurely without General Allenby's knowledge and consent, to guarantee his action, there will be the very devil to pay later on, which might upset the whole apple cart. So use all your restraining influence, and get Lawrence to do the same, to prevent Feisal from any act of rashness in the north, which might force our hand and in the wrong direction. The situation is completely in our hands now, so Feisal need have no fear of being carted, provided he will trust us and be patient. Only let him on no account move north without first consulting General Allenby – that would be the fatal error.'[23]

Throughout this crucial period, Faisal's stature with the people of the area continued to grow. His army had assumed almost mythical proportions amongst the peasantry of southern Syria, and his commanders became household names. 'The people of Shaikh Saad [a village in the Hawran district north of Dera'a] came shyly to look at Feisal's army which had been a whispered legendary thing, and was now in their village, led by renowned or formidable names – Talal, Nasir, Nuri, Auda,' wrote Lawrence of the passage of the Northern Army through one of the villages of the Dera'a district.[24] Rustum Haidar in his diaries describes how Faisal was obeyed in all matters by his followers, and his entire camp was solici-tous of his comfort.[25] The collapse of the Ottoman front brought out the people of the small towns and villages of southern Syria into an open revolt against the retreating Turks, and emissaries from Damascus arrived regularly at Faisal's camp at Azraq. 'We used to plead with people to join the revolt. But now, whoever wants to stay at home can do so, and whoever wants to fight with us is welcome,' Faisal said to a delegation of Druze notables.[26]

On 22 September, Faisal, accompanied by Dr Ahmad Qadri, Nuri al-Sha'lan and Lawrence, visited the front, returning only on the 25th with news of the disintegrating Ottoman armies and risings throughout the area. Nearly four thousand stragglers from the Ottoman armies were holed up in Dera'a. A thousand of them had been stripped of their clothing by Bedouins during their retreat into Dera'a. The ten days between the launch of Allenby's offensive and the capture of Damascus saw Turkish forces collapsing at all levels and withdrawing in panic from long-held positions. The Turkish retreat was everywhere stymied by the destruction wrought on the Hijaz railroad, forcing the soldiers to take to the roads. Columns of retreating troops were waylaid by Bedouins or armed peasants. The front line was indistinct, confused and jumbled. Mustafa Kemal, the commander of the defeated Ottoman Seventh Army and later the founder of the modern Republic of Turkey, was one of those who were nearly captured by Arab army troops as he beat a retreat northwards. Kemal had actually been corresponding with Faisal for some months, part of Faisal's continuing engagement with senior Ottoman officers, and he may have evaded capture by being allowed to escape by Faisal.[27] He could prove a useful ally to the Arab cause as he was known to believe that Turkey should prepare itself for the Arabs' eventual separation from the empire: 'Mustafa Kemal . . . [promised Faisal] that when the Arabs were installed in their capital, the disaffected in Turkey would rally them and use their territory as a base from which to attack Enver and his German allies in Anatolia. Mustafa hoped that the adhesion of all Turkish forces east of the Taurus would enable him to march direct on Constantiniple.'[28] Faisal would later prove a strong supporter of Mustafa Kemal in his struggle for the control of Turkey. Meanwhile, the Arab army, continuing on its march northwards towards Damascus, fell on retreating Turkish soldiers. Atrocities followed atrocities as the Arabs took their revenge against the carnage committed against helpless villagers by the Turks. At Tafas, a small village near Dera'a, a particularly gruesome massacre of retreating Turkish troops took place.

On 29 September 1918 Faisal entered Dera'a in a Vauxhall motor car, followed by the armoured cars of the Arab army. He installed himself in the railroad station. The day before, General George Barrow, commanding the Indian army's Fourth Cavalry Division, had taken control of the town in scenes of mayhem and looting. Rustum Haidar, who was with Faisal in Dera'a, wrote in his diary: 'What great joy . . . Peasants carting off wooden doors, windows, wheels, carriages, cupboards, chairs . . . Looters breaking down doors to steal the wood . . . The town council lost its roof . . . The Turks had burnt it together with Jamal Pasha's (the Younger) house ... dead horses lying in pits ... wounded Turks lying in alleyways ... destruction ... the horrors of war everywhere ... a shame on a barbarous humanity.'[29] The Turks had abandoned the town and were streaming in disorganisation northwards. Barrow sent out a cavalry force for the march to Damascus with the elements of the Arab army under Nuri Pasha al-Sa'id providing protection for his right flank – or trying to get to Damascus first. There was a conscious desire on the part of Faisal to have his forces be the ones to capture Damascus.

The roads north to Damascus held harrowing scenes of death and devastation. The destruction of the retreating Turkish Fourth Army was complete: 'The roads were scattered with enemy who had died from exhaustion and dead horses and broken down vehicles were strewn in every direction. It is estimated that two thousand of the enemy must have been accounted for between Dera'a and Damascus.'[30] Serious planning now started for the government of Damascus and the parts of Syria that would be administered by an Arab authority. Faisal sent out emissaries to the major towns of Syria and Lebanon.

The capture of Damascus

Allenby had given orders to the Desert Mounted Corps, under the Australian Lieutenant General Henry Chauvel, to seize Damascus but with the caveat to 'let the Arabs go first, if possible'. The entry of Faisal's forces into Damascus was not a gift from Allenby designed to provide the Arabs with a symbolic but undeserved victory.[31] The reality was that it was more in the form of recompense for an earlier decision of 20 September 1918 that explicitly forbad Faisal from marching on to Damascus when he had the means to do so. 'The Commander-in-Chief [Allenby] wishes you [Joyce] to ensure that Amir Faisal ... does not embark on any enterprise to the north, such as an advance on Damascus, without first obtaining the consent of the Commander-in-Chief. (In this connection you can, if necessary, quote King Hussein's definite statement that Amir Faisal and his Army are directly under the orders of the Commander-in-chief.) ... Close cooperation with the E.E.F. is essential and there must not be any independent or premature action by Amir Faisal.'[32] So read the order from Allenby's chief of staff, Major General William Bartholomew, to Joyce.

Allenby's good intentions towards the Arab Revolt were constrained by the terms of the Anglo-French agreements on the future of the Arab territories of the Ottoman Empire. Soon after Allenby's September offensive, the French began to badger the British about their mutual commitments under the Sykes–Picot Agreement. Balfour cabled Wingate on 24 September to the effect that Allenby's advance on Damascus should be within the terms of the 1916 agreement. If an Arab administration were to be installed there, the interface between Allenby and such an administration had to be through a French liaison office.[33] Before the month was out, both Wingate and the Foreign Office had sent Allenby instructions to abide by the terms of the Sykes–Picot Agreement. But the British were still holding out for a French relaxation of their demands under the agreement, and even though the two sides met on 30 September to hammer out the arrangements for the occupying authority for territory designated to be under French influence, the British convinced the reluctant French to co-author a declaration that eschewed any annexation claims on Arab lands.

Damascus, comprising 300,000 people, was of great symbolic and political significance to the Arabs. It was a relatively modern city and a leading economic and cultural centre. In the last decades of Ottoman rule it had benefited from considerable expenditure on its public buildings, educational and religious institutions, markets and thoroughfares. The wealthy Damascene classes lived in considerable splendour in elegant stone houses with shaded courtyards. It had immense historical and religious significance as the centre of the Umayyad dynasty that ruled over the largest empire of its time, from Spain to India, and was the site of one of Islam's earliest and biggest congregational mosques, the Umayyad Mosque. Damascus was the key to the Arab nationalist cause and to Faisal. Everything until then had paled in significance.

Damascus was also an important military prize. It was at the centre of communications for the entire Ottoman armies south of Anatolia, and held large caches of weapons and stockpiles of supplies. Its defences were strong, bounded as it was to the west by the mountains of the Anti-Lebanon range, and surrounded by the Ghuta oasis. An attacking army would have to march through rough mountain terrain to the south or through desert to the east. In the event of battle, the city was replete with narrow streets and alleyways, and walled housing that would have provided ample cover for its defenders. The Turks, however, chose not to preserve their control over the city, even though a determined line of defence running from the south of Damascus to Beirut could have held up Allenby's advance. By the end of September 1918 the Ottoman administration in the town had simply disintegrated. The governor and the main city officials had departed and the city's traditional local leadership was absent. Allies of the Ottoman administration, such as the notable Fawzi al-'Azm, and the largest landowner in Syria, 'Abd al-Rahman al-Yusuf, were either in Istanbul or travelling. Some supporters of the revolt had left Damascus to join Faisal in the preceding weeks, while a number of dissident Syrians were in exile or in prison.

The remnants of the Damascene political class were divided into two very distinct camps. The first was led by the Jaza'iri brothers, Amir Sa'id and Amir

'Abd al-Qadir. Their base of support was the 15,000-strong Algerian community in Damascus. The two brothers were exiled to Bursa in Anatolia during the war, partly because of their perceived pro-French inclinations. (Another brother, Amir Omar al-Jazaiiri, had been executed by Jamal Pasha for suspected nationalist activities). Amir Sa'id was allowed to return to Damascus, but his brother 'Abd al-Qadir had escaped and made his way to Mecca at the start of the Arab Revolt. There, Hussein had welcomed him and had given him considerable funds to spend on fomenting rebellion against the Turks in Jebel Druze. 'Abd al-Qadir embarked for Aqaba to join Faisal and thereafter proceeded to Jebel Druze, carrying the banner of the Arab Revolt before him. However, upon reaching Jebel Druze, 'Abd al-Qadir bolted and switched sides, returning to Damascus and proclaiming his loyalty to the Ottoman government. 'Abd al-Qadir, by all reckoning a wildly adventurous and recklessly courageous man, even bordering on the lunatic, harboured a deep ambition to have his family govern Syria. With the Ottoman administration collapsing all around them, the two brothers seized their moment. They had already organised a militia composed of their Algerian followers to be deployed in the city after the departure of the Ottoman army had been completed.

The other main party in Damascus were supporters of Faisal, led by Ali Ridha Pasha al-Rikabi[34] and Shukri Pasha al-Ayubi.[35] However, al-Rikabi had made his way to Barrow's headquarters so he was not in Damascus at this time. On 29 September 1918, the few remaining notables assembled in the town hall – the Dar-ul-Hukuma – and exercised their limited authority by electing the Amir Sa'id al-Jaza'iri to head a government.[36] The flag of the Arab Revolt, which 'Abd al-Qadir claimed had been given to him personally by King Hussein in Mecca, was raised in the town hall, replacing the Ottoman standard.[37] Sa'id proclaimed the establishment of an Arab government under the overall tutelage of King Hussein. He formed a consultative council comprising several local notables, and appointed heads for the Damascus town government, the gendarmerie and internal security. He also fired cables to all the heads of municipalities in Syria and Lebanon announcing the formation of the new government. 'Following the withdrawal of the Turkish State, an honourable Hashemite Government has been established. Becalm the populace and proclaim the new government under the title "The Arab Government", read Amir Sa'id's cable. As head of the government in Beirut, he appointed Omar al-Da'ouk from a notable local family.[38] Shukri al-Ayubi, who had already been charged by Faisal to establish an Arab government, had no choice but to go along with the Sa'id brothers' *fait accompli*, and agreed to work with the new authority. Al-Ayubi must have been disoriented, as he had just been freed from jail. Earlier in the day, a major demonstration, led by one of Faisal's followers, the Golan tribal leader Ahmad al-Maraywid, had taken place in the Midan district of Damascus. The demonstrators raised the flag of the

Arab Revolt and attacked the prison at Khan al-Pasha, releasing Shukri al-Ayubi and a number of his colleagues. The demonstrators, now led by al-Ayubi, marched to the citadel where they released four thousand prisoners.[39] Another of Faisal's followers, Faris al-Khuri, a Christian, who later filled several posts in Faisal's Syrian government, also agreed to serve in the Sa'id government. The Jaza'iri brothers wasted no time in proclaiming their authority. They seized the printing presses of the former Ottoman newspaper, *al-Sharq*, and renamed it *al-Istiqlal al-Arabi* (Arab Independence). The issue of 1 October 1918 praised King Hussein and Faisal, but was mainly concerned with declaring the virtues of the Jaza'iri brothers and claiming that Faisal himself had entrusted the administration of the city to them.[40]

On the same day, Amir 'Abd al-Qadir visited Jamal Pasha the Younger, the commander of the Ottoman forces, who was still at his headquarters at the Victoria Hotel in Damascus. 'Abd al-Qadir wanted to see the back of the Turkish forces so that his Algerian militia could secure the city to his and his brother's advantage. Jamal had already decided to evacuate the city and recognised the authority of the Arab government of Sa'id. Meanwhile, German soldiers attached to the Ottoman army blew up the huge stockpiles of ammunition and even tried to burn down the main terminus of the Hijaz railroad.[41] The ensuing fires lit up the night sky over Damascus.

Despite numerous accounts regarding the events of the night of 30 September 1918, it is still unclear who was the first to enter Damascus. The Declaration to the Seven had made it clear that the Arabs had the right to establish a government over all the territory that they had liberated. Some advanced units of the Arab army may have entered the city on or before 30 September, particularly as it may have been known to them that there were few Turkish defenders left. Australian cavalry units that were deployed to block the retreat of the Turks northwards may have also entered the city from its northern suburbs. Chauvel, however, was more concerned about the military aspects of preparing the city for its assault rather than the political glory that came with being its liberator.[42] On 1 October at 7:30 a.m., Sharif Nasir and Nuri al-Sha'lan entered Damascus. Lawrence, who had been detained outside Damascus by Indian troops of the Bengal Lancers in a mix-up of identity, could only join Nasir and Nuri later. The streets were 'nearly impassable with the crowds, who yelled themselves hoarse, danced, cut themselves with swords and daggers and fired volleys into the air. Nasir, Nuri Sha'lan, Auda abu Tayi and myself were cheered by name, covered with flowers, kissed indefinitely and splashed with attar of roses from the house-tops,' wrote Lawrence to the general staff of Allenby's army.[43] The Arab Army's entry into Damascus was described by Subhi al-'Umari, a Syrian officer, in even more evocative terms: 'On the morrow of October 1, 1918 we [regular] units of the Arab Army marched towards

Damascus and entered it from the Bawabat-Ullah (The Gate of God) and taking
the road of al-Midan-Bab al-Jabiyya-Sanjaqdar-Marja.⁴⁴ The populace were
gathered all the way from Bawabat-Ullah to al-Marja in their thousands, on the
streets, on rooftops, men, women and children. All were greeting us with clap-
ping, songs and anthems, ululations, flowers, rose-water sprayed on us, [the
latter being] a Damascene custom of greeting. I cannot describe the feeling that
possessed me on that hour. My tears were flowing and my heart nearly stopped
from excitement . . . The type of joy that we were experiencing amidst the thousands of the people was a different type of joy, greater than all the joys that a
human being may normally experience in a lifetime. I do not believe that I can
describe it, neither could anyone else who has not experienced and tasted it.'⁴⁵

Faisal, meanwhile, was preparing to leave Dera'a for Damascus by train.
While in Dera'a, he began to map out the skeletal structure of the new Arab
government, making a few local appointments in Dera'a and in nearby towns
and districts. The problems of administering the newly liberated territories
were formidable. He now had to concern himself with the details of local
government, security, supplies and services, especially the provision of drinking
water, in an environment of uncertain authority and dire lack of funds. The
Ottoman currency had collapsed and his source of revenue was restricted to
the British subventions to the revolt. On 2 October 1918, Haidar noted in his
diary the desperate shortages of staples such as wheat, lentils and rice the provision of which Faisal's nascent government was now responsible for and the
absence of an acceptable circulating currency. Faisal's train passed through a
number of small stations, most of which had been destroyed as had a considerable amount of rolling stock. On board the train Haidar described how Faisal,
observing through his binoculars a group of Bedouins separating horses from
camels, related a story about the way the Bedouins worked: 'Once I was travelling at night when the guide stopped and cried out, "People! We have lost our
way". He then dismounted, took a handful of dirt, inspected it and smelt it.
"Stay hopeful", he said to us. After travelling for a while, the guide dismounted
and repeated his previous operation. He then said, "Now, we have reached
the correct way!" On another occasion, a Bedouin from Nejd came to me and
said, "O Amir, I had an infant camel that I had lost four years ago, and now, as
I came to town, I noticed its trace. I followed the traces until I found my lost
camel amongst your herd." I told him to describe the camel. He described it
[accurately], so I paid him its price!'⁴⁶

Lawrence made for the town hall and found Nasir, Nuri al-Sha'lan and
Auda were already there, confronted with the Jaza'iri brothers' new administration. Nasir's apprehensions about the Jaza'iri brothers' actions were mollified to some extent by Amir Sa'id's acknowledgement that he was only acting
on behalf of King Hussein. Lawrence, however, was not prepared to accept the

authority of the Jazai'iri brothers. He held a deep antipathy to them, considering them insane and the worst sort of religious fanatics.[47] Dr Ahmad Qadri had also entered Damascus and was familiar with the inner workings of the main Damascene families. He also warned Nasir and Nuri al-Sa'id about the Jaza'iri brothers' ambitions and the potential threat they posed to the Arab government.[48] Taking matters into his own hands and pronouncing himself Faisal's true representative, Lawrence declared the provisional civil administration of al-Jaza'iri dissolved and appointed Shukri al-Ayubi as the temporary military governor of Damascus, until the return of the permanent governor, al-Rikabi, to the city.[49] An altercation ensured when 'Abd al-Qadir drew a dagger and attacked Lawrence, only to be blocked by Auda. Nuri al-Sha'lan declared that his Ruwala tribe were for Lawrence, and this clinched the matter in favour of Lawrence and Faisal's men. The Jazai'ri brothers skulked away, spewing venom against Lawrence.[50] When Chauvel finally arrived at the town hall, Lawrence and his allies had already despatched the Jaza'iris. Lawrence introduced al-Ayubi to him as the military governor. Chauvel thought that al-Ayubi was in fact the Ottoman-appointed wali of the town, but was later told by Lawrence that al-Ayubi had been appointed by him under the authority of the king of the Hijaz. This dissimulation, together with the fact that Lawrence, a relatively junior officer, had unilaterally taken charge in Damascus, led to considerable tension between Chauvel and Lawrence.

'Abd al-Qadir and his armed Algerian retinue continued to pose a threat to the new regime. On the night of 1 October the Jazai'ri brothers attempted a rebellion, which was quickly put down by the Arab army. Sa'id surrendered and was sent to exile in Haifa. 'Abd al-Qadir, however, went on the run and a few weeks later was gunned down by police while evading arrest. The death of 'Abd al-Qadir may have been instigated by Lawrence and Nuri al-Sa'id. According to Subhi al-'Umari, he was asked to come to the Victoria Hotel on 2 October 1918, where he met Nuri al-Sa'id in the company of Lawrence:

> He [Nuri al-Sa'id] told me that 'Abd al-Qadir al-Jaza'iri is trying to foment a rebellion, acting on the instructions of the French. His presence is a serious threat to the security of the country and its independence and we want to get rid of him in an unofficial manner. I told him do you want me to kill him. He said "Yes". I then said that this order is outside normal military conventions, as it involves an assassination. If you order me to bring him to you alive I will do so, and if he refuses arrest I will bring him under duress; if he forcibly resists I will kill him and bring him to you dead. As for assassinating him, this has nothing to do with me and cannot be part of any military order issued to me. After a little reflection, he [Nuri] agreed to my suggestion and instructed me to ask the chief of police, who was aware of the issue, the whereabouts of 'Abd al-Qadir's house.[51]

However, on the appointed day, al-'Umari was called elsewhere, and thus was not part of the police action that ended in 'Abd al-Qadir's death.

The first day of Damascus's liberation was given over to joy and celebration. British and Arab troops marching through the town were cheered, and exultant gunfire could be heard all over the city. Throngs gathered at public squares to hear emotional speeches. The mood of jubilation was genuine. The years of Jamal's iron rule had been unpopular and the deprivations of war were now at an end. In some neighbourhoods there was concern regarding the intentions of Faisal and the sharifians, but these were mitigated by the presence of large British forces.[52] But the night of 1 October 1918 was a night of lawlessness and widespread looting. Druze peasantry and Bedouins descended on the city, intent on plunder and riot. Turkish-run hospitals, supply depots and shops were looted. Casualties, were low, however, reaching only a dozen before the riots ceased. Units of the Arab army under Nuri Sa'id's command were deployed and order quickly restored. Al-Rikabi, who by then had returned to Damascus and had assumed the post of military governor, set up mock gallows in the public square at Marja and announced that he would execute anyone caught breaking the peace. These incidents of lawlessness have frequently been exaggerated to demonstrate the ineffectiveness of the new Arab administration in maintaining law and order and keeping public services running. In fact, the skeleton Arab government that was set up on 1 October quickly proved its mettle, in spite of the fact that conditions in the city left behind by the Turks were indeed dire. With little assistance from the British, the Arab administration had got the electrical generating system working again by 2 October. The tram service, idle since 1917, was also restarted. The relative effectiveness of the new government was attested by Clayton a few days later in a cable to the Foreign Office.[53]

Faisal's plan for establishing an Arab authority wherever the Turks had withdrawn was far wider in scope, extending well beyond Damascus. This is amply established by diaries and memoirs of the times, which talk of feverish activity in Faisal's camp with a stream of visitors and delegates seeking instructions or guidance from the new power centre.[54] As the centuries-old Ottoman ascendancy began rapidly to unravel, a great number of Arab officers and officials, hitherto loyal to the Ottoman state, began to gravitate towards his camp. However, Faisal had to rely at first on the small core of supporters that had been firm in their commitment to him and the Arab cause. Most of these came from al-Fatat society, which had been instrumental as Faisal's arm in Damascus and in other Syrian and Lebanese towns and cities. They probably did not amount to even a few dozen individuals, to which were added Faisal's personal relationships with the notable families of Syria. The other main bulwark of support came from the Arab officers who had joined the revolt, or who had sought contact with Faisal's army in the last few weeks before the fall of Damascus. In these very early days, the overwhelming desire on the part of nearly all the participants, setting aside their own ambitions and desires, was to establish the credentials and power of an Arab government.

The Turks began to prepare to withdraw from Beirut on 30 September, leaving the administration of the city in uncertain hands. On the same day, before he was ousted from his post, Amir Sa'id sent a message to nationalists in Beirut to proclaim an Arab government. Soon thereafter, Shukri al-Ayubi was sent by the new Arab administration to Beirut in his capacity as the military governor for the Syrian coast. The Arab Revolt had encroached on territories whose administration was not clearly within their mandate. It was a direct challenge to the French, who thought they had an indubitable claim on the administration of the Syrian littoral, according to the terms of the 1916 Anglo-French agreement. Lawrence, presciently, considered this move premature and to be a mistake, believing that it would cause a great deal of trouble with the French later.[55]

Faisal enters Damascus

With the city becalmed and the attempted rebellion by the Jaza'iri brothers crushed, Faisal was now able to enter Damascus in triumph. His train had stopped at Deir Ali, a Druze village, where it was met by a group of peasants who brought the news that the Arab army was now in Damascus and had beaten the British forces to it. But according to them it was the Druze who had been the first to enter the city! Reaching al-Kiswa, about twenty kilometres from Damascus, the train stopped. Faisal ordered Rustum Haidar and some of his own house servants to ride to Damascus to inform Sharif Nasir, the field commander of the Arab forces, of Faisal's arrival. Riding horses, the party made for the Serail (the main government building), but Nasir had already left. Proceeding to the house of the Bakris, Faisal's old friends, they found Sharif Nasir there. They informed him of Faisal's presence at al-Kiswa, and the need for Nasir and Nuri al-Sa'id to proceed there forthwith, to accompany Faisal into the city. After consuming endless cups of coffee, Haidar rushed back to Faisal, but found that none of the accompanying party had yet reached him. Shortly thereafter, however, the welcome party arrived on horseback, by camel, in wagons and in motor cars. The crowd gathered around Faisal, kissing his hands and congratulating him on this great victory. Amongst the crowd were veterans of the war and the Arab cause, as well as opportunists who saw their chance in the new order. Faisal greeted them all. Riding his horse, and followed by Sharif Nasir on his mount, he led the huge procession into the city.[56] He entered it from its southern approaches through the Midan route, surrounded and followed on horseback by the tribal leaders from the Howaitat,

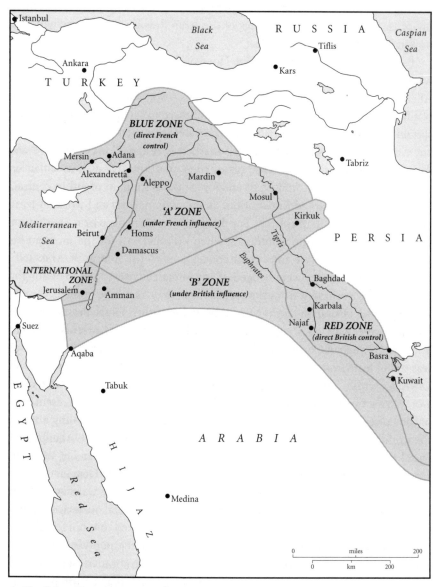

Istanbul

Black
Sea

R U S S I A

Caspian
Sea

Tiflis

Ankara

Kars

T U R K E Y

BLUE ZONE
(direct French control)

Mersin ● Adana
Alexandretta

Aleppo Mardin

Mosul

Tabriz

'A' ZONE
(under French influence)

Kirkuk

P E R S I A

Mediterranean
Sea

Beirut Homs

Tigris

Damascus

Euphrates

INTERNATIONAL
ZONE

'B' ZONE
(under British influence)

Baghdad

Jerusalem ●

Amman

Karbala

Suez

Najaf

RED ZONE
(direct British control)

Aqaba

Basra

Kuwait

Tabuk

E G Y P T

A R A B I A

H I J A Z

Red Sea

Medina

0   miles   200
0   km   200

4. The Sykes–Picot Agreement of 1916

Ruwala and Druze. Behind them were tribesmen on camels and on foot, numbering thousands.[57] It was a magnificent spectacle. All of Damascus appeared to have turned out to greet the hero. Faisal slowly made his way through the mass of people, waving and saluting the townsmen, in scenes of great jubilation and joy. The crowds were deliriously acclaiming him and their unaccustomed freedom.[58] The flags of the Arab Revolt were everywhere. For now at least, the city was at his feet.

Faisal headed for the Victoria Hotel for a prearranged meeting with Allenby, who had arrived by car from Jerusalem with his staff earlier on 3 October 1918. Allenby had just received detailed instructions from Whitehall about the type of administration that the Arabs should be allowed to set up and the attitude he should take towards Faisal and the Arab cause. He was to recognise and support any Arab authority established in areas marked as 'A' and 'B' in the Sykes–Picot Agreement, and respect the symbols of such an authority, such as a flag or emblem. 'Our policy should be to encourage the setting up of either central, local or regional Arab administration, as the case may be, and work, at least ostensibly, through them entirely. For this purpose, there need be no hesitation to accept a merely nominal authority when no other can for the moment be established.'[59] These were important concessions to the notion of Arab self-determination, but they were hedged. If any foreign advisers were to be sought by the Arab government from the Syrian coast, they had to be French.

Allenby and Faisal met for the first time at the Victoria Hotel. Present at their meeting were Nuri al-Sa'id, Sharif Nasir, Chauvel, Joyce, Lawrence, Hubert Young and Kinahan Cornwallis, the latter from the Arab Bureau in Cairo. Faisal was still in tears from the ecstatic welcome he had received from the crowds. As Lawrence wrote, 'They were a strange contrast: Feisal, large-eyed, colourless and worn, like a fine dagger; Allenby, gigantic and red and merry, fit representative of the Power which had thrown a girdle of humour and strong dealing around the world.'[60] No full records have been kept of the meeting between Allenby and Faisal at which Lawrence acted as interpreter. In the *Seven Pillars of Wisdom*, Lawrence devotes a scant number of sentences to the event, but General Chauvel did keep more detailed notes of the meeting, although they were written up several years after the event. Nuri al-Sa'id regrettably kept no record of the meeting.

According to Chauvel, Faisal was informed that France was to be the protecting power over Syria; that the Arab administration in Syria was to operate under French guidance and financial support; that Lebanon, which was defined as the entire Syrian coast from Tyre to the Gulf of Alexandretta, would be administered directly by the French; and finally that Faisal was to have a French liaison officer. Chauvel noted that 'Feisal objected very strongly. He said that he knew nothing of France in the matter; that he was prepared to have British assistance; that he understood from the Adviser whom Allenby sent him that the Arabs were to have the whole of Syria including the Lebanon but excluding Palestine; that a country without a port was no good to him; and that he declined to have a French Liaison Officer or to recognise French guidance in any way.'[61] Allenby then turned to Lawrence and asked him whether he, Lawrence, had told Faisal about a French protectorate over Syria and the French position on Lebanon. On both issues Lawrence stated that neither he nor Faisal knew about these arrangements, in effect denying that either had any knowledge of the Sykes–Picot Agreement. This cannot stand scrutiny, as by October 1918 the details of the Sykes–Picot Agreement were widely known, even though Faisal did not receive any official notification about it. However, the clear message that France was determined to assert its rights under the agreement must have come as an unpleasant jolt. The meeting ended after slightly more than an hour. Lawrence stayed on to inform Allenby of his wish to go on leave immediately and go back to England. Allenby reluctantly agreed. The following day, 4 October 1918, Lawrence was driven away from Damascus, never to return. His official biographer wrote, 'His wartime mission was now fulfilled: Turkey was defeated and the Arabs were established in Syria . . . Ahead lay a more difficult task: to persuade the Allies to let Feisal keep what had been won.'[62]

Faisal left the Victoria Hotel and headed for the town hall where a huge reception committee was waiting for him. His arrival was met with deafening calls of acclamation by the assembled throng of dignitaries: government officials, tribal and religious leaders and the city's notables. The mufti of Damascus came forward and gave his allegiance through Faisal to his father Hussein: the very same mufti who had issued a fatwa in Ottoman times for the killing of Faisal.[63] Faisal then gave a speech to the crowd, the outline of which Haidar recorded in his diary: 'Syria had to proceed on the path of development; were it not for the gallows [of Jamal Pasha] matters would not have come to this end; the necessity to remain true to the cause; the necessity to pursue the war until the Turks leave Aleppo and move beyond the Taurus mountains; all transgressors will be severely punished.'[64] Later in the day Faisal moved to the house of Mahmud Fakhri al-Baroodi, a local dignitary and long-time supporter of the Arab Revolt, where he established his temporary base. On the night of 3 October, Faisal attended a banquet hosted by Allenby. At the table was Nuri al-Sa'id, who sat between Clayton and Captain Mercier, a French liaison officer. Nuri casually mentioned to the Frenchman that the Arabs had captured Beirut and had hoisted their flag over the city. This was enough to set alarm bells ringing with Captain Mercier, who quickly left the dinner table to cable Paris about the Arab challenge to French authority in the Lebanon.[65] This was merely a foretaste of things to come for the French.

For the moment, Faisal was the undisputed leader of the Arabs of Syria. He had arrived at this desired goal after more than two years of hard warfare, marked by high drama, setbacks and dangers. The revolt had prevailed, but Faisal could not rest on his laurels. Immense problems were lying in store. The battle for Syria, but even more, the battle for the essence of the Arab cause, had in fact just begun.

PART III

A SHATTERED DREAM
Syria and the Paris Peace Conference
(1918–1921)

CHAPTER 9

••••••✠✠✠••••••

THE RUDIMENTS OF A STATE

THE FALL of Damascus abruptly shifted the focus of attention from the military aspects of the campaign to the administration of the occupied territories. Faisal now found himself at the heart of the complex tangle of interlocking interests and ambitions, both domestic and foreign, each of which sought to impose its own priorities and control the pace and direction of events in Syria. On the one hand were Faisal and his Syrian and Arab nationalist allies. Faisal had asserted his primacy in Damascus by the appointment of his allies, with Allenby's essential acquiescence, to the key posts of the evolving administration of Syria. Ali Ridha Pasha al-Rikabi became the military governor, and Faisal's supporters were seeded throughout the new government of Syria. The *coup de main* that had unseated the Jaza'iri brothers removed the immediate potential opposition to Faisal's power and authority in Damascus. Allenby chose to accept these appointments and ratified them, but he still had a campaign to fight. Although Allenby wanted to minimise any decisions on his part that would have major political consequences and might prejudice the negotiations at the Paris Peace Conference, in Syria he implicitly accepted Faisal's claim to some authority inside the occupied territories. Nevertheless, his instructions to Faisal, in the latter's capacity as a lieutenant general in Allenby's army, were to recruit more troops and refit them to continue the advance into the rest of Syria. Allenby also advised Faisal to avoid involvement in the civil government of Syria, an obviously impractical suggestion, and to leave the tangled mess of administration to the likes of al-Rikabi, over whom Allenby had direct authority.

But Allenby also revealed, perhaps inadvertently, the extent of France's ambitions in the Levant and its determination to oblige the British to adhere strictly to the terms of the Sykes–Picot Agreement. France, whose efforts in the campaign against the Turks were minimal, was now racing to impose its control over the territories that were marked to be under its direct influence according to the agreement, the so-called Blue Zone, which included coastal Syria. It was also determined to influence the administration of the Syrian interior (the 'Zone A' of the agreement). The seeds of an independent Arab government in Damascus were thus a direct, even mortal, threat to the claims of the French in the Levant. At the same time, Faisal's evolving power structures in Damascus were not altogether welcome to the traditional Damascene elites who had sided with the Turks in the war. At present they were in no position to influence events, but they were biding their time to regain and assert their traditional authority, in partnership with, and if necessary in opposition to, Faisal. The emergence of open political activity and the rise of political parties further complicated Faisal's desire to create a broadly united front to press for Arab demands. The division of the nationalists into moderate and radical camps, with the latter pressing for maximalist demands in spite of the Allies' over-whelming military and political power, was an almost inevitable outcome of the fall of Ottoman rule. From its inception Faisal's government in Syria was beset by grave crises. How Faisal managed and navigated these crises would determine the outcome of his rule in Syria.

The Arab military government in Syria

The rudiments of the government for the occupied territories were discussed at the meeting between Faisal and Allenby at the Victoria Hotel. In fact the main purpose of the meeting was to allow Allenby to relay the guidelines that he had earlier received from the British War Office on the administration of the occupied lands. These had already been agreed between the British and the French and substantially hewed to the Sykes–Picot Agreement.[1] 'The authority of the friendly and allied Arabs should be formally recognised in any part of the areas "A" and "B" as defined in the Anglo-French Agreement of 1916, where it may be found established, or can be established as a result of the military operations now in progress,' read the instructions in part. The Arabs of Faisal were granted belligerent status, granting them some formal recognition and paving the way for their possible inclusion in the peace conference. At the same time Allenby's instructions called for 'the regions so liberated [to be] treated as Allied territory enjoying the status of an independent state (or confederation of States) of friendly Arabs . . . and not as enemy provinces in temporary military occupation.'[2] Allenby was to recognise the flag of the Arab Revolt as a symbol of 'native' Arab rule, and in fact 'to encourage the setting up of either central, local or regional Arab administration, as the case may be, and work, at least ostensibly, through them entirely.' These were important concessions to Arab self-rule, but they did not extend to the Blue Zone of the Sykes–Picot Agreement: Mount Lebanon and coastal Syria. Allenby was also obliged to remind Faisal that if he were to seek the assistance of European functionaries in the running of the Arab government in the A Zone, such personnel had to be French. Although the meeting ended inconclusively and was at times acrimonious, Allenby himself had formed a positive impression of Faisal. Writing to his wife that evening, he said: 'You would like Faisal. He has a lean body with clear features, with a nervous disposition. His hands are as fine as a woman's, and when he talks his fingers move in a nervous way. But he is a strong-willed man with upright convictions.'[3]

These measures were subsequently formalised by Allenby in a note that was sent to the War Office on 23 October 1918, which divided the occupied territories in the eastern theatre of war – excluding Mesopotamia and the Hijaz – into three separate occupation zones.[4] All ultimately reported to Allenby and roughly followed the administrative boundaries of the collapsing Ottoman state. The first zone of occupation, Occupied Enemy Territory – South (OETS), included the Jerusalem autonomous district (Sanjaq), and the provinces of Acre and Nablus and their districts. These were equivalent to the yellow area of the Sykes–Picot Agreement, involving Palestine, which, under the stipulations of the agreement, were to be governed under some form of international arrangement. In the interim, however, they were to be under direct British administration. The second zone of occupation was Occupied Enemy Territory – North (OETN). This was later renamed Occupied Enemy Territory – West (OETW) and included Mount Lebanon and the entire Syrian coast from Acre to Iskenderun (Alexandretta). This was to fall under direct French administration. The last zone of occupation, Occupied Enemy Territory – East (OETE), was placed under direct Arab administration and was the core of Faisal's Arab government. It included the province of Damascus, reaching south into the lands east of the river Jordan, and most of the southern areas of the province of Aleppo.

Faisal did not immediately comment on Allenby's measures, but he revealed his true feelings much later in the interviews that he gave to Mrs Steuart Erskine in the early 1930s: 'The first deception occurred when Field Marshal Lord Allenby announced that Syria had been divided into three zones under the pretext that this arrangement was purely temporary and administrative. The second blow levelled against the Arab's happiness was the confirmation of the secret Sykes–Picot treaty which had been denied in 1917. I have seen with my own eyes the map of the country under three colours, revealing the different fate of the three zones. In this way we had to face the bitter truth.'[5]

The new Arab government in OETE, as well as the Northern Army, were in a peculiar legal and administrative position. Faisal's forces were still technically under the command of Allenby and were part of the Allied forces. Faisal, as the head of the Northern Army, was responsible for all military matters to Allenby's GHQ. The government itself, a blend of military and civilian figures, and headed by Ali Ridha Pasha al-Rikabi, drew its resources from the Allies, while claiming fealty to Faisal, and beyond, to King Hussein in Mecca. From the onset, Faisal and his government sought to ignore or belittle their dependence on the Allies, working assiduously to establish the government's authority and extend the territory under its control. Faisal seized whatever opportunity arose to proclaim the independence of the Arab government as something separate from an interim military administration and to create facts on the ground to pre-empt any counter-moves by the Allies, especially the French, and the many groups that disputed Faisal and the nationalists' claim to power.

On 5 October 1918, Faisal issued his first proclamation to the people of Syria. In ringing tones, he exclaimed that 'an absolutely independent, constitutional Arab government has been established in Syria in the name of our Lord King Hussein'. Faisal announced that a military administration had been formed and that he had appointed al-Rikabi as the head of the government.[6] Faisal had earlier presented the gist of the proclamation to assembled Damascene notables and dignitaries at a banquet the day before. He affirmed that the reach of the Arab government would include areas 'not yet freed from slavery', with reference to Arab lands still under Ottoman rule.[7] Predictably, the French saw these statements as direct challenges to their own ambitions and in open contravention of their agreement with the British. There was no mention of the French role in 'advising' the new Arab government, and the action of the nationalists in asserting their rights in areas clearly assigned to France was another major challenge to French plans for controlling Syria. Faisal had pre-empted the arrival of the French in Beirut by sending his emissary Shukri al-Ayubi to proclaim the authority of the new Arab government. In effect, the attempt by the Arab nationalists to confirm the authority of the new government over Lebanon had begun a few days earlier.

Acting on a cable that was sent out by Amir Sa'id al-Jaza'iri to all Arab officials of the Syrian Ottoman provinces, calling on them to proclaim the formation of the new Arab government, the head of the Beirut Municipality, Omar al-Da'ouk, visited the Ottoman governor of Beirut. He showed him the contents of the cable, and after some hesitation the Ottoman governor, Ismail Haqqi Bey, agreed to recognise the authority of the Arab government and handed over power to him. On 1 October 1918, in a ceremony presided over by Da'ouk as the representative of the Arab government, the Arab flag was hoisted over the main government building in Beirut.[8]

At midnight on 4 October 1918, Shukri al-Ayubi – with a hundred soldiers and accompanied by Jamil al-Alshi, a Syrian officer in the Arab army, and Rustum Haidar – left Damascus for Beirut with instructions from Faisal officially to proclaim the Arab government in Beirut and Mount Lebanon.[9] The train tracks from Damascus to Beirut had been disabled by German detachments with the Ottoman army, forcing the party to travel on horseback. Passing through various villages and towns, where they were received with loud acclamation, the party finally reached Beirut on 6 October 1918.[10] The following day, Shukri al-Ayubi met the Christian leader Habib Pasha al-Sa'ad at the main government building in Ba'abda, on the foothills overlooking Beirut. (Ba'abda had served as the main seat of government during the war.) Sa'ad had been the last leader of the autonomous Mount Lebanon administration before its dissolution in 1915 at the outbreak of war. Habib al-Sa'ad then took the oath of office, as the head of the new administration of Lebanon, swearing loyalty to Faisal's government in Damascus.[11] However, this was a case of overreach for Faisal and the nationalists. The conditions of Lebanon were altogether different from Syria, and the stage was set not only for a serious altercation with the French but also with a substantial portion of the Christian population of Lebanon, in particular its Maronite community.

Confrontation over Lebanon

Faisal had always exhibited a very accommodating attitude to the Christians of the Arab world. During the war Faisal and his father tried to allay the fears of Arab Christians regarding the post-war order and the possibility of the imposition of Muslim religious rule over them. The new Arab state would be based on national rather than religious considerations. Faisal took every opportunity to state his well-known adage that 'The Nation belongs to all: Religion belongs to God', while refusing to countenance any discrimination against Christians, either in his entourage or in the Arab government. A number of prominent Lebanese Christians, including the Maronite leader Iskandar Ammun, did join Faisal, serving as his minister of justice in Damascus, but many Christians, especially Maronites, were suspicious of Faisal's intentions. His move into Beirut and Mount Lebanon was thus determined by his concern that if the Sykes–Picot Agreement were to be implemented in its broad form, Lebanon would be lost to the new Arab state. A separate Lebanese state, dominated by the Maronites and under French protection, would undermine the territorial integrity of Syria and even affect the other main Christian denominations that were supportive of the idea of a broadly based Arab state. Other minorities such as the Druze and the Alawites could also then claim a separate status for their territories, reducing the idea of a single country to at best a loose confederation of sectarian states. On the other side were the mass of Sunni and Shi'a Muslims of Beirut, Tripoli, Sidon, Tyre and the Beqa'a Valley, who would not easily countenance the idea of living in a predominantly Christian state under French protection. Faisal could not abandon his claim to these regions without subjecting himself to accusations of abandoning the Muslims of Lebanon to Christian and foreign rule.

He was well aware of the particularities of Lebanon, with its complex mix of sects and denominations, both Christian and Muslim. Its population was estimated at about 520,000 people before the war, with a Christian population of about 345,000.[12] The Maronite Christian community was the largest single denomination and had historic and religious links to Europe, in particular to France. It was led by its very powerful clergy, who saw a chance of wresting control over the entirety of Lebanon by carving out a state that would include Mount Lebanon as well as the coastal littoral and the Beqa'a Valley with their predominantly Muslim population. This 'Greater Lebanon' could not come into being without the support of France and the establishment of some form of a French protectorate over its territory. But in early October 1918, French forces were nowhere to be seen, while Faisal, allied to the British, was ensconced in Damascus and was seizing the initiative, declaring the authority of the Arab government over all of Lebanon. The Maronite patriarch Elias Huwayik received a cable from Amir Sa'id al-Jaza'iri asking him to declare his support for the Arab government, but he assiduously ignored it. Instead, he urgently contacted the French requesting their guidance on the matter. The French sent back a two-word response to the patriarch: 'Nous venons' (We are coming).[13]

Faisal's move into Lebanon set alarm bells ringing with the British. Lawrence himself, however, attributed the move not to Faisal but rather to the hotheads who surrounded him, specifically al-Rikabi and the al-Bakri brothers.[14] However, Lawrence's claim does not stand scrutiny as Faisal was directly involved in the decision to assert the authority of the Arab government over Beirut and the rest of Lebanon. The diaries of Faisal's close confidant Rustum Haidar are clear about this, although the actual instruction to proceed to Beirut was indeed given by al-Rikabi and not Faisal.[15] Allenby called the move 'unexpected', while General Clayton, Allenby's chief political adviser, thought the move peremptory. It was designed to use the Declaration to the Seven of June 1918 as justification to occupy as much territory as possible. The captured lands would fall under the category of lands liberated by the Arabs themselves and therefore be part of the self-administered areas of the Arabs.

The French, of course, were not satisfied with muttering protests. Upon hearing the news of the movement of Faisal's men to secure the authority of the Arab government in Lebanon, and the symbolic flying of the flags over the main government buildings, Captain Coulondre,[16] the French representative in Syria, urgently requested his government to send troops to take over Beirut and the coastal towns.[17] Coulondre then protested to Clayton, demanding the immediate appointment of French officers to the coastal towns. When Clayton demurred, saying that it was only Allenby who could give such an order, Coulondre took his protests to Faisal. But Faisal refused to countenance the claim that his forces broke any prior agreements, saying that they were only there to prevent disturbances and assist in expelling the Turks.

Allenby meanwhile, sensing the gravity of the situation and the possibility of confrontation between the French and the Arab forces in Lebanon, instructed the Twenty-First Corps under General Edward Bulfin, deployed along the coast south of Beirut, to accelerate their advance to the city. They reached the town of Sidon, thirty miles south of Beirut, on 7 October 1918. Allenby also agreed to the appointment of French military governors in Sidon and Beirut, a move that was resisted by Faisal's representatives. On 7 October French naval units, under Admiral Varney, landed troops in Beirut. The troops had left Port Said a day earlier and were part of the special French detachment for the Levant.[18] Upon reaching Beirut, Bulfin ordered al-Ayubi to give up his position as military governor and bring down the Arab flag. Al-Ayubi refused to do so without explicit instructions from Faisal. Clayton had also sent a message to Faisal in Damascus warning him that the Arab case would be seriously prejudiced if Faisal attempted to control areas that were part of the Blue Zone, and also stressing the special conditions of Lebanon. Faisal rejected all these pressures, including a request from Allenby that al-Ayubi should surrender his position.[19] He also sought assurances from Allenby that any military arrangements for the coast would be temporary and would not jeopardise the final status of these territories.[20] On 16 October 1918 Allenby wrote to Faisal, saying 'that whatever arrangements may be made now for districts in the coastal area, these are of a military nature and without prejudice to the final settlement which will be decided by the Allies in a Peace Conference.'[21]

However, in Beirut the French were adamant about stripping al-Ayubi of any official status and demanded that the Arab flags be lowered from all public buildings. A compromise suggestion made by Clayton and Bulfin that al-Ayubi should remain as a civil administrator under a French military governor was not acceptable to Coulondre. Allenby relented and confirmed the appointment of the French governor-designate, Colonel de Piepape. Al-Ayubi vigorously protested, but in the end took to his room at his hotel while Piepape assumed the authority of military governor. During the night of 10 October 1918 British officers in Beirut lowered the Arab flag from all public buildings. It was a grave blow to Faisal and the Arab movement, and one that he would not allow to be forgotten. Faisal fired off an incendiary cable to Allenby protesting this move. 'I see no need to explain or elaborate to you what disgrace befell the Arab flag in Beirut, the very same standard of the nation that you told me recently was included by his Majesty King George V as part of Britain's allies . . . I might have erred by sending Shukri al-Ayubi to that place [Beirut], but I believe, nay, I know, that this standard was not raised by me or by Shukri al-Ayubi or by any military force. But it was raised by a nation that chose this flag for itself and represents their commitment to their own kith and kin; and asked us to send without any compulsion, one to govern them ... The people of coastal Syria wanted [independence] and sought to join their Arab brethren. Is it just or equitable that they be denied this desire?'[22] While the French – and to some extent the British – saw the assertion of the Arab government's authority in Lebanon as a crude power grab, for Faisal and the nationalists it was symbolic of their commitment to a state uniting all Arabic speakers in Syria. At the same time, it confirmed to Faisal the implacable opposition of the French to the idea of a united Arab government covering all of Syria, and France's insistence on the strict implementation of the Sykes–Picot Agreement. In other parts of coastal Syria within the so-called Blue Zone, representatives of the Arab government of Damascus were also obliged to withdraw. In Latakia, as in Antakya in Cilicia, the French landed forces to assert their authority and lowered the Arab flags.

No sooner had the issue of the administration of the Syrian coastal littoral been settled, another issue involving disputed territories arose. The Beqa'a Valley, separating the mountains of Lebanon and the Anti-Lebanon, with a mixed population but with a Muslim majority, was ruled in the Ottoman period as part of the wilayets of Beirut and Damascus. The valley was divided into four separate districts, but none was part of the autonomous Maronite-dominated Mount Lebanon administrative council, although Maronites had continually demanded its inclusion in their autonomous area. The Sykes–Picot Agreement, however, designated the Beqa'a Valley as part of the Blue Zone, and this was to come under direct French control. The French, fresh from their 'victory' in Beirut, now sought to assert their rights in the Beqa'a Valley.

On 16 October 1918 Coulondre, acting on instructions from the French Foreign Minister Stéphen Pichon, asked Clayton to inform Faisal that France intended to exercise its rights in the Beqa'a Valley and occupy the area. Clayton reported to the Foreign Office that Faisal and the nationalists were not prepared to give way to the French challenge. None of the contested districts belonged to Lebanon and the Arabs would oppose their annexation to areas under French control. But the French would have none of it, and when Allenby announced his plans for the administration of the occupied territories, the Beqa'a Valley was placed in OETW, or inside territories that came under direct French administration. However, Faisal vigorously protested to Allenby and even threatened resignation.[23] In spite of French protests, however, Allenby reversed his decision and placed the Beqa'a Valley, with the important towns of Zahle and Baalbek, in the Arab-administered occupation zone, OETE. He also gave Faisal full political authority in OETE, reducing the status that had previously been given to al-Rikabi.

The last days of Ottoman Syria and the new order

Tentative outlines of an Arab state were emerging in Syria, congruent with the boundaries of OETE, and beginning to take a recognisable shape. The western boundaries included, importantly, the Beqa'a Valley, giving Faisal an important perch from which to continue to press his claim in the rest of Lebanon. To the south and east, the territories of OETE included most of the 'A' and 'B' zones of the Sykes–Picot Agreement: internal Syria and Transjordan. In the north, the boundaries shifted with the retreating Ottoman armies and only stabilised north of Aleppo after the Armistice of Mudros, which ended the hostilities between the Allies and the Ottoman Empire, was signed on 30 October 1918. After the fall of Damascus the Arab army had been mainly deployed for internal security, but Faisal could still offer 1,500 regular troops under Sharif Nasir, together with thousands of locally raised tribal forces, for the ongoing campaign against the remnants of the Ottoman armies. The capture of Damascus greatly boosted the morale of the Arab forces and even lent them a certain cockiness. After the main political issues had been tended to in Faisal's meeting with Allenby at the Victoria Hotel, Faisal had fallen into a pensive mood.[24] Allenby asked what was on his mind. 'We shall move on to the Taurus [Mountains of Turkey],' said Faisal. 'Our infantry are fast and they can live hard. If your army comes with us, so much the better. We can keep you stocked with forage and supplies. The only thing that we cannot provide is ammunition.' Faisal then conveyed his intention to proceed alone if necessary.

Of course, Allenby was not going to allow the Arab army to march north-wards on its own. That was the task of the Fifth Cavalry Division under General Henry John Macandrew. But British fighting strength had been seriously depleted by illness, and the Fifth Cavalry Division did not number more than 2,500 men. Barrow's Fourth Cavalry Division, the other main force that could be used in the campaign for the north of Syria, was now reduced to 1,200 men. The Arab forces, under Nuri al-Sa'id, were to march alongside the British units, covering the right flank of the advance. The contribution of the Arab forces to the campaign north of Damascus was proportionately much greater than it had been previously, comprising a third of the fighting forces of the Allied armies. On 16 October 1918 Macandrew, together with the Arab units of Nuri, entered the town of Homs to the tumultuous reception of its inhabitants. While Macandrew was awaiting reinforcements from Allenby, Arab forces pushed north towards the town of Hama, which Nuri occupied on 20 October and then moved towards the other great city of Syria, Aleppo. On 23 October the Arab forces met up with Macandrew's division a few miles outside the city, but thought that they were too weak to dislodge the defenders. The Ottoman army in Aleppo was under the command of the formidable Mustafa Kemal and calls on him to surrender were ignored. But a reconnoitre by Nuri found the Turkish defences abandoned, and the city was then occupied by Arab forces on 25 October.[25] The Arab flag was raised over Aleppo and Nuri made the necessary appointments to cover local administration. On 26 October 1918 Macandrew formally entered the city without opposition and the combined British and Arab forces were met with wild demonstrations of support and joy. Nuri drew on whatever Arab forces were available and pushed further north, occupying the Muslimiya rail station where the Baghdad and Istanbul lines join with the main line through Syria.[26] Beyond that lay the formidable defensive positions on the frontiers of Anatolia that Mustafa Kemal had prepared. Breaking through these lines was beyond the capabilities of the British and Arab forces in the Aleppo region. This was the limit of the Arab advance. On 31 October 1918, at noon, following the Armistice of Mudros, hostilities came to an end between the Allies and the Ottoman Empire. Four centuries of Ottoman rule of the Arab Near East had come to an end.

Faisal's capital of Damascus had escaped major war damage, but rubble and litter filled the streets. Basic services were slowly re-established after the seizure of the city, but the railroads and the post and telegraph system remained under the control of the British. They were not prepared to hand over key elements of the communications infrastructure to an untried administration while the war was still continuing. Finances were also an issue. The monthly expenses of the government were considerable and estimated to range between £E150,000 to £E200,000 (Egyptian pounds, the main authorised currency in circulation) while Faisal could only dispose of a few thousand pounds from taxes that had already been collected by the Turks.[27] The Arab government was now responsible for the civil administration, army, police and gendarmerie, as well as direct costs for refugee relief. Large numbers of people displaced by war or who were refugees in Syria, such as Armenians, had to be supported during these critical times. It was not until December that the British subsidy of £E80,000, barely sufficient to meet the most pressing needs of the government, would reach Faisal. The financial condition of the Arab government, its dependence on outside money and its limited revenue-generating capacity dogged Faisal throughout his time in Syria.

Al-Rikabi as the military governor held the reins of government and functioned under the supervision of Faisal and Allenby, acting through Clayton, his on-the-spot representative. Clayton, however, did not interfere in the details of government and only exerted his power in exceptional circumstances. The departure of most of the Turkish civil government's departmental heads obliged the new government to appoint Arabs quickly as replacements. A new cadre of director generals were installed, replacing the ministries in Istanbul to which the former department heads reported. They were mainly Syrian or Palestinian

Arabs, but also included a number of Iraqis. A new appellate court (court of cassation) was also established, but in the main the old Ottoman legal code and structure continued in operation.[28] Freedom of speech and assembly were recognised and respected. The language of the state quickly changed from Turkish to Arabic, and employees had to be taught the composition of official documents and correspondence in the new language.[29] Old Ottoman-era titles, such as Pasha, Bey, Khawaja and Agha, were formally replaced by simpler Arabic equivalents. A new consultative council was also appointed, drawing on a number of notables from Syria and Lebanon, both Muslim and Christian. It was tasked with reviewing and proposing laws and regulations for consideration by the military governor and approval by Faisal. The old Northern Army was dissolved and replaced by a new Arab army, drawing on the large number of Arab officers who were still with the Ottoman forces in their final weeks, as well as, of course, the Arab officers in Faisal's regular army. Three under-strength brigades were formed, based in Damascus, Aleppo and Dera'a. Yasin al-Hashimi headed the council for the military. Internal security was delegated to a British officer with Arab antecedents, Colonel (later General) Gabriel Haddad. New governors for provinces were appointed, including 'Ala al-Din al-Durubi for Damascus. The Damascus municipal council included twelve members, two of whom were Christian and one Jewish. After a short interlude in which Shukri al-Ayubi acted as military governor, Aleppo was run mainly by Iraqi appointees – Ja'far al-'Askari as military governor and Naji al-Suwaidi as the chief administrative officer.[30] The rudiments of the new state emerged quite rapidly, in spite of the great difficulties of wartime conditions and resource and manpower scarcities.

However, the seeds of contradictions and rivalries were also sowed at this time. Faisal was aiming at nothing less than building an Arab state in the broadest meaning of the word, whether a unitary state or a confederation of states, but he had to contend with regional and local considerations. He himself was Hijazi, not Syrian. His special status and background, and fitness to rule could not be challenged. But his commitment to the Arab nationalist cause obliged him to draw on all available talent in the new state, including those who might have been hostile to the nationalist cause, and not overtly to discriminate in favour of Syrians when offering jobs in the new government. The number of Iraqis, Lebanese and Palestinians in key positions of administration and the military was at first accepted as part of the process of building a broad Arab state, but in time it became a source of serious conflict, between 'Syria firsters' and pan-Arabists.[31] At the same time, although Faisal's authority and influence on the government was recognised in practice, he was still outside the administrative structures of OETE. The Arab government was still beholden to Allenby's general headquarters, and in the final analysis al-Rikabi had to report to them. This overlap in authority at times led to the reversal of the government's decisions by Allenby's GHQ, and on other occasions the government was obliged to implement directives that were not of its making.[32] Al-Rikabi was a capable administrator but a complex man who would often switch loyalties. His relations with Faisal were by and large cordial and cooperative, at least while Faisal was physically in Syria, and together they agreed on the key appointments in the Arab military government. His Damascene origins were also initially an important asset, and helped to allay the early mutterings about the role and power of non-Syrian officials in the government.

Political life in the new Arab state

Faisal's commitment to Arab nationalism as a political ideology was both qualified and to some extent expedient. Arab nationalism itself was an evolving idea and its adherents ranged across the entire spectrum of political opinion. At one end were those Arabs whose revolt against the Ottomans was justified by the empire's break with supposed norms of Islamic government, such as the abandonment of the Sharia, a charge that was commonly levelled against the unionists. Hussein used this argument most extensively in justifying the revolt against the Ottoman caliphate.[33] His political vision was moulded within the traditional Islamic forms of the state. Arab pre-eminence was not a precondition but a coincidence, as others, in this case the Ottoman Turks, had failed to live up to the responsibility of leading an Islamic state. His son 'Abdullah also believed in the validity of an Islamic basis for government, but with the essential difference that the Arabs, qua Arabs, had a privileged role to play in reviving Islamic government. Arab nationalism in this instance was closely intertwined with the idea that Arabs had a special role to play in the revivification of Islamic rule. They had been the original bearers of the Islamic message and were responsible for its first great wave of propagation. 'Abdullah's views on the Arabs and their role in Islam were cast in the same mould as the Islamic reformers of the late nineteenth and early twentieth century – such as Muhammad 'Abduh and his disciple Rashid Ridha – and paralleled that of the Syrian writer 'Abd al-Rahman al-Kawakibi. Writing in 1900 in his tract *Umm-ul-Qura*, al-Kawakibi envisaged the creation of a caliphate based in Mecca and led by an Arab.[34]

Faisal, however, though not entirely secular in outlook, understood Arab nationalism more in ethnic and cultural terms. He was not an advocate of the political unity of all the Arab peoples, and in fact his political landscape at first hardly strayed from the Hijaz and Greater Syria. He chose Arab nationalism as a satisfactory political programme and tool to gain support in areas outside his family's historic reach in the Hijaz. At the same time there is no doubt that

Faisal genuinely believed in the aspirations of Arab political independence, a tendency which was certainly reinforced during the Arab Revolt. His continued membership in al-Fatat society was testimony to this. He understood that the foundations of legitimate rule in the Arab lands of the Near East after the collapse of the Ottoman Empire had decidedly shifted from both the narrow dynastic principle and purely traditional and religious formulations. His natural inclination was thus towards a moderate and pragmatic nationalism, tempered by sensitivity to local power relations. However, this was not always manifested in his response to events and circumstances in Syria.

At the beginning of the twentieth century, Syria, with a population of nearly one-and-a-half million, had become an increasingly urbanised society, and this process accelerated during the war. It was a predominantly Sunni Muslim country, with significant Christian, Druze and Alawite minorities. The Christians of Syria, unlike Lebanon, were fairly distributed throughout the country, but both the Druze and Alawite communities were geographically concentrated. The vast majority of Sunni Arabs were rural dwellers with ill-formed political opinions or none at all. In some areas, such as Aleppo and Hama, they were beholden to large landlords. By and large they had little or no interaction with the state, except through tax collectors and the much-hated Ottoman conscription drives. The traditional elites of Syria, on the other hand, were mainly from wealthy, landed families or from a long line of religious scholars and high administrators. Very few gravitated towards a career with the Ottoman military. With the exception of a few urban Christian notables, they were overwhelmingly Sunni Muslim. Although often critical in private of the Ottoman government, they were nevertheless broadly supportive of Ottoman rule. With the collapse of the Ottoman Empire, the traditional elite became unmoored, unable either to affect the policies of the new government or to realistically call for a restoration of the old order. In any case the Allies would not have countenanced any reformulation of the Ottoman state, and Syria's fate, as a separate entity from Turkey, was sealed.

The new order in Syria was dominated by Arab nationalists. The epithet of Arab nationalist itself applied to a diverse group. At its heart were those members of the pre-war secret societies who now occupied high positions in Faisal's government. Their ranks were greatly expanded by the addition of a flood of new members who joined out of conviction or expediency. The nationalists had varying backgrounds, but most came from relatively wealthy and privileged backgrounds and tended to be professionals such as doctors, lawyers and journalists. Most also had had some form of advanced education, either from Istanbul, Beirut or the European capitals. Not only Damascenes but other Syrians and non-Syrian Arabs gravitated towards the new capital of the Arab nationalist cause. Some had been Ottoman functionaries in Istanbul or elsewhere in the Empire; others were officers who had loyally served the Ottoman cause until the end. Tribal shaikhs mixed with provincial dignitaries in Damascus, all trying to find, in one form or another, their role in the new state. Damascus was also the centre for those who had fallen foul of colonial authorities elsewhere in the region, whether they were Lebanese at odds with the French or Iraqis at odds with the British. Faisal's Damascus was undoubtedly the heart of the Arab nationalist movement, a veritable 'Kaaba for the Arabs', as the memoirist As'ad Daghir called it.[35]

By far the most significant political grouping in the Arab government was al-Fatat, into which Faisal himself had been inducted just before the Arab Revolt. Twelve of its members, including the chief military administrator al-Rikabi, the new commander of the Arab army Yasin al-Hashimi, and the chief of police Muhammad al-Tamimi, occupied high positions in the government. Five of Faisal's personal staff, such as Awni 'Abd al-Hadi, his private secretary Rustum Haidar and Nasib al-Bakri, were al-Fatat members. Faisal trusted and sought the advice of the society's central committee members, leading many observers, contemporary as well as later historians, to conclude that al-Fatat actually controlled the Arab government. That, however, would be carrying the argument one step too far. The connections between al-Fatat and the nascent Arab state certainly helped in making al-Fatat the most powerful and best funded of the political parties in Damascus, but at the same time it had to bear the responsibility and frequent criticism for policy decisions that were beyond its control.[36] It was also subject to debilitating divisions between its leading lights and suffered from poor leadership and often chaotic, paralysing and acrimonious internal debates. In essence, it failed to build the institutional structures necessary for it to project its power effectively whether inside the state or at large, and to develop a coherent and sustained policy framework to assist Faisal in the challenges of the times. Neither did Faisal try to impose his own vision or control and leadership on al-Fatat, using it more as a consultative and support body and a sounding board, until the end of 1919 when his relationship with al-Fatat deteriorated.[37] The rush of new members into al-Fatat significantly weakenend the bonds that had existed when it had been a much smaller and cohesive group. In a specially convened meeting which included all its Arab branches held in Damascus on 17 December 1918, it voted for a new central committee. It also kept its secret status 'in the light of present circumstances', but formed a front political party, the Istiqlal (Independence) Party, to act as its public arm.[38] In time the popularity of the Istiqlal party would eclipse that of its founding group.

The other main pre-war political grouping that emerged in the Faisalian era in Syria was al-'Ahd Party. The party had managed to keep its structure alive during the war, and a number of its main figures joined Faisal, either at the outbreak of the revolt or just before the fall of Damascus. Al-'Ahd was dominated by Iraqi officers and was essentially confined in its membership to the military. The seeds of divisions between its Iraqi and Syrian members were evident even during the revolt, but became a reality after the establishment of the Arab government in Syria. The divisions were not only caused by regional rivalries but were also exacerbated by the increasingly divergent paths that Iraq's and Syria's politics were taking. Al-'Ahd basically split into two parts: a Syrian 'Ahd and an Iraqi 'Ahd. The Syrian and some Iraqi members of the pre-war 'Ahd joined up with al-Fatat society, while the bulk of the Iraqi al-'Ahd members focused their concern and activities on influencing events in Iraq.[39]

The third main node of political activity in Damascus was al-Nadi al-'Arabi (the Arab Club), modelled to some extent on the Arab literary club the Muntada that was active in Istanbul in the pre-war years of Istanbul. The club was organised as a literary and social club, and one of its founders was the military administrator, al-Rikabi. He also served as its honorary chairman. Supposedly pan-Arab in scope and ambition, it was effectively a Syrian organisation, with its head office in Damascus and branches in Aleppo and Homs. Although non-political in its charter and aims, it soon attracted extreme nationalists and hotheads of various kinds, becoming 'the centre of the Arab nationalist movement and a school for national, political awareness.'[40] Most public protests were launched at its meetings, as were calls for marches and demonstrations. Its significance as the main intellectual centre for the nationalist movement was confirmed when important foreign visitors, such as Mark Sykes, François Georges-Picot and Gertrude Bell, were asked to address its meetings. But the activities of the club often got out of hand, leading to serious rioting and even sectarian disturbances. Faisal tried to influence and even control its direction, but he also needed it as a reflector of nationalist opinion and a potential ally – and foil – for his manoeuvrings with the British and French.

Aleppo and the 8 November declaration

After the situation in Damascus had stabilised to an extent, Faisal sent a letter to his father detailing developments to date. By this time Hussein had reconciled himself to the reality that it was Faisal who had to carry the burden of day-to-day decision-making in Syria, and even to the possibility that Faisal might carve out a domain for himself outside Hussein's immediate control and influence. Faisal was always scrupulous in maintaining the appearance that he was acting on behalf of his father, sometimes referring to Syria in his correspondence with his father as Hussein's 'kingdom'. But Hussein's status in Syria and OETE was not explicitly recognised by the Allies. He was regularly informed of developments in Syria, either through Faisal's correspondence or more often by communications with Wingate. But the news reached him late and he recognised that he had to cede near total control over decisions in Syria to Faisal. The French mischievously insisted on calling Faisal's Arab government 'the sharifian government'. This was designed to belittle its legitimacy as well as to raise doubts in the minds of the Syrian elite about their role in a state dominated by outsiders from the Hijaz. The barbed inference was that Hijazis were from a desert backwater and associated with Bedouins and all that was retrograde in Arab tribal culture. They were not fit to rule the supposedly worldly Syrians.

Faisal's letter to Hussein described the tensions with the French and then the British regarding Beirut, the treatment of his representative, Shukri al-Ayubi, and the lowering of the Arab flag from the main government buildings in Lebanon. He was obviously embittered by the whole experience and poured out his sentiments to his father. His letter also showed his deep distrust and dislike for the French and their policies in Syria and Lebanon.

As for France in Beirut, she rules in her own name, in spite of the assurances from the commanding officer [Allenby] that there will be no identifying names attached to the governments [of Syria]. Their politicians spread the French idea [of control over Lebanon and Syria] and the people of the land [Lebanon and Syria] are deeply upset [at French actions] especially the Muslims and a great part of the Christians. They are holding us responsible for the country and its future. They say that the people chose its future but you [the sharifian family] agreed with France and handed the people over to them [the French] as well as the coast . . . I am hobnobbed and I don't know what to do. I could resist France by force. But the prestige of the British and especially the commander-in-chief [Allenby] and his statements and promises, have stopped me from doing this . . . I will observe the situation . . . and [if necessary] I will leave my official position and defend my personal honour even if I am alone. As for the people of the country, we are responsible for them. We gave them promises of security and definite commitments, guaranteed with our lives and the honour of our family . . . Either an honourable life or death! We cannot hand over coastal Syria to the French . . . If it is left to me, I will fight anyone who wants to take our land and destroy us.[41]

On 4 November 1918, Faisal left for a tour of his newly liberated country. He had felt confident enough that the situation in Syria had stabilised and that it was now opportune for him to visit the other major cities of Syria. The public had to know him better and he needed to acquaint himself with local leaderships and issues. He also needed to demonstrate his popularity with the masses. His youthful entourage in Damascus was also keen to have him tour the country, and Aleppo was their main target.[42] It was the major city of the north of Syria, probably bigger in size than Damascus, and the capital of an Ottoman province. Shukri al-Ayubi had recently been installed as governor after the debacle in Beirut, and this would also provide the technical excuse for Faisal's visit. But only a few motor vehicles were available to allow for the journey by road. The entourage left before Faisal by a circuitous route that took them via Zahle in the Beqa'a Valley, then Homs and Hama. The entourage then rendez-voused with Faisal at Ma'arat an-Nu'man, before Aleppo. Faisal himself followed by car, accompanied by Dr Ahmad Qadri, and headed first for Homs, where he was received by the illustrious 'Azm family. The route to Homs was crowded with well-wishers. In the Beqa'a Valley, the entire route of his journey was decked out with Arab flags. In Hama, his next stop, he held a large public reception. Faisal used the occasion of his presence in Hama to push for better and more modern educational standards, and managed to raise the large sum of £E4,000, augmented by his own commitment of £E8,000, in support of educational reform. On 6 November 1918, Faisal, now accompanied by his Damascene supporters, entered Aleppo in triumph. The entire city turned out in support and praise for him, showering him with scented water and flowers.[43] On 11 November Faisal delivered his first purely political speech in Syria at the Arab Club hall in Aleppo. It was profoundly important because it set out for the first time Faisal's vision of the future Arab state, and his understanding of what Arab patriotism and nationalism meant.

Faisal started his speech by reviewing the centuries of Turkish rule and what drove his father to declare the revolt. He then continued:

The Turks departed from our lands and we are now as children. We have no government, no army and no educational system. The huge majority of our people have no understanding of patriotism or freedom, or the meaning of independence – even the little that they ought to know ... That is why we have to make them understand the blessing of independence ... and endeavour to spread education, for no nation can survive without education, organisation and equality. I am an Arab and I have no superiority over any other Arab, not even by an atom ... I call upon my Arab brethren irrespective of their different sects to grasp the mantle of unity and concord, to spread knowledge, and to form a government that will do us proud, for if we do what the Turks did [in misrule] we will also depart from the land, God forbid; but if we act in a responsible and dutiful way, history will record our deeds with honour. I repeat what I have said in all my previous positions. The Arabs were Arabs before Moses, and Jesus and Muhammad. All religions demand that [their adherents] follow what is right and enjoin brotherhood on earth. And anyone who sows discord between Muslim, Christian and Jew is not an Arab.

I am an Arab before all else. I swear by my honour and that of my family and by all that I hold sacred and dignified, that I will not unjustly turn from those with rightful grievances, nor will I forgive those who sow discord ... The Arabs are diverse peoples living in different regions. The Aleppan is not the same as the Hijazi, nor is the Damascene the same as the Yemeni. That is why my father has made the Arab lands each follow their own special laws that are in accordance with their own circumstances and people ... We should have started first by organising a congress that would have set out these laws [the constitution for the Arab state]. But the Arabs now living abroad are better fit to formulate such laws, and that is why we have postponed this matter until the exiles can meet. Those I have recalled from abroad are people who are competent in drafting good laws that are in the spirit of the land and the characteristics of its people. They will meet in Damascus or elsewhere in the Arab world for their congress.[44] I ask my brothers to consider me as a servant of this land. You have given your fealty to me in all sincerity and trust. In return I will make the great oath that I will not shirk from always defending the truth and fighting oppression and will act in all ways to raise the status of the Arabs.[45]

Faisal's speech was carefully crafted: measured in tone, modest in his personal assumptions, instructive in the ways that he envisaged the future and very well received. It set out the bases of an inclusive and moderate Arab nationalism that would form the backbone of a federal, constitutional state or a group of such states loosely tied in a confederation. Faisal also marked out his and his family's special role in the new order, but qualified this by insisting that status was matched by deeds and success. The allegiance that he presumed the Syrians had given him as their rule was contingent upon his actions and performance.

A few days earlier Faisal had received notice of an important Anglo-French declaration that appeared to put paid to the Sykes–Picot Agreement and to vindicate the Arab position on the question of self-rule and independence for the Arab lands of the Ottoman Empire. He referred to this declaration at the onset of his speech, and effusively supported it. Some form of declaration that would assuage Arab nationalist opinion had been mooted since August 1918, and the Foreign Office believed that it would calm anxieties regarding the Allies' true intentions. The French went along *pour la forme*, at the same time as their high commissioner in the Levant, François Georges-Picot, who had landed in Beirut on 6 November, was demanding that the British hand over all of Syria to the French. Nevertheless, the declaration was worded in ways that, though legalistic, carried the strong implication that the Arabs would be granted the right of self-determination. But there was a sting in the tail. The final sentence of the declaration gave the Allies the right to 'ensure impartial and equal justice for all; to facilitate economic development of the country by encouraging local initiative; and to put an end to the divisions too long exploited by Turkish policy.'[46] Of course, behind the 'functions' that the Allied claimed for themselves, all forms of direct and indirect rule could be envisaged. These nuances were lost on the populace in the Arab lands, and there were large demonstrations of support for the declaration, including in Beirut and Damascus. People believed that the Sykes–Picot Agreement was finally dead and that the Allies were determined to offer the Arabs self-determination. Otherwise why issue such an emphatic declaration when the war was well and truly over, and there was no need to prevaricate about Allied intentions?[47]

Preparations for the Paris Peace Conference

Faisal's tour of northern Syria coincided with important developments taking place in London that would affect the course of events in the Levant. Lawrence reached London in the last week of October, and after a short respite began a round of meetings with senior officials. It was increasingly apparent in Whitehall that the Sykes–Picot Agreement was not workable in practice, but there was a limit as to how far the British were prepared to go in confronting the French on this matter. The French position was simple and clear: it was an agreement entered in wartime, and now the war was over it was essential to abide by its terms. Sir George Macdonough of the War Office, greatly influenced by Lawrence, wrote a detailed memorandum dated 28 October 1918, setting out the reasons why the agreement should be discarded. The memorandum was addressed to the highest policy-making committee of the War Cabinet dealing with Near Eastern Affairs, the Eastern Committee, headed by Lord Curzon. In the memorandum, Macdonough laid out nine developments, ranging from the outbreak of the Arab Revolt, the conquest of Palestine and Syria by the British with practically no support from the French but with important assistance from the Arabs, to the entry of the Unites States into the war, the condemnation of secret treaties and Wilson's proclamation of the rights of peoples to self-determination. Macdonough called for the Arabs to be represented at the peace conference on a par with the other belligerents, the US, Britain, France and Italy.[48] He also suggested that Mesopotamia should be divided into two areas: Northern Mesopotamia under Amir Zaid, and Southern Mesopotamia under Amir 'Abdullah. Syria would remain under the control of Faisal and would include the Mediterranean coastline from Tripoli to Tarsus. Britain would stay as the pre-eminent power, while French influence would be contained to Lebanon and an enclave around Alexandretta.

The following day Lawrence addressed the Eastern Committee in person. He outlined a number of positions regarding the division of the Arab lands of the Near East that closely followed Macdonough's previous note. Lawrence was then asked by Curzon to put his ideas more formally in a note to the Eastern Committee. The Eastern Committee also asked for formal depositions on the Near Eastern issues from Arnold Talbot Wilson, the acting civil commissioner in Mesopotamia, and from Sir Arthur Hirtzel of the India Office. Hirtzel's main focus was Mesopotamia and his note called for turning it into a virtual colony, to be run by the India Office. He was dismissive of Lawrence's call for the division of Mesopotamia. He was also unsympathetic to the sharifian cause and to all Arab nationalist claims, as well as to Faisal's position vis-à-vis the French in Syria. Further contributions to policy-making were made by David George Hogarth of the Arab Bureau in Cairo and from General Clayton. Apart from the India Office, there was near unanimity amongst those who had to deal with the 'Arab question'. The Sykes–Picot Agreement had to be seriously amended or abandoned: Faisal's government in Damascus should be encouraged and supported, and its territory should be extended to include the coastal strip running from Tripoli northwards, while French ambitions should be confined to Lebanon. The French reply came in the form of a long note from their foreign minister, Stéphen Pichon. 'On no point, whether at Damascus, Aleppo or at Mosul, is [France] prepared to relinquish in any way the rights which she holds through the 1916 Agreement, whatever the provisional arrangements called for by a passing military situation.'[49] The British were in the increasingly uncomfortable position of having to carve out a policy that would suit their interests, assuage the French and meet their minimal demands, and be acceptable to Britain's Arab allies.

The Paris Peace Conference was fast approaching and the issue of Arab representation came to the fore. The British were keen to see the Arabs at the peace conference, both to act as a counterweight to French demands and to put the gloss of international endorsement on any deal affecting the Arab lands that might emerge. In early November 1918, the Foreign Office cabled Allenby, Wingate and Clayton asking if the time was propitious to invite King Hussein to a peace conference that would tackle the issue of the Arab lands of the Ottoman Empire. The understanding was that Hussein would nominate a person who would deputise for him and represent the Arab case at the conference. Both Allenby and Wingate agreed that such an invitation should be made and concurred that Faisal was the best person to undertake such a task and to head an Arab mission. On 8 November Lawrence cabled Hussein informing him that conversations regarding Arab issues were likely to be held in Paris within fifteen days. 'General Allenby has telegraphed that you will want to have a representative there. If this is so, I hope you will send Feisal, since his splendid victories have given him a personal reputation in Europe which will make his success easier. If you agree please telegraph him to get ready to leave Syria at once for about a month.' Lawrence also asked Hussein to notify the British,

French and Italian governments that Faisal would be proceeding to Paris as his representative.[50]

Faisal received Hussein's cable instructing him to leave for Paris on 11 November, while he was still in Aleppo. Hussein continued to believe that the best policy for the Arabs at any international meeting was to follow the British line closely, and to hold them to what Hussein wilfully believed were iron-clad promises of Arab statehood and independence. The cable read: 'Our loyal ally Great Britain has requested your [Faisal's] presence as representative of Arab interests . . . And since our only link is with British might – for we have no other relationship or occasion [to have one] with others . . . all your observations should be relayed to their leaders and honourable representatives, whether your colleagues at the conference or their appointed officers. And you should abide by what they ask you to do or say, whether in the meeting or elsewhere, and avoid all else. This is the limit of your permitted powers during the meeting.' It was a tight, even constricting, term of reference, but Faisal accepted it and prepared to leave for Europe. Whether he would consider himself bound to the rather demeaning terms, which precluded any initiative and judgement on his part, was another matter.

Before leaving Aleppo, Faisal asked his father to send 'Abdullah to deputise for him in his absence, but 'Abdullah could not be spared as he was still involved in the siege of Medina. Fakhri Pasha, the Ottoman commander, continued to hold out and refused to surrender to the forces of Hussein, in spite of the Armistice of Mudros. Fakhri did not acknowledge that his besiegers were legitimate combatants, and would only surrender upon written instructions from the sultan himself. It was only three months later that Medina's surrender took place.[51] Nevertheless, Faisal proceeded forthwith to Beirut, travelling via Homs and Tripoli. It was also an occasion for him to demonstrate his popularity in areas under French control. In Tripoli he was met by the mufti of the city, 'Abd al-Hamid Karami and other leaders. In the welcoming speeches the dignitaries all stressed Tripoli's links to the rest of Syria. They also gave him the right to represent them in Europe.[52] He arrived in Beirut on 19 November 1918, where he was met with wildly enthusiastic crowds. The youth of the city turned out in force and physically pulled his carriage through the streets of the city to shouts of *'Ma bnardhi ghayrak sultan* (We accept no other than you as our king)' and *'La nardhi illa al'Arab* (We accept none [no government] except an Arab [one]).' The British commanding officer, Sir Edward Bulfin, who was responsible for Faisal's travel arrangements to Europe, was also there to greet him. But in an indication of French feelings towards him, Faisal's car, on which his pennant was flying, was deliberately stopped by French troops and his driver mistreated. Fortunately Faisal was not in the car at the time.

Faisal was apprehensive about his journey to Europe, especially as it came at a critical time in the affairs of Syria. He had written to Allenby on

17 November 1918 protesting at French activities such as the banning of literary meetings and severe press restrictions, but in a second letter to Allenby shortly thereafter, he expressed his concern at leaving at such an important juncture to attend a preliminary conference. Secret agents of the French had already informed the Druze shaikhs of the Hawran district to expect a French protectorate. 'I cannot stay to see my country sacrificed to the ambitions of a nation that I do not believe has our interests at heart,' he wrote to Allenby.[53] The administration of the country was not yet in place, and faced enormous challenges in terms of security, resources and the maintenance of law and order. Faisal also brought up the issue of how certain provisos of the Anglo-French declaration were going to be implemented. In particular, he queried the matter of how the opinions of the people of the Arab lands were going to be canvassed. For the first time, the possibility that the United States might be a neutral arbiter in determining the future of the Arab lands was raised. Faisal hoped that an unbiased Allied nation 'such as the liberal and just American government' could canvass opinion in both Syria and Lebanon.[54]

The day before his departure for Europe, Faisal addressed a letter to his father, describing his reception in Beirut and his thoughts about policy towards the Allies.

The population of Beirut, especially its Muslims, came out in droves. They demonstrated in ways that I cannot describe, even as the French governor put obstacles in their path and banned all demonstrations . . . Their [enthusiasm] and what I saw of their commitment to the throne of Your Majesty is beyond any description I can provide. The French here are strongly against us [the sharifian family], and are against the Arab idea and against even their allies, the British. Our situation within is very disturbed and I don't know what will transpire between us in France. I see the British as greatly supportive and helpful. I refused all French help because I saw them as greedy for occupying our lands. Our bonds with England must be definitive, for there is no way for the Arabs but in steadfastness and loyalty to them [the British]. I don't know if what the British do is merely for political ends or is genuine, but whatever may be the case, we have to stick to [supporting] their policies because our interests are intertwined with theirs. I was ordered by His Majesty [Hussein] to proceed to the conference and I obeyed the order in spite of my great reservations. I am proceeding without knowing what the foundations upon which I am walking are. There is no doubt that the French would demand their rights in the country and claim that the Christians wish to join France. We will have to organise a plebiscite to prove that the country is with us . . . but the Christians are divided in three parts: The Greek Orthodox are with us in all meaning of the word, and you can consider them [in their support] as you would the Muslims. The Protestants and [Greek] Catholics are hesitant and demand that any government be under international supervision. And the Maronites – in effect the people of [Mount] Lebanon – are mainly with France. The Syrians generally are 80% – or even 90% – with us . . . I will offer England a definitive alliance between herself and the Arabs, on the condition that no other foreign power has any involvement with us. In this way we will guarantee the British all their interests . . . and we will ask from her all that we lack, in advisers, officials, money and arms on the condition that we will not lose one iota of our independence and that we will be a nation that rules itself by itself . . . I am sure to be worried during my stay in Paris because the government [in Syria] has not yet been organised properly . . . but the presence of Zaid here [Amir Zaid, who was chosen to deputise for Faisal] gives me some peace of mind.[55]

The viewpoints expressed in these letters are those of a person who was much wiser than his thirty-five years would suggest. This was Faisal's first trip to Western Europe, but he held views that were far more liberal and accommodating than the French would have others believe, or that their officials themselves held. This was no caricature of the fanatically minded religious bigot that the French were so fond of applying to the sharifs of Mecca. Remarkably, Faisal had no feeling of religious or racial intolerance and instinctively respected democratic ideals and the need to have popular sanction for Arab rule. He also firmly believed in the idea of total independence, but tempered it with a realistic appreciation that this was not forthcoming without an alliance with, and the protection of, a great power. To him, Great Britain was still the power to contend with and the one that held the best opportunity for the Arabs to be allied with.

The ship carrying Faisal to Europe was delayed somewhat and Faisal motored to Damascus where he gave his instructions to the young Zaid who was to deputise for him in his absence. On 22 November 1918 Faisal embarked on the small British cruiser HMS *Gloucester*, sailing from Beirut for Marseilles. He was accompanied by his aide-de-camp Nuri al-Sa'id, his chief of cabinet, Rustum Haidar, his personal secretary Faiz al-Ghusain, his private companion Tahsin Qadri, and Dr Ahmad Qadri, his personal physician and special counsellor. These were Faisal's most loyal group of advisers and friends who were not Hijazis, and they included an Iraqi, two Syrians, a Lebanese and a Palestinian. He was planning for a short visit, not to exceed a few weeks. Lawrence had earlier written to him to expect to spend about six weeks in Europe and to come 'wearing Arab clothes', presumably to stand out in the crowd of top-hatted diplomats, bemedalled officers and statesmen in frock coats whom he was now preparing to meet.

CHAPTER 10

✦✦✦✦✦ ✧✦✧ ✦✦✦✦✦

FIRST FOOTSTEPS IN EUROPE

F AISAL LEFT for Europe with his status and the purpose of his visit still unclear. He had reluctantly agreed to travel, ostensibly to attend a preliminary conference on Syria and the other occupied Arab lands, but this was rapidly being superseded by events. The venue for the peace conference had been set and Allied leaders were preparing to assemble in Paris within a few weeks. The imminent arrival of President Woodrow Wilson in Europe to launch the peace conference added a significant new dimension to the thorny issues of the Near East. The Eastern Committee, meeting on the day the *Gloucester* sailed, had agreed that Faisal's presence at the peace conference was essential for persuading the Americans to accept British claims in Palestine and Mesopotamia. A distinguished Arab would add considerable weight to their argument if he was seen to endorse British primacy in these two countries. Conversely, the Americans would also be forced to take note of Arab objections to French control over Syria. The French, however, were incensed that Faisal had embarked on his journey without their being notified as to his intended mission. A mix up in the flow of cables between London, Cairo and Jeddah added to the confusion.

First days in France

The French were only officially notified by the Foreign Office of Faisal's arrival, as the *Gloucester* was almost reaching Marseilles. They well knew of Faisal's attitude to their ambitions. His presence in Europe as an advocate for Syrian independence was unwelcome, doubly so now that he could influence a powerful new player in the settlement in the Middle East: the United States. But there was little the French could now do to stop his visit. It was a *fait accompli*, so they scrambled to control his visit and manage its outcomes. They agreed to receive him not as an official diplomatic representative of his father, but as a distinguished military leader and son of a friendly sovereign king and ally. His itinerary would include a visit to Paris and to the battlefields of northern France.

The journey from Beirut to Marseilles was a short one and by all accounts uneventful. On board, Faisal maintained the decorum and courtesies of an Arab Muslim prince. He refused alcohol and would not have it served on his table.[1] The *Gloucester* docked in Marseilles on 26 November 1918. Waiting to receive him was Emmanuel Bertrand, a retired French foreign service official, under strict instructions to stick to an innocuous schedule of visits and events. There were to be no substantive political discussions with Faisal. Bertrand was to accompany Faisal in a planned sojourn in France and to stop him heading directly for England. The Foreign Office would have much preferred that Faisal not linger too long in France, but Bertrand artfully deflected the attempts by British officials to put Faisal on a train to Paris and then London. Meanwhile Lawrence had arrived in Marseilles a few hours after the *Gloucester* had docked, but was told by the French in no uncertain terms that he was not welcome. He was wearing glittering white Arab robes and headdress, attire that was guaranteed to annoy the French. Nevertheless, he attached himself to Faisal's entourage and travelled with the party as far as Lyons. Colonel Brémond, head of the French military mission to the Hijaz during the revolt, was also inducted to chaperone Faisal during his visit to France. Brémond, who was on leave in France when Faisal arrived, received an urgent message to come to Paris where he received verbal instructions from Jean Gout, the deputy director for the Asia department at the French Foreign Office. Brémond was ordered to join Bertrand and Faisal's entourage, who by then were heading for Lyons. He was told to treat Faisal as a general and a distinguished personage, but in no way accord him any diplomatic status.[2] Faisal reached Lyons on 28 November and was installed at the Terminus Hotel. He visited the Chamber of Commerce and the University of Lyons, which was then mooting the idea of sponsoring an Arab university in Damascus. Lyons was historically associated with the silk trade in the Levant, and its merchants and clerics were strongly in favour of the creation of a Maronite-dominated state in Lebanon.

Faisal felt both apprehensive and confined by the unusual turn of events. A visit that was supposed to revolve around the issues of Arab independence and representation at the peace conference was now deflected towards staged meetings and events. He sent Nuri al-Sai'd to complain quietly to the British consul in Lyons. Nuri told the consul that Faisal 'felt himself rather like a prisoner in the hands of his French hosts, and though it had been expressly enjoined upon him not to do anything to cause annoyance, he wished to know whether he should assert himself, with a view to cutting short his French tour'.[3] It must have been daunting for a person with only a smattering of French and a group of advisers not fully experienced in international affairs to be at the mercy of hosts who did not think too kindly of him or his actions and plans. Recalling this episode to Mrs Steuart Erskine in 1933, Faisal summarised the French position as follows: 'France has no information concerning the official mission with which you are charged at Versailles; consequently it is undesirable for you to continue your journey to Paris.'[4]

But Faisal acquitted himself well throughout almost a fortnight in France. Ahmad Qadri describes how Faisal's noble deportment in his flowing Arab robes, headdress and ceremonial dagger gave him a great presence, affecting many of those who came into contact with him. Some even compared him in bearing and looks to images of Jesus.[5] On 30 November the party left for Belfort in a special rail wagon, in preparation for visiting the main battlefields of France. They were joined there by the chief Arabic interpreter for the French, the Moroccan Qaddour ibn Ghabrit, who was already familiar with the shari-fian family from previous visits to the Hijaz. He would feature in many of Faisal's later interactions with the French.[6] From Belfort, the party headed for Strasbourg, but it was still uncertain as to whether and when the French would officially invite Faisal to Paris. While in Strasbourg, Faisal called Brémond aside. 'We fought the war together, we are comrades-in-arms,' Faisal said, 'I have confidence in your expressions of friendship and loyalty. Tell me frankly the situation. If the French government does not wish me to come to Paris, then let me know. I have placed in Damascus as my representative my brother Zaid. He is young and inexperienced. The situation is difficult and I am worried. If I am going to waste my time here, it is better if I return to Damascus.'[7] Brémond replied that he would try to get definitive answers as soon as possible, and communicated Faisal's concerns to the Foreign Ministry. The answer came back that President Raymond Poincaré would receive the Amir Faisal on 7 December 1918. Faisal, reassured, could now continue with his ceremonial visits to the battlefields of the French front. The party visited Metz and Verdun, and took a short detour to visit Wiesbaden and Frankfurt in Germany. French officers accompanying the party explained to Faisal the details of the terrible battles at Verdun and the heroic leadership of Marshal Petain.[8] Trudging in the shell-torn and muddy fields of the western front in full Arab regalia, Faisal was greatly affected by the awful scarred landscape of war.[9] On 5 December at an impressive military ceremony in Strasbourg, Faisal received a high French military decoration, the Croix de La Légion d'Honneur. Present at the ceremony was General Henri Gouraud, later to become Faisal's great nemesis in Syria.

On 7 December Faisal and his group left Bar-le-Duc for Paris in a wagon that was used by the kaiser in his pre-war trips to Alsace. Faisal was received by a welcoming party at Paris's Gare de l'Est and then taken to the Hotel Continental. At the hotel, a new recruit to his entourage, 'Awni 'Abd al-Hadi, was brought in to meet him. 'Awni , a Palestinian member of al-Fatat, had been in Paris as a student. He was a friend of two of Faisal's companions, Dr Ahmad Qadri and Rustum Haidar, and it was they who introduced him to Faisal. 'Awni relates in his memoirs how he came across Faisal in his hotel suite, seeing him resplendent in his Arab dress and carrying his ceremonial gold dagger. 'Awni was immediately accepted by Faisal, who asked him to give his opinion on the French and their views about the Arabs. 'Awni thought the French were misled by their government and elites, who depicted Arabs as a backward people, and that France had a civilising mission in the Arab lands that they occupied. Even though the Arabs had fought on the side of the Allies in the war, the French continued to justify their involvement in Syria as part of their civilising destiny, and were unlikely to abandon or modify their intransigent policies regarding its future control. After this interview, Faisal appointed 'Awni as the head of the administrative office for the Arab delegation to the peace conference.[10] Later that afternoon, Faisal, accompanied by the Moroccan interpreter ibn Ghabrit, made a courtesy call on President Poincaré at the Élysée Palace. That evening, Faisal attended the comic opera *Marouf*, with its Arab themes.

On 9 December, the day for his departure to London, Faisal visited the French Foreign Office where he had a lunch meeting with the foreign minister, Stéphen Pichon.[11] It was more a getting-to-know-you meeting, and nothing of substance was broached or discussed. Later in the day the French took him to a theatre in the Champs-Élysées, where a dancing troupe was performing. Faisal ignored the act, believing it a ploy to distract him from the more pressing political matters, which the French had studiously avoided discussing during his visit. On leaving the theatre, Faisal turned to 'Awni 'Abd al-Hadi and said, 'Do the French think they can entice me with their dancers? I did not come here for play and sport. I came to serve my country.'[12] In the evening, Faisal and his party, which included Brémond, took the night train to Boulogne for the channel crossing. Awaiting them was Lawrence wearing his white Arab robes, as if he 'were a Catholic choir boy'.[13] Faisal was certainly happy to see him for, outside his Arab entourage, Lawrence would be the only familiar and trusted face as the party made its way to England. Lawrence had been in France for two days, preparing for Faisal's trip to England. Witnessing a detachment of khaki-clad women telegraph operators preparing to board the ship to England, Faisal commented to Brémond, 'It is necessary to see such a scene to actually understand the European idea of equality between men and women. In our country, women are idle, and the idea of equality is merely a pleasantry. Here, women work as men.' Brémond noted in his memoir regarding this incident that few in France have the understanding and the fairness of the Amir Faisal.[14]

The two weeks that Faisal spent in France were a whirlwind of meetings, activities and events. But Faisal's suspicions of the French could not be allayed.

Writing to his father on 12 December soon after arriving in London, Faisal surmised that they should expect the worst from the French. He wrote,

> As for France, she has no intention of accepting only what the 1916 treaty [the Sykes–Picot Agreement] offered her in terms of the lands between the Mediterranean westwards and Acre in the south, and all of Damascus and Lebanon (that is, Mount Lebanon eastwards with the Beqa'a Valley), and the railroad to Aleppo eastwards and Malatya in the north. France actually wants to rule over all of interior Syria that is in Damascus, Aleppo and Homs, and not simply to exert its political influence there as per the agreement. In summary, France wants the coast as well as the interior of Syria; or in another way, all of Syria without any part staying outside of its control ... They are afraid of British competition in the East because [France] knows that the Arabs naturally prefer the British, even though I told them [the French] that the Arabs love those who love them in return and guard [Arab] interests.[15]

To his brother Zaid, Faisal wrote on the same day, 'Political warfare is going to start between us and France because she has exhibited enmity [towards us] ... I might return [to Damascus] if necessary before the end of the [Peace] Conference and appoint you my representative here in Paris ... But we might also have to declare war on France ... Be prepared!'[16]

Coming on top of the ongoing crisis in Syria and the anticipation of momentous events to come, the burden on Faisal to navigate successfully through these dangerous waters was immense. His native intelligence and experience in the arena of the politics of the Arab Revolt and then Syria served him well, but these assets were still insufficient in the complex and treacherous world of international politics and great power rivalries and ambitions. He rather amateurishly tried to elicit the views of the myriad foreign politicians and diplomats who were staying at the Hotel Continental.[17] However, apart from the French and the British amongst them, no one else seemed to know much, let alone care, about Arab issues.

His predicament was best described by 'Awni 'Abd al-Hadi, writing decades later to his daughter.

> His Highness [Faisal] came to Paris with nothing in his armoury that would facilitate his work in the larger world that was Europe. Neither did [Faisal] have any prior personal experience of [Europe], nor did his father give him any political directives that would illuminate the path in front of him ... He [Faisal] was a politician by instinct but he was not yet a master of political manoeuvrings, and had not yet become acquainted with the main political leaders. His exposure to political issues and especially to western politics was

limited until then [the time of the peace conference.] His visit to Europe at the end of 1918 was the first of its kind. All this has to be factored into consideration. All that he [Faisal] knew until then was that his father had fought alongside the Allies to rid the [Arab] lands of Turkish rule and his father had sent him to Paris to represent him at the Peace Conference. Faisal was a very intelligent man with a great capacity to appreciate and understand what he heard and saw. But he especially had a great ability to quickly develop and adapt.'[18]

His intelligence and political skills were now to be tested to the limit.

New Year in England

Faisal's departure for England took place as important developments had occurred that would dramatically affect the future of the Arab lands under Allied occupation. On 1 December 1918, Georges Clemenceau had arrived in London to meet with the British prime minister David Lloyd George, to discuss their policies and positions before the start of the peace conference. At a private meeting at the French embassy in London, the two leaders agreed far-reaching changes to the Sykes–Picot Agreement. Clemenceau accepted Lloyd George's demand that control over the Mosul area, designated as being under French influence in the agreement, should be given over to the British. Clemenceau also agreed to the transfer of control over Palestine to the British, abandoning the idea of an international administration over the country. In return, Clemenceau demanded that Britain should not oppose French administration over the whole of Syria. Lloyd George readily agreed.[19] Meanwhile the Eastern Committee, which had not been informed of this 'gentlemen's agreement', was still debating the scrapping of the entire Sykes–Picot Agreement.[20] The Clemenceau–Lloyd George agreement, however, prevailed. Britain would not pressure the French to drop the agreement as the foundation document for the post-war disposition of Arab lands of the Ottoman Empire.[21]

Faisal arrived in London without knowing that the British, whom he had to rely on as his only ally at the peace conference, had cut a deal that gave the French a clear path to control over Syria. The British would not stop Faisal from pleading the case for an independent Arab state with the Americans, and they would also be supportive if he were to engage the French and seek to modify their administration and control over Syria, but they would not confront their wartime ally by actively supporting the Arab agenda. The French never lost an opportunity to remind the British of their fundamental obligations and to refrain from talking to Faisal on matters of substance relating to Syria.[22]

The British had deposited Faisal inside a complex maze of commitments, promises and subterfuges. The Foreign Office recognised the difficulties that might arise if Faisal became aware of the fact that the British had effectively cut him loose at the peace conference. It was to Lawrence that they now looked to guide and influence Faisal, so that vital British interests were not ignored or threatened by Faisal's actions. Lawrence, at the Foreign Office's instigation, was to be attached to Faisal's entourage, but would be listed as an advisory member to the British delegation to the peace conference. He was now engaged in the difficult balancing act of making sure that British interests were met, while at the same time advocating the cause of Faisal and Arab independence. It was a case of living a lie while simultaneously trying to change the circumstances so that the lie itself was eliminated, or at least its consequences were diminished.

Lawrence was now Faisal's virtual shadow. It is futile to speculate over the real motives and drives of Lawrence as it related to Arab issues – a veritable industry has grown around the analysis of Lawrence's character – but their outer expression fell into two, often contradictory, aspects. At one level he was bound by the overall instructions and guidance given him by higher authorities, whether the cabinet, Foreign Office or the military. However, he filtered them through his own idiosyncratic and brilliant personality, and peculiar agenda. At another level, he felt a sense of duty to the 'Arab cause' – which he conflated with his own interpretation of it – and to the person of Faisal. Lawrence thought of Faisal more as a ward who had to be chaperoned in the halls of state and protected against the schemes of politicians, the ambitions of governments, and the vicissitudes and complexities of international affairs – at least until Faisal would 'grow' into the role that he, Lawrence, envisaged for him. Faisal was too intelligent and alert not to be aware of Lawrence's conflicted position, but his relative inexperience in international affairs at that juncture left him little choice but to rely on Lawrence's advice and representation. Faisal undoubtedly trusted Lawrence, believing that his concern for the Arab cause and to the sharifian family was genuine. He also needed to trust the British government. Not only were these the instructions of his father, but Faisal had no other allies elsewhere as the peace conference began. Faisal thought that the Americans might be brought to the side of Arab independence if the British failed to confront the French on behalf of the Arabs. He wrote to his father, '[The British] do not want to declare war on the French [regarding the scrapping of the Sykes–Picot Agreement] if France insisted on its implementation. That is why they want America to become involved in and to adjudicate the matter in its capacity as a referee for all parties. And the hope is that President Wilson would render judgement justly and according to the principles [the Fourteen Points] that he enunciated and to which he had abided by until now.'[23]

Faisal and his party, which included Rustum Haidar, Nuri al-Sa'id, Dr Ahmad Qadri and 'Awni 'Abd al-Hadi, were put up in one of London's grandest hotels, the Carlton. *The Times* carried a few lines on his visit, symptomatic of the low political importance in which it was held. The paper referred to him as the 'Hero of the Arab Epic' and spoke of his 'Romantic exploits as Commander-in-Chief of the Arab Northern Army'. Faisal had come to England to 'present the respects of his father to the King', but not a word about Syria and the ongoing problems with the French.[24] On 12 December, Faisal accompanied by Lawrence, who also acted as interpreter, called in the evening on Arthur Balfour, the foreign secretary. Earlier in the day, Faisal had received an Armenian delegation that wished to thank him for the great support he had shown the displaced Armenians in Syria who were driven there by the massacre of their community in Anatolia during the war.

Faisal's visit to Balfour also revealed the extent to which Lawrence allowed his own personal wishes to intervene in the reporting of events. The accounts of the visit, in which Lawrence acted as translator, differ sharply with both the version that Faisal reported to his father and what Balfour later recorded in his own official memorandum. Both Faisal and Balfour were, of course, relying on the veracity and accuracy of Lawrence's translation. Balfour confines most of his memorandum to describing Faisal's hostility to the French and his promise to fight them if they continued in their aggressive tactics. But Faisal's letter expresses in no uncertain terms the increasingly profound unease that he was sensing regarding Britain's true policies and intentions towards the Arabs. Faisal reminded Balfour that the sharifians had to carry the obloquy and condemnation of large parts of the Islamic world when they rose against the Turks. They did so because of the assurances on independence that were given by McMahon, as well as the commitments made under the Declaration to the Seven that all lands liberated by Arabs would remain under Arab rule. Because of the Arabs' belief in British commitments, 'they surrendered part of such lands to powers that were covetous of them. We have surrendered . . . the coast of Syria on the bases of General Allenby's assurance and statements that these were but temporary arrangements.' According to Faisal, Balfour then replied that, 'it was not the British government that helped the Arabs but rather the Arabs who aided Britain [in the war] and that the British will always be a helper and friend of the Arabs'. To which Faisal retorted, 'I have doubts about this matter because of what I know of the secret 1916 treaty [Sykes–Picot Agreement] that effectively destroys the life of Arabs. We accept no occupation. I have read in *The Times* that M. Clemenceau has said that he wishes to keep Syria intact and not to partition it. This sounds all very well, but this really means that he wishes to keep it whole the better to swallow it. And were it not for the British armies and General Allenby's presence, we would have been settling our scores with them by now. If you don't help us [in confronting the French] we will declare to the world your treacherous actions and we will fight whoever seeks to occupy our lands . . . I want Britain to tear up this agreement and I find no excuse not to do so.'[25]

Balfour sought to calm Faisal's anxiety, and lamely offered, on his honour, that 'the Arabs will emerge smiling from the Peace Conference having recovered all that they hoped for of those glories that all humanity is proud of'. In Faisal's own words, written immediately after his meeting with Balfour, he clearly reveals that he was not quite the innocent that Lawrence might have wished him. The letter expresses the nagging fear that something was afoot which was going to prove detrimental and very costly to the Arabs; and the hope (against hope?) that the British would be prevailed upon, or might see the necessity, to side firmly with Faisal against the French on matters of Arab independence.[26] Faisal also sensed that British politicians were hesitant about committing to any policy positions regarding the Near East before the arrival of President Wilson, whom Faisal thought of as the final arbiter in these disputes.[27] The following day Faisal met with King George V in Buckingham Palace, where he was awarded the Royal Victorian Order, in recognition of the 'common blood spilled by the Arabs and the British fighting side-by-side on the battlefield'. George V then continued by assuring Faisal of Britain's support and commitment, but also queried why Hussein was always repeating the demand for independence and self-sufficiency. These remarks appeared to be aimed at the British and questioned their intentions.[28] In reply, Faisal repeated his previous day's assertions to Balfour that the Sykes–Picot Agreement was iniquitous and that the Arabs could not settle for anything less than complete independence for Syria. At the same time, Faisal continued to stress his confidence in British friendship and promises.

After his meeting with the king, Faisal left on a four-day visit to the north of England and Scotland, where he inspected the fleet and boarded the battleship HMS *Orion*, and also visited several industrial complexes. It may have been a deliberate ploy on the part of the Foreign Office to keep him away from journalists and prying eyes in London, but more likely it was to expose Faisal to the country and its industrial and military might. Faisal was greatly impressed by the scale and reach of British industry, and especially noted with approval the role of women in the industrial workforce. 'I saw with my own eyes . . . the participation of women in the labour force especially in the large munitions plants for heavy shells.'[29] At a civic function during the visit, Lawrence, who accompanied Faisal during his tour, later made the ridiculous claim that Faisal addressed the assemblage by reciting excerpts of the Quran, which Lawrence then rendered into an impromptu speech. This was one of Lawrence's mischievous claims that cannot possibly be true, for two reasons: first, there were many Arabic speakers in the audience who would have commented on the matter; second, Faisal who had great respect for religion and scripture, could not possibly have made light of the Quran in this way in front of a foreign audience.

Outline of the Arab case

Returning to London, Faisal went through the rounds of meetings at the Foreign Office and India Office, where he met the secretary of state for India Edwin Samuel Montagu. Faisal had been planning to meet Prime Minister Lloyd George, but the meeting could not be arranged. He was informed officially that Britain could not refuse the French if the latter insisted on their rights under the Sykes–Picot Agreement.[30] According to the notes kept at the meeting, Faisal replied that he 'recognised the exigencies of the Anglo-French Alliance, and the obligation upon Great Britain to keep faith with her ally. But this obligation should be discharged at the expense of Great Britain herself, not of the Arabs.'[31] On Saturday, 28 December Faisal met privately with Lord Curzon at the latter's home. Rustum Haidar accompanied Faisal during the visit and kept notes of the conversation between the two. Curzon affirmed Britian's support for Arabs, but wanted a detailed note from Faisal as to what constituted Arab demands. He also sought some concessions from Faisal regarding French interests in the Levant. Faisal resisted giving the French anything but a symbolic presence in Syria, and then only because of British representations. The meeting ended well, with Curzon exclaiming that 'England wished to help you with all its strength and she is with you in your demands. Be sure of this.'[32] Coming from such a high-ranking and influential personage as the head of the Eastern Committee, Curzon's comments could not but have a positive impact on Faisal, especially after the previously dry recitations of the India and Foreign Offices. He now set out to write the memorandum that Curzon sought to set out the Arab position for the peace conference.

The memorandum was worked on by Lawrence and Faisal in the last days of 1918. It went through several revisions, at least if one relies on the amended English-language draft of the note that still survives in Lawrence's own hand-writing. This note was of great significance because it would be the main submission by the Arab delegation to the peace conference. Its tone was meas-ured and moderate, possibly reflecting the Foreign Office's recommendations, as expressed through Lawrence, to couch the Arab position in reasonable terms. Nevertheless, the burden on Faisal to produce a key negotiating docu-ment upon which would rest the Arab opening position was immense. His father had given him very few instructions, while the Foreign Office wanted a bland position paper that could be remoulded any which way. At the same time, Faisal was keenly aware of his own limitations, his inexperience in inter-national diplomacy, and his lack of language skills beyond Arabic and Turkish. The French were ranged against him; the British were equivocating behind a façade of support. Having to rely on an ally whose real agenda and options were unclear, and might very well be fundamentally at odds with Faisal's, was an uncomfortable position to be in. Faisal had no experience whatsoever of Americans, but nevertheless he placed a great deal of hope on Wilson's public statements regarding self-determination and the rejection of secret treaties.

The note carried an idealistic undertone, no doubt aimed at the absent Americans, and designed to appeal to the Wilsonian sentiments that Faisal believed would infuse the peace conference.[33] According to the official British historian of the peace conference, Faisal had said privately before the conference that 'he proposed to submit to [the Conference] a project for a Confederation of Arab States, free of Turkish domination, and placed under the guidance and protection of the United States'.[34] The note began by defining what Faisal meant by the Arab nation and the aims of the Arab nationalist movement. 'The country line from a line Alexandretta-Persia to the Indian Ocean is inhabited by "Arabs" – by which we mean people of closely related semitic stocks, all speaking the one language, Arabic. The non-Arabic-speaking elements in this area do not, I believe, exceed one per cent of the whole . . . The aim of the Arab nationalist movements . . . is to unite the Arabs eventually into one nation.' He did not seek to impose unity by force but neither would he accept the division of the 'area as spoils of war among the great Powers'.[35]

The note struck all the right tones. It carefully navigated through the thicket of competing claims and ambitions, but never lost sight of the ultimate objective: independence for the Arab states within a loosely federated structure. It addressed British concerns for guardianship over Mesopotamia, gave an indirect acknowledgement of the special status of Palestine, and legitimated an international trusteeship over that country. However, lurking in the wings were the ever-intransigent French, and they would not be swayed by the fine sentiments of the note. It contradicted their most fundamental assertions. On 29 December 1918, Pichon addressed the French Chamber of Deputies on Syrian policy. He affirmed that French rights in Syria, Lebanon and Cilicia were based upon historic relations, treaties and contracts and the wishes of the inhabitants, who were 'clients' of France.[36]

The Zionist movement

Ever since the British government had encouraged Weizmann's visit to Aqaba to meet with Faisal, its plans were to draw its Arab and Zionist allies towards a common acknowledgement and support for British control over Palestine. The Zionists needed no convincing, for British control over Palestine would allow the unfettered implementation of the Balfour Declaration. At the same time the British recognised that the ambiguities regarding the nature of the Jewish

National Home in Palestine, the centrepiece of the Balfour Declaration, might prove an insurmountable obstacle for Arab opinion. It was in this vein that Hogarth was dispatched to see Hussein in November 1918, charged with convincing him that Zionist projects in Palestine were altogether benign to Arab interests. At the same time, both Sykes and Lawrence were effusive about the role that Zionist money and the technical acumen brought by Jewish settlers in Palestine would play in transforming the economic landscape of Palestine and improving the lot of the Arab peasantry. Sykes's long and rambling letter to Faisal of March 1918 referred to the power of international Jewry, if mobilised in support of the Arabs, as being the key for the success of Arab plans for independence. These factors were constantly repeated to Faisal by his British interlocutors: that a Jewish National Home did not mean the establishment of a Jewish state and would not jeopardise Arab rights in Palestine; that Jewish immigration to Palestine would be limited and non-threatening to the local population; that the Zionists commanded a great deal of resources and technical knowledge that could be put to use in Palestine; that the Zionist lobbies in the US and Britain were formidable and could tip the balance at the peace conference in favour of the Arabs.

Until he had reached Europe, Faisal did not have the necessary sophistication in international affairs to appreciate the range and depth of Zionist ambitions in Palestine. Naturally tolerant of other religions and creeds, Faisal at first was attracted in a fashion to the Zionist idea of Jewish colonists helping to build the lands of Palestine. Arab Jews were an integral and welcome part of the Arab national project, and the ideal of fraternal bonds between European Jewish immigrants and the settled Arab population of Palestine, under Arab rule, was an appealing prospect.[37] However, Faisal began to sense with increasing disquiet that the Zionist project might not be as benign to Arab interests as portrayed, a view that was no doubt reinforced by his retinue of Arab advisers, and this unease crept into his public remarks. This tension between his earlier, rosier conceptions of Zionism and the apprehensions regarding the true intent of political Zionism bubbled to the surface during his European visit. Both the British government and the Zionists sought to nullify the anxieties that they knew he was experiencing, and their effects on their own plans. The British government meticulously micro-managed and guarded his schedule, and only exposed him to what they wanted him to see and hear. A persistent political 'massage' was applied to Faisal, and had the effect of, at times, smothering him. This task was made immeasurably easier not only because of Faisal's utter dependency on the British while in Europe but also because of the immense discrepancy between the resources of a great power, emerging victorious from a world war, and the puny advisory team that Faisal could muster for his European foray. The Zionists wanted to secure from him some favourable agreement acknowledging their projects in Palestine, knowing that while Arab representation at the conference was still loosely defined – only the Hijaz was to be seated at the conference – Faisal was its effective Arab face. Any positive statement or agreement on his part could therefore be construed as an Arab agreement to the Zionist position on Palestine. The fact that a Zionist team, headed by Chaim Weizmann, was twice invited to see Faisal during his London stay is indicative of the importance that both the British and the Zionist movement saw in securing Faisal's acquiescence to Zionist representations regarding Jewish national and historical rights in Palestine.

Weizmann first called on Faisal at the Carlton Hotel on 11 December 1918, soon after the latter had arrived in London, and in fact before Faisal left to visit Balfour that day. Lawrence was present and acted as interpreter. Following their earlier meeting in Aqaba, Faisal had formed a positive view of Weizmann as a person, a sentiment that Weizmann reciprocated in his memoirs.[38] According to Weizmann, who, knowing no Arabic, could only report according to Lawrence's translation, Faisal started the meeting by showing Weizmann the map of the Sykes–Picot Agreement and stating that its terms were unacceptable to the Arabs and Jews. Faisal bitterly complained of the French and said that he was pinning his hopes on the Americans. Weizmann then responded that he expected the peace conference, and Faisal, to acknowledge the historic and national rights of the Jews in Palestine, and that the Zionist movement would push for a British mandate over Palestine. He assured Faisal of Jewish technical and financial support for the Arabs. The Jews intended to purchase their lands in Palestine from feudal landlords and urban effendis, and they would improve them to the extent that Palestine could accommodate a further four or five million Jewish immigrants. Faisal then responded that Arab lands were wide enough to accommodate new migrants, and asked for Jewish help in meeting his aspirations.

However, Faisal's report on the visit differed substantially. Writing to his father on 12 December 1918, Faisal said that it was Weizmann who asked for the meeting and that at the onset of the meeting Weizmann said that 'the Jews do not have as their purpose to govern in Palestine. The extent of their objectives is to found a refuge there and they do not have the least ambition of establishing a government [in Palestine]'. Weizmann then dismissed the Sykes–Picot Agreement and stated that if 'the Arabs and Jews marched side-by-side no nation can deny them their rights.' Faisal then wrote that Weizmann repeated his insistence that the Jews did not seek to establish a government of their own in Palestine. 'Rather they want to stop anyone blocking their right to emigrate there and to establish companies, roads and railroads . . . They want to see the Jews in Palestine recognised as nationals with a right to enter the local and national councils ... They have funds that can be made available to the Arabs to strengthen their government and reconstruct and build their country.' Faisal had responded, 'This not be scoffed at if [these sentiments] are genuine ... The Arabs will oppose the idea of occupation with all their power and might, and if England, which put them in this spot, or America would not help them, then we will fight the French until death so that no one can say that we sold our country cheaply ... The Arabs are in need of resources to rectify what has been destroyed in their lands and they seek from you [the Jews] political support with the powers.' At that point Weizmann extended his hand to Faisal and said, 'I promise you in the name of all the Jews that we will either die or survive together.' Faisal then concluded by saying, 'If you honour what you have told me, I will honour what I have told you: the Arab realm cannot be divided.'[39] The gaps between the two reports of this meeting are too wide to explain in any other way than as translation deficiencies, deliberate or otherwise, on the part of Lawrence. These deficiencies would appear in a more damning form a few weeks later when Faisal met Weizmann for a second time.

On the following day, 12 December 1918, *The Times* carried a statement from Faisal, no doubt instigated by Lawrence and the Foreign Office. It read: 'The two main branches of the Semitic family, Arabs and Jews ... understand one another, and I hope that as a result of interchange of ideas at the Peace Conference, which will be guided by ideals of self-determination and nationality, each nation will make definite progress towards the realization of its aspirations. Arabs are not jealous of Zionist Jews, and intend to give them fair play; and the Zionist Jews have assured the Nationalist Arabs of their intention to see that they too have fair play in their respective areas. Turkish intrigue in Palestine has raised jealousy between the Jewish colonists and the local peasants, but the mutual understanding of the aims of Arabs and Jews will at once clear away the last trace of this former bitterness, which indeed had already practically disappeared even before the war.' It is unclear whether Faisal read the statement in its Arabic version, if any were in fact made, or agreed to it on the say-so of Lawrence. There is no mention of it in his detailed letters to his father or Zaid. Later, at a banquet given in his honour on 29 December 1918 by Lord Walter Rothschild, a leader of British Jewry and a prominent Zionist, Faisal said:

No true Arab can be suspicious or afraid of Jewish nationalism. The Turks ruled by encouraging discord and enmity between their subject peoples and creeds, and I regret that others are doing the same now. I have been told by people who regard themselves as civilized that the Jews want our Mosque in Jerusalem as a temple, and to grind down and stamp out the peasantry of

Palestine. For my part, I know that no true Jew holds these views. These insinuations have no effect on any of us. We are demanding Arab freedom, and we would show ourselves unworthy of it, if we did not now, as I do, say to the Jews – welcome back home – and cooperate with them to the limit of the ability of the Arab State . . . Dr. Weizmann's ideals are ours, and we will expect you, without our asking, to help us in return. No state can be built up in the Near East without the goodwill of the Great Powers, but it requires more than that. It requires the borrowing from Europe of ideals and materials and knowledge and experience. To make these fit for us, we must translate them from European shape into Arab shape – and what intermediary could we find in the world more suitable than you? For you have all the knowledge of Europe, and are cousins by blood.[40]

The sentiments expressed by Faisal on this occasion regarding Arab–Jewish amity were not very different from the memorandum that he drafted for the peace conference; but they were different in tone and emphasis from the statement that was sent to *The Times* carrying his name, which appeared to accept the notion of Jewish national rights in Palestine.

The second meeting between Faisal and Weizmann in London took place on 3 January 1919, also at Faisal's quarters at the Carlton Hotel. This time Weizmann was accompanied by Nahum Sokolow, the secretary general of the World Zionist Congress, and Herbert Samuel, the postmaster general in Asquith's wartime cabinet and a dedicated Zionist. Once again Lawrence was the sole translator between Faisal and the visiting party. Weizmann presented Faisal with a handwritten 'agreement', in English, whose contents Lawrence then proceeded to explain to Faisal. The text of the agreement covered the racial and ancient bonds between Arabs and Jews, the necessity of cooperation between them for the progress of the new Arab state and Palestine, the establishment of 'duly accredited agents' in their respective territories, and the provision of guarantees for the implementation of the terms of the Balfour Declaration, and for freedom of worship. In the important Article 4, the agreement stipulated that 'All necessary measures shall be taken to encourage and stimulate the immigration of Jews into Palestine on a large scale, and as quickly as possible to settle Jewish immigrants upon the land through closer settlement and intensive cultivation of the soil. In taking such measures the Arab peasant and tenant farmers shall be protected their rights, and shall be assisted in forwarding their economic development.'

Faisal, bending to Lawrence's representations and to the accumulating pressures on him by the British for formal recognition of Zionist claims, and without being able to read the English text, consented to sign the agreement. But he then added a codicil in his own handwriting, which was couched in such broad and categorical terms that it had the effect of negating the agreement. In effect, Faisal's signature was conditional on the British government fulfilling its promises regarding Arab independence, as expressed in Faisal's memorandum to the Foreign Office a few days earlier. The codicil read as follows, 'Provided the Arabs obtain their independence, as demanded in my Memorandum dated the 4th of January, 1919, to the Foreign Office of the Government of Great Britain, I shall concur to the above articles. But if the slightest modification or departure were to be made [in relation to the demands in the Memorandum] I shall not the be bound by a single word of the present Agreement which shall be deemed void and of no account or validity, and I shall not be answerable in any way whatsoever.'[41] Lawrence's rough translation of Faisal's codicil that he gave Weizmann was very poor and possibly deliberately deceptive. He did not refer to Faisal's specific demands for Arab independence in the codicil, which obviously included the Arabs of Palestine. The agreement was not made public until 1936, when Weizmann first revealed it in a letter to *The Times*. But it was given to the American delegation at the peace conference by the Zionist movement, without either Faisal's codicil in Arabic or Lawrence's (mis)translation of it, and played its part in the conference's favourable position on the Zionist demands.

When Faisal left the meeting with Weizmann to explain his actions to his advisers who were in a nearby suite of offices at the Carlton Hotel, he was met with expressions of shock and disbelief. How could he sign a document that was written by a foreigner in favour of another foreigner in English, in a language of which he knew nothing? Faisal replied to his advisers, as recorded in 'Awni 'Abd al-Hadi's memoirs, 'You are right to be surprised that I signed such an agreement written in English. But I warrant you that your surprise will disappear when I tell you that I did not sign the agreement before I stipulated in writing that my agreement to sign it was conditional on the acceptance by the British government of a previous note that I had presented to the Foreign Office . . . [This note] contained the demand for the independence of the Arab lands in Asia, starting from a line that begins in the north at Alexandretta-Diyarbakir and reaching the Indian Ocean in the south. And Palestine, as you know, is within these boundaries . . . I confirmed in this agreement before signing that I am not responsible for the implementation of anything in the agreement if any modification to my note is allowed.'[42]

Irrespective of Faisal's protestations to his advisers that by writing the codicil he had avoided any traps that could have been set for him, it was nevertheless a dangerous, if not quite damning, act. It was one of two documents signed by Faisal that the Zionists later used to demonstrate that their plans in Palestine had the prior knowledge and approval of the Arabs.[43] Faisal later recognised the folly of his appending his signature to the agreement with

Weizmann, even with its codicil, and might have felt duped by Lawrence and the British. Speaking to a journalist in March 1920, when his knowledge of the merciless realities of international affairs had grown by leaps and bounds, Faisal admitted to his earlier haziness about Zionist intentions. He believed that grounds could be found for Arab–Jewish cooperation in Palestine, especially after the serial assurances given by Hogarth, Weizmann and Lawrence that the Zionists did not seek to establish an independent state in Palestine, and that their goal was to enable a flourishing Jewish presence there without encroaching whatsoever on Arab rights and interests.[44] Faisal's dependence on Lawrence in those early days in Europe was unavoidable, but Lawrence was also ultimately responsible for ensuring that Faisal did not stray too far from key British policy positions. Lawrence may have cursed and criticised the ambiguities, confusions and dissimulations of British policy in the Near East – which he mercilessly mocked in his private correspondences – but he still shared their underlying precepts. The preservation of British interests and the extension of British power and influence in the Near East were never too far from his mind, even though he pursued them in his own idiosyncratic way. For Lawrence, the remaking of the Near East was in the way of an adventure, and the Zionist project in Palestine, in spite of its inherent incompatibility with Arab independence, could be presented as an important source of support for the Arabs. Writing to Alan Dawnay later in 1919, Lawrence expressed the fanciful notion that the Zionists could finance the entire east, and not just Syria and Iraq, as Palestine was too small a territory to be of more than of passing interest to their big financiers![45] With allies of this power and influence, Faisal would be greatly strengthened in his stand-off with the French.

Faisal's days in London left a mark on his personal deportment. 'Awni 'Abd al-Hadi wrote in his memoirs,

> The few days that Prince Faisal spent in London were sufficient to greatly affect him, for it moved him from being a noble Arab prince steeped in the Bedouin way to a modern-minded prince. In my opinion, the Prince's mixing with the class of lords in London, and his mingling with the English in their private gatherings and over the dinner table, and the leisure life of the English generally, left their imprint on him. We noticed this obviously in the way that the prince altered his mannerisms. The prince whom we know would not enter any meeting except in his Arab robes, and into his presence no one would enter except formally attired, and to whom no one would speak unless given personal permission, began to wear odd-shaped hats instead of the headdress [of the Arabs]. [He] took to wearing the *bonjour* or frock coats instead of the formal Istanbuli coat and the *abaya* [cloak]. He would rest on a companion's arms as he took his leisurely walks in London's streets or hotels,

1 Young Faisal (l) with brothers and their tutor Ahmad Safwat. Safwat later followed Faisal to Syria and then Iraq (Istanbul, probably 1895).

2 Nuri al-Sa'id (r), Ja'far al-'Askari (c) and Ali Jawdat (l) as Ottoman officers, 1909. They were Faisal's three most important Iraqi collaborators during the Arab revolt.

3 Faisal with Lowell Thomas, the American reporter, 1917. It was Thomas (r) who popularised the Lawrence of Arabia image.

4 Nasib Bakri with Bisha during Arab revolt.

5 Faisal and Zionist leader Chaim Weizmann, Aqaba, 1917. Faisal was noncommittal but wary regarding Weizmann's representations on the objectives of Zionism in Palestine.

6 Faisal during the Arab revolt, 1918.

7 Faisal emerging from the Victoria Hotel, Damascus, 1918.

8 Faisal with Allenby, Damascus, 1918. Allenby was sympathetic to Faisal but was bound to implement Allied policies in the Arab east.

9 Faisal en route to England, 1919. Captain Pisani is second from left.

10 Faisal with T. E. Lawrence, Nuri al-Sa'id (2nd from l), Rustum Haidar (l) and Tahsin Qadri (r), Paris, 1919. Nuri would later become Prime Minister in Iraq.

11 Faisal, 1919.

12 Faisal with Nobel Laureate Anatole France, 1919, St Cloud, France. Dr Ahmad Qadri is standing at the front (2nd from l) as is Rustum Haidar (2nd from r).

13 Celebrations in Damascus for the coronation, 1920.

14 Lawrence and Amir Abdullah in Jerusalem, 1921, after the Cairo Conference where Britain's empire in the Middle East finally took shape.

15 British troops entering Baghdad in 1918.

16 Ja'far Abu al-Timmen, a key leader of the nationalist opposition in Iraq. His relations with Faisal were correct.

17 Faisal with Zaid in Baghdad, 1921.

18 Coronation as King of Iraq, 1921. The throne chair was inappropriately large, dwarfing Faisal.

19 Sir Percy Cox, first high
commissioner in Iraq. His plans for
British control over Iraq through
indirect rule were resisted by both
Faisal and the nationalist opposition.

20 Grand Ayatollah Abul Hassan al-Isfahani, supreme leader of Iraq's Shia Muslims, at prayer in Najaf, Iraq.

21 Faisal, Baghdad, 1923. Gertrude Bell (r), and Saiyid Hussein Afnan, cabinet secretary (l).

the same as would be the case of the many sons of the monarchs of Europe, who thronged London's streets.'[46]

This could be read as a caricature of the potentate from a backward land absurdly mimicking western ways. However, while he was in Europe, Faisal sought recognition as a modern-minded person and to dispel any impression amongst Europe's leaders and peoples that he was somehow representative of a backward family or society. He needed to impress as well as to signal to the world that the Arabs had come into their own as a 'modern' people.

As the New Year beckoned, the whirlwind of social activity in the last days of 1918 saw Faisal attending a lunch hosted by the Lord Mayor of London on 30 December 1918. Among the guests were Sir Arthur Henry McMahon and Lord Rothschild. *The Times,* reporting on the function, wrote: 'The Lord Mayor, proposing the Prince's health thanked him for the brilliant services his gallant troops had rendered in freeing the Holy Land from the detested rule of the Turk. The Prince, in reply, said that the Arabs were fighting for those great principles of freedom and justice which were so sacred to the Allies, and which were the antithesis of the Turkish sway. He rejoiced that, in that mission and cause, they had the true sympathy of the British people.' But the lands that he had left behind were never far from his mind. His last letter of 1918, dated 31 December 1918, was addressed to his brother Zaid in Damascus. He assured him of Britain's good intentions and loyalty, the high hopes that he placed on the coming of the Americans, and the firm support for independence that he was receiving from the Syrian community in America. He ended the letter with reference to the gloom of London in winter, the long nights with the sun setting at 3 p.m., and the clouds and fog blotting out its rays during the day. He sighed with the refrain, 'My land will always be dearer to me, even when it mistreats me.'[47]

CHAPTER 11

AT THE PARIS PEACE
CONFERENCE I

O N 9 January 1919 Faisal and his entourage arrived in Paris by the boat train from London. The Paris Peace Conference was scheduled to open formally on 18 January, but the question of the representation of the Hijaz delegation was still unsettled. Faisal had entered an arena that was implacably hostile to Arab claims to independence. The French government petulantly refused to recognise Faisal's status, and the Quai d'Orsay saw him as nothing more than incorrigibly anti-French and manipulated by the British to further their own interests in the Near East at the expense of France.[1] The French press was equally unfriendly to the presence of the Arabs at the peace conference, and represented Faisal in the worst light, both as an ambitious Hijazi interloper in the affairs of Syria and as an obstacle to France's civilising mission in Syria and its claims for a special protectorate status over its supposedly vulnerable (and pro-French) populations. Faisal was also acutely aware by now that the British, who would often publicly endorse his positions and give him encouragement, might easily modify and even reverse their positions in their private negotiations with the French. The bare instructions from his father were fatuous as they carried no constructive brief as to how to conduct the negotiations with the Allies – apart from a reliance on British good will – and press for the main objectives of the Arab Revolt. To top it all, the peace conference was mainly concerned with the reconfiguration of Europe after the defeat of Germany and Austria and the dissolution of their empires. The issues of the Arab Near East were of secondary importance and could occupy only so much of the leaders' time.

Preparations and planning

Formally, of course, the French government accorded Faisal the proper courtesies due to a visiting dignitary, albeit one without as yet the full panoply of diplomatic credentials. He and his staff and aides were lodged at the palatial home of the Comtesse de Kellermann off the Champs-Élysées.[2] (Lawrence, however, was installed at the Hotel Continental, some distance from Faisal's headquarters as well as the main hotels where the British delegations were staying, the Astoria and the Majestic.) Thus began nearly five months of arduous discussions, meetings and negotiations that Lawrence described as 'the worst I have lived through: and they were worse for Feisal. However, he learnt the whole art of politics from them.'[3]

The first task facing Faisal was to ascertain France's intentions towards his delegation and to remove the French objection to the seating of the Arab delegation at the conference. Only then would he have the opportunity to present the Arab case to the Allied leaders. His first meetings with French leaders and officialdom were not encouraging. Soon after arriving in Paris, Faisal paid a courtesy call on Clemenceau, who made some general remarks about the Arabs being recognised as co-belligerents.[4] However, on 16 January, two days before the scheduled opening of the peace conference, the assistant director of the Asian section of the French Foreign Ministry, Jean Gout, paid Faisal a call. 'Awni 'Abd al-Hadi, who was present at the meeting, later recalled what had transpired. Gout informed Faisal that France welcomed him as a visitor, but he greatly regretted that France was unable to agree to allocate a place for him at the conference. His explanation for this snub was that the Allies as a whole had not recognised the kingdom of the Hijaz, nor did they recognise his father as king. This was technically true, as neither the US nor Japan had yet formally recognised the sovereignty of the Hijaz. However, in a feeble attempt at mollification, Gout informed Faisal that France would have no objection if Faisal had one of the powers deputise for him.[5] Gout's assertions were very disturbing to Faisal. 'This news came as a great blow to Faisal; he had left his native lands to present his people's case, for their unity and independence, and he began to feel that his coming to the Conference was going to end in failure.'[6] However, Faisal's anguish was short-lived. Lawrence impressed on Britain's foreign secretary, Arthur Balfour, the need to act firmly on the issue of the seating of the Hijaz delegation when he was to meet with Pichon, his French counterpart, and with Clemenceau. After some protestations, the French grudgingly acceded to the Hijaz being represented at the conference with two delegates.[7]

Faisal's fear of the French and their machinations came through clearly in a detailed letter he wrote to his father on 19 January. It was his belief that 'France wanted to excise Syria from its Arab roots and to rule there unchallenged.' The French were deploying all types of arguments to pursue their ends, not least by painting the Hijazis as interlopers and stressing wherever they could the 'special' nature of their relations with Syria. Faisal complained that his father had given him little in the way of documentary evidence to buttress his case,

and as a result his negotiating position was very weak.[8] Faisal had no knowledge of the details of the Hussein–McMahon correspondence and therefore
could not use them to reinforce his case for Arab independence. Faisal was
aware of the documents and had asked his father for them. But Hussein had
replied that the text of these documents was in London and that Faisal had no
real need for it.[9] It is inexplicable why Hussein did not see fit to brief Faisal of
their import before his departure to the peace conference. Surely it could
not have been simply his faith in the absolute trustworthiness of the British
to reflect what he thought he had agreed with them? More likely it stemmed
from Hussein's need to keep the tightest control over the negotiations, and to
drip-feed vital information to Faisal only when absolutely necessary.

In spite of the absence of the vital texts of the Hussein–McMahon
correspondence, Faisal had to evolve a negotiating strategy in dealing with the
Allies. In the same letter to Hussein, Faisal went on to outline the case he was
going to make to the Allies.

> I am the representative of my father and of the Arab Army that all three
> powers have recognised as a co-belligerent. I came to Europe to defend the
> Arabs and demand our rights, in the name of the king [Hussein] and the
> fighting army that is composed of all Arabs . . . I ask the powers not to deter-
> mine anything that concerns my land whose [boundaries] are defined north-
> wards by the Taurus mountains and Diyarbakir, except after the opinions of
> the people of the land of whom the Arab army is composed are taken into
> account. The people of this land have the right to elect the government that
> they want, and the powers have to acknowledge their independent decision
> . . . Any decision that contravenes this principle will not be accepted by us. I
> will say that because the principles of the American government, its leader,
> Wilson, and the rest of the powers confirm that it is the people – not govern-
> ments – that have the right to determine their future. In this way, no one, not
> least the French, can exhibit the slightest objection. I believe that such words
> will conform precisely to the general trend of public opinion, and I will push
> for it with great vigour. And I will say that his Majesty [Hussein] does not
> wish to force the Arabs to accept his authority, but he will abide by decisions
> freely reached, and will demand with all his strength that the Arabs should
> have a clear right to determine their future and dispose of their resources. He
> [Hussein] will not accept that any government should interfere in their
> [Arabs'] affairs and impel them to accept a government that does not arise
> from their clear will. The land is no one's private preserve, but is in the hands
> of its people, as your Majesty told Messrs. Sykes and Picot when they came to
> Jeddah, and you impressed on them the necessity to allow the people their
> absolute freedom.[10]

Faisal's political sophistication had immeasurably increased over the past few weeks as he became immersed in the labyrinthine world of international diplomacy and great power rivalries. 'Awni wrote: 'His Highness [Faisal] showed great concern about the policies of European powers, and especially France's. I found that His Highness was not too concerned about the vagaries of European politics, but was absolutely prepared to delve into the bases underlying the formulation of their policies. He thought well of Britain's policies in light of his father's instructions regarding the importance of his abiding by their advice.'[11] Faisal's letter to his father, barely six weeks after his arrival in Europe, indicates a maturity and understanding of the levers of European politics that is quite remarkable for a person who had never previously been exposed directly to European ways. His strategy reflected the need to hold the Allies accountable for their proclamations regarding the self-determination of peoples, and his appeal to public opinion indicated a more than intuitive understanding that ultimately politicians in democracies could not stray too far from their electoral base. In the battle for public opinion, however, Faisal knew he was at a considerable disadvantage, particularly with the French. He bitterly complained that the French public had been fed a diet of lies and half-truths about the Arab case by politicians and the press. This in turn fed into the widespread disdain for the Arabs that was held by the public, and helped to reinforce the image of France as a civilising power of backward people. He quoted to his father the authoritative *Les Temps* newspaper that scoffed at the idea that an 'uncivilised' country such as the Hijaz should ever be given rule over Syria.[12] Faisal knew that France would be his most formidable adversary at the conference, and planned that rather than castigate the French press and public opinion for their bigoted ways, he would patiently try to overcome their prejudices by example, by interviews and by accommodating statements and policies that would lessen their fears about an independent Arab state in the Near East.

On 18 January 1919, the Paris Peace Conference officially opened at the splendid Salle d'Horloge at the Quai d'Orsay in Paris. The date was carefully selected by Clemenceau for its symbolic significance. It coincided with the enthronement of Kaiser Wilhelm I at Versailles, as the first emperor of a united Germany, following France's defeat in the Franco–Prussian War of 1870–71. It was now France's turn to sit in judgement on Germany. The Hijaz delegation took its place at the conference. The two delegates, Faisal and Rustum Haidar, were the only Arabs admitted to the conference when it formally opened at 3 p.m. Later that day, Gout visited Faisal and apologised for his intemperate comments a few days earlier.

Anglo-French tensions

The conference opened with tensions between Britain and France on the resolution of the Syrian question. The official British position was that of neutrality between France's claims and those of Faisal, and Britain refused to take any definitive stand on the matter lest it prejudice the decisions of the peace conference. At the same time, there were rival currents within the British delegation at Paris that pulled in different directions. The majority felt that it was the future of Europe that mattered, and that the Syrian issue was of secondary importance as no vital British interests were at stake. If France insisted on its rights under the Sykes–Picot Agreement, then Britain could not do much to block it. The Anglo-Indian lobby, led by Sir Arthur Hirtzel, wanted to turn Mesopotamia into an outright colony, and in as much as this paralleled to a great extent France's intentions in Syria, then this lobby's policy recommendations were to accommodate France in its quest to wrest control over Syria and Lebanon. Arab demands for independence could safely be ignored as the realities of imperial power asserted themselves on the Near East. A third current, best represented by Lawrence, Gertrude Bell[13] and General Gilbert Clayton, Allenby's political adviser, sought to reconcile Britain's conflicting promises, commitments and interests with support for an independent Arab state or states, but nevertheless tied to Britain;[14] Clayton addressed the dilemma that Britain faced in the Near East in a detailed memorandum.[15] Britain, Clayton wrote, was committed to three distinct but incompatible policies: the agreements with Hussein encompassed by the Hussein–McMahon letters, which committed Britain to support an Arab state or confederation of such states; the Sykes–Picot Agreement, in which Britain acknowledged France's predominance in Syria and Lebanon; and the Balfour Declaration, which committed Britain to support the Zionist project in Palestine. The realities of the situation on the ground, however, Clayton wrote, made the realisation of these policies impossible. The Arabs of Syria, apart from the Maronite Christians and a small minority amongst other segments of the population, simply refused any French control over the country. The idea of a single Arab state was not workable if the area was divided into spheres of control by imperial powers whose administrative systems and political culture were entirely different. And there was also a growing hostility to the Zionist project on the part of the majority of the Arab population of Palestine and Syria.

France, on the other hand, was determined to exercise untrammelled control over Syria and Lebanon. The modifications to the Sykes–Picot Agreement that were accepted by Clemenceau during his December trip to London had been the limit of what the French were prepared to concede. One of the greatest obstacles to French plans was the British commitment to an independent Arab state, and this the French were determined to frustrate. No effort was spared to disparage and insult Faisal in the French press, and the French Foreign Ministry regularly sent out memoranda to its British counterpart accusing Britain's military in Syria of anti-French bias and working to undermine French interests and claims.

The United States also posed a looming problem for the French. The American calls for self-determination as the basis for establishing national governments in the new states emerging from the post-war rubble might derail France's prospects of establishing its control over Syria. Any plebiscite or referendum in Syria would surely call for independence free from any entanglements with France.

For his part, Faisal recognised the importance of securing the support– or at least the goodwill – of the United States for an independent Arab state or states. 'My work these days is focused on the Americans,' Faisal wrote his brother, Zaid. 'I have agreed to meet with their key figures and I shall meet privately soon with President Wilson, and will conclude the matter with him in the appropriate way, God willing. I will remind him to implement his declared plan: namely to canvass public opinion in the country, and by that I mean a plebiscite in all the lands freed from the Turks, and I have no doubt that he will agree to that.'[16] On 20 January, Faisal and a few of his intimates, including Rustum Haidar, met with Colonel Edward House, President Wilson's chief adviser in Paris. Faisal presented the outline of the Arab case. He asked for a plebiscite to ascertain opinion in the Arab lands, in the event that there was no common agreement on the disposition of these countries. On 23 January Faisal met with Woodrow Wilson. Faisal was not particularly satisfied with the outcome of the talks he had with Wilson, as the latter was non-committal regarding Faisal's demands. Wilson merely promised that he would stand by his principles and do what was right.[17]

Address to the Council of Ten

Faisal was invited to present his case in person to the main policy-making body of the conference, the Council of Ten, on 6 February, nearly three weeks after the opening of the talks.[18] Prior to this all-important address, Faisal had circulated the memorandum of 1 January 1919 to the delegates of the great powers that he had earlier sent to the Foreign Office. A précis of this memorandum was presented to the conference on 29 January, to which Faisal added that he had based his case on the principles enunciated by President Wilson, and especially the second point of his speech at Mount Vernon on 4 July 1918 in which he called for the right of self-determination of nations.

Faisal used the period after the opening of the conference, while awaiting the invitation to address the Council of Ten, to intensify his contacts with the delegates, and to try to influence French opinion positively. Rustum Haidar records in his diary an interminable round of meetings with senior officials from the Allied countries and of dinners where Faisal was the star guest. Faisal made the rounds with ministers, generals, newspaper editors, university professors and Arab dignitaries living in Paris. Amongst the latter was Izzat Pasha al-Abid, Sultan 'Abd al-Hamid's *éminence grise*, who gave his own version of the events that had led to the demise of the empire, and amused his listeners with his caustic views on the 'reformers' and the CUP.[19] Faisal was visited once again by Gout, with the ubiquitous ibn Ghabrit in tow. Faisal acknowledged that Lebanon might have a separate status, but was insistent that the only legitimate rule for Syria must be based on the will of the people expressed through a plebiscite. Gout's protestations about the need to protect minorities were swept aside by Faisal, who pointed that the Allies were preparing to establish many national states with significant ethnic minorities, none of which required the formal protection of a foreign power. The Arabs were as advanced as the Greeks or Romanians, who had their own national states, and had no need for a foreign mentor. Advisers and experts would be welcomed, but this was a far cry from requiring the imposition of foreign rule over the country. The conversation with Gout appeared to have had its effect, as ibn Ghabrit came the following day to announce to Faisal that the French government would soon declare its official policy on Syria, providing the impression that France might retreat from the idea of direct control over the country.[20] On 30 January, the Big Four and Japan decided to sever the Arab lands and Armenia from Turkey, implicitly accepting that they had an independent identity, but the powers qualified that independence by requiring that mandatory powers be appointed to guide and counsel the new states towards genuine independence. Apparently the Arab lands and Armenia were seen as 'a sacred trust entrusted to civilisation', according to the communiqué of the great powers. The loaded terms of mandates and mandatory powers now entered the lexicon of the post-war order.

The invitation to address the Allied leaders came suddenly on 5 February, giving Faisal only one day's notice. Haidar recorded in his diary that 'the news [to address the Council of Ten] came in the afternoon [of February 5] saying that the Conference wished to hear the representatives of the Hijaz regarding their territorial demands . . . In reality, we had been awaiting this [invitation] on a daily basis but we did not anticipate that it would be so sudden, thinking that they would give us a day or two to prepare for it.' Faisal had wanted to write out a note that would help him to organise his thoughts for the upcoming presentation, but nothing had been prepared beforehand. Both Sykes and Lawrence then arrived at Faisal's quarters with their own notes, but Faisal asked his own team of advisers to prepare his address. Working through the night, Haidar, 'Awni 'Abd al-Hadi, Dr Ahmad Qadri and Nuri al-Sa'id, with Faisal frequently dropping in to see their progress, produced a draft that Faisal found acceptable. 'The Amir came in from time to time to hear what we had written, agreeing to parts, amending others, and adding his thoughts. At midnight he went to bed, but I don't know if he slept that night. He was disturbed because he was aware of the gravity of the situation. For it was time to talk plainly and that is why he was agitated . . . And how can a person not be agitated when the time had come to garner the fruits of his labour. This would need great courage in presentation.'[21]

On 6 February, a historic day because it marked the debut of the Arabs on the international stage, Faisal met with Haidar to finalise the draft of his speech.[22] Later that morning, Lawrence and Sykes came in to add their comments, and to improve the English and French-language versions of the draft, as Faisal was to deliver the address in Arabic. Sykes was concerned that Faisal did not antagonise the French and general Catholic opinion by including Lebanon in his demands for an independent Arab state, while Lawrence wanted to ensure that Palestine was not mentioned by Faisal in the context of Arab demands for independence.[23] By the early afternoon, the English and French-language drafts had been completed and Faisal, in the company of Haidar, Nuri al-Sa'id, 'Awni 'Abd al-Hadi and Lawrence, set out for the Quai d'Orsay where the Council of Ten was awaiting them. The party met Clemenceau, Pichon and President Wilson in the great hall of the building, who then preceded Faisal and his group to the conference room where the Council of Ten was to meet. Faisal and his party were then invited to enter the conference room. Awaiting them, seated at the conference table, were: President Wilson; Robert Lansing, the American secretary of state; Lloyd George; Balfour; Vittorio Orlando, the Italian premier; and the Japanese delegation headed by Prince Saionji Kinmochi, a former prime minister. Faisal was met by Clemenceau at the door, who then introduced him to the seated leaders. Faisal took his place at the middle of the conference table, and after a short pause, Clemenceau said, 'The floor belongs to Prince Faisal!'[24]

Faisal stood up and gave his address, based on an expanded version of the 29 January memorandum that had earlier been sent to the conference. He started by saying, 'I am pleased to be in this company that includes the great leaders of the world and I believe that this higher forum will treat the Arab nation equitably, as they [the Arabs] seek to defend their natural rights.' He then delivered the main body of his speech. Faisal paused at regular intervals to give time for Lawrence to deliver the English translation, which was then simultaneously translated into French for the benefit of Clemenceau by an aide seated next to him. As he approached the end, Faisal asked for permission to read the entire speech without any interruptions to the end. The continuous flow of Arabic, delivered in strong and measured tones, with varying intonations, had the desired effect on the audience. Haidar noted in his diary that, 'They [the assembly] were spellbound as they had never heard a speech or any length of text read in Arabic. I cannot say how the guttural Arab sounds affected them melodiously, but the signs of astonishment were clearly on their faces.' Lawrence then read the English version aloud, followed by a French officer reading out the French version. Wilson nodded his head in acknowledgement to the main points of the speech, while Lloyd George was smiling and Orlando shaking his head in agreement. Only Clemenceau and Pichon were frowning, with Pichon's face becoming ever more sullen as the speech progressed.[25]

Faisal's speech stuck closely to the contents of his 1 January memorandum. As the representative of his father, the leader of the Arab Revolt against the Turks, he demanded that the powers acknowledge the Arab populations of Asia, from a line running from Alexandretta to Diyarbakir northwards, to the Indian Ocean southwards, as a sovereign people, so recognised by the League of Nations. Faisal excluded the Hijaz, which was by now a separate and recognised kingdom, as well as the British crown colony of Aden. He repeated the reasons why the Arabs were a sovereign people: the glories of their past civilisations and what they could contribute in the future; the fact that they all spoke a common language; the natural frontiers that separated them from other nations; the resources that a common statehood could dispose of; the increasing transport and communications links between the various regions of the area. It would be difficult to find any other group of people with such commonalities. Faisal's concluding remarks were: 'The Allies promised the Arab nation its freedom and independence at the end of the war. Now they have emerged from the war victorious, it is necessary that they abide by their promises. I am confident that the great powers will be more interested in the welfare of the Arab people than in their own material interests [in the Arab countries] ... Arab national demands conform completely to the principles enunciated by President Wilson and which were agreed to by all the states of the world.'[26]

After Faisal had finished, the conference room fell silent. Clemenceau then asked if there were any questions. Lloyd George inquired about conditions in Iraq, to which Faisal replied that most of his regular troops and officers were Iraqis and that they had fought loyally alongside the Allies for Arab independence. Wilson then asked a loaded question. 'Whether, seeing that the plan of mandatories on behalf of the League of Nations had been adopted, would he [Faisal] prefer for his people a single mandatory or several?' Faisal responded, 'I am hesitant about expressing my opinion on this matter because of the immense responsibility attendant to it. It is my father who has the right alone to answer this question. As for me, I came to Paris to represent my father at the Peace Conference and to demand the complete independence and undivided unity of the Arabs' lands that were detached from the rule of Turkey.'[27] Wilson insisted, 'But if I ask your opinion.' Faisal replied, '[My] principle is Arab unity. It was for this that the Arabs had fought. I will not accept any division of our lands and I seek independence [for the Arabs].' At this point Faisal asked for an international investigative committee to be sent to the Arab countries to determine the views of the inhabitants as to the type of government that they sought.[28]

Lloyd George re-entered the questioning and asked Faisal as to what exactly the Arabs had done in the war. Faisal then described to him in some detail the beginning of the Arab Revolt, the campaigns against the Turks in the Hijaz and then in Transjordan, and finally the entry into Damascus and the campaign in Syria. In response to one of the delegates' inopportune remarks regarding the Arabs, Faisal became impassioned. 'My nation has a great civilisational legacy, and when it was at its height of civilisation, the nations that you represent were in a state of chaos and barabarism. I ask you not to betray this nation that had served the cause of all civilisations.' Faisal's parting words had its impact on the audience, who nodded their heads in agreement. The London *Daily Mail* reported the following day that 'the Prince [Faisal] did not shirk from reminding the delegates that his nation was already civilised when their nations were still in a savage state.'[29] After a round of questions, Faisal stood up, shook Clemenceau's hand and left the room.

Faisal had been hampered by the absence of any documents that could specifically pin down the British to a set of commitments made to his father. His father had breezily told him to ask the British for such documents, who had not been forthcoming about their existence in the past. Writing to his father on 28 February, Faisal had complained, 'I submit to Your Majesty that I had written you several letters to which you only replied with telegrams. I am still awaiting the instructions that you had previously mentioned, and about which I have so far received nothing. I hope they have not been lost in transit (!)'[30] However, the day after Faisal's address to the Council of Ten, *Les Temps*, in a scathing attack on Hussein and his 'imperialist' strategy of dominating the Arab East, alluded to the Hussein–McMahon correspondence. This led to an exchange between *Les Temps* and 'Awni 'Abd al-Hadi, in which 'Awni sought to refute the allegations of the newspaper. 'Awni brought the altercation to Faisal's attention, who denied all knowledge of the contents of the exchanges between Hussein and McMahon. Faisal then instructed 'Awni to proceed forthwith to London and ask the Foreign Office for copies of such letters, if indeed they existed. The Foreign Office acknowledged the correspondence and complied with Faisal's request. 'Awni was given a full set, in Arabic, of the correspondence. Faisal was shocked that his father had withheld such vital documents from him. The only explanation that 'Awni could muster for Hussein's extraordinary secrecy was that 'King Hussein believed that no one, not even his son

Faisal, had the right to know what had been agreed in consequence of these exchanges between himself and a great power, Great Britain, as he had full trust in the intentions of the British.'[31]

Faisal was not the only person who was asked to address the Council of Ten on the matter of Syria. Dr Howard Bliss, President of the Syrian Protestant College in Beirut (later renamed the American University of Beirut), was asked by the state department to make a formal presentation on Syria to the council. Bliss was a much respected academic and university administrator, with a deep knowledge of, and experience in, the Middle East. Faisal thought highly of both Howard's father, Daniel Bliss, who was the founder of the college, and of Howard himself. He called Daniel Bliss the 'grandfather' of Syria, and Howard Bliss the 'father' of Syria.[32] Bliss addressed the council on 13 February and made an impassioned plea for a commission of inquiry to ascertain the views of the people of the Syria.[33] He had earlier written to the American delegation in Paris to say that he expected the Syrian people would first choose the US as the mandatory power, then Britain.

Following Bliss's statement, the French had engineered that Shukri Ghanem, a French national of Syrian origin who had lived outside Syria for forty years, should also address the Council of Ten. Ghanem was head of the French-sponsored Comité Central Syrien (Syrian Central Committee). The Syrian committee had emerged out of a French-backed conference in Marseilles, organised by Ghanem in early January 1919, which passed a resolution to place Syria under the protection of France. Faisal was greatly upset when he heard that Ghanem had been invited to address the council. He despatched Haidar to complain formally to the conference about the invitation to Ghanem, and demanded that he, Faisal, be present at Ghanem's speech. His request was declined, even as Faisal protested that he was there by formal invitation as an official delegate to the peace conference, while Ghanem came at the behest of another party and had no official status.[34] Ghanem made a long, flowery speech, aimed mainly at undermining Faisal's claims to represent the Arabic speakers of the Near East. He also called for the establishment of a mandate over Syria without consultation, and simply dismissed the idea of a formal plebiscite to canvass public opinion on this vital issue.[35] Ghanem's speech, which lasted two-and-a-half hours, was very poorly received. Wilson started to pace the room while Ghanem went on interminably. Clemenceau turned to Pichon, angrily asking him, 'What did you get the fellow here for, anyway?'[36]

The fact that the Council of Ten had agreed to listen to other representations on the Syrian issue gave Faisal some concern. He needed to reaffirm and differentiate his status, especially from the likes of Ghanem. On 15 February he wrote to his brother Zaid in Damascus asking him to have Syrian dignitaries send telegrams to Paris, authorising Faisal to represent them at the peace conference.[37] A large gathering of notables, religious leaders, intellectuals and officials gathered at the government centre in Damascus, the Dar-ul-Hukuma, where they were addressed by Ali Ridha al-Rikabi. Al-Rikabi told the audience about Faisal's task in Paris and his need to have his negotiating position bolstered by a clear statement of support from the leading lights of Syria. A consensus emerged on the need to strengthen Faisal's hand by giving him a broad base of support from the natural leadership of Syrian society and government to his demands for the complete independence of Syria. Telegrams were then drafted and sent to the peace conference, and to the leaders of the Great Powers, affirming that Faisal was authorised to speak on their behalf at the conference and reiterating their demands for the independence of Syria.[38] The signatories included those of the chief rabbi and the Greek Catholic patriarch.

On the same day, Faisal lost his private secretary Faiz al-Ghusain, who was asked to leave for Syria. Al-Ghusain's departure came under a cloud. Haidar in his diary accuses him of theft and of being in the pay of the French. Al-Ghusain was not popular with Faisal's entourage, who saw him as humourless, pompous and narrow-minded, but he had been with Faisal since the Arab Revolt. In the end Faisal was glad to let him go.[39] He used the occasion of al-Ghusain's departure to strengthen his delegation by adding two luminaries from Syria and Lebanon, the politician Faris al-Khoury, a Christian, and the Druze prince Amin Arslan. He also prepared to send a mainly Christian delegation to the Americas to reach out to the Syrian and Lebanese communities in the diaspora.

Impressions of Faisal: David Lloyd George and Robert Lansing

In spite of its small numbers and peripheral status, the Hijaz delegation stood out at the conference. The duo of Faisal and Lawrence were more than a match for the Big Four in terms of their publicity interest, and the press gave them good coverage. The outlines of the legend of Lawrence of Arabia were already formed, and Lawrence cut a dramatic presence in his Arab headdress. Nearly everyone who had written about the conference noticed Lawrence's presence, but Faisal's bearing and dignity left an equally profound effect on those who came across him. David Lloyd George in his *Memoirs of the Peace Conference* wrote:

> The Amir Feisal presented his case to the Peace Congress at the Quai d'Orsay on the 6th of February, 1919. He was accompanied by Colonel Lawrence. These two remarkable men were arrayed in the flowing robes of dazzling white in which they were apparelled when they led their mounted warriors to battle against the Turks. Feisal, whose intellectual countenance and shining eyes would have made an impression in any assembly, added to the distinction of his appearance by the picturesqueness of his oriental costume. He

stated his case with clarity, conciseness and dignity. He spoke in quite restrained tones. He only fired up once. A clumsy observation made quite unintentionally by one of the delegates seemed to treat the Arabs as if they were an uncultured or semi-civilised people. He immediately flashed out in stern and ringing tones: 'I belong to a people who were civilised when every other country represented in this room was populated by barbarians.' Signor Orlando [the Italian prime Minister], as a representative of Ancient Rome, bridled at this attack. Feisal sharply retorted: 'Yes, even before Rome came into existence.'[40]

However, it was Robert Lansing, Wilson's Secretary of State, who left an intricately wrought profile of Faisal at the Conference.[41] Writing in 1922, Lansing said of Faisal:

Of the many prominent representatives of race, nationalities and creed who gathered in Paris to negotiate the treaties of peace and to restore, as far as possible, the political and social order shattered by the war, there was none more striking in appearance than this prince from the sacred City [Mecca] . . . Slender and erect, seeming to be taller than he actually was, his flowing black robe and golden turban, with a richly-embroidered veil falling gracefully over his shoulders from beneath the turban's edge, enhanced his dignity of carriage and the serious expression which never left his face. No one could look at the Amir Feisul without the instinctive feeling that here was a man whom nature had chosen to be a leader of men, a man who was worthy to be a leader of men.

The features of the Arab Prince were clear-cut, regular and typical of his race. His hair and beard were black and slightly curling. His lips, which were partly hidden by a small moustache, were red and full, but did not indicate grossness or sensuality. His complexion was sallow and slightly mottled . . . His face was thin and, though with few lines and wrinkles, was strong and earnest in expression. His dark eyes were serene and kindly, but one could easily imagine that they would flash fire under the excitement of conflict or the impulse of violent emotion. Candor and truth were in the straight-forward look from his eyes. He had none of that subtlety of expression, that ill-concealed craftiness, which is so often the characteristic of the facial lines of the natives of South-western Asia.

The movements of the Amir Feisul were always unhurried and stately. He moved and spoke with deliberation and dignity. One felt his reserve of power and his strength of character, while there was the feeling that he possessed a profundity of thought which raised him above the common man . . . Everything about the Amir commanded respect. In him one seemed to see nobility of character and nobility of purpose. That was the impression that he made upon me . . . and that is the impression that remained unchanged when I came to know him better and to appreciate the intellectual force which harmonized so entirely with his physical characteristics.[42]

Lansing gave due credit to Lawrence in the Arab Revolt, but then went to say that this

in no way lessens the credit due to the Amir Feisul for the success of the Arab arms. It was about him, a Moslem that the tribesmen gathered. It was for his sake that they rushed into battle against the Turks. He was the personification of a cause, the living inspiration to Arab unity and independence. Without him success would have been impossible. . . . The Amir Feisul came to the Peace Conference with the purpose, and I believe with the expectation, of founding an Arab kingdom extending northward from the desert wastes of the Arabian Peninsula to the Taurus mountains and the borders of old Armenia, and from the Euphrates to the Mediterranean. The vast majority of the inhabitants of this region were Arabian and Aramean stocks and with few exceptions believers in the Koran. The capital of this new state was to be Damascus . . . The Amir's desire seems to have been to include Palestine within the boundaries of the proposed state, a not unreasonable desire in view of the fact that nearly nine tenths of the population of that territory are today of Arab blood, though I think that he could not have been sanguine of achieving this wish in view of the Zionist Movement which had received the unqualified support of the British Government.

He presented the Arab claim and the aspirations of the Mahommedans of Syria before the Council of Ten of the Peace Conference. Unquestionably he impressed his hearers strongly with the soundness of his arguments and with the calm and judicial way in which he gave his reasons for the rebirth of Syria as an independent state . . . The Prince spoke with solemn dignity, perhaps it would be more accurate to say with stateliness, and with an ease of utterance which denoted familiarity in addressing public assemblages. One longed to be able to understand the language which he used, for there is no doubt that his sentences lost much through translation, particularly in the vividness of expression where the Arabic idiom found no direct counterpart in the European tongues.[43]

Lansing continued with an extraordinary admission regarding the real underlying causes why Faisal's hopes were going to be dashed. He went beyond great power rivalries and conflicting commitments to the deep-seated animus against Islam and Muslims that prevailed amongst the western powers. 'The Amir Feisul met in Paris forces more powerful and less easy to overcome than the Turkish armies which he had battled so successfully. There had existed for generations throughout the Christian world an antipathy toward the Mahomeddan faith . . . The collapse of the Ottoman Empire offered this opportunity [to restore the fortunes of the Christians of the east] and the European delegates to the Paris Conference were generally determined to prevent a restoration of the power of the Mussulman in the territories which had been subject to the sovereignty of the Sultan . . . The atmosphere of hostility to Moslem rule made the purpose of the Amir Feisul to create a new Kingdom of Syria – which, remember, was to be a new Moslem kingdom – difficult of accomplishment.' Nevertheless, Lansing concluded that a new Arab state under Faisal might have been materially different from the Ottoman Empire in its relations with the western powers. 'The manner of the man in the circumstances was so admirable that his dignity and poise were emphasized and made a deeper impression because he was striving against irresistible forces. It was a test of character and of temperament which enhanced the high regard in which he was held by the delegates to the Conference. Prince Feisul made the impression of one who comibned the best and finest traits of Oriental character. Nobility and dignity, honesty and candor, reserve and wisdom, were manifest in his conduct and words.' But then Lansing let through his own deeply held prejudices against Faisal's religion in a statement that, in its time, was perfectly acceptable to be aired openly. 'He seemed so eminently fitted for success even though he was of a religion that has been a curse rather than a blessing in so many lands.'

Lawrence and Faisal had invested a great deal of effort in cultivating the Americans during the Paris Peace Conference.[44] The idea that the US would hold the balance between the interests of France and Britain in the Middle East, and the immense moral authority of President Wilson upon whose principles of self-determination the edifice of the peace conference was supposed to be constructed, made the Americans a most desirable ally for the Arab case. American accounts of both Lawrence and Faisal of the time were tinged with a degree of romanticism – in one case Faisal's appearance was compared to that of Christ – but it should be noted that Lansing was writing his profile of Faisal several years after the proceedings in Paris, with the benefit of hindsight and with great events intervening in the while. It was hardly the fleeting impressions of a dazzled spectator.

Faisal in French society

Faisal's presence in Paris quickly became known to the political classes and to the literati, intelligentsia and hostesses of the city. The Comtesse de Kellermann herself took charge of introducing Faisal to the leading lights of French culture and letters, and within a short while an invitation to meet Faisal was much coveted. De Kellermann used to call regularly on 'Awni 'Abd al-Hadi at the mansion to ask him to extend an invitation to Faisal for a lunch or dinner party or some reception. 'Abd al-Hadi records in his memoirs that 'French high society fiercely competed with each other to meet with Faisal. They were smitten by his personality, his Arabian clothes and his attractive face, and what they saw as his integrity, tolerance and gracious conduct. These convinced them of his greatness.'[45] Faisal's bonds of friendship with the leading lights of French society deepened, but none more so than with France's literary giant (and subsequent Nobel Prize winner), the writer and novelist Anatole France. The latter would often appear at Faisal's residence in the morning or evening, knock on the door, and finding Faisal accommodating to his unexpected visits would continue to take liberties and visit at odd hours. It was Anatole France who took to comparing Faisal's visage with that of Christ. Anatole France also generously reciprocated and would often invite Faisal and his group for lunch or dinner at his quarters when he was in Paris, the Hotel Bellevue, or at his suburban home. Alongside Faisal he would invite many of the country's leading journalists and editors of influential newspapers, such as *Les Temps*, *Le Matin* and *Le Figaro*. Anatole France would dominate the conversation in such gatherings, and would steer it towards his praise of Faisal's intelligence and good sense, his respect for France the country, and the merits of the Arab case. He would then encourage the newspapermen to support Faisal in his national demands.[46]

Faisal's success with the intelligentsia and high society owed a lot to the novelty of the exotic and an idealised, neo-orientalist vision of the Arabs that infused the cultured classes. Rustum Haidar records in his diary a visit by Faisal and his entourage on 26 February 1919 to the home of Anatole France in St Cloud, in Paris's western suburbs.

We met with Anatole France, an old man of 76, a mixture of Victor Hugo [the nineteenth-century French novelist] and al-Mutannabi [one of the greatest poets of the Arabs who lived in the tenth century]. [France] looked at the Amir appreciatively, commenting on how splendid his clothes were and how they matched his looks ... He then opined about how the Arabs love commerce and thus continued to survive even after their empire had ended, unlike the Romans who, because they only had martial virtues, disappeared after their military collapse ... Every time France looked at the Amir his mind went back to the *Thousand and One Nights* ... How common is this view in Europe. As if the entire civilisation of the Arabs, which is unknown even to their greatest thinkers, has left no trace except for the book of the *Thousand and One Nights*. The imaginative and exotic storytelling of the *Thousand and One Nights* has left westerners, even their literary figures, believing that the entire East is like that.[47]

The day continued with Haidar being asked to recite a poem to Anatole France, composed by Faisal and called 'Al-Qasida al-Khanjariya'.[48] At a later occasion, though, Haidar softened his views of Anatole France and saw him as a true champion of Faisal and the Arab cause. At a lunch party hosted by Faisal, to which the writer and dramatist George Bernard Shaw and his wife Charlotte were also invited, Anatole France gave a moving tribute to Faisal and the Arabs. Responding to Faisal's praise of him, Anatole France said, 'I salute you as the leader of an army of a nation which had the better share in uplifting and serving humanity . . . The Arabs have served humanity in the past and for that I hope that they will achieve their desires so that they can serve humanity once again in future generations.'[49]

Faisal also visited France's leading educationalists and scientists, hoping to impress on them the justice of his case and hopefully have them write or speak publicly in favour of the Arab cause. One such figure was Professor Aular, the head of the Sorbonne, whom Faisal met at the latter's offices.[50] Faisal spent more than an hour outlining the right of the Arabs to self-determination and the imperative for the peace conference to admit this right and grant the Arabs their independence. The following day, Aular wrote an article for the newspaper *Le Journal des Débats*, and supported Faisal's call for the freedom and independence of the Arab people. But the occasional article in the French press supporting the Arab case was insufficient to combat the overall negative tone regarding Faisal, the sharifians and the calls for Syrian independence. The French press was suffused with the notion of France's entitlement to a privileged position in Syria, legitimated by both the Sykes–Picot Agreement and as a just reward for France's heroic struggle in the First World War. It was also influenced by the colonial lobby that wanted to assert France's interests in Syria, as well as by Catholic opinion that reflected the maximalist position of the Maronites of Lebanon. Added to these hostile factors was the widespread antipathy, frequently degenerating into outright racism, against Arabs and Muslims.

This relentless assault on the culture, religion and aspirations of the Arabs, maintaining somehow they were not fit for independence and had to be guided into the modern world, was not limited to the French press. It had its effect not only on public opinion but also reinforced stereotypes and prejudices even inside the supposedly cool and collected minds of diplomats at the Quai d'Orsay. Jean Gout confided, remarkably, to an American diplomat that 'he [Gout] thought the Moslems were gaining in strength and believed there was great danger in a large Arab empire. The French wished to nationalize the Moslems [that is, strip of their primary allegiance to Islam] . . . He believed that the Amir Feisal was very much interested in the preservation of the Ottoman Empire.'[51] Faisal was well aware of the depth of these prejudices, but he coped with them, frequently behind a shield of humour, as, for example, at a dinner

party given in his honour by Professor James Shotwell of the American delegation. To the assertion that the Parisian public saw him as half-civilised because
he carried a ceremonial dagger, he replied that French officers must be
completely uncivilised because they carried ceremonial swords![52] Faisal was
too secure in his background and identity to feel the need to prove himself as
an equal in front of a sceptical audience, but he did at times adjust his dress or
habits to accommodate himself to the expectations of westerners. Invited to
dine with Faisal, Shotwell reported on the regrettable outcome of these compro-
mises. 'Unfortunately, the Arabs have come to the conclusion that unless they
dress like Europeans their cause will suffer, for people have been talking as if
they were half-civilised, so the Amir had a Prince Albert coat cut like a clergy-
man's around the neck and a stiff white collar. [But] he looks dignified in
anything and his gracious manner was able to counteract the atrociousness of
his attire.'[53] Faisal's sartorial sense would improve with time. In fact he would
become quite a fashionable dresser in his well-cut European clothes. Rustum
Haidar caught the spirit of this change. In his diary entry of 16 December 1919,
he recorded that Faisal ordered a frock coat to be tailored for him after he had
attended a dinner invitation in Paris that included the Shah of Persia. Faisal
had worn traditional clothes but all the other guests, including the shah's
retinue, wore frock coats. Faisal had felt uncomfortable in this situation and
had confided to Haidar that 'no person should attend a banquet that includes
kings unless they were wearing the most suitable clothes'. Whereupon Haidar
said to him, 'Sire, if someone had come to you three months ago and suggested
you should have a frock coat tailored for you, you would have thrown him out!
But now you think it is necessary.' Faisal smiled and said, 'Yes, that is true. But
necessity now rules.'[54]

CHAPTER 12

AT THE PARIS PEACE
CONFERENCE II

THE HEROIC efforts by Faisal to convince the Council of Ten, especially the triumvirate of Lloyd George, Clemenceau and Wilson, of the viability and indeed desirability of an independent Arab state or confederation of states was ultimately dependent on achieving the good will of the powers for such an outcome – if not all of them at least Britain and the United States. The lasting personal impression that Faisal had left on the peace conference meant little in practice if it did not establish the conditions under which his, and, by extension, Arab, demands could be satisfied. Wilson's high principles were gradually being whittled away as the conference progressed. The realities of international relations obliged him to bargain down, or misplace, his principles, as these faced the ambitions and interests of the European imperial powers. Faisal's belief that he could hold the United States accountable to its declared aims for the post-war order could not be seriously sustained as French demands proved intractable, and Britain was caught in increasingly contorted twists between its own ambitions and its conflicting commitments to its French, Zionist and Arab allies. Nevertheless, the United States had considerable residual power to influence the outcome of events in the Middle East. The principle of national self-determination was still potent and one that the European powers had acknowledged, perhaps insincerely, as forming one of the bases upon which the Ottoman Empire would be partitioned.

The genesis of the Inter-Allied Commission of Inquiry

The conference had listened to four presentations on the Arab lands: Faisal's was by far the most significant, and there were three more from Dr Howard Bliss, Shukri Ghanem and Daoud Ammun.[1] The latter headed a mainly Maronite Lebanese delegation that had the backing of France. It also received official status at the peace conference and was heard by the Council of Ten on

15 February. Ammun called for the establishment of an autonomous state in Lebanon within its pre-1860 frontiers and loosely confederated with Syria.[2] Faisal was clearly aware that the thicket of claims and counter-claims regarding the future disposition of the Arab lands might significantly weaken his case with the United States. His attitude to the latter had become increasingly positive, to the extent that he contemplated a possible American mandate over Syria. But he was also convinced that his position was the one that had the greatest following in Syria and that this could easily be confirmed by an impartial commission of inquiry. Faisal had already advised the military representatives of the Supreme Council that 'the Associated Powers should send a commission to Syria to establish the facts and ascertain the wishes of the people.'[3] In fact Faisal had brought the matter up earlier in a meeting that he had had with Professor W. L. Westermann, chief of the Western Asian section of the intelligence division of the American delegation. Faisal had explained to Westermann that his plan was to ask the conference to send an investigative commission to examine the situation to Syria and to ascertain the opinion of its people. He needed American backing for such a proposal.[4]

It was Dr Howard Bliss, however, who was the most effective in helping to convince Wilson and the American delegation of the need for such a commission.[5] Bliss had written to Wilson on 7 February 1919 saying that the people of Syria were counting on the Americans to carry out the principle of self-determination, and that the reports that he had heard of a possible American commission to investigate the situation in the Middle East were most welcome.[6] Bliss also reiterated his position to Lansing on 26 February, by which time the American delegation had come round to accepting that the findings of a commission of inquiry would form an essential prerequisite for any settlement in the Near East. The French had already rejected earlier American feelers to this effect, but this time the US was determined to put the matter of a commission of inquiry firmly on the agenda of a future meeting of the Big Four.[7] Nothing, however, could be resolved until Wilson returned from the United States. He had left Paris on 14 February and was scheduled to return on 14 March. Faisal stayed in Paris awaiting the return of the American president, upon whom a great deal of his hope for Arab independence now rested.

The Supreme Council, with the Big Four in attendance, met in a secret conference on 20 March 1919 at Lloyd George's flat in Paris to discuss the Syrian question. Significantly, General Allenby had been invited to attend the meeting. Allenby had earlier informed Lloyd George about the anxieties in Syria generated by rumours about ceding the country to French control.[8] The meeting was heated, with the French insisting that the Sykes–Picot Agreement gave them a free hand in Syria and Lebanon. The British only narrowly accepted French claims as they related to Lebanon, but not to interior Syria.

The disposition of the government there had to take into account their own agreement with Hussein. Pichon rejected the notion that France should be bound by the terms of the Hussein–McMahon correspondence, to which they were not a party, and complained that the French had only received copies of the exchanges a few weeks earlier. Lloyd George then retorted that it was the British who fielded over a million men in the Middle East theatre of war, and that it was they with their Arab allies who had finally defeated the Turks. Allenby concurred that Arab help was invaluable to the campaign. Wilson, clearly exasperated by the feuding powers, finally intervened by stating that the US was indifferent to the claims of both Britain and France over peoples. ' . . . One of the fundamental principles to which the United States adhered was the consent of the governed . . . and to discover the desires of the population of these regions'. He then went on to propose that an Inter-Allied Commission go to Syria and elsewhere in the former Ottoman territories to determine the views of the people.[9]

Clemenceau only grudgingly accepted the idea of an inquiry 'in principle', saying that 'Orientals were very timid and afraid to say what was at the back of their minds'. He also wanted a French military presence in Syria to counterbalance the British and Arab military presence there, as the 'Amir Feisal was practically a soldier of England'. Lloyd George accepted the idea of a commission to cover all the former Ottoman territories that were to be placed under a mandate system, including Palestine, Mesopotamia and Armenia, and requested that the American delegation draft the terms of reference of the commission.[10] The apparent agreement on the Inter-Allied Commission, however, was insufficient to cover up the often acrimonious discussions at the meeting. It left Wilson confused and upset. 'President Wilson came out of the meeting cursing everybody and everything saying that he had done nothing but talk for forty-eight hours and was getting disgusted with the whole business.'[11]

No one was more elated than Faisal about the decision to send a commission of inquiry to the Near East.[12] He wrote to President Wilson on 24 March of his gratitude and appreciation for the opportunity given the Arabs to express 'their own purposes and ideals for their national future'.[13] A few days later Faisal, together with Lawrence, called on Colonel House and told him that the idea of sending a commission to Syria was the best thing he had ever heard. Faisal was by now ever more enthusiastic about forging a relationship with the United States, and in this he was supported by Lawrence. The latter in fact had sought to 'manage' the American connection, drawing on his own relations with leading figures in the American delegation and the spread of his fame in the United States. He insisted that contacts with the Americans in Paris be strictly limited to Faisal and himself, and barred any other members of the Hijaz delegation from having any individual dealings on political issues with the American delegation.[14] At the meeting with House and in view of the Anglo-French friction on the issue of a mandate for Syria, Faisal asked House if the US would itself consider being the mandatory power for Syria. The Arabs, Faisal said, 'would rather accept death than a French mandate'. Lawrence also went along with the idea of an American mandate for Syria, as the British could not take it lest they be accused of being hypocrites by the French. Lawrence also felt that an American mandate over Syria would be welcomed by Arab Americans.[15] House, however, questioned whether the US would accept a mandate over Syria.

The commission was scheduled to leave for the Middle East by the end of May 1919. The Americans were the first to announce the composition of their delegation. Wilson's choice for commission members fell on the president of Oberlin College, Dr Charles King, who was then in France, and a well-known Chicago businessman, Charles Crane, who had some knowledge of the Near East.[16] However, matters were not to be so smoothly arranged for the British and French contingent to the Inter-Allied Commission of Inquiry. The French were in no hurry to move and were in fact finding a way to stymie the operations of the commission and abort it. As far as the French were concerned the 20 March meeting of the Big Four only agreed in principle to the despatch of the commission, and the American desire to move to the Near East as soon as possible was simply impracticable. Putting on world-worn airs, they condescendingly informed the Americans that they 'were too honest to deal with Orientals'.[17] The ultimate status of the commission remained in abeyance for the following two months, mired in confusion and intrigue, and played out against rapidly evolving circumstances in the Near East.

Faisal and the Zionists

The Zionist Organisation had been officially acknowledged by the peace conference, and Sokolow addressed the Council of Ten on 25 February 1919. He called for the implementation of the Balfour Declaration, the establishment of a British mandate over Palestine, together with a local administration that would guarantee the continuing immigration of Jews to Palestine. The Zionist Organisation, alarmed by the implications of a commission of inquiry on the Zionist project in Palestine, exerted its influence to abort the despatch of the commission, or at least to exclude Palestine from its remit. Felix Frankfurter, a professor at the Harvard Law School and an adviser to the Zionist Organisation, called on Colonel House in late March. As House recapitulated his impressions of the meeting with Frankfurter, 'The Jews have it that the Inter-Allied Commission which is about to be sent to Syria was merely a device to cheat Jewry of Palestine.' House assured him that there was no such intention and that the Balfour Declaration was to be honoured.[18] Frankfurter continued in his campaign to block the commission from investigating opinion in Palestine by writing directly to Wilson. 'The controlling Jewish hope has been – and is – your approval of the Balfour Declaration and your sponsorship of the establishment of Palestine as the Jewish National Home. The appointments of the Inter-Allied Syrian Commission and the assumed postponement for months, but particularly beyond the time of your stay here, of the disposition of Near Eastern questions, have brought the deepest disquietude to the representatives of the Jewry of the world.'[19]

Faisal's partly benign view regarding the Zionist project in Palestine was being eroded as details emerged as to the true extent of Zionist political ambitions. These were clearly pointing towards the establishment of a Jewish state in Palestine. The tactical alliance that he had with Weizmann, based firmly on the twin beliefs that the Zionists would help the cause of Arab independence and that their programme in Palestine precluded the establishment of a Jewish state, had now become a liability. His entourage were deeply suspicious of the Zionist claims in Palestine, a position that seemed vindicated by the statements and positions of the Zionist delegation at the peace conference that veered considerably from Weizmann's earlier measured comments. On 12 February 1919, the French newspaper *L'Information* carried an interview with Faisal in which he mentioned Palestine three times in the context of those Arab countries for which he sought independence.

On 1 March Faisal had another interview with *Le Matin* in which he outlined his position on the matter of Jewish immigration to Palestine. According to Rustum Haidar, Faisal told the paper's reporter that 'the Jewish people can find refuge in Palestine, the centre of their people and religion. However, the majority of Palestine is Arab and the government there has to follow the interests of the majority. The foundation of government must be the equality of rights of the people.' However, *Le Matin* published the interview with the following text attributed to Faisal. 'We will be pleased, in the name of humanity and chivalry to see the immigration of oppressed European Jews to Palestine, on the condition that they settle there aware of their national duties under a Muslim power or a foreign Christian power mandated by the League of Nations.'[20]

The interview caused no end of trouble with the Zionist delegation in Paris, who rushed to vent their displeasure with Lawrence. A meeting was then hurriedly arranged between Faisal and Frankfurter, with Lawrence in attendance, to defuse the impact of the interview. Lawrence then drafted an effusive letter to Frankfurter, to be signed by Faisal. The letter became the subject of much future controversy as it was later effectively disowned by Faisal and his entourage. Lawrence's draft went far beyond what Faisal had ever expressed before, either privately or publicly, regarding the Zionists. 'We Arabs, espe-cially the educated among us look with the deepest sympathy on the Zionist movement. Our deputation here in Paris is fully acquainted with the proposals submitted yesterday by the Zionist Organisation to the Peace Conference, and we regard them as moderate and proper. We will do our best, in so far as we are concerned, to help them through: we will wish the Jews a most hearty welcome home.' The letter went on waxing lyrical about Arab–Jewish cooperation and the similar objectives of the Arab national and Zionist movements. Frankfurter 'responded' to this purported letter by thanking Faisal for considering these proposals 'moderate and proper', and that Faisal was now 'a staunch supporter of their realisation'. *The New York Times* of 5 March, in a despatch from its Paris correspondent, printed Faisal's letter to Frankfurter, and the body of the letter found its way into the British archives.[21]

Subsequent controversy over the authorship of the letter emerged in 1929, when Sir Lloyd Friedman, acting on behalf of the Zionist Organisation, tabled a copy of the letter in its English language version, and with Faisal's signature in English, to the Shaw Commission on Palestine. 'Awni 'Abd al-Hadi, who was by then a member of the Palestinian Arab delegation meeting with the Shaw Commission, had his suspicions that the letter was a forgery and cabled Faisal in Baghdad inquiring about the authenticity of the letter. Rustum Haidar, then the royal chamberlain in Baghdad, cabled 'Awni back, saying, 'His Majesty [Faisal] has no recollection that he wrote anything of the sort.' In a letter of 25 January 1930 to the Baghdad newspaper *al-Bilad*, which had translated the letter into Arabic, Haidar said that Faisal 'finds it exceedingly strange that such a matter is attributed to him as he at no time would consider allowing any foreign nation to share in an Arab country'. Not quite a complete denial, but a dissociation with the letter and its implications nevertheless.

However, it was 'Awni 'Abd al-Hadi who, in his memoirs, would strongly reject the authenticity of such a letter. First of all, 'Awni, as secretary of the Hijaz delegation, states categorically that such a meeting never took place – at least not with his knowledge. Second, the absence of any Arabic-language version of the letter would imply that Lawrence was its sole author, and that it was concocted between Lawrence, Weizmann and Frankfurter without Faisal's awareness of its details and its over-accommodating tones. 'I am unaware that a meeting on that date [1 March 1919] had taken place between the Amir Faisal, Dr. Chaim Weizmann, Mr. Felix Frankfurter and Lawrence. I also did not witness, in my capacity as secretary to the Amir Faisal, any such meeting ... I believe that this letter, assuming that it is authentic, was written by Lawrence, and that Lawrence signed it in English on behalf of Faisal. I believe this letter is part of the false claims made by Chaim Weizmann and Lawrence to lead astray public opinion.'[22]

The balance of evidence would indicate that 'Awni 'Abd al-Hadi's observations are the closest to the truth, but not necessarily the whole truth. Faisal was indeed becoming increasingly concerned about Zionist plans for the settlement of Palestine and the dangers these would pose to Arab independence in Palestine. The content and tone of the letter to Frankfurter carries none of the urgency that Faisal had felt regarding the dangers for the Arabs of Zionist plans for Palestine. In fact a few weeks after the purported letter to Frankfurter, Faisal composed a draft memorandum that Lawrence brought to Stephen Bonsal, a member of the American delegation. The memorandum was a clear reflection of Faisal's anxieties regarding the future of Palestine, a sentiment that is opposite to the one that emerges in the Frankfurter letter. Faisal wrote,

If the views of the radical Zionists as presented to the [peace conference] should prevail, the result will be a ferment, a chronic unrest, and sooner or later civil war in Palestine. But I hope I will not be misunderstood. I assert that we Arabs have none of the racial or religious animosity against the Jews which unfortunately prevail in many other regions of the world. I assure you that with the Jews who have been seated for some generations in Palestine our relations are excellent. But the new arrivals exhibit very different qualities from those 'old settlers' as we call them, with whom we have been able to live and even co-operate on friendly terms. For want of a better word I must say that new colonists almost without exception have come in an imperialistic spirit. They say that for too long we have been in control of their homeland taken away from them by brute force in the dark ages, but that now under the new world order we must clear out, and if we are wise we should do so peaceably without making any resistance to what is the fiat of the civilised world.[23]

Moreover, in mid-April 1919, while meeting a French academic delegation, Faisal commented on the dangers posed to the Arabs of Palestine by the more extremist Zionists. 'Such people exaggerate in their statements and take extremist positions in ways that raise Arab ire. And it is for the Jews to avoid comments that raise our emotions. We do not want to abandon our land and leave it to the Jews, as one of their [extremist] writers has said: "Give the Muslims [of Palestine] the cost of travel and they will carry their belongings on their backs and leave," as if the people are nomads.'[24] The most likely explanation for the purported Faisal–Frankfurter exchanges is that a meeting did indeed take place between the protagonists, and that Lawrence drafted a letter in English whose contents were not entirely made clear to Faisal. He then may or may not have been induced to sign it, or it is likely that Lawrence simply signed it in English on his behalf. Lawrence may have also impressed on Faisal a sense that if the Zionist delegation were not appeased, the Arab cause would lose a potential ally and source of influence with the Allies. But it is clear that the contents of the letter ran diametrically against Faisal's public and private statements at the time regarding the dangers to the Arabs of Palestine inherent in the Zionist project.

Faisal and the French

The French, whose public position had been to belittle Faisal and the calls for Syrian independence, recognised early on that they could not completely ignore him and his followers. They had to reckon with the implications of Faisal's demanding complete independence for Syria, even if he enjoyed only limited British support. Their rejection of Faisal's version of Arab independence in the Near East did not necessarily translate into refusing to acknowledge that he might have some role to play in a French-dominated Syria. Up to the date of Faisal's speech to the Council of Ten on 6 February, France was reluctantly prepared to concede to Faisal some measure of power in Syria, if for no other reason than to assuage its British allies, thus allowing the British to claim to have met its obligations to its sharifian allies and meet the spirit of the Anglo-French Declaration of 6 November. Faisal, on the other hand, raged in private and public against the French and what he saw as their ultra-colonial bent, and sought allies wherever he could find them to thwart France's determination to implement the Sykes–Picot Agreement in Syria.

His address of 6 February to the Council of Ten was received with hostility by the French, and soon thereafter violent attacks against him multiplied in the French press. The French were expecting a more conciliatory, even accommodating, position from Faisal, but what they got instead left them with a sense of bitterness. This contributed greatly to the *idée fixe* in French official circles of Faisal as an untrustworthy double-dealer.[25] The Quai d'Orsay fired off a roughly worded note to the British about Faisal's speech, drawing a protest from Curzon as to its language. 'Amir Faisal, chief of nomads, transformed into a mandatory of all the Arab speaking peoples, is terrorising a population which by its culture and historic traditions should oppose domination by Bedouins', the note read.[26]

The British had become alarmed at the bitter tones of the French towards Faisal. The India Office, true to form, questioned whether Arab claims should be supported to the point where Britain's relationship with France was jeopardised, and suggested that Britain act as an honest broker between Faisal and the French. Clemenceau was the key figure, as he was seen to be more liberal and open-minded, though still sceptical, about Arab claims than the professional Foreign Ministry bureaucrats and diplomats. Lord Milner, by now the colonial secretary, was despatched by Lloyd George to convince Clemenceau to hold a meeting with Faisal. Milner explained to Clemenceau that the British were dissatisfied with the Sykes–Picot Agreement and, as allies to both, sought to reconcile French and Arab demands. Allied commitments to the 'complete enfranchisement for the people of Syria' could not be squared with a mandate over Syria, and their best bet was to reach a deal with Faisal.[27]

However, before this meeting with Faisal could take place, Clemenceau was shot and wounded on 19 February, and the meeting had to be postponed. Its prospects were not improved when Clemenceau, while convalescing, heard of the massacre of French-protected Armenians in Aleppo on 28 February. The branches of the Arab Club in Syria had organised mass demonstrations against French claims that the Syrian people willingly sought France's protection. In Aleppo, the demonstrations quickly turned into anti-Armenian rioting, partly fuelled by reports of the mistreatment by the Armenians of Cilicia of surrendering Arab troops of the Ottoman army. The rioting lasted for over two hours and targeted Armenian-owned buildings and a French-sponsored orphanage. Nearly two hundred Armenians were killed or injured, some by rioters in uniform, before British and Arab troops restored order.[28] This incensed Clemenceau and drove him to break off the proposed meeting with Faisal.

With Wilson away in the US, and not expected back until the middle of March, and the peace conference focusing on German matters, Faisal undertook a tour of Alsace, the Rhineland and Belgium, the latter after he received an official invitation from King Albert I. He left by car for Nancy on 10 March for the start of his visit, which was to last for ten days. He was accompanied by Dr Ahmad Qadri and Colonel Pisani. Faisal returned to Paris on 20 March, arriving in the late afternoon at the Gare du Nord. 'Awni 'Abd al-Hadi and Rustum Haidar met him at the station and filled him in on the events of the intervening period. Faisal was especially pleased to learn that Allenby was in Paris. Turning to his trip, Faisal said, 'My tour was very useful. I now know the greatness of the German nation and how it was able to face off the entire world. I have never seen such a built-up country before. The French and the British should seek German teachers to tell them how to reform their lands.' Haidar told him that Balfour had joked with Lawrence that Faisal would return from his trip enthralled by Germany. Faisal laughed and said, 'That is the truth of it. Are they aware of it?!' Faisal then continued in praising Belgium and its king, 'who is lovable, nay an enchanter who seizes hearts by his good graces and courteous conduct'. The Belgian press was also very favourable to Faisal and the Arab cause, calling on the Allies to grant the Arabs their independence.[29]

By the end of March 1919, France was studiously ignoring Faisal and was unwilling to deal with him formally on matters relating to Syria. Faisal was exasperated and was determined to leave for Syria in preparation for the arrival of the Commission of Inquiry. The British then redoubled their efforts to bring the two parties together, and a backdoor channel was opened to air the issues. On 25 March, Wickham Steed, the editor of *The Times*, hosted a dinner which was to have an important influence on the course of diplomacy in Paris. Steed was a significant behind-the-scenes player and had a special interest in Arab and Near Eastern affairs. The meeting was called partly to smooth over the cracks that were growing between the French and British positions on Syria and the alienation between the French and Faisal. Present at the meeting were Jean Gout and Robert de Caix, a leading light of the French colonial lobby and an adviser to the French peace conference delegation on Middle Eastern affairs. Lawrence was also one of the invitees, as was Gertrude Bell. Surprisingly, Lawrence warned of the dangers that a commission of inquiry would pose for France's ambitions in Syria. It would very likely confirm the widespread belief that France was an unwelcome power in the country. He instead suggested that France should seek an accommodation with Faisal. With Faisal on board, the Syrians might very well be convinced to call for a French mandate. (Lawrence reversed his position a few days later when he supported the call for an American mandate in Syria during his and Faisal's meeting with House.) Lawrence's arguments carried the day and de Caix recommended to the Quai d'Orsay that France should reach a deal with Faisal.[30]

The French Foreign Ministry continued to prevaricate until once again Lawrence entered the fray and wrote a note on 7 April 1919 to Clemenceau, who had by now recovered from the attempted assasination, on the desirability of a meeting with Faisal. The following day, Georges-Picot called on Faisal, who had already set 12 April as his departure date for Syria. According to Picot's notes on the discussions, Faisal offered to lead the population of Syria in accepting French cooperation in exchange for a specific commitment by France to Syrian independence. He also complained that his presence in Paris was no longer necessary as decisions were taken without consultation with the Arab delegation. It reminded him of 'the Ottoman Parliament, where one was only convoked when something was decided by the Committee [CUP] with the order to sanction the decision taken by it.'[31] He made it clear to Picot that he would, nevertheless, agree to extend his stay in Paris if a meeting with Clemenceau could be arranged.

The arrangements were made and on 13 April Faisal met Clemenceau at the Ministry of War.[32] Clemenceau had grown tired of the interminable disputes with the British on Syria and finally accepted that a settlement with Faisal was greatly preferable to canvassing Syrian opinion on a French mandate. Faisal was accompanied by 'Awni 'Abd Al-Hadi while Clemenceau had alongside him the official French interpreter, ibn Ghabrit. Several versions of the conversation between the two are available, including the notes kept by 'Awni 'Abd al-Hadi and a later reconstruction of the events given by Faisal to Sati' al-Husri. Clemenceau began by saying that France had no colonial ambitions in Syria and that he had fought colonialism for over fifty years in his writings and speeches. Faisal said he trusted Clemenceau, but that he could not say the same about the French politicians who might succeed him. At that point Clemenceau talked about the long-established bonds between France and the Syrian people. Now that the British were withdrawing from Syria, there was no alternative but to replace them with French troops. Faisal, of course, rejected this premise and denied that Syria required any foreign troops on its soil. 'I assure you that if Syria requires any foreign troops in the future, I will not hesitate in asking you for assistance,' he added. But Clemenceau insisted that the presence of French troops was essential if France were to meet its obligations to the Syrians. The meeting ended with Faisal stating that he was leaving for Syria to arrange for the arrival of the Commission of Inquiry.[33] Faisal had immediately recognised the dangers for Syrian independence by acceding to the presence of French troops. Nevertheless, he seized upon Clemenceau's affirmation that he was vigorously anti-colonialist as a sign of his support for Syrian independence.

Faisal's meeting with Clemenceau also raised his suspicions that the matter of the Commission of Inquiry was not yet settled. Clemenceau seemed to have left Faisal with the impression that it was the British rather than the French who were hesitating about sending a commission to the Near East. These anxieties were exacerbated by Lawrence's report about the difficulties of reaching a consensus amongst the Big Four regarding the despatch of the Commission of Inquiry. The following day Faisal sent off a note to Lloyd George that sought clarification as to the British position regarding the commission, and informing Lloyd George of his decision to leave as soon as possible for the east. He noted to Lloyd George that if the commission was not to come, then he, Faisal, would be faced with a crisis of credibility in his own country, returning in effect with nothing to show for his efforts. He also warned Lloyd George that he might not be able to contain the disturbances and violence that would surely follow in the wake of any news about the cancellation of a commission of inquiry.[34]

At this point, Lawrence, in one of his bouts of frenetic background diplomacy, met with Lloyd George, who then telephoned Faisal and informed him that the commission was now definitely scheduled to leave for the Near East. Faisal was elated at the news, and was in a celebratory mood when ibn Ghabrit called on him in the afternoon of 14 April carrying his own message from the Quai d'Orsay. He told Faisal that the French were now supportive of the Commission of Inquiry and wanted to see it depart as soon as possible. However, the French had asked for assurances that the expected plebiscite of the Syrian people should not favour the Americans. Faisal replied that the people of Syria would only vote for complete independence and that they would delegate to him the right to negotiate it on their behalf. He would not negotiate with anyone before he reached an agreement with the French. Ibn Ghabrit left the meeting saying, 'C'est fait! – It's done!' It would appear that the French had agreed to Syrian independence under a French mandate of limited duration.[35]

On the following day, 15 April, Clemenceau sent Robert de Caix to meet with Faisal and possibly reach an agreement. It is not surprising that Clemenceau preferred to use such a back channel rather than the rigid bureaucrats of the Quai d'Orsay. The discussion turned to the issue of the Commission of Inquiry. Faisal stressed that its significance lay precisely in that it would set out the clear views of the people on matters of the gravest importance for them. 'I do not believe that the Commission would resolve the matter, but at least the will of the people will be known. I know that the future [of the Arab territories] would not be settled until after the Commission returns to Europe . . . I will ask for the total independence of my country for I am an Arab before all else. I will return to Europe and defend this principle. I know that our countries need outside assistance but first we have to agree to the principle of independence. Only then can the country choose who will assist her. I promised Clemenceau that I will not speak to anyone before I spoke to him. I hold to my promise that I will not speak to any state or allow anyone else to do so until I have settled the matter with the French government.' De Caix then questioned whether the British would ever leave the countries under their control [meaning Mesopotamia and Palestine], even if the Commission of Inquiry found against them. Faisal said that this was another issue. 'If England denied the people their rights, I will know what to do and how to defend the rights of my nation. Either I will die doing so . . . or I will become a Bolshevik!' De Caix then asked for a second round of meetings with Faisal to try to settle the outstanding matters so that the French could clarify their final position inside the Commission of Inquiry.[36]

The Faisal–Clemenceau Correspondence

On April 16, ibn Ghabrit called on Faisal carrying a message from Clemenceau: France would recognise Syrian independence in exchange for a statement from Faisal acknowledging France's interests in the country. Faisal was overjoyed at the first official French recognition of the Syrian people's right to self-determination. The following day, de Caix visited Faisal with a proposal to bring the matter to a formal conclusion through an exchange of notes between Clemenceau and Faisal. De Caix proposed that Clemenceau send a brief draft of the proposed letter to Faisal, to which Faisal would respond, and the two drafts, once agreed and finalised, would form the basis of France's policy position on Syria and could continue even if Clemenceau were to leave office. In the evening of that day, de Caix returned with the draft of the planned letter from Clemenceau for Faisal's comments before it was rendered in its final form.

Faisal, who was earlier minded to accept its main tenets, changed his views when he closeted himself with his advisers. They were unanimous in their opinion that the draft was unacceptable. It imposed a mandate on the country in exchange for the right of independence, a right that had already been acknowledged by the Allies. De Caix and ibn Ghabrit tried to change Faisal's views, finally relenting and affording Faisal the time to draft his own reply that would be the basis of the Arab position.[37] In any case, Faisal was awaiting the return of Lawrence from England and a meeting with Lloyd George to ascertain Britain's position on the exchange of drafts with Clemenceau. He postponed his departure to the East once again. Writing to Zaid in Damascus on the same day, Faisal said, 'I have delayed my trip because of an important exchange of notes. Perhaps France has finally agreed to the complete independence of Syria.'[38]

Faisal returned satisfied from his meeting with Lloyd George. Rustum Haidar noted in his diary that Faisal might have had a false sense of security about British intentions. Britain was not entirely the honest broker, let alone the unflinching ally that Faisal saw in the county. Haidar seemed to have seen through all the machinations and had reached a conclusion that made Faisal quite angry. He concluded that Britain had already decided in favour of its alliance with France, and that the Commission of Inquiry would not work to further British interests. In fact Haidar surmised that the purposes of the commission were widey rejected – by the French, the British with respect to Palestine and Mesopotamia, the Armenians, the Italians, the Greeks and the Zionists. Only the Arabs and possibly the United States, which was considering taking up a mandate for Armenia, were in favour of the commission.[39]

Faisal's advisers wanted to compose a strongly worded draft that would leave no room for equivocation as to the Arabs' demand for independence. Faisal was willing to accept such advice, even though he would have preferred a more lenient position with the French. Fearful that Lawrence, who had just returned from England, would influence Faisal in a contrary direction, Haidar, with a note of exasperation, wrote in his diary, 'Lawrence arrived in the evening from England and the Amir related to him the issues at hand. [Faisal] was blindly dependent on him, even though Lawrence was nothing more than an instrument in the hands of the men-in-power. He [Lawrence] promoted his policies [with Faisal] regarding the Jews that were in total accordance with the position of the British government and now he is promoting the policies of Lloyd George, even though his heart may have been with the Amir. But as he often said friendship has no part to play in political issues . . . Lawrence used to speak with the Amir directly relying on [Faisal's] position of weakness. He did not like any one of us arguing with him, to protect his standing with the Amir, as if he would not deign to talk to anyone except the Amir. In this way, the Amir's reliance on him was great.'[40]

Lawrence, true to his complex and enigmatic personality, engendered different personal reactions from Faisal and his advisers, and these became especially apparent in the enforced proximity of weeks together during the peace conference. Suspicion of Lawrence's true allegiances and plans mixed with great respect and admiration – even love – for this most puzzling of men. On 7 April 1919, Lawrence was told that his father was mortally ill. He immediately left for England, arriving too late and a few days later he returned to Paris. Faisal wrote:

The greatest thing I have seen in him, which is worthy of mention as one of his principal characteristics, is his patience, discretion, zeal, and his putting the common good before his own personal interest. When he came to take leave I asked the reason for his departure. He said, "I regret to say that my father has died and I want to go and see my mother." I enquired when his father had died and he said, "A week ago – I received a telegram saying that he was ill, and left straightaway, but when I arrived I found that he had died two hours previously. I did not stay in England until the funeral because I realised that you were here alone and that there is much work to be done. I didn't want to be far from you, in case things happened in my absence. I didn't tell you this at the time in case it upset you. So I tell you now. I shall return on Friday." Consider such honesty, such faithfulness, such devotion to duty and such control of one's personal feelings! These are the highest qualities of man, which are found in but few individuals.[41]

Haidar, who often had harsh words for Lawrence, wrote the following entry in his diary when Faisal told him of the death of Lawrence's father.

I went to commiserate [with Lawrence] and he was very distressed, but he then returned to the conversation carrying his habitual smile . . . I have never seen a man like him who always has a smile. He always says to the Amir: It's done! Irrespective of what it cost him, as if the word No! did not exist in his dictionary. And each time I asked him for something, he used to say: I will do my best. The truth is that he struggled mightily for the Arab cause. Yesterday, he told the Amir that the British know nothing. I take a blank sheet of paper and write on it what I want and they will abide by it and execute it . . . He told me one day in the presence of the Amir: The journey is far better than the arrival. As if he wanted to say that man has to struggle and suffer since it is through struggle and suffering that a good life is earned. For if man reaches his goal, he will feel happy for a moment and then his life's journey will stop. He was afraid that if he had reached his goal he would stop in his tracks and it is in action that he finds the joy of living . . . .[42]

When the Arabic draft of Faisal's reply to Clemenceau was shown to de Caix the following day, de Caix was extremely upset with its contents and undiplomatic tone. The draft called for recognition by the powers of the complete independence of Syria as a democratic federation. Its status would be guaranteed by the League of Nations. Syria would welcome the help of advisers, but on Syria's own terms. France would receive its moral recompense by supporting Syria's call for independence, and this would assist it in extending the scope of its interests in Syria. De Caix, seeing the draft as an affront to the person of the premier and to France, categorically refused to accept it and considered it a rupture in the negotiations. Faisal was forced to reconsider his position once again, this time relying more on Lawrence's arguments than on his advisers. Lawrence was making the case for a milder draft based on demanding independence for Syria, recognising France's interests, especially on the Syrian coast, and relying on the vagaries of French politics, deteriorating economic conditions inside France, and the possible arrival of anti-colonialist socialists to neutralise the power of the colonial lobby.[43]

Lawrence also wrote to Clemenceau urging him to deal with Faisal and accept the term 'independence' for Syria. In return, Lawrence promised that he would convince Faisal of the need to seek a solution to the imbroglio through France, and to cement French interests in the form of a treaty of alliance or mandate. But Faisal was determined to leave for the Near East and the time was running out for detailed negotiations. Haidar caught Faisal's dilemma. 'The Amir was fearful of the consequences of taking an inflexible stance, and saw the need to moderate the Arab position, bringing it in line with the British. But we [his advisers] warned him of the dangers of flexibility and weakness towards France's policies and ambitions . . . which would pull the country towards servitude and divisions. But Lawrence stood behind the Amir, and the Amir believed that Lloyd George was behind Lawrence.'[44]

Faisal then drafted another letter to Clemenceau that tried to reconcile their positions: complete independence for Syria and a special status for France in the country. The new draft was seen by Faisal's advisers as being too accommodating to France and as opening the door for a French protectorate over the country. This view was not well received by Faisal, who had an altercation with Dr Ahmad Qadri on the matter retorting that he himself was responsible for what he signed. He then called in Lawrence to adjudicate the dispute with his advisers. Lawrence naturally took Faisal's side, saying that it was best to conciliate France at this stage so as to gain time. But Faisal's advisers stood their ground. Haidar told Lawrence that they were deeply suspicious of France and its intentions, and that in any case France was not the type of country that would be a good ally for the Arabs. It was selfish, oppressive and would sow divisions in Syria. Referring to the eight hundred members of al-Fatat, Haidar said that they could mobilise thousands around them to fight off France if it came to it. Seeing the unanimity of opposition to the draft by Faisal's Arab advisers, Lawrence relented somewhat and the decision was finally made to abandon it. Instead, Faisal sent Clemenceau a farewell letter that spoke in generalities, leaving the final status of Syria still to be negotiated.[45]

On 21 April, with the negotiations doomed to fail, Faisal prepared for his departure for the east. Before he left, he made a farewell call on Colonel House, and returned pleased with the meeting. House had confirmed that the Commission of Inquiry was scheduled to leave soon. Faisal also insisted on making his personal farewells to Clemenceau, and the latter found a few minutes to receive Faisal. The short conversation, as recorded by Haidar who was present, started with an exchange of courtesies, but Faisal was determined to extract some form of recognition from Clemenceau regarding the departure of the commission for the Near East. Clemenceau refused to be drawn into the discussion and deflected Faisal's repeated questioning. On the evening of 21 April, Faisal set off for Rome by train from Paris's Gare de Lyon. Seeing him off were Lawrence, Gout, Georges-Picot, de Caix and those of his entourage who had stayed behind to continue the work at the peace conference, including 'Awni 'Abd al-Hadi and Rustum Haidar. There were also a large number of Syrian and Lebanese Christians at the station to bid him farewell. A few days earlier, Shukri Ghanem had visited Faisal, probably prompted by the French, and had offered him his fealty and support in the most extravagant language.[46]

Before he left, Faisal gave Haidar and 'Awni 'Abd al-Hadi written instructions as to the position they had to take with the French on various issues: denunciation of all secret treaties (meaning, of course, the Sykes–Picot Agreement); recognition and endorsement of the full independence of Syria; withdrawal of all foreign occupation forces at the time of the Arabs' choosing; respect for the autonomy of Lebanon; independence for all Arab lands with international guarantees; and the option for the Syrian government to keep part of the foreign occupying forces. In exchange for these conditions, the Syrian government would lean towards accepting assistance from France.[47] Faisal's departure was keenly felt by his friends and advisers. Returning to an empty mansion, Rustum Haidar wrote, 'The mansion had no vitality as if the life had gone out of it.'

Faisal had planned to pass through Rome to meet with Italian officials before he was to board the French battleship *Paris* at Taranto that was to take him to Beirut. Faisal had met with the Marquis Salvago Raggi, a senator and member of the Italian delegation to the peace conference, to discuss issues affecting Italy's position in the Near East. The visit to Italy was not altogether welcome by either Britain or France, who were both concerned that a third party, extraneous to the Near East, would be drawn into the debate. The Italians had informed Faisal that they wished to support him and the Muslims generally, as they had done in Tripolitania.[48] The Italians were in favour of the Commission of Inquiry, and all they sought in Syria was to ensure their economic interests and the country did not fall under the control of a single foreign power. Faisal was received with great honour in Rome. He met with the king, the deputy prime minister, and the ministers of foreign affairs, marines and war, as well as the minister for the colonies. He also called on the pope, with whom he was closeted for over an hour. The pope sent, through Faisal, his greetings to the Christians of the east.[49] The Italian government also assigned a general and colonel to accompany him to Taranto.

On 27 April Faisal left for Beirut. On board with him was the French liaison officer Colonel Toulat. According to Toulat's report on the voyage, Faisal was fearful of France's ambitions in Syria. The violent tone of the French press had left a deep impression on him. An article in *Le Matin* on the day of his departure from Paris referred to the establishment of a French protectorate over Syria as a matter that had already been settled.[50] If Clemenceau, whom Faisal thought of as a liberal and anti-colonialist, could agree to such a measure, what were Faisal's chances with the more reactionary elements in French government and society? *Le Matin* also made certain assertions regarding Faisal's willingness to work with the French and to follow a common policy. These were simply untrue. As Lawrence commented on the article in *Le Matin*, 'There is hardly a word of truth in these statements. Feisal did leave in a French cruiser (after making his will) but will probably not return to France . . . He made no agreement with Clemenceau, and is persuaded that France is the only nation in Europe determined to refuse independence to Syria.'[51]

Faisal left a strong personal impression with French officialdom and society. De Caix in particular developed a great respect for Faisal. He contrasted him favourably to the native rulers of French North Africa. 'In him we find no Bey of Tunis or Sultan of Morocco, disposed by his character and tastes to resign himself without pain to lead an easy and gilded existence as a client of France.' De Caix went on to say that Faisal was not a sensualist but a nationalist, and his conceptions of the role of Arabic cut out the core of the French civilising mission in the Levant. Rather than submit to French rule, Faisal might withdraw entirely from Syrian affairs. He could not accept 'a political regime – and we accepted him as the [head of] the Amirate of Damascus – that can only work for a mandate inspired by local realities and the French national interest.'[52]

Faisal's last weeks in Paris were fraught with ambiguities and disappointments, but behind them all was the inherent weakness of his position, and his extremely constricted room for manoeuvre. The British were hamstrung by their commitments to the French, more so in fact after they had obtained France's agreement to the transfer to them of supremacy in Palestine and Mosul. There was a built-in limit to what they could do to bolster Faisal's claims in Syria proper. They had, in effect, cut Faisal off, even though it was they who had the greatest power on the ground and ability to influence the outcome in Faisal's favour. Clemenceau, whatever his liberal and anti-colonial instincts, could not offer Faisal anything more at the time than a relationship of dependency, with the theoretical possibility that time and events might ameliorate this condition. America might have acted as Faisal's mentor, but only if Wilson were prepared to stake America's moral and financial power in favour of Arab self-determination. The instrument to do so, in Faisal's view, was the Commission of Inquiry, but its potency was being daily degraded by the stonewalling of the French and the British, and by regular disputations as to its terms of reference and whether it was a fact-finding, advisory or policy-making body. It is no wonder that dealing with the French, no matter how unpleasant and risky, was Lawrence's advice to Faisal. An agreement with the French would resolve Britain's moral dilemma and would receive America's blessing, but Faisal was not prepared for that.

The negotiations with the French were broken mainly because what the French were offering in the form of self-government was less than what Faisal already had on the ground in Syria. Faisal did not negotiate with the French in bad faith. Both sides stuck to their position: Faisal that of immediate recognition of Syrian independence, with the possibility that France would be allowed privileges in the new Syrian state; France that of a formal recognition of French pre-eminence in Syria, in the form of troops and the raising of the French flag alongside the Arab flag in a Syria that would at first enjoy only limited independence. Faisal could only await the arrival of the Commission of Inquiry, whose findings he hoped would tilt the balance in favour of immediate independence.

However, another huge issue was looming as Faisal arrived in Beirut on 30 April 1919. During his prolonged absence the political situation in Syria had changed markedly and passions had risen to dangerous levels. Faisal now had to contend with this new and unstable factor in his quest for Arab independence in Syria.

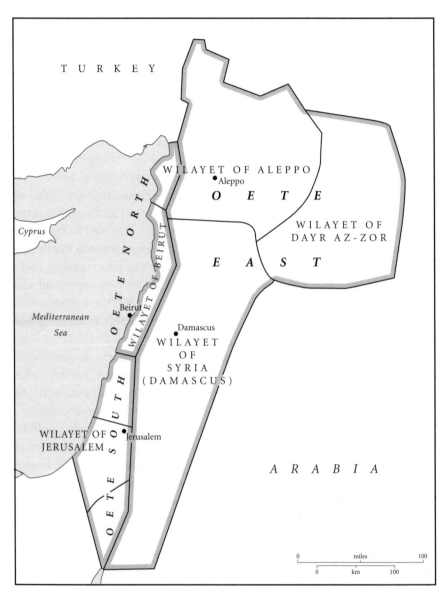

TURKEY

WILAYET OF ALEPPO

O   E   T   E

●Aleppo

WILAYET OF
DAYR AZ-ZOR

Cyprus

E   A   S   T

O E T E N O R T H

WILAYET OF BEIRUT

Mediterranean
Sea

●Beirut

●Damascus

WILAYET
OF
SYRIA
(DAMASCUS)

WILAYET OF
JERUSALEM

●Jerusalem

O E T E S O U T H

A R A B I A

| 0 | miles | 100 |
| 0 | km | 100 |

5. The Arab government of Syria (OETE), 1918–1920

++++++◆╳◆++++++

CHAPTER 13

THE STRUGGLE FOR SYRIA

T HE BATTLESHIP carrying Faisal docked in Beirut harbour on 30 April 1919. Two French admirals boarded the ship to welcome Faisal before he went ashore. Receiving him on the docks were the British and French commanders in Lebanon, and a large crowd organised by the Beirut representative of the Arab government in Damascus, Jamil al-Alshi. Faisal made his way through the crowds and then by car to the Beirut headquarters of the Arab government at the Daouk Building.[1] After receiving a parade of Syrian and Lebanese notables, foreign dignitaries and well-wishers, Faisal made his first public comments after his prolonged absence in Europe. He chose his words carefully. His speech had to contain the right balance between keeping hope alive for the cause of Arab independence, and the anxieties that he acutely felt about French ambitions, British ambiguities and American dithering. He pinned his hopes on the expected arrival of the Inter-Allied Commission of Inquiry. This was at least one concrete achievement that he could claim as a result of his five-month sojourn in Europe. And in a clear nod to the Christian minorities of Syria, in particular the Maronites, Faisal concluded with the remarks: 'You will be free in your own lands and homes and each component [of Syrian society] can manage their own affairs with due respect for your customs and traditions.'[2]

Later in the day, though, when addressing delegations from Syria at the Arab Government's offices in Beirut, Faisal's tone was more forceful. 'The world has prepared for us the conditions for us to demand our independence, and has helped us in this regard. But independence is something that is taken and not simply given. And persons who seek their independence from westerners without struggling, preparing and working for it, are as if they are building their thrones in the skies. Yes, we do not deny that we need the assistance and support of Europeans, and we shall agree on this help with whomever we want and according to our interests . . . But we must not take everything from them and refer to them in our affairs; and only after we have taken our complete, undivided independence, whose foundations we have to build with our own hands. And we have to take our independence free of any ambiguities.' Faisal's comments left a great impression on his audience, and fired their expectations that independence was only a matter of time. Unusually, delivering a *khutba* (sermon) at Beirut's Great Mosque during Friday prayers, Faisal talked of the absolute necessity of cooperation between Muslims and Christians if independence were to be attained. 'Unite so that Europe will know that Syria wants to have independence.'[3]

Throughout his short stay in Beirut, Faisal's actions and comments accorded with the promise that he had made to Clemenceau, that if Syria were granted independence, he would respect France's interests and legitimate concerns. He had kind words for Clemenceau, calling him a great humanitarian, and invited the acting French high commissioner, whom nearly all in Beirut had studiously ignored, to dinner. He had left France without an agreement with Clemenceau, but had at least planted the seed of a possible deal with the French. Faisal had no serious supporters in the French government, but some leading exponents of France's policies in the Near East, such as Georges-Picot, believed that France's interest would be better served if a deal could be struck with Faisal for the running of Syria.[4] As Faisal prepared to leave for Damascus, he was well pleased by the results of his reception and meetings in Beirut.

On 3 May Faisal's train departed Beirut for Damascus. He was seen off by a multitude of well-wishers and hundreds of Syrians boarded the train to accompany him on his journey. As his train approached the Ma'alaqa station in the Beqa'a Valley, he was cheered by throngs demanding independence under his banner.[5] He disembarked for a while, resting at the mansion of the Beqa'a notable Yusuf Namour, where he met with streams of visitors. Faisal's train left the Beqa'a Valley in the afternoon, reaching Damascus later that day. Crowds lined the route of the train, all shouting out his name and calling for independence. An eyewitness described the reception that met Faisal as he alighted from the train. 'When he [Faisal] reached the capital Damascus, he was met with a reception that had little equal. The eye could not discern anything but vast crowds along the entire route from the station to the palace. The ear could not hear any sound but the cries to the heavens calling for the Prince's victory.'[6] Colonel Toulat cabled the Quai d'Orsay that Faisal's reception in Damascus 'was extraordinary [*formidable*]. I have seen nothing like it. Here he is with his own people, surrounded by his own nation; he is truly the leader of this nation and its most illustrious personage. Whoever sees these huge demonstrations would know the status of this Prince. It is enough that one sees the cinematographic film of these demonstrations to be convinced that there is no need for a commission of inquiry in these parts.'[7]

During Faisal's long absence in Europe, Syria had been run on a day-to-day basis by the military administrator, Ali Ridha al-Rikabi. He reported directly to Allenby, who was still based in Cairo, or through the British liaison officer to the Arab government, Colonel Kinahan Cornwallis. The latter conducted his relationship with the Arab government with great discretion and as a matter of principle avoided involving himself in the running of the country's affairs, leaving the task entirely to al-Rikabi. This in turn strengthened al-Rikabi's authority and dignity, allowing him the claim that he had the explicit support of the British military in the running of the country. By most reckonings the Arab government barely acquitted itself in the first few months of its existence. Several measures were undertaken to ensure its popularity, such as the re-instatement of Ottoman-era welfare programmes, which had been suspended during the war. In addition, the Arab government resumed the payment of pensions to war widows, orphans and former Ottoman functionaries and their families. The government also tried to ensure – not altogether successfully – the stability of food prices by buying grain directly from farmers, and estab-lishing distribution centres in most cities. Free grain was often given to the urban poor and free seeds to impoverished farmers. This largesse was under-taken by government officials, who made sure that the beneficiaries were aware that it came from Faisal's Arab government.[8] Al-Rikabi himself undertook extensive tours of the main Syrian cities and the countryside, inspecting government facilities, distributing cash handouts, checking on prices and announcing amnesties of one type or another. The government didn't limit its support to the urban poor and the peasantry. In time-honoured fashion, it used the subventions provided it by the British to buy the loyalty of the wealthy and powerful as well.

A motley collection of Syrians, Lebanese, Iraqis, Hijazis, Palestinians and Transjordanians ran the uncertain and ramshackle new state.[9] The govern-ment's authority outside the capital was tentative. In the provincial towns, the Arab government had to compete with the de facto (and sometime *de jure*) powers of local notables, who were resentful of the centralising policies of the Arab government. There were too few competent and honest officials in the government and too many conflicting and confusing lines of authority and responsibility, reflecting the patched-up nature of the government itself, a strange military and civilian mixture of unclear status. Above all, the Arab government was tightly constrained by its total dependence on British finan-cial and fiscal support. This amounted at first to £E150,000 per month. This subsidy, together with the money spent by British occupying forces, trade restrictions and embargoes, transport bottlenecks and the widespread specula-tion and hoarding, had the effect of igniting an inflationary spiral. The Arab government's revenue-generation abilities were greatly restricted and bore no relationship to its heavy expenditure.[10] Financial record-keeping was abysmal and the British-appointed financial adviser to the Arab government, Sa'id Shuqair, frequently complained to his British overseers about financial irregularities and bureaucratic incompetence in the accounts department of the government.

Faisal in Damascus

Damascus was a microcosm of Syria. Its population was mainly ethnically Arab, with a large number of Arabised Kurds, Circassians and Albanians. It was overwhelmingly Arabic speaking, although there was significant minority of Armenians who had fled persecution in Anatolia. It was also mainly Sunni Muslim, while nearly a fifth of the population comprised heterodox Druze and Alawites and the various Christian denominations of the east. It probably had a Jewish population of about five thousand. But the city that Faisal had left in November was now a different place. Damascus was seething with political activity. The main political groupings – al-Fatat, al-'Ahd and the Arab Club – were all very prominent, but they were now augmented by all manner of ad hoc committees that had sprung up to reflect the prevailing moods and concerns. There were committees promoting Arab unity, pan-Syrian solidarity, and the defence of Syria's independence. A semi-official committee dealt with the stream of visitors (and adventurers) from Arab lands who gravitated towards the Syrian capital to seek jobs, vaguely participating in defending Syria's new-found freedoms or to advance their political fortunes. Most of the prominent people were lodged at the Orient Hotel, which served as the de facto headquarters and meeting place for all types: politicians, officers, government employees, spies and informers, as well as a fair sprinkling of British and French officers. Expectations had risen to a dangerously high level, and hotheads and extremists were everywhere. Faisal had now to craft his position inside this combustible brew of passions, ambitions and anxieties. He called on al-Rikabi to convene a public meeting in the hall of the government building, to which were invited the leading political, secular, religious and tribal figures of Syria, as well as representatives of the Allied powers. On the appointed day, 5 May 1919, Faisal stood up to deliver his address.

It was a long speech that began with the causes of the Arab Revolt. Deflecting the blame put on his father and himself by those who thought their actions treacherous to the Ottoman and broader Muslim communities, Faisal said, '[Hussein] felt that if the Arabs continued the war on the side of the Turks who were allied to the Germans, they would share the same fate of defeat and dismemberment . . . The Arabs had been yearning for a long time to escape from the yoke of subjection . . . and wanted to regain their historic position.'[11]

He then turned to the agreements that his father thought he had with the Allies and on the basis of which he had gone to war against the Turks. And when the war ended with the Turks defeated, Faisal 'went to claim our due at the Conference which was meeting in Paris . . . I was permitted to speak freely and explain the people's desires to the best of my ability.'

Here Faisal was confronted with the uninformed notions held of the Arabs by the West. 'I soon realised that the Westerners were profoundly ignorant about the Arabs and that their information was derived entirely from the tales of the Arabian nights. They thought the Arabs were the same as the ancient Arabs, being unaware of the existence of the modern Arab peoples, their political thinking and renaissance. They looked upon the Arabs as Bedouins living in the desert; they didn't consider the city-dweller Arabs at all.' Faisal had spent a long time at the conference simply explaining basic facts about the Arabs and the lands they inhabited. 'I told this to the Conference and revealed the goals, intentions and actions of the Arabs to relieve the oppressed. Once the Allies understood the purposes, claims and accomplishments of the Arabs on their behalf during the war, they recognised the independence of the Arabs in principle . . . and they saw fit to appoint an international committee to investigate the situation at first hand.' Clearly, the despatch of the Commission of Inquiry was Faisal's most significant claim for success for his mission in Paris. 'When the Committee returns to Paris [after its fact-finding mission], the League will consider all arguments and reveal the thoughts of the different peoples who were under the domination of the Turks. It will state the demands of the Arabs and others either for subjection or independent self-rule, according to the degree of knowledge and capacity of the nations freed from the Turks.' The latter point was an indirect allusion to the mandate.

Faisal then artfully swung around the issue of Arab unity, expressed by some as the desire for a single Arab state. This was a demand of the extremest nationalists who had taken a strong position against division of the Arab lands of the Ottoman Empire. He justified the division of the Arab lands into states on the ground that though the territories were indivisible, there were nevertheless substantial differences in terms of levels of economic, social and educational development that would make a single state impractical. He depicted the carving out of states in Iraq and Syria as a victory for the Arab cause, and as a step towards a single, unified state as the regions developed and drew close to one other. Faisal now swung to the legitimacy of his claim to public support 'The leaders of the Revolt acted without consulting the people simply because the time did not permit it. They took the entire responsibility upon themselves and functioned accordingly until today. However, this is now a matter of history. I want those present here – under the circumstances they represent the people morally not officially because of the special standing in their communities – to voice their opinions frankly and tell me whether what we have done is good or not.' It was a clear call for a renewal of his mandate by some form of public acclamation by the attending notables and leading figures of Syria. Faisal was not disappointed as the hall rang to loud applause and cries of 'Agreeable, agreeable! (*Muwaffiq, muwaffiq*)' and 'Yes, yes, complete approval.' He then asked rhetorically whether the audience wanted him to be still in command. 'Do you want us to continue our work or not? Do the people trust those in charge of their affairs or not? ... Will the people allow me after today to direct the external and internal affairs of the movement or not?' The response from the hall was effusive and loud, punctuated with cries of 'Long live Amir Faisal!'

Faisal now sought a direct affirmation of his mandate and his continuing legitimacy as the representative of the Syrian people.

This present body should ask the question: Do the people support by word and deed all my actions at home and abroad? Will they help me by granting unconditionally everything I request or not? This is what I want ... It will be the instrument of the person and persons or body who are to direct the affairs after today until the Syrian Congress [a proposed elected body] meets, which will be soon. Meanwhile, in order to work I must have authorisation and this I ask of you. Give it to me and I shall work ... I want the people to look upon me as before. I expect them not to deceive themselves and say: 'The nations gave us our independence.' Such recognition is only figurative; we get nothing except what we take with our own hands. It is up to the people and they must act ... I want them to back their words with deeds. This is all I want – it is very little. Since I do not know what else to ask, I cannot say anything more. But after I obtain your confidence and support, I shall ask for the nation's co-operation to the degree deemed necessary.

It was a brilliant passage and entirely captured the psychological moment. It captivated the audience. Pandemonium broke out as one after another of the delegates stood up and exclaimed his own, his region's or tribe's undying support and love for Faisal. Representatives from Palestine, Iraq, Hawran, Hama, Homs, Aleppo, Sidon, Beirut, Amman, Salt, Baalbek, Tripoli, South Lebanon and even Mount Lebanon vied with each other in their praise of Faisal and their willingness to sacrifice all in the cause of freedom and independence. The representatives of all the religious communities were no less enthusiastic. The Shi'as of South Lebanon were represented by Shaikh 'Abd al-Hussein Sadiq, who said, 'In the name of the people of Jabal 'Amil (South Lebanon) I pledge you our fealty to the death.' The Roman Catholic patriarch said, 'At your command Your Highness. Command what you wish!' The Orthodox patriarch said, 'Your Highness concluded an agreement with us. We shall abide by it,' a sentiment that was shared by the Syrian Catholic archbishop. The Nestorian archbishop emphatically pronounced, 'Speaking for the Nestorians of Syria, we pledge ourselves to obey your orders, take the oath of fealty, and support you.' The chief rabbi of Damascus said, 'Our wealth and our lives are in your hands.' The Armenian archbishop, speaking in Turkish, thanked the Arabs for the sympathy and humanity they had showed the Armenian people during the four years of war. 'Our history will inscribe the name of the Arabs in gold ink. I bless you and thank you.' Amir As'ad al-Ayubi, speaking on behalf of the Sunni Muslims of Lebanon, said, 'We give you blanket authorisation; whatever you deem good is good.'

As the audience quietened, Faisal, obviously satisfied, replied, 'I have obtained what I wanted. There is no doubt that with the support I have received from this body, I shall continue to labour as before until the General Congress meets and enacts laws to regulate the affairs of all Syria.' Before concluding, Faisal repeated his call for toleration and accommodation between the various sects and religions of the Near East. It was also an obvious ploy to defuse the fear of the Christians of the Levant regarding their marginalisation in a future Muslim-majority state, an issue that the French had seized upon to justify their role as 'protectors' over the Christians of the Levant. 'In my thoughts about the administration of Syria the claims of the minority groups will definitely be given preference over the views and wishes of the majority . . . I ask everyone, big and small, to rely on the Creator, glory be to Him, then on one who is from their midst, this humble individual, because I shall protect and treat them all alike regardless of religion. They are the same in my eyes but I prefer the good and the educated. I swear this by the honour of my father and forefathers . . . Let everyone know that I shall show no favouritism to a person because he comes from an important or powerful family. I shall consider ability, not social status. I shall use a man in the position for which he is most qualified because personal dignity has a purely abstract value, whereas work is of tangible benefit to the whole nation.'

Faisal may have become, for the moment, the undisputed leader of the Syrian independence movement, but this fact did not stop the feverish political activity and intrigue that had marked the country while he was in Europe. He now sought to take command of the situation by imposing his writ on the administration of the country and controlling the pace and direction of political life. Bypassing al-Rikabi, whose powers Faisal now sought to diminish, Faisal gave instructions to the heads of the main government departments to report directly to him, while giving them also considerable leeway in the management of their affairs.[12] He also began to receive official delegations from all corners of the country, and placed his own men to oversee the provinces. Sharif Nasir was already based in Aleppo and Faisal now appointed

Sharif Jamil, another of his *ashraf* relatives, to the Hawran region as its governor. A tight group of advisers now coalesced around Faisal, including his relatives – his brother Zaid and Sharifs Nasir and Jamil – and his long-standing companion, Nasib al-Bakri,[13] and the two Iraqi officers, Nuri Pasha al-Sa'id and Ja'far Pasha al-'Askari. He brought in his old Istanbul tutor Safwat al'Awa, whom he implicitly trusted, as the head of the finance department. Other confidants of his in this period were: Fouad al-Khatib, a poet and former associate of his father; Issa al-Issa, head of the cabinet office; Fakhri al-Baroodi, his personal aide; and the Qadri brothers, Ahmad and Tahsin. Both Rustum Haidar and 'Awni 'Abd al-Hadi formed part of the close group around Faisal, but they had stayed behind in Paris to oversee the work of the Hijaz delegation in the final months leading to the signing of the Treaty of Versailles.

Trying to draw all the political strands into his hands, Faisal began to pursue a dual strategy in his relations with the main political parties and groups. He sought to keep the issue of full independence firmly at the front of the agenda while avoiding openly breaking with the Allies or openly supporting the extremists. The Allies for their part were driven by other considerations: that the Arab government was not a government-in-waiting but the administrative arm of an occupation authority, OETE; that the issue of Syria and broader Arab independence was a matter for the peace conference to decide; that a mandate system was already an announced policy for the former territories of the Ottoman Empire. Faisal had to work around these obstacles of form and substance, while manoeuvring to push forward his key demands. The Nadi al-'Arabi (the Arab Club), so often the scene of passionate speeches and nation-alist ferment, was instructed to limit itself to discussing only cultural matters. A notice was pinned to its walls banning political meetings, but clearly the definition of what constituted 'cultural' issues was stretched to accommodate all manner of subjects. Political activity was formally 'banned' in OETE, while nothing was done to control the activities of political parties and groups. As General Clayton wrote to Curzon regarding these spurious banning orders, 'It would be easier to dam the Falls of Niagara than to stop the Syrians from talking politics, and he [Faisal] will, therefore, allow discussions to continue in the houses of members.'[14] Trying to reconcile the conflicting positions of those who sought independence for Syria only, and those who it for all Arab territo-ries, Faisal gave instructions to the officials of the government to spread the word that the people should ask for independence for Syria and express their hope that the same could be offered to other Arab lands. Faisal believed that it was critical that opinion in Syria be channelled in a single direction prior to the arrival of the Commission of Inquiry.

Nevertheless, Faisal was treading a very fine line. His gestures towards France could not hide his own deep ambivalence about France's intentions in the Levant,[15] nor were they a salve to the profoundly anti-French sentiments in Syria. Soon the French would demand concrete measures to bring Faisal's actions in line with his remarks, and Georges-Picot, seated in Beirut, was poised to confront Faisal on this very issue. At the same time, Faisal could not skirt around the decision by the Allied powers to adopt the mandate system. This would compromise his call for independence and put him at loggerheads with the nationalists, whose ideas of independence precluded a special position for any of the powers.[16] The matter of the future of Palestine exercised the nationalists and the Palestinians in Damascus no end, and Faisal began to distance himself clearly and publicly from the Zionist project. As Clayton wrote, 'Feisal has begun to realise the difficulties which he will have in reconciling the Palestinians and Zionists, and no longer treats the question as a minor one . . . He will also try to induce the Zionist Commission to moderate its demands, and will probably propose a conference to the Peace Commission.'[17]

Faisal, Allenby and Georges-Picot

May 1919 was a month of intense activity for Faisal. Not only was it necessary to plan for the expected arrival of the Commission of Inquiry, but he had to manage the increasingly complex relations with the British and the French in Syria. On 12 May Allenby arrived in Damascus to hold discussions with Faisal. Faisal intimated to Allenby that he intended to call for a general congress of Syrians at which complete independence would be declared. Allenby, alarmed at the implications of such a prospect, took strong exception to it, and Faisal dropped the proposal of using the congress to present the world with a fait accompli. Faisal was also hesitant to ask that Britain be the mandatory power for Syria in case the French got wind of this and thwarted it. He was also unsure whether Britain would accept such a mandate. But he told Allenby that while he would publicly call for complete independence for Syria, he recognised that the decision to impose a mandate might have been already taken. He would then inform the commission that if complete independence were not possible, he would accept that Britain be the mandatory power for Syria. Throughout his meeting with Allenby, Faisal exhibited profound concern about France's course of action. Were France to impose its control over Syria by force, he would identify himself with the active opposition.[18] Earlier Faisal had asked Allenby for armaments and equipment for the Arab army in Syria, no doubt concerned about the state of military preparedness in case a confrontation loomed with the French. He also, tellingly, asked Allenby if the Arab army could use the services of American military experts as trainers.

A few days later, on 16 and 17 May, Faisal met with Georges-Picot in Damascus. By this time the brew of contradictory impressions, perceptions,

actions and intentions that characterised Faisal's difficult relationship with
France had reached another turning point. Faisal was certainly taken aback by
the virulence of anti-French sentiment in Syria, a circumstance that made him
review the wisdom of his attempts to placate France by words if not deeds. The
principle of a mandate over Syria, which he had only just accepted as being
probably inevitable, had to be squared with the loud calls for total independence. The idea that the mandatory power might be France was simply anathema,
and many people in Syria began to feel that Faisal's conciliatory remarks about
France concealed the possibility that he had made a secret deal with the
French.[19] Faisal confided to Clayton in Damascus that his overtures towards
France during his discussions with Clemenceau and later in his public remarks
in Beirut and Damascus were only a measure to buy time until the arrival of the
Commission of Inquiry. Faisal now banked on the commission for a breakthrough that would cut through the thicket of conflicting issues and offer Syria
a path to complete independence.

The meeting with Georges-Picot settled nothing. Both parties traded accusations that each was involved in underhanded measures to discredit the other.
Georges-Picot complained of the anti-French activities of Faisal's followers in
Damascus, while Faisal confronted the French high commissioner with
evidence that some on his staff were stirring the Druze and other minority
groups against Faisal and the Arab government. Faisal reminded Georges-
Picot of the profoundly anti-French feelings in Syria, which obliged him to stop
making any statements about France's role in Syria until after the Commission
of Inquiry had made its investigations.[20] Georges-Picot attempted to placate
Faisal by stating that France had agreed to Syrian independence in principle,
but did not elicit the expected statement of thanks from Faisal. Rather, the
latter asked that France formally renounce the Sykes–Picot Agreement and
withdraw its forces from coastal Syria, after which an Arab administration
would take over all of Syria. France could then be asked to help the Arab
government in financial and technical matters, but Faisal refused to countenance any protectorate status over Syria akin to the one that France had over
Tunisia and Morocco. Faisal also asked for French support to unite Palestine,
Cilicia and the Mosul wilayat with Syria, together with a public statement from
France that it supported the Arab cause.[21] This was a tall order but Georges-
Picot did pass on the request to Paris, informing Faisal a few weeks later that
the French government was prepared to issue a general statement in support of
the Arab cause for independence. But by that time events had moved on,
rendering such a statement practically meaningless.

While Faisal was confronting all these challenges in Syria, disturbing news
had reached him about the defeat of his brother 'Abdullah's army at Turaba in
the Hijaz by the Wahhabi forces of ibn Saud. The Battle of Turaba, fought in late

May 1919, was a military disaster for 'Abdullah, who barely escaped with his life, but it was a catastrophe for the sharifians of the Hijaz. King Hussein's power and prestige were fatally compromised; the sharifians were now on the defensive in their stronghold of the Hijaz, with neither the Ottoman sultan nor the British there to help them to regain their foothold. This had a terrible effect on Faisal, for his ancestral base, no matter how enfeebled, was now being removed from under him. The tribes of Arabia, the stalwarts of his army, were now of two minds; some had gone over to ibn Saud, while others were biding their time to see which way the wind blew. It also turned his brother 'Abdullah, embittered by defeat and with no practical role left for him in the Hijaz, into a potential rival.[22] Calls for a Muslim army to be raised from Syria to support King Hussein in the Hijaz were simply pipedreams. All Faisal could do was to send a few selected officers and men, with some artillery and machine guns, to his father.

Faisal visited Aleppo in early June 1919, as part of his campaign to unite Syria's elites behind his leadership. He addressed the city's leaders and notables at the Arab Club of Aleppo, where he stressed the bonds of fraternity that joined Syria's many communities. 'We must learn that we shall not succeed unless we cling to brotherhood, sincerity, oneness of language, and prove to the world that we are people fit to enter civilised society. Each of us must come before this Commission [of Inquiry] and frankly and fearlessly tell what is in his heart if he wishes to promote the welfare of his people . . . We are a single body. The actions of the temporary government clearly show that there are no religions or sects, for we were Arabs before Moses, Jesus and Muhammad . . . The new Arab government [of an independent Syria] that will be formed with the help of those nations who supported us will do its utmost to hold up the rights of minorities through written pledges; and I am confident that the minorities themselves will tear up these pledges because they will see that the majority will abide by them, and even more so [than the minorities].'[23] At the end of his speech, Faisal made a call for a recruitment drive to staff the nascent state's security and military forces, in clear anticipation of the possible troubles that lay ahead.

The Syrian General Congress

The speech that Faisal gave on 5 May at the Municipality of Damascus referred to the need to have a properly constituted assembly that would reflect the opinions of the people of the people of Syria. An elected assembly would play a large part in convincing the Inter-Allied Commission of the breadth of support in Syria for the idea of independence. At the same time, the leaders of the national movement in Syria had felt that the presence of such a body might have helped in securing Faisal's case in Paris, and that his demands for independence were not merely based on his personal or dynastic interests. A properly elected body might have strengthened Faisal's bargaining position in Paris and helped him in overcoming the tremendous political pressures to which he had been subjected. A congress would also give the Arab government in Syria a democratic gloss, further enhancing its credibility and its law-making functions. Accordingly, Faisal gave his backing to a group from the al-Fatat-affiliated Independence (Istiqlal) Party that had approached him with a suggestion to call for elections for a national congress, with representatives drawn from the three administrative units into which Syria had been divided.[24] By aligning himself with the calls for an elected assembly, Faisal undoubtedly had also sought to strengthen his domestic position against claims that he had been too accommodating to the Allies.

However, there were formidable obstacles to the election of an assembly. Syria was effectively divided into three administrative areas, and the writ of the Arab government only carried in OETE. The French on the coast would certainly not collaborate with any plan to hold elections on their territories; the British were not prepared to entertain elections in their areas either. Allenby had earlier issued an order banning any election rallies in the southern and western areas, but did countenance the holding of elections in the eastern territories. He also sought to circumscribe the powers of any elected assembly while a formal military administration was already in place.

Nevertheless, elections were held in the eastern territories, entirely relying on the previous Ottoman electoral register and according to the old Ottoman election laws. A two-stage electoral process led to an electoral college, which in turn chose the delegates to the congress. Most of those elected to the congress had in fact previously been deputies in the Ottoman assembly. In the southern and eastern parts of occupied Syria, deputies were chosen by a process of consultation with notables and tribal shaikhs. The French did their utmost to block the departure of some of these deputies to the congress in Damascus. The composition of the Syrian Congress had its fair share of the old families of Syria, as well as a number of the rising classes. Proportionally, the Christians were over-represented compared to their percentage composition in the general population. However, they were over-whelmingly drawn from the pro-Faisal camp. There were no representatives from the communities that supported a French mandate over Syria. Sixty-nine out of a total of eighty-five deputies eventually assembled in Damascus for the opening of the Syrian Congress on 3 June at the headquarters of the Arab Club of Damascus.[25] The congress elected Hashim al-Attasi from Homs as its first chairman.

Even though the congress had been hastily assembled with an imperfect and incomplete electoral process, it was nevertheless fairly representative of the political currents in Syria, and its decisions and decrees reflected the general sentiments in the country. Two broad currents dominated. The first included supporters of the Independence (Istiqlal) Party, who demanded self-determination for all the Arab lands; the second revolved around a newly established party, the Syrian Union Party (Hizb al-Ittihad al-Suri), which was connected to the Syrian exile community in Egypt. It was headed by the formidable Dr 'Abd al-Rahman al-Shabandar. A third group, built around the old aristocracy of Syria, and concerned mainly with local issues, coalesced into what became known as the Syrian National Party (Hizb al-Watani al-Suri). Faisal's sentiments were clearly with the first group, some of whom had worked with him during the revolt, and the preponderance of al-Fatat members was evident. Its pan-Arab tendencies were also in line with Faisal's thinking at that time, but the close cooperation between Faisal and this group generated considerable resentments amongst other deputies, who felt excluded.

The establishment of the Syrian Congress was an important element in Faisal's strategy of presenting a united front to the Inter-Allied Commission of Inquiry. However, it might have had the opposite effect by highlighting the divisions within the Syrian political elite regarding the country's future, particularly as it related to the mandate system and the role that France was to have in the management of Syrian affairs. Already the traditional families, represented by 'Abd al-Rahman al-Yusuf and Muhammed Fawzi al-Azm, had distanced themselves from Faisal and his partisans, sensing their marginalisation in the evolving order in Damascus. Others, particularly France's supporters, were biding their time for a change in the political climate in their favour. The ambiguous position of the Arab government in interior Syria could not be reconciled with the realities of French power on the coast and the increasing determination of Britain to exert its authority in Palestine and Iraq. From the point of view of Faisal's adversaries, it was a matter of time before the realities of imperial power would impose themselves on the situation in Syria and the pretensions of the Arab government would then be reduced to naught. At the same time, the divisions within Faisal's camp were also becoming sharper. Incessant rumours that he had struck a secret deal with Clemenceau had followed Faisal to Damascus as he sought to explain the meagre rewards that he had obtained from the peace conference. The more volatile nationalists in his camp, confronted with the seemingly imminent imposition of colonial rule on Syria and Iraq disguised as a mandate, were incensed that Faisal appeared to acquiesce with the mandate system. In effect, Faisal was accused of deviating from the goals of full independence for Syria, a charge that was levelled against him at the frequent political meetings that were held in Damascus before the arrival of the Commission of Inquiry.

The nationalist writer As'ad Daghir was an eyewitness to one of these incidents.

This change of policy in the Palace and its entourage had generated great agitation amongst patriots, driving the political parties and others to meet to discuss these changes. Most of these meetings were presided over by Faisal himself. I recall that I attended in one night two such critical meetings at the house of the Bakris ... The first was a general meeting at which hundreds of concerned Arabs were present; and the second was a private meeting held in one of the salons of the house. This was attended by leaders of the Istiqlal Party and its advisory body. After lengthy and often acrimonious discussions, Faisal spoke and repeated the line to which I had earlier referred. He based his argument on the discussions that were held between him and British and American politicians as well as on documents that he had received from key figures. In this way, he succeeded in convincing the majority to lean towards his views, or at least to reduce their opposition by weakening the bases upon which they made their arguments ... However, Ahmad Muraywid [a nationalist leader from the Golan area] insisted that the Commission of Inquiry should hear of no case except for the demand for the total independence of Syrian lands, and I supported him in this demand. I addressed Faisal and said that what he spoke was of the utmost importance. However, politicians who habitually ignored their commitments cannot be relied upon in such a vital case. If they would renege on their commitments to Your Highness and to your father, what are we to do; and with what justficiation could we then confront France? Faisal said, 'The only recourse we would then have would be the use of force; and we have to prepare ourselves for that.' At that point, Muhammad Pasha al-Azm turned to me and whispered in my ear, 'I am afraid my son that you will reach a point where you will regret what you did to the Turks!'[26]

This comment is very telling. The traditional elite continued to harbour pro-Turkish sentiments, and these would later intensify with Mustafa Kemal's successful campaign to cement the independence of Turkey.[27] Anxiety and confusion prevailed in Syria and the sense of drift and foreboding reached even faraway Paris, where Rustum Haidar noted in his diary entry of 6 June 1919: 'News from [Syria] talk of growing political awareness but public ethical standards have deteriorated to filthy levels: frenzy for official jobs and higher salary scales; medals and decorations; corruption; envy; backbiting; Syrian versus Iraqi; Woe to this nation ... the country needs an iron hand. Where is it? Leniency is harmful and the strong hand is missing. If the Commission continues to delay its departure then the situation will deteriorate further.'[28]

The King–Crane Commission

The Commission of Inquiry was vitally important for Faisal's strategy in pressuring the Allies for an independent Syria and fending off French ambitions to dominate the country. The intermittent delays that accompanied its formation and departure greatly added to Faisal's anxieties. At one point he fired off a telegram to Rustum Haidar in Paris to be passed on to all the delegates at the peace conference. He wanted immediate confirmation of the departure date for the commission, and warned of dire consequences if its mission were postponed or aborted. Behind the scenes in Paris, the United States was the only power backing the despatch of a Commission of Inquiry. The French had already convinced themselves that the commission was a nefarious plot to deprive them of their rights under the Sykes–Picot Agreement. The British, who had initially made a number of affirmative noises regarding their intention to participate in the commission, eventually distanced themselves from it under a combination of pressures: the need to allay French suspicions; and concern about the possible findings of the commission and its effects on British policy. The Zionist lobby was dead set against the Commission of Inquiry. On 21 May 1919, President Wilson decided to act unilaterally and instructed the American members of the commission to prepare for their departure to Syria. It was now formally known as the American Section of the International Commission on Mandatory Turkey – or popularly, the King–Crane Commission, after its leaders – and it arrived at Jaffa on 10 June. It set to work immediately. For forty-two days its members worked indefatigably, gathering information, receiving petitions, interviewing key political leaders and ordinary people, meeting with religious dignitaries, civil and professional societies, syndicates and municipal leaders. The commission travelled through all of Greater Syria – from Palestine to Lebanon and Syria proper – visiting thirty-six towns and cities and receiving nearly 1,863 petitions.

Prior to the arrival of the commission in Damascus, the Syrian Congress had passed a general resolution on 2 July, which was to form the basis of its representations to the King–Crane Commission. The congress declared itself the true representative of the Syrian people and the proper interlocutor with the forthcoming commission. It also marked out its position in favour of the total independence of undivided Syria, and rejected any calls for any form of lingering occupation disguised as a mandate. There were a number of anti-French resolutions, and a complete rejection of French claims to influence and control Syrian affairs.[29] If a mandate were to be granted over Syria, it should go to the Americans, and failing that, to the British. The congress also called for a decentralised government over all of Syria that would respect local particularities and the rights of ethnic and religious minorities. Significantly, it called for a monarchical government to be headed by Faisal as king, 'as he has striven so nobly for our liberation and enjoys our full confidence and trust to be our King.'[30] The congress also rejected outright 'the claims of the Zionists for the establishment of a Jewish commonwealth in that part of southern Syria which is known as Palestine.'[31] The decisions taken by the congress constituted the single most important statement of the Syrian and Arab position that was presented to the King–Crane Commission. On 17 July Faisal addressed the congress, where he praised President Wilson and his anti-colonialist stand and urged the delegates to present their case to the commission faithfully, headed by 'his good friend, Mr Crane.'[32]

The King–Crane Commission arrived in Damascus on 2 July and, after a protocol visit to Faisal at his palace quarters, its members set themselves up at their hotel to receive the numerous delegations that descended on the capital. Sentiment in the city was mobilised in favour of nationalist demands, and thousands of leaflets were printed and distributed demanding total independence.[33] Amongst the first visitors to the commission was a twenty-man delegation from the Syrian Congress, headed by its leader Hashim al-Attasi. The delegation formally delivered the resolutions of the Syrian Congress and verbally reiterated its main demands (now known as the 'Damascus Programme'). Later Faisal spoke to the commission for over an hour-and-a-half, repeating the call for an undivided Syria, qualifying his understanding of the mandate system as a matter of providing technical and financial advice to the country, and demanding that the educational and commercial systems in Iraq and Syria be kept uniform to facilitate the future drawing together of Arab lands. He also rejected the call for an independent Lebanon, stating that it was the product of French machinations in league with reactionary religious elements. The solution for the problem of minorities was through a democratic and decentralised government and not through division of the Syrian lands. Faisal closed his presentation by dramatically declaring that if the conditions deteriorated further in Syria 'he would prefer to be imprisoned with others of his people rather than be free alone.'[34] The commissioners were greatly impressed by his presentation, which was both statesmanlike and convincing.[35]

The commission then proceeded to other parts of Syria, including Transjordan and the Beqa'a Valley, and the coastal zone. French propaganda, money and mobilisation of government employees, together with the support of the Maronite and Greek Catholic communities for a French mandate over Syria, broke the near unanimity that prevailed in Damascus and Palestine in favour of a united, independent Syria with an American or British mandate.[36]

Opinion in Aleppo and Beirut mirrored that of Damascus but with less enthusiasm, as did opinion amongst the Greek Orthodox communities of Syria. The Alawite community in the mountains behind Latakia also stood out in favour of a French mandate. All in all, though, the majority opinion, in some cases the overwhelming majority, was in favour of the programme of the Syrian Congress. Crane cabled President Wilson on 10 July affirming the commission's preliminary impressions that the vast majority of the population was in favour of the unity and independence of Syria and Palestine, and rejected the idea of a French mandate.[37] After briefly visiting Cilicia, the commissioners retired to Istanbul where they drew up their final report, which they deposited with the US delegation in Paris in late August 1919; but it was kept under wraps for over three years and not released for publication until December 1922, well after the mandate system had been established and the Near East effectively partitioned. When it finally saw the light of day, it was clear to all that the King–Crane Commission's assessments and recommendations would have proved most embarrassing to the British and French peacemakers assembled at Paris who were designing their own settlement for the Arab provinces of the former Ottoman Empire.

The King–Crane Commission report is marked by a dispassionate and clear-eyed reading of the situation in Syria at the time. Although the commissioners came out in favour of a mandate system for both Iraq and Syria, they recommended that this be of strictly limited duration. They also called for the preservation of the unity of Syria (including Palestine), with Lebanon being granted a degree of autonomy within a united Syria. They determined that the form of government in both Iraq and Syria should be a constitutional monarchy, with Faisal as king of Syria. They rejected the idea of a French mandate for any part of Syria and recommended that the US be granted a mandate over Syria and Britain over Iraq. If the US were unable to take up the mandate for Syria, then Britain should be granted it. Although the commissioners had started their mission predisposed to the Zionist plans for Palestine, they concluded by recommending that Zionist ambitions be strictly curtailed. They had reached the conclusion that the Zionist project could only be achieved at the expense of the rights of the indigenous Arab population, and then only by force of arms.

Anglo-French rivalries and the evacuation decision

The King–Crane Commission took place at a time when Anglo-French rivalries in the Middle East were reaching crisis point. Clemenceau had become increasingly suspicious of British intentions in Syria, and saw the tangled web in the country as part of a British plot to scupper French interests and to deny France the mandate over the country. Britain's actions, and their apparent concern with finding a resolution to the pledges they had made to their sharifian allies, pointed to an abandonment of the principles of the Sykes–Picot Agreement. Matters came to a head in a heated meeting of the Council of Four held in Paris on 21 and 22 May, when Clemenceau openly accused Lloyd George of breaking his promises regarding the future disposition of Syria.[38] French pressure on Britain had now become relentless. The field reports of the King–Crane Commission on the broad popular rejection of a French mandate only added to French anxieties regarding Britain's true intentions. Robert de Caix, France's policy coordinator for Syria, wrote a particularly vitriolic article in the *Bulletin de l'Asie Française*, which had wide coverage, in which he denounced Britain's supposed double-game in the Levant. De Caix openly accused the British of fanning anti-French sentiments to drive France from Syria. The British were using Faisal as their cat's paw in this game.[39] French diplomatic pressures, the clamour of the French colonial lobby, and an intense anti-British press campaign had their effect in concentrating British minds as to their priorities in Syria. By August 1919, Lloyd George had become exasperated by the intractability of the 'Syrian question' and moved to extricate Britain from its web of conflicting commitments by acceding to French demands over Syria. On 13 September, Lloyd George and Clemenceau reached an agreement whereby the British forces in Syria would be evacuated by 1 November 1919, to be replaced by French troops in Cilicia and along the Syrian coast, and by forces of the Arab government in the four cities of Damascus, Aleppo, Homs and Hama. Superficially, it appeared that one Allied force had replaced another, but it was an implicit endorsement of the Sykes–Picot Agreement as the underlying basis for the settlement of the question as to which power was to prevail in Syria.

Faisal had little inkling of Britain's decision to pull out of Syria. He was nevertheless perturbed by the confusion and uncertainties that surrounded the mandate issue and the unclear responses he was receiving from both the British and the Americans as to whether they were prepared to take up a mandate for Syria. Faisal had already been notified by Allenby's chief of staff that Britain intended to accept a mandate over Palestine, a development that set off alarm bells for Faisal. Not only would that imply the division of geographic Syria, but it also carried the risk that Syria's mandate would be divided between two or more powers. The King–Crane Commission may have reached conclusions that were favourable to Faisal's position, but it was glaringly obvious that the absence of the British and the French made the enforceability of its recommendations very doubtful. Faisal spent sleepless nights worried that the French now saw him as the villain in the piece, as the person most responsible for swaying the King–Crane Commission against a French mandate for Syria. The British themselves were none too happy about the progress of the commission's work in Syria. Several Syrian newspapers were openly hostile to the British, forcing Allenby to warn Faisal about their continued circulation.[40] Newspaper reports from Europe fed the anxieties in Damascus about an impending Anglo-French deal that would surrender Syria to France.

On 17 August Faisal fired off a letter to Allenby threatening resignation if a mandate were imposed on Syria against its people's wishes. 'If there is any possibility of the Peace Conference making a decision which is contrary to this desire [one mandatory power over all of Syria and Palestine] and which involves division of the country, Feisal cannot remain in his present position which would render him liable to the accusation that he consented to the ruin of his country', said the summary of Faisal's letter that was sent on to Curzon.[41] The note went on to say that 'Feisal believes His Majesty's Government have come to an Agreement with the French. He threatened to issue in a few days a call to his people to fight but has been persuaded to withdraw it. He insists however that he must send someone to England or go himself to present his case.'

The situation in Syria started to deteriorate as rumours multiplied about the Allies' intentions amidst the continuing uncertainties about the fate of the country. Partly to strengthen his domestic situation, Faisal approved the formation of a new six-man cabinet, which would report directly to him and in his absence to al-Rikabi as the military administrator. The Iraqi general Yasin al-Hashimi was appointed the military affairs secretary – a fateful decision as it turned out – and General Gabriel Haddad was put in charge of internal security. Hashimi began to lay plans for the enlisting of volunteers into the army of the Arab government in anticipation of trouble to come. The cabinet was empowered to issue decrees with the force of law, but these had to be ratified by Faisal. For the first time, Faisal took over responsibility for the direct administration of the country, even though he was still technically bound by the orders emanating from Allenby's headquarters. On 31 August Faisal once again met with Allenby's chief of staff, General Pawles, in the company of Colonel Richard Meinertzhagen, General Clayton's replacement as the chief political officer to Allenby. Faisal made a long statement describing the position of the Arabs ever since they raised the standard of revolt against the Turks, relying on the pledges of Britain. The entire Islamic world was now watching to see what they would gain from Britain after they had revolted against the caliphate. They had not fought to see their lands divided up between France and Britain. They would reject this humiliation and would fight to regain their dignity. He, Faisal, would fight alongside them. This was neither bluster nor a threat but simply a reminder for the British, for who would ever believe them again if Britain did not honour its promises to King Hussein?[42]

On the same day, Faisal wrote a long letter to Lloyd George, to be passed on to him by Allenby. He repeated many of the comments he had made to General Pawles, but with greater passion and urgency.[43] Allenby handed the letter over to Lloyd George on 9 September, but the British prime minister paid scant attention to Faisal's warnings and admonishments.[44] Faisal was needed in Europe to put the final touches to Britain's plans to withdraw from Syria, and in the hope that a deal could be struck between Faisal and the French for the governing of interior Syria. On 11 September Lloyd George cabled Faisal, inviting him to Paris to be present as the discussion of the Syrian question was imminent. Faisal received the cable the following day. It was simply not possible for Faisal to arrive in Paris in time to join the critical discussions between Lloyd George and Clemenceau. Nevertheless, within six hours he had completed his preparations for the departure for Europe. He took the train for Alexandria via Haifa, where he boarded a British warship, the *Speedy*, for Malta. His entourage included Dr Ahmad Qadri and his adjutant Tahsin Qadri, together with his political adviser Fouad al-Khatib,[45] and General Gabriel Haddad,[46] amongst others. Toulat was also on board. On the train in Palestine, Faisal wrote to his brother Zaid, fearful lest the British agree to the replacement of their troops by French troops in interior Syria. 'If, God forbid, this does happen, I shall return forthwith and declare my opposition. You should declare the country's independence and start military conscription in defence of the country.'[47]

The *Speedy* was indeed a fast ship. It raced through rough waters, but before reaching Malta it inexplicably slowed down, raising Faisal's suspicions that his arrival in Europe was being deliberately held up. In Malta, the ship had to refuel and undergo minor repairs. The commander suggested that Faisal await the arrival of a cruiser that would carry him to Marseilles in greater comfort, but Faisal insisted that the journey continue on board the *Speedy*. He hoped to reach Paris before the scheduled departure of Lloyd George on 16 September.[48]

Ominous talks in London

Faisal's arrival at Marseilles was hardly auspicious. He was met by a low-rank official party who bundled him and his entourage on a train headed for Boulogne for the crossing to England.[49] The deliberations in Paris between France and Britain over Syria had ended, and he was not even afforded the courtesy of being allowed a stopover in Paris, in spite of being an official delegate to the peace conference. The French government was making its intentions to him absolutely clear: he was seen as a force working against French interests and was not welcome in France. In any case, France had already agreed to Lloyd George's aide-memoire and was putting its own gloss over its more contentiously ambiguous terms. No sooner had Faisal arrived in London on 18 September, after a long and tiring trip, than he was plunged into a series of meetings with Britain's highest officials. On 19 September, Faisal met with Lloyd George at Downing Street. Present at the meeting were Acting Foreign Secretary Lord Curzon, Leader of the House of Commons Bonar Law, Field Marshal Allenby and the assistant political officer of the Egyptian Expeditionary Force Colonel Cornwallis. Faisal was accompanied by Fouad al-Khatib and

General Haddad, who also acted as interpreter. Lloyd George had invited Faisal mainly to 'induce him to accept the proposal about occupation as assented to in Paris'. The meeting went on for several hours, with Lloyd George explaining the reasons behind Britain's decision to evacuate its forces from Syria – while retaining them in Mesopotamia and Palestine – and Faisal trying to hold Britain to its promises made to his father and the various pronouncements it had made regarding its support for Arab independence. This time Faisal was provided by his father with the key correspondence between Hussein and the British. He used it to maximum effect to try to change British policies.

However, partly relying on his father and 'Abdullah's say-so, Faisal constantly referred to a 'treaty' between his father and the British as forming the backbone to the alliance between the two parties. There was, of course, no such treaty, a fact which became embarrassingly obvious when Faisal raised it with Lloyd George. The prime minister simply said that this was the first time he had heard of any definite treaty with King Hussein. Lloyd George kept reiterating that the aide-memoire was a provisional document and that the final disposition of all the Arab lands of the former Ottoman Empire could only be resolved at the peace conference.[50] Faisal was not appeased by Lloyd George's comments about the provisional nature of the agreement, or by his remarks that Britain intended to meet all its obligations to the Arabs. He vehemently resisted the Anglo-French deal on Syria if it prejudiced the final outcome, which he saw only in terms of the unity of the Syrian lands, with a single mandatory power if necessary. Repeating his oft-made comments, Faisal said that 'he could not stand before the Moslem world and say that he had been asked to wage a war against the Caliph of the Moslems and now see the European powers divide the Arab country.'[51] That evening, no doubt as relief from the wearying meetings, Faisal went to the theatre.

Two days later, Faisal sent Lloyd George a formal response to the aide-memoire. He rejected the entire basis of the agreement, namely the Sykes–Picot Agreement, saying that the Arabs would never consent to the division of their lands. He vigorously objected to the division of the Syrian territories before the peace conference had concluded its work. Even though the Anglo-French deal had been presented as provisional, there would nevertheless be firm boundaries between the various zones, which might form the basis for the final disposition of frontiers. 'In conclusion,' Faisal wrote, 'I ask that this proposed engagement between the French and British governments shall be entirely cancelled as it is contrary to the ideals of the League of Nations and is also contrary to our other engagements which were based on national honour. It is, moreover, an unjust return to the policy of ambitious imperialism which after this war should be swept forever.' And in an aside addressed to Allenby, hoping to gain his influential voice, Faisal wrote, 'I cannot understand how the Commander-in-Chief, who is aware of all these facts [of popular resistance to the division of Syria], could consent to expose the country he liberated to internal disorder. It would surely be much more advisable to leave the status quo as it is or withdraw all European troops until the final decision [of the peace conference].'[52]

Faisal had another meeting with Lloyd George on 23 September in Downing Street, with the same participants as at the earlier meeting on 19 September. The issue of the 'treaty' that Hussein and Faisal had alluded to was discussed at length. It transpired that what was referred to was almost certainly an addendum that Hussein had attached to a letter he had sent to McMahon in August 1918, which gave Hussein's understanding of the various commitments that Britain had made. The enclosure was sent to London and no further action had been taken on it. It hardly qualified as a treaty in the conventional sense, as the British did not in any way sign or even acknowledge it. What Curzon emphasised during the meeting was there was no signed treaty between the British and Hussein, only a set of correspondences. In any case, the British had taken issue with Hussein's summary and had refused to accept that it accurately reflected the pledges that were made to the Arabs. An important prop of Faisal's negotiating strategy was thus undermined, leaving him perplexed as to why he had been misled to believe that such a powerful tool had actually existed. 'What was I to do? My hopes were dashed with the loss of my most powerful tool . . .'[53] It also marked an important change in Faisal's own position. Previously acting as his father's representative and spokesman for a broad Arab cause, he was now increasingly his own man, speaking on behalf of his own legitimacy and status as the representative of the aspirations of the population of Greater Syria. He now signed documents in his own capacity, with only formal reference to his father as the nominal head of the Arab cause. He did not abandon the old Hashemite cause of a confederation of Arab states, but his diplomacy now focused on Syria.

For the next few weeks, Faisal awaited the formal response of the British government to his note of 21 September. Meanwhile he continued to receive a stream of visitors at his quarters at the Carlton Hotel. The Zionist leader Weizmann visited him twice, on 24 and 26 September, as did Herbert Samuel, the former minister in Asquith's War Cabinet and the future high commissioner in Palestine. On his first visit Weizmann offered Faisal's government a five-year loan of £30 million in exchange for his support for the Zionist programme. Faisal would also receive Zionist support in the media for his stance against the French.[54] During his second visit, however, Weizmann was more explicit about what he meant. Rustum Haidar wrote in his diary, 'Weizmann said there are 14 million Jews in the world, and all of them wish to see Palestine Jewish, but only 6 million want to actually go there. He [Weizmann] was a moderate man and his moderation has raised others' ire against him. He does not think it right or reasonable that Palestine should be now under a Jewish government, for there are only 60 to 70 thousand Jews there at present [while Arab] Muslims and Christians are 600,000. He wants to see [Jewish] immigration and with time if Jews become a majority then they can establish a democratic government on the basis of equality [with the Muslims and Christians]. They [the Jews] desire to be brothers to the Arabs. The Arab lands have now a population of 13 million, but they can support 50–60 million. There is therefore no danger on the Arab lands, which are very wide, in the arrival of 6 million Jews.'[55]

But Faisal had grown increasingly apprehensive about the implications of the Zionist project on the prospects for Arab independence, a change of heart noted by British despatches from the Near East. It was a fine balancing act to acknowledge and even welcome Jewish immigration into Palestine – on economic, religious and humanitarian grounds – while rejecting outright the political implications that might arise from an increasing Jewish population in the country and the attendant demands for a separate political status or even state. On 3 October 1919 the London *Jewish Chronicle*, the semi-official organ of British Jewry, published an extensive interview with Faisal on the Zionist question. In the interview, Faisal made cordial remarks regarding Dr Weizmann. 'I found Dr. Weizmann's proposals quite moderate and practical. As I understand it, he is working towards a regulated immigration into the country, for conditions in which the Jew will have equal rights with the Arab, shall take part in the government of Palestine ... There is nothing to object to that.' But he refused the idea of unrestricted Jewish immigration into Palestine, stating that the country could not absorb more than 1,000 to 1,500 migrants annually. Faisal also warned against the possibility of Arab–Jewish clashes if Zionist extremists planned to seize the country and set up a Jewish state. Faisal's remarks to the *Jewish Chronicle* alarmed a number of leading Zionist figures in London, who met with Faisal on 15 October to establish whether his reported comments had accurately reflected his views. The meeting was attended by Herbert Samuel, Harry Sacher, the lawyer and Weizmann collaborator, and Nuri Pasha al-Sa'id. Faisal stated that his remarks were prompted by the correspondent's assertion that the Jews intended to establish a state in Palestine.[56] The Zionist delegation was prepared to take Faisal's explanation at face value. However, Faisal's position on Zionism was actually moving ever closer to the nationalist line of complete rejection of any Zionist claims on Palestine, even as he tailored his remarks to conform to the expectations of different audiences.

Faisal began to feel the ground giving way beneath him. On 26 September he wrote a letter to his father summarising his view of events to date and the position of the British. Although the latter tried to empathise with his perspective, they were nevertheless driven 'by material gains and interests which to them are the bases of all actions.' Anticipating trouble ahead, Faisal urged his father to narrow his differences with tribal shaikhs and leaders and make new alliances with them. Faisal was most apprehensive that events would now be determined by 'fait accompli, and policies based on imposition, the sword and force.'[57] To Zaid, he wrote the next day, 'By God! By God! Force! And Force! The stronger we are and the more we are able to show a military vitality the more they [the Allies] would respect us and agree to our demands.'[58] He also asked 'Awni 'Abd al-Hadi to contact officials in Damascus to prepare to take over positions evacuated by the British and to strengthen the Arab government's military capabilities in the Beqa'a Valley.[59] Faisal continued to base his strategy on the rightness of the Arab cause and in this he pinned his hopes on a special gathering of the Big Three. If need be, he would travel to America. He wrote to Lloyd George on 9 October, saying that 'The withdrawal of the British would be a great catastrophe for the whole Arab world . . .' and calling for the Anglo-French evacuation agreement to be postponed. The whole issue should be presented to the peace conference or to a special Anglo-Arab-French commission, chaired by an American, to present its findings and recommendations to the peace conference.[60]

On the same day, Faisal received a letter from Lord Curzon in reply to his note of 21 September. Curzon recapitulated the pledges and commitments that Britain had made to Hussein, and set out the reasons behind Britain's decision to withdraw from Syria. The eastern front had cost the British Treasury £750 million and the deployment of 1,400,000 troops. The British taxpayer could not be expected to continue to sustain this burden. Curzon also reminded Faisal of the sacrifices of France on the western front, which, by destroying German power, removed the Turks' ability to sustain the war and made Arab freedom possible. He therefore urged Faisal to accept that 'the best course for the Arab peoples is to accept the temporary arrangement proposed and to enter into friendly working arrangements for its execution with their Allies, Great Britain and France.'[61]

Whatever hopes that Faisal might have had for changing the British decision to evacuate Syria were dashed when, on 10 October, he finally received Lloyd George's response to his various letters. Lloyd George rejected Faisal's requests that the issue be put to the peace conference or to a special commission. Britain was not prepared to undertake any mandate for Syria and the prime minister reiterated that Britain's decision to evacuate Syria was final. Lloyd George did 'concede' that representatives of the concerned parties would meet to facilitate the process of withdrawal by 1 November.[62] The pressure thus piled up on Faisal to meet with the French and to put the best light on the Anglo-French evacuation agreement. Lawrence, who might have somewhat ameliorated these pressures and given Faisal moral support and political advice, was absent from the scene. Prompted by the Foreign Office, he had written a number of articles in the newspapers expressing lukewarm support for the Sykes–Picot Agreement: 'a covenant for the Arabs,' he had called it.[63] But he had also written to Curzon suggesting that the Allies formally recognise the Arab government in Syria. 'My own ambition is that the Arabs should be our first brown dominion and not our last brown colony,' he wrote.[64] Lawrence's recommendations to Curzon, however, were not acceptable and he was asked not to meet Faisal.

There followed a series of exchanges between Lloyd George and Clemenceau, some of them quite heated. Clemenceau accused the British of trying to solve their tangled problems with the Arabs by sacrificing French interests. Clemenceau also charged the British with arming the Arabs, arms which could then be used to fight the French. The only solution as far as Clemenceau was concerned was for the British to impress upon Faisal that he must enter upon serious talks with the French regarding the situation after the British evacuation. Lloyd George was deeply upset by the tone of Clemenceau's cables – 'monstrous calumnies' is what Curzon called them – and composed a long note justifying British actions throughout the period. Nevertheless Lloyd George found Clemenceau's opening to Faisal a means to overcome the latter's objections to dealing with the French. On 16 October Curzon and Allenby met Faisal and convinced him to accept Clemenceau's invitation to open discussions. Faisal had little choice but to go to Paris. The British were about to wash their hands of the entire Syrian affair and the Americans were in no mood or state to play the white knight. On 20 October Faisal arrived in Paris in circumstances that bore little relationship to his earlier visit.

Faisal in Paris

Public opinion in France had shifted noticeably against the Arabs and Faisal. On the day of Faisal's arrival in Paris, a well-known author and deputy in the National Assembly, Maurice Barres, wrote a vitriolic article in the Echo de Paris strongly critical of both Britain and Faisal. He stressed that France had a right to receive a mandate for the four cities of interior Syria. 'The Feisal comedy has gone far enough,' he pronounced. Continuing, Barres wrote, 'No nation other than France possesses in so high a degree the particular kind of friendship and genius which is required to deal with the Arabs. The British theory of installing in Syria an Arab Government of the Hedjaz is untenable. The Amir Feisal has no right to be in Damascus, Homs, Hama or Aleppo . . . What is Feisal to us or to the Syrians? A man of straw set up by England without a title, without influence . . . If England wishes to give a kingdom to this Amir, let her set him up in Baghdad.'[65]

Faisal stayed in Paris for the next two-and-a-half months, meeting a host of French officials including Clemenceau, Philippe Berthelot, who was the secretary general at the Quai d'Orsay, Gout and General Gouraud. The meetings were held in either the Quai d'Orsay or at Faisal's quarters, and were mostly led by Faisal himself. He delegated some of the negotiations to Rustum Haidar and 'Awni 'Abd al-Hadi, but kept close watch and control over their activities. The meetings with the French were difficult as the French were in no way minded to listen to Faisal's arguments. He tried to enlist the British and American governments' support for his position, but to little avail. To Lloyd George, Faisal wrote, 'I came to Paris as you advised, and have been here for about fifteen days. I have done my best to keep on good terms with the French government, endeavouring to eliminate misunderstandings and to meet our mutual interests.'[66] But Faisal saw no equivalent response from the officials he met and he informed Lloyd George that he intended to bring the matter of the British evacuation from Syria to the Supreme Council of the peace conference. Faisal also met with Frank Lyon Polk, the head of the US delegation to the peace conference, but the discussions with him led nowhere. The US was simply not prepared to adopt a position on the Syrian issue.[67]

Faisal also had exchanges of correspondence with Clemenceau. 'Awni 'Abd al-Hadi took charge of drafting the French translation of Faisal's letters to Clemenceau. The former's main intent at this stage was to convince Clemenceau to delay or cancel the planned evacuation of British troops and to accept modifications to the Anglo-French agreements of September. He presented the familiar arguments about the division of historic Syria into separate states and zones of influence, the uncertainties that this would entail, and the resistance that was to be expected if it came about.[68] Clemenceau's reply aimed to calm Faisal's anxieties by stressing that neither Syria's political future nor its final boundaries were at issue at the present time. Faisal now turned to the Supreme Council. On 6 November he addressed a detailed note to the council where he enumerated the risks and problems that would arise if the Anglo-French agreement were to be put into effect. He denounced the division of the country into three separate zones in the name of military expediency, when in reality it was a politically motivated decision. 'Has any country in the world been able to make any progress under such obstructive circumstances?' he asked rhetorically. The basis of the aide-memoire, he reminded the council, was the hated Sykes–Picot Agreement, 'which dealt with the country as if it were a private estate or a mere parcel of goods.' Faisal also brought out the spectre of rising religious antagonism as 'the people will think that there is a definite intention to persecute Islam.'[69] But his appeal to the Supreme Council led nowhere. Clemenceau, writing to Lloyd George on 9 November, said, 'The Peace Conference will have nothing to do but to sanction our agreement for the French mandate in Syria and the British mandate in Mesopotamia.'[70]

Faisal was also deeply concerned about the true allegiances of the people of Syria, and whether they would fight against occupation if it came to it. He was aware that the Arab government was not universally popular, especially amongst a large segment of the traditional elites, whose power and influence had been greatly undermined since the demise of the Ottoman Empire. The loyalties of the Christian minorities were still in doubt. The Maronites of Lebanon were squarely ranged against the possibility of being ruled by a Muslim government, even one whose religious credentials had been supplanted by nationalist ones. France had stirred up trouble with the Druze and Alawites, who were apprehensive enough already, so that their loyalties to the shaky Damascus government were also in question. Toulat had warned Faisal that the reports that were reaching the Quai d'Orsay about the situation in Syria and Lebanon all spoke of the shallowness of Faisal's support and the increasing turmoil, lawlessness and confusion in the territories under the control of the Arab government. Zaid, who had been left behind to oversee the government, did not endear himself either by his alarmist reports about the deteriorating conditions inside the country or by insinuating that the population was about to explode in anger.[71]

Another crisis was about to break out while Faisal was still in Paris, as the date of the withdrawal of British troops from Syria by 30 November was fast approaching. The French were determined to deploy their troops to take over the Beqa'a Valley, whose status as part of the territories under the Arab government's control was disputed by the French. General Gouraud had issued orders for the occupation of these areas by French troops, but Faisal was determined to keep them under the control of the Arab government. He wrote to Lloyd George warning him that the Arab troops stationed there would resist any French encroachments by force. The British prevailed on Clemenceau to delay the deployment of their troops in the Beqa'a Valley. In any case, Clemenceau had already began to see the virtues of striking a deal with Faisal as the best course open to France to achieve its objectives while avoiding the use of force and intimidation. An agreement was reached with Faisal that the Arab troops would be withdrawn from the Beqa'a Valley while the French troops would not enter these territories. France would also withdraw its token artillery detachment in Damascus in deference to Faisal's request that it should respect the authority of the Arab government in those territories under its control.

Faisal was now desperate to return to Syria as the political and military situation was in a state of complete flux. A major crisis had broken out in late November when the British had arrested the Arab government's military head, General Yasin al-Hashimi, on the grounds that he was recruiting troops to resist the French in the Beqa'a Valley. He was also suspected of being in touch with the Turkish nationalists under Mustafa Kemal, who were gaining greater ground and support in their struggle against the Allies. Riots and demonstrations had broken out in Damascus in protest at Yasin's arrest. The British had completed their final withdrawal from Syria by the first week of December. Their comforting presence would no longer be there to provide a theoretical counterweight to French power, and the options available to Faisal had dwindled to almost nothing. Faisal had little choice but to agree to postpone his return until some form of agreement had been hammered out between himself and the French. The British and French were already locked in meetings to try to arrive at the final status of Syria, and their final agreement would be the basis for the deal that would be offered Faisal.

The agreement that was known later as the Faisal–Clemenceau Agreement, called in essence for the creation of an independent Syrian state within borders to be finally determined by the peace conference. This state would agree to rely on France for technical, military and administrative support, and would delegate its foreign diplomatic representation to France. A separate and independent Lebanese state, under a French mandate, would be carved out of historic Syria. Even though Faisal had been exhausted by weeks of incessant meetings and negotiations, abandoned by the British, wary of the value of armed resistance and with a crumbling domestic front, the agreement was by no means a capitulation to French demands. Most of his advisers, Dr Ahmad Qadri being a notable exception, also agreed to its stipulations. Faisal had been preparing to initial it, but in the end decided not to do so without consultation with his government and before gauging the public's acceptance of the agreement. His father had also sent an emissary to warn Faisal that he should not sign any agreement that contradicted British promises to the Arabs. Faisal was content to let the French know that he would push for having the agreement accepted in Syria and would then return to France to sign the final agreement, which would be presented to the peace conference.

The agreement was not simply one imposed on Faisal by force of circumstance. Both sides received and made important concessions, as the progress of the negotiations clearly indicated. France had agreed not to fly its flag over Damascus, and had even conceded parts of the Sykes–Picot 'Blue Zone' to the Syrian government. French advisers were to be employed by contracts that could be terminated at will by the Syrian government, but with an indemnity. Instead, their previously envisioned powers would be held by the Syrian government ministers. The French also agreed to a Syrian parliament, but without explicitly accepting Arab demands that it should have wide legislative powers. Not all French officials accepted this agreement, seeing it as a dangerous concession to Arab demands. These included, notably, Gouraud himself, who rejected the idea that French troops could only be deployed in Cilicia rather than in Syria proper, as well as his new political adviser, Robert de Caix. But the French had a change of heart regarding the terms of the agreement after the elections of 20 January 1920, in which Clemenceau was defeated for the post of France's president, and a new cabinet, under Alexandre Millerand, came into power. It was far less accommodating to Faisal than Clemenceau would ever have been. But what mattered to Faisal now was the attitude of his compatriots in Syria, especially the nationalists. The agreement fell far short of the idea of a united Syria in confederation with other independent Arab states. It ran counter to nearly all the nationalist manifestos, notably the one that formed the political basis for the Arab Revolt: the Damascus Protocol of 1915.

It was to this much-changed world that Faisal now returned. On 7 January 1920 Faisal left Paris for Syria.

CHAPTER 14

THE COLLAPSE OF THE KINGDOM OF SYRIA

THE SITUATION in Syria during Faisal's nearly four-month absence in Europe had become ever more confused and turbulent. Zaid, who had deputised for Faisal in the interim, was inexperienced and often overwhelmed by the enormity of developments cascading on the country and its people. His letters to his father and Faisal are ample testimony to that. They carry the hallmark of one who can barely manage to stay afloat in these churning waters. French cynics went so far as to say that Clemenceau had deliberately kept Faisal back so that the Syrians would have their fill of the meandering administration of the Arab government under the leadership of an earnest but hapless Zaid, who yearned to leave for Cambridge to pick up his interrupted education, or failing that to go back to the Hijaz.[1] Neither was the mild-mannered military administrator Ali Ridha al-Rikabi able to imprint his authority on the myriad factions vying to channel, or benefit from, the increasing public frustration and bitterness at the unfolding events. He preferred compromise to confrontation, and was not prepared for meeting the rising tide of extreme, and often irresponsible, nationalists.

Faisal was aware that sentiment in Syria had shifted against him while he sojourned in Paris. Haidar relates in his diary that on 17 December 1919 Faisal met with Amin al-Tamimi, who had recently arrived from Damascus. Al-Tamimi told Faisal that the nationalists in Syria had began to question Faisal's motives and that a number of the extremists were opposing and undermining the Arab government. Visibly angry, Faisal responded, 'They can think what they want but they have no right to attribute ill intentions to me or question my sincerity. Are they to lecture me about patriotism? Oh these extremists! What sons of bitches are they who think they can trade their nationalism with me? I will show them what patriotism means!' Haidar then quietened Faisal down by reminding him that even if the extremists wished to pursue the wrong policies, they would nevertheless be in the front ranks of those who would support him if he chose war.[2]

The agitation and uncertainty that affected all groups in Syria spilled over into a rise in anti-sharifian sentiment. As Meinertzhagen wrote to Curzon on 2 December 1919, 'The feeling against the Sharifian family has undoubtedly been growing in strength for some time. They have failed to appeal to the classes, who merely desire security owing to the miserable ineptitude of the Administration, and the encouragement, or at least tolerance extended to the Bedouin . . . On the other hand, they are not sufficiently extreme for the more ardent Nationalists and the irreconcilable anti-French party.'[3] The growing hostility to the sharifian cause had not quite extended as yet to the person of Faisal, but it was to this much more fraught environment that Faisal returned in January 1920.

Syria in the autumn of 1919

Yasin al-Hashimi, whom Faisal had appointed the de facto defence minister of the Arab government, became the focal point for organising the opposition to the 15 September evacuation decision. Yasin himself, though a late adherent to the cause of Arab independence, saw the evolving crisis as an opportunity to bolster his power and his nationalist credentials. He had also assumed the leadership of the Iraqi wing of al-'Ahd Party, thus bringing under his direct influence a large number of former Arab officers of the Ottoman army.[4] An intense propaganda campaign against the presence of the British, and particularly the French, was launched by al-'Ahd. Yasin also joined with other officers in sending a cable to the Foreign Office in June demanding the immediate application of the Anglo-French declaration of November 1918. Immediately after Faisal's departure to Europe, Yasin, on his own initiative, had started a 'Committee for National Defence' and had begun a major conscription campaign aimed at raising an additional twelve thousand troops for the Arab government's army. Allenby soon put a stop to this, however, and warned Yasin to cease unauthorised activities, but balked at arresting him as the French had wanted.[5] The Arab government disavowed Yasin's committee and denied that there was any military conscription. However, secret recruitment continued for informal militias and armed political groups. On 28 October 1919 a major demonstration organised by the nationalists took place in Damascus, ending with the handing over of a petition addressed to the government and foreign delegations 'against any settlement that aims to divide our country and deny it independence and turns its southern reaches into a homeland for Jews.'[6] In Paris Faisal responded to the demonstrators by asking them to be patient and await the results of his deliberations.[7]

In this hothouse environment, where numerous armed groups and radical political parties were vying for leadership of the nationalist cause, a new figure arose to consolidate the popular committees under his leadership. Shaikh Kamil al-Qassab was a cleric from a modest background, a fiery speaker and skilled agitator.[8] He helped to organise the 'Higher National Committee' (al-Lajna al-Wataniya al-'Ulya – the Lajna), an organisation that arose at the end of a series of meetings held in Damascus by nationalist figures.[9] Each of Damascus's forty-eight districts chose four representatives, who met in early November 1919 at the house of the president of the Damascus Municipality Council.[10] Al-Qassab addressed the gathering and presented the assemblage with the manifesto of the Higher National Committee. He then prevailed on all those at the gathering to sign a covenant binding them to a nationalist course that rejected all compromise and half-solutions to the demands for independence. It is possible that Faisal himself had encouraged al-Qassab to this action. According to the writer and journalist Muhib al-Din al-Khatib, who was then the editor of the Arab government's newspaper *al-'Asima*, Faisal had given instructions to various figures prior to his departure for Europe to build the capabilities of the army. Faisal had also told al-Qassab that he 'expected from him [Qassab] and from his nationalist comrades to start a popular movement to transform the people into an armed people . . . and to change the nation into a military barracks.'[11] The organisation started to accept volunteers and train them in various camps, financed by wealthy supporters. The training was haphazard as some of the volunteers would soon lose their enthusiasm and desert, while others resisted military discipline and often mutinied against their officers' orders. Nevertheless, the Lajna was broadly acceptable to public opinion. The leading religious lights of Damascus, both Muslim and Christian, gave it their blessing and even attended some of its meetings. It played an important part in raising public consciousness regarding the need to prepare for the defences of the country if required.[12]

While in Paris, Faisal had been kept abreast of developments in Syria, mainly through the regular cables from Zaid but also from travellers, emissaries and newspaper reports. In early November he despatched Nuri al-Sa'id to Syria to brief its leaders about developments in Europe, and especially the implications of the Anglo-French accord. Nuri was also charged with ascertaining the state of opinion in Syria and the degree to which the country would be prepared to rise in opposition to French control. Nuri met with most of the leading figures in the country and opinion divided. A majority led by younger officers such as Yusuf al-'Azma stood firm in their opposition to a French mandate, promising to resist it by force if necessary. A minority, built around Ali Ridha al-Rikabi, sought some form of compromise and based their argument on the imbalance between the Arab forces and the French, especially now that the British had withdrawn their support from the Syrians. Zaid, who had attended these meetings, then offered that the entire issue should be referred to the Syrian Congress.

By November 1919, Yasin had become the undisputed leader of the ultras. 'Yasin Pasha, the leading spirit in Syria, is now known to be in correspondence with Mustafa Kemal,' wrote Meinertzhagen. 'Yasin is aiming at reinstating Turkish rule in Syria, not so much on national or pan-Arab grounds, as on those of personal power . . . There is little doubt that at the present moment Yasin's influence has replaced for the bad the more moderate and reasonable influence of Feisal. He now carries with him the army and the majority of the people. It is even doubtful now whether Feisal can assume control over an administration which must move with public opinion or disappear.'[13] The British became greatly concerned by Yasin's power games, especially when he failed to heed their warnings not to reinforce the Arab government's troops in the Beqa'a Valley. Not only did he now threaten the British and French positions and policies in the Near East but he also threatened their putative ally, Faisal, and his claim to primacy in Syria. Furthermore, Yasin's growing contacts with the Turkish nationalists and Mustafa Kemal added another dangerous dimension to his rise. Neither did Yasin's involvement in Iraqi affairs, by organising Iraqi officers and helping to foment resistance to Britain's rule, endear him to the British. All these factors were more than enough to clinch his fate. On 22 November 1919, Yasin was invited to tea at the headquarters of the British commanding officer in Damascus. There he was kidnapped, put into an armoured car, and spirited off to Palestine, being moved from location to location, not quite imprisoned but certainly not free, until he was finally allowed to return to Syria via Egypt in early May 1920.[14]

Yasin's arrest prompted large demonstrations in Damascus and the closure of all the shops for a day in protest. On the day of his arrest the Syrian Congress had met to hear al-Rikabi give a mild speech regarding the main duties of the Arab government, couching it in conciliatory terms to the French. The speech made a poor impression on the delegates who were far more interested in making or hearing ringing statements about independence and their duty to struggle for it. On 24 November the Syrian Congress met again and reaffirmed the commitments that it had made to the King–Crane Commission regarding Syrian independence and the establishment of a constitutional monarchy. It was not a declaration of independence but a preparation for such an eventuality. By the end of November 1919, as the British were putting their final touches to their withdrawal from Syria, war fever had taken hold in Damascus, even affecting Zaid. The French in Beirut had deliberately blocked a crucial cable from Faisal to Zaid informing him of the details of Faisal's agreement with Clemenceau on the Beqa'a Valley. Zaid was left in the dark as to the true state of affairs. He vacillated between preparing for war and counselling moderation on the more militant nationalists. Eventually he bit the bullet and directly confronted the extremists. He ordered the Syrian Congress adjourned, to be reconvened when the government so wished, presumably after the return of Faisal.[15]

Meanwhile, Gouraud had arrived in Beirut on 18 November. The new high commissioner and commander of all French forces in the Levant was determined to extend French influence and control to the entirety of Syria. Gouraud, who had little faith in Faisal as a potential ally of France, chose to ignore the agreement reached between Faisal and Clemenceau. He began to pressure the Arab government in Damascus to accept the deployment of French troops in the four districts that made up the Beqa'a Valley.[16] The Arab government hurriedly despatched Nuri al-Sa'id to meet Gouraud and try to strike a deal with him that would not result in a violent clash between French troops advancing to replace the withdrawing British and the Arab government's troops already in the Beqa'a Valley. Gouraud, however, got the better of Nuri, who agreed to a deal that was at odds with the Faisal–Clemenceau compromise on the Beqa'a and gave Gouraud nearly all that he wanted. Faisal, on hearing the news, was incensed with what Nuri had done. He even accused him of treasonous dealings with the French.[17] In essence, France was given a military presence in the Beqa'a Valley, whereas the Faisal–Clemenceau compromise had called for a standstill until the peace conference ruled on the matter. But Gouraud pushed his advantage beyond the concessions that Nuri had agreed. At Mu'allaqa, withdrawing Arab troops were quickly replaced by a large French force, contrary to the stipulations of the agreement between Gouraud and Nuri. A mob from the mainly Christian town of Zahle, at the edge of the Beqa'a Valley, then descended on Mu'allaqa, rioting and pillaging and desecrating a mosque.[18] A counter-reaction set in, forcing Christian families to flee to the coast. The important regional centre of Marja'youn in the south of Lebanon came under siege, and everywhere armed bands sprung to life, some focusing their ire on the French, while others were simply bandits. In Baalbek, the Beqa'a Valley's largest town, a group of Shi'a Muslims attacked a French officer who was forced to flee to Zahle. Gouraud demanded a formal apology from the Arab government, suspecting that it was behind this incident, and, failing to receive it, ordered three thousand French troops to occupy the town, in clear violation of his own agreement with Nuri. Chaotic conditions prevailed in many regions and a climate of fear and lawlessness began to grip the country.[19]

The unity of the political class of Syria, superficially evident in the early days of the Arab government, began to fray, and divisions sharpened between those who sought accommodation with France and those who demanded outright independence. It was the radicals who were gaining the upper hand, especially after news of the Faisal–Clemenceau agreement began to filter into Syria. The better terms that Faisal had received from Clemenceau meant very little to the radicals, who saw in the agreement a capitulation to French demands and a drastic retreat from the aims of the nationalist movement. 'Revolution is at the gates . . . Deep resentment [at the Agreement]', Zaid cabled Faisal on 16 November.[20] A chasm arose between the extreme nationalists and Faisal, some going as far as to accuse him of treason. They now focused their outrage on the pacific and cautious al-Rikabi.[21] Pressures grew on him to resign, but he put up resistance. He wrote to Zaid that 'he could not follow the divisive policies of irresponsible individuals' who would lead the country to ruin. On 10 December, following an acrimonious meeting with Zaid and his advisers, al-Rikabi was pushed to resign.[22] Significantly, al-Rikabi handed his resignation to Zaid and not to his titular boss, Allenby, an indication that al-Rikabi at least acknowledged the independent status of Syria.

Zaid now appointed Colonel Mustafa Ni'ma as the chief military administrator, with Yusuf al-'Azma as head of the Military Council. Ni'ma's nationalist bluster quickly gave way to the harsh realities of power as he was faced with the acute imbalances between the resources at the disposal of the French and those of the Arab government. Nevertheless, a few days later, the Council of Ministers issued their order for general conscription because 'volunteer forces were insufficient to establish order after the pullback of the British . . . and . . . funds were not available to pay in full the wages of the volunteer soldiers.'[23] The order appealed to the demands of the nationalists that preparations be made to confront the French. But the general call for conscription badly failed to raise the military preparedness of the Arab government. Wealthy individuals could buy their exemption from military service and the effective blockade of Syria would mean that arms, ammunition and supplies would be extremely scarce for the army. The Arab government was in dire need of funds. The British stipend had been held back, and the French, of course, resisted making any significant transfers to its coffers.[24]

The Arab army was rife with desertions and poor discipline and morale, and wise counsel knew that it was no match for the French. It numbered about seven thousand, out of a permitted total of eight thousand, and was over-officered, primarily with Iraqis. Recruits were paid a miserable £E3 a month, which often went unpaid for weeks on end.[25] The crucial Beqa'a Valley was commanded by a veteran of the Arab Revolt, Ali Jawdat, who was preparing his forces to confront the French. However, Ni'ma would not send him any reinforcements. The officers in the Arab army had another purpose: to train, arm and provide logistical support to the guerrilla bands that were being raised to harass and confront the French. In this they were supported by the Lajna, which also aided the guerrilla forces independently, as well as by the political parties, principally al-Fatat.[26] By December 1919, guerrillas were active along the entire frontier zone between the Arab government's OETE and the French-controlled OETW. They also spread into Lebanon proper and as far afield as

Latakia, on the Syrian coast, and Antioch. Some of these bands were also motivated by brigandage. All in all, the French provided themselves with ample
justifications both to denounce the Arab government for surreptitiously
backing the armed groups and to promote their own French-allied armed
bands in opposition to the Arab government.

Elsewhere in Syria it was the British who were the target of nationalist
bands and armed tribal groups. At Deir el-Zour in mid-December 1919, on
the as yet non-demarcated frontier between Syria and Mesopotamia, a tribal
band led by a minor shaikh, Ramadhan Shalash, occupied the town and
took its small British garrison hostage. Shalash was acting under the previously
issued instructions of Yasin, as well as secret orders from Zaid to mobilise
the tribes.[27] The plan was concocted by the Iraqi al-Ahd society as a precursor
to a broader rebellion in Syria and Iraq. Faisal, who was still in Paris, distanced
himself from the attack and issued a statement denouncing it as a violation of
the spirit of the alliance between the Arab movement and Britain.[28] The
crisis was defused when the British agreed with Ja'far Pasha al-'Askari, then
governor of Aleppo, formally to withdraw from the town, but the echo of
Shalash's 'victory' reverberated around the country. Although officially
London had accepted Faisal's entreaties that he was not involved in the attack,
the feeling persisted amongst the British officials in Mesopotamia that Faisal
was behind it.

Another unexpected element was added to the dangerous polarisation that
was taking place in Syria by the end of 1919. The Turkish resistance to Allied
demands and the collaboration of the remnants of the Ottoman government
had fed the growth of a powerful national resistance movement led by Mustafa
Kemal. The struggle of the Turkish nationalists against the French in Cilicia
had drained most of Gouraud's fighting strength. At the same time channels of
communication were opening up between the Turkish nationalists, the Arab
government and various radical Arab groups. Public opinion had also veered
sharply in favour of the Turks, and the resurgence of pro-Turkish sentiments
was evident everywhere in Syria. This was skilfully exploited by Mustafa Kemal
with his propaganda aimed at undermining the French in Syria by playing on
its pan-Islamic sentiments and portraying the war against the French as a
joint Arab-Turkish struggle against European hegemony. Faisal himself was
ambivalent about these connections with the Turks. On one level, he was
concerned that, if pursued, they would be discovered by the British and
he would lose the support of his most valuable ally. At another level, the success
of the Turkish nationalists and the evident popularity of a pro-Turkish policy,
if it were pursued by the Arab government, would help him in his struggle with
the French.[29]

Faisal and the nationalists

Faisal had left Europe from the port of Toulon on board the French warship the *Waldeck-Rousseau*. He landed in Beirut on 13 January 1920 and was grandly welcomed by an official reception party of senior French officers led by General de la Motte, Gouraud's deputy. After meeting his followers and well-wishers at the Beirut quarters of the Arab government, he was entertained in the evening by General Gouraud at a lavish banquet in Beirut's municipal park. Gouraud pointedly walked a few paces ahead of Faisal, no doubt to impress on the public the superiority of his status,[30] but there were other matters on Faisal's mind than Gouraud's posturing. Faisal was at pains to impress on the delegations that came to visit him of his commitment to the agreement he had reached with Clemenceau. The terms were the best that could be obtained, and he, Faisal, would consult with the country's notables and political leadership before returning to the peace conference and signing on the final document. Nevertheless, an undercurrent of disquiet about the terms of the Faisal–Clemenceau agreement was already evident in Beirut, a prelude to what Faisal was to expect in Damascus. Members of al-Fatat whom Faisal had met expressed grave misgivings with the agreement.

Driving from Beirut to Damascus through the pelting winter rains, Faisal arrived on 16 January 1920. There he was met by large crowds, but they were more restrained than during his earlier triumphal return. The following day, the Lajna and Arab Club organised a large demonstration. Though ostensibly in support of Faisal, the demonstration also reflected the widespread unease regarding the agreement. Faisal addressed the crowds directly, calling for unity and calm. His speech was well received but he knew that the agreement he had initialled was far from being acceptable to a broad swath of public opinion. In his long speech to the Arab Club ten days later, Faisal directly addressed the issue of his leadership of the Arab cause. He had been preceded by 'Abd al-Rahman al-Shabandar, who had given a rousingly nationalist speech. Faisal was not a rousing orator, and his flow was often interrupted by lengthy pauses and hesitations. However, he was determined to seize the initiative. 'I am not afraid of the strength of governments or political groupings,' Faisal said, 'but only of the judgement of history; and that in the future people will say that such-and-such acted in ways that were not appropriate to his antecedents who had worked for independence . . . The people should know that I was the same person in the West . . . I did not change my views either in front of politicians or even in the most dire circumstances. My principle was always to have my country independent and return our stolen glory . . . God is my witness that I had worked for this. No one wishes to see the foreigner to lord it over us . . . All feel as one in demanding total independence.'[31] But he then went on to remind his audience that the Arab government had no international recognition, and that it stood or fell on the strength of his own personal support for it, until a formal basis for its legitimacy was established. 'I am the spirit of the movement, and the people by relying on the government rely on me. Until the opportunity arises and we form our own assemblies that people can rely upon, I will not allow [undue criticism] of the government. I am the responsible person until a national assembly is elected whereupon I shall relinquish my responsibilities and hand it over to the people.'[32]

Faisal's immediate tasks were not only to regain public confidence in his leadership and goals, but also to reassert his authority over the government. The affairs of the country had drifted dangerously during his absence and he now set upon the task of reorganising the government. A large number of senior officials were removed and Zaid's role was formalised as the chief director, responsible for routine administrative affairs. Al-Rikabi returned to the government as head of military affairs. He had met with Faisal few days after the latter's return, and gave his version of the events that had led to his resignation. Faisal appeared satisfied with al-Rikabi's explanations. In any case Faisal wanted al-Rikabi's moderating influence in the cabinet partly as a counterweight to Yusuf al-'Azma, who was brought in as a chief of staff of the army.[33] 'Abd al-Rahman al-Yusuf, the leading public figure of Damascus, was made head of the consultative assembly. Yusuf and other notables had drifted back towards Faisal partly in response to the growth of the influence of al-Qassab and his Lajna. But reorganising the government was still a long way from regaining the political initiative, let alone control over the political situation.

Radical nationalists were now far more in evidence and their political agenda categorically rejected Faisal's conciliatory and pragmatic policies. Faisal's prestige and domestic and international support still assured him his place at the top of the Syrian political landscape, but the radicals were not content to allow him unfettered leeway in the making of policy. The heart of the divide between Faisal and the radicals was not so much regarding the issue of striving for unity and independence – there had already been agreement on this objective – but rather as to the means by which this could be achieved. In particular, opinion was divided as to whether the Arab government had the means – financial, diplomatic, but above all military – to confront the French. No one seriously believed that Faisal or his supporters sought a French mandate for its own sake. The moderates were working towards a settlement that would satisfy both the medium-term goals of unity and independence as well as one that could be realistically achieved. The radicals, on the other hand, had already settled on a maximalist position of rejecting any French claims and the recourse to military action if necessary. They were certainly affected by the relative weakness of the French military position in Syria, given that most of Gouraud's fighting strength was tied up in the war in Cilicia. The feeling was that the regular Arab government's army, buttressed by the guerrilla bands, could make the French position untenable.[34] Other nationalists saw a confrontation with the French as necessary even if this led to military defeat, because of the imperative of preserving the honour and dignity of the Syrian people and their commitment to the cause of Arab nationalism.

However, there was little doubt that the deal that Faisal had struck with Clemenceau was suspect and deeply unpopular. Even moderates saw it as a bitter pill, and few would publicly back its terms. Faisal himself referred to the agreement in these terms. 'The agreement was largely distasteful to him [Faisal], and would be unpopular with his people but that attitude of British authorities gave him no choice and that he had been handed over tied by feet and hands to French', said a despatch from Meinertzhagen, quoting a meeting in Beirut between Faisal and Colonal Waters Taylor, the British liaison officer to Gouraud.[35] Faisal tried but failed to convince the leadership of al-Fatat, supposedly more accommodating after the arrest of Yasin al-Hashimi, to support his agreement with Clemenceau. In early February 1920 Faisal called the central committee of al-Fatat to a meeting at which he set out the details of the agreement. 'This is the best [deal] that I could get. There is no doubt that the raising of the Syrian question at the Peace Conference and at the League of Nations will work to our benefit, and that my efforts in this regard will bring success.' But the central committee members were adamant that it was better to risk war with France and Britain than end up as a miserable protectorate like Tunisia and Morocco.[36] With this scale of opposition, at least in public, Faisal began to reconsider his commitment to the agreement, more so now that Clemenceau, its other author, was out of power and the new Millerand government was in no mood to compromise with the Arab nationalists. Nevertheless, Faisal did feel that the agreement with Clemenceau was the best that could be hoped for, and might have formed the basis for an acceptable settlement with France. In later years, he would remember it as a lost opportunity for the Arabs. Al-Shabandar, writing in the Egyptian magazine *al-Muqattaf* in 1933, said, 'Faisal stayed consistent in his regard for the agreement. He reminded [al-Shahbander] of it in 1926 in Baghdad, with deep regret ... increasingly so when he compared it to the terrible situation into which Syria had since descended.'[37]

Faisal was trying to steer the ship of state inside these swirling political currents. Polarisation between the factions, loosely termed as radical and moderate, now took on a certain class character. The old notable families of Damascus, feeling alienated from the populist groups and threatened by their rise, began to organise themselves through a separate political formation. Faisal instigated the founding of this party and his old friend Nasib al-Bakri took the lead in this matter, founding the Syrian National Party as a counter-weight to the Lajna and other popular committees. Faisal allowed his relative Sharif Nasir to join the party's founding committee.[38] He certainly expected to benefit from its formation, as it might prove a useful ally against the radicals. Faisal had grown noticeably cooler to the Lajna since his return, seeing in the demonstrations that they had organised a veiled threat to his authority. Nevertheless, working on the assumption that it is best to keep your enemies close to you, he agreed to serve as its honorary president. It was one way of keeping the radicals under check and maintaining a modicum of credibility with them, but it did carry risks.

Faisal's links with radical organisations, though formal and limited, opened him to the charge that he was consorting with extremists and men of violence. But, more damningly, he would develop an undeserved reputation of being duplicitous and willing to deal with all and sundry to achieve his ends. In reality, it would have been impossible for Faisal to choose one side over the other without compromising his own programme and freedom of action. He had to preserve his position as being above the fray in Damascus, sharing with the nationalists their goal of complete independence, but at the same time tempering these demands with an essential pragmatism and awareness of the international ramifications of the Syrian issue. Faisal also knew that he had to deal with the social strains arising within the new Syrian political class, and the fear of the notables and landed elements of the rising power of the populist groups. His own social standing would have pushed him in the direction of the old landed groups and notables, but he was an outsider and did not fit into their social hierarchy. His friends and allies in Syria were partly drawn from this class, but he had many others who were either from humbler backgrounds, or who, like him, were outsiders. The latter group, especially the large corps of Iraqi officers who had gravitated to the service of the Arab government, were a formidable force in their own right. The management of this complex array of groups and forces in a turbulent political arena, beset with pressures from all sides – from the British, the French, the Turks under Mustafa Kemal, the gravely deteriorating domestic economy, lawlessness, roving armed bands, and acute financial crises – was daunting. In addition to this sea of troubles, Faisal now had to contend with thinly veiled attacks on his policies from his father. In early February 1920, Hussein had fired off a cable to the Egyptian newspaper al-Ahram, denouncing anyone (that is, Faisal) who negotiated away the Arab right to self-independence. This, of course, played into the radicals' hand in Damascus. Delegations descended on his quarters demanding that Faisal accede to his father's statement. Faisal sent them packing, rejecting any criticism of his nationalist credentials and affirming his commitment to his own policies.[39]

Henri Gouraud

Clemenceau's liberalism did not sit well with the colonial party, who were suspicious of his stewardship of France's colonial interests in the Levant. The colonial party was centred on the Comité Lyonnais des intérêts français en Syrie, a grouping led by Lyon's Chamber of Commerce and supported by Jesuit educational interests in Lebanon. The Comité was determined not to forfeit France's claims in the Levant and its own substantial investments in Lebanon. So it was something of a surprise when Clemenceau appointed General Henri Gouraud in October 1919, both as the new high commissioner in Syria and Lebanon and as the head of France's Army of the Levant. Gouraud was a devout Catholic and his early career had been intimately connected with the consolidation of France's control over West Africa. He had also served in Morocco under France's great colonial administrator, Marshall Lyautey. During the First World War, he had served as commander of the French Fourth Army on the western front, where he lost an arm in battle. Gouraud had openly advocated a French military presence in the interior of Syria, and promised to protect France's, and especially Lyon's, commercial and educational interests in the Levant.[40] For Gouraud, the expansion and consolidation of French power and commercial dominance in the Levant was an essential aspect of its overall imperial policy, not to be compromised by any messy deal with a ramshackle Arab government in Damascus of dubious legality. The new French government under Millerand was of the same mind and kept only the minimum channels of communication open with Faisal. It was immaterial that their policies would push Faisal into a corner with the extremists. The French were biding their time until the moment was ripe to put their plans into effect.

Faisal had written to Gouraud informing him that he intended to implement the terms of the agreement with Clemenceau, and in spite of widespread opposition from his own entourage, he travelled to Beirut in February to meet Gouraud and to try to settle some of the outstanding issues.[41] Gouraud had committed most of his forces to counter the Turkish nationalist threat in Cilicia, and the battle to control the town of Maras was already raging. The French therefore were in a relatively weak position militarily, and Gouraud acceded to most of Faisal's suggestions to defuse the tensions between the French and the Arab government. He agreed to remove French troops from the contentious parts of the Beqa'a Valley and to allow the flying of the Arab flag in the French zone of occupation. In turn, Faisal promised to stop attacks on French targets by Arab irregulars and to discipline those who were accused of these acts. Faisal also agreed that the Arab government would no longer block the use of the Aleppo–Rayyaq section of the railroad, which ran through territory controlled by the Arab government and which France needed to transport its troops to the Cilician front. But none of these concessions were actually implemented in their entirety and the situation soon reverted to the status quo ante. Both sides adopted a wait-and-see attitude, but the feeling was growing that something had to be done to break the impasse.

Faisal was now in a most unenviable position. He had initialled an agreement with Clemenceau but his co-author was no longer in power to ensure that its terms could be met. The radicals and most of the moderates in Syria had rejected the agreement out of hand, while the new French government and Gouraud did not feel themselves bound to its terms in any way. Caught in the middle, Faisal had little choice but to manoeuvre constantly between the French and the radicals in Damascus. He sought from the French at least some concessions, even cosmetic, to the pride of the nationalists and the authority of the Arab government, while he counselled the radicals against any ill-considered move against the formidable power of France. At the same time, he had to prepare for the worse contingency, war with France, together with only the most meagre of resources, with a fractious and disputatious political class and the effective abandonment of his most important foreign ally, Great Britain. It was a circumstance fraught with risk, to his leadership, cause and stature. Reflecting on Faisal's situation, the French traveller and author Berthe Gaulis wrote during her visit to Syria in the winter of 1920, 'He [Faisal] lost his prestige in interposing himself between them [the extremists] and us; he would have a triumphant popularity the day he turned away from France.' To her perceptive eyes Faisal had become an increasingly isolated and solitary figure.[42] In the midst of all his troubles in Syria, Faisal concerned himself with events in Iraq and Palestine and how they would impinge on his own situation in Syria. He did not wish to appear to have forgotten the other causes for which the Arab Revolt stood. On 23 February 1920, he wrote to Allenby asking him for some official statement of assurance regarding British intentions in those countries to assuage public opinion in Syria. He did not want to ignore their plight. 'I wanted them [Iraqis and Palestinians] to know that I have not ignored their condition because of my involvement in Syrian affairs. I am accused of being involved in [Syrian] matters only for my personal benefit. I am confident that you are aware of my uncomfortable situation in front of my father and the entire Arab nation.'[43]

By the beginning of March 1920, Faisal was beset by massive problems from all sides which he could do little to resolve unilaterally. Trying to find a mooring for his increasingly precarious position, he finally threw in his lot in parallel with the radicals, not quite yet their ally and with enough distance between them to keep some hope alive for a moderate course of action. He could not possibly rule the country in direct opposition to the radical nationalists. They could easily outflank him by reminding him of his own words that 'independence is taken and not granted', and he might lay himself open to their charge of treason if he persisted in openly calling for an understanding with the French. He could only regain his nationalist credentials and thus his influence by drawing closer to the radicals and adopting their slogans and their programmes. In a later interview with the British journalist J. M. N. Jeffries recalling the events of the times, Faisal said that he could not ask his people to wait much longer for the decisions of the peace conference. They were agitated by the ambiguities regarding the future of their country and were coming under the influence of anti-Allied propaganda. He was worried that if he returned empty-handed from another journey to Europe, his own position would be untenable and chaos would reign in the land.[44] He began to speak out publicly against the French and adopt the nationalist plan for strengthening the government's military capabilities by conscription. But this change of tack incensed Gouraud, who saw nothing in it but insincerity and duplicity, a confirmation, if any were needed, of the futility in dealing with Faisal and the nationalists. Faisal's letters to Gouraud disassociating the Arab government from the increasingly frequent guerrilla attacks on the French sounded hollow when Gouraud knew full well that the Arab government was providing logistical and material help to the armed bands.

The reconvening of the Syrian Congress and declaration of independence

Both radical and most moderate nationalists had despaired of achieving their ends through negotiations with Britain and France. The withdrawal of the US from European and international entanglements was another contributory factor to the nationalists' anxieties, as the US was the originator of the principle of self-determination of nations and peoples.[45] Faisal was prevailed upon to abandon his planned journey to Europe and in its stead recall the Syrian Congress. Its members had scattered after its adjournment in December, but Faisal decided to reconvene it, 'so as the Amir could inform them of developments and leave it to the [Congress] to decide on [Syria's] future.'[46] Faisal's decision was very much influenced by al-Fatat's representations that something had to be done to pre-empt any decisions affecting Syria's future emerging from the peace conference. The Syrian Congress was the only collective body that had the credibility and legitimacy to embark on such a course. While the delegates were assembling in Damascus from various parts of Syria, a large number of Palestinians had already gathered in the capital to discuss the future of their country. On 27 February they organised themselves into the 'Palestinian Congress', composed of leading political figures and notables. They set out an uncompromising position on the independence of Palestine inside a united Syrian state, denounced the Zionist project in Palestine, and demanded an end to Jewish immigration. They also rejected the idea that Syria's independence should be beholden to any foreign state. The radical character of the Palestinian Congress's resolutions set the stage for the forthcoming meeting of the Syrian Congress, and made it difficult to circumvent the content and tone of the resolutions. The Syrian Congress may not have been hostage to the resolutions of the Palestinian Congress, but there was a great deal of sympathy for the Palestinians' resolutions.

The formal opening of the Syrian Congress took place on 6 March 1920, at the Arab Club in Damascus, after a sufficient number of delegates had assembled in the capital. Faisal and all his government attended the opening session, and he gave the opening speech, delivered for him by 'Awni 'Abd al-Hadi. The speech reviewed the Arab case and the various Allied promises, statements and declarations that acknowledged and supported the Arabs' right to independence, especially Wilson's Fourteen Points and the Anglo-French Declaration of November 1918. 'The Arabs have earned their freedom and independence by dint of their blood that was shed and the hardships and oppression that they have endured . . . I do not want Europe to grant us anything that is not ours in any case, but only to confirm our clear right which they have already acknowledged, to live as a vital nation that seeks to have a free life and complete independence, as for all other civilised nations.' Faisal then called on the congress to give Syria its constitutional form and concluded by reminding his audience not to neglect their brethren in Iraq who were undergoing similar issues, and to declare their solidarity and support for them. Although his speech was avidly nationalistic he did not close the doors to further negotiations. In fact, he was quite gracious regarding the Allies' intentions. 'During my many official visits to Europe, and the discussions and exchanges that I had with their leaders, there is no room in me for doubt or hesitation about the good intentions of their governments.'[47]

The congress then delegated to a nine-man committee the task of formulating a response to Faisal's speech. Shaikh Kamil al-Qassab delivered the reply, calling for the establishment of a constitutional parliamentary democracy in a decentralised unified Syria.[48] It reconvened on 7 March under the direction of Hashim al-Attasi, and a number of key resolutions were unanimously passed. The preamble to the resolutions summarised the position of the nationalists regarding the total independence of Syria within its natural frontiers, including Palestine, drawing on the right of the people to self-determination, the promises of the Allies and Wilson's Fourteen Points. The congress rejected the Zionist plan for a Jewish National Home in Palestine and called for administrative decentralisation and a special status for Lebanon. The resolution then declared Syria to be a fully independent state within its natural boundaries and offered the crown of Syria to Faisal as its constitutional king. 'We have unanimously chosen Your Highness to be the constitutional king of Syria because of your wisdom, soundness of judgement, and other exceptional qualifications, immortal deeds in war and diplomacy, love of freedom and the constitution, and devotion to the country and its people.'[49] the resolution floridly announced. The formal investiture of Faisal through a public declaration of *baya'a* (allegiance) would take place the following day, 8 March, at the municipal building.[50]

The declaration of independence and Faisal's investiture took place amidst scenes of widespread joy and celebration. Cannon fire and the raising of the flag of independent Syria – the Arab Revolt emblem to which a white star was added – accompanied the ceremonies. Members of the congress, religious dignitaries, municipal officials and other notables pledged their allegiance to Faisal and their commitment to government by law, religious toleration and the maintenance of order and security.[51] Later that day Faisal was feted at the Arab Club of Damascus, where he was formally given the new flag of the state and a commemorative banner written over with patriotic slogans. Standing beside Faisal at the military parade after the ceremonies were, surprisingly, the chief French liaison officers, Cousse and his deputy Toulat, and the American consul in Damascus. Absent was the British liaison officer, who had deliberately left the city to avoid any embarrassment or confrontation. Toulat was a good-natured officer who had learnt Arabic while serving in Algeria. He had become close to Faisal, often accompanying him on his visits to various parts of Syria and to Europe, but his influence on him was in no way comparable to the one that Lawrence had once wielded. The two French officers were present at the ceremonies of their own volition, acting without express orders from Gouraud. In fact, Gouraud later claimed that the two officers were cleverly deceived, having been invited to tea only to find themselves in the midst of a military parade. But the fact remained that Cousse had been informed earlier of the intentions of the congress to declare Syria independent, and Gouraud himself was aware of the general drift of events. Most likely Gouraud allowed the declaration of independence to go ahead without hindrance, knowing that it would seriously alarm the British and alienate them from the new Syrian state. Faisal, however, did send Gouraud a cable on 8 March informing him that the Syrian Congress had declared independence and would offer him the crown of Syria. He attributed this action to the people's exasperation with the delays in settling the future of Syria, and that the independence of Syria was in any case an outcome that the Allies themselves desired.[52]

The declaration of independence was a hazardous decision. It directly threatened the interests not only of France, which saw itself challenged throughout the Levant, but also of Britain. The declaration abolished the occupation zones, theoretically bringing them all under the authority of a single state. It explicitly rejected the division of Syria into the three territories of interior Syria, Lebanon and Palestine. The British occupied Palestine, whose fate had already been determined in Britain's favour by the deal that had been struck between Lloyd George and Clemenceau over a year previously. The simultaneous declaration of independence by the Iraqi Congress ('the 29 Mesopotamians' as Curzon dismissively called them) greatly angered the British, notably the India Office, who were beginning to discern the first stirrings of rebellion in Iraq. The Arab government had no means by which to enforce its ringing statements and was still critically dependent on the Allies for supplies and financial, operational and logistical support. By any reckoning, the decision unilaterally to declare the independence of Syria in its widest definition could bring nothing but trouble from the Great Powers. It united Britain and France in joint opposition, removing any space that might have existed between them in their respective treatment and consideration for the Arab government. There is no doubt that the declaration of independence was immensely popular, but cooler and wiser heads might easily have discerned the dangers inherent in this course of action. Faisal, who had hitherto been working towards finding an accommodation with the powers while trying to prepare his government and people for a possible confrontation, had suddenly switched course. He had now not only accepted the policies of the radicals but had adopted them as his own. He had put himself at the head of an unstable coalition of forces that was pushing the nascent state into an unequal confrontation.

Faisal certainly could not be accused of craving glory or personal aggrandisement by seeking a crown. None of those who came across him ever noted that he sought fame for himself. In fact some went further, to note that Faisal seemed indifferent to worldly ambition and acted selflessly and with a profound sense of duty.[53] The crown of Syria, though of great symbolic value, could not have motivated him in this dangerous direction. In spite of later claims to the contrary, Faisal was not duped or deliberately entrapped to pursue independence, a path that he must have known would put him in collision with the Allies. The French had allowed members of the Syrian Congress to cross their territories, and Gouraud had authorised a payment to the Arab government a few days before its convening. These actions would imply that the French facilitated the holding of the congress with the knowledge that it would take action that might work against their interests. However, Gouraud had earlier counselled Faisal not to take unilateral action, as did the French liaison officers in Damascus. The best explanation for France's wavering position in the days before the declaration of independence was a genuine concern that an openly hostile position on their part would aggravate their critical military situation in Cilicia and might open another front for the overstretched French forces.[54] But above all it was Faisal's concern that he could be left behind by the build-up of nationalist momentum to declare independence, and the tremendous popular appeal of such a move. The decision was almost a foregone conclusion, with or without his approval. If he had resisted the measure and the decision had taken place anyway, he would have been dangerously, or possible fatally, isolated. The likes of Shaikh Kamil al-Qassab had the street and the mob on their side, and they were in no mood to accept conciliation. The success of the Turkish nation-alists also encouraged the ultras, and gave rise to visions of an independent Arab state, uniting with the forces of Mustafa Kemal to drive the enfeebled French out of the Near East. There were still a large number of pan-Islamists, former Ottoman officials and officers and members of the Syrian Congress who yearned for such an eventuality.[55]

After the declaration of independence, Faisal moved quickly to reassert his control over events and restore relative moderates such as Ali Ridha al-Rikabi to power. A new cabinet was formed under al-Rikabi, a signal to the Allies that Faisal intended to pursue a reasonable course of action. The new government announced a raft of reformist measures and declared a general amnesty for most classes of criminals. It also set in motion a number of measures that asserted Syrian sovereignty. These included the flying of the new flag, issuing new postage stamps and mentioning Faisal's name as king in the Friday call to prayer. Faisal downplayed the significance of the declaration to the Allies, portraying it in almost incidental terms. He had no desire to challenge the Allies and was wary of the possibility that he might be thought of as a rebel, working against the Allies and the decisions of the peace conference. Allenby wrote to Curzon on 13 March 1920 that he had received a note from Faisal in which he 'assures His Majesty's Government that neither proclamation of independence nor his own advent to the throne will change the friendly relations between Syria and Great Britain . . . The Declaration of the Congress was merely a statement of the will of the people and a request to the Peace Conference to fulfil its promises.'[56] Faisal was equally hesitant with his father. The declaration of Syrian independence decisively broke Syria from any connection with the future of the Hijaz. It made Faisal a figure of equal stature to his father, a circumstance that was bound to create its own issues with both Hussein and 'Abdullah. Faisal in fact avoided telling his father officially of the decision to take the title of king, only addressing him on this matter on 20 March, nearly a fortnight after the date of the declaration of independ-ence. In his letter, Faisal sought to set Syrian independence in the context of the wider aims of the Arab Revolt to form a confederation of states under King Hussein. 'With the help of God, we have started the work and have declared Syria and Iraq independent under the overall kingship of your majesty.'[57]

Fury in London and Paris

The declaration of independence was quickly followed by a campaign to gain diplomatic recognition for the new state. Faisal and al-Rikabi wrote to Curzon, Berthelot and Gouraud to express their friendship and good intentions, while Nuri al-Sa'id, who had developed a relationship with Gouraud, sent off messages of a similarly conciliatory nature. Allenby, ever concerned with the internal security situation in Syria, had at first tried to make the best of the dramatic developments in Damascus. On 8 March he cabled Curzon to permit 'Faisal to announce to [Syrian] Congress that Powers accepted him as representative of Arab state including British provinces of Mesopotamia and Palestine and French provinces of Lebanon and littoral. Remainder of Arab provinces under direct control of Feisal.' He then asked Curzon to authorise him to send such a message to Faisal. Curzon wrote, 'Do nothing' on the margins of the note.[58] On 13 March, Curzon sent Allenby a cable to be relayed to Faisal. It reflected the official British response to the declaration of independence and was harsh and angry in tone. 'H.M. Government cannot recognise right of Damascus Congress, of whose composition or authority they know nothing, to settle future of Syria, Palestine, Mosul or Mesopotamia. These countries were conquered by the Allied Armies, and their future . . . can only be determined by the Allied Powers acting in concert . . . H.M. Government cannot recognise the right of a self-constituted body at Damascus to regulate these matters, and H.M. Government together with the French Government are compelled to say that they regard these proceedings as null and void.'[59] Curzon did, however, leave a small door open for further negotiations. He asked Allenby to renew his invitation to Faisal to come to Paris to place his case before the peace conference. The French sent a similar cable to Gouraud to relay to Faisal. France and Britain were now acting in unison. Earlier, on 7 March, they had sent a joint message to Faisal advising him to desist from his course, but the message had reached Damascus a day later and had no effect on the proceedings of the Syrian Congress. Privately Curzon blamed the French for escalating the conflict with their unreasonable demands and pressures, both on Faisal and on Britain. 'In deference, however, to the insistent pressure of the French Government, we had in November last evacuated both Cilicia and Syria, not without warning the French Government of the serious results that might arise if they attempted to extend their military occupation of the latter,' Curzon had written to the British ambassador in Paris, Lord Derby.[60]

Faisal's conciliatory responses to both Curzon and the French failed to cover up the fact that his options in facing the Allies' categorical rejection of the decisions of the Syrian Congress had dwindled. Curzon may have been prepared to see Faisal as king of Syria, and in a belated response to Allenby's message to recognise Faisal as 'representative of the Arab state', Curzon wrote: 'While we have no objection to Feisal being declared King of Syria by a properly constituted Syrian authority and while we would willingly recognise him as such ourselves, we could not regard decision of Congress as superseding duties and decisions of Peace Conference . . . or as entitling Feisal to force our hands.'[61] The decisions of the congress had to be ignored or reversed – an impossibility – and Faisal had to come to Europe if Curzon were to reconsider his position. Allenby, closer to the ground, continued to argue in vain for an accommodation with the 'Damascus Congress', which he considered as 'representing the vast majority of Syrian feeling'. He also presciently warned that if the peace conference continued to deny the validity and legitimacy of the Syrian Congress, hostilities would be inevitable.[62] But Faisal stuck to his position and refused to come to Europe unless the Allies made some important concessions. On 28 March he wrote to Curzon refusing the latter's request that he came to Europe. After repeating the Arabs' rights to independence and setting it in the context of Allied promises and declarations, Faisal wrote, 'I assure you of my desire to come to Europe in response to your invitation, but only after I receive official assurances from the British Government – even though privately expressed – in which it announces that it has accepted our independence.'[63] The makings of a stand-off were already there, leaving the only way out of the impasse the resort to arms, or at least the threat of arms.

The French army in the Levant, of around 35,000 troops, was heavily engaged in fighting the Turks and was generally getting the worst of it. The soldiers were mainly conscripts from France's North African colonies and Senegal, and were mostly Muslim. Gouraud was therefore in no position to launch hostilities. His messages to Faisal were firm but not yet belligerent. Gouraud also had to contend with the views of Cousse and Toulat, France's liaison officers in Damascus, who were both advocates of a friendly policy with Faisal and the new Syrian government. Toulat often wrote to his superiors in glowing terms about Faisal and the need to cooperate with him. 'We had before us a convinced patriot, nearly a fanatic, profoundly dedicated to the kingship just attributed to him, and one could feel him ready to return to the simple insurgent Bedouin chief, fighting for a cause whose apostle he was and in which he engaged his personal honour. More than even [sic] I persist in believing that France has a good opportunity to seize in working with our English allies to find a conciliatory ground which would avoid, for the Amir, turning to a gesture of despair that he considered necessary to save honour.'[64] Cousse, the senior liaison officer, also shared these views. Paris and Gouraud had no time for their recommendations, but allowed them to continue in conciliatory talks with Faisal. It gave Faisal comfort that a diplomatic solution was still possible, and bought time until France had sorted out its troubles in Cilicia.

The main issue that Faisal now faced was his representation at the fourth-coming conference of the Supreme Council, scheduled to be held in San Remo, Italy, in mid-April. It was a decisive conference for the issue of the mandates, and their allocations were on the agenda. The British felt grievously embarrassed by Faisal's actions, which ran counter to their specific warnings, and Faisal lost much-needed sympathy and support in London. But in spite of this Curzon had wanted Faisal to attend, and a formal invitation was extended to him.[65] Faisal was still resistant to the idea of attending the conference without something tangible in place from the Allies that would acknowledge the decisions taken by the Syrian Congress. He wanted France to reaffirm its commitment to the agreement he had struck with Clemenceau and to agree that the Syrian Congress's declaration of independence did not breach its terms. He sought different assurances from Britain: that it reaffirmed its promises and declarations regarding Arab independence. Faisal was also particularly concerned that Zionist policies should not be imposed on Palestine and wanted a British statement to this effect. But his policy of extracting concessions before journeying to Europe was not leading anywhere, and the messages flying between Damascus, London, Paris and Beirut were no substitute for face-to-face diplomacy. Nevertheless, Faisal was wary of embarking for Europe so soon after the new state was declared. There were urgent matters of state to attend to and his position inside the country, though pre-eminent, might still be threatened. The radicals might easily undermine his base at home by claiming that he would make unacceptable and unauthorised concessions to the Allies.

Under such inauspicious circumstances, the San Remo Conference of the Supreme Council opened on 19 April 1920. The only Arab representation was an unofficial delegation composed of Nuri al-Sa'id, Rustum Haidar and Najib Shuqayr. They arrived nearly a week late and had difficulty finding lodgings. They were effectively ignored by the Allies and remained isolated from the main decisions of the conference.[66]

The San Remo Conference and its aftermath

The Allied Supreme Council met at San Remo from 19 to 26 April, with Lloyd George and Millerand in attendance. The first sessions were devoted to the drafting of a treaty that later became the Treaty of Sèvres, which dealt with the peace terms offered to Turkey. On 25 April, the conference recognised that Mesopotamia and Syria were independent states, but in the same breath assigned mandates for Mesopotamia, Palestine and Syria. Syria was given over to France, and Palestine and Mesopotamia to Britain. The boundary lines for these mandates were left to the mandatory powers to sort out, and these were settled by Britain and France in a convention on 23 December 1920. The utter cynicism of the mandate system was not lost on anyone. Even Lloyd George called it a 'substitute for the old Imperialism'.[67] Article 22 of the Covenant of the League of Nations, which was used to justify imposing the mandate system on the Near East, emphatically stated that 'The wishes of these communities [the people of the Near East] must be a principal consideration in the selection of the Mandatory.' But these ringing tones were conveniently set aside as the powers divided the lands and resources between themselves. Britain and France also struck a grubby deal at San Remo to divide the spoils of Iraqi oil. The British government undertook to give France a 25 per cent share in the oil company organised to exploit this resource. In return, the French agreed for the passage of a pipeline from the Iraqi oil fields through French-controlled territory in Syria to the Mediterranean Sea.

The announcement of the mandate system and its implications for Arab nationalist aspirations had now to be stage-managed for the anxious public of Syria and Iraq. Curzon, writing to Lord Hardinge, the permanent under-secretary at the Foreign Office, on the day after the mandates were allocated, was particularly concerned with Faisal's reaction and the prospects for his rule in Syria. He insisted that Faisal should come in person to the peace conference to set out his case as well as to legitimise his kingship. Palestine had now been formally severed from Syria, and there was no chance that Faisal's rule would extend over it. If Faisal wanted to be king of Syria, he would first have to obtain the approval of the peace conference for such a status and the French would have to agree with him the modalities of his rule and power. It was Allenby who was given the task of informing Faisal about the decisions of the San Remo Conference. On 27 April Allenby cabled Faisal to tell him that Syria had been placed under a French mandate, and Mesopotamia and Palestine under a British one. Allenby sugar-coated the decisions by stating that Syria and Mesopotamia were recognised as independent states, but immediately added the 'proviso that they be aided by a mandatory power until such time as they are able to stand alone.'[68] He also urged Faisal to come to Paris, where the Allied Supreme Council was to meet again in late May, and to set out his case. In the same cable, Allenby reiterated the British government's commitment to imple-ment the terms of the Balfour Declaration, a requirement of the mandate given to Britain over Palestine.

Faisal's response to Allenby came in the form of a note which barely concealed his disappointment at the decisions of San Remo. While welcoming the Allies' declaration that Syria and Iraq were independent states, he could not accept the mandate system. 'I have no right to discuss it, the people being aware of the danger which it may entail upon their future safety and independence, have bitterly protested against it and refuse to accept it.' He rejected the separa-tion of Palestine from Syria, as well as the suggestion that he accepted the

Zionist project in Palestine. 'All that I have admitted is to safeguard rights of Jews in that country as much as rights of indigenous Arab inhabitants are safe-guarded and to allow same rights and privileges. Arabs of Palestine both Christian and Muslim have repeatedly availed themselves of every opportunity to protest against any agreement or pledge that they would make their mother-land the national home of Israelites.'[69] Faisal concluded by demanding that any visit to Europe be preceded by a declaration from the Allies that Palestine would not be separated from Syria.

Arabs received the news of the French mandate for Syria (and the British mandate for Iraq) with great dismay. It divided Arab lands into unnatural and potentially adversarial states, saddled with different forms of government. The Hijaz delegation, still the only official Arab presence at the peace conference, vigorously protested the San Remo decisions. Haidar and Nuri al-Sa'id, who were at San Remo, were shocked at the outcome. It was a disastrous setback for Arab national aspirations and left the moderates, who were banking on Allied good will and counselling an accommodation with the French, completely exposed. There were strikes and demonstrations in all Syrian towns. Angry crowds denounced the mandate and demanded that the government take steps to defend Syrian independence. The al-Rikabi government could not face the onslaught of questioning from the congress, and was forced to submit its resig-nation less than a month after its formation. Faisal was closeted in his quarters with various nationalist figures led by Shaikh Kamil al-Qassab. They impressed on Faisal the need to form a unity government that would face the challenges ahead with a programme that would emphasise resistance and national defence.[70] On 3 May a new government was sworn in. It was led by the veteran politician and speaker of the Syrian Congress, Hashim al-Attasi. Its first state-ment, read for it by the foreign minister Dr 'Abd al-Rahman al-Shabandar, virtually mirrored Faisal's reply to Allenby. The new government authorised the raising of a national loan equivalent to £1.5 million against the mortgage of state-owned land in various parts of Syria. The government also extended conscription to a year of service and suggested that the penalty for its evasion should be flogging. The matter was brought to Faisal's attention, who often met his cabinet ministers on an individual basis on Sundays. Faisal signed the proposal to extend conscription, but only after he had struck off the article that called for the penalty of flogging for draft dodgers.[71]

Senior political figures in Europe began to recognise that the San Remo decisions might weaken Faisal's position in favour of the radicals, and narrow the space for resolution of the growing impasse in Syria. Daladier, a leading French parliamentarian, spoke in the National Assembly on 25 May in defence of Faisal: 'He is a moderate man who is using all his means to convince the Arab radicals to compromise with France.' Lloyd George also spoke in favour of Faisal as he addressed the House of Commons. His remarks helped to change Faisal's perception about the advisability of continuing to refuse to journey to Europe. Faisal wrote to his father on May 20, 'I may proceed to Europe in response to the wishes of the Peace Conference and especially in light of Lloyd George's recent comments in Parliament.'[72] This time Faisal planned to take with him representatives of the nationalist radicals such as Shaikh Kamil al-Qassab and Yasin al-Hashimi. His cabinet had also changed its views about his return to the peace conference. Even people such as 'Abd al-Rahman al-Shabandar came around to the view that he should go to Europe after Faisal gave him a copy of the agreement that he had struck with Clemenceau.[73] Only the war minister, Yusuf al-'Azma, persisted in his opposition to returning to the peace conference. The Syrian Congress, in spite of the hesitation of some of its members, also backed the idea of sending a Syrian delegation headed by Faisal.

However, by the time the official decision to send the delegation was taken by the cabinet and Faisal in early July, the situation had drastically changed. France was no longer willing to deal with the Syrian government, let alone recognise it. Neither was it in any way prepared to entertain the counsel of its British ally when it came to dealing with Faisal and the Syrians. Curzon had in fact laid the groundwork for a French maximalist position if Faisal did not come to Europe in response to the summons from the Allies. In a note of 18 May to the French ambassador, Curzon wrote of the consequences if Faisal did not heed the demands that he come to Europe. The invitation could not again be renewed; Faisal would no longer be recognised by the conference as the Hijaz representative; all financial assistance from the British and French governments would terminate; and France would be at liberty to occupy the Aleppo–Rayyaq railroad, a crucial supply link to their forces in Cilicia.[74]

France's position was becoming ever more confrontational and even belligerent. Faisal's clumsy attempt to engage France with a new alliance based on the Faisal–Clemenceau agreement failed miserably. He had drafted a note of such a deal to Gouraud, asking that France recognise the sovereignty of Syria and evacuate its troops from all of Syria except for Lebanon, as defined by the peace conference. In exchange Faisal would agree to accept French advice and assistance in Syria and help France to secure the borders of Syria against Turkey.[75] The proposed deal was rejected out of hand by both Gouraud and the French Foreign Ministry. Gouraud replied frostily on 3 June that 'the declaration of the [French] government was sufficient, as it satisfied the Syrian peoples whose independence [France] had recognised.'[76] Gouraud was fortified by the improvement in the French military situation in the Levant. He signed an armistice with the Kemalists in early June 1920 and could now redeploy his forces from the Cilician front to Syria.

Escalating tensions

The declaration of Syrian independence coincided with the escalation of fighting in Syria and Lebanon between armed groups and French and French-backed forces. Even though these never reached the point of a national insurgency, they nevertheless gave Gouraud pause for thought in his dealings with Faisal. The French had to contend with a number of local uprisings in their zones of occupation, some originating in a reaction to their own policies of setting up local administrations under French officers with wide latitude. The most serious of these were in the 'Alawite regions of Latakia and Banias. These were led by a local figure, Shaikh Saleh al-'Ali, and were mainly driven by local considerations and rivalries between the Ismaili and 'Alawite communities. Shaikh Saleh had only the most tenuous of links with Faisal, but this did not stop Gouraud from accusing Faisal of indirectly supporting the uprising.[77] There was strife elsewhere in territory controlled by the French. In the south of Lebanon, the Shi'a of Jabal 'Amil rose in revolt against the French and their Maronite allies. A number of Maronite villages were sacked and the town of Tyre was besieged. It was only after the arrival of large French forces that the revolt was put down. French reprisals were brutal: thirty-six of the leaders received death sentences and the town of Bint Jbail was razed to the ground in retaliation. Many of the rebels fled to British-occupied Palestine and to interior Syria. Faisal complained bitterly to Lloyd George about French action in Jabal 'Amil. 'French artillery and aeroplane's explosives are promiscuously and without pity destroying the villages and tearing to pieces the defenceless inhabitants.'[78] However, the Jabal 'Amil uprising was also only tangentially connected with Faisal. Other revolts had broken out in the north of Syria. Subhi Barakat, a notable from the Antioch region and later a member of the Syrian Congress, had been leading a band of rebels in harassing French troops since May 1919. A more serious revolt, led by another congressman, Ibrahim Hannanu, broke out in the Idilb region north of Aleppo and stretched to include nearly all the territory between Alexandretta and Tripoli. Hannanu was coordinating his operations both with Shaikh al-'Ali and with the Turks. In all these revolts the Arab government denied its involvement, but there is considerable evidence that Faisal helped them with money and arms and allowed his army units to provide surreptitious support for particular operations where possible. At the same time, Faisal had his own litany of complaints against Gouraud. In a letter of 16 May, al-Shabandar, acting on the instructions of Faisal, accused the French of arming the Christians of Jabal 'Amil, encouraging separatist feelings amongst the 'Alawites and Druze, engineering defections from Faisal's military, and tolerating insults against Islam and the person of Faisal amongst Christian volunteers in the French army.[79]

The French were also faced with splits within the Maronite community that had hitherto been seen as monolithically united behind a French mandate, and which gave France its greatest excuse for extending its control over Lebanon. An important group of Christian leaders had been secretly negotiating with Faisal to switch their allegiances publicly to the Syrian government if it accepted an independent Lebanon linked with Syria. These leaders were no doubt impressed by the lack of sectarian sentiment and the protections given to minorities by Faisal's government. But they were also acting on rumours that Faisal was prepared to grant Lebanon the independence that they sought provided Lebanon maintained a confederal arrangement with Syria. On 10 July a delegation of Maronite leaders, including seven members of the administrative council, led by the Maronite patriarch's brother, Sa'adallah Howeik, were on their way to Damascus to reach their own agreement with Faisal. They would then head towards Europe, where they intended to present their own case for an independent Lebanon without a French mandate. The group, however, was arrested in the Lebanese town of Zahle, and then exiled to Corsica. Gouraud dissolved the administrative council and pushed the Maronite patriarch to send a cable to France, proclaiming his continuing loyalty. The French held Faisal personally responsible for this incident and accused him of bribing the delegates.[80] Had they made it to Europe, France would have been seriously embarrassed by the presence of this high-powered delegation in the midst of the peace conference, giving the lie to its claims that it was best positioned to protect the Christians of Lebanon.

Other seemingly minor issues also soured the relationship between the French and Syrian governments. The flying of the new Syrian flag on top of the Syrian liaison office in Beirut was prohibited, and Gouraud put a stop to the name of Faisal being mentioned in public prayers. Muslims in Lebanon saw this as a direct interference on the part of the French in matters of religion. But it was the disposition of the Aleppo–Rayyaq railroad, which ran through Syrian territory that caused the greatest problems. The line was crucial for the effective movement of French supplies and men to the Cilician battlefields, but the nationalists were determined to deny France its use. Faisal knew that the railroad was vital for the French war effort in Cilicia, and blocking its use would be seen as a grave threat by Gouraud. At the same time, it was not lost on him that acceding to France's demands would be deeply unpopular. The result was a vacillating policy that sporadically allowed the French the use the line for the transport of supplies (but not troops or war materiel), while French transport was disrupted by frequent freight inspections, line closures and demonstrations along the tracks. By 21 May even this limited usage was stopped, as the Syrian government, bowing to public pressure, temporarily denied the French any use of the line. Gouraud was incensed, treating the matter as a hostile act. He held

Faisal personally responsible for this policy, brushing aside Faisal's denials that it was not his personal wish but that of the government that was behind the move.

However, the entire landscape in Syria changed after the Franco–Kemalist truce was signed. Nationalists foolishly interpreted the ceasefire as a Kemalist 'victory', but cooler heads understood that it would not augur well for Syrian independence and sovereignty. Faisal made a hurried trip to Aleppo to assess the situation first hand and to gauge the extent of his support. He was also reported to have met with Mustafa Kemal's emissaries. But any attempts to launch an alliance with the Turks were doomed to fail. Faisal himself had always hesitated in tying his cause with that of Mustafa Kemal, and after the terrible events of the Great War, the Arabs of Syria were divided about the wisdom of a new Turkish alliance. Faisal's room for manoeuvre had now shrunk to insignificance and he was faced with a belligerent Gouraud, strengthened by the release of troops from the Cilician front. Extremely anxious about Gouraud's next moves, Faisal sent a cable to Curzon on 19 June: 'I was greatly surprised to hear of armistice between French and the Turks under Mustafa Kemal, which leaves greater part of northern Syria and Cilicia to Turks . . . The concentration of French troops which have evacuated Cilicia and Syria leads one to believe that their Commander in Chief [Gouraud] intends to find some excuse for starting military operations against my government and to inflict deep injuries upon it.'[81]

Standing behind Gouraud was the equally belligerent Millerand, who saw no merit in either an alliance with Faisal or in the agreement that Faisal had struck with Clemenceau. Millerand had effectively set the stage for the final denouement with Faisal. He charged Gouraud with the task of bringing Faisal and his government in line with the San Remo decisions, occupying the Aleppo-Rayyaq railroad, and Aleppo itself if necessary, and ordering the Syrian government to put a stop to the activities of the guerrilla bands. If Faisal did not comply with these demands, Gouraud would then occupy Damascus, disarm the population and arrest the militants. The stage management of the operation against Faisal and its timing – sooner rather than later – was left to Gouraud to determine.[82] Meanwhile, reinforcements were on the way to strengthen Gouraud's forces in the Levant. Millerand announced in the National Assembly that France was prepared to send 30,000 troops to occupy Damascus and Aleppo, while Robert de Caix talked about 60,000. Even the ultra nationalist Yasin al-Hashimi, only recently returned from exile in Palestine, was sobered by the size of the French military force being assembled.[83]

France's intentions were now absolutely clear. The country was determined to exert its direct authority over all of Syria and to interpret the terms of the mandate in neo-colonial terms. Britain could only watch these developments silently. France had allowed Britain free rein in the management of affairs in

Palestine and Mesopotamia, and expected Britain to reciprocate in Syria. Whatever residual obligations that Britain had felt towards Faisal had been compromised by the declaration of independence and by France's determination to impose its rule on Syria, by force if necessary. All that Britain could do was vaguely to call for moderation and counsel Faisal to cut the best deal that he could with the French. Faisal now switched tack. Rather than taking exception to French actions, he offered to have his army assist the French in Cilicia, but Gouraud firmly declined. He then asked Gouraud point blank whether France intended to attack Syria. Gouraud gave him a non-committal answer that avoided any direct confirmation or denial.[84] With only few options left open to him, Faisal saw his best hope to lie in travelling to Europe as soon as possible. He needed to present his case at the peace conference in the vain hope that he could avert imminent action against Syria. France might be induced or pressured to suspend, or even cancel, its preparations for war. But Gouraud would have none of this. He was not going to allow Faisal the opportunity to reverse by diplomacy what he was certain France could achieve by war. Gouraud told Faisal that after ignoring requests to come to Europe for two months, the latter now wanted to depart immediately, without adequate logistical preparations and notice, for the peace conference. This was simply not possible and Gouraud had to await further instructions from Paris. If Faisal insisted on travelling to Europe other than via Beirut, France might refuse to receive him officially.[85]

Faced with Gouraud's increasingly threatening position, Faisal sent Nuri al-Sa'id to Beirut in early July to ascertain at first hand Gouraud's intentions. Nuri was also charged with eliciting from Gouraud a formal recognition of Syrian independence with Faisal as king. But rather than acceding to Faisal's requests, Gouraud sent Nuri back with a verbal ultimatum. Gouraud demanded an immediate occupation of the Aleppo-Rayyaq railroad, the recognition of France's mandate over all of Syria, approval and free circulation of the French-sponsored Syrian pound currency, and the abandonment of military conscription. Nuri, travelling back to Damascus on 11 July, was delayed for several hours by ominous French military movements along the route. Without waiting for Faisal's reply, French units occupied the Aleppo–Rayyaq railroad on 12 July. The excuse was that Arab units had reinforced the small outpost near 'Anjar in the Beqa'a Valley. Faisal's protest went unheeded, as did Faisal's subsequent offer of reducing the garrison at 'Anjar if the French pulled out of the Aleppo–Rayyaq railroad.

The ultimatum

Emboldened by the feeble Arab response to his military initiatives, Gouraud issued a formal ultimatum on 14 July, addressed to Faisal. Ten pages long, it

broadly followed the lines of the verbal terms carried by Nuri, with additional
demands including a reduction in the size of the army and the punishment of
those deemed guilty of hostile acts against France. Faisal was given four days to
accept the terms of the ultimatum unconditionally. If no response was forthcoming, Gouraud would impose its terms by force. Faisal immediately sent his
advisers 'Adil Arslan and Nuri al-Sa'id to Haifa to seek the advice and support
of Allenby. British public opinion, and even parliamentary opinion, was in
favour of some action to deter French aggression, but this had little effect on
government policy. The British government was washing its hands of the whole
affair. Lord Hardinge cabled Allenby: 'I am afraid that it is impossible for us to
intervene. Since grant of mandate for Syria to French at San Remo they have
possessed a prior right with reference to purely Syrian affairs which it would be
neither right nor expedient for us to contest ... If their present attitude to
Feisal lands them in trouble, the responsibility will be exclusively theirs.'[86]
Faisal also sought the support of Italy, which felt short-changed by the decisions at San Remo. The Italian ambassador in Damascus gave Faisal plenty of
sympathy but little practical help.

Domestically, Faisal's position was also becoming increasingly isolated. He
had given a long speech on 28 May, on the occasion of the end of Ramadhan at
the Royal Palace in Damascus. He tried to find a course other than capitulation
or despair. He rejected the principle of a mandate as it blatantly contradicted
the idea of Syrian independence. 'The word mandate has no definition or clear
meaning to it and has been totally rejected by the nation. It is a malleable term
that is at times interpreted as the worst form of colonialism and at times in the
lightest way that doesn't affect independence. Whichever way it is, it is a
disgrace on a nation that wants to live [free]. I wish the nation to know that its
leader, ruler or king that it has elected believes in this. He [Faisal] will not
accept what might be said that the kingdom of which he is the head is under
the tutelage of another kingdom ... Despair should not spread to a single
person; and it is up to our thinkers, opinion leaders and newspaper publishers
not to spread [despair] for we shall live and no one can harm our independence
... No one will pass a death sentence on us; such a sentence has not [been]
passed and will not pass.'[87] It was a powerful and emotional speech, but offered
only hope rather than a clear way out of the crisis. The divisions in Syria had
already hardened between those who were effectively seeking martyrdom and
those advocating compromise. The Syrian Congress, whose powers and
frequent mischief-making Faisal was seeking to curtail, had become the platform for the nationalists, and pushed for an aggressive line with the French.
Many notables, seeing the impossibility of the situation, were trying to reorganise the congress through new elections, hoping to reduce the influence of
the radicals on its decisions. The cabinet, on the other hand, was closer to

Faisal in sentiment. With the exception of Yusuf al-'Azma, the war minister, who was personally close to Faisal, they generally adopted moderate views.[88]

In spite of the strong desire to avoid hostilities, Faisal and his government pushed for preparations for war. On 13 July, Yusuf al-'Azma addressed the congress and announced emergency measures. A state of siege was declared, press censorship imposed, and the army was given the power to requisition vehicles. The leaders of the various guerrilla groups were summoned to Damascus and left with instructions to support the army in case of hostilities. Gouraud had estimated that there might have been upwards of 30,000 irregular forces available to support Faisal's army, but this was probably an exaggeration. The Arab army itself consisted of about 15,000 troops, but was rife with poor discipline and morale problems. The officers expected a fifth of the army to desert in the event of hostilities. It was also undersupplied and poorly armed. Faisal's government had signally failed in finding new sources of weaponry, and neither Britain nor France was prepared to arm the Arab government with up-to-date weapons. Al-'Azma was leading the military preparations. He was youthful, energetic and devoted to Faisal. But he was also enamoured with Mustafa Kemal and his successful campaigns against the French, believing he could replicate that experience in Syria.[89] He called for raising the army to 25,000 men and the establishment of fortified positions overlooking the Beqa'a Valley. But he was wildly over-optimistic about the fighting capabilities of the army. It was not until the return of Yasin al-Hashimi, chastened from his enforced stay in Palestine, that a note of realism was introduced into military planning. After inspecting the frontline formations, al-Hashimi informed Faisal that the army was in no position to encounter the French. For instance, it had enough ammunition for only a few hours of battle. The War Cabinet met under Faisal on 16 July to consider al-Hashimi's report. Al-'Azma was visibly upset by al-Hashimi's allegations, but relented when confronted with the evidence that each rifleman had less than 270 rounds of ammunition and each artillery piece had only eight shells. These could barely last for one battle. Nevertheless, the officers all declared themselves duty-bound to fight a war.[90]

On the following day, 17 July, Faisal called the Syrian Congress to a secret meeting at the Royal Palace. The general belief was that the congress would be asked to declare that war was imminent. Faisal posed the question of whether they should enter a war against a powerful enemy or seek a compromise. Opinion was divided, with most of the delegates keeping silent, while those from the western and southern districts (Lebanon and Palestine) calling for a defensive war against France. Faisal was aware that no consensus could be achieved with the congress. The delegates later met separately and, without the moderating influence of Faisal, passed a resolution that accused the government of acting treacherously by preparing to accede to the French ultimatum.[91]

As the date of Gouraud's ultimatum drew close, Faisal again met with his cabinet on 18 July. They reached a fateful decision to which all, with the exception of Yusuf al-'Azma, concurred. They refused to enter a war with France and agreed to pull back the troops that al-'Azma had deployed in the hills and ridges overlooking the Beqa'a Valley and the Beirut–Damascus road. When Faisal ratified the cabinet decision, al-'Azma rushed to agree and immediately ordered the withdrawal of the Arab soldiers from 'Anjar and its environs. At this juncture, the British liaison officer in Damascus, Colonel Easton, returned to Damascus from Beirut, and informed Faisal in no uncertain terms that he must accept the terms of the French ultimatum. Faisal cabled Gouraud that the cabinet had agreed to a withdrawal of forces from the 'Anjar region, but Gouraud cabled back that the conditions of the ultimatum had to be accepted and implemented in their entirety. In spite of this, he extended the ultimatum to 20 July. On 19 July Faisal wrote to Cousse, the senior French liaison officer in Damascus, that the Syrian government now unconditionally accepted the ultimatum.

On the same day, the Syrian Congress under its new leader, the influential religious figure Rashid Ridha, convened and unanimously passed a resolution to the effect that any government that accepted France's conditions was illegitimate. The resolution was printed and widely distributed, appearing in the official newspaper al-'Asima. A delegation from the congress now visited Faisal at his palace to inform him of its decision. An altercation then occurred between Ridha and Faisal. Faisal angrily asked him, 'Who are you people? It is I who created the state of Syria.' Whereupon Ridha replied, 'Is it you who created Syria?! Syria was there before you were born!'[92] It was symptomatic of the heightened state of public anxiety and tensions that were gripping the capital as a result of Gouraud's ultimatum. Things were careening to a climax. On 20 July the cabinet, not as yet aware of Faisal's earlier communication with Gouraud, finally agreed to accept the terms of the ultimatum and officially notified Cousse to this effect. Cousse in turn encoded the cabinet's decision, and around 6 p.m. gave it to the Damascus telegraph office to send to Gouraud. It was a decision that was unavoidable if the cabinet was realistically to weigh its options and avoid bloodshed. Orders went out to demobilise the army, and units already in Damascus were immediately disbanded. The defensive lines at 'Anjar were finally evacuated. The roads in the area were littered with abandoned weapons and ammunition crates.[93]

As the news of the disbandment of the army and the acceptance of the ultimatum reached the populace, a storm of rejection swept the capital, which entered into the throes of an uprising. A description of the events of the day was given by the director of general security, Taha al-Hashimi, Yasin's brother. Writing in his memoirs, Taha al-Hashimi said, 'On July 20, a number of soldiers left the Baramka barracks [in Damascus] brandishing their weapons and shouting that the government has surrendered to the French . . . They were then joined by other soldiers and the mob swelled. They attacked the Citadel and the arsenal, releasing prisoners and wildly firing.'[94] At that point Zaid, Faisal's brother, exhibited unusual alacrity and courage. Armed with a machine gun, and with only one aide, an Iraqi lieutenant, Baha al-Din Nuri, Zaid drove his car into the demonstrators and fired at them, scattering them in all directions. Subhi al-'Umari, who had witnessed these events, wrote, 'were it not for this bold move on the part of the Amir Zaid and the personal risk that he took, chaos would have engulfed the whole of Damascus and its environs.'[95] After order was finally restored the casualty toll was very high. Nearly two hundred people were killed in the riots of that day.

However, the French army did not pause in its march. Gouraud did not receive Cousse's telegram informing him of the acceptance of the ultimatum on the appointed day. The telegraphic lines between Damascus and Beirut had been cut and the cable only arrived the following day, 21 July.[96] French troops under General Goybet, spearheaded by the Senegalese and the North Africans, advanced towards Damascus, capturing the bridges over the Litani River and reaching their goal for the day at the foot of the Anti-Lebanon mountains. The size of the French army deployed dwarfed that of the opposing Arab forces, even before the unruly demobilisation and disbandment order had been given. Ten battalions of infantry were joined by cavalry and artillery units, numbering in total over twelve thousand fighting men. They were supported by tanks and bombers.

The news of the advance of the French army, in spite of the acceptance of the ultimatum, was received with great alarm by Faisal and his cabinet. Faisal made the strongest possible objection to what he considered to be treacherous French action. It was a betrayal, pure and simple, of the promises made by Gouraud. Fighting could no longer be avoided. It became a matter of honour for Faisal, the officers of the Arab army and the people at large. Faisal made an appearance at the Grand Umayyad Mosque of Damascus, where he addressed the people: 'I had sought to stop the advance of the enemy army by agreeing to their demands but they betrayed us . . . If you want your country then go out and defend it.'[97] Orders went out to the disbanding forces coming out of 'Anjar to reorganise themselves in a defensive line west of Khan Maysaloun, a mere twenty-five kilometres from Damascus. Command of the defensive positions was given to General Hassan al-Hindi, with a direct order from Faisal to defend it to the end.

Popular enthusiasm for war gripped the populace, but most drifted away from committing to the front after it became clear to them that a rabble was no match for a regular, modern army. The popular committees of Shaikh Kamil al-Qassab also fared no better. In spite of bombastic promises, they could only muster a thousand volunteers at most for the front.[98] Shaikh Kamil al-Qassab boasted to Faisal that he could field ten thousand fighters, but when it came to it, he produced a few hundred bullets and £300 gold pounds as his contribution to the war effort. Yusuf al-'Azma presided over the final disposition of the defending forces at Maysaloun. At best the Arab forces defending the lines amounted to three hundred regular troops, the remnants of al-Hindi's division a few hundred along with other soldiers mustered by al-'Azma and irregular forces and volunteers, including Bedouin and camel cavalry, amounting to probably another thousand men. Faisal's essential mission was now to buy time to stop the unequal battle from taking place.

The cabinet now deputised one of its members, the minister of education, Sati' Al-Husri, to travel to the mountain town of Aley, Gouarud's headquarters. Al-Husri was accompanied by Jamil al-Alshi, Faisal's former Beirut representative, and Colonel Toulat. His task was to try to convince Gouraud to halt the French advance. Gouraud was in a belligerent mood and insisted that the French advance was prompted by the fact that the reply to the ultimatum had not come at the appointed time. Gouraud then read out new set of conditions that the Syrian government had to abide by if war were to be averted. The most egregious of these new conditions was the demand that a French mission be installed in Damascus to oversee the implementation of the ultimatum and to chart out a way for the application of the mandate. Gouraud also agreed to extend the truce a further day, until midnight on 23 July. Al-Husri immediately left Gouraud's presence to return to Damascus. He also carried with him a personal letter from Gouraud to Faisal. Al-Husri gave the letter to Faisal, who appeared to be exhausted. He read the letter and listened to al-Husri's report, but said nothing. He called for a cabinet meeting the following day.[99] On 23 July Faisal again met with the cabinet to consider Gouraud's new demands. During the meeting, Cousse came in with a request from Gouraud that the French army be allowed to advance to Maysaloun, where water was plentiful. This was sufficient evidence, even to the waverers, that France was determined to occupy Syria by force. The cabinet decided to send an urgent appeal to all the powers, but for purely symbolic effect. It had rejected Gouraud's latest demands because it considered their acceptance would be a prelude to civil war.

The Battle of Maysaloun and the end of the Kingdom of Syria

The French launched their attack just after dawn on 24 July, towards Wadi al-Qarn and the wells of Maysaloun. The assault was led by tanks, which attacked the centre of the hastily prepared Arab positions while cavalry and other units attacked from the north and south. At first, the resistance from the motley collection of regular Arab troops and volunteers was enough to slow down the tank charge. Fierce fighting raged for the first few hours, with two companies of Senegalese troops surrounded by Arab troops. But the Arab trenches in the centre were finally overrun and the battle turned decisively in favour of the overwhelming superiority of the French. Yusuf al-'Azma, with his reckless bravery, was directing the defence. He had planned to mine the trenches to stop the French advance but was killed at his command post before he could set off the explosions. The Arab forces disintegrated and their retreat turned into a rout when French planes harassed and bombed their lines. By 10 a.m. the battle was over. It was a military disaster, but its name has gone down in Arab history as a synonym for heroism and hopeless courage against huge odds, as well as for treachery and betrayal. The French prepared to advance on the city of Damascus. A day earlier, Aleppo had surrendered peacefully to French forces under General Goubeau.

Faisal had been at the front along the second lines of defence at the village of Alhamma, and he could see the progress of the fighting. As the debacle unfolded, it was decided that the government should withdraw to the town of Kisweh, twenty kilometres south of Damascus and on the Hijaz railroad. Faisal was to go there by car, while the rest of the cabinet would join him by train from Damascus. All the cabinet turned up at the railroad station with the exception of the minister of interior, 'Ala al-Din al-Durubi. He gave a barely credible excuse that he should stay in the capital. In fact he had been in touch with the French who had offered him the post of prime minister in their new government. The party remained in Kisweh, in specially fitted out carriages that served as their sleeping and working quarters, awaiting the arrival of Faisal. At sunset, 24 July, Faisal drove up to Kisweh station in his car with his retinue. He refused to engage in any serious discussion about the next steps for the government. He was subdued and appeared to be awaiting some important news. This finally came in the form of a cable from Nuri al-Sa'id with some falsely reassuring news regarding French intentions, calling Faisal back to Damascus. Faisal appeared comforted by the message, reading into it a cause for some optimism.

The following day, 25 July, more apparently encouraging news reached him from travellers from Damascus, and he made the decision to ask al-Durubi, known for his accommodating attitude with the French, to form a new government. He despatched the royal chamberlain, Ihsan al-Jabiri, to assess al-Durubi's willingness to form a government. But al-Durubi had no compunctions in this regard; he had already cut his deal with the French and had formed a new cabinet, with their knowledge and approval, on the same day. He kept some of the old cabinet members, removing those whom he considered offensive to the French, such as al-Husri, and bringing in others who were considered to be cooperative with the new order. Amongst those was Faisal's former representative in Beirut, Jamil al-Alshi, and the Damascene grandee 'Abd al-Rahman al-Yusuf. Al-Jabiri also met with the sympathetic Italian consul general, the Marquis de Paterno, who informed him that the French were preparing a declaration declaring Faisal's regime illegal and that Faisal's investiture was null and void. The marquis advised al-Jabiri to stress to Faisal the importance of his return to Damascus to counter these moves. Faisal agreed and returned by train to Damascus with a number of his former cabinet members.[100]

Damascus's conqueror, General Goybet, now assembled a new cabinet and read out a prepared statement that damned Faisal and his policies: 'Amir Faisal dragged the country to within an inch of destruction and his responsibility for the bloody disturbances in Syria during the past few months is so clear and so great that it is utterly impossible for him to remain in the country.' When notified of this statement, Faisal immediately sent a telegram to Gouraud, vainly protesting this action and demanding that any communications or instructions given to the government should be made through him. But it was only a matter of time before the French would tire of these legal tussles and take decisive action against him. On 27 July, Colonel Toulat, Faisal's friend and sometime confidant, brought him a short message ordering him to leave the country. The note read: 'I have the honour to inform Your Royal Highness that the Government of the Republic of France has decided to request you together with your family and retinue to leave Damascus as soon as possible by the Hijaz Railroad. A special train will be at the disposal of Your Highness and party.' It was signed by Gouraud. Faisal formally rejected the note. He refused to acknowledge France's right to annul his authority to administer Syria or to abolish his title, 'which was granted by the Syrian people.'[101]

Nevertheless, Faisal knew that his protestations were to no avail. He left Damascus on the night of 27 July by train, heading south towards Dera'a. The only former cabinet officer travelling with him was al-Husri. Before his departure a crowd of people, including a group of young nationalists from notable families, visited him at his palace. Faisal told them that he was not prepared to follow in the footsteps of the Egyptian ruler, the Khedive Tawfiq, who had made a deal with the British to keep his throne. Faisal would not reach an agreement with the French at the expense of his countrymen. He then continued, 'I am leaving now for Dera'a and I don't know where I will be heading afterwards – to the south or to the west. I asked for the support of the country many a time, but they [his detractors] said that I am seeking a position or that I have made secret deals. I told them to trust me and not to disobey me, so that I can find you the right path, but no one was interested . . . When I saw the danger with my own eyes, and pointed out that we had to pursue a policy of moderation and wisdom, no one listened to me. My opinions were scattered to the wind, but no matter. For God will bring ease after discomfit.'[102]

Faisal arrived in Dera'a at night and slept on the train, and his companions waiting for him there were not aware of his arrival until the following morning. The writer As'ad Daghir describes his reaction when he saw Faisal alighting from the train in the morning. 'The King descended from the train with his habitual smile but it concealed great pain. We joined him at the station cafeteria for breakfast which we ate in silence. There was none of his friendly banter. We then left the cafeteria for the town hall where one of its grand salons was prepared as his temporary accommodation . . . His majesty sat at one of the tables and started to write for about fifteen minutes. He then got up and paced the room, repeating the lines of the poet:

> For one who herded sheep in the Lion's domain
> And neglectfully slept,
> Allowed the Lion to be the shepherd[103]

Faisal and his party stayed three days in Dera'a. He used the time to meet local leaders and tribal shaikhs, and a special tent was set up for him near the train for this purpose. Many tribal chiefs and local dignitaries called on him, all proclaiming their allegiance and loyalty, but Faisal knew that the support of the local tribes for resistance to the French would be tepid. It depended entirely on the degree of support that such resistance would generate from the British. The new government was also wary of his movements. The new minister of war, al-Alshi, sent a message to the commander of the Arab forces in Dera'a to keep a close watch on Faisal's movements and not to extend him any assistance.[104] Faisal was now faced with two choices; either to head south towards Transjordan and the Hijaz, or to head west towards Palestine. If he chose the former, this would have indicated his intention to continue to rule over a portion of Syria, and stay in touch with both the Hijaz and the interior of Syria proper, and possibly to organise resistance to the French from a base in Amman. If he moved west towards Haifa, he would have indicated his intention to proceed to Europe, where he would bring his case to an international audience and try to recover his position. Each course had its supporters and detractors, and Faisal hesitated between the two. The Iraqi members of his entourage tenled to push him towards organising resistance in the Hawran, and to continue in guerrilla warfare against the French. Others, partly because they were unsure of the loyalty of the Hawran tribes and the Druze, sought a more diplomatic policy based on reaching an agreement with the French, or, failing that, to bring Faisal's case to the peace conference.[105] But Faisal did not have the luxury to debate the matter extensively. Many of his advisers and supporters had scattered, some to escape the wrath of the French, others to reach an accommodation with the new order.[106] He badly needed to consult with Hussein as well as with his erstwhile allies the British. Faisal was also in dire need of funds as he had left Damascus with no money, and had to ask his father for financial help.

Faisal's staying in Dera'a disturbed the French, as they thought he might be planning to raise a tribal revolt against them. They instructed al-Durubi to send a cable to Faisal, under al-Durubi's signature, demanding that Faisal depart for either the Hijaz or Haifa. Al-Durubi pleaded in the cable for Faisal 'to hurry in order to save the Hawran from disaster and ruination'. On the same day, a French plane dropped leaflets over Dera'a and other towns of the Hawran, calling on the people to drive Faisal out of the region. If Faisal refused to leave, the French warned the inhabitants, they would bomb his encampment. They gave the inhabitants a deadline of ten hours for Faisal's train to leave the country. Under these circumstances, Faisal had little choice but to prepare to leave Syria. He chose to go to Haifa.

Faisal then asked 'Adil Arslan, who was already in Palestine, to contact the new high commissioner in Palestine, Sir Herbert Samuel, to authorise his journey to Haifa. The British welcomed Faisal's turn towards Palestine rather than towards Transjordan. A move south would have alerted the French that Faisal might be planning to initiate hostilities against them, from a base that was secure inside British-administered territory. But the British were not prepared to accept such an eventuality.

Faisal's train left Dera'a for Haifa, arriving there on 1 August 1920. He had left Syria and its crown for good.

Thus ended two and a half tumultuous and event-laden years in which Faisal had sought an independent state for the Arabs in Syria. He now turned away from Syria towards new horizons, chastened by the denouement of the last few weeks of his kingdom, but wiser in the ways of the Great Powers and the treacherous currents of Arab political ambitions and rivalries.

CHAPTER 15

ADRIFT

FAISAL'S IMMERSION in the merciless, cynical world of great power rivalries and interests, and the disastrous end to his kingdom in Syria, would have embittered and even broken other men. The expectations and hopes raised by the Arab Revolt lay in ruins all around him. When it came down to it, the Sykes–Picot Agreement and the Balfour Declaration, the two emblematic statements of real Allied intentions, had easily prevailed over the calculated vagueness of the McMahon letters and the other declarations by the British and French that seemed to give credence to the idea of Arab independence. Syria and Lebanon were now firmly under French control. Five weeks after the fall of Damascus to French forces, Gouraud announced that Lebanon would be granted its formal, separate status, with the addition of the Beqa'a Valley and the coastal littoral including Tripoli. Maronite ambitions for their 'Greater Lebanon' state, carved out of historic Syria, were now realised. Palestine was pointedly excluded from any connection with Syria proper, with a high commissioner who was a committed Zionist charged with implementing the terms of the mandate that specifically called for the realisation of the idea of a Jewish National Home. Iraq, the other great territory of the former Ottoman Empire, was in the throes of a rebellion, whose outcome could only be the further deepening of British control. In Syria, Faisal's allies amongst the nationalist forces had been often more dangerous to his rule, in their recklessness and disregard for political realities, than his erstwhile enemies the French. There was a legion of disgruntled notables and ambitious politicians who had no compunction with regard to cutting deals with the French to advance their personal goals. The Hijaz itself, impoverished and under constant financial pressure, was ruled by a sulking and increasingly erratic Hussein, threatened by the forces of ibn Saud on the one hand, and on the other by ever more exasperated and testy relations with Britain, its main foreign benefactor.

But Faisal was determined to learn from the bitter experiences of the recent past. He would not allow the scale of the betrayals and volte-faces of his erstwhile friends and allies, notably the British, and the ruinous outcome in Syria to overwhelm him. This was the first real indicator that he had developed profound statesman-like qualities, and it would colour his persona until the end of his life. Faisal had not changed his overarching goal – the establishment of an independent confederation of states for the Arabs – but after Syria he would be extremely wary of allowing nationalists and radicals to outflank him, and he would not easily concede to their ill-considered, maximalist positions. He developed a healthy scepticism regarding the assertions of politicians and religious leaders who claimed that they spoke for the public interest and that they could mobilise hundreds of thousands of people. The feeble response to calls for mobilisation and to confront the French had been amply demonstrated in the Maysaloun debacle. Faisal became more self-confident, aware that his own instincts would have been a far better guide for action than the course that he had been obliged to follow. These instincts involved a healthy respect for political realities and for power on the ground, for appreciating the weaknesses of Arab societies entering the modern era, saddled with limited resources and a backward political culture, and for understanding that divisiveness and fragmentation were an ever present threat and could only be transcended by strong leadership that provided purposeful direction. Faisal was also aware that force and coercion had to be available to a ruler faced with internal dissension and external threats. The patent inadequacies of the Arab Army in Syria were a constant refrain; no state could possibly expect to survive in the area without a properly constituted fighting force. These themes would determine his position on a host of issues as he prepared to confront his predicament, adrift in a world where the Great Powers ruled the roost.

His first challenge was to re-establish his alliance with Britain, the only power that had the means to affect the course of events and to remedy, even if only partly, the ruinous outcome of the Syrian interlude. The British were seriously discomfited by the declaration of Syrian independence and had become passive observers of the last days of the Syrian kingdom as it fell to France. They were alarmed by the rumours that France wished to maintain a form of monarchical rule for Syria, and that the French were prepared to invite Amir Sa'id al-Jaza'iri back to Damascus to take up the now vacant throne. '[It] had occurred to me that the French might contemplate putting the Emir Mahommed Sa'id in the place of Feisal. This would be a very unfortunate selection and one which His Majesty's government could not regard with equanimity', wrote Curzon on 31 July 1920 to the British ambassador in Paris, the earl of Derby, in an early response to the fall of the Arab government.[1] The British, however, were remarkably composed about the brutal way in which France had

exercised its prerogatives. Curzon had met Berthelot, the leading French official at the Quai d'Orsay, in Boulogne on 27 July, to review the situation in Syria.
Curzon was considerate of the French response. Even though it might have
been a trifle too forceful by his reckoning, he nevertheless accepted it because
of their historic alliance and mutual commitments. 'We [the British] should
adhere as faithfully to that engagement as I was convinced the French
Government would to the corresponding settlement in Mesopotamia and
Palestine', he wrote to Sir George Grahame, the British ambassador in Belgium.[2]
As for Faisal, Curzon haughtily acknowledged some residual concern for him:
'[Faisal] was brought into certain relations with us, both in connection with the
pledges we had given to his father as to the independence of the Arab countries, and also because of his connection with the areas for which we had
accepted a mandate.'[3] These were now the main reasons of state for which
Britain continued to hold out some prospects for Faisal. But another had
recently been added for the first time. The acting civil administrator for
Mesopotamia, Arnold Talbot Wilson, had sent a cable on 31 July from Baghdad
to the Foreign Office in which he brought up the possibility of Faisal being king
of Mesopotamia. 'Will His Majesty's Government consider possibility of
offering him [Faisal] Amirate of Mesopotamia? Objections entertained on this
for Amir [Faisal] have hitherto been primarily that no suitable person could be
found. We have always regarded Feisal as being booked for Syria. Nothing that
I have heard during the last few months has led me to modify my views of
unsuitability of 'Abdulla and our experience of last few weeks in Baghdad
makes it fairly clear that no local candidate would be successful in obtaining
sufficient local support to enable him to make good. Feisal alone of all Arabian
potentates has any idea of practical difficulties of running a civilised government on Arab lines.'[4]

But the throne of Mesopotamia was hardly on Faisal's mind as he made his
way from Dera'a to Haifa.

Preparations for a return to Europe

Faisal arrived in Haifa on 1 August and was cordially received by its British-
appointed governor, Colonel Edward Alexander Stanton. On the journey, the
train stopped at Affoula, a small station inside British-administered Palestine.
Faisal was offered some tea from the canteen. However, later in Haifa the penny-
pinching accounting department of the British army in Palestine presented him
with a trifling bill for the refreshments.[5] It was a salutary, if startling, lesson to
remind him of his now much reduced circumstances. Faisal, with a few of his
followers, was accommodated at the house of a Mrs Newton, a staunch supporter
of the Arab cause. The governor continued to be accommodating towards Faisal

and Zaid, but he was less so to the stream of visitors who sought a meeting with
Faisal. 'Faisal and Z and their ADC's are no trouble, but it is the other notables
who are round the place and in and out like a swarm of bees, and one never
knows how many meals are required for lunch or dinner', wrote the governor to
Ronald Storrs, then the British-appointed governor of Jerusalem. He listed the
entourage that wanted to go with Faisal to Egypt, en route to Europe, and
groaned, 'They cannot stay here indefinitely.'[6]

For the next few days in Haifa, Faisal sought to reconnect with the powers
that be in the Near East, and above all with Allenby, who was then in Alexandria.
However, Allenby avoided meeting Faisal at all costs. He cabled Curzon on 2
August regarding Faisal's requests for a meeting: 'I have no advice to give to
Feisal, being unaware of future attitude of His Majesty's Government towards
him, and any reception of him would certainly make a bad impression on
French. I suggest he should be conveyed to some station on Hedjaz Railroad,
such as 'Amman, and from there to proceed to Medina. If you consider it
desirable Feisal should be received on behalf of His Majesty's Government, I
submit under all circumstances it is preferable that High Commissioner
Jerusalem [Samuel] should receive him.'[7] It was an uncharitable and inglorious
statement coming from Allenby towards his wartime ally and co-combatant,
but it reflected the widespread sentiment amongst senior British officials in
the Near East that Faisal should voluntarily remove himself from the scene to
avoid any possible embarrassment to the British by his lingering presence.
Faisal suspected as much, and he notified Samuel that he wished to proceed to
Europe at his own expense. Faisal also stressed to Samuel that he did not
seek to complicate the relations between Britain and France, nor was he
planning any move against the French.[8] Curzon instructed Samuel to inform
Faisal that the British government valued his statement that he did not wish to
sow discord between the British and the French. Furthermore, the British
government 'are fully aware that he [Faisal] had made every effort to sustain
a difficult position . . . and that they trust they may in the future have an opportunity of showing to him that his loyal attitude to the British Government
has not been forgotten.'[9] It was enough of a signal from Curzon that he could
still try to salvage his position, and that not all the doors had been slammed
shut against him.

On 9 August, Faisal wrote a detailed letter to his father about the tumultuous events of the past few months that had ended in the tragedy of Maysaloun.
He began by admitting that

duty obliged us to be flexible with the great powers because of their ambitions
and our weaknesses. But two matters stopped us from achieving this end:
Firstly, the principles [that Hussein had enunciated] meant totally refusing

compromise and flexibility on any issue affecting the call for the independence of the Arab lands. Secondly, those hot-headed youth demanding independence adamantly opposed any compromise, especially with the French government . . . I could have struck at these [radical] parties but I feared the judgement of history. Whenever I had agreed on some matter [with the Great Powers] irrespective of its favourable conditions [it] ended up with me being blamed and condemned . . . The greedy foreign power was simply awaiting the right opportunity to pounce, massing its forces and the [Syrian] nation just watching transfixed as if it had no implications for it. I regretfully must admit that the nation talks and does nothing . . . We introduced conscription to develop a 30,000 strong army, but those fleeing from service were greater in number than those who served. The nation ran away from any financial contributions to the war effort.

Under such impossible circumstances, Faisal wrote, he had no choice but to seek a political way out of the impending debacle. But he was blocked in this endeavour by Gouraud. 'Western countries falsely saw us as a nation that could defend itself and had prepared itself for a long struggle, but I knew that we could not fight for more than three days . . . On this basis, we reluctantly had to accept the [French] ultimatum . . . especially because the British government had informed that they would not interfere and advised me to deal with the French.' Faisal now turned to the reprehensible role of the radical parties that did so much to reduce whatever fighting chances the Arab government had. They encouraged a chaotic atmosphere of violence and mayhem in the capital, a day before the ultimatum was due. 'While the enemy was at the gates, the armouries were being looted and we ended up fighting between ourselves. The mob was at the beck and call of the radical parties and firing could be heard everywhere. But the government showed its mettle and deployed machine gun units at critical junctions. My life and that of the government was in real danger.' Faisal then bitterly complained of Gouraud's duplicity. The news of the French march towards Damascus had hit the capital like a thunderbolt. 'Even those who sought compromise knowing of our weaknesses now became agitated, favouring death over surrender. People chaotically started moving towards the front, with no weapons, and I could not stop them. I was reduced to saying that we cannot properly defend ourselves but we could not ban the people from war either . . . I was at the second line of defence [at Maysaloun] and I witnessed with great sorrow the routing of the people who fled the battlefield, and I knew it was all over . . . I then returned to Damascus to stop the French from taking advantage of my absence from the capital and announcing my overthrow, but only after I ascertained that we had no weapons left and we could not transport the heavy equipment.'

Faisal then described his stay in the Dera'a area, where he saw for himself the reluctance of the Hawran people to fight on. In any event Faisal knew that 'the matter [of Arab independence] was one that could not be gained by force of arms but only by political means. I was then determined to demand our rights in front of the international conclaves rather than stay in Southern Syria such as Amman or Ma'an ... I nevertheless sent Sharif Muhammad Ali al-Bedaiwi [one of Faisal's distant relatives] to Amman to serve as a rallying point for us.'[10] It was a remarkably frank letter, and Faisal neither embellished his record nor sought to escape from the terrible consequences of the Syrian catastrophe. It was part of the difficult self-assessment that Faisal was undertaking. As 'Awni 'Abd al-Hadi wrote in his memoirs about this period, 'Faisal was critically reviewing past actions, showing his regret at some of them, and openly criticising the actions of others.'[11]

Faisal was in dire need of funds. He had left Damascus with very little money and had to look after his entourage and fund his journey to Europe. He could not and should not ask the British for any handouts. This was unacceptable under the circumstances. He wired his father for money and Hussein responded with unaccustomed alacrity. He sent Faisal £25,000, which Faisal received in Haifa, to cover his immediate expenses and to prepare for the journey to Europe.

Faisal remained in Haifa until 18 August. The news from Syria was uniformly depressing, of the deprivations of the French and the traitorous acts of former supporters. Sati' al-Husri, who was with Faisal in Haifa, wrote in his narrative *Yawm Maysaloun*, 'We received a good deal of news, most of it highly unpleasant, about the oppressions of the French and the acts of traitors and paid agents. We also obtained details of the fines imposed by the French on various parts of the country and the texts of the death sentences meted out to many nationalists by military courts. We read articles in the hired press in Damascus which harshly criticised the Arab government and praised the French. Military courts passed sentence without a trial, without even calling for a trial ... Every day we met a number of [political] refugees in Haifa.'[12] Faisal was greatly distressed at the news from Syria and at the cascade of death sentences passed by the French. The list of condemned men included some of his closest collaborators, such as 'Awni 'Abd al-Hadi, Ahmad Qadri and Ihsan al-Jabiri.[13] (In fact, they had already escaped from Syria.) Faisal had now made up his mind to go as soon as possible to Switzerland, where the peace conference was meeting and where Lloyd George was expected. But as passage through France was impossible, he had to await a ship that would sail to Italy, whence he would then proceed to Switzerland. Faisal was also determined not to sail on any French or British-flagged ship. The first available sailing was on 20 August from Port Said in Egypt, steaming for Naples in Italy.

The train for Egypt carrying Faisal and his small party left Haifa in the morning on 18 August. Before he left, Faisal gave Colonel Stanton £1,500 to cover his expenses. Faisal was met at Lydd station on the Palestinian coast by the high commissioner Herbert Samuel, and by Ronald Storrs. The latter, writing in his memoirs, described the scene in the following terms: 'I went with Sir Herbert to greet Faisal and Zaid when the train of exile passed through Ludd, where we mounted him a guard of honour a hundred strong. He carried himself with dignity and the noble resignation of Islam: *Nor called the gods with angry spite / To vindicate his helpless right*, though the tears stood in his eyes and he was wounded to the soul.'[14] At Qantara on the Suez Canal, Faisal was met by 'Abd al-Malik al-Khatib, the representative of the Hijaz government in Egypt. He gave Faisal and the rest of his party passports of the kingdom of Hijaz, to facilitate their passage to Europe. Al-Khatib also passed on a message from Hussein. The letter instructed Faisal not to go to France, not to discuss matters of high policy with anyone except the British government, and that any discussions or negotiations must be entirely based on the Hussein–McMahon letters. Hussein also admonished Faisal for declaring a separate kingdom and not being content to remain as Hussein's representative. He based his remarks on the spurious grounds that the Allies would have respected Faisal more as they had already recognised Hussein as a friendly power.[15] After al-Khatib had left, Faisal and his party had to await another train from across the Suez Canal to take them to Port Said. Several of Faisal's group took leave of him, as Faisal simply did not have the funds to take a large entourage. Ahmad Qadri, whom he would have normally taken, excused himself as he was personally in need of funds and had to take up his medical practice in Egypt to make ends meet. Others who stayed behind were assigned a small stipend to be funded by the Hijazi government's budget for Egypt. The final group that Faisal selected to accompany him to Europe included Zaid, Nuri al-Sa'id, Sati' al-Husri, Ihsan al-Jabiri and Tahsin Qadri, Faisal's aide-de-camp. As the Egyptian government did not officially recognise his status, he was left unescorted at Qantara station; there Faisal was espied, sitting alone on top of his luggage and awaiting the departure of his train.[16] On the morning of 20 August, he and his party boarded the cargo ship *Strobi*, which had room for passengers, at Port Said, destined for Naples.

The sailing was calm and provided ample time for reflection and assessments. Sati' al-Husri, writing in *Yawm Maysaloun*, described conversations with Faisal.

'The five days on board ship provided a relaxed atmosphere in which King Faisal could both analyse the past and think about the future. They also enabled me to have long talks with him and study his psychology. In truth, these sessions were a continuation of the conferences began in Haifa. There the King was distracted by the many foreigners as well as Syrians and Palestinians whom he had to meet. Our conversations were often interrupted and only rarely completed. On shipboard, however, the peaceful mood was conducive to sustained thinking . . . When reviewing the past King Faisal critically exposed the right and the wrong in our policies and did not hesitate to express his regret and indignation at the actions and attitudes of certain people. But in general his thoughts were focused on the future and his plans to rectify the errors of the past. He showed his concern for the future particularly during the last days of the voyage, when he gave me a new assignment . . . The King asked me to go to Istanbul and make contact with the Kemalists in order to learn how much aid we might expect from them in our struggle against the French.'[17]

Faisal arrived in Naples on 25 August. His immediate plan was bare: to make an appearance at the highest Allied forum and with his presence confront the Allies with their unfulfilled promises and re-present the case for Arab independence. He had lost whatever legitimacy and power he had had as king of Syria. He had not been in high-level communication with the British. The interlude in Palestine was spent more in receiving visitors and well-wishers than in discussing matters of high policy. The only serious discussions he had with a senior British official were with Herbert Samuel at Lydd station. Samuel was interested only in the Palestine mandate and extending its territory to include southern Syria, in effect, Transjordan.[18] He had had little time or inclination to advance Faisal's cause beyond ensuring that Transjordan did not become a platform for anti-French agitation. Faisal had to manoeuvre in this environment of collapsed power and constrained prospects. He developed a two-pronged strategy to confront his dilemma. The first was to reach out to Mustafa Kemal, both to seek out the prospects for an Arab–Turkish alliance in the event that widespread armed resistance to French and British ambitions became necessary, as well as to raise his 'nuisance' value to the Allies. The second part of his strategy was to influence as much as possible the direction of British policy in the Middle East, especially the manner in which they were to administer their mandates in Mesopotamia, Palestine and Transjordan.

Faisal had charged Sati' al-Husri with the task of establishing contacts with the Kemalists. Faisal himself had made a number of sympathetic remarks regarding the resistance of the Turks to Allied occupation. He always made a careful distinction between the aims of the Arab Revolt against the Ottoman Empire, and the right of the Turks to self-determination in their own lands. In Syria, of course, the Arab government effectively denied the use of the Aleppo–Rayyaq railroad to French forces, and thereby indirectly supported the Kemalist war effort in Cilicia. Al-Husri himself was a good choice of envoy to the

Kemalists. He had been a loyal Ottoman functionary, spoke Turkish better than Arabic and knew some of the leading players in the Kemalist camp. Al-Husri took the first boat from Italy to Istanbul, met in secret with a number of Kemalists, and returned soon thereafter to Italy, which also served as a base for the Kemalist leadership. But these meetings did not produce any significant results, partly because the Kemalists saw the British rather than the French as their mortal enemies, and partly because of the lingering resentments about the Arab Revolt.[19] In fact, when Faisal first arrived in Naples, a news agency confused him with his father and circulated the news that King Hussein had arrived in Europe. The erroneous news item was picked up by a Turkish newspaper, *Yeni Gun*, owned by a member of the Turkish Grand Assembly who was close to the Kemalists,[20] which ran a scathing article denouncing King Hussein and accusing him of the vilest crimes against the Muslim people and allowing Muslim territory to fall into foreign occupation. The resentment against the Arab Revolt was deeply ingrained in the Turkish psyche, irrespective of whether one was a defender or opponent of the Ottoman cause.

Stuck in Italy

Faisal immediately left Naples for Rome, from where he took a train to Milan and thence a train northwards to Switzerland. He had met briefly with a British embassy official in Rome, who had expressed some disquiet about his upcoming journey. Also he seemed to have received a hint from the embassy official that he should reconsider his trip to Switzerland, which soon materialised into a firm demand. As Faisal's train approached the Swiss frontier, he was met by General Haddad Pasha, his representative in London, with a verbal message from General Clayton, whom he had met at the Foreign Office, to the effect that Faisal should stay in Italy and not proceed to Switzerland. Faisal later reported to his father what Haddad had told him. 'The British government would be deeply appreciative if you remain in northern Italy for several weeks more. They advise you not to proceed to Switzerland because it is a country full of foreigners intriguing, and it is not appropriate that you should find yourself in such an environment. At the same time, they do not wish to see you in the same country at the same time as the British Prime Minister, because if you were there you would no doubt have to meet him. And he is not prepared at this point to consider your demands, and this might make you regret your meeting and doubt the intentions of the British government towards you. On this basis, the British government asks you to agree to postpone your visit until the Prime Minister returns. The British government would then have had more time to consider your case and you will be advised to come to England for further discussions.'[21] However, there was another reason why Faisal was discouraged from going to Switzerland: the British must have got wind of his attempts to reach out to the Turkish resistance. In a note of 30 August 1920, Lord Hardinge recorded that he had informed the French chargé d'affaires in London that '[the British] had done our utmost to prevent Feisal from coming to Switzerland, where it would be very undesirable that he should be in touch with the Young Turks and other disloyal sections.'[22]

Faisal acceded to Haddad's message and re-routed his journey to Varese, a suburb of Milan. He and his entourage stayed there for a few days and then headed for Como, north of Milan and close to the Swiss border. Meanwhile, Faisal's lieutenants who had remained in Europe for the peace conference were frantically searching for him. Rustum Haidar had left Paris on 28 August for Lucerne, where Lloyd George was supposed to be on vacation, accompanied by George Lutfallah, brother of Habib Lutfallah who was head of the Hijaz peace delegation in Paris.[23] Arriving at the National Hotel in Lucerne, they found out that Faisal's entourage had reserved and then cancelled their rooms. Confusion reigned as Haidar could not locate Faisal's whereabouts. In the evening, however, the hotel manager showed him the name of Ihsan al-Jabiri, who was staying at the hotel, and who told him about the change in plans following Haddad's interception of Faisal's train. Finally, on 1 September, Haddad cabled George Lutfallah to tell them to proceed to Como where Faisal was expected the following day.[24] Faisal had been booked to stay at the Metropole, a rather dingy establishment in Como, but had then relocated to the Villa d'Este Hotel in Cernobbio, on Lake Como. His entourage remained in the Metropole and Faisal had no further funds to give them to relocate to a more suitable hotel. All those who wished to change hotels had to bear the difference in costs themselves.

For the next three months, Faisal was ensconced in northern Italy. He was awaiting developments from the peace conference, from the Near East, and above all from Britain, to clarify his position and to allow him to plan for subsequent events. He had not quite given up on recovering the lost ground in Syria, this time by recourse to international law. While in Rome he met a well-known professor of international law, Professor Bonfanti of Rome University, whom he asked to prepare a legal disposition on the Syrian case and the actions of the French government. Faisal promised to give Bonfanti all the necessary documents and information to pursue action against the French. Bonfanti produced his report, which was supportive of the Arab cause, but Faisal could find no opportunity to pursue its recommendations.[25] The public acknowledgement by the British government of France's actions in Syria had simply precluded any possibility of his return there.

The day-to-day routine in Como was tedious, and there was frequent bickering and back-biting between members of Faisal's entourage. Haidar records in his diaries the increasing ennui felt by him and a sense of despondency that descended on the group. Faisal himself was affected by the anxiety-inducing drift. At one point he announced that he would become a revolutionary Bolshevik if he were forced to return to the Hijaz empty-handed. 'My father is asking me to return to the Hijaz and settle in Wejh. What is the use of this? I will be one of the many who are stuck there like my brothers. It will be said that the Arab idea is now a hopeless case. My departure [for the Hijaz] would put an end to the Arab idea, at least for the moment . . . But my presence here [in Como] is pointless. What must I do? I don't believe the British would do anything under present circumstances. There is nothing left for me but . . . Arabs fight well if they are sure of foreign backing but . . .?'[26] Faisal showed his worry in a cable to Haddad in London. 'I want you to do your utmost to get me out of this place.'[27]

Haidar noted that no one was sure where Faisal actually stood. He could not meet Allenby in Egypt; he had come to Europe without prior agreement with the British. And here they were, sitting in a lakeside resort out of season, not quite sure what to expect. 'Our daily existence is miserable,' noted Haidar, 'And one would wish to leave all of this and depart, but a sense of obligation keeps us here to bear this tedium. We are staying at a modest hotel where our food and rooms are paid for [by Faisal's father], but anything else – coffee, tea, beer (!), laundry, we have to pay for. Others [presumably referring to the wealthy Lutfallahs] smoke cigars and walk around in new suits . . . We are cut off from the world's news. We read about it in the newspapers but these only arrive intermittently.'[28]

There were unpleasant incidents and strange occurrences during their stay in Como. For instance, a blonde femme fatale had insinuated herself into the entourage. Faisal, who appeared fascinated by her, challenged her directly and asked her if she was spying for anyone. The woman denied that she was a spy, but Faisal arranged for her to meet with a young Italian staying at the hotel who plied her with drink. While inebriated, the woman blurted out that she was working undercover, but in time she was to be replaced by a more professional agent. The woman was most likely a con artist. In the same period, a sum of £E175 and 6,000 Swiss francs was stolen from Faisal's room, but far more valuable jewels and other cash had been overlooked. They amounted to more than £15,000 sterling. A man was seized but an accomplice had driven off in a car.[29]

In the middle of this enforced retreat, a delegation from the Indian Khilafat movement, led by Maulana Muhammad Ali, visited Faisal in Cernobbio.[30] The group was in Europe to influence the Allies not to abolish the caliphate. It was a curious meeting as the Khilafat movement's leadership had generally supported the Ottoman cause and was highly critical of the Arab Revolt.

Nevertheless, Faisal met them, partly to gain support from the large Indian Muslim community and partly to deflect blame from the Hashemites for breaking a supposedly united Muslim front during the war. Haidar wrote in his diary: 'An Indian delegation led by [Maulana] Muhammad Ali and his colleagues met with His Majesty and a long discussion ensued along old lines: the need for Muslim cooperation, transcending the ill-will between Arab and Turk ... the necessity for the Arabs to acknowledge the caliphate. [Faisal] answered them that indeed Muslims must work together, but the call for the Caliph's success [after the ritual prayers] were not terminated until the Turks had emptied the coffers of the Prophet's Mosque in Medina. His father [Hussein] had warned them against doing that. His Hashemite Majesty [Hussein] does not want the Caliphate and this is a matter for the Muslims to decide. It is the Turks now who are avoiding helping the Arabs. Faisal then strangely added: the news that there are negotiations [between the Arabs] and the Turks and Jamal are correct but ... there ought to be a conference of all Muslims either in Mecca or Medina during the upcoming Haj.' The discussions, according to Haidar, were testy, and harsh words were exchanged that did not become Faisal. 'Muhammad Ali asked [Faisal] if it was true that he had accepted the idea of a mandate. Faisal answered him that it was a lie. If he had accepted the mandate there would have been no bloodshed. Muhamad Ali then said that they wished that all the lands of the Arabs would be a refuge for Muslims from the deprivations of foreigners. Unfortunately, when al-Sayyid Hassan [Mahmud al-Hassan, an important Indian Muslim leader] was in Mecca, he was arrested by the Sharif [Hussein] and handed over to the British.[31] This left a bad impression amongst Indian Muslims.' With the meeting ending on this sour note, Faisal was in no mood to entertain his visitors. They dined alone at the Villa d'Este, their bill being picked up by George Lutfallah.

With plenty of time on his hands, Faisal wrote two long and important notes, one to his father and the other to Lloyd George. The letter to Lloyd George was written early in his stay at Como. Dated 11 September 1920, its purpose was to present the details of the Arab case, its inherent justice and the events that had led to the debacle in Syria. The letter, which was hand-carried to London by General Haddad, was also intended to counter French propaganda that portrayed Faisal as duplicitous and driven by illegitimate dynastic desires, and the Arab government as chaotically incompetent and working against Allied interests. It was couched in chivalrous terms regarding his family and its tireless work for the Arab cause. It was his family's honour and dignity that were now compromised by the defeat in Syria, for the Arabs had gone to war because of his father's leadership of the cause, and he in turn relied on British promises. Faisal then launched a detailed condemnation of French designs on Syria and the aggressive intentions of General Gouraud. The occupation of Damascus was illegal and France had acted throughout as an occupying power. However, Britain was different. 'We [the Arabs] negotiated with the British and with no one else. The promises that were made to us were made by the British and no one else . . . It is up to the British only to see that they keep to their promises.' Faisal then said that he wished to visit London as his father's representative, carrying with him the authorisation to discuss the entire gamut of issues affecting the Arab cause.[32]

The letter to his father, dated 10 November 1920, was more analytic and prescriptive. To some extent it was in response to his father's message, relayed through 'Abd al-Malik al-Khatib, that Faisal had grievously erred by declaring the kingdom of Syria.

> I do not wish to blame this party or that, or take the entire responsibility on myself or deny any . . . I only wish to present the truth and examine the main reasons that brought us to this condition. Firstly, the switch in British policy and its disregard for the promises it made to Your Majesty. And the principle factors that drove British policy in this direction were French ambitions in Syria and the focus of World Jewry on Palestine . . . Secondly, the disunity of opinion in Arab lands made it easy for foreigners to divide and belittle our cause. Thirdly, the Syrians' penchant for talking and not acting. We had placed our hopes on the people of Syria as they were the main props of the nationalist movement and it was they who pushed us to rise [against the Ottomans] . . . They could have been that [the drivers of the Arab movement] if they had not exaggerated in their bravado and had done their duty . . . but with the greatest regret this experience was deeply painful.

Faisal then went on bitterly to describe their prevarications, fooling not only themselves with regard to their capabilities and courage, but also fooling Faisal. The newspapers also played their part in irresponsibly agitating the public. 'It is easy to call for war, but it is an altogether different matter to wage it . . . I had sensed that the people as a whole were not desirous of war . . . and I knew that the truth would reveal itself at the critical moment and this was what I had feared . . . And if [the revolt in] Iraq had not happened [the Syrian debacle] would have been a shameful episode . . . But it is an Arab trait not to forget . . . The present situation in Syria will not last and there is bound to be a violent reaction soon. Abandoning any notions of despair and continuing in our struggle is the best power that we have for the future.'

Faisal continued by complaining to his father about the actions of Habib Lutfallah, who had given several newspaper interviews in France, appropriating for himself the role of Hussein's representative in Europe. 'I had asked

Your Majesty to cancel whatever previous authority you had given [to Habib Lutfallah] and to clearly designate me in that role to dispel any rumours and misunderstandings. It has reached the point that in Egypt it has been said that your trust in me was shaken and that it now resided with Habib Lutfallah.'[33] Faisal was also aware that the British government had sought to convince Hussein to ratify the Treaty of Versailles. Hussein, however, had adamantly refused to do so, insisting that Britain first meet its commitments to the Arabs. In addition, his attitude to the British had markedly changed from cooperation to obstruction, and this change was critically noted in British despatches. In the letter, Faisal implored his father to reconsider his position vis-à-vis the Treaty of Versailles, on account of the obvious benefits that would accrue to the Hijaz state by its formal membership within the League of Nations. Of course, Article 22 of the Versailles Treaty dealt with the matter of mandates, but Hussein could express his reservations about this article while approving the treaty as a whole. Hussein's position of linking the signing of the treaty with the fulfilment of Britain's promises to the Arabs was bound to be ineffectual, and, moreover, might alienate the British. Faisal's entreaties to his father were also probably influenced by his need to show the British that, in this instance at least, he was also working in their interests. In addition, Faisal advised his father to establish contacts with the Bolsheviks who were then reaching out to the Muslims of the east. Faisal's letter was hand-carried to Hussein by Zaid, who was returning to Mecca at their father's insistence. Faisal had become very attached to Zaid and thought highly of his capabilities and qualities. He had asked his father that Zaid be allowed to remain in Europe, to complete his studies at a British university, and for Faisal to groom him for further tasks in the service of his family and the Arab cause generally.

At last, Faisal's wait in Italy was about to end. On 21 October, Faisal had sent a letter with Nuri al-Sa'id to Curzon to the effect that he wished to visit London in a private capacity if the British government found it difficult to receive him officially. He wished to meet King George V and thank him personally, on behalf of his father, for the gifts that George V had given to Hussein. Meanwhile, Hussein had formally appointed Faisal as head of the Hijaz delegation in Europe, which facilitated his reception in London. Curzon acknowledged Faisal's new role and on 11 November instructed the British consul general in Milan to inform Faisal that George V was in a position to receive him. Faisal could not proceed through France because of the hostile French attitude towards him. He had to plan a circuitous route to England that passed through Austria, Germany and then Belgium. On 28 November 1920, Faisal set off to England with his small party. His motorcade passed through Verona and then through the Brenner Pass to Austria and thence to Munich. The German authorities were notified of the passage of Faisal's motorcade and assigned

a young foreign service officer, Fritz Groppa, to accompany them. Groppa
would later become an ambassador in Baghdad in the 1930s, achieving
prominence – and notoriety – in his advocacy of close collaboration between
Iraq and Germany.

Groppa describes his journey, which had its moments of high drama,
through Germany with Faisal and his entourage in his memoirs. Unexpectedly,
the train had to pass through a French-occupied part of Germany, and had to
stop for the passenger wagons to be examined.

> We turned off the lights in our two cabins. The King was a bit anxious, pacing
> to and from in the wagon. As for Amir ʿAdil Arslan, who had a death sentence
> hanging over him, passed *in absentia* by the French for his activities in Syria
> against them, he held in his hand his gun with the safety clutch off [, saying]
> 'The French will not take me alive'. As we reached Hennef, the French troops
> in their metal helmets and with their rifles slung against their shoulders, came
> out to guard and inspect the train. They checked on the various cabins but did
> not search ours as the lights had been turned off. The stop at Hennef took
> nearly 15 minutes and then the train started on its journey again. We reached
> the British zone after a short while, and we all let out a great sigh of relief.
> After Cologne, where we had dinner in one of the restaurants, I accompanied
> the King to the Belgian frontiers. There he took off his Longines watch and
> gave it to me.[34]

Intimations of a new kingdom

Curzon's invitation to Faisal to come to London had very little to do with
allowing him to thank George V personally for his gifts to Hussein. It had been
a carefully considered matter and came at a time when the British were seriously debating the form of government for their mandate in Iraq. The India
Office, which was then directly responsible for the administration of Iraq
through its Baghdad Residency, had little truck with the idea of Arab independence or self-government. Sir Arthur Hirtzel, head of the India Office
Political Department, had caustically noted that '[the Arabs] are no more
capable of administering severally or collectively than the Red Indians'.[35]
However, the India Office's adamant opposition to any 'native' government in
Iraq came to an end following the rebellion in Iraq in the summer of 1920. It
became a matter of urgency to find a political solution to the crisis in the
country that would protect Britain's interests and meet the clamour for an
indigenous government.

Faisal and his party arrived in England on 1 December 1920, by the boat
train from Ostend to Dover. There they were met by Kinahan Cornwallis,

General Haddad and Fahmi al-Muddaris, and drove to London where they were put up at Claridge's Hotel.[36] Faisal was apprehensive about his forthcoming meetings in London, having become suspicious of Curzon's true intentions. After all, the disaster that had befallen him in Syria had come under Curzon's watch at the Foreign Office. Faisal felt that Curzon could have put up a more spirited defence of his rule in Damascus, and could have ameliorated, if not stopped, the French destruction of independent Syria. But in fact Curzon was a great supporter of the idea of a continuing British alliance with the Hashemites, to extend to all the lands that fell under a British mandate. Curzon also held Faisal in the highest regard. He refused to give any credence to French charges regarding Faisal's character and duplicity. In a note to Hardinge, Curzon brushed away the French claims against Faisal. 'We have always hitherto contended that the French were mistaken in imputing to Feisal a desire to play us off against them . . . As we know, he was forced by pressure of public opinion in Syria to identify us with the French in his propaganda for complete independence, but this was in order to get rid of them from Syria . . . Even if he went so far as to urge that both British and French mandates should be cancelled, neither he nor his party ever contemplated siding with the French against us.'[37] Curzon did not recognise Faisal's kingdom, not because he was inherently opposed to the idea or because of any dislike for Faisal, but because he was insistent that Faisal's position in Syria could only be confirmed by the peace conference and not by some unilateral action. Lloyd George was also a partisan of Faisal and wrote about him in glowing terms in his memoirs. After the debacle in Damascus, Lloyd George could see no reason why Faisal should not be offered the throne of Iraq.

Curzon was far from being the lone advocate for Faisal at the Foreign Office. The permanent undersecretaries Charles Hardinge and Sir Eyre Crowe, who replaced him in November 1920, were both supporters of the Hashemites and thought highly of Faisal. The influence of Lawrence was felt throughout the lower rungs of the foreign policy establishment, and his sympathies in favour of Faisal were clear. 'I should like to emphasise the importance that the Foreign Office attaches to Colonel Lawrence's views, which rest upon a thorough knowledge of the Arab countries, including Mesopotamia . . . and he has immense influence with Feisal,' wrote Louis Mallet.[38] Moreover, two of those who knew and had worked with Faisal during the Arab Revolt and after, Gilbert Clayton and Kinahan Cornwallis, had joined the Foreign Office in the summer of 1920 on a temporary basis. They could only strengthen the group that was influenced by Lawrence's perspectives on the Hashemites in general and Faisal in particular. In addition, Hubert Young, a decorated war hero who had been attached to Faisal's Northern Army, had become the resident Foreign Office desk officer on Arab issues. He, too, was a great admirer of Faisal.[39]

Faisal's name was being considered for Mesopotamia only a few days after he had been ousted from Damascus. C. G. Garbett, the Foreign Office's expert on Mesopotamia, wrote that 'if the Entente could stand the strain, Faisal would make an Amir such as we desire.'[40] The cabinet had decided on 3 August to back Faisal for a role in Mesopotamia, but were aware that the French would take violent exception, and their objection had to be carefully managed. On 8 August, Curzon and Lloyd George approached the French government to find out what they would think if Faisal were to be placed on the throne of Mesopotamia, and it was made clear that the installation of Faisal in Mesopotamia would be considered 'an unfriendly act'. Sir Eyre Crowe noted on 8 August, in a record of his discussions with the French chargé d'affaires in London, the deep misgivings, bordering on hatred, that official France had for Faisal.[41] With such a determined French stance against Faisal, in August 1920 the British cabinet decided to keep the matter of Faisal's candidacy for the throne of Mesopotamia on hold, until public opinion in Mesopotamia had coalesced around his candidature and the French had removed their objections.

Lawrence had re-emerged from his temporary disappearance in the spring of 1920, leading a public campaign for the consolidation of all Middle East policy-making in a single department. He also launched a vitriolic campaign in the newspapers against Britain's Mesopotamian polices, and in particular the administration of A. T. Wilson, which he held responsible for the deterioration of circumstances that had led to the Iraqi rebellion. However, in a series of articles in *The Times*, *Sunday Times* and the *Observer*, he turned his attention to praising Faisal and the virtues of ruling the Middle East through friendly allies rather than the direct administration favoured by the India Office, which had led to such disastrous results in Mesopotamia. He described Faisal as imbued with 'prophetic fire and with eloquence, enthusiasm and knowledge'. Faisal was 'honest and tactful and knew more about war than any Arab in the Hedjaz'. He was 'a moderate who kept his hotheads from troubling us', and was 'the most democratic of men'. However, the cause of Faisal was not served by the ever more insistent accusations emanating from Wilson in Baghdad and from the British military commander in Mesopotamia, General Aylmer Haldane, that the Iraq revolt was partly instigated by Faisal. These accusations could not be conclusively substantiated and the Foreign Office's position on this matter was best expressed by a minute written by Young. 'I do not believe that Feisal is himself in any way responsible for the trouble . . . though he is probably winking at it.'[42]

The hardening lines between the India Office and the Foreign Office on the administration of the British mandates in the Near East – especially in Iraq – were becoming a serious obstacle to the formulation of a common British government position on Faisal and the sharifians generally. The India Office had brought in Richard Marrs, an old Mesopotamian hand who had worked under Wilson, as well as N. N. Bray, who had served both in Mesopotamia and in Arabia during the revolt. Bray, who was charged with examining the causes of the rebellion in Mesopotamia, had reached an unfavourable conclusion on the role of Faisal in fomenting the rebellion: 'Feisal can hardly be called friendly ... It is impossible to believe that Feisal was ignorant of the various anti-British activities that took place ... he was therefore implicated either actively or passively.'[43] But Bray went further in his analysis of the causes of the rebellion by imputing it to a vast conspiracy hatched in Moscow and Berlin, with pan-Islamic and Bolshevik overtones. These reports simply divided opinion even further between the Foreign and India offices, with Curzon's advisers now submitting themselves 'once more to the hypnotic influence of Feisal,' according to Hirtzel.[44] The India Office had convinced itself that Faisal was behind the troubles in Mesopotamia, while the Foreign Office blamed the retrograde policies of A. T. Wilson in Baghdad.

Matters came to a head on the last day of 1920, when Lloyd George confronted the issue of who was to control policy-making in the Middle East. The cabinet decided to create a new department in the Colonial Office that would be primarily responsible for policy-making in the Middle East. Mesopotamia and Palestine would now be run by the Colonial Office. The following day, Lloyd George offered the Colonial Office to Winston Churchill. Faisal could have been only vaguely aware of these critical struggles taking place behind the scenes in Whitehall. However, he was not innocent of the opportunities that might come his way with the events that were occurring in Mesopotamia, but he had to tread very gingerly. He had only indirect and insufficient indications of the trends in British policy-making, and he was also very careful about overstepping the mark in case he fell foul of his father or his brother 'Abdullah. He had first broached the idea of his availability for Mesopotamia during his meeting in Egypt in August with 'Abd al-Malik al-Khatib. According to a despatch from General Headquarters in Egypt, reporting on the discussions between Faisal and 'Abd al-Malik, 'He [Faisal] heard vague rumours [about Iraq] ... If the British government wished him to go he was ready either as ruler or as regent for 'Abdullah. And whichever of them was selected he should go at once in order to stop the troubles now resuming in that country.'[45] Marrs from the India Office wrote in his minutes of 17 October 1920: 'Meanwhile, there is sufficient evidence that Faisal has aspirations for Mesopotamia. His agent in London, Haddad, approached Foreign Office, and failing in his object there, War Office (this from a conversation with Major [Hubert] Young) with a view to securing permission for a representative of Faisal to address the Mesopotamian families exiled from Syria before they are conveyed from Egypt to Basrah.'[46] Haddad had also earlier met with Colonel Frank Balfour in London, and had discreetly informed him that

'Amir Faisal had decided to take a keen interest in the throne of Mesopotamia, which would make up for the loss of his one in Damascus.'[47] However, there were other, more personal, indications of Faisal's willingness to consider the throne of Iraq. In a diary entry of 14 September, 1920, Haidar noted a conversation with Faisal. 'F [presumably Faisal] told me that he would prefer death to [a life of irrelevance in] the Hijaz. He still held hopes for Iraq as he believed that the British do not want 'Abdullah. If events quieten down now [Iraq was in the throes of a rebellion] who will guarantee its future?'[48]

But Faisal reached London still uncertain as to how the British government was to receive him. In a letter of 27 November 1920, addressed to Zaid and written while Faisal was en route to England via Germany, Faisal laid out his anxieties but also his hopes:

Every day that passes brings what is far near and makes our cause stronger and more successful. But we have to be patient and steadfast and not lose any opportunity, great or small, and seize whatever we can – the weaker will become stronger and the stronger will become more constrained. I do not know what the British government's plans towards me are, and whether they are prepared to negotiate or not. But I am not despairing. If they agree to negotiate then my desire will have been met; if not I would then appeal to public opinion in Britain and to the League of Nations and to British society. The English newspapers are friendly to us and will force the government, willingly or not, to negotiate with us. And if all this fails I would be then free to do what I must. If a door closes, God will surely open another. In short, the opportunity is there and the timing is right, but success will only come from God.[49]

✦✦✦✦✦◆❈◆✦✦✦✦✦

CHAPTER 16

A KING IN WAITING

F AISAL KNEW that his presence in London, the third such visit since the end of the First World War, would prove critical for his future political life. His ambitions for a commanding role in Iraq were now far more evident, reinforced by the apparent drift of British policy in his direction. The rebellion in Iraq had been put down with considerable loss of life and the issue of how and who would govern the country was now preoccupying Whitehall, as were the other messy outcomes caused by the disintegration of the Ottoman Empire: the boundaries of Palestine; the disposition of the territories of Transjordan lying between the Hijaz, French-dominated Syria and Palestine; relations with Hussein; and the ascendancy of ibn Saud in central and eastern Arabia. The only thing that seemed settled was France's brutal imposition of its supremacy in Syria and Lebanon.

The British were tiring of the huge costs involved in maintaining a large army and an occupation administration in the Middle East, as well as with the difficulties of forming workable governments and alliances that would secure their interests and meet their wartime commitments. In such an environment, the proponents of a 'sharifian solution' to Britain's predicament became more and more insistent. Those who opposed this idea – mainly those in the India Office – were wrong-footed by the outbreak of the rebellion in Iraq, which put paid to the idea that Iraq could be ruled directly by London or India. Ibn Saud's ambitions were focused on Arabia and thus he could not be the partner that Britain was seeking in the administration of its mandated territories. Neither could the British rely on the motley collection of often unreliable tribal allies, local functionaries, minority community leaders and urban notables that it had amassed in Iraq and Transjordan to do this job. Without a sharifian buffer, there would be no middle ground between the British and the radical nationalists who could make stable rule well nigh impossible. Although the British had to take this risk in Palestine, where they were committed to the implementation of the terms of the Balfour Declaration in the teeth of huge opposition by the local Arab population, Iraq, and to a lesser extent Transjordan, were altogether another matter. With this confused but nevertheless favourable background, Faisal could discern a pathway to power in Iraq. However, there were still many formidable obstacles he had to overcome: France's deep suspicions regarding his person; his brother 'Abdullah's ambitions for the throne of Iraq; his father Hussein's increasing belligerence displayed towards the British; and Faisal's own limited support in Iraq.

London once again

Faisal's first official duty, as the personal representative of the king of the Hijaz, was to call on King George V and to extend to him Hussein's thanks for his gifts and his appreciation of George V's support for the Arab Revolt. He had been primed by the Foreign Office not to raise any sensitive subjects with the king, such as the loss of Syria, the hostility of the French and the promises made to the Arabs during the course of the First World War. He was also told not to make any public statements to the press or to accept any representations on matters of concern unless they came from Curzon himself. At the audience with George V, Faisal stuck to the cues that he was given. George V, however, did not appear to have been given any talking points, and launched into a direct exposition on all the forbidden topics, which greatly amused Faisal. George V also added that Faisal should not be worried as the British were firmly behind him.[1] The audience was attended by Curzon, and Faisal later recalled a short conversation he had with Curzon at the time.[2] Curzon noticed that Faisal was not wearing his Arab cloak, the 'abaya that he had customarily worn on formal occasions. 'Where is your delightful 'abaya, Your Majesty?' Curzon asked. 'You have stripped me of my country, your lordship, so I took off my 'abaya!' replied Faisal. 'Don't worry,' said Curzon, 'You will wear better than that.' At that point, Faisal recounted that he was suddenly struck by what Curzon had said. It seemed to indicate that the British were seriously contemplating offering him the throne of Iraq. It is highly improbable that this was the first time that Faisal had been given the intimation that he might accede to the throne. Nevertheless, it was a broad enough hint that it was a more than a chance possibility, and something that would require his continuing presence in London until matters were successfully concluded.

Soon after his arrival in London, Faisal moved out of Claridge's to long-term accommodation in London's Berkeley Square. His stay in London was going to be lengthy and he needed less conspicuous premises to conduct his meetings and convene with his advisers and supporters. Two of the first people to call on him were Lawrence and Hogarth, apprising him of developments in

Whitehall and in particular the implications of Winston Churchill's new assignment at the Colonial Office. Lawrence had already met Churchill, who was trying to convince him to join the new Middle East department at the Colonial Office. Churchill, whose previous position had been minister of war, had been responsible for overseeing all the military dispositions in the empire, including the Middle East. He held strong views about the area and how the British could ensure their continued military and political supremacy. He was also a great proponent of Zionism and an unabashed philo-Semite. Lawrence met Churchill in early December, and though not too enthusiastic about harnessing himself to a desk job, agreed to help Churchill in the new Middle East department.[3] The possibility of Faisal acceding to the throne of Iraq was already on Churchill's mind, but he wanted to elicit Faisal's reaction if such an eventuality materialised. Lawrence was the ideal person to ascertain this, and in his first meetings with Faisal on 9 December 1920 the issue was gingerly broached. Haidar recorded in his diary: 'We had lunch with Lawrence and Hogarth . . . . It would appear from Lawrence's statements that Britain will act in Iraq. He [Lawrence] asked our Lord [Faisal] about his views. There is no doubt that at heart he [Faisal] wants this [position] even if it would lead to conflict with his family.'[4]

Other visitors came to see Faisal in the last weeks of December, including a group of British parliamentarians, one of whom presented Faisal with a ludicrous scheme, supposedly approved by Bonar Law, the lord privy seal, of turning Iraq into a commercial prize administered by a chartered company along the lines of the East India Company.[5] The former governor of Haifa, Colonel Edward Alexander Stanton, who oversaw Faisal's stay there in August, also visited him. He had been retired because he had clashed with the high commissioner in Palestine, Herbert Samuel, about the extent of the Palestine government's support for the Zionist project. According to Stanton, Palestine was incapable of supporting large-scale Jewish immigration.[6] General Edward Bulfin, the commander of British forces, who first entered Beirut in October 1918, was another visitor. He attended a lunch hosted by Faisal that included other allied officers. Bulfin was fulsome in praise for Faisal's prowess and his valuable military contributions as Allenby's right flank in the advance through Palestine and Syria. Faisal was deeply moved by Bulfin's remarks, and addressed the gathering not as a political leader but as a comrade-in-arms. 'I am embarrassed in your presence because I believe, with a remorseful heart, that I did not fulfil my obligations towards my people and land in the recent period. I am not speaking from the political but from the military point of view. As a soldier I am deeply embarrassed [about the Syrian debacle], but I had to listen to the advice of my friends [the British] and avoid conflict with those who had earlier been my and my nation's allies [the French]. Otherwise, it would not have been so easy for the country to fall under French rule. I did not bear arms against the French and did not seek to fight them for a single moment. From a military point of view, my conscience bears on me; but from a political perspective, I consider myself to have done what was required for the general interest. I say this in front of you because I fought alongside you and I knew you and you knew me. The friendship that was forged between us during the difficult war years is the strongest bond that a person could achieve.'[7] Faisal was no doubt hoping that his words would reach the British government and that they would appreciate his moderation in Syria by not choosing to continue to fight the French. But equally he wanted his visitors to be aware that it was not because of a lack of Arab military competence that the French were able to dominate Syria. Rather, it was due to a disastrous miscalculation by which Faisal relied on the representations of the British to stop the French from the use of force.

The Zionist leader Chaim Weizmann was also a regular visitor to Faisal's quarters during the last days of 1920. Weizmann was, of course, extremely concerned about the form of government that was to be established in the mandated territories, especially the one in Transjordan, which would affect the territorial boundaries of Palestine. At the same time he believed himself to be a friend of Faisal and sought, whenever he could be given the opportunity, to represent the benign and even beneficial aspects of the Zionist programme to Arab aspirations. Faisal's entourage went along with these visits. It did not make sense to antagonise the Zionist leader openly given his considerable influence in Whitehall, but nevertheless they and Faisal were very sceptical about Weizmann's declarations of good will. Haidar recorded in his diary the feeling of disbelief regarding Zionist intentions after a dinner with Weizmann: 'As for Weizmann and the Zionists, their policy is one of subterfuge (*mudahanna*), and they are consistently against the Arabs. Their policy is close to that of France. The latter is against the rise of the Arabs in Syria because of France's fear that the idea [of independence] could spread to [French colonies in] North Africa. And the Zionists are equally against it because of their fear of it [the idea of independence] spreading in Palestine. We have to be wary of them.'[8]

At a dinner party that Faisal gave for Weizmann, to which Lord Lothian (Philip Kerr) was also invited, the conversation turned to the character of T. E. Lawrence. Kerr was the private secretary to Lloyd George and had been present at the peace conference. Kerr himself was a proponent of the Zionist cause and had assisted Weizmann and Ze'er Jabotinsky, the militant Zionist leader, in obtaining Lloyd George's support for the establishment of a Jewish battalion and the Balfour Declaration. Kerr asked Faisal what he thought of Lawrence. Faisal spoke well of him, saying, 'He [Lawrence] has a broad perspective, and he acts in accordance with the circumstances and the needs of the hour. He does not limit himself to "European" ways of doing things. If he found himself in a new situation that did not lend itself easily to a conventional way of acting, he would use his native intelligence unlike many Europeans ... He takes up the challenge and does not tire or easily lose. He was also truthful in his promises, a matter that made the Arabs [the Bedouin] trust him. He lived with them and did not patronise them. That is why they loved him.'9 Faisal used the opportunity of Philip Kerr's presence to question him about the prospects of an indigenous Arab government in Iraq, but Kerr would not be drawn into this discussion. He limited himself to generalities. Nevertheless, Faisal persisted in his pitch for an indigenous Iraqi government. 'The situation in Iraq is at present quiet but only because of the change in policies [of the British government]. It would be even more tranquil if a competent national government is elected. The agitation of the people would be then much reduced.'10

The Foreign Office had other issues apart from Iraq to discuss with Faisal. The most immediate was the situation in Transjordan. 'Abdullah had moved to the town of Ma'an, which lay inside of the Hijaz but on the boundaries with southern Syria. From there he was threatening to raise an army to drive the French out of Syria. Both the British and the French were seriously alarmed by reports about his activities, and the issue became a factor in the increase in Anglo-French tensions. The French had little doubt that 'Abdullah's actions were known to the British, and even condoned by them. Herbert Samuel wrote to Curzon to the effect that de Caix, Gouraud's adviser, believed the British were allowing 'Abdullah to prepare to attack the French so that the Arabs would be preoccupied with the French rather than direct their attentions to the British in Palestine.11 'Abdullah was making bellicose remarks about recovering Syria in league with Mustafa Kemal in Turkey, but in fact he was far more interested in establishing his claim to a possible principality in Transjordan than in pursuing a war with the French. Nevertheless, the British government took the matter seriously and impressed on Faisal the need to restrain 'Abdullah and end any talk of recapturing Syria by force of arms. Faisal sent his father three cables in quick succession between 7 and 16 December, pleading for Hussein to intercede directly with 'Abdullah to stop any launch of hostiles against the French. Faisal told Hussein that any hostilities on the Hijaz border with Syria would jeopardise negotiations in London.12 Faisal's name was appended to one of the cables, which read: 'I hear rumours of anti-French movements and actions ... I request you to take immediate steps to prevent all hostile movements of any kind against anyone. Trouble in Transjordan will ruin our negotiations in London which otherwise will go well. I take complete responsibility for this statement, which please forward at once to 'Abdullah.'13

The urgent missives had their desired end, and 'Abdullah stopped his belligerent movements. It is also possible, however, that privately Faisal saw the benefit of some turmoil in Transjordan, all the more in that it would strengthen his negotiating hand. But he was not able to communicate these views directly to either his father or brother except by hand-carried messages. All of Faisal's cables to Hussein were liable to be intercepted by the British. In fact Faisal often had to take recourse to a British-provided cipher to send sensitive messages to his father, and he took it for granted that his communications with Hussein would be read by the British. As such, there is a marked difference in tone and content when one compares Faisal's communications with his father by cable and by letter. The former always appear to be accommodating and are often rendered in stiff Arabic after being translated from English. Faisal's letters, however, are critical and reveal far more of his true feelings and intentions.

Other issues that were troubling the British were conditions in the Hijaz and Hussein's refusal to sign the Treaty of Versailles. Hussein for his part wanted tangible confirmation that the British were committed to the terms of the Hussein–McMahon Agreement as he understood them. Faisal wanted a confirmation from his father that he was indeed authorised to discuss these matters with the British, but Hussein was hesitant in giving him such an authorisation. Eventually Hussein did send Faisal the necessary authorisation. On 19 December, a few days before the set date for the first substantive talks with the Foreign Office, Faisal received the necessary empowerment from his father. On 23 December, Faisal, accompanied by Rustum Haidar and General Haddad, met with Sir John Tilley, a senior Foreign Office diplomat, representing Curzon. Tilley was accompanied by Young and Cornwallis. The discussions ranged along familiar grounds, with Tilley insisting that the British were determined to meet their obligations to the Arabs by establishing independent Arab governments, and Faisal repeating Hussein's demands that the letter and spirit of the exchanges with McMahon be fully respected.[14] Faisal was not at his best with Tilley, undoubtedly exasperated by the oft-repeated claims of the British that they were actually fulfilling their obligations to the Arabs. He could not control his impulse to tear into Tilley's presentation, frequently interrupting him and stopping him from completing his case. What made matters worse was Tilley's mild-mannered character. Haidar described him as being drowsy all the time. He had only the barest knowledge of Arab matters, even though he reviewed eastern papers before sending them on to Crowe.[15]

Secret negotiations over Iraq

By the end of December 1920, the approaches from British officialdom regarding Faisal's availability for a leading role in Iraq markedly increased. Apart from Lawrence's soundings, Lloyd George had asked Philip Kerr to elicit

Faisal's views on Iraq, and Curzon sent Young to the same end. In both cases, Faisal's reply was adamantly insistent – perhaps disingenuously – that he would not consider the throne of Iraq as his brother 'Abdullah had already been nominated for the post. At the same time, he left the matter open in case 'Abdullah withdrew and the Iraqi people, through a referendum, selected Faisal for the throne of Iraq.[16] However, on the night of 7–8 January 1921, the matter of Faisal's availability for the throne of Iraq was officially broached. Kinahan Cornwallis, whom Faisal knew and trusted, had been asked by Curzon to approach Faisal and to ascertain his position, more as a friend than as an official emissary. Cornwallis had been given five pages of detailed instructions by Curzon as to how to approach Faisal on the matter.[17] Cornwallis appeared at Faisal's apartments in Berkeley Square, on the evening of 7 January, but Faisal was at the theatre. Cornwallis waited for Faisal, and once the latter returned around midnight the two immediately plunged into a four-hour discussion about Iraq and other matters. Cornwallis left a detailed hand written note, which also ran into five pages, on the meeting.

Faisal listened to Cornwallis's representations, but initially categorically refused to entertain the prospects of being king in Iraq, because the kingdom had already been offered to 'Abdullah.

> My father in truth wants to send 'Abdullah to Iraq and he will not accept it [Faisal's nomination for the crown]. He [Hussein] and people generally will think that I am working for myself in league with the British and not for my country. I will not seek to nominate myself because my honour is more dear to me than being a king. I will not let people accuse me of opportunism. I have caused enough dissension between Muslims . . . I will go to Iraq only if the British government rejects the candidature of my brother 'Abdullah and asks me to bear the responsibility, and if the people of Iraq want me. In that case I believe that my father and 'Abdullah would agree under these circumstances. I do not believe that they could stand against the wishes of the people, but I will not take the initiative. I was driven out of Syria, so how can I accept that it be said of me that I am seeking a throne at the expense of my brother?

However, Cornwallis's note also revealed that Faisal was doubtful of 'Abdullah's prospects in Iraq. He let on that his position on the issue of the mandates might be accommodating, but only because he believed in Britain's good will and sense of justice, and because they had been wartime allies. Nevertheless, his support for the mandate system was heavily hedged. 'But do not expect me to agree to the mandate conditions before I have had a chance to examine them. I cannot possibly go to Iraq without knowing the type of government that Britain envisages establishing there. And I need to be convinced that its foundation would be based on the spirit of our relations at the outset [of the Arab Revolt], as I am sure that in fact it would be so. But I cannot accept anything blindly.'[18] Faisal then ended with a declaration that neither he nor his family had any selfish interests. His sole concern was to further the cause of Arab independence and to build a solid relationship with the British without compromising his personal dignity or the principles that he believed in. Cornwallis's message was clear: Faisal would not intrigue against 'Abdullah for the throne of Iraq. But if the throne remained unobtainable for 'Abdullah – which appeared to be a realistic possibility – then he would accept the nomination. Faisal's position on the mandate was such that it could be interpreted as an acceptance of it in principle, and thus meet one of the essential British conditions for offering him their support for Iraq. But his position also allowed him enough room to question and challenge the terms of the mandate when the circumstances were right. It was a reflection of the position he would increasingly assume in the future: accepting what was on offer and what was at that time non-negotiable, and then working towards extracting more concessions with time and effort. It was a typical 'Faisalian' stance that would generate a great deal of suspicion and controversy later about his true intentions. Faisal must have discussed the outlines of the discussions he had with Cornwallis with his advisers, at least with Haidar. The latter recorded in his diary: '[Cornwallis] said that he had come to find out [Faisal's] views on events and to prepare a personal report to the Foreign Office. The [British] government had no knowledge of this visit (!) . . . He impressed on Amir Faisal the necessity that he nominates himself for Iraq, but [Faisal] would not accept that . . . It is now clear that the [British] government wants to install him in Iraq but within legally defined grounds.'[19]

On the same day that Cornwallis ended his visit to Faisal, 8 January 1921, Faisal set out to the country home of Edward Turnour, the Earl of Winterton, fifty miles from London. The guests included Lawrence, and the Conservative MPs William Ormsby-Gore and Walter Guinness. Winterton, an Irish peer, was a personal friend of Faisal and had served with the Northern Army in the march from Aqaba to Damascus. Faisal spent the weekend at Winterton's home, and there the conversation turned towards Iraq. Winterton, who had been primed by Curzon, also broached the subject of Faisal's nomination for the Iraqi throne. He reminisced about these events later. 'King Feisal was a brave, most talented and charming man, and one of the greatest gentlemen I have ever met, but like most geniuses he was temperamental. For hours, to all our collective persuasion, he made the same answer. He was sick of politics, especially European politics, and indeed of all Europeans except personal friends such as ourselves. He had been abominably treated in Damascus; was there any reason to believe we should treat him any better in Baghdad? At last he assented to our request and said he believed Iraq and Britain could and should work together, which would be his great aim in his new position.'[20]

Winterton's biographer describes a five-hour discussion between Faisal, Winterton and the other guests that went on until midnight. 'Finally, after long hours of discussion, Faisal agreed to become king of Iraq . . . Convincing him was not an easy matter. He felt a deep bitterness about the way that he had been treated by the British and the French, and he made some wounding remarks about the British character generally.'[21] Cornwallis, who was also a guest at Winterton's country home that weekend, once again pitched in about the necessity for whoever was to be king of Iraq to acknowledge and accept the terms of the mandate. Faisal replied that 'he could not accept the mandate unless he knew its terms completely. [Faisal asked] What is this mandate? If it was in the country's interests then we could discuss it, but I cannot accept it blindly.'[22] The late-night sessions at Winterton's country house could not be the final word on the issue of the throne of Iraq. This would have to await other portentous developments taking place in London and the Middle East. The next few weeks would define the structure of the state system that was being put in place to replace the old Ottoman hegemony, and would mark out the future for Faisal, Iraq and the entire Middle East.

Towards the Cairo conference

By mid-January it had become obvious to Faisal that official London had decided on his nomination for the throne of Iraq. On 10 January, Faisal met with Lawrence, William Ormsby-Gore and Walter Guinness.[23] Ormsby-Gore was a close friend of Churchill's. The meeting was in line with the discussions that Faisal was regularly having with the Foreign Office on Arab issues. This time the talks revolved around the expected changes in the department responsible for British Middle Eastern policy, as well the measures that Hussein needed to take in the Hijaz to cement his control and authority in light of the challenge from ibn Saud and the still lingering matter of the Idrisi in the 'Asir. Finally, Lawrence broached the subject of Faisal's candidature for the Iraqi throne, and impressed upon Faisal the need to present his name for consideration formally. Faisal continued to demur, and stated that the British government should arrange to publicise his suitability for the throne of Iraq.[24] Lawrence later reported to Churchill on the meeting, but could not yet confirm that Faisal would accept the nomination for Iraq if the British government made him a formal offer.

On 13 January 1921 Faisal, accompanied by General Haddad, met with Curzon at the Foreign Office, but the discussions did not touch upon Iraq. Faisal was very anxious about the Wahhabi encroachments in the Hijaz, and the difficult situation that could arise if ibn Saud attacked Mecca or Medina. Hussein's forces had recently prevailed in battle over the Wahhabis, but the danger was still there. Faisal wanted to establish the British government's position as he was extremely suspicious about the actions of the India Office, which appeared to be fully supportive of the ambitions of ibn Saud.[25] Curzon shifted the responsibility onto Hussein, whom he maintained threatened his own security by refusing to sign the Treaty of Versailles. Faisal asked for armaments for the Hijazi forces and reinstatement of the subsidies paid to Hussein, but Curzon would not oblige him.[26] The subsidies were a function of the war and Hussein could not expect them to be maintained at that level after the war had ended. Faisal left the meeting very upset, appalled that Curzon wished to see the Hijaz under constant pressure from ibn Saud, the better to control Hussein's actions.[27] Faisal wrote Curzon an angry letter pointing out the dire financial condition of the Hijaz and the relentless pressures from the Wahhabis who still received generous subsidies from the India Office. Partly in response to this letter, Curzon asked Sir Ronald Lindsay, a senior official at the Foreign Office, to meet with Faisal. Apart from his other functions, Lindsay held the extraordinary title of chairman of the inter-departmental committee on Bolshevism as a menace to the British Empire.

On 20 January Faisal met with Lindsay, in the company of Haddad and Haidar. Lindsay had with him Young and Cornwallis. Lindsay's knowledge of Arab affairs was limited, despite his previous experience in the Egyptian government, and he was evidently unprepared for the meeting. His personality was gruff, which did not endear him to Faisal, and Haidar found him 'unfortunately ignorant of [Arab] issues'.[28] The meeting soon degenerated into a shouting match. Faisal raised the issues of the Hussein–McMahon correspondence, the promises made to the Arabs, the Syrian debacle, Palestine and the situation in the Hijaz. Lindsay had only perfunctory understanding of the historical record, and prefaced all his remarks by repeating the instructions given to him. He could not discuss with Faisal the matter of Syria and Palestine, and the Hijaz and other related issues could be better addressed if Hussein signed the Treaty of Versailles. The acrimonious meeting did achieve one unintended consequence, however. It led to a misunderstanding that would later be used against Faisal. Churchill later claimed to parliament that, during the meeting with Lindsay, Faisal had acknowledged that the territory of Palestine was specifically excluded from the promises of support for an independent 'Arab Kingdom' that Britain had given to Hussein during his exchanges with McMahon. In fact the minutes of the meeting show that Faisal only accepted that this could be the British government's interpretation of the exchanges as they related to Palestine, without necessarily agreeing with them. This became a fundamental accusation levelled against Faisal by certain nationalist writers who were hostile to the Hashemites.[29]

It was during these days that Faisal's candidature to the Iraqi throne became consolidated.[30] In later discussions with 'Awni 'Abd al-Hadi, Faisal refers to a 'secret' meeting that he had with Curzon, where the matter of the throne of Iraq was directly broached with him. It is unclear whether this meeting was the one that Faisal had with Curzon on 13 January, or whether it was another, earlier session that was off the record. In any case, Faisal recounted this meeting in the following way:

I received an invitation the following day to meet with Lord Curzon at the Foreign Office. He told me that he discussed the matter [the throne of Iraq] with the government, and the entire Cabinet agreed that it was impossible to install 'Abdullah as king over Iraq. Curzon said: 'You [Faisal] are the only one who is known to the European powers and they know nothing of your brother 'Abdullah. I implore you to think seriously of this matter and not to lose the opportunity given you.' At this point, I could not immediately respond to what Lord Curzon had said, and I was in a real dilemma. Should I insist on my refusal to countenance the offer and stay adamant until the end, or should I accept the facts on the ground and deal with them? The matter, as you know, 'Awni, is dangerous and complex. Should I have rejected the throne and left Iraq drifting towards an unknown destiny until the British find another person? Lord Curzon hinted to me that there was someone else who would gladly take up the throne. [In this way] the Hashemite family would lose all that it had struggled for in the service of the Arab countries.

Faisal asked Curzon for a day to reflect on the matter and to give his final answer. 'I could not sleep a wink that night, and spent all night thinking about this dangerous issue ... I asked myself: should I accept the throne of Iraq, even though the throne of Iraq is in my brother's right, or should I refuse? If I accepted the crown my brother would consider it an affront to his rights. On the other hand I told myself that my rejection of the offer would result in the loss of Iraq to the Hashemites and the isolation of the family from the possibility of serving the Arab cause. I met with Lord Curzon again on the third day and told him my acceptance of what was offered me. God knows that I only wanted what is good for the whole of the Arab nation and I did not seek any personal gain.'[31]

The outlines of Churchill's new policy in the Middle East were becoming clear by February 1921. It was premised on two main considerations. The first was to base the preservation of British primacy and control in the Middle East through the notion of indirect rule rather than direct government. In practice this meant supporting Faisal for the throne of Iraq, and 'Abdullah in Transjordan, and relying on their alliances as the cornerstones of British policy. In this way, British interests would be preserved by friendly princes who would be kept dependent and beholden to British advisers. The second consideration was motivated primarily by costs: how to maintain stability and security in Iraq without the huge outlays that would be incurred by a large military presence. The revolt in Iraq had cost the British Treasury nearly £40 million – a staggering sum in 1920 – and a very great deal more than what Britain had spent on supporting the Arab Revolt. The prospects of maintaining a large army in Iraq was something that Churchill knew would be a source of continuous contention with the Treasury and would not be supported by an increasingly critical parliament and public. Churchill's solution was to rely on the Royal Air Force (RAF) to provide the essential security for establishing a viable state in Iraq. A few strategically located bases would be enough, so Churchill thought, to enforce control throughout the country. Hugh Trenchard, the chief of air staff, fully concurred with the plan. Revolts of tribesmen, the greatest source of instability in Iraq, could be subdued by aerial bombing, and the RAF could patrol the lines of communications and supply without the need for large numbers of ground troops. To put the final touches to his Middle Eastern grand plan, Churchill called for a meeting in Cairo of all of Britain's experts and senior administrators involved in Arab affairs.

A great deal of preparatory work had gone to ensure that the Cairo conference would reach the desired conclusions. Churchill himself did not take up his new post at the Colonial Office until 14 February 1921. A day before he had drawn up the list of appointments for the new Middle Eastern department. J. E. Shuckburgh, a senior official from the India Office, was appointed the permanent under-secretary, Lawrence was the adviser on Arab affairs on a one-year contract, and Hubert Young headed the political and administrative branch of the new department. It was Lawrence who was the main planner of the Cairo conference. In spite of the concern shown by some officials that he was uncontrollable and unfit for bureaucratic rigour, Churchill nevertheless gave him wide latitude and followed his advice on key issues, notably the support of Faisal's candidature for the throne of Iraq. Lawrence had been meeting with Faisal regularly during February, and keeping him apprised of developments at the Colonial Office and the preparations for the Cairo conference.[32] Faisal had grown confident that the British would formally acknowledge his candidature for the throne of Iraq, and though not yet a 'done deal', his observations to his friends and advisers clearly reflected this assurance. On 4 February, Haidar noted in his diary, 'Our Lord [Faisal] had felt this [the approach to become king of Iraq] and he was partial to Iraq, saying that he had tried the Syrians and does not want to work with them any further.' Faisal also let on, incautiously, that he had supported the revolt in Iraq. 'Our Lord said that the Iraq Revolt has had a great effect and that he [Faisal] had expended £40,000 in its support.'[33] Faisal had obviously said this with one eye cocked at courting Iraqi nationalist opinion. It was a dangerous admission to make, even in front of trusted aides, one that the British would not have looked kindly upon.

Lawrence's crucial meeting with Faisal was on 16 February. 'I explained to him [Faisal] that I had just accepted an appointment in the Middle Eastern Department of the Colonial Office . . . I then spoke of what might happen in the near future, mentioning a possible conference in Egypt . . . in which the politics, constitution and finances of the Arabic areas of Western Asia would come in discussion . . . These were all of direct interest to his race, and especially to his family, and I thought present signs justified his being reasonably hopeful of a settlement satisfactory to all parties.'[34] Faisal had just returned from a weekend at Chatsworth House, the grand estate of the Duke of Devonshire. He was greatly impressed. He told Haidar that he had met an aristocratic youth [presumably the Duke's son], 'who was a lieutenant in Palestine and [had] fought in the Dardanelles. His fortune was that of kings and his father was now the Governor General of Canada. He was the only son. The youth told Faisal of the huge number of his relatives that were lost in the war. [Faisal] then said: Would any of our rich people do something like that? We deserve the mandate! When one sees such things, one feels small indeed. That is how real nations live and are governed. If such a fortune was held by any one of our wealthy people he would move heaven and earth to make sure that none of his family was conscripted.'[35]

The draft agenda for the Cairo conference was worked on by Lawrence and Young, and prominently featured was the plan to offer Faisal the throne of Iraq. Lawrence saw his assignment at the Middle Eastern Department as a means to redress the obvious sense of betrayal that was widely shared in the Arab world. Lawrence felt acutely that Britain had not kept its promises to the Arabs, no matter how the matter was dressed up. The Cairo conference was the instrument to demonstrate to the Arabs that in spite of the catastrophe in Syria, in spite of the severing of Palestine from the rest of Syria, in spite of the mandates, there was still a pathway for Arab unity and independence. This path passed through the establishment of sharifian governments in Iraq and Transjordan that were friendly to Britain, and that might then form the core of independent states around which other Arab countries could eventually coalesce. An interdepartmental committee of the Colonial Office approved the conference agenda on 26 February, very much along the lines that Lawrence and Young had developed. Lawrence was determined that the Cairo conference should achieve these ends and staked his career and reputation on its outcome, threatening to resign if his goals were not achieved. 'I'll get my way or resign,' Lawrence wrote to the ageing Wilfrid Scawen Blunt as he embarked for Egypt.[36]

The Cairo conference opened on 12 March 1921 at the Samiramis Hotel. Churchill had invited all the main players in the Middle East, including the high commissioner in Mesopotamia, Sir Percy Cox, and his oriental secretary and adviser Gertrude Bell, and all the senior staff of the Middle Eastern Department at the Colonial Office. In all, nearly forty officials attended the conference, during which dozens of sessions were held. But the issue of Faisal for Iraq was quickly settled after the first day. Lawrence had won over all the sceptics regarding Faisal's candidature, not least Gertrude Bell, who hitherto had been unsure as to whether Iraqis would accept an outsider as their ruler. The conference dismissed the idea of a republican regime for Iraq, a proposal which had only a few adherents amongst British officials in the country, notably St John Philby. At the first meeting of the political committee of the conference on 12 March, chaired by Winston Churchill and including Cox, Young, Bell and Lawrence, a range of candidates for the throne of Iraq were considered. They included: the naqib of Baghdad,[37] the head of the Gailani religious dynasty, who was then heading the interim Iraqi government; Sayyid Talib of Basra, a powerful political boss; Shaikh Khaza'al, leader of the Arabs of the Muhammara region in southern Persia; ibn Saud; the Agha Khan; and Burhan al-Din, a prince of the Ottoman dynasty. All of these candidates were deficient in one way or another according to the conference participants.

Cox then spoke of the virtues and experience of Faisal, and was immediately supported by Lawrence. The meeting concluded with the notation that 'If the Amir Faisal decided to offer himself [as candidate for the throne of Iraq], and was favoured by the people of Irak, His Majesty's Government would offer no obstacles to his selection.'[38] The formula that Lawrence had worked out for the unfolding drama was that Faisal's followers in Iraq would call for his enthronement and he would then respond to this call, with British government support. Churchill cabled Lloyd George, asking the cabinet to approve Faisal's candidature for the throne of Iraq, now officially Mesopotamia's new name. Churchill wrote: 'The formula would be "In response to enquiries from adherents of Amir Feisal the British Government have stated that they will place no obstacles in the way of his candidature as ruler of Iraq, and that if he is chosen he will have their support." On this, Feisal will at once proceed to Mecca, passing through Egypt on the way. We do not want any announcement, even in guarded terms, of the formula if it can be possibly avoided until Feisal is at Mecca and Sir P. Cox at Baghdad about the middle of April.'[39]

There is no evidence from contemporary records or from the memoirs and reminisces of Faisal's companions in London that Faisal was privy to the stage-management of his 'call' to Iraq. Lawrence might have briefed him on the outlines of the Cairo conference's agenda and on the British Government's intention to stand solidly behind his candidature once the cabinet had approved the plan to nominate him as king of Iraq. However, Haidar in his meticulous diary provides no hint that Faisal was aware of the conference's agenda, neither does Faisal allude to it in his letters of this period to his father or to Zaid. In his letter of 1 March 1921 to his father, Faisal does state that agreement had been reached 'on a semi-official basis . . . to establish an independent Arab government in Iraq and to lift the mandate from this government, leaving it free to act externally.'[40] However, in an extensive passage in the same letter, Faisal sets out in detail to his father the opportunities that might now arise after the devastating blows that were delivered to the Arab cause by events in Syria and the division of the Arab lands. The rebellion in Iraq that resulted in a dramatic shift in British policy there had opened up new possibilities. 'Before, these setbacks could have completely destroyed the prospects for Arab unity. The previous policy [of the Allies] had aimed at division and partition, not only in terms of the lands but also as it affected the economies, education and morals [of the Arab countries]. But God Almighty defeated the plans of those in charge of these policies, and the cause has now a new course to march upon. But the opposition remains strong, and we have to confront it with patience and sincerity.' Faisal then went on to justify the formation of an independent government in Iraq, which could not, at this stage, be united either with the Hijaz or with Syria. In the former case, the Iraqi people themselves had to decide on linking the country to the Hijaz. As to Syria, the French were opposed to Faisal and had embarked on a path to separate Syria and Lebanon from its Arab context along the lines of what they did in Algeria. However, an independent government in Iraq would unite the lands of Mesopotamia and there could be no objection in the future if the new independent Iraqi state linked itself to other Arab states. Faisal seemed to be outlining a vision for the new Iraqi state, under his leadership, to act as the catalyst for realising the ambitions of Arab unity to be achieved through the Hashemites.

Faisal also sought to remove any family objection that might be raised to his candidature for the Iraqi throne. He did not actually renounce his claim to the Syrian throne, but couched his present focus on Iraq in purely political considerations. France would not countenance his return to Damascus, nor would it consider him acceptable for any position of authority in southern Syria [Transjordan]. The same considerations applied to Zaid. Without actually saying so, Faisal clearly implied that the only viable candidate for southern Syria had to be 'Abdullah. With 'Abdullah established in Transjordan the cause of Arab unity through the Hashemites' installation in key Arab countries would be immensely strengthened. It was a carefully crafted appeal for his father's support for Faisal assuming the Iraqi throne, and it was to have the desired effect.[41] Faisal repeated his perspectives on events in his letter of 1 March to his brother Zaid. The Cairo conference would confirm the policies already reached in London and the new proposed governments in Iraq and Transjordan would improve the prospects for Arab unity: 'Reaching Damascus and beyond will be now much easier after the government is formed in Baghdad.'[42]

Meanwhile, Faisal had in fact been preparing his position for another conference that was meeting in London before the Cairo conference. The Allies (Britain, France, Italy and Japan) were meeting in London on 22 February to discuss, inter alia, the issue of Faisal and Syria, and the peace treaty with Turkey. A Turkish delegation was also expected at the meeting. Faisal had written to Lloyd George a day earlier reiterating his father's position on the Treaty of Sèvres, which was planned to form the basis for the final settlement with Turkey. Hussein had refused to sign the treaty because it did not meet the Arabs' demands, nor was it a foundation to secure the peace in the Middle East. Faisal asked that a Hijazi delegation be allowed to attend the deliberations in London, as the Hijaz was still technically at war with Turkey.[43] Lloyd George tabled Faisal's letter at the meeting, but was met with fierce resistance by Aristide Briand, the French prime minister. Briand exclaimed that Faisal could not be allowed to address the meeting because of his stated hostility to France and his direct responsibility for the shedding of French blood. The French delegation would simply refuse to sit on the same table as Faisal. Lloyd George then made a spirited defence of Faisal and his crucial role in the military campaigns in the eastern theatre of war. Eventually, Briand accepted to have General Haddad deliver Faisal's note to the conference. On 10 March, Haddad presented Faisal's paper to the assembled leaders of the Allies, in the presence of Lloyd George, Briand and Curzon. It did not go beyond the familiar litany of complaints regarding broken promises and the unnatural division of Arab lands, and justified Hussein's refusal to sign the Treaties of Versailles and Sèvres because both treaties referred to the unacceptable notion of mandates.

Preparations for Iraq

Faisal's path to the Iraqi throne had been cleared by the Cairo conference, except for the resistance of a few holdouts, mainly Cox's security adviser in Baghdad, Harry St John Philby. However, there remained the matter of the French and their deep hostility to Faisal, as well as 'Abdullah, ensconced in Amman and still claiming to rally the people of southern Syria to recover Faisal's crown in Damascus. Briand had become aware of Britain's insistence on nominating Faisal for the throne of Iraq during the London meeting of the Allies in March. There was little the French could do to block the passage of Faisal to the throne in Iraq. After all, their key argument in asserting their control over Syria and driving Faisal out had been that the area assigned to them under the mandate gave them, in effect, unbridled rights. Britain enjoyed the same privileges in Iraq, and the French could not undermine the legitimacy of any unilateral action that the British chose to take in their zone of control. But the French could protest diplomatically and raise whatever arguments they could to try to dissuade the British from implementing their decisions. On 23 March 1921 Curzon received the French ambassador in London, who proceeded to denounce Faisal for his anti-French actions, and repeated the allegations that Faisal sought to conspire with the British against France. He also said the if Faisal were to become ruler in Iraq it would be interpreted by the French public as an anti-French move encouraged by the British government. Curzon would have none of this, however, and dismissed the ambassador's arguments. Britain did not raise one finger to oppose the measures that France took in Syria and he expected the French to reciprocate on the issue of Iraq.[44] The French ambassador again met Curzon on 6 April. This time he fell back on the idea that France would consider that Faisal had been chosen as king of Iraq solely because of his anti-French credentials. It was an absurd argument and Curzon summarily dismissed it. Peeved, the French ambassador exclaimed that France would always consider Faisal an enemy and would not extend him any courtesies in his passage from England to the Middle East.[45] This ended formal French attempts to scupper Faisal's candidature.

The Cairo conference never seriously considered the possibility that 'Abdullah should rule in Iraq. The consensus was that Faisal would be a much better ruler, but the issue of what to do with 'Abdullah remained. Although it had been agreed that Transjordan would have a separate political status, the presence of 'Abdullah in Amman created a quandary. Would 'Abdullah be satisfied with a role in Transjordan, causing him to renounce both his claims in Iraq and his posturing related to liberating Syria? If not, how would the British handle his obduracy, as armed conflict with him was out of the question? In the end, Lawrence was despatched to Amman to meet 'Abdullah and explain to him the details of Britain's policies in the area, including, of course, Britain's backing of Faisal to be king of Iraq. Lawrence then left with 'Abdullah to meet Churchill in Jerusalem. There, 'Abdullah agreed to relinquish any claims to the Iraqi throne and to halt any anti-French activity. In exchange he was offered the rule over the principality of Transjordan, and would receive British financial and military help. The arrangement was meant to be a holding pattern until Faisal could establish his legitimacy in Iraq, after which 'Abdullah would be confirmed in his permanent status.

However, the truth of 'Abdullah's relinquishing his 'rights' to Iraq are more complex than descriptions in official despatches. 'Abdullah was incensed at Britain's decision to back his brother Faisal, but had to swallow what must have been a very bitter pill. He was driven by a mixture of sibling rivalry, jealousy and sheer anger at the loss of what he thought of as his legitimate right to rule in Iraq. 'Awni 'Abd al-Hadi was in Amman during this period as one of 'Abdullah's key advisers, and he recalls in his memoirs 'Abdullah's outburst when told the news of Faisal's candidature for the throne of Iraq. 'Awni had rushed to meet

Faisal in Egypt while he was on his way to the Hijaz after leaving London. He was carrying with him letters to Faisal from his brother 'Abdullah. Faisal read the letters out loud and then turned to 'Awni and said: 'My poor brother [*Maskin akhi*]. He doesn't know me and it seems my father does not know him. He had instructed him to meet me at Port Said [but 'Abdullah had not come]. He ['Abdullah] thinks that I have usurped from him the throne of Iraq, and that I tore with my own hands the decision by the Iraqi members of the Syrian Congress to take Amir 'Abdullah as the king of Iraq. I have heard all that he has said about me, and I always used to say "May God forgive him". Faisal then went on to outline the course of events in Syria and then Europe that finally pushed him towards the Iraqi throne. He was obviously expecting 'Abd al-Hadi to relay this perspective to 'Abdullah, who was convinced by what Faisal had said that he had sought neither to undermine his brother nor to connive at the Iraqi throne. 'Abd al-Hadi told Faisal, 'What Your Majesty did was correct. If you had not accepted the Iraqi throne, Britain would have found someone else to replace you and he would have been no more than a pliant instrument in her hands.'[46]

'Abd al-Hadi then rushed back to Amman to report to 'Abdullah on the discussions he had had with Faisal. 'King Faisal asked me to kiss your hands on his behalf . . . and asked me to tell you all that I know regarding the position of the British government on the throne of Iraq, and his [Faisal's] own resistance to his nomination [for the throne of Iraq], his insistence on its rejection, and his demand that you ['Abdullah] should take the throne on the basis of your acclamation by the Iraqi members of the Syrian Congress.' 'Abd al-Hadi then went on to justify Faisal's actions while he was in London, saying that Faisal did not go to London to seek the Iraqi throne but to organise a redress for what had occurred in Syria. The matter of the Iraqi throne came up only because Britain had found immense difficulties in establishing its authority as a result of the 1920 rebellion in Iraq. 'Abd al-Hadi then asked 'Abdullah to accept what had happened. But 'Abdullah was adamant in refusing to countenance this line of argument. "Awni, I know my brother. He had earlier mounted the throne of Syria and had become a head of state. After this, nothing would matter to him in life except ascending other thrones. My brother Faisal is no different than other heads of state in these matters. History has taught us that whoever amongst the Arabs had become a head of state, he would insist on the perpetuation of this condition even if it would have led to his demise. And that is why my brother has preferred to ascend the throne of Iraq even if this throne was the right of his brother. All I can do here is to ask him to seek God's forgiveness.'[47] 'Abdullah's attack on Faisal masked a great deal of jealousy as to what his brother had accomplished.

Faisal's views on 'Abdullah were that he was basically an indolent dilettante. He told 'Awni 'Abd al-Hadi as the latter was preparing to join 'Abdullah's service, 'I want to give you an idea of my brother's characteristics as this might help you in your work with him. My brother is good company, attractive and delightful in speech and enjoys joking and laughing. He is a connoisseur of poetry and literature, especially ancient literature, and enjoys chess and the jokes of his friends. He likes horse-riding and shooting at targets that he selects, sometimes on top of a heap of rocks and sometimes at an apple that he places at the head of one of his servants. As for general affairs, he scarcely pays them any attention. Otherwise, he meticulously prays the five daily prayers, and meets all its obligations, even if the prayer time falls when he is in the middle of the desert or in a place full of dust, thorns or rocks or in foreigners' palaces.'[48] It was not much of a testimonial as to 'Abdullah's statesman-like qualities. Faisal's own claims of selflessness and bowing to the inevitable regarding the throne of Iraq are plausible up to a point, but for them to ring completely true would require a person devoid of any personal ambition. Faisal was seen to be such by many of his friends and supporters. 'Abd al-Hadi, writing much later to his daughter in 1959 when he had cause to reflect on the events of past times, said of Faisal: 'Faisal was not a prophet who was inerrant, or one who was not affected by his passions. But I can confirm that he was the most sincere person I have known in his loyalty to his nation. I have witnessed him passing hours where he entirely forgot he was a king, and all he could think then was of his patriotic duty.'[49]

With the work of the Cairo conference completed, Lawrence cabled Faisal in London: 'Things have gone exactly as hoped. Please start at once for Mecca by the quickest possible route . . . I will meet you on the way and explain details. Say only that you are going to see your father and on no account put anything in the press.'[50] Lawrence's telegram had reached Faisal before the cabinet was officially notified of the call to Faisal to proceed to the Hijaz. It clearly revealed Lawrence's (and Churchill's) confidence that the matter was finally settled in Faisal's favour. On 22 March 1921, the cabinet ratified the decisions of the Cairo conference. The minutes of the meeting read in part: 'Feisal will be told privately that there is no longer any need for him to remain in England, and that he should return without delay to Mecca to consult his father, who appears from our latest reports to be in a more than usually unamiable frame of mind. Feisal will also be told that if, with his father's and brother's consent, he becomes a candidate for Mesopotamia and is accepted by the people of that country, we shall welcome their choice, subject, of course, to the double condition that he is prepared to accept terms of mandate as laid before League of Nations, and that he will not utilise his position to intrigue or attack the French . . . If above conditions are fulfilled, Feisal would then from Mecca make known at the right moment his desire to offer himself as candidate, and should make his appeal to the Mesopotamian people.'[51]

Faisal left England for Port Said in early April, obviously elated at the turn of events. Lawrence, who had been with Churchill in Jerusalem, flew to Port Said to meet Faisal's ship. The two had a long, secret meeting on 11 April, where Lawrence briefed Faisal of the results of the Cairo conference and discussed the next steps with him. Lawrence wrote to Churchill to say that:

> Feisal expressed his appreciation of the general policy outlined and promised to do all he could to make his part of it work. He will guarantee neither to attack nor intrigue against the French . . . He will agree to establish friendly relations with ibn Saud on condition of Hedjaz immunity from Wahabi attack. He thinks that if he is given a free hand for the first few weeks after Ramadhan in Bagdad and neighbourhood, there should be little doubt of the success of his candidature . . . He asks for a British adviser on his personal staff. This must not be an official of the Mesopotamian Government for many reasons, but it must be a person of weight in whose judgement he can trust, and he asks for the loan of Colonel Cornwallis from the Egyptian Government to accompany him to Mesopotamia. He makes this a condition of his going . . . he regards the people of Irak as not fitted yet for responsible Government, and if he is left at the mercy of the local people in all things there will be a disaster.[52]

Faisal, however, was not prepared to accept the permanent conditions of the mandate and its humiliating implications of dependency and colonial status. He said that at his first public declaration after reaching Iraq, he would say that the mandate terms would be renegotiated after Iraq's basic law, in effect its constitution, came into effect and after appropriate negotiations between the British and Iraqi governments. Faisal then left for Cairo, where he stayed at the Shepherd's Hotel, awaiting an opportune time to leave for Suez and thence to Jeddah.

A stream of visitors passed by Faisal's quarters at his hotel, ranging from his advisers and stalwarts from Damascus days, such as 'Adil Arslan and Shukri al-Quwattly, to the leading lights of the Egyptian nationalist movement, such as Sa'ad Zaghloul and Shukri Yakan. Faisal was partial to the Egyptian nationalist leadership, but was disappointed by the Egyptians' parochialism and lack of knowledge or interest in Arab affairs. At the dinner parties that he gave, most of the guests would leave the table still hungry. Faisal's constant smoking meant that he would quickly consume the first course and leave the table to roll out his cigarettes. The staff would then clear the table, leaving his guests still famished. Most who knew of Faisal's habits would consume their meals before reaching his dinner table. At these gatherings Faisal gave his views on power, the art of politics and his prospects in Iraq. Faisal noted to 'Awni 'Abd al-Hadi, 'I accepted to be nominated for the throne of Iraq in spite of my knowledge that all kinds of accusations, both from Iraq and from outside, will be levelled against me, whether from good or ill intentions. But I felt that I would betray my country if I chose to sleep in my bed in the Hijaz, fearful of what people might say, and knowing all the time that it is in my power to serve my country. In my opinion, the traitor is not only the one who consciously betrays his country, but also the one who refuses to serve his country even though it is in his power to do so.'[53]

Referring to his prospects in Iraq, Faisal said,

I am very confident that this time, with the help of the Almighty, our efforts [in Iraq] will be crowned with success, and we can avoid what befell us [in Syria] because of our lack of experience in political matters. The Syrians used to insist on meeting all the Arab goals immediately; the unity of all of Syria including Syria, Lebanon and Palestine, the total independence of Syria and the removal of all the obstacles that stood in the way of immediate and total independence. We have learnt from the great experiences that we have had in international politics and in the [formulation of] proper policies. Politics in my opinion is not to insist on achieving all that a politician wants to achieve, but rather to achieve what is possible. And the true politician is not the one who knows what he wants but rather the one who knows the limits of what is possible and [who can] accept these limits. If he is unable to know the highest limits of what he can achieve, and accepts what is less, he will have lost to a greater or lesser extent what he is capable of demanding, and if he ignores the upper limits of what is possible, and demands more than he can achieve, he will have lost everything.[54]

Faisal continued with his ruminations on politics:

I believe in the policy of 'Take and then ask'. These two expressions define all the arts of flexible politics. In other words, take what is offered at the moment and then pursue a flexible policy that will allow you to cover, step by step, the way forward until the lights shine clearly in your eyes and it becomes possible for you to achieve yet another of the rights for your country . . . In this way you, by accumulating rights, by demanding the possible and taking it, will gain complete independence for your country. This, ideally, is the politics that I will want to pursue in Iraq. The Syrians lost independence for Syria by insisting on the policy of all or nothing; or in other words, either complete independence or complete subservience, or, either the patient survives or dies. I do not want to rule Iraq with a foreign hand lurking over me. And if I accept to rule under this foreign tutelage, it is only because I will work tire-lessly to get rid of this tutelage, and I and the people of Iraq live under an honest Arab government. This will not happen to us unless we follow a wise and flexible policy, or the policy of 'Take and then Ask', until victory is assured for the Arabs and the country achieves its promised independence.[55]

On 21 April, Faisal left Cairo for Suez to embark on the ship that took him to the Hijaz. In Suez, he had another unpublicised meeting with Lawrence, but it is not known what transpired between them. A few days later Lawrence left for England, having completed his mission in the Middle East. Faisal was now securely in the running for king of Iraq, but his support in Iraq was untested and he needed the backing of the British Residency in Baghdad if his candidature were to prevail. Faisal had already established a beachhead of sorts in Baghdad. Ja'far al-'Askari, who had returned to Iraq after the fall of Damascus, was now the defence minister in the interim Iraqi government, and had attended the Cairo conference in that capacity.[56] He was in close contact with Faisal and was aware of the decisions of the conference, including the establishment of an Iraqi army. Nuri al-Sa'id was already in Baghdad and organising the groundwork for Faisal's expected arrival in Iraq.

Faisal sailed on board the khedival boat *Jantu*, reaching Jeddah on 25 April 1921. The Egyptian government had obviously got wind that something was brewing in Iraq and that they should pull out all the stops for a future ruler of the country. It was a far cry from Faisal's previous visit to Egypt, when he had had to wait for his train at Qantara while sitting on his luggage and being ignored by the Egyptian government. Faisal was clearly apprehensive about the reception he would receive from his father, but to his astonishment he was received as a hero. Hussein was very welcoming and threw a huge lunch party in Faisal's honour after his ship had docked at Jeddah.[57] Faisal then departed for Mecca, where he and his father began the process of communicating with Iraq's leaders offering Faisal as the prospective king of Iraq. Hussein addressed a cable to the naqib of Baghdad, the prime minister of the interim government: 'And as I see your invitation [to Faisal] as a genuine, patriotic call, I shall send to you Faisal to assist you in [the running of] Iraq.' Faisal sent a similar message to the naqib as well as to Sayyid Talib, the minister of interior in the interim government. 'When in Europe, and for a long time before that, it had become clear to me that the people of Iraq want me to participate in the management of their affairs. I have now returned to Mecca and have consulted with my father, and he has agreed that I should help my nation and its people to the best of my abilities. If the people of Iraq wish for my presence, then I am prepared to come. And I wish with all my heart that your Excellencies will assist me and not deny me your support and fatherly advice.'[58]

On 5 June Faisal received a cable from Major Marshall, the British Consul in Jeddah, advising him that the cruiser *Northbrook* would be arriving in Jeddah and would carry him and his party directly to Basra. On 12 June Faisal embarked on the *Northbrook* heading for Basra. On board with him were a group of prominent Iraqis who had taken refuge in the Hijaz after the collapse of the 1920 rebellion. They were now returning as part of the amnesty that had been declared by the British authorities in Iraq. They included the Shi'a religious figure Sayyid Muhammad al-Sadr, Yusuf al-Suwaidi, 'Abd al-Muhsin Abu-Tabikh, 'Alwan al-Yasiri, Rayih al-'Atiya and Ali Jawdat. Faisal also had his own close group of advisers, including Rustum Haidar and Tahsin Qadri. Cornwallis, his newly appointed adviser, a giant of a man and a distinguished athlete in his college years, was also on the *Northbrook*. He was on loan from the Egyptian government for three months, but in fact he remained in Iraq, with a few interludes, for over twenty years. His last posting in Iraq was as ambassador during the Second World War. He had Faisal's confidence and was his trusted conduit for his dealings with the British authorities. Faisal exchanged messages with the naqib of Baghdad while on board the cruiser. The naqib, in a volte-face from his previously guarded position on Faisal, sent him a cloyingly effusive message.[59]

The *Northbrook* reached Basra on 23 June. A motorboat flying the British flag approached the cruiser, carrying the defence minister, Ja'far al-'Askari, and St John Philby, the adviser to the Ministry of Interior. On land were hundreds of notables from Baghdad and Basra awaiting to greet the prospective new king.

For the first time ever Faisal disembarked on Iraqi soil. It was the start of another extraordinary episode in his life.

PART IV

A NEW BEGINNING
Iraq (1921–1933)

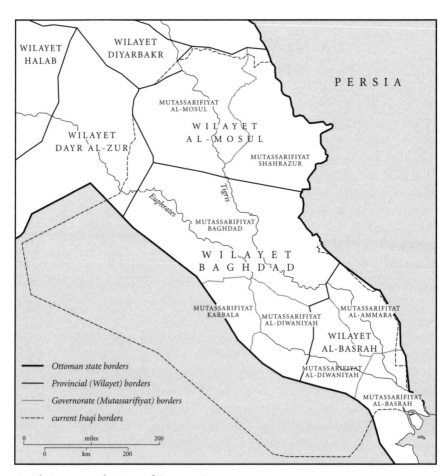

6. Administrative divisions of Ottoman Iraq

CHAPTER 17

FROM MESOPOTAMIA TO IRAQ

F AISAL ARRIVED in a country that had undergone years of warfare and
upheaval. The Ottoman years had not welded the three provinces of
Baghdad, Basra and Mosul into a coherent political entity. The mixed population of Arabs and Kurds, Shi'as and Sunnis, town dwellers and tribesmen, and
the sizable contingent of Jews and Christians and resident Persians, had been
mostly detached from even the minimal certainties provided by the Ottomans.[1]
Further additions to the country's mix came from the thousands of Assyrian
refugees who, fleeing from their failed uprising in eastern Turkey, were relocated by the British to the northern reaches of Iraq. The country was occupied
by a British army of over 100,000. This force had been hard at the task of fighting
the Ottomans, and when the armistice was declared it found itself in effective
control over the three former provinces of Mesopotamia. Very soon afterwards,
however, the British were confronted with a serious tribal uprising, encouraged
by the Shi'a religious hierarchy in the holy shrine towns that convulsed most of
southern and central Iraq. This had been preceded by Arab nationalist agitation
in some western Iraqi towns, inspired and led by the Iraqi officers of Faisal's
Arab army when the Arab government in Syria was crumbling.

The British provided whatever sense of security and order existed in the land,
and by the reckoning of most did a better job than the Ottomans ever had. They
also provided the rudiments of administration, put together as a matter of necessity. They were the only party that could take on the responsibility of government as the old order fell apart. The British had promoted the formation of an
Iraqi cabinet, an all-Sunni affair led by the venerable naqib of Baghdad, which
tried to put a local face to what was in fact an occupation. It issued its own decrees
and edicts, but real power lay with the high commissioner.

Unlike his experiences in Syria, Faisal had precious little direct knowledge
of the internal workings of the country or previous access to its leading figures.
The Iraqis with which he was most familiar were the former officers of the

Ottoman army who had joined the Arab cause during the war or who had later joined his government in Damascus. With very few exceptions they were parvenus, drawn from the lower echelons of Iraqi society, and were viewed suspiciously by the notables of Baghdad and Mosul. The political landscape was extremely unsettled and various currents were vying to assert themselves. The Ottoman years had left a potent residue of loyalty to the sultan, and now that the empire was being dismantled this loyalty was partly being transferred to the rising state of Turkey. The old Sunni notable classes were cosying up to the British, hoping to regain their primacy under the new dispensation. Tribal chiefs who had stayed loyal to the British during the 1920 uprising expected recognition and compensation for their stance, while others who had joined or led the rebellion were awaiting an uncertain fate in the new state. The Shi'a religious hierarchy was sullen and mostly unreconstructed in its opposition to British rule. The Kurds, concentrated in the former wilayat (Ottoman province) of Mosul, were hoping for the breakthrough that would ensure their independence. A growing nationalist or crypto-nationalist political class, driven by ambitious politicians and effendis, was making itself felt by noisy opposition to the dominance of the country by the British. The large groups of urban Jews and Christians, the former in Baghdad and the latter in Mosul, were eager to bind the future of Iraq with Britain, seeing in this the best safeguards for their own security and prosperity. There were even separatist regional tendencies. Key figures in the wilayat of Basra were jostling to sever the province from the rest of Iraq and declare it a separate state, aligned with Britain, along the lines of the principalities of Kuwait and Muhammara.

Faisal had to deal with this jumble of conflicting views and tendencies, of ethnic, sectarian and social divisions, an occupied country emerging from centuries of rule by a distant empire, and build a political community and state where none had existed before. It was a formidable challenge, far greater than his first failed attempt to build an independent Arab state in Syria. However, this time round he had the support of a great power, which had already determined that establishing the kingdom of Iraq with Faisal at its head was the best way forward to preserve its power and interests in the country. But Faisal had his own ideas, which included building the institutions of a modern state that would achieve its independence. These had to be set against the demands of the great power, which to all intents and purposes in 1921 held most if not of all of the cards.

Britain, Mesopotamia and the war

The outbreak of war between Britain and the Ottoman Empire was preceded on 3 August 1914 by the drums of mobilisation, heard in all of the major towns of the Mesopotamian provinces. The brutal Ottoman conscription drives, known as the *safarbalik*, were followed by wholesale desertions by Iraqi conscripts. These in turn were followed by draconian Ottoman reprisals, which did little to uphold the morale of the fighting troops. In the end, most of the hard fighting was carried out by the stolid but ever loyal Anatolian troops. Ottoman forces in the three provinces amounted to a scant four divisions, two of which were quickly dispatched to fortify the Sinai fronts, while the Baghdad division was sent to the Caucasus. The only force left in the country to meet any contingency was the Basra-based division. It was appallingly equipped. The army had one feeble armoured river boat, the *Marmaris*. There was only a single map of the country with the appropriate military scale.[2] The British had assembled a division-size force in Bahrain under General Walter Sinclair Delamain and prepared for a naval landing in the Shatt-al-Arab waterway. The command was under the government of India and was formally known as the India Expeditionary Force (IEF) 'D'. The intention of the landing was to secure Basra and the headlands of the Gulf. There was no plan to occupy the entirety of Mesopotamia. After a series of small skirmishes, IEF 'D', now under the command of General Barrett, marched towards an undefended Basra. The Ottoman army had withdrawn from the town towards Qurna, at the confluence of the Tigris and Euphrates rivers. Within a few weeks the remnants of the Ottoman forces in Qurna were roundly defeated and their commander captured.

The fall of Basra was preceded by a call for jihad throughout the Mesopotamian provinces. The Ottoman government sent a high-level delegation to the shrine towns of the Shi'a to persuade the *mujtahids* (Shi'a Muslim legal doctors) to support the Ottoman war effort. This was no time to continue the quarrel between the sects of Islam when Islam itself was in danger from the British invasion. The *mujtahids*, led by the Grand Ayatollah Kadhim al-Yazdi, concurred that Islam was in danger and called on the people to rise and support the war effort. A great tribal army was raised, led by the *mujtahids* themselves, some well into their seventies, which marched southwards to assist the Ottoman forces in repelling the invaders. On 12 April 1915, the Ottoman forces, under the command of Suleyman 'Askari and supported by up to 50,000 tribesmen, launched an attack on the entrenched British forces. The battle lasted for three days with vicious hand-to-hand fighting, but first the tribes broke and then the regular Ottoman units.[3] The Battle of Shu'ayba seesawed, but eventually ended with a decisive British victory. Suleyman 'Askari, a valiant commander, could not withstand the shame of defeat and committed suicide in front of his aides.

With the British position in the Basra region now fully consolidated, the expeditionary force pushed northwards along the Tigris towards 'Amara and Kut, 250 miles to the south-east of Baghdad. General Charles Townsend, now commanding the advancing forces, occupied 'Amara on the Tigris on 3 June

1915, after a series of river boat battles. Emboldened by his easy victories, he pushed on to Kut, which fell to his forces on 25 September 1915. Baghdad now became an irresistible target. But his forces were checked at the Battle of Ctesiphon by the Ottoman Fifth Army and retreated to Kut where they were besieged. With exhausted supplies, rampant disease and an increasingly hopeless position, Townsend surrendered to the Ottoman army on 29 April 1916. Nearly 11,000 British Empire troops were taken prisoner. It was a major military disaster for the British. The War Office in London took charge of the Mesopotamian war and a new commander, General Stanley Maude, was sent out to replace the old guard. His orders were to hold the gains in Basra wilayat and to protect the oil fields of Persia. Any advance northwards had to be explicitly authorised. But Maude was not content to play a waiting game. He wanted to smash the Ottoman army in Mesopotamia, and wipe out the shame of the Kut disaster. It was only a matter of time before he would launch his offensive.

Responses to the British invasion of Mesopotamia

The British advances in Mesopotamia elicited varying responses from different parts of the population. The initial outburst of support for the Ottoman cause led by the religious classes quickly turned into a wait-and-see position. By far the most volatile in their loyalties were the tribes of southern Mesopotamia. The majority of the tribes adhered to the Shi'a sect, and those whose territories were proximate to the shrine towns were directly influenced by the decisions and positions of the *mujtahids*. But the tribes were above all concerned with their material welfare and power, and their shaikhs carefully weighed the rewards that might emanate from the Ottomans or the British as a price for their support. Entire tribes switched support from the Ottoman cause to a neutral position, then to a pro-British course and back again, depending on the local military preponderance of the protagonists, and the money, land titles and materiel that they could offer to the tribal leaders.

The Sunni religious establishment was, by and large, solidly in favour of the Ottomans. They were mostly state employees and shared with the Ottoman state the strict interpretation of Sunni Islam. The Shi'a religious hierarchy was an altogether different matter. It kept itself as far as possible from the Ottoman government and dealt with it only in matters of necessity. The Ottoman state was at best indifferent to the Shi'a. However, for a brief moment following the CUP coup of 1908 and the promise of a return to constitutional rule in 1908, the Shi'a glimpsed the possibility of removing the age-old barriers against them. The *mujtahids* of Najaf had been broadly supportive of the 1908 revolution, having previously played an important part in the events leading to the Constitutional Revolution of 1906 in Iran. But the Ottoman state was institutionally predisposed against the Shi'a, and the reforms that the CUP introduced only tangentially affected the Shi'a community. They were allowed to open their own 'modern' educational establishments, but no Shi'a could realistically aspire to either a military or bureaucratic career in the Ottoman Empire. Nevertheless, at the outbreak of war, the Arab *mujtahids* of Iraq ruled in favour of defending the lands of Islam from foreign invasion and declared for a defensive jihad. Those that didn't were mostly of Persian origin and used the arguments regarding the unpreparedness of the people for war.[4]

The Sunni notables of Baghdad and Mosul were to a large extent non-committal or backed the Ottomans until the British army was nearing Baghdad. In earlier times, the grand families had forged close ties with the sultan and they were not too enthusiastic about the constitutional revolution or the CUP. Their support for the Ottoman cause was qualified by their suspicions of the CUP's intention, but they were too closely integrated into the structures of Ottoman rule to countenance active opposition to the Ottomans, at least while the war was raging. The Arab nationalist movement in Mesopotamia was weak, and its few civilian adherents in Baghdad, mostly minor functionaries and journalists, had made an ineffectual attempt to contact the British, but they had been blocked in that by the naqib of Baghdad, 'Abd al-Rahman al-Gailani.[5]

However, the Iraqi officers of the Ottoman army, all Sunni Muslims, were another matter altogether. They formed an important element of the Ottoman army.[6] They mostly came from middling backgrounds and saw a career in the Ottoman army as a pathway to personal and professional advancement. Although a large number of them had been organised before the war in al-'Ahd secret society, they had mostly remained loyal to the Ottoman cause. But as the war progressed and Ottoman reverses multiplied, a number found their way to the forces of the Arab Revolt, either through desertion or having been transferred to the Hijaz after a stint at the British prisoner-of-war camps. Most, though, remained deeply sceptical of British motives and designs on the Arab territories of the Ottoman Empire. This factor bedevilled the relationship between the British and the Iraqi officers who had defected to the Arab Revolt.

The Jews and Christians of Mesopotamia generally welcomed the prospects of an Ottoman defeat at the hands of the British Empire. In spite of the promises of a common citizenship held up by the return of constitutional rule and an adequate representation in the Ottoman parliament, there was nevertheless a widespread belief that the structures of the empire were determinedly Islamic. Additionally, during the war Jewish merchants of Baghdad were under constant watch for hoarding and profiteering, and were regularly harassed to contribute to the Ottoman war effort. Several Jews were publicly hanged for avoiding military service in the Ottoman army. A British victory in the war would be more of a deliverance for them. There was little doubt in the minds of the Jewish and

Christian communities of Mesopotamia that direct British rule would safeguard their interests far more effectively than the continuation of Ottoman rule.[7]

There were also regional forces at play. The port of Basra had always had a more open and cosmopolitan mix of populations then the rest of Mesopotamia. The large community of merchants, with its vital trading interests with India, was naturally supportive of the British. On 1 January 1915, six of Basra's leading citizens sent King George V a New Year greeting and called for the establishment of Basra as a British protectorate. Their enthusiasm for British rule might have been encouraged by the temporary eclipse of power of the Basra political boss and tough, Sayyid Talib al-Naqib. At the outbreak of war he contacted the British and offered them his support if he were to be appointed the governor of Basra and given a sizable stipend. But the government of India did not trust his constant prevarications and switches of loyalties, and engineered his exile to India where he sat out the war.[8]

The fall of Baghdad

Following the inconclusive Battle of Ctesiphon and the surrender of the British army at Kut, a false sense of security permeated the Turks in Iraq. Khalil Pasha, the governor of the Baghdad wilayat and overall commander of the Ottoman armies in Mesopotamia, was a debauched character, frequently found in cabarets and in the company of prostitutes.[9] The fall of Kut had taken place during his watch and he took credit for the victory, in which he had played no part. His British counterpart, General Stanley Maude, displayed very different characteristics. He was single-minded, a ferocious worker, and a stickler for detail.[10] Maude moved his forward headquarters near Kut, and carefully prepared for his offensive. By December 1916, he was ready to march. Battle was joined for nearly three weeks, but Maude had brought overwhelming force to bear on the Ottoman defences. He could now deploy seven divisions, in contrast to Townsend's one. His firepower was also immeasurably greater and he had several planes at his disposal for reconnaissance, strafing and bombing.

By February 1917, the Ottoman lines forming the forward defences of Baghdad had collapsed. Khalil Pasha bowed to the inevitable and ordered a general evacuation of the town. Storehouses, weaponry, files, furniture and the miscellany of the Ottomans' presence in Baghdad trudged northwards on all forms of transport: train, mule, lorries, carriages and river transport. Central authority vanished and with it came the bane of Mesopotamian towns when law and order recede. Baghdad and its sister town of Kadhimain were given over to looters.

On 11 March 1917, units of the British army entered Baghdad and the Union Jack was flown from the famous clock tower in Qishla Square. After nearly four centuries, Ottoman rule had come to an end. The Ottoman withdrawal from Baghdad was followed by the evacuation of the mid-Euphrates area to the vicinity of Fallujah and Ramadi in the Western Desert of Iraq. The new Ottoman lines now stretched from Sammara, north of Baghdad, to Ramadi. But any thoughts of recapturing Baghdad were laid aside in the face of the overwhelming preponderance of the British.

The administration of occupied Iraq

The status of occupied Iraq had been a concern of the British ever since war had loomed with the Ottoman Empire. By 1915 the government of India and the India Office had already staked their claim to the territory, and it was an article of faith with them that the provinces of Basra and Baghdad would be directly ruled by India or even annexed to the Raj. But London was averse to settling the matter of the future of Iraq in such peremptory fashion before a general peace agreement had been reached. Instead, a committee under Lord Curzon was organised in 1917 soon after the fall of Baghdad and charged with the interim oversight over the country. The committee included Sir Mark Sykes as well Sir Arthur Hirtzel of the India Office. The viceroy of India was explicitly informed in a note of 29 March 1917 that the government of India would have no hand in the administration of Iraq. Rather, the country would be ruled directly, for the time being, from London. The boundaries of the province of Basra were delineated and Basra was expected to be run as a British dependency. Baghdad Province, on the other hand, would be placed under indirect British protection or tutelage, but with an Arab face. This arrangement fell roughly within the stipulations of the Sykes–Picot Agreement. Both Maude and Percy Cox, the chief polititcal officer in Mesopotamia, however, opposed the immediate implementation of these decisions and counselled that there should be minimum interruptions to the pattern of government established in the Ottoman years.

The matter of Iraq's government came to the fore a few weeks following the capture of Baghdad, when there was a falling out between Maude and Cox. Maude had little inclination to share power with his senior political officer, and in any case saw little merit in any civilian authority, preferring to maintain the military, otherwise himself, as the ultimate arbiter of the administration of the country. The British government interceded in the dispute and a middle ground was chosen. Maude's powers would remain undisputed, but Cox would be entrusted with the day-to-day civil administration, reporting to London through the commander-in-chief. This left enough leeway for Cox to put together the rudiments of a separate administration for Iraq, which he, and then his successor, A. T. Wilson, began gradually to extend. The power of the civil administration was greatly expanded following the sudden death from cholera of General Maude in November 1917. The evolution of a strong civil administration in Iraq allowed both Cox and then Wilson to distance Iraq from the various schemes, mostly emanating from Mark Sykes's indistinct plans for an 'Arab government' to run the conquered Near Eastern territories of the Ottoman Empire. The separate status of Iraq from the rest of the Near East became a firmly established reality.

In contrast to the problematic conditions of Syria and Palestine, Cox sought to create the impression that the people of Iraq positively welcomed British rule.[11] In a note to the Eastern Committee of the War Cabinet entitled 'The Future of Mesopotamia', he presented a detailed analysis and plan of action for the future of Iraq. Cox's main concerns were to remove any vestiges of Ottoman rule in the country and to consider the two provinces of Basra and Baghdad as essentially one. British influence could then be applied uniformly over the territory of Iraq. Without this tutelage Iraq could never be properly governed, nor could its resources be successfully exploited. Cox presented two proposals for the shape of this government: the first would be rule through a British high commissioner to whom the heads of governmental departments, presumably British appointees, would directly report; the second would be the installation of a figurehead 'native ruler', with a status lesser than that of a king. He dismissed the idea that Sharif Hussein or his sons could play any part in the running of the country. '[Sharif Hussein] is a figure who carries no weight in Iraq, where only the most distant interest is taken in him.' On the other hand, Cox suggested that the naqib of Baghdad could fulfil this role.

Cox then outlined the three groups in the country upon whom Britain could rely to smooth its administration of Iraq. The first would be the class of urban notables of Baghdad and Basra. The second group would be the landed classes and the prominent tribal leaders. In addition, the British should encourage and promote Iraq's minorities, especially its Jews, who presumably would be more amenable to working with the British. In this regard, Cox advised that Weizmann, or his representative, should be invited to Baghdad to encourage the Jewish community to extend its support and cooperation to a British-led civil administration.[12] This in effect would be the basis of subsequent British policy in Iraq. The Eastern Committee formally approved Cox's note and authorised him to realise it in its broad outlines. The task for its implementation, however, fell to Cox's successor, A. T. Wilson, as Cox had been reassigned to Iran in July 1918.

Arnold Talbot Wilson, Cox's deputy, was appointed acting civil commissioner for Mesopotamia in April 1918, and his administrative policies – or maladministration – had a profound bearing on the course of events in Iraq during the turbulent years between 1918 and 1920. Wilson, a colonel in the

Indian army, was committed to the notion of Britain's imperial mission and its civilising effect on native populations. He was also a firm believer in the 'muscular Christianity' so beloved of late-Victorian imperial administrators. Iraq was a perfect laboratory and locus for his imperial bent. Paternalistically concerned for the people of Iraq, Wilson had little but disdain, even contempt, for the elites and their ability to govern the country.[13] He worked energetically to establish an administrative structure that would facilitate Britain's imperial rule.

Wilson's resistance to independence for Mesopotamia set him against the policies advocated by Lawrence of installing Sharif Hussein's sons over the former Arab territories of the Ottoman Empire.[14] Initially Wilson dismissed the idea of a 'sharfian settlement' for Iraq,[15] but later he reversed his position and proffered a number of alternative arrangements for the governing of the country. These included the possibility of selecting a son of the sharif of Mecca amongst three other possible candidates to become the titular head of the country.[16] He also recommended to the cabinet the holding of a plebisicite, to canvass opinion in the country. There was no question but that ultimate authority would reside in a British high commissioner, whom Wilson expected to be Percy Cox. Wilson in fact offered a fifth alternative, namely the direct rule of the country for at least five years by a British high commissioner, with no Arab amir or head of state.

The plebiscite of 1918–19

On 27 November 1918, the cabinet authorised Wilson to organise a plebiscite whose wording revolved around three basic questions: do Iraqis support the establishment of a single Iraqi state from Mosul to the Gulf, under British tutelage? If so, would they want an Arab at its head? And, if so, who would that Arab be? Wilson instructed his district political officers throughout the land to canvass the opinion of the leading personalities in their areas; there was no question of holding a general referendum. The population was deemed too ignorant and illiterate to have any serious understanding of the issues. Only the shaikhs, urban notables, religious figures and the educated classes were approached for their views. The plebiscite was to some extent intended to reflect genuine local opinion, but the principle of continuing British primacy was not to be contested. Wilson certainly used the occasion of the plebiscite to push for his own proposals, namely the willing acceptance of the populace of direct British rule and a clear separation of the future of Iraq from the nationalist currents then affecting other Arab lands.

The plebiscite was organised by Wilson's deputy political officers throughout Iraq, and in many instances Wilson himself would travel to various towns and districts to meet with local leaders. Opinion was solicited through open

meetings, which were then expressed in the form of *madhbatas*, signed statements that expressed the position of the signatories regarding questions raised
by the plebiscite. In most of the tribal districts of the south of Iraq, the tribal
leaders were susceptible to British pressure. They were dependent on the
British for their land claims and for subsidies. The local political officers were
often on friendly terms with the shaikhs of the tribes.[17] The *madhbatas* from
the southern tribal towns of Nasiriya, 'Amara, Diwaniya, Kut and Musayab
were uniformly in favour of continuing British rule – in fact, whatever the
political officers deemed appropriate for Iraq. It was only in the shrine towns
and urban centres that dissent emerged. Not surprisingly, the Shi'a centres of
Najaf, Karbala and Kadhimain were mostly hostile to the idea of foreign tutelage. In Najaf, Wilson himself pleaded the case of British oversight to the grand
ayatollahs, using the Persian language at which he was adept. At first, Grand
Ayatollah Kadhim al-Yazdi himself went along with British rule, 'as the people
are ignorant, and if Arab bureaucrats were imposed on them, the result would
be chaos ... There is no single person that the people can accept as their
Amir.'[18] But opinion quickly divided and two *madhbatas* from Najaf emerged,
one supporting British rule and the other demanding an independent Arab
state with an amir. Karbala, on the other hand, was firmly on the side of an
independent Arab government, ruled by one of the sons of Sharif Hussein.[19] In
Kadhimain, the atmosphere was even more hostile to British rule. Here, leading
town notables and ayatollahs from the al-Khalisi and al-Sadr families took the
lead in rejecting British rule and demanding an independent Arab government. The *madhbata* called for the installation of one of the sons of Sharif
Hussein of Mecca as amir over the country, with the stipulation that his powers
be constrained by a parliament.

It was in Baghdad, though, that the worth of Wilson's plebiscite would be
most tested. It was the major city of the country and the centre of anti-British
sentiment. Here the fledgling intelligentsia of the country could combine with
the *ulema* (Muslim clerics) and independently minded notables to push for
their own vision of an independent Iraq. Wilson attempted to pack the Baghdad
convention so as to produce a pro-British *madhbata*, but failed. Jews and
Christians stayed away from the resultant gatherings and the declaration that
was produced after two inflammatory meetings was decidedly anti-British in
tone. 'We being of the Muslim Arab nation and representing the Muslims of
the Shi'a and Sunni communities inhabiting Baghdad and its suburbs, resolve
that the country extending from northern Mosul to the Persian Gulf to be one
Arab state, headed by a Muslim King, one of the sons of our Sharif Hussein,
bound by a local Legislative Council sitting at Baghdad, the capital of Iraq.'[20]
The anti-British vehemence of the declaration prompted a number of notables
and landowners, who were clearly worried about its adverse effects on their

own interests, to deliver a more appropriately worded *madhbata* to the acting civil commissioner.

Not all Iraqis welcomed the plebiscite. Several notables thought that a public airing of the issues of sovereignty and government would hide people's true feelings. The naqib of Baghdad thought it foolhardy, and a source of instability and discord. The idea that a conquering world power would ask the public for its opinion on government was startling, even ludicrous, to many Iraqis.[21] The results of the plebiscite itself were ambiguous, but they were manipulated to fit the outcomes desired by Wilson. The selection of the participants who were invited to the plebiscite conclaves, the intimidating presence of political officers, the selective filtering of expressed opinions and the anxiety felt by the *madhbata* signatories that contrary opinion would become known to the authorities could all be used to satisfy the ends sought by Wilson. Wilson actively managed the process and the results to impress London with the breadth of support for British rule. But there was an uglier side to the plebiscite. Wilson deported known opponents of British rule from Baghdad, and summarily dismissed religious opinion expressed in the *madhbatas* as unrepresentative of the 'enlightened' classes. In Mosul, the views of a *madhbata* with only twenty signatories were deemed an accurate reflection of the views of the entire Muslim population of the city. There was no doubt that many saw immediate British rule as necessary to maintaining security and establishing the basics of a civil administration. Pro-British sentiment was strong in the city of Basra and amongst minorities. But this was a far cry from accepting the inevitability of continuing British rule over a new state in Iraq. Simmering tribal resentments were smothered by the apparent unanimity of feelings amongst pro-British tribal shaikhs; religious fears, especially with the Shi'a *mujtahids*, that Iraq was going to fall to a non-Muslim power, were ignored; Arab nationalist sentiment was dismissed as negligible or irrelevant; and the first stirrings of an Iraqi-based national movement were overlooked. All these countervailing currents could have seriously challenged Wilson's views and by the middle of 1919 were gathering for a powerful eruption.

The genesis of the Iraqi national movement

The tortuous mix of promises, claims, alliances, interests and ambitions that drove Britain's actions had become increasingly tangled. The redrawing of the map of the Middle East had to abide, above all, with the alliance with France and its claims on Syria. This gave Britain an essentially free hand in Iraq, to which the province of Mosul could now be added after the Clemenceau–Lloyd George deal. The province of Basra was explicitly designated as British-run territory under the Sykes–Picot Agreement, and the Hussein–McMahon correspondence was interpreted by Whitehall as giving substance, if not legitimacy, to Britain's claims of primacy in Mesopotamia. Curzon himself was vitally concerned with creating a chain of friendly states in the Middle East that would straddle the borders of India, and it would have been inconceivable for Britain to relinquish its hold over Iraq, especially after its hard-won victory over the Ottomans.[22] But the Anglo-French declaration had raised nationalist expectations everywhere in the Arab east, and Iraq was not immune to the calls for independence. Britain's intention to rule over Iraq, whether directly or indirectly, had to be somehow reconciled with the rising tide of demand for self-government. Wilson's plebiscite afforded Britain the possibility of navigating itself out of this complex maze by claiming that continued British involvement in the affairs of Iraq was a popular demand.

Accordingly, the India Office cabled Wilson on 14 February 1919 to prepare a constitution for Iraq that would give 'full play to different elements of population and recognizing and incorporating local peculiarities and idiosyncrasies[!]'[23] Wilson's constitution was ready within a week and he flew to Paris and London to present it to the government. Essentially it called for the establishment of direct British rule under a high commissioner, the incorporation of Mosul, including southern Kurdistan, and the disputed areas around Deir el-Zour into Iraq. The country would be divided into four provinces, each with a deputy high commissioner, and Kurdistan would form a separate region inside Iraq. British officials would be seeded throughout the administrative structures of the country, although 'Arabs of good birth and education would be given, from the outset, positions of executive and administrative responsibility.'[24] The government gave its approval to Wilson's constitution, but removed Mosul and any autonomous Kurdistan region from his brief. The British government was not yet prepared to settle the issue of Mosul province, even though Wilson viewed the inclusion of Mosul into Iraq as fundamental to the implementation of his constitutional proposals. However, by the second half of 1919, events in Iraq were taking an unexpected turn contrary to Wilson's representations. In May 1919, the Kurds under Shaikh Mahmud had risen in rebellion and occupied the town of Suleimaniya. Police reports were reaching the Foreign Office that anti-British sentiment was growing, no doubt exacerbated by news that a mandate was to be imposed on Iraq. Wilson's openly imperial posture was alarming the Foreign Office and pressure began to mount for his replacement.

The petitioners who chose independence were not content with stopping at the plebiscite. They organised meetings in mosques to demand independence and some of their leaders were arrested and exiled to India. Two secret parties emerged: the 'Guardian of Independence' (Haras al-Istiqlal) and an Iraqi branch of al-'Ahd, then active amongst Iraqi officers in Damascus.[25] The Haras Party in particular soon lost its effendi and elitist tag, and began to accept recruits openly from all ranks and groups of society. It also extended its reach into the shrine towns and tribal lands. A third formation seeking independence, the 'Society of Jaafari Youth' (Jamiat al-Shabiba al-Ja'fariya), more closely aligned with the Shi'a, also emerged in this period. Throughout the summer and autumn of 1919, agitation in Baghdad and elsewhere had increased against the plans for a mandate and the likelihood that independence would be an ever-distant goal. Demonstrations and marches against the mandate increased in intensity, posters denouncing British rule were plastered on the walls of Baghdad and schoolchildren marched to the ditty: 'Protectorate or mandate / They all mean enslavement: And a life of dishonor / We will never accept.'[26]

In the shrine towns the high-handedness of British officials, and the great anxiety induced by the possibility that Iraq could lose its Muslim identity, drove Grand Ayatollah Muhammad Taqi Shirazi of Karbala to send a message in April 1919 to the American legate in Teheran asking for American support for an independent Arab state in Iraq. At the same time, Grand Ayatollah Shirazi and his equal in rank, Grand Ayatollah Isfahani, sent a message to President Woodrow Wilson gently reminding him of his Fourteen Points and stating that 'the desire of Iraqis and the prevailing opinion is that, as they are a Muslim nation they should [enjoy] legal freedoms and install a new independent, Arab and Muslim state with a Muslim king constrained by a national assembly.'[27] This drove the British authorities to deport a number of the ayatollah's followers in Karbala, which in turn prompted the grand ayatollahs to send a letter to Acting Civil Commissioner Wilson in August 1919, complaining of the British action. Wilson responded by justifying British measures, and laying the blame on agitators and trouble-makers.[28]

Disquiet and unease also spread into the tribal heartlands of the mid-Euphrates valley. The area was agriculturally rich and many tribal leaders had grown wealthy on the cultivation of rice. They had the wherewithal to dabble in nationalist politics. The partly settled tribes of the region, strongly committed to their Shi'a identity and closely linked to the religious hierarchy of the shrine towns, still held many of their former nomadic values, not least an exaggerated concern with honour and lineage. The need to respect the decorum and dignity of the tribal shaikhs was frequently lost on the British political officers with whom they came into contact. A well-known tribal figure, Sayyid 'Alwan al-Yasiri, had been shabbily treated by an arrogant British officer. The aggrieved al-Yasiri harboured a deep grudge against the British and became their implacable enemy.[29] Throughout the summer and autumn of 1919, al-Yasiri led a campaign amongst the tribal leaders of the region to rise against the British. By the end of the year he had succeeded in drawing a large number of converts to the cause of rebellion, the most important of whom was al-Yasiri's elder cousin,

Sayyid Nour al-Yasiri, and 'Abd al-Wahid al-Haj Sikkar, paramount chief of the Fatla tribe.

The Arab Revolt had little resonance in Iraq and few people were aware of its occurrence when it happened.[30] The Ottoman authorities naturally sought to downplay it, portraying it as an insignificant rebellion that would be soon put down, and Sharif Hussein as nothing but a British tool. The British paradoxically also failed to use the news of the Arab Revolt in their propaganda in Iraq against the Turks. The Indian government was loath to incite feelings amongst Indian Muslims that the caliphate itself was under threat. By the end of the war, popular sentiment was that the Arab Revolt was a contributing factor to the destruction of the Ottoman Empire and thus Muslim rule. It had few supporters, and for a long while the Arab Revolt, in the mind of the empire's supporters, and even religiously minded people in Iraq, could not be separate from the notion of *Arab Khiyanat*. This was a contemptuous Turkish term, literally translated as 'treacherous Arabs', applied to all those who opposed the empire during the war. The Arab Revolt had its greatest impact, of course, amongst Iraqi officers in the Ottoman Empire. These nationalist and frequently anti-British officers turned their attention to their homeland from their base in Syria. They would form yet another component of the unstable alliance that led to the Iraqi rebellion of 1920.

Sharif Hussein, Faisal and the Iraqis

Syria was the lynchpin of the Arab nationalist cause. Iraq, though not quite peripheral to the ambitions of Arab nationalists, had its own peculiarities. Its future disposition was in any case of great interest to Britain, and its 'exceptional' status was recognised in the Hussein–McMahon correspondence. The Arab Revolt itself had expanded from the Hijaz and into Syria rather than Iraq, and the subsequent establishment of the independent Arab state in Syria further concentrated Arab minds on Syria. All of these facts have helped to obscure the extent of the relationships between the sharifs of Mecca and developments in Iraq in the war years and immediately thereafter.

Faisal had come across the few Iraqi parliamentarians who had been members of the Ottoman Majlis (assembly) but no lasting relationships between Faisal and those Iraqis in Istanbul had apparently developed from those years. Sharif Hussein had also had little contact with Iraqi notables in the years before the war, although Iraqi pilgrims did call on him during the Haj season. Hussein was visited by a number of leading Persian ayatollahs resident in Iraq, but these were mainly ceremonial and courtesy calls with little political significance. Hussein harboured no ill will to the doctrines of Shi'a Muslims, and refused to countenance any of the discriminatory practices that used to afflict Shi'a pilgrims on Haj. The rise of ibn Saud and the fiercely anti-Shi'a bias of the Wahhabis pushed a lot of Iraq's Shi'a religious leaders into tacit support for the sharifs of Mecca against the Wahhabi danger.

By the end of the war, however, the sharifian cause became more widely known – and popular – in Iraq, as were Faisal's efforts in Paris to induce Arab independence. In April 1919, the three main protagonists of rebellion, Sayyid 'Alwan, Sayyid Nour al-Yasiri and Shaikh 'Abd al-Wahid, met secretly with others in Najaf, and discussed approaching Sharif Hussein in Mecca to ask him to install one of his sons as king of Iraq. They informed him that they had signed petitions to that effect during Wilson's plebiscite and now sought his support to counter British opposition to their goals. They designated Muhammad Ridha al-Shibibi, a young man of literary promise who had participated on the Ottoman side in the Battle of Shu'ayba, to carry their message to Hussein. Al-Shibibi took with him signed declarations by dozens of leading religious figures, tribal leaders and nationalist youth, all confirming their commitment to independent rule in Iraq under one of Hussein's sons.[31] Avoiding the British authorities, who had caught a whiff of his mission, al-Shibibi crossed the desert on nomadic trails from Zubair in southern Iraq to the highlands of Arabia. The arduous journey took a month to complete. In Wadi Fatima, on the way to Mecca, al-Shibibi met with the Amirs Ali, 'Abdullah and Zaid, who arranged for him to meet their father. In Mecca, al-Shibibi presented Hussein with the signed petitions and laid out the situation in Iraq. Hussein replied in person to all the letters from Iraq, and give an especially endearing response to Grand Ayatollah Muhammad Taqi Shirazi, whom he called the 'Perfect Pontifex' (Al-Hibr al-Kamil).[32] His letter was couched in vague generalities, but still clearly supportive of the demands of the petitioners.

Hussein also instructed Faisal, then in Paris, to defend the cause of Iraq's independence at the peace conference.[33] Al-Shibibi noticed Hussein's heightened anxieties about the future of the Arab lands and the obvious signs of his disillusionment with the Allies. He was also struck by the confusion, lassitude and mismanagement that characterised the independent Hijazi state. Al-Shibibi spent forty days in Mecca after which he departed for Damascus, riding on the trains of the partially destroyed Hijaz railroad. He spent several months meeting with the expatriate Iraqis, and on numerous occasions meeting with Faisal and Zaid at Faisal's house in the Muhajireen district of Damascus. Faisal had by then returned from Paris and had informed al-Shibibi that all the petitions that al-Shibibi had brought with him from Iraq had been presented at the peace conference by the Hijaz delegation. Al-Shibibi stayed in Damascus for a while and attended the Iraq Congress on 8 March 1920, which was held simultaneously with the Syrian Congress at which independence was declared.

The Iraq Congress of March 1920

Following the fall of Damascus, al-'Ahd split into separate Iraqi and Syrian components. Although this was mainly a result of personal animosities, there was also the recognition amongst the Iraqi officers who were the backbone of the organisation that the possibility of a united Arab state rising from the wreckage of the Ottoman Empire was remote. They needed to organise themselves for the separate state that was to emerge in Iraq. At the same time, Iraqis had begun to outgrow their welcome in Syria. There was increasing Syrian animosity against them, as they were perceived to have taken a disproportionate share of the Arab state jobs in Damascus. In January 1919, four Iraqi al-'Ahd members, acting on behalf of 385 Iraqi officers and civil servants working in Syria and the Hijaz, sent a letter to the British government demanding the formation of an independent, constitutional Iraqi state under one of the sons of King Hussein. They asked that this state be linked in a confederal arrangement with other independent Arab states. They also pledged that this Iraq would be allied to 'Great Britain, with its noble principles and which has been the Arabs' supporter.'[34] The signatories received no more than a curt acknowledgement of the receipt of their letter. On 23 April 1919, they sent another letter along similar lines to the Allied liaison officer in Aleppo, to be sent on by him to the Foreign Office. This time the letter carried the added signature of Ja'far al-'Askari, the military governor in Aleppo.

This string of letters had its desired effect on Curzon, who considered it prudent and politic to respond to the anxious inquiries of these 'Baghdadi' officers. The Foreign Office drafted a response to the officers, which was to be relayed to them by A. T. Wilson. However, the latter took strong exception to even deigning to reply. He considered them no more than an insignificant clique of ambitious officers. The Foreign Office took Wilson's caustic observations into account when it sent the officers a reply that was non-commital regarding Iraq's status, merely repeating the formal British position that the fate of Iraq would be settled in the final peace treaty. The Iraqi officers in Syria were further estranged from Britain after a number of incidents had convinced them that London was not serious about granting Iraq independence. Throughout the spring of 1919 they were clamouring to return to Iraq, but Wilson was convinced that they were behind the escalating nationalist agitation in the country.[35] Nevertheless, the Iraqi officers were mostly in agreement on the leading role that Britain was expected to have there. As late as November 1919, Yasin al-Hashimi, the arch-nationalist, was openly calling for a key position for British advisers in the development of the Iraqi state.[36] But by the end of the year the situation had changed for the worse. Ignored by the Foreign Office, facing a hostile civil administration in Baghdad, and seduced by

Kemalist nationalist agitation, most of the Iraqi officers in Syria turned against Britain and began to advocate and plan for military action. It was at the disputed frontier region of Deir el-Zour in the opening months of 1920 that the Iraqi officers of al-'Ahd first encouraged armed opposition to British control. Faisal was, of course, aware of the change of mood amongst the Iraqi officers in Syria, and strove to influence it in ways that would strengthen his position with the British. He was also very supportive of the wholesale repatriation of Iraqi officers in Syria. He saw them as the most important allies of the sharifian cause in Iraq, and understood they could strengthen his brother's rule if 'Abdullah succeeded in ascending the throne of Baghdad.[37]

The shift of the Iraqi officers in Syria towards greater radicalism encouraged al-'Ahd society to convene the Iraq Congress in March 1920, and to call openly for Iraq's independence. The opening of the Iraq Congress in early March in Damascus was arranged so as to coincide with that of the Syrian Congress. It had Faisal's blessing because he believed it would bolster his own precarious position in Syria, as well as anoint 'Abdullah as king over Iraq. This might diffuse a potentially serious family rupture over the throne of Syria, which 'Abdullah was entitled to claim by right of being the elder of the two brothers. Al-'Ahd had carefully prepared the ground for such a congress. It engineered signed declarations from Iraqi notables in Baghdad and Mosul, delegating its leadership to represent them in a congress to be convened by the organisation. Twenty-nine Iraqis who were then in Syria were chosen to represent Iraqi opinion. Seven were former Ottoman army officers and the remainder were writers, lawyers and merchants resident in Syria. They were all Sunnis, except Muhammad Ridha al-Shibibi, who was inducted into the congress as the only Shi'a. He was the only person at the congress who had any contact with the growing opposition to British rule in the tribal areas of southern Iraq and who had any relationship with the Shi'a religious hierarchy. The congress was opened by Tawfiq al-Suwaidi, a French-trained Baghdadi lawyer. It unanimously approved a statement that called for the independence of Iraq 'from the north of Mosul wilayat to the Persian Gulf.' The declaration also called for 'Abdullah to be Iraq's constitutional king with Zaid as his deputy. It 'dissolved' the British military occupation and called for a responsible national government. And for good measure the declaration reaffirmed, 'in the name of the Arab nation of Iraq' the commitment to Iraq's allies and friends (presumably Britain).

But events on the ground were spinning out of control. The Iraqi officers in Syria demanded from Faisal that measures be taken to confront the British in Iraq. After all, they had fought the Turks to liberate Arab lands, not to replace one set of occupiers with another. Faisal reluctantly agreed to support the opening of a front against the British in the Mosul area, and provided £E5,000, a paltry sum, to help arm the Iraqi contingent in Deir el-Zour. A raiding party led by Jamil al-Midfa'i entered Iraq in the vicinity of Mosul, supported by tribesmen from the Shammar and Dulaim tribes, and by members of al-'Ahd society in Mosul. It attacked British lines of communication, and on 4 June 1920 occupied the town of Tel 'Afar, on the road to Mosul. However, the town was soon recaptured by the British and the raiding party retreated into Syria. No sooner had this happened than the entire edifice of the Arab government in Syria was swept aside by Gouraud's army. Starved of funds and military backing, the few remaining Iraqi officers concentrated in the northern Syrian village of Raqqa, but their efforts to confront the British from this base were doomed. The Raqqa pocket disintegrated within a few weeks.

The rebellion of 1920

The rebellion of 1920 is a seminal event in Iraqi history, and is one of the few founding stories about which most of Iraq's population can agree. At its height, the rebellion, a mix of armed tribal uprisings and civil disobedience in towns, covered large parts of the mid-Euphrates valley, the shrine towns and Baghdad. It required large military and financial commitments by the British to put it down. A great deal has been written on the rebellion by both Iraqi and non-Iraqi writers and historians. It played a major part in the elevation of Faisal to the Iraqi throne, it changed the balance of power inside the country, it shifted British policy towards indirect rule, and it created a powerful narrative of resistance and struggle that was exploited by subsequent oppositionists and radical nationalists.

Throughout the spring of 1920, resentment and unease in Baghdad spread amongst the educated and administrative classes regarding the implications of British rule. The award of the mandate for Iraq to Britain at the San Remo Conference in April 1920 simply confirmed to these groups the subsidiary role that they were to play in the new Iraqi state. In May 1920, coinciding with the fasting month of Ramadhan, mass meetings took place throughout Baghdad with the aim of denouncing the mandate and demanding independence. A novel feature of these meetings was the unprecedented degree of cooperation between the Shi'a and Sunni communities, who held joint meetings in their respective mosques and places of worship. These meetings combined the predominantly Sunni celebration of the Prophet's birthday with the Shi'a rites of mourning for the martyrdom of Imam Hussein, the Prophet's grandson. The Guardians of Independence Party played the largest role in organising and monitoring these meetings. At a particularly large gathering at the Hyderkhana Mosque in late May 1920, a delegation of fifteen people was selected to represent the throng to the British authorities. Wilson agreed to meet the delegation, and in consequence removed all restrictions on the holding of mass meetings. Such meetings proliferated throughout June 1920. Poets, orators, politicians and even notables (though reluctantly) all vied to impress the crowds with their patriotic zeal. The blind cleric and poet Muhammad Mahdi al-Basir was particularly celebrated for his impassioned speeches, and was dubbed the 'Mirabeau of Iraq'.[38] The British became increasingly concerned with the clamour and spread of these rallies. Gertrude Bell, Wilson's senior political adviser, wrote to her father on 1 June 1920: 'We are in the thick of violent agitation and we feel anxious . . . The extremists here [have] a handle which they are using. They have adopted a line difficult in itself to combat, the union between Shi'ah and Sunni, the unity of Islam. And they are running it for all it's worth.'[39]

From Karbala, the son of Grand Ayatollah Shirazi, Muhammad Ridha al-Shirazi, was actively assisting in the spread of anti-British propaganda and exhorting the tribes to join in launching a rebellion. The grand ayatollah himself stood openly in support of the agitation in Baghdad and sent delegations to the capital to report on developments there. He also wrote a letter to Faisal in Damascus, praising him for his work on behalf of Arab unity, 'the fount of Islamic unity', and asking for his help against the British in Iraq. 'You are surely aware of the oppression experienced at every instant by the suffering Iraqi people . . . This oppression has reached unbearable levels.' He then called on Faisal to bring the plight of the Iraqi people to the attention of the world's press and to the European and American governments.[40] Meetings were organised in Karbala and Najaf under the grand ayatollah's auspices, to select delegates to present their case to the British authorities.

Increasingly concerned with the trend of escalating events, Wilson sent a large force at the end of June 1920 to Karbala to arrest the key leaders of the agitation in the mid-Euphrates region, at the head of which was Muhammad Ridha. They were all deported to the island of Henjam at the head of the Gulf of Basra. Wilson thought that by these firm measures he would avert the risk of further trouble, but the opposite was the case. The news of the arrest of the grand ayatollah's son spread far and wide, and, with the prompting of the grand ayatollah himself, a major tribal conclave in the mid-Euphrates town of Mishkhab took place. Leading the gathering were Britain's old enemies, Sayyid 'Alwan al-Yasiri and Shaikh 'Abd al-Wahid. A delegation was then sent to Major Norberry, the chief political officer of the mid-Euphrates valley, demanding the release of Muhammad Ridha. Norberry prevaricated, as did other British political officers who were approached by tribal delegations demanding his release and holding Britain to its promises of Iraq's independence. In the town of Rumaitha, a minor tribal figure, Sha'lan Abul Jawn, chief of the Dhawalim division of the Bani Hachim tribe, was arrested and locked up in the town hall jail by the local British political officer. He was sprung from jail by his tribesmen to the accompaniment of general mayhem in the town. Returning to his tribal territory, Sha'alan knew that there was no turning back and raised the cry for a general uprising. On 1 July 1920, the town of Rumaitha was besieged by tribal forces. A relief column was badly mauled by tribesmen. Sir Aylmer Haldane, the commanding officer of British forces in Iraq, knew that he might have a general tribal uprising on his hands and telegraphed London for urgent reinforcements. He had nearly 60,000 troops under his command, 56,000 of which were Indians. Many of the latter were Muslim and thus might be hesitant to crush a partly religiously inspired uprising. But no reinforcements could be sent to him before the end of July at the earliest.

For nearly two weeks, because of deep tribal rivalries and fearful of the consequences of taking on a great power, none of the other tribes in the region joined Sha'lan in his uprising. Grand Ayatollah Shirazi, concerned that the hesitancy of the other tribes might abandon the Dhawalim to their fate, tried to open discussions with Wilson to settle the siege of Rumaitha peacefully, but Wilson would have none of it. The grand ayatollah then issued a fatwa authorising resistance to the British, by force if necessary, to regain the legitimate rights of Iraqis.[41] The Fatla tribe under Shaikh 'Abd al-Wahid raised the flag of revolt on 13 July 1920, and with other tribes who joined the rebellion laid siege to the town of Abu Sukhair. Nearly two hundred soldiers were billeted there, but they were allowed to retreat unscathed from the town. A truce between the rebellious tribes and the British did not last long, however, and by the end of July the entire mid-Euphrates valley was in the throes of a widespread tribal uprising. The town of Kifil fell to rebellious tribesmen, and Diwaniya, a major railroad depot and the chief military base of the British in the mid-Euphrates area, was threatened. At Rarinjiya, the rebels won a famous victory over a large British force.

But the rebels' momentum was drastically curbed by the disastrous defeat of the tribal forces trying to capture the important town of Hilla, and by relentless bombardment of their positions by the RAF. By August 1920 the British, reinforced by two Indian divisions, had regained the initiative in the mid-Euphrates valley and had retaken the town of Musayab and the barrage at Hindiya. They were now poised to assert their control over the centre of the rebellion, the shrine town of Karbala. Fortuitously for the British, Grand Ayatollah Shirazi, the spiritual and political head of the rebellion, died on 17 August, greatly affected by the parade of coffins of fallen tribal warriors coming to their burial place in Karbala. Grand Ayatollah Isfahani in Najaf was then nominated by general acclamation to be his successor. Isfahani issued a hortatory declaration, calling on the people to continue in their uprising, but he also authorised the opening of truce talks with Wilson. The latter had sent out peace feelers to Isfahani, and British planes carried this appeal to the insurgents by aerially dropping leaflets carrying Wilson's message over a wide area.[42]

The rebellion, however, continued. There was no consensus about whether Wilson's calls for peace were sincere. The rebels also sent out an appeal to the major powers and the League of Nations setting out their case.[43] But the rebellion never achieved the wide traction needed to sustain itself beyond the summer. Major tribal figures had stood by the British throughout. The tribes along the Tigris did not participate at all in the uprising, and neither did the effendis and hotheads of Baghdad who had earlier flocked to the mosques demanding the end of British tutelage. Although there were scattered tribal risings in the Diyala region, north-east of Baghdad, they were of short duration and were quickly quelled. West of Baghdad, Shaikh Dhari of the Zawba'a tribe killed Colonel Leachman, the British political officer for the western region of Iraq, but here again the revolt was short-lived. British forces soon recovered the town of Fallujah, the epicentre of the revolt in the west. They were helped in no small part by the position of the paramount chiefs of the Dulaim and Aniza tribes in preventing Dhari's revolt from spreading. The rebellious tribes of the Euphrates region were left to themselves. They began to suffer from shortages of money and ammunition, and were taking very large losses in the fighting. Wilson's truce calls also had their effect in splitting the ranks of the insurgents, with some questioning the wisdom of continuing the fight against very high odds. By the autumn of 1920 the rebellion had petered out, but the British had paid a high price for their victory. Nearly 2,500 British Empire soldiers were killed, wounded or missing in action. The rebellion cost the Treasury nearly £40 million, a vast sum for the times. Tribal losses, however, were higher. Nearly 8,500 people were killed or wounded during the uprising.[44]

The uprising was the final nail in the coffin of the policy that sought to turn Iraq into a protectorate directly ruled by Britain. Whitehall was now completely won over to the idea of an 'Arab government', run by locally recruited civil servants, albeit advised by the British. Britain's influence would now be indirect and allusive, exercised subtly through a high commissioner. Iraq would be bound by the terms of the mandate but the illusion, and part substance of independence, would be maintained without serious jeopardy to Britain's interests. Britain would still represent Iraq internationally, a condition of the mandate. Britain would maintain a residual force in Iraq for the purposes of internal security and external defence, and would keep an eye on the country's finances. Otherwise the 'Arab government' would be free to act in its own interests. This policy was debated and agreed during the summer months while the insurgency was raging, and it fell to Percy Cox to put the new policy into effect.[45] The India Office instructed Wilson to prepare the country to receive Cox as the new high commissioner. Wilson was effectively discredited. He left Iraq, and later left government service entirely. After a lengthy period of consultations in London, Cox arrived in Baghdad on 11 October 1920. A day later he set the

wheels in motion to form an 'Arab government', and offered the premiership to
the venerable Naqib of Baghdad 'Abd al-Rahman al-Gailani. The naqib formed
his first cabinet on 23 October 1920, comprising eight ministers, including the
Jewish notable Sassoon Effendi Heskei as minister of finance,[46] Faisal's old
friend Ja'far al-'Askari as minister of defence, and a lone Shi'a as minister of
education. The new cabinet was entirely dependent on the British: for money,
security, expertise and advice. It was this cabinet that began the formal overtures to Faisal, but not before the ground had been carefully laid out in London
and Cairo, and in Baghdad by Cox.

CHAPTER 18

KING OF IRAQ

FAISAL LANDED in Iraq precariously poised between the demands of the British and the demands for Iraqi independence. It was a difficult and uncomfortable perch from which to rule, but there was no plausible alternative. If he had been the uncompromising champion of immediate independence, he would have had no chance of achieving power. Britain would simply have vetoed his appointment and that would have been that. If he had turned himself into a British tool, his credibility would have been shattered with the independence party. He had to tread a fine line between these two poles: remaining true to his alliance with Britain without compromising on his goal of independence for Iraq. And this tension, to a greater or lesser extent, would mark his years in Iraq. The British had won a Pyrrhic victory over the insurgents; the price had been the abandonment of any suggestion that Iraq could be treated as a direct colony of Britain. A formula had to be found that would secure Britain's strategic interests and present the country with a reasonable path to independence. At the same time, a moderately nationalist government led by Faisal might be a buffer against the radicals and a bulwark against the spread of Bolshevist and Kemalist notions into Iraq. The Bolshevik threat was a particular preoccupation of the Foreign Office at that time.[1]

Faisal's popularity in Iraq was untested. The announcement of his imminent arrival in Iraq concentrated minds, and British intelligence reports of the time generally indicated a friendly interest in his candidature. But as he prepared to disembark from the *Northbrook*, Faisal was apprehensive about the welcome he was to receive from a population with which he had had little contact or first-hand knowledge. Even the British, the supposed architects of Faisal's candidature, were unsure as to the probable success of their venture. Gertrude Bell wrote to her father on 23 June 1921, the day of Faisal's arrival. 'We've thrown our die – the next few days will show whether it's a winning number. His [Faisal's] adherents anticipate that his coming will be the sign for a great popular ovation. Heaven send that it may be so for it will immensely simplify matters for us. Meantime there can be no question that it is regarded with anxiety by the magnates.'[2]

The British had done their best to reduce the number of serious contestants to the throne of Iraq. Sayyid Talib al-Naqib, the erstwhile minister of interior, had started to proclaim his candidature loudly, but the British had become alarmed at his bombastic behaviour and belligerency. On 16 April while returning from a tea party at Lady Cox's residence he was arrested and deported to Ceylon, and thereby a powerful and unscrupulous rival to Faisal had been safely removed from the scene. The effect of Sayyid Talib's unceremonious exile on the sulking notables of Baghdad, especially Prime Minister 'Abd al-Rahman al-Naqib, was immediate. Their tone of measured hostility to Faisal quickly changed to one of acceptance. Other would-be candidates also began to waver and withdraw. Shaikh Khaz'al of Muhammara switched from being a candidate to a fierce supporter of Faisal. He announced to Gertrude Bell that '[Faisal] was an infinitely more suitable candidate than himself and he would henceforth devote all his efforts to supporting him!'[3] Gradually, there built up a growing sense of the inevitability about the choice of Faisal as king of Iraq. 'Abd al-Rahman al-Naqib had become a firm advocate for Faisal, no doubt influenced by his frequent talks with Cox and Bell, who indicated that Faisal was also Britain's preference. A moderate pro-Faisal party had now coalesced and could count on the support of a number of prominent personalities as well as newspapers. Even amongst the radicals, Faisal had become an acceptable candidate. They had been angered by Churchill's speech in parliament on 12 June, made before Faisal's departure for Iraq, which reasserted that Britain would introduce a mandate government to Iraq. But they were not inherently anti-monarchist. The radicals' main point of contention was that an elected national congress should be convened first, at which Faisal would be chosen as a constitutional king.[4] Several Baghdadi newspapers, such as the *Dijla* (Tigris) and *al-Istiqlal* (Independence), reflected this point of view.[5]

In Baghdad, arrangements were hastily made to ensure that Faisal received a proper welcome. The cabinet had decided on 16 June to extend Faisal an official welcome and to receive him as a guest of the government. A few days before the *Northbrook*'s arrival, a number of Faisal's supporters in Iraq, led by Naji al-Suwaidi,[6] formerly the assistant military governor of Aleppo, and the governor of Baghdad, convened a large gathering at the Royal cinema in Baghdad, held with the knowledge and approval of the high commissioner. At the meeting, Naji solicited members of the audience to form a sixty-person welcoming party and to travel, at their own expense, by train to Basra to greet Faisal officially.[7] The welcoming party was joined by two government officials, the defence minister Ja'far al-'Askari and Philby. This was a deliberate decision by Cox to create the impression of impartiality, as Philby was known to be an opponent of Faisal and an advocate of a republican regime for Iraq. Cox also thought that an exposure to Faisal's charm and pleasant temperament might soften Philby's republicanism and even make him a convert to his cause. However, Philby was not a person to be easily swayed from his predispositions, and in fact he played an insidious part in undermining Faisal's reception. Wherever the train stopped en route to Basra, the local political officers, accompanied by the area's notables, would visit the train and ask Philby for instructions on to how to act when Faisal reached their districts. Philby told them that Faisal was merely a candidate for the throne of Iraq, not yet king, and that they were free to receive him as they saw fit. There had been no special instructions from the high commissioner in this regard.[8]

Basra and the journey to Baghdad

Faisal rode the motor launch from the *Northbrook* to shore. Alongside were dozens of small river craft and other launches flying the flag of the Arab Revolt. Along the riverfront were crowds of local farmers and workmen, calling out Faisal's name in greeting. Alighting at the 'Ashar district along the Shatt-al-Arab waterway, Faisal was confronted with banners hailing the 'Iraqi Confederation' and proclaiming 'Long live Basra'. These were not-so subtle reminders of the struggle going on behind the scenes between the advocates of an autonomous status for Basra and those calling for a centralised Iraq. Only a week before Faisal's arrival, a petition carrying the signature of 4,500 people was presented to the high commissioner by a Basra delegation. The delegation, mainly merchants and landowners headed by the notable 'Abd al-Latif al-Mandil, though not quite seeking independence for Basra, had demanded wide autonomy for the province. Basra's merchants had done well during the war. They sought to maintain their prosperity, which they equated with distance from Baghdad and autonomy, based on firm ties to the British.[9] However, the petitioners were by no means representative of all opinion in Basra; Cox had reservations about their demands and politely declined to support them.

Faisal spent only a day in Basra, at the house of the governor, Ahmad al-Sani'i. On the morning of his departure he received a large delegation of local notables, where poems and paeans were recited in his honour. Faisal extemporised a lengthy response, dwelling on his desire to serve his country and to follow whomever the people chose as their ruler.[10] In the evening, he and his entourage boarded the train that was to take them to Baghdad, stopping at most of the towns of the lower and mid-Euphrates valley. In Faisal's private car sat his personal adviser Cornwallis, with Philby. They spent most of their time arguing politics and drinking whisky and soda. Faisal was, of course, aware of Philby's personal hostility to the sharifian cause and his republican inclinations, but he was nevertheless angered by Philby's brusqueness. To a question from Faisal as to the chances of his candidature, Philby was alleged to have replied: 'It rather depends on your own attitude. So far as the people in general have any policy, it sums up in the one word – independence. The rebellion was led and fought on that single issue. It was discontinued in response to the British government's acceptance of a change of policy on the basis of independence. Now, if you are to base your campaign on the fact that you are the accepted nominee of the British government, I think your chances are extremely slender. If on the other hand you declare that you seek the suffrage of the people as a champion of their complete independence, then I think you have a better chance than anybody.'[11] This rather dry but balanced response has been contradicted by others who witnessed the conversation. They recalled that Philby had advocated a republican form of government to Faisal.

Faisal had been nonplussed by his reception in Basra, with its mixture of staged enthusiasm, a formal but cold official welcome, and local calls for autonomy. His bewilderment increased as he experienced contradictory impressions throughout his journey in southern Iraq. At Nasiriya, the first stop, the official welcoming party was small and formal. At Samawa he was received rather more warmly by groups of local shaikhs and tribesmen, but the audience at Diwaniya was much smaller and showed little enthusiasm.[12] Arriving at Hilla, Faisal was met by a welcoming party composed of only two individuals: Bertram Thomas, the deputy local administrative officer and Philby acolyte, and 'Abd al-Razzaq Sharif, the mayor. Ja'far al-'Askari, witnessing this humiliating reception, exploded at the hapless mayor for his apathy and organisational incompetence, but of course the mayor had no say in the matter. The reception formalities were the responsibility of the political officers, who had been primed by Philby to adopt a measured indifference to Faisal's presence. Ali Jawdat, who had accompanied Faisal on the *Northbrook*, was also on the train with him. He recalls in his memoirs that Bertram Thomas walked into Faisal's waiting room and rudely asked him, 'Why have you come to Iraq?'

Faisal replied, 'And why are you asking me this?'

Thomas said, 'Because the people don't want you.'

Faisal said, 'And why do you want to interfere between me and my people?'

'Only so as to inform you,' said Thomas.

'I have no need of your information. You will soon know whether the people want me or not,' replied Faisal. At which point, Thomas left the room.[13]

Hilla was Faisal's alighting point for the all-important journey to the shrine towns, which he could reach only by motor car. There, he and his entourage stayed at the house of the local dignitary, Sayyid Muhammad Ali al-Qazwini. A number of visitors called on the house to welcome the prince, in marked contrast to the miserable public reception that Faisal was accorded at the Hilla railroad station.[14]

On the following day, 26 June, Faisal left Hilla in a motorcade for the shrine towns of Najaf and Karbala. Cornwallis and Philby stayed behind. Philby's negative effect on the journey unexpectedly terminated: he was struck with malaria while still in Hilla. Faisal arrived in Najaf in full Arab regalia, no doubt symbolising to the people that the goals of the 1920 rebellion and Iraq's independence under an Arab king were near the point of realisation. Throughout his visit to Najaf he was accompanied by Muhammad Ridha al-Shibibi, the emissary to Faisal and the Arab government in Damascus. Al-Shibibi had become a great advocate for Faisal amongst the leaders of the 1920 rebellion.[15] Faisal's first act was to visit the imposing shrine of Imam Ali, the person from whom all *sayyids*, including the sharifs of Mecca, descend. A large gathering was organised for him at the home of Sayyid Hadi al-Naqib, where Faisal delivered a speech extolling the achievements of the Arab Revolt and the Iraq rebellion. Baqir al-Shibibi, brother of Muhammad Ridha, stood up to welcome Faisal. 'We have been eagerly awaiting the visit of Iraq's great guest, Prince Faisal, to the epicentre of the revolt, where we hope its objectives will now be achieved. . . . We seek God's support in ensuring that the goals of His Majesty King Hussein for the independence of the Arab lands and the unity of all the Arabs will be achieved.' In the evening Faisal was regaled at a banquet organised by the gatekeeper (*kilidar*) of the shrine, Abbas al-Kilidar. Faisal gave a speech calling for the reconstruction and development of the country. This was followed by a rousing speech given, once again, by Baqir al-Shibibi. This time, however, Shibibi chose some unfortunate turns of phrase: 'We have sacrificed all that is near and dear to us, and we cannot be expected to hand over the fruits of our long struggle except to trustworthy hands that would be jealous of protecting the country's independence and our national goals and interests.' Whether or not al-Shibibi was deliberately alluding to Faisal was immaterial. Faisal took the statement as a personal affront, and it clouded what up to then had been a successful visit to Najaf.[16]

On 27 July, Faisal proceeded by car to Karbala. There the governor, an Indian, Hamid Khan, had earlier decamped to Baghdad because he did not want to be present when Faisal arrived there. He had obviously been influenced by Philby's admonishments. Cox, however, sent him back to Karbala, where he hurriedly tried to make up for the absence of an official reception for Faisal. In Karbala Faisal visited the shrines of Imam Hussein and his brother al-Abbas, and met various religious figures. But it was an awkward, and not altogether successful, visit. The leading *ulemas* of the town had stayed markedly aloof. Returning to Hilla, Faisal was received far more enthusiastically this time round. Crowds of people, perhaps shamefaced at their earlier reticence, now thronged the streets, hailing him and crying out, 'Welcome to King Faisal!' Hordes of visitors descended on the house at which he was staying, and poets vied with each other in singing his praises.[17] On 29 June Faisal's train left Hilla for Baghdad. Faisal was undoubtedly disappointed by his reception in the south, where the country's Shi'a majority lived, and the lack of enthusiasm surely added to the insecurity of his position and his precarious standing as an outsider.[18] He openly blamed Philby for his poor reception, but there must still have lurked the suspicion that it was the British authorities who were behind this. After all, by inviting him to Iraq, they were also responsible for ensuring the cordiality of his welcome.

Arrival in Baghdad

Whatever misgivings Faisal might have had about the fervour of his reception in southern Iraq, they were soon overcome by the immense crowds and the displays of support and affection that met him when he reached Baghdad. His train was supposed to arrive in the early morning, but it was delayed until the late afternoon. This only increased the anticipation of his arrival. Rumours swirled in Baghdad that the train had been deliberately held up by the British so that the crowds would disperse and his reception would be muted,[19] but the delay was more probably due to a breakdown along the tracks. Whatever the case, the crowds only grew larger. Gertrude Bell wrote to her father about the events of the day, June 29: 'Colonel Joyce [formerly the military adviser to the Northern Army] and I motored to the station together . . . The whole town was decorated, triumphal arches, Arab flags, and packed with people, in the street, on the housetops, everywhere. At the station immense crowds.' Returning to the station in the early evening, Bell noted that 'the town was unbelievably more crowded than before – I scarcely thought we should get through. However we did, and arrived to find the station similarly much fuller of people.'[20] It was a particularly hot day in the middle of a Baghdadi summer, hardly the type of weather that would encourage crowds to come out, which must have added more significance to Faisal's reception.

Faisal was received by High Commissioner Percy Cox, General-Officer-Commanding Sir Aylmer Haldane, the minister of justice representing the prime minister and a large coterie of officials and notables. Gertrude Bell wrote: 'Sidi [My Lord] Faisal stood at the carriage looking very splendid in full Arab dress, saluting the guard of honour. Sir Percy [Cox] and Sir Aylmer [Haldane] went up to him as he got out and gave him a fine ceremonious greeting, and all the people clapped. He went down the line of the guard of honour, inspecting it.'[21] Delegations from all the provinces of Iraq were also on hand to greet him. Faisal then drove through the decorated streets and triumphal arches to his lodgings. His car was mobbed at several points by the dense crowds. The poet, and one of the heroes of the 1920 rebellion, Muhammad Mahdi al-Basir, wrote in his narrative of the times, 'The city received him most tumultuously and never was Baghdad more attractive with its festive decorations. The people that day showed their true love for the prince.'[22]

Baghdad had not been a true capital city since the collapse of the Abbasid Empire in 1258. There were only three bridges, mounted on boats astride the Tigris River. The main street, cut by the Turks during the war, was still unpaved. Along its route were abandoned houses that had been shorn in half with pieces of furniture lying about. When it rained, infrequently, but then often torrentially, the streets became impassable. Porters would then line up to ferry people on their backs across the inundated streets. Most of the houses in the city were poorly constructed mud-and-brick dwellings. The great families of the city lived in large, rambling houses, hidden behind heavy doors opening on narrow lanes. It was a private world where the patriarchs of these families presided, dressed in long robes, beturbanned and uniformly bearded. Their sons, often partly westernised by virtue of their modern Ottoman education, tended to wear suits and fezes. Women were cloistered and hardly ventured out of their private domains except to go to the public baths.

There were no public utilities to speak of. Lighting and sanitation were rudimentary, and water had to be carried to the houses from the river, by donkey or by hand in leather skins, where it was stored in large earthenware jars. Public transport was primitive, relying on a fleet of ancient carriages run by ill-tempered and foul-mouthed drivers wearing the Iraqi workman's headgear, the *charawiya*. The famed arts and crafts of Baghdad had vanished, although there were guilds of artisans in the jewellery, silversmith and coppersmith trades. Faisal's new capital was to all intents and purposes a medieval city with a smattering of modernity superimposed on it.

Faisal stayed at Dar-al-Mashiriya, the official residence of the former Ottoman governors of Baghdad. It formed a wing of a large building called the Qishla, part of the complex of Ottoman governmental buildings known as the Serai, on the left bank of the Tigris. Faisal's apartments overlooked the river. On the day after his arrival, poets in time-honoured fashion called on the future king, welcoming him in verse and competing in praise of his virtues. The leading poet of Iraq at that time, Jamil Sidqi al-Zahawi, composed a particularly well-known poetic greeting. Its first line ran: 'All of Iraq resounds in greeting / You, O Noble King'.

Faisal wasted no time in approaching the Shi'a community, the people whose ambivalent welcome had perplexed and worried him. On the following day, he visited the overwhelmingly Shi'a town of Kadhimain, a few miles to the north of Baghdad. Kadhimain was the site of the shrines of Musa al-Kadhim and Muhammad al-Jawad, the seventh and ninth imams of the Shi'a. His reception was fervent and sheep were slaughtered at his feet in welcome. A large banquet hosted by the notables of the town was held in his honour. He prayed at the shrine of Musa al-Kadhim, and was later received at the homes of the religious leader Sayyid Muhammad Hussein al-Sadr and the Kadhimain notable 'Abd al-Hussein al-Chalabi. On 1 July Faisal attended Friday prayers at the main centre of Sunni Islam in Baghdad, the shrine of Imam Hanifa, one of the founders of the four schools of Sunni Islam. Later he visited the shrine of 'Abd al-Qadir al-Gailani, the eleventh-century founder of the Qadiri Sufi order, whose descendant 'Abd al-Rahman al-Naqib was now the prime minister of Iraq. The entire neighbourhood of the shrine, the Bab al-Shaikh district, which was decked out in flowers, came out to greet him. Faisal then visited the naqib's home, and was received by the naqib's eldest son Mahmud, who said, 'The family of the Naqib, O Prince, are your right hand which you can use any way you wish in the service of the country.'[23]

A few weeks later Faisal moved to a house in the Kasra district of Baghdad, rented for him by the Ministry of Interior to serve as his permanent residence. The house belonged to a wealthy Jewish merchant of Baghdad, ibn Sha'shou'.[24]

Building support

Faisal was well aware of the complex make-up of Iraq, with its mixed tribal and settled population, its Shi'as and Sunnis, Arabs, Kurds and Turcomen, and bewildering array of smaller communities, from Jews to Christians, to Yazidis and Sabaeans. Iraq also had a fairly large group of settled Persian residents, mainly in the shrine towns, as well as deserters and stragglers of different nationalities from the former Ottoman army. His greatest challenge at first was to establish his legitimacy and to sink roots in the country. This could not be done, however, without establishing a modicum of support from the Shi'a. By a small margin, they outnumbered the rest of the population. The politically conscious Shi'a were divided into different groups. Some were involved in, and even led, the nationalist movement. Their attitude to Faisal was a cautious welcome, respectful of his leadership of the Arab Revolt and his rule in Syria. But respect was tinged with concern that he would fall under British influence and would bargain away or jeopardise the cherished nationalist goals of complete independence and sovereignty.

The mostly Shi'a leaders of the 1920 rebellion who had taken refuge in the Hijaz had first-hand knowledge of Faisal and were generally supportive of his candidature. Faisal benefited from the wide-ranging discussions on Iraq that he had with them, which deepened his understanding of sectarian issues. Muhammad Ridha al-Shibibi, in a letter to Sayyid 'Alwan al-Yasiri, talked of this interaction between Faisal and the leaders of the rebellion. 'And of those matters that give satisfaction . . . are the agreements that drew you to Faisal and he to you. There is no doubt that you poured out your views and concerns to him [Faisal] and informed him of the flow of events in Iraq, and gave him of your valuable advice and worthy opinions . . . This will give him a fulsome understanding and insights into the conditions of Iraqis, their habits and traditions, religion and practices and their other circumstances.'[25] However, the group of Shi'a exiles in Mecca had split, with one faction supporting Faisal and accompanying him back to Iraq on the *Northbrook*. This split was to some extent engineered by Hussein who exhibited blatant favouritism between the Iraqi exiles. The dissenting group included Ja'far Abu al-Timmen, a leading figure in the Haras al-Istiqlal, who had fled to the shrine towns after a deportation order was made against him by A. T. Wilson. Abu al-Timmen later made his way to the Hijaz after the British succeeded in suppressing the 1920 rebellion. This faction was not prepared to give Faisal their unconditional allegiance without some assurances as to the limited nature of the proposed mandate. They stayed behind in the Hijaz and reached Iraq later by a different route.[26]

The *ulema* were the other politically significant group that Faisal had to contend with. The *mujtahids* of the Shi'a mainly looked askance at their entanglements with politics, but they had nevertheless taken a leading part in the rebellion of 1920. Some of the lesser *ulema* had become highly politicised, and their goals did not differ in substance from those of the nationalist movement. Faisal had enough experience with tribal politics to deal with the paramount chiefs of the Shi'a tribes, but he was still unable to manage or influence the strong bonds that they had with the leading *mujtahids* of the shrine towns. All the Iraqis in Faisal's army were Arab (or Arabised) Sunnis, and his engagement with the Shi'a dignitaries of Iraq was of very recent origin, dating from the last days of his rule in Syria. Rustum Haidar, one of his closest advisers and a Shi'a from Lebanon, could only give Faisal general guidance about the policies that he should adopt with the Shi'as of Iraq. He himself was a committed Arab nationalist and highly secular in his outlook, and was unable to relate fully, at least in 1921, to the religiously charged world of Iraqi Shi'as

Faisal could count on the help and advice of those Iraqi Shi'a figures whom he could trust, but not those with whom he had only recently come into contact. He therefore had to rely mainly on his own intuition and innate resources. These were, however, quite formidable. He was acutely conscious of the sectarian sensitivities in Iraq and had already determined that he needed to reach out to the Shi'a. His progress through southern Iraq and his deliberate halting at the shrine towns were indicative of his concern in this regard. The coolness of his reception by the *mujtahids* may have dismayed him, but it did not deter him from continuing to find common ground with them. Faisal also benefited from his lineage. There was no doubt of his illustrious line, which he could trace back to Imam Hassan, the eldest son of Ali, the Prophet's cousin and son-in-law and the first of the Shi'a imams. Faisal's religious views were known to be liberal for the time. Though formally a Sunni of the Hanafi school, he held no doctrinaire or dogmatic positions. In fact, British intelligence reports of the period mention that there was a widespread belief that he was a closet Shi'a![27] He was an early exponent of inter-faith and inter-sect toleration, and for the Shi'a, emerging from the Ottoman centuries of indifference and marginalisation, this would have been a welcome change of perspective from a ruler.

Faisal's support in the Sunni community was not that much deeper, but he had a natural base, small though it was, amongst the sharifian officers who had served in the Northern Army and those who had later accompanied him to Damascus. However, these officers were regarded with great reserve and suspicion by the traditional Sunni elites of Iraq. The main Sunni tribal confederations in the western and northern parts of the country were solidly behind the British, who were to all intents and purposes their paymasters, and could be expected to take their lead from the high commissioner. The nationalist movement, on the other hand, was dominated by ambitious politicians, mostly drawn from the former Ottoman functionary class. At this time their interests had not crystallised into an anti-monarchical stance. They were primarily concerned with ensuring that the country's politics were not totally dominated by the British and that Faisal was bound by the terms of a constitution. Their goals overlapped with those of Faisal, whose idea of legitimacy precluded subservience to the British. Faisal was determined that his relationship with Britain be defined by a treaty rather than by the unilateral terms of the mandate. That left the naqib of Baghdad, whose earlier hostility to Faisal and the whole idea of sharifian rule had abruptly given way to acceptance. Faisal had to mollify the naqib and establish the basis of a sound working relationship with him. He was a sensible and wise personage, who carefully chose his positions on the basis of a pragmatic disposition that recognised the realities of power, mixed with a reverence for the traditional religious office that he had inherited. The naqib was now predisposed to open a new chapter with Faisal.[28]

On 7 July the naqib hosted a large banquet at his house in honour of Faisal. It was widely seen as a good-will gesture and a peace offering. The neighbourhood was adorned with flowers, and as Faisal arrived at the house the naqib was there in person to welcome him, leaning his frail body on his personal physician. They embraced and entered the house hand in hand in the traditional Arab demonstration of friendship. Faisal took his place at the head of the assembly, between the naqib and the high commissioner. The poet Ma'arouf al-Rusafi delivered a poem in praise of Faisal and the naqib. Al-Rusafi, a brilliant poet, but a mercurial and complex person, had only recently been given a sinecure in the government, which may explain his enthusiasm for the powers that be.[29]

On 11 July the Iraqi cabinet convened and unanimously passed a resolution that called for Faisal as king of Iraq, with the stipulation that his government would be 'constitutional, democratic, representative and limited by law'.[30] By this time the naqib had fully converted to Faisal's cause. The cabinet decision was prompted by background manoeuvring by Percy Cox, who had become concerned that a growing climate of uncontrolled enthusiasm for Faisal might lead to his proclamation as king by acclamation of the radicals, a *coup d'état* that would draw them into the centre of power and cast a shadow over Faisal's legitimacy. Cox had delayed the promulgation of an election law that would have allowed for the establishment of a constituent assembly, ostensibly because of the difficulties involved in organising elections in the Kurdish areas of the country. In any case, it would take several months before a constituent assembly could meet, thus delaying the issue of who should rule Iraq. Cox sent a letter on 8 July to the cabinet, setting out the reasons why a referendum would be more suitable under the circumstances. 'There appears to be an increasingly insistent demand on the part of the public for an immediate opportunity to decide who shall be ruler,' he wrote.[31] Cox informed the cabinet that he could only approve their resolution offering Faisal the crown if a referendum was organised that would confirm the wishes of the people. Faisal himself was markedly in favour of a referendum, and was equally sensitive to the idea that his rule should be based on popular sanction. Bell found Faisal in high spirits as a result of the cabinet resolution and Cox's calls for a referendum: 'I found him radiant – it was very different from my first early morning visit the day after he arrived! But eagerly insisting on the need of a referendum through the machinery of the Ministry of Interior which, I was able to assure him was exactly what Sir Percy wanted . . . His anti chamber was a sight to gladden one – full of Baghdad notables and shaikhs from all parts of the country.'[32]

Faisal's campaign to build up his support was paying off. In the two months between his arrival in Iraq and his coronation, he attended countless banquets, parties and gatherings organised in his honour. Only a day after his arrival in Baghdad, the municipality held a large banquet at the Maude Gardens, attended by all of the senior British officials and leading Iraqi figures. The poet al-Zahawi stood up and recited: 'We have invited you as our king / We will never accept anyone but you.'

The audience cheered and he was called upon to recite these lines three times.[33] A professional reciter of lamentations for the martyred Imam Hussein, or *rawzakhun*, brought the audience nearly to tears. Bell, who did not understand his words, was nevertheless moved: 'And then there stepped forward into the grassy space between the tables a shi'ah in white robes and a black cloak

and big black turban and chanted a poem of which I didn't understand a word
... but nevertheless it was wonderful. The tall robed figure chanting and
making time with an uplifted hand, the starry darkness and the palm trees
beyond the illuminated circle – it hypnotized you.'[34] Another person compared
Faisal to the great heroes of history, calling him 'the Napoleon of the Adnanis'
and the 'Bismarck of the Qahtanis'. The Adnan and Qahtan were the two mythical founding tribes of the Arabs. Faisal thanked the speakers, but mildly chas-
tised them for their exaggerations and hyperboles. The incessant speechifying,
here and elsewhere, was quite a burden for him. He confided to Bell, 'I used to
do all I could to avoid speeches in Syria and I'm afraid that they are going to be
much worse here!'[35]

Another significant event was at the Ja'fariya School, located in the Souk
al-Ghazzal neighbourhood of Baghdad, a predominantly Shi'a area. This school
had been founded in 1906 by leading Shi'a notables of Baghdad to provide a
modern education for Shi'a children who had been denied access to Ottoman
state schools. It was a point of pride for the Shi'a community, and a large
number of the future leaders of the Shi'a – professionals, merchants and
politicians – were schooled here. It was an important and symbolic setting for
Faisal to visit. After the usual rounds of speeches and poetic recitations, Faisal
stood up and replied, 'I swear, by God, by God, by God, I did not make this
move seeking any worldly gain or any material reward. I have not acted because
I sought fame or station or position. And neither have I nor my father nor any
one of my family arisen because we were greedy for anything, but only because
we did our duty seeking the mercy of God . . . I swear by my honour and the
souls of my ancestors [the Prophet's household] that were it not for the insistence of my friends and the Iraqi nation, I would never have considered coming
to Iraq.' At which point, Ahmad al-Shaikh Dawood, a local dignitary, stood up
and in a loud voice demanded the audience swear fealty to Faisal as king. They
roared back their assent.[36]

A few days later, on 18 July Faisal attended a banquet given by the chief
rabbi of the Jewish community of Baghdad, a large and commercially significant part of Baghdad society. Gertrude Bell was there and wrote of the occasion, 'Faisal was clapped to the echo when we came and we all sat down to a
programme of 13 speeches and songs interspersed with iced lemonade, coffee,
tea and cakes and ices! It took two hours by the clock, in sweltering heat . . . The
speeches on this occasion are all set speeches . . . But yet they were interesting
because one knew the tensions which underlay them, the anxiety of the Jews
lest an Arab government should mean chaos, and their gradual reassurance, by
reason of Faisal's obviously enlightened attitude.'[37]

The chief rabbi presented Faisal with the Rolls of Law in their golden cylin-
ders and a bound the copy of the Talmud. He was also given a plaque with

Hebrew inscriptions reading, 'Give him strength O Lord, and accept his work, and destroy the power of his enemies so that none can resist him.' The ubiquitous poet al-Zahawi was also in attendance, this time giving a speech on the need for brotherhood between human beings. Faisal replied, citing the common ties that should bind all Iraqis. 'I do not want to hear about Muslims, Christians and Jews. For Iraq is a national homeland, and there is only one nation here and it's called the Iraqi [nation].'[38]

On 30 July it was the turn of the Chaldean Christian community to host Faisal. He gave a speech that emphasised his tolerance of all sects and religions: 'I do not differentiate between sect and sect for we are all Iraqis . . . Let all know that in this land there are no minorities or majorities, for a minority is a majority and a majority a minority.' He then went on to speak of the renaissance that he looked forward to in Iraq. He would lead the country in rapid development after seven hundred years under foreign tutelage. But 'we must not hurry and err, and let not our hot blood and nationalist sentiments boil over precipitously.' He then expressed his support for the British alliance, saying that there were Britons who were more loyal to Iraq than some Iraqis. He then added, rather incautiously, that he might be mistaken in his assessment of the British, but that no one should stand against the policy of alliance and friendship with Britain.[39]

The Sunni Arab tribes of western and northern Iraq, led by Ali Suleiman of the Dulaim, were the next to host Faisal. They were solidly aligned with the British and took their cue from the Residency. It is probable that the invitation to Faisal was prompted by the British, partly no doubt to remind him of the power that they wielded behind the scenes with the tribes. Gertrude Bell, a close confidante of Ali Suleiman, attended the banquet, which was held in the open desert. In a letter to her father of 31 July, Bell describes the events of the day and its extraordinary demonstration of Britain's influence on the tribes.

> Under the steep edge of the Syrian desert were drawn up the fighting men of the Anazeh, horsemen and camel riders, bearing the huge standard of the tribe. We stopped to salute it as we passed. Ali Sulaiman the Chief of the Dulaim, and one of the most remarkable men in Iraq came out of the Ramadi to meet us. He has been strongly and consistently pro-British . . . We drove to the Euphrates bank where Ali Sulaiman had pitched a huge tent about 200 ft. long with a dais at the upper end and roofed with tent cloth and walled with fresh green boughs. Outside were drawn up the camel riders of the Dulaim, their horsemen and their standard carried by a negro mounted on a gigantic white camel; inside the tribesmen lined the tent 5 or 6 deep from the dais to the very end. Faisal sat on the high diwan . . . Faisal was in his own country with the people he knew. I never saw him look so splendid. He wore his usual white robes with a fine black *abba* over them, flowing white headdress and

silver bound *Aqal*. Then he began to speak, leaning forward over the small
table in front of him, sitting with his hand raised and bringing it down on the
table to emphasize his sentences. The people at the end of the tent were too far
off to hear; he called them all up and they sat on the ground below the dais
rows and rows of them, 400 or 500 men. He spoke in the great tongue of the
desert, sonorous, magnificent – no language like it. He spoke as a tribal chief
to his feudatories. 'For four years,' he said, 'I have not found myself in a place
like this or in such company' – you could see how he was loving it. Then he
told them how Iraq was to rise to their endeavours with himself at their head.
'Oh Arabs are you at peace with one another?' They shouted, 'Yes, yes, we are
at peace.' 'From this day – what is the date? and what is the hour?' Someone
answered him. 'From this day the 25th July (only he gave the Mohammedan
date) and the hour of the morning (it was 11 o'clock) any tribesman who lifts
his hand against a tribesman is responsible to me – I will judge between you
calling your Shaikhs in council. I have my rights over you as your Lord.' A grey
bearded man interrupted, 'And our rights'. 'And you have your rights as
subjects which it is my business to guard.' So it went on, the tribesmen interrupting him with shouts, 'Yes, yes,' 'We agree . . . Yes, by God.' It was the
descriptions of great tribal gatherings in the days of ignorance, before the
Prophet, when the poets recited verse which has come down to this day and
the people shouted at the end of each phrase, 'The truth, by God the truth.'

When it was over Fahad and Ali Sulaiman stood up on either side of him
and said, 'We swear allegiance to you because you are acceptable to the British
government.' Faisal was a little surprised. He looked quickly round to me
smiling and then he added, 'No one can doubt what my relations are to the
British, but we must settle our affairs ourselves.' He looked at me again, and I
held out my two hands clasped as a symbol of the Union of the Arab and
British Governments. It was a tremendous moment, those two really big men
who have played their part in the history of their time, and Faisal between
them the finest living representative of his race – and the link ourselves. One
after another Ali Sulaiman brought up his shaikhs, some 40 or 50 of them.
They laid their hands in Faisal's and swore allegiance.[40]

Irrespective of the gloss that Faisal had put on it, it was an embarrassing
declaration by two of the most powerful shaikhs of western Iraq about their
dependency on the British and their good will, and the need to ensure Britain's
commitment to Faisal before they in turn would give their allegiance to him. It
also revealed a distrust of the type of government that Faisal was going to lead.
The tribes of the western desert were more comfortable with the British as
their paymasters and advisers than the urbanised and secularised elites that
they thought would dominate the government of an independent Iraq. It

reflected the deep divisions between traditional Bedouin Arabs and the alien ways of a 'modern' government. (When asked later, after Gertrude Bell's death, by the Lebanese writer Amin Rihani about the veracity of Bell's reminiscences of these events, Faisal replied, 'Miss Bell was true in what she wrote, but did harm in what she did, May God rest her soul.'[41])

The process known as *baya'a*, or giving a binding allegiance, was the traditional way by which Muslims affirmed their loyalty to a new ruler. Faisal gave this measure its due importance, especially with religiously minded communities. A commitment of this type could carry equal, if not more, weight with these groups than the formal process of a referendum. Faisal in particular sought the *baya'a* of important religious figures who had stood aloof from his candidature, and none was more significant in this regard than Ayatollah Mahdi al-Khalisi of Kadhimain, one of the leading Arab ayatollahs of Iraq, though not quite of the first rank as a *mujtahid*. Al-Khalisi had taken a strong position against the Arab Revolt, which he saw as giving support to infidels against a Muslim state. Al-Khalisi's son, Muhammad Mahdi, a power in his own right, was even more implacably hostile to Faisal. He saw him as an interloper and a master of deception. Faisal, soon upon his arrival in Baghdad, started to woo the ayatollah, sending him messages of greetings and asking about his welfare. He also visited the Khalisiya School, an important religious academy in Kadhimain, where he had audiences with the ayatollah. Faisal finally obtained the *baya'a* of al-Khalisi, which was published in the local press on 13 July 1921, though it was not exactly what he had sought. It read in part: 'Praise be to God who has unfurled the banner of truth over his creation, and gave them victory under the leadership of one who has won honour and dignity, the king who must be obeyed, and incumbent upon us to obey . . . his high majesty Faisal the First . . . and hasten to give him allegiance . . . we are ones who have accepted this ruling and give him allegiance in private and public, to be king over Iraq.'

But Ayatollah al-Khalisi ended his declaration with a major qualification to his *baya'a*: 'On the condition that as king of Iraq he would be constrained [in his powers] by a constituent assembly, separate from the power of the others [the British], independent alongside him in its decisions and rulings.'[42]

The public display of the ayatollah's conditional allegiance was of profound significance and played a large part in mobilising the nationalist movement to question the installation of Faisal as king before a constituent assembly had been elected. Two days before, on 11 July, the people of 'Adhamiya, where the main Sunni shrine of Baghdad was located, had given their *baya'a* at a public gathering where the district's notables and tribal leaders of the surrounding lands were present. No such preconditions to the *baya'a* were made in this instance. The Jewish community of 'Adhamiya, meeting at another house, also gave their *baya'a* to Faisal.[43]

It is hard to discern the extent of Faisal's true popularity in Iraq on the eve of the referendum that was to establish his legitimacy. He led a tireless campaign that took him into the countryside, to the desert lands of the tribes, to the minor towns of south and central Iraq. Nevertheless, he was still an outsider with no natural constituency. His support was wide but shallow; yet there was no real alternative, a fact understood by even the radical nationalists. The path of revolt had ended in abject failure; the other candidates for the throne had scattered and in any case had been non-starters; the republican option was a conceit of only a few urban intellectuals, promoted by the quixotic Philby. (Cox had asked for his resignation after his less than constructive behaviour with Faisal during his travels through the south of Iraq.[44])

Faisal's personal traits, dignified bearing, impeccable manners and careful diplomacy no doubt helped to improve his standing amongst the Iraqis as well as the British. 'What helps everything is that Faisal's personality goes three quarters of the way,' wrote Bell. A British intelligence report of the time praised his 'personality and statesmanship which had made an admirable impression. The consideration he had shown for the local deputations, which had come to Baghdad to welcome him, had captured their suffrage and many of the *Ashraf* of Baghdad are already prepared to consider his election as King as settled.'[45] But the fact remained that the single most important factor behind Faisal's support in the country, especially amongst its political and social elites, was the evident support of the British for his candidature. It is not so much that Faisal was 'imposed' on Iraqis, as later radical nationalists would claim, but rather that most of Iraq's elites were thoroughly in awe of Sir Percy Cox, and had a healthy respect for British power. Cox had imposed his authority on all strata of Iraq's society. Bell practically hero-worshipped him, but then so did many Iraqis who came into contact with him and fell under the thrall of his authority and pro-consular presence.[46]

The radicals who opposed Faisal's nomination by referendum were partly driven by genuine concerns about the country's independence, but a good many were simply office seekers who could, and did, switch their loyalties when the occasion arose. Whatever their motives, al-Khalisi's conditional *baya'a* had a galvanising effect on them and they gathered at Baghdad's Royal Cinema to hear the governor of Baghdad invite them to support Faisal's nomination. The audience, however, loudly approved demands that Faisal's government be independent of all foreign powers, and that Faisal should call for a constituent assembly within three months of his coronation. The incident at the cinema incensed Cox and he removed the unfortunate governor from his post.[47] A similar incident happened in Kadhimain at the house of the politically minded Sayyid Muhammad al-Sadr, a scion of the powerful al-Sadr religious family. Al-Sadr had invited a large number of dignitaries and clerics to consider signing a petition that would have called on Faisal to denounce the proposed mandate. One of the attendees slipped away to tell Faisal that a plot was being hatched against him at al-Sadr's house. Faisal despatched an aide to bring al-Sadr over to his quarters. He told him in no uncertain terms that he [Faisal] was king for all practical purposes and that he would not tolerate untoward actions and disturbances to the public peace.[48]

The plebiscite

The plebiscite to gauge public opinion on the installation of Faisal as king was organised over about two weeks, commencing at the end of July 1921. It was based on soliciting the views of a wide group of people, ranging from local officials (and their British advisers), notables and dignitaries in Baghdad and the provinces (*liwas*), and involved arranging meetings, mainly presided over by the British or trusted government officials, at which selected representatives would make their views known. These declarations would be brought in front of an election committee that would draw them up in *madhbatas* or petitions. The form of these *madhbatas* was already fixed and printed, and no deviations to its wording were allowed.[49] The process was not too dissimilar from Wilson's earlier referendum. Riders to the *madhbatas* were allowed, primarily to encourage the inclusion of declarations in favour of British support and the mandate system. Every effort was exerted by Cox and his administration to ensure that the desired outcome would be achieved. Nevertheless, there were enough dissensions and qualifications to make the results of the process contentious. The official form of the *madhbata* was rejected by Ayatollah al-Khalisi and other Shi'a leaders. An altered version of the form, calling on Faisal to be a constitutional king, independent of a foreign power and subject to a constituent assembly, was widely distributed in Baghdad. There were more such *madhbatas* in Baghdad other than the officially sanctioned ones.

In Kirkuk *liwa*, with its large Turcomen and Kurdish population, opinion as expressed in the official *madhbatas* was against Faisal, but only by a small margin. In Suleimaniya, an overwhelmingly Kurdish province, no referendum took place. In Mosul, the *madhbatas* had riders that called on Faisal to respect the rights of Kurds and Christians. In Basra, the signatories to the *madhbatas* withheld their support until they were assured that the British mandate would continue and that Basra's call for autonomy would be considered. Elsewhere, however, the plebiscite proceeded according to plan. In the tribal areas of western Iraq, the mid-Euphrates valley and the lower Tigris, many of the *madhbatas* had riders that made their support for Faisal contingent upon the continuation of the British mandate. In the shrine towns of Najaf and Karbala, the official form of the *madhbata* was signed without any riders.

The plebiscite was certainly flawed but it was not completely unrepresentative of public opinion in the circumstances and conditions of the summer of 1921. British officialdom sought to represent its results as an outpouring of popular support for Faisal. Bell talked of his being elected unanimously with one exception (Kirkuk), which, though technically true, overlooked the qualifying riders from Baghdad and elsewhere. The Ministry of Interior announced that 96 per cent of the 'electorate' had assented to the election of Faisal as king of Iraq. But it was not the farce that some nationalist writers later claimed it to be. It broadly reflected the views of Iraq's leading classes, pulled as they were towards Faisal by his qualities and character, as well as by a realistic assessment of the continuity of British control. Most wanted to be on the right side of the high commissioner. There was also a studied vagueness regarding the mandate and whether it would in fact be abrogated by the proposed treaty that Faisal was insisting upon in its stead. It is a moot point whether the outcome would have been different if a constituent assembly had been elected before the referendum had taken place. It certainly would have confronted the full reality of Britain's intention to implement the mandate system. The prevalent mood of broad, but shallow, support for Faisal could then easily have been undermined.

Faisal was conscious of the fact that he owed his election as king of Iraq to British manoeuvring. At the same time, he intended to pursue his own agenda. His interests and political ambitions meant that he had to pay due attention to the clamour of both the Shi'a religious hierarchy and nationalist groups, both demanding the weakening, even dissolution, of Iraq's ties to Britain. As king, he would have a far more authoritative perch from which to balance these competing interests, and he was looking forward to making a clear statement of his position and responsibilities as king, as well as a convincing declaration regarding the substitution of a treaty between two sovereign nations instead of the mandate.[50] Faisal had broached the subject with Lawrence in Port Said and believed that he had Churchill's assurances that this would indeed be the case. He was therefore aghast when he learned that Churchill had telegraphed the high commissioner instructing him that Faisal should announce, on his accession, that his 'rulership depends on continuance of our exclusive support and assistance'. Churchill also wanted an explicit confirmation from Faisal that 'the Mandate has been accepted by him and until it is replaced by some other relation he must work with it'.[51]

Faisal immediately protested and threatened to pull out if Churchill's instructions were not modified. He pointed out to Cox that he had accepted the candidature for king of Iraq on the understanding that the mandate would be replaced by a treaty of alliance between the two countries. It was critical that his dignity and prestige be safeguarded; no king could earn the respect of his people if he started out by declaring his dependence on his allies publicly. Faisal was equally concerned that Churchill's demands heralded a change in Britain's attitudes towards himself and the way the country ought to be run. His understanding was that he and his government would have the last word on matters domestic, and that his accession should be seen by the people as an important step towards the goal of full independence. He argued with Cox that it was in Britain's interest to strengthen his person and that his position should not show any overt signs of dependency. 'H.M. government and I are in the same boat and we must sink or swim. Having chosen me you must treat me as one of yourselves and if you wish me and your policy to succeed it is folly to damn me permanently in the public eye by making me an obvious puppet.' he told Cox.[52] Cox himself forcefully supported Faisal's stand, and through skilful mediation prevailed upon Churchill to change his instructions. Faisal also pulled back by agreeing to postpone the definition of his functions to a later date.[53] With a full-blown crisis averted, Faisal and the high commissioner could now agree on a coronation date, which was set for 23 August 1921.

Coronation

The date, personally chosen by Faisal, was of great symbolic significance. It coincided with 18 Dhul Hijja of the Hijri calendar, the Day of al-Ghadir. The Shi'a consider it a day of celebration when, according to their beliefs, Imam Ali was nominated by the Prophet, at the gorge of Ghadir Khum, to be his successor. Faisal wanted to remind the Shi'a of his lineage as a direct descendant of the Imam Ali. It gave an Islamic sheen to his rule. The coronation ceremony was held at the Qishla Square, near the clock tower. A dais was set up for Faisal and his entourage, and a distinctive high-backed chair was brought in for Faisal.

Bell described the setting in a letter to her father of 28 August 1921.

The enthronement took place at 6 a.m. on Tuesday, admirably arranged. A dais about 2ft. 6in. high was set up in the middle of the big Serai courtyard; behind it are the quarters Faisal is occupying, the big Government reception rooms; in front were seated in blocks, English, Arab Officials, townsmen, Ministers, local deputations, to the number of 1,500.

Exactly at 6 we saw Faisal in uniform, Sir Percy in white diplomatic uniform with all his ribbons and stars. Sir Aylmer, Cornwallis and a following of A.D.C's descend the Serai steps from Faisal's lodging and come pacing down the long path of carpets, past the guard of honour (the Dorsets, they looked magnificent) and so to the dais . . . We all stood up while they came in and sat when they had taken their places on the dais.

Faisal looked very dignified but much strung up – it was an agitating
moment. He looked along the front row and caught my eye and I gave him a
tiny salute. Then Saiyid Hussain [Afnan, the cabinet secretary] stood up and
read Sir Percy's proclamation in which he announced that Faisal had been
elected King by 96 per cent. of the people of Mesopotamia, [then he cried]
Long live the King! With that we stood up and saluted him. The national flag
was broken on the flagstaff by his side and the band played 'God save the
King' – they have no national anthem yet. There followed a salute of 21 guns
... It was an amazing thing to see all Iraq, from North to South gathered
together. It is the first time it has happened in history.[54]

Faisal then stood up and read out a long speech. He saluted the martyrs of the
'Arab renaissance', subtly mixing the Arab Revolt with the 1920 rebellion. But
he also praised the British and emphasised his commitment to the Britsh alliance and its importance to the regeneration of Iraq. Reaching the end of his
speech, he promised that his first task as king would be to arrange the elections
for a constituent assembly.[55]

The coronation ceremonies did not take a long time. Bell went to her quarters where she received a stream of visitors. Ali Suleiman, the paramount chief
of the Dulaim, in his comments on the proceedings was more enamoured with
Cox than with Faisal. 'Sir Percy Cox was like the moon amongst them, and his
face was like heaven.' It showed where his true loyalties lay. Faisal retired to his
modest quarters. On 25 August, acting on the suggestion of Sayyid Muhammad
al-Sadr, he visited the shrine of Imam Musa ibn Ja'far in Kadhimain. Celebrations
were organised for him in the forecourt of the shrine, where he was presented
with a sword with a golden inlay. The poet Rashid al-Hashimi stood up to
recite a poem, which appeared to anger Faisal. Its opening lines read:

Congratulations O wearer of the crown / If you had come to seek
independence
Grace it with knowledge and complete justice / And not with pearls and
rubies.[56]

Faisal's troubles had barely begun.

Faisal had arrived in Iraq barely two months previously. Within this very
short period of time he had managed to stamp his presence and influence on
the country, helped in no small measure by the weight of British support for his
candidature. But his personality and character also played a significant part in
confirming to the largely sceptical or indifferent elites that he was a satisfactory, and to some an inspired, choice to lead the country. Faisal was aware that
the road ahead was fraught with complex problems and issues that might be

difficult to reconcile, let alone resolve. The loyalty of his new countrymen to the new kingdom was essential, but so was his ability to manage adroitly the claims of the various groups vying to determine the shape and direction of the country. He now had his stature confirmed. His name was inserted in the Friday sermon – the *khutbah* – in addition to the Ottoman caliph. He was the undisputed king of Iraq, but he was not, yet, pre-eminent in the country. This would have to be hard-earned over the next few years as he painstakingly built up his power base and authority, and drew away more and more power from the British to expand the scope of Iraq's independence. How his reign would fare, and how Iraq would progress as an independent state, would depend entirely on the outcome of this prolonged struggle.

CHAPTER 19

FAISAL, COX AND THE RISE OF
THE OPPOSITION

F AISAL WAS now installed as king of Iraq through an extraordinary set of
circumstances. He had experienced revolt against the Ottomans, tenuous
rule over Syria, defeat at the hands of the French, with the prospects of a
prolonged and impotent exile. He had undergone great changes during this
period. At thirty-eight years of age he had become an experienced statesman,
schooled by adversity and disappointments, and it was as a mature and astute
person that he sat on the throne. The one constant in the past few years had
been his alliance with the British. They had provided him with vital materiel
and resources to fight the Turks, had given him diplomatic cover in Paris, and
throughout his confrontations with the French and had engineered his nomination to the crown of Iraq. Faisal wished for nothing more than to anchor
these relationships through a formal treaty with the greatest power in the
Middle East. However, his idea of the shape of such a treaty ran against what
his would-be allies expected. As king, he felt that he had to rule, and to do that
he needed to draw from the British, gradually but surely, the powers that they
attributed to themselves as conquerors of Iraq and as the mandatory power
sanctioned by the League of Nations. The British might not have seen him as
merely a puppet in their scheme for control over the country, but Churchill had
come very near to this when he had asked for Faisal publicly to acknowledge
his dependence on the high commissioner. There loomed the possibility that
an unbridgeable chasm would open between Faisal's interpretation of the treaty
as a clear signpost pointing towards independence, and the British understanding of the treaty as merely a byword, a camouflage, for a mandate. The
installation of Faisal as king would give Britain the legal basis to sign a treaty
with him, as he would be acting in his capacity as head of state. Politically
conscious Iraqis thought that a treaty would displace the hated mandate system
with its connotations of an infantile race guided by a benevolent but stern and
civilised power. A treaty is contracted between two sovereign nations, and to

their eyes was synonymous with independence. It was this fundamental divergence of views that would mark Faisal's reign and beneath which lay the root of the conflicts between Faisal and the British.

Faisal also had other issues to contend with. Iraq was not a nation state formed over a long period of history with a common ethnicity and shared religious and political culture. Its boundaries were artificially drawn and it had a heterogeneous and mainly discordant population. The political system proposed for the country was based entirely on western models of representative government: of elections, parliaments and constitutions. The formative experiences of Iraqis had been of governments that were autocratic and distant, including the short Ottoman interlude of parliamentary government. Legitimate authority was based more on traditional patterns of duties and obligations: to notables, landowners, tribal shaikhs and religious figures. Faisal had to create the framework of a modern state in a context in which the old order had crumbled but where deep bonds of obligation still maintained their hold on a large part of the population. He was not indigenous to the country, and the looming presence of the British made such a task doubly difficult. However, Faisal had no desire to build a state on the traditional mould of non-territoriality anchored to a foundation of an Islamic dynastic order. He accepted the forms of the modern state, even the need to utilise the language of modern Arab nationalism as one of the tools that would unite his country. But he also claimed legitimacy from his sharifian lineage and could not afford to alienate the traditional classes or ride roughshod over the bonds that bound Iraq's communities together. He was no Mustafa Kemal, who would ferociously build a brave new world on the total destruction of the old order. At the same time Faisal shared the aspiration of most Iraqis of getting rid of the mandate system and delivering the country from the suffocating embrace of a western power. He needed power and legitimacy to govern effectively and to prevent the country from slipping into disorder and chaos, and had constantly to manoeuvre between these contending forces while keeping sight of his goal, a difficult process under more benign circumstances, but especially difficult given the present circumstances in Iraq. His manoeuving gave rise – with the British, with Iraqi political, religious and social leaders – to bafflement, anger and confusion regarding his true intentions.

Sir Percy Cox

Before Faisal could begin to stamp his authority over the country, he had to contend with the formidable presence of Sir Percy Cox, the person who embodied the might and power of Britain in Iraq. Cox had attended Harrow school and later Sandhurst, from which he received his commission in 1884. He left England for India soon afterwards and started on the first rung of a long career in Britain's imperial service, filling increasingly important posts in Oman and the Trucial States. At the end of his tenure in the Gulf, Cox could rightly be said to have set up the sinews of Britain's imperial presence in the area. At the outbreak of war between Britain and the Ottoman Empire, Cox became the chief political officer of the British army in Mesopotamia, a position he held until 1918 when he was assigned as Britain's ambassador in Teheran. In October 1920, he returned to Iraq as the British high commissioner.[1]

Cox had a long preparation for his last and most difficult posting. He was a patient, determined and insightful man, and his knowledge of Arab affairs was probably greater than that of any other person, including Lawrence. He also had the rare ability to see into the motives of people from a radically different culture, but could be forceful and resolute where Britain's vital interests were at stake. *The Times* obituary of Cox spoke of his 'steady, passionless, methodical energy with which he met each successive problem. Above all his standard of accuracy was astonishingly high.'[2] He attracted the loyalty of many talented people, and his choice for his deputies and advisers was inspired. He was quite liked by ordinary Iraqis, who saw him as kindly, wise and tolerant, and many parents named their children 'Kawkuss', an Iraqi mangling of his surname. Iraqi politicians and tribal leaders who supported the British presence were often in awe of him, while the opposition attributed to him all manner of superhuman guile and artful manipulation.

The first matter that the new king had to contend with was the appointment of a new prime minister and cabinet. The naqib had submitted his resignation after Faisal's coronation, and while Cox had wanted to reappoint this reliable man, Faisal sought a different candidate, one not so beholden to the British. Faisal asked one of the leaders of the 1920 rebellion, Shaikh 'Abd al-Wahid Sikkar, to approach the religious leaders in Najaf and ask for their help in selecting the new government, and he met with leading ayatollahs and relayed to them Faisal's 'good Islamic intentions'. The ayatollahs entrusted to Faisal the task of selecting the cabinet, but cautioned him to select a prime minister who was known for his religious observance, and to be particularly conscious of the choice of minister of interior.[3] The latter, of course, had power over all the provincial and local governments. Faisal agreed to the re-nomination of the naqib, and recommended Naji al-Suwaidi for the post of minister of interior. Cox, however, would not agree to Naji's candidacy. He did not fully trust him on account of his role in the 1920 rebellion, and thought him too independent for the job. Instead he suggested Tawfiq al-Khalidi, but Faisal rejected him as, being too close to the Turks. The altercation between Faisal and Cox went on for three weeks, with Faisal threatening to depart for London to put the matter in front of Cox's superiors. Bell and Cornwallis, however, prevailed upon Faisal to abandon his plans to depart for London, as it would send dangerous signals inside Iraq about his irreconcilable differences with Cox. Finally, a compromise candidate, Haj Ahmad Ramzi, the officer in charge of the army's recruitment, was agreed upon. Naji al-Suwaidi was selected for the Ministry of Justice. Only one Shi'a, the cleric 'Abd al-Karim al-Jaza'iri, was chosen for the cabinet as minister of education. It was a worrying sign that Faisal's cabinets were to be dominated by Sunni Arabs, who were former Ottoman officers and functionaries. Al-Jazai'ri turned down the appointment, however, and another Shi'a had to be found for the Ministry of Education, Hibbat-ullah al-Shahristani from Karbala.

Bolstering alliances

Talks on the treaty between Faisal and Sir Percy Cox began in October 1921. Hubert Young, from the Colonial Office, was also present at the discussions. The negotiations fell at an inauspicious time. Tensions were mounting with Turkey. The nationalist forces under Mustafa Kemal, flush from their victories over an invading Greek army, were increasing their pressure on the north of Iraq. The Treaty of Sèvres, which had not be signed by the Turks, was now a dead letter. Mustafa Kemal was renewing his claims on northern Iraq and continuing to prop up the Turkish ex-candidate for the Iraqi throne, Ahmad al-Sanussi of Libya. Al-Sanussi had sent a number of emissaries to the tribes of the Euphrates, urging them to rise against Faisal and the British in the name of Islam.[4] Cox was genuinely afraid that the Turks would commence hostilities to recover the wilayat of Mosul. There was still considerable opinion inside Iraq expressed by pro-Ottoman and pan-Islamic forces in favour of an alliance with, if not rule by, Turkey. The outpouring of joy in Iraq at the Turkish victories over the Greeks was symptomatic of this. Baghdadis were openly discussing the possibility of the Turkish army moving on to Baghdad. Partly to counter the rise in pro-Turkish sentiment in the north of Iraq, on 9 October 1921 Faisal embarked on a tour of the northern districts and the city of Mosul. His tour was by all reckoning a success. He was enthusiastically received by crowds wherever he stopped, including the town of Samarra, where he visited the shrines of the tenth and eleventh imams of the Shi'a. The visit seemed to have galvanised his supporters amongst local officials and notables, and helped to dampen pro-Turkish sentiments in the province.[5]

The other matter that worried Faisal as he began negotiations on the treaty was the status of Kurdistan. This had been left deliberately vague by the British, a stance that had many advocates at the Cairo conference. There was a strong feeling that Kurdistan should not be brought under an Arab government in Baghdad. At the very least it was thought that the Kurdish-majority areas should have some form of local autonomy and be run entirely by Kurdish offi-cials. But a case was also made for the Kurds being a buffer between Iraq and a resurgent Turkey. Faisal had no way of influencing the outcome of the discus-sions affecting the Kurds. He also had to rely on British military power to consolidate his state and to ward off any threats to its integrity. This was an extremely uncomfortable position to be in, and drove his determination to build up his military capabilities at the earliest opportunity.

There was another reason why Faisal was vitally concerned about the status of the Mosul wilayat and the Kurdish-speaking territories of Iraq. The absence of these predominantly Sunni lands from his frontiers would turn Iraq into an overwhelmingly Shi'a country, raising awkward issues regarding the long-term viability of an outsider monarchy relying greatly on Sunni Arab elements and ruling a country with a Shi'a majority. This was not so much a sectarian stance, but rather a cold calculation regarding the feasibility of an Iraq that would be overwhelmingly Shi'a but ruled by a Sunni Arab elite. Faisal's attitudes towards the Shi'a were complex and finely balanced. He had no sectarian prejudices and was not particularly concerned with the dogmatic niceties that underlay the sectarian divisions in Islam. He knew that British officialdom was generally hostile to the Shi'a, especially to their religious leadership whom they held responsible for the 1920 rebellion. Bell in her letters intimates the dislike, even disdain, that the British had for the Shi'a. It was obvious where her sympathies lay: the kindly naqib who was well disposed to the British, as opposed to the fanatics of Shi'a Islam. The old Ottoman prejudices against the Shi'a infected a goodly part of the exclusively Sunni officer and functionary class, who saw in the new kingdom a continuation of the privileged status that they had enjoyed in the Ottoman days. Bell records in a letter to her father how 'Abd al-Majid al-Shawi, the mayor of Baghdad, unprompted, simply declared to Bell that he hated the Shi'a.

However, in those very early days of the new state of Iraq, Faisal was trying his utmost to increase the presence of the Shi'a throughout the administration, but was stymied because very few of them had any modern qualifications. After discussions with his advisers, in particular Rustum Haidar, now Faisal's private secretary, it was agreed that all efforts would be made to increase the number of Shi'a in the newly reopened Law College. Tawfiq al-Suwaidi,[6] who was appointed to head the Law College in November 1921, recalls in his memoirs that he gave instructions, at the insistence of Faisal, to accept the qualifications of the Shi'a schools in lieu of the normal secondary-school certif-icates. Another example of Faisal's reach to the Shi'a in the early days of his reign was his concern with their rites of Muharram, which commemorate the martyrdom of Imam Hussein. In 1921, the month of Muharram fell on 4 September, two weeks after Faisal's coronation. Faisal financed a number of the processions and attended several of the commemoration sessions. The new Iraqi flag, partly based on that of the Arab Revolt, was flown at these processions for the first time.[7]

Even after the unhelpful publication of Ayatollah al-Khalisi's conditional *baya'a*, Faisal continued to find ways to work with him and to defuse his evident lack of sympathy with the new order. An early test of Faisal's policy towards al-Khalis came soon after Faisal had become king. Al-Khalisi had sought to appoint one of his candidates to act as the district governor of Sammarra, a predominantly Sunni town that holds one of the main Shi'a religious sites. Al-Khalisi had chosen an Indian resident in Kadhimain for this job, and sought to prevail on Faisal to accept his appointment. Faisal was pondering this issue when he was visited by Ali Bazargan, a leader of the 1920 rebellion and a friend of King Hussein. Bazargan recalls in his memoirs what then transpired:

> I went one day to visit King Faisal I at the Sha'shou' mansion. I used to call on him with no prior appointment. I saw him in his room as he was having tea, and when he noticed me he said: 'Look Ali,' and he handed me a letter from Imam Mahdi al-Khalisi to King Faisal asking him to appoint Mirza Muhammad al-Hindi, the political adviser to the deputy governor of Kadhimain, to the post of district governor of Samarra for the services he had rendered to Muslims. His Majesty then commented on the letter. 'What would people say if I appointed an Indian national to this post? And did you undertake your rebellion against the English simply so that I appoint Indians in the offices of state? Is there no one in Iraq fit for this job?' His Majesty then smiled and said to me, 'If you can change Shaikh Mahdi al-Khalisi's position regarding the appointment of this Indian, you will put me in your debt.'

Bazargan then called on al-Khalisi to convince him to change his mind and to seek an Iraqi candidate for the post. The latter finally relented when Bazargan produced an Iraqi Kurd, Jalal Baban, for the post, and al-Khalisi then wrote another letter to Faisal withdrawing the Indian's nomination and asking him this time to select Baban. Faisal happily accepted, telling Bazargan that he had saved him from the unenviable dilemma of either accepting al-Khalisi's earlier nomination of the Indian, and then being criticised for it by Iraqis, or refusing the candidate and earning al-Khalisi's enmity.[8]

In late November 1921, Faisal visited Najaf and Karbala once again. He went on to visit the tribal heartlands of the Euphrates valley, where he was cordially received. Faisal used these visits to strengthen his position with the high commissioner and as regards the ongoing discussions regarding the treaty. He told Cox that the Shi'a *mujtahids* were prepared to back him as an Islamic monarch, but not if he was merely an instrument of British policy.

Wahhabi raids

Faisal and the Shi'a, however, did share a common enemy. On 11 March 1922, a large raiding party of the Ikhwan, fanatical Wahhabis under the leadership of Faisal al-Duwaish, attacked Iraqi tribes who were herding their livestock in the desert south of Nasiriya. The raiding party came into Iraq from the territory of ibn Saud in Nejd. The attack on the herdsmen and their families was lethal. Nearly seven hundred people were killed by the Ikhwan and huge numbers of livestock were taken away by the raiding party.[9] There was an immediate and intense reaction to the incident, noticeably amongst the tribes of the Euphrates valley. The enmity between the Wahhabis and the Shi'a was long-standing, dating back to the eighteenth century when the Wahhabis attacked Karbala and killed thousands of its inhabitants. The panic that this new raid engendered was widespread. People spoke of a Wahhabi invasion of Iraq that would slaughter the Shi'a and destroy their holy shrines.

The Wahhabis were the mortal enemies of the Hashemites. They were poised, after the disastrous Battle of Turaba on the Hijaz's shrunken frontiers, to bring Hussein's kingdom down. Faisal was incensed and personally affronted at the raid. He became even more concerned when Cox's response to this flagrant violation of Iraqi territory was at best tepid. Cox had hesitated because the RAF had lost a plane as it was reconnoitring the area of the raid. The British deterrent force in Iraq was dependent on the RAF, and Cox was not prepared to risk further losses without specific instructions from London. Iraqis, though, saw Cox's hesitancy in a different light, as part of a deliberate plan to keep Iraq weak and off-balance, thereby affirming the need for the British mandate and for Britain as the ultimate guarantor of Iraq's safety. After all, was Cox not friendly with ibn Saud, and would the latter have acted in such a brazen fashion without British acquiescence? The incident further confirmed Faisal in his resolve to build up his armed capabilities, pushing him both to accelerate the development of the Iraqi army and to arm the overwhelmingly Shi'a southern tribes. At that time Faisal had drawn towards him the key tribal leaders of the 1920 rebellion, including 'Abd al-Wahid Sikkar, Sha'lan Abul Jawn, al-Muhsin Abu Tabikh and 'Alwan al-Yasiri. They were all clamouring for arms to confront the Wahhabi menace. Faisal sent a note to the cabinet on 27 March 1922, urging it to increase the budgetary allocations for the Ministry of Defence. However, the cabinet split on the matter, with Faisal's supposed ally Naji al-Suwaidi refusing to support the request, claiming that the Wahhabi raid had little to do with Iraq and was part of the Wahhabi–Hashemite struggle for supremacy over the Arabian Peninsula. In any case, Britain was responsible for Iraq's defence against external threats. Four other ministers supported Naji's position and tuned down the request, much to the chagrin of Defence Minister Ja'far al-'Askari. Faisal had no doubt that the Residency was behind the intransigence of the ministers.[10]

Meanwhile Cox had received a belated apology from ibn Saud regarding the raid, claiming that Faisal al-Duwaish had acted without his approval or knowledge, but it was insufficient to mollify public opinion inside Iraq. A fact-finding mission despatched by the cabinet to the scene of the raid laid responsibility for the failure to anticipate or counter the raid squarely on the government, and in particular on those ministers who had refused to countenance an increase in the defence allocations. A newspaper campaign against the ministers (and by inference those behind them, namely the Residency) ensued, led by *al-Istiqlal* newspaper. On 31 March 1922 the recalcitrant ministers submitted their resignation from the cabinet, which Faisal immediately accepted.[11]

Cox was angered by Faisal's decision, which had been taken without consulting him. He fired a cable to Churchill in London complaining of Faisal's impulsive actions and its repercussions on the standing of the resigning ministers in their own communities.[12] Churchill replied in a similar vein, expressing his astonishment that Faisal had acted without consulting the high commissioner. In reply, Cox went so far as to raise the question of Faisal's 'Abdication should he persist in his unilateral decisions. 'It is not the policy of HM Government nor my personal inclination to destroy his prestige as a King and to oblige him to 'Abdicate by compelling him to do ill-advised or hasty acts, which he has taken without consultation, but if he shows an undue tendency in that direction my policy is to ask him to be relieved and to make known the reasons.'[13] Cox's sudden recourse of threatening Faisal with 'Abdication must have been stirred by latent doubts about his malleability. But this was merely a forerunner of the crises to come between the Palace and the Residency, as Faisal tried to expand his space for manoeuvre while the British sought to limit his actions to those they could control or direct. Of course, Faisal's attempts to expand his powers were broadly welcomed by the nationalist opposition, who nevertheless showed little concern about the risks that this might entail to Faisal's overall position.

The Karbala conference

The leading *mujtahids* of Najaf, Grand Ayatollahs Abul Hassan al-Isfahani and Mirza Hussein al-Na'ini, were gravely concerned about the Ikhwan raid. They decided to convene a conference in Karbala that would include leading tribal figures and urban notables to discuss the response to the Wahhabi incursions. Britain's tardy response to the raid could also afford those who attended the conference the opportunity to consolidate their anti-mandate opinion. The grand ayatollahs also invited Ayatollah Mahdi al-Khalisi.[14] Al-Khalisi sent out an invitation to 1,500 people to attend the conference, and on 8 April he set out from Kadhimain to Karbala, accompanied by over 20,000 followers.[15] All the major ayatollahs of Iraq had now assembled in Karbala except for Grand Ayatollah al-Na'ini. Inexplicably, he withdrew and refused to attend the conference.

There is strong evidence that the Karbala conference was organised with Faisal's support behind the scenes. British intelligence reports attribute this to his efforts to draw close to the Shi'a clergy and to play the leading part in coordinating the anti-mandate forces.[16] Faisal also sought to draw public anger at the Ikhwan incursion to his advantage by reminding them of his own family's long hostility to the Wahhabis. In this way, his credibility with the people as a confirmed opponent of the Wahhabis would enhance his popularity in the country. Al-Khalisi extended Faisal a formal invitation to attend the conference, but even though he had intended to attend in person, the Residency's pressures on him not to do so meant he had to reconsider. He sent Tawfiq al-Khalidi, the new minister of interior, as well as Nuri al-Sa'id, whom he trusted more, to represent him. The two would also exert a moderating influence on the conference,[17] which had by now grown in size and scope. Leading figures of the Sunni Arab community, organised by Shaikh 'Abd al-Wahhab al-Na'ib, had met at the Khaldiya Tekke (an important Baghdad Sufi centre), and were also considering their position on the Wahhabi incursion. The conference attendees all concurred that the Wahhabis were nihilists and a mortal threat to Islam, and that it was their duty to support the conference in Karbala.[18] They then issued a fatwa authorising war against the Wahhabis, and hundreds joined al-Na'ib and other Sunni *ulemas* in a procession to Karbala. Another large group of delegates reached Karbala from the north of Iraq, including a number of sharifian officers led by Mawlud Mukhlis, and notables and tribal leaders from the Mosul area. It was a remarkable example of intersectarian and interregional cooperation in a common goal to stop the Wahhabi raids on Iraq, and at the same time to express a position on the issue of the mandate.

The conference opened on 9 April 1922. Nearly 200,000 people had descended on Karbala, eager to support the conference and be present when its decisions were announced. Petitions were drafted, to be circulated for signing to as wide a group as possible. After a long preamble denouncing the Wahhabi incursions, the statement read: 'We have united in a common cause in what serves the interest of our nation and the defence of our holy sites and tombs . . . We shall push back and fight the nihilist Ikhwan with the support of our King's army, based on our commitment to the throne of our great monarch Faisal the First and acting on his orders as to how to defend and fight against the nihilist Ikhwan . . . and to organise revenues for our monarch [to that end].' The conference was, on the surface, a resounding affirmation of Faisal's position and an encouragement for him to continue in his demands for strengthening Iraq's defence capabilities. However, it was not all words and proclamations. British intelligence noted that a secret unit was formed to penetrate the army and assassinate both pro-British shaikhs and British officers.[19]

On 13 April 1921 Faisal sent a telegram of thanks to the delegates, which was read out by Ja'far Abu al-Timmen, who had returned to Iraq in the autumn of 1920 'We have heard of your historic meeting in which noble sentiment, true patriotism and wisdom have been manifested and we thank you for your loyalty,[20] the statement read in part. Abu al-Timmen was a star in the nationalist opposition to the British mandate. He was passionately in favour of reducing British influence and curtailing the number of British advisers in the government. He had toured several Islamic countries drumming up support for the nationalist cause. Though not fundamentally opposed to Faisal, Abu al-Timmen had been greatly concerned by the coterie of officers and Syrian officials who were surrounding Faisal, and whom he thought were compromising the unity of Iraqi resistance to the British mandate.[21] The Residency was very wary of this rising politician, and was not particularly enthused when he won a seat on the Baghdad municipality with a sizable majority. Nevertheless, he was destined to become a major political figure throughout Faisal's reign.

Abu al-Timmen had played a large part in reconciling the position between those who sought immediate action against the Ikhwan and those who were more cautious in their approach and more cognisant of the realities of power. The latter were not prepared to confront the Residency or dismiss its attempts to extract an apology from ibn Saud, or even some disciplinary action against the Ikhwan. Abu al-Timmen had in fact called for the conference at Karbala to give Faisal the wherewithal to strengthen his position and create room for independent action. Faisal was greatly taken by Abu al-Timmen's willingness to defend the king's position and to seek common grounds between the various factions in Karbala. He overlooked Abu al-Timmen's previous guardedness towards him and asked him to become minister of commerce, replacing 'Abd al-Latif al-Mandil. However, the Residency soon counterbalanced Abu al-Timmen's appointment by supporting the nomination of 'Abd al-Muhsin al-Sa'adoun, known for his pro-British policies, to the post of minister of justice.

The Residency was also determined to undermine the Karbala conference and any decisions that emanated from it. Cox had called it 'ill-advised and dangerous', and believed the Bolsheviks and the Kemalists were secretly behind it. Several pro-British tribal leaders declined to attend, including Ali Suleiman of the Dulaim. Others who did attend, such as 'Adai al-Jaryan of the Albu-Sultan tribe and Murad al-Khalil of the Jabour, refused to sign the petitions. At a subsequent meeting in Hilla they produced a counter-manifesto denouncing the involvement of religious leaders in political matters and affirming their commitment to the British mandate. They established contact with Ali Suleiman who agreed to meet them in Baghdad, in preparation to calling on Cox. Cox wisely advised them not to organise the counter-manifesto, as it would be seen by the public as a Residency-inspired document, which would undermine its credibility. Rather, he suggested that they call on Faisal and outline to him the dangers inherent in following the path of the radicals.

Ali Suleiman, accompanied by forty tribal chiefs, called on Faisal on 22 April 1922. They reminded him in no uncertain terms that their oath of loyalty to him was conditional upon Faisal accepting the advice of the Residency. The following day the tribal leaders visited the naqib, who, contrary to Cox's advice, urged them to publicise their manifesto. The naqib was deeply concerned about the Karbala conference, and thought that Faisal could fall into a trap engineered for him by the radicals and the Shi'a. The proposed counter-*madhbata* was replete with insults and accusations levelled against the organisers of the Karbala conference. 'After we [the pro-British tribal leaders] have examined the paper that we were asked to sign, we found that the listed demands were of no value to the government or country . . . And we noticed that behind the scenes, the intentions of those who were asking for our signatures were harmful to the interests of the Iraqi government and would bring disasters and troubles to this country, as had happened before [as a result of the 1920 rebellion]. From the onset, we gave our allegiance to His Majesty King Faisal in ways and with conditions that were known to all, and these would never alter, and that is why we have refused to sign the paper concerned as we are for the safety of this country and the dignity of its government.' They then went on to list their own demands, which included reliance on Britain for assistance and advice, support for the mandate and the replacement of government ministers with people known to the tribes.[22] Once again, when the tribal chiefs presented their draft to Cox, he strongly advised them not to publish it, as it would encourage dissension in their own ranks.

Only a few months into his reign, the crisis over the Karbala conference reflected the tightrope over which Faisal had to walk and the myriad conflicting forces through which he had to navigate if he were ever to reach his goal. If he was pulled in one direction, he would more than likely be forced to modify or reconsider his position so as not to alienate a powerful opposing player or constituency. The Karbala conference was an opportunity for the radical nationalists and the anti-mandate Shi'a *mujtahids* to galvanise their forces under the pretext of stopping the Ikhwan raids. The *mujtahids* were also concerned about the direction in which the Iraqi state was developing, in effect a continuation of the rule by a Sunni establishment under a new dispensation. The king could be an important ally in their quest, but then again it was unclear to them to what extent Faisal could be coaxed or pushed into becoming their collaborator. He was still an unknown quantity and he could not realistically be expected to distance himself totally from the Residency. In turn Faisal needed to burnish his nationalist (and non-sectarian) credentials so as to establish his own position as an independent force.

But the extent to which he could go as an ally of anti-British forces had to be carefully calibrated so that it would not lead to an irreparable rupture with the British. They were the masters of the situation, at least militarily and financially. The pro-British tribesmen (and the naqib) were concerned above all with their loss of power or status in the new order. But they also had to contend with the growing power of the Palace and the king, who owed his crown to the willingness of Britain to back his candidature. The Residency was concerned that Faisal should not overstep his mark and become associated with the cause of radicals. The Residency could not conceivably compromise with these forces. Faisal was an important ally to the British in their quest for a stable and secure political order that would have the hallmarks of independence but would nevertheless be bound to the ultimate power arbiters in the country: themselves. In their early dealings with Faisal, the Residency had to attune their responses whenever he tried to extend or exert his authority. The Residency did not object when Faisal appointed one of his staunchest followers, Ali Jawdat, to the governorship of Hilla in October 1921. Ali Jawdat's main task there, which he performed well, was to draw the area's tribes and religious leaders to Faisal's cause. But the Residency effectively blocked Faisal from extending his power in Karbala when he removed Britain's appointee 'Abd al-Hamid Asad Khan and replaced him with his own candidate. Before Faisal's man could assume his post, Cox had sent out a posse to return him forcibly to Baghdad. The ensuing tensions between Cox and the king were only resolved when a compromise candidate, 'Abd al-Aziz al-Qassab, was agreed upon.[23]

The Karbala crisis was the first test in the new kingdom of Iraq as to how these forces were going to align themselves and resolve their contradictions and conflicts. The Residency could not stop the conference, but it could dilute or block its results. Faisal's dilemma was how to take advantage of the conference and its manifestos of support for his rule and defence policies, without alienating the Residency and the important pro-British constituency of influential tribal leaders. Soon after the conference, Faisal began to make amends with the Residency. He sensed that the decisions of the conference could be misinterpreted by the British and that his support for the conference's resolutions – even though couched in generalities – might open up a divide between himself and the Residency. Cox was aware of Faisal's dilemma, but of course saw it primarily through the lens of Britain's interests. In a series of cables to London in late April 1922, Cox spoke of Faisal's concern that his relationship with Britain might have become badly strained, and that he wished to clear the air by reaffirming his alliance with Britain. Faisal had admitted to a number of errors, but he acted out of concern that financial and manpower constraints on the British might have limited their commitment to the defence of Iraq. Faisal also admitted to the high commissioner that he had underestimated the extent and range of moderate opinion, presumably referring to the petition of the pro-British shaikhs, and that he, Faisal, should be counted amongst those who were firm proponents of the British role in Iraq.[24] How much of this was genuinely felt and how much dissimulation is a matter of conjecture. Faisal undoubtedly believed that Iraq could not survive without British support, but he equally believed that Iraq's independence had to be assured and that he would make all the necessary alliances to achieve that end. The bobbing and weaving that this inevitably entailed had always been a feature of Faisal's policies, even in Paris and Syria, and gave those who wanted their rulers or allies to be simple and direct in speech and action cause to complain of his famed 'duplicity'.

Negotiations over the Anglo-Iraqi Treaty of 1922

Cox's suspicions regarding the Karbala conference did not stop him from tackling the problems arising from the Wahhabi incursions. There is no evidence that the British conspired with ibn Saud to generate a crisis that only they could resolve. A few weeks after the conclusion of the Karbala conference, Cox initiated a meeting between representatives of ibn Saud and the Iraqi government to demarcate the frontiers between Iraq and ibn Saud's Nejdi state. They met at Muhammara on the Shatt-al-Arab. A treaty was signed between the two parties on 5 May 1922, known as the Muhammarra Treaty. But ibn Saud refused to accept the treaty, blaming his representative for conceding too much. He loudly complained to the visiting Lebanese writer, Amin Rihani, that the British were abandoning him, their true friend, in favour of the Hashemites. Cox agreed to reconsider the terms of the treaty and arranged to meet ibn Saud personally, this time on the eastern coast of Arabia, at 'Aqeer. Ibn Saud demanded that the border between Iraq and his state should be the Euphrates River. Cox was infuriated by his intransigence and exploded in uncharacteristic anger, whereupon ibn Saud completely collapsed and, on the verge of tears, loudly exclaimed his loyalty to Britain and to Cox in particular.[25] He dropped his insistence that the frontier should be at the river's banks. The frontiers between Iraq and the Nejdi state (and later its successor state, Saudi Arabia) were then settled, with Iraq gaining most of the territories it had sought and the frontier being pushed far to the south of the Euphrates River. Faisal had been kept abreast of the negotiations, and was clearly concerned about the final border demarcations. But he

could not affect the final outcome of the negotiations. The credit for this beneficial outcome for the nascent state went entirely to Cox.

Another ordeal awaited Faisal in the tortuous process that led to the Anglo-
Iraqi Treaty of 1922. The start of the process was not encouraging. The British
MP, H. A. L. Fisher, who was also Britain's delegate at the League of Nations,
had unexpectedly announced in Geneva on 17 November 1921 that the treaty
was merely another name for the mandate.[26] Fisher's statement was mainly
prompted by Britain's needs to stay publicly in step with France, which saw its
mandate in Syria and Lebanon in far more sweeping terms than did the UK.
Nationalist opinion in Baghdad, however, was incensed. Faisal, who needed
the treaty both to bolster his position inside the country and to point to some
positive steps towards independence, was greatly upset when he saw the first
draft of the treaty. Bell, commenting on the reaction in Baghdad to Fisher's
remarks, wrote: 'The word "Mandate" produces the same effect here as the
word "protectorate" did in Egypt. Fisher's declaration has raised a minor hurri-
cane, even Faisal was taken aback ... The Mandate he understood was to be
dropped and it was reappearing in another form.'[27] Many British officials in
Baghdad also thought that the mandate should be dropped. Cox himself recognised the sensitivity of the matter and asked the Colonial Office to stop using
the term and refrain from referring to it in their communications with Faisal.
Even so, London was not prepared to abolish the principle of the mandate.
When Faisal saw the provisional draft of the treaty on 16 November 1921,
he 'nearly went through the roof ... and asked why ... his treaty with us
should be based on a draft of a Mandate which has not been approved by
anybody.'[28]

The draft treaty was a wide-ranging document that set out the relations
between Britain as the mandatory power and King Faisal acting on behalf of
the Iraqi government. Several of the articles simply reflected their equivalent in
the mandate document, and the overall thrust of the draft was to establish
Britain's pre-eminence in Iraq in nearly all fields of state and government.
Article 3 referred to Britain's right to vet Iraq's representatives abroad and to
agree to the presence of foreign diplomats in Iraq. Article 8 talked about the
establishment of a judicial system to safeguard the interests of foreigners.
Article 12 talked about the freedom of missionary activity. A special article,
Article 4, was inserted to define the position of the high commissioner, who
would now be given formal powers as adviser to the king of Iraq. The king was
obligated by treaty to be guided by his advice. There were subsidiary agreements involving the employment of British officials and advisers in all the Iraqi
ministries, including defence, justice, interior, finance and public works. The
military agreement, subsidiary to Article 7, called for Iraq's defence capabilities
to be based on lines approved by Britain. British forces would remain in Iraq,

and their commanding officer would be given the dual function of inspector general of the Iraqi forces. The treaty was to be valid for twenty years. The word 'mandate' was never used, but the treaty reflected all the essential parts of the mandatory document.

The draft treaty, at best a modified form of colonial control, has to be viewed in the context of the times and circumstances of the country. Even diehard nationalists recognised that immediately cutting the British umbilical cord was impractical. Britain was simply not going to abandon its pre-eminence in the country, won through war and at immense human and financial cost. But there was also a genuine desire to regain national honour and dignity that could only come in the wake of real independence, and not one so baldly subservient to Britain's interests. Cox presented the draft treaty to Faisal as just that, a draft that would be subject to further discussions. The Colonial Office had sent out Major Hubert Young on 15 October 1921 to assist in the talks, and the difficult process of negotiations began in earnest in December 1921. For the next few months, discussions went on in near total secrecy between the Palace, the Residency and the cabinet. Every time Faisal made amendments or comments on the draft articles, the process of passing the document back to the Residency and the cabinet had to recommence. It was a tortuous process that neither Faisal nor Cox found easy. Cox complained to London of the strain, and, referring to Faisal's constant objections and amendments, went further: 'Considering the impossibility of adopting any costly policy in Iraq it seems in view of attitude of British taxpayer more prudent to secure goodwill of Iraqis by giving them what they want than to adopt policy which will probably have contrary effect.'[29] Cox was in fact advocating that Britain reach an agreement with Faisal with which he could live, and abandon the idea of an intrusive treaty that would underline Britain's control over the country. Churchill, however, would not countenance this change of tack. The mandate was Britain's only legal claim to a special position in Iraq and the treaty would need to reflect this fact.

Faisal, on the other hand, was driven by a totally different understanding of the mandate and its function, drawn from what he thought were his agreements with Churchill. He confided to Amin Rihani that, prior to the Cairo conference, Churchill had made him wide-ranging promises. 'Churchill made me two promises: that he would abandon the Mandate, and that he would recognise Iraq's independence. He has now brought us a treaty replete with references to the Mandate and the League of Nations. If we are going to be subject to a mandate, then what is the point and use of a treaty? And if it's is a treaty why have a mandate? There is no need to point out that the one of the two is neither necessary nor useful. We are determined to stick to what Mr. Churchill had promised us, and this is what Iraqis want, the moderates as well as the extremists. And I still am hoping that he will fulfil his promises. Otherwise the situation is difficult my friend, very difficult.'[30]

Faisal was also aware of his deep debt of obligation towards the British, and he needed to balance this debt with Britain's promises to him. He could only push the British so far. He told Rihani,

If I started to look for an ally for Iraq now, where would I find it? In France? The French are my enemies. In Turkey? The war between us and Turkey is not yet over [referring to Mustafa Kemal's claims on Iraq]. In Persia? The government of Persia adds to our problems and concerns by its constant interference in the affairs of Iraq's Shi'a. Where do I find the ally? In Nejd? Ibn Saud's plans are still more bellicose than peaceful. They are equally dangerous to us as they are to him. Don't you see that we are surrounded by enemies and we have no friends but the British?[31] This is the truth my friend, and if I accept it and try to modify it towards what is better, I am accused of being partial to Britain and serving their interests. And as for the British? God help us! They are asking me to sign a treaty that will stop me from forming a strong and patriotic government, a treaty which will not allow us even to meet our obligations. Take the army as an example. We want a strong national army. But no one will join the army if the country is under a mandate. The evidence is clear. Iraqis will say: If the British are staying in Iraq let them then defend it with their armies. That is true and it is also logical.[32]

Rihani describes Faisal in those days as speaking to him 'in a calm collected tone, but full of wisdom. I noticed its power even as he spoke quietly, and its discernment when he paused in speech, and in his movements and gestures. He took off his ring and played with it to quieten his nerves. And every time he mentioned Churchill's name, there were clear signs of agitation on him. He took off his *sedara* and placed it next to him on the table.'[33]

Rihani was obviously captivated by Faisal. Early in Faisal's reign, before the ravages of ruling in Iraq had consumed his health and aged him prematurely, Rihani described him as he doffed his *sedara*:

'This was the first time that I had seen him bareheaded ... As I looked at his face, I remember what a Frenchman once said, that he looked like Christ. The hair above his high and lustrous forehead was thick with no flecks of grey. His face was clear and open, and full of meaning. The eyes appeared larger than they actually were, far-seeing and full of light. His mouth betrayed his anger and disappointments, while his angular cheekbones reminded me of the hollows of Abraham Lincoln's face. The beard only added dignity to his bearing and to his noble heritage ... Is it strange therefore that Faisal had this magic quality that few who knew him – and even those who didn't – could ever escape his captivating bearing and presence ... Even Sir Percy Cox, that haughty Englishman, respected Faisal and honoured him but took his precautions by closing his heart whenever he was in Faisal's presence so that Faisal's magic would not percolate into him ... His disputes with Faisal were entirely political; he left the charm and magic to effect? Miss Bell, drawing energy to her work in her waking hours, and embellishing her letters to her mother ... In short the dispute over the treaty between Faisal and Sir Percy Cox was a dispute between one who has an intelligent heart and one whose intelligence has no heart.[34]

The negotiations over the treaty continued in secrecy until May 1922, when Churchill, in a statement to the House of Commons, claimed that Faisal and his government had never informed Britain that the Iraqi people rejected the idea of a mandate. This was reported in the Baghdadi press and uproar imme-diately ensued. It was the first inkling that the imposition of a mandate was still a real possibility. On 28 May 1922 a public gathering organised by the nation-alist opposition was held at the Wazir Mosque, near the government offices at Qishla Square. The date coincided with the first day of the Muslim holiday after the fast of Ramadhan. Later in the day, the meeting was reconvened at the Hyderkhana Mosque, where a large crowd elected six representatives to present their protests against Churchill's statement. The delegates included Shaikh Muhammad al-Khalisi, Muhammad al-Sadr, Mahdi al-Basir, Yasin al-Hashimi and Hamdi al-Pachachi.[35] The delegates, followed by the crowd, marched to Faisal's official quarters, but he was not there. He agreed to see them at his private residence the following day.[36] Al-Hashimi, recently returned from Damascus and on probation with the British, slipped away from the meeting with the king. The five came away with a sense that the king supported their notion that the people of Iraq totally rejected the mandate and sought complete independence for Iraq. When they composed a cable to this effect, to be wired to capitals around the world, the telegraph office refused to send the telegrams without the explicit approval of Faisal. Caught in a quandary between the demands of the delegates and the wrath of the British, Faisal procrastinated but finally decided to block the despatch of the cables. Muhammad al-Khailisi, who was already ill-disposed towards Faisal, saw this as another example of his deviousness and double-dealing. But Faisal was coming under increasing pres-sure from the British, a fact no doubt lost on al-Khalisi and other radicals. Churchill had grown exasperated with Faisal's prevarications, going so far as to write Cox that 'reception of the same argument of Faisal again and again is useless in view of the international obligations and the trouble involving the prospects of additional expenses arise in Iraq. I am sure that the cabinet will order an immediate evacuation. Faisal should be under no delusion in this matter, he will be a long time looking for a third throne.'[37] Faisal took Churchill's threats to heart. He wrote to Cox in early May 1922, 'I can tell you with certainty that the dangers and injuries to myself and my country which would result from sudden and unnatural abandonment [of Iraq] . . . I never expected such a thing from you at all.'[38]

Faisal's balancing act was becoming ever more difficult. He had told the high commissioner that he was not prepared to sign the treaty and would delegate that responsibility to the naqib. But the combination of events that culminated at the Karbala conference and the resignation of the ministers had raised serious questions in the Residency and in London about his true intentions and his reliability as an ally. The tone of official communiqués between London and Baghdad when discussing Faisal's motives and character began to change during this period. There was a note of frustration that Britain's erstwhile ally might not always toe the line or play the role that it had marked out for him. Even Gertrude Bell, whose regard for Faisal bordered on hero worship, became noticeably exasperated with Faisal's abrupt twists and turns. In a letter to her father of 4 June 1922, she came close to calling him duplicitous. 'Faisal is one of the most loveable of human beings but he is amazingly lacking in strength of character. With the highest ideals, he will trip every moment over the meanest obstacle – he has hitched his wagon to the stars, but with such a long rope that it gets entangled in every thicket. You can't do anything with him except by immense personal sympathy – it isn't difficult to give it to him, but one must remember that he veers with every breath.'[39] But as the crisis abated, Bell's tone and changed, and it is hard not to conclude that Faisal's standing as far as she was concerned rose and fell to the extent that he was acting in line with British policies and demands. Later in that month, Bell wrote another letter to her father.

> Next day I went to tea with the King and had one of the most interesting talks I've ever had with him. We began about Yasin [al-Hashimi] whom I said I was drawn to but thought I didn't feel I understood him. H.M. said that was exactly his feeling – he had never understood Yasin and then we went back over the whole tale of the Paris Conference. Faisal's gradual conviction that we were going to hand him over to the tender mercies of the French . . . then the renewed hopes roused by the American delegation – Crane and his colleague – dashed once more by the complete suppression of their report. Finally his determination to get on with the French as long as he possibly could so as at any rate to found and establish an Arab Govt which even if he were turned out would be difficult to obliterate; then his hand forced by the hot heads on his own side and French rigidity. And all the time his own family bitterly jealous of him, never giving him a hand's turn of help – and he clinging to our

vanishing skirts. I sat listening with breathless interest – it was a contribution
to history and I've put it all down at length – but what I can't reproduce is
the psychology of it. If you could have watched him for five minutes you
would have understood it – his face narrow and eager between the folds of
his white kerchief, reflecting every turn of his thought with its wonderful
mobility of feature; the shining eyes of the idealist, deepened by sorrow and
disappointment and yet no reproach in them. I felt as he told that tragic
tale – for it is nothing short of tragic, though we are not yet, thank Heaven, at
the last act of it – that no amount of patience and forbearance that we might
be called upon to exercise towards him now was more than what he had
deserved at our hands. When, if ever, we come up to eternal judgement . . .
Faisal on that day will come out very high.[40]

British irritation with Faisal was matched by the nationalist opposition. His
frequent statements of support for some of the nationalist positions were belied
when he later had to act, mostly under British pressure, to nullify their implications. Co-opting some of their leaders, such as Abu al-Timmen, and bringing
them inside the government did not assuage the radicals who continued
to view Faisal with considerable apprehension. Faisal's dilemma was well
described by Rihani: 'People were unable to understand Faisal's position in
those days. Neither the British nor Iraqis have been just to him. The British
have said that Faisal turned against them after his coronation; while the nationalists claimed that Faisal worked for the British and served their interest. In
truth King Faisal was neither this nor that. On the one hand, he wanted to
preserve his crown; and on the other [he sought] to oblige the British to fulfil
their promises'[41]

In the middle of these tumultuous events, Faisal found time to meet with a
visiting dignitary, Lord Apsley. Apsley was a director of the *Morning Post*, a
leading British Tory newspaper. He was also a strong opponent of the Zionist
project in Palestine. His presence in Iraq was hailed by the local press and he
was invited to attend a meeting with the chief leaders of the opposition in
Kadhimain. Bell wrote to her father on 8 June 1922 regarding Apsley's visit:

In conversation with the King he was quite admirable . . . We talked over the
whole mandate question with complete amity. Lord A. developed the reasons
for which we had to have recourse to a mandate – a means of obtaining the
consent of the Powers to our treaty, of persuading the British nation that we
had accepted a responsibility and were bound to fulfil it etc. The King asked
whether he saw any objection to a combined protest on the part of ourselves
and the Arabs to the League of Nations against the mandatory relation once
the treaty was an accomplished fact. Lord A said, on the contrary, the *Morning*

Post would do all it could to help us, but they must get the treaty through first, otherwise all our enemies in Europe would declare that the Arab nation did not want us. The King enthusiastically agreed and I added that it was a programme in which we must be able to count on their help . . . At the end Lord Apsley, who really is a diplomat of the highest order, said that now he wanted to come to something really serious. They all pricked their ears – Yes, he said, a thing of real importance – when are you going to have a polo team? They were all delighted. Ja'far [al-'Askari] assured him eagerly that the Iraq Army was getting a team together, while the King said he understood that in political negotiation golf was more useful – but on second thoughts he did not think he could bear to play golf with Mr Lloyd George.[42]

Building towards a crisis

The tempo of the anti-mandate campaign picked up in June 1922. The cabinet received the draft treaty on 22 June, starting a laborious process of internal deliberations. Faisal had sent several secret messages to the cabinet, asking them to include a proviso in the draft treaty that would specifically repudiate the mandate. Five of the ministers agreed, but Sassoon and al-Sa'adoun stood firm in support of the British.[43] The naqib had sat in silence throughout. Abu al-Timmen insisted that the matter should be discussed only by a constituent assembly. The cabinet deliberations seeped out, and on 24 June Baghdad's shops and markets were closed in protest. Processions involving the various trades and guilds marched towards the naqib's residence. The aristocratic naqib barely deigned to receive them, questioning their right to speak on behalf of anyone. Angrily, he said, 'And who are you to claim to speak on behalf of the country? I am the leader of this country and I am more knowledgeable of the country's needs and purposes. Go back to your homes and workplaces.' The protesters left sheepishly.[44] Later in the day the naqib was visited by a delegation led by Ayatollah Mahdi al-Khalisi, seeking to influence the naqib, on Islamic ground support the anti-mandate campaign. The naqib protested his allegiance to Islam. He claimed that now that he was nearing his deathbed, he would do nothing to compromise its integrity. But his protestations of frailty were belied by his inordinate appetite. At a meal later, al-Khalisi's son recorded that the naqib ate more than four people put together.

Pressure from the Residency on the cabinet was relentless. On 25 July, the cabinet accepted the draft treaty.[45] The naqib, however, managed to insert a proviso that the treaty had to be ratified by a future constituent assembly, and refused to relent even when Cox tried to prevail on him to abandon the clause. On the following day, as Baghdad and Kadhimain became aware of the cabinet's decision, the atmosphere became highly charged. Cox made it publicly known that he had inquired from the British consulate in Bushire how many prisoners the island of Henjam could accommodate, in a not-too-subtle move to frighten the opposition. A newspaper campaign against the treaty was launched, with British intelligence reporting that it was Faisal who was financing it. Faisal continued to apply pressure on the ministers to modify their position regarding the treaty and had reservations regarding the language used in the Arabic version of the treaty. It was a tactic that was designed to buy time until public pressure grew to the point where the British might reconsider the terms of the treaty. Faisal also sent four of his supporters, led by Nuri al-Sa'id, to Najaf to collect signatures denouncing the treaty.

Faisal's subterfuges naturally affected Cox's relationship with him and the latter began openly to accuse Faisal of double-dealing. Bell was equally distraught by Faisal's behaviour, which she saw as reckless pandering to the extremists. In a fit of pique, she decided to break off all contact with the king, but relented after strong representations from her friends. By August, the situation was rapidly spilling out of control. Rumours were flying thick and fast that the leaders of the 1920 rebellion were on the verge of rising again. On 12 August a huge mass of people, said to number over 300,000, descended on Najaf, ostensibly to celebrate the Ghadir festival. Faisal had sent his closest aides, led by Ali Jawdat, to Najaf to lend Faisal's support to the gathering. The king was increasingly relying on his own men to circumvent the British officials and pro-British shaikhs. Yasin al-Hashimi was sent out to Nasiriya as its governor, and he and others directly connected to the Palace were taking their instructions from Faisal rather than their nominal chief, the minister of interior, Tawfiq al-Khalidi. He was charged with maintaining order in the Euphrates valley, but tendered his resignation, citing the impossibility of doing his job while the king was lending his support to the radicals and the demonstrators. The cabinet, sympathising with the resigning minister, sent a note to Faisal asking him publicly to affirm his support for the cabinet. Faisal replied that he saw no reason why he should change his policies, thus implying that he wished to see the cabinet's resignation. Nearly all the ministers resigned, but the naqib, supported by Cox, asked the king to reconsider his position. Faisal, however, would not budge, thereby pushing the naqib himself to resign, and bringing the whole cabinet down. The situation had become critical. An intelligence report spoke of the deteriorating conditions inside the country: 'For the last ten days there had been signs of disintegration in the country due to lack of common purpose in the government and the consequent lack of uniformity in the manner in which the government officials conducted affairs under pressure from the extremists, and the main cause of divergence had arisen from the treaty.'[46]

Faisal was throwing a serious challenge to Cox. His support for the anti-mandate forces and his engineering of the cabinet's resignation deeply angered

Cox. In a cable to London at the end of July, Cox wrote, 'I found it difficult to have any confidence in him. If a solution to the present difficulty can be found, it is only the hope that he will turn over a new leaf and play the game.'[47] In another despatch Cox commented on Faisal's character: 'It is of course he has not the moral courage to give his people a lead instead of weakly pronouncing his position as king.'[48] Cornwallis spoke at greater length on Faisal's character during these difficult August days. 'I think his character is more to blame than anything else . . . I think that his nature is too unstable for anyone to be able to succeed in keeping him within bounds at any rate.'[49] It is remarkable how British officialdom, when faced with Faisal's intransigence regarding the mandate, could only see a 'weakness' and 'instability' in his character. It is far more a reflection of their disillusionment, or astonishment, that their supposed ward was unwilling to play their game unconditionally.

Faisal's manoeuvrings were, nevertheless, bordering on the reckless. Encouraging opposition that might degenerate into lawlessness and even rebellion was a step too far and could rebound against him and the throne. His control over the opposition was limited. Faisal had neither the wide popular base nor the independent power which would have given him a strong platform from which to guide and direct the opposition. There were too many indigenous leaders with their own power bases and agendas to delegate willingly the direction of the movement to Faisal. Challenging Cox locally could be misconstrued in London and turned into a firm anti-British posture from which undesirable conclusions would be drawn about him. In fact, London was actively considering a draconian response to Faisal's alignment with the nationalists, including an enforced 'Abdication and handing the throne of Iraq to 'Abdullah or even the naqib.[50] The British might also pack up and leave, abandoning the maintenance of security and law and order to ill-equipped Iraqis. As the anniversary of Faisal's coronation beckoned, he was confronted with a deteriorating situation and possibly the fatal alienation of his only outside sponsor, the British. The debacle of Syria might now be repeated in Iraq were this situation to continue unabated. Nuri al-Sa'id felt that Faisal should step back, and told him so – that he was forfeiting Britain's trust and that his policies were leading to disaster. But Faisal still refused to change tack. Matters came to a head on 23 August 1922, exactly one year after Faisal's enthronement.

A few days earlier Faisal had sent a letter to Cox that warned of a rising and disclaiming any responsibility for it. He told Cox that either he should take on the responsibility of running the country or that he himself should be given a free hand to do so. Cox drafted a strong reply, in effect blaming Faisal for the deterioration of events, but did not send it lest it marred the upcoming anniversary of Faisal's accession. The opposition groups had recently organised themselves into two political parties, the Hizb al-Nahdha (the Renaissance Party) and the Hizb al-Watani (the National Party), both led by Shi'a Baghdadi political figures. Al-Nahdha was co-chaired by Amin Charchafchi and 'Abd al-Rassoul Kubba; al-Watani by Ja'far Abu al-Timmen, and backed by Ayatollah Mahdi al-Khalisi. A third party, Hizb al-Hur (the Free Party) was led by the naqib's son and was broadly supportive of the British. One of its main backers was the tribal chief Ali Suleiman of the Dulaim.[51] The two opposition parties organised a joint meeting on 20 August, presided over by Muhammad al-Sadr, in which they demanded the elimination of British influence, the suspension of negotiations over a treaty until a constituent assembly was elected, and the formation of a cabinet of 'patriotic' (presumably opposition) elements. They also called for a public demonstration on the anniversary of the king's accession at which they would present the king with their joint demands.

On the appointed day, as the king was receiving well-wishers at his official quarters at the Qishla, the demonstrators, numbering nearly ten thousand, descended on the square facing the royal offices. Speeches were made by the leading figures of the opposition, including the blind poet Shaikh Mahdi al-Basir. As al-Basir was talking, Cox, accompanied by Gertrude Bell and others, was ascending the stairs that led to the king's quarters where he was receiving callers. One of the demonstrators, a certain Hassoon the Cheesemaker,[52] shouted out: 'Down with Britain; Down with colonialism!' The chant was taken up by the crowd, to Cox's great anger. He continued up the stairs into the king's presence, gave his greetings and left. Cox was deeply affronted by the crowd's outburst, and saw in it the hidden hand of the king's entourage, especially his anti-British chamberlain, Fahmi al-Muddaris. In his report to London over the incident, Cox claimed that the king's entourage had deliberately arranged for the demonstrators to be at the Qishla Square before Cox's arrival, and for al-Basir to deliver an anti-British harangue designed to stir up the crowds.[53] The following day, Cox's secretary sent a strongly worded letter to Faisal demanding that he apologise for the insulting behaviour that Cox had been subjected to, that he dismiss al-Muddaris, and that disciplinary measures be taken against the instigators of the demonstration. Faisal, himself nervous about the actions of the demonstrators the previous day, dismissed al-Muddaris forthwith and instructed Rustum Haidar to script a fulsome apology to Cox.[54]

Faisal's illness; Cox takes charge

A day after the anniversary of his accession, 24 August, Faisal felt sharp 'Abdominal pains. Doctors were called in, including the chief surgeon at the Royal Hospital Noel Braham, the king's own doctor Colonel Maalouf, and Harry Sinderson, a young doctor attached to the General Hospital. Maalouf was not prepared to accept Sinderson's diagnosis of appendicitis, but this was confirmed by Braham.[55] In the early 1920s appendicitis was an extremely serious ailment and required immediate surgery. Any delay could prove fatal. Faisal was informed of the need to operate and 'accepted the decision with serenity, and even with apparent relief'.[56] The operation was set for 25 August, to be performed by Noel Braham, and a room in the king's palace was selected as an operating theatre. Cox, on hearing that Faisal was to undergo an operation, demanded to see him before and and informed Sinderson that he would be at the palace in the early morning. Faisal's condition deteriorated overnight, and his mental state was not helped when Maalouf consulted a crowd of mostly Ottoman-trained Iraqi doctors, many of whom reached a different diagnosis. (Sinderson attributed their contrary diagnoses to xenophobia rather than medical opinion.) But the British doctors prevailed, and the operating theatre staff assembled for the surgery. Braham was to be assisted by G. S. Woodman, another surgeon at the Royal Hospital.

Before the operation began, Cox and Cornwallis entered Faisal's room for their discussion with Faisal. The conversation was carried out in private. There are two versions of what subsequently transpired: from Amin Rihani, as related to him by Faisal; and from Philip Graves, Cox's biographer, as related to him by Cornwallis. Rihani's version of events is as follows:

> In the morrow following the anniversary of the accession, as Faisal was surrounded by doctors and nurses, and their surgical implements, the High Commissioner Percy Cox arrived, took out an order from his pocket and presented it to Faisal for his signature. It was an order to arrest seven of the opposition leadership and to exile them from Iraq. The King read it as he was lying down, shaking his head. Cox elaborated on why this order was justified, but the King said nothing. One of the British doctors approached Cox and said, 'This is not the time, High Commissioner, for such matters'. Cox answered him, 'The matter is urgent to secure law and order. The country is in danger'. The doctor answered, 'Postpone it until the surgery is over. It is essential to save the King's life, and we have to start it now'. The King, with the order in his hand, addressed Cox, 'In a few moments I will be in the hands of these doctors, and I might not return to life. Are you asking me Sir Percy, that signing this order is the last thing I do when alive? Do you expect me, before my death, to exile these people, the people of this land, from their country? By God, this is not possible, not possible'. He said that as he pushed the order back to the High Commissioner, who put it in his pocket and left the operating room without saying a word.[57]

Graves's account provides more detail as to an altercation between Cox and Faisal. According to Graves, Cox described to Faisal the sensitive situation, and told him that they, the British, had reached a crossroads with him. He urged Faisal to abandon the extremists and take the side of the British; otherwise he would have to face the consequences of allying himself to what Cox called a destructive minority. Cox then urged Faisal to agree to the arrest of the seven opposition leaders. Faisal refused, stating that such an action would lead to a general uprising, and that he was not going to his death with this on his conscience. Cox and Faisal continued in their argument until the surgeon intervened and insisted that Faisal be placed on the operating table.[58]

The operation took place in view of Faisal's heavily armed personal body-guards, bondsmen and attendants, who had come with him from the Hijaz. Several Iraqi doctors were also in the room to observe the proceedings, some no doubt to pounce on the surgeons if there had been a misdiagnosis. As Sinderson said, 'Our chances of survival should anything go wrong seemed so remote that they were made the subject of playful satire with which to cloak our feelings of tension as zero hour approached.' The British surgeons were proved right. 'However, no sooner was the diseased appendix removed and its gangrenous tip revealed than the disbelievers slunk away. Colonel Maalouf resigned and left for Egypt two days later.'[59] Faisal's operation had been in the nick of time; a few hours' or days, delay, and the appendix would have ruptured with fatal consequences. Sinderson subsequently became the de facto personal physician to the royal household. Faisal's condition had been kept secret from the public and rumours abounded that he was feigning illness in order to hand the affairs of the country to the British. An embittered Muhammad al-Khalisi continued to insist years later that Faisal was merely pretending, yet another example of his deviousness and immorality.[60]

The king's convalescence proceeded rapidly, but it was more than a month before he could assume his normal duties. One of his first acts after his recovery was to award his British surgeon with Hijazi medals, as no Iraqi ones had yet been struck. Faisal spent his last week of recovery at his newly acquired estate near Khanaqin, close to the Persian frontier.[61] Meanwhile, Cox made full advantage of the king's illness and took matters into his own hands. Using Faisal's incapacity and the absence of a working government as pretexts, he declared himself to be the chief executive authority in the country and assumed full power. On 26 August Cox addressed a long communiqué to 'All the People of Iraq', full of blandishments and promises, and announcing that he had assumed full executive powers. He followed this in quick succession by closing down the two opposition parties and banning the main opposition newspapers, al-Mufid and al-Rafidain. Three of the opposition leaders, including the blind Shaikh Mahdi al-Basir, and the heads of al-Nahdha Party, Kubba and Charchafchi, were arrested at home. When Abu al-Timmen and Hamdi al-Pachachi went to the CID headquarters to protest these measures, they were also arrested. In total, seven of the opposition leaders were exiled to Henjam Island at the head of the Gulf of Basra. A few other opposition leaders disappeared or made their way to Iran. Cox also fired Ali Jawdat from his governorship of Hilla and removed several district governors who were loyal to Faisal or the opposition. He also sent the RAF to make a few perfunctory raids in a show of force on recalcitrant tribes of the Euphrates valley. On 28 August Cox made his move against the religious opposition. He sent an Indian Muslim aide, Muhammad Hussein Khan al-Kabuli, to Kadhimain to the homes of Ayatollah Hussein al-Sadr, father of Muhammad al-Sadr, and Ayatollah Mahdi al-Khalisi, warning them that their sons, the two Muhammads, had to leave Iraq within twenty-four hours. If they didn't, then Cox would take measures against the ayatollahs themselves. The two sons of the two ayatollahs, whom Cox considered to be the spearheads of the opposition, left by train for Iran on the following day.

Cox's shock tactics were broadly approved by those Iraqis who were considered Britain's friends and allies. Hizb al-Hurn, the party of the Gailanis, saw a huge expansion in its membership, and wavering politicians descended on the Residency and on Gertrude Bell, offering their support and congratulations. The dour and secretive Yasin al-Hashimi visited Bell and seems to have captivated her with his energy and charismatic presence: the Man of Destiny, she called him. Yasin praised the draft treaty. He complained of Faisal's prevarications and blamed the British for not doing enough to control him. Later, however, Bell changed her view of Yasin after coming across a letter sent by him to one of his supporters in which he cursed the British and called them oppressors and occupiers.[62]

As Faisal was beginning his convalescence, his political future was being debated between the Residency in Baghdad and the Colonial Office. Cox wrote in his 27 August despatch to Churchill, 'It is obvious on the one hand that if he dissociates himself from the actions taken by me either he or I must retire from the stage. If he publicly endorses my actions on the other hand such action would put him in theory right with us … He now has a last opportunity to change his attitude, and to come out openly on our side by public announcement that the steps taken by the High Commissioner have his approval and support.' Cox then continued in another attempt to decipher Faisal's character. 'He does not appear to me to possess any of the qualities which are necessary to make him a good King. He is morally weak and unstable. He gives his word and evades his fulfilment of it with equal readiness. He is a subtle and accomplished schemer and a very bad judge of men . . . He aspires with the help of his entourage to become an irresistible autocrat.'[63] Cox's solution to Faisal's supposed personal weaknesses was to limit his powers, reduce the influence of his entourage and turn him into a docile constitutional monarch. Cox's message was partly bluster, as the British still needed to work with Faisal. Their entire

Iraq policy was based on indirect control exercised through an alliance with the king. To retreat from this policy would have been a catastrophic and humiliating retreat for Britain from a position on which too many actors had staked their reputations and careers.

Churchill was also not predisposed to force Faisal's departure, in spite of his own misgivings about the pliability of the king. He approved of the broad outlines of Cox's policies towards Faisal, working with him as reformed character rather than seeking to oust him from the kingship of Iraq. He cabled Cox on 29 August 1922, 'It should be made clear to him [Faisal] that we will not allow his obstinacy to wreck our whole policy . . . He was brought to Iraq not to play the autocrat but to settle down into a sober and constitutional monarch friendly to us.'[64] In a follow-up cable, Churchill predicted that Faisal would lose his crown for a second time if he forced the British to withdraw from Arabia, leaving it to the mercy of ibn Saud.

Armed with London's support for his actions and policies, Cox, on 10 September 1922, visited the king during his convalescence. He told him in no uncertain terms that the British government would not countenance any further delays to the signing of the treaty and would not accept Faisal's dallying with the opposition. Faisal should distance himself from his past actions and come out in support of Cox's decisions. Faisal could only reply that he took the actions he did because there was no constitutional framework within which he could work, and that cabinet was a divided body. Once a treaty and a constitution were in place, he would then be able to act within their terms. Cox then handed Faisal a draft of a letter that read: 'Now that by the will of Providence I am restored to health and permitted by my medical advisers to deal with affairs of state, I feel it is my duty before taking up the reins of affairs to tender to Your Excellency my cordial thanks and to express to you my appreciation for the prompt policy and necessary measures adopted by you as representative of His Majesty's Government in order to maintain public interest and preserve order and peace in that sudden coincidence of my sudden illness with the interval between the resignation of one Cabinet and the formation of another.' Faisal signed the letter, and approved the formation of another cabinet under the naqib. He did extract some concessions from Cox, notably that the naqib's appointment would be of short duration, because Faisal saw the naqib as too beholden to British interests and was still uncertain of the extent of his loyalty to the king. Faisal also convinced Cox that he should have a free hand in nominating his chief secretary and chamberlain, and not leave their selection to the cabinet, which Cox had earlier proposed. On 13 October the treaty was published in Baghdad carrying the king's signature. Faisal issued a declaration to the people. He praised the treaty, based as it was on the mutual interest between Iraq and Britain, and promised that it would deliver great benefits to

Iraq. It was a necessary volte-face on the part of Faisal; there was no question that he could maintain his equivocal position, given that London had thrown down an unambiguous challenge. It would have been an unequal match. He had to reaffirm his alliance with the British if his fragile rule were to continue. Any continuation of his policies of encouraging the anti-mandate opposition were now doomed. The opposition was routed, its leaders in exile and its newspapers closed. Faisal was determined not to lose his crown again. He came very close to it in August 1922. He now had to change his tactics markedly, but his goal remained the same.

As in Syria, when the battlelines became clearly demarcated, the most vocal of the opposition took cover. Reflecting on those difficult times, Faisal related a telling episode to Rihani. 'People before my illness used to come to me with great enthusiasm declaring, "Raise the flag, we are your men, we will sacrifice our lives for you!" . . . Faisal then recalled the case of one of those *fedayeen* [self-sacrificing zealots] who was one of the great leaders of the opposition, and the most vocal. But he disappeared before Cox had begun to exile the opposition leaders. He had returned recently and came to congratulate the King on his recovery. The King asked him, "And what did you do with the British?" The man answered immediately, without hesitation, "They told us that they had exiled you, so we kept quiet".'[65]

CHAPTER 20

THE REBELLION OF THE AYATOLLAHS

W ITH THE crisis that nearly cost him his throne behind him, Faisal settled into a pattern of dealing with Britain that became the hallmark of his reign in Iraq. He rarely referred to the mandate, treating it in ostrich-like fashion as if it did not exist. As far as he was concerned, it was a stain that would be removed in due course. It was a bitter, but unavoidable, pill to swallow, given that Britain was determined to secure its rights in Iraq in legal form. He had done his utmost to challenge the British plan, often in a clumsy and under-handed manner, but ultimately the unstable combination of domestic forces opposed to the treaty could not carry through their resistance. The byzantine manoeuvrings of Faisal broke against the inflexible British resolve to have their treaty relations confirmed. That battle was now over and Faisal had learnt a valuable lesson. His task was constantly to probe, test and, it was to be hoped, shape the boundaries of Britain's position in Iraq, but he could not ignore Britain's power or its understanding of its own security interests. He could, however, push to frame the British in the context of increasing his own authority, at first domestically and then internationally. It was futile to chal-lenge Britain's authority directly if the groundwork had not been carefully prepared beforehand. Otherwise the challenge would be resisted, threatening the very ends towards which Faisal was driving. What mattered most was that the British were held to their promise to support the admission of Iraq into the League of Nations, as an independent sovereign nation, in as short a period as possible.

The crisis also improved Faisal's understanding of Iraq's complex domestic, political and social scene. Opposition to the treaty was based on a very narrow common ground of resisting British rule, but there were deep fissures within the myriad groups that comprised the opposition. The Shi'a religious hierarchy was broadly opposed to non-Islamic rule, but the grand ayatollahs of Najaf and Karbala were themselves divided as to the extent to which they should call for resistance to the evolving order. Some even favoured monarchical rule, as most befitting an Islamic country.[1] The wing led by Ayatollah Mahdi al-Khalisi was deeply politicised and rejected any form of foreign tutelage. It was this wing that sought to transcend, in part, the sectarian divides and make common cause with other elements of the opposition. This wing was also far more equivocal regarding rule by a Hashemite king, and there was deep animosity towards Faisal himself on the part of Muhammad al-Khalisi, the ayatollah's son. The tribally based groups were also deeply divided. The tribes of western and north-western Iraq, led by Ali Suleiman, were unabashedly pro-British, as were a number of their counterparts in the southern regions of the country. Their views of the king were dependent on what the British thought or told them. The tribal leaders of the 1920 rebellion in the mid-Euphrates valley, however, seem to have made their peace with the new order and gravitated towards Faisal as their best chance for advancement. Other southern tribes, oddly, saw the British as their protectors against predatory tribal chiefs who were grabbing the best agricultural lands for personal gain. Their leaders were allied to the government and the evolving political class that had the power to entitle them with these misappropriated lands.

The Sunni religious hierarchy, which was much weaker as historically it had been dependent on the Ottoman state, was unsure where it stood. Its best bet was to establish an incontrovertible Sunni authority in Baghdad from which its members could draw their own power and privileges. Sunni urban notables, the best positioned to have benefited from the Ottoman Empire, were now unmoored, awaiting the evolution of the political order and by and large supporting the Residency. Very few joined the nationalist Sunni Arab groups that were clamouring for an end to British rule; after all, the leaders of these groups came from humble backgrounds, unworthy of the magnate families of Mosul and Baghdad. The urban-based nationalist effendis were mainly drawn from the new professions and trades: lawyers, journalists, functionaries. Their nationalist drive for independence might have been genuine, but they were also hungry office-seekers jostling for positions of power and influence in the new state. Faisal was either the implacable foreign-imposed enemy, or an ally who could lead them to the promised land of independence – or jobs.

Last were the still unresolved regional issues, domestic and foreign, whose resolution was vital to the identity of Iraq: the smouldering calls for autonomy, and even independence, in Basra; the undefined status of Kurdistan; and control over the former wilayat of Mosul. In Kurdistan a serious uprising broke out, led by Shaikh Mahmud Barzanji. He had declared himself king and sought nothing less than full independence. Kemalist claims on northern Iraq were insistent and were now shaping into ever more frequent armed incursions into these lands. The successes of the Kemalists against the invading Greeks also gave a strong fillip to the large constituency of people inside Iraq who favoured a return of Ottoman rule. Each of these regional concerns might have a profound bearing on the shape of the country that was to be Iraq, its population mix and its chances for stability and survival. Faisal was also faced with a still hostile French authority in Syria and with the menace emanating from the Wahhabis of Nejd. Iran, only recently emerging from the chaos of revolution and war, was very leery of the new country, with running disputes regarding the frontiers between the two countries and the treatment of Persian subjects in Iraq. To the south, Hussein's kingdom of the Hijaz was tottering under the threats from ibn Saud, the weight of mismanagement and the permanent financial crisis that affected its government. It was hardly a propitious environment in which to construct a modern state, or to threaten Iraq's relations with its sole military and diplomatic backer, Britain.

A new cabinet under the naqib was formed on 2 October 1922, with Sa'adoun in the all-important interior ministry. Although the naqib had signed off on the Anglo-Iraqi Treaty, the document still had to be ratified by a constituent assembly. The assembly would also be charged with approving Iraq's constitution, the so-called Organic Law. On 20 October orders were issued to the provincial governors to prepare for elections for a constituent assembly. But trouble was awaiting Faisal just around the corner.

Cox's draconian measures against the opposition did not decisively check them. Instead, the overall leadership of the anti-treaty agitations now shifted to the *mujtahids* of Kadhimain and Najaf. It is the wont of senior *mujtahids* to address the issues of the hour by responding to questions from their followers requesting religious guidance and the appropriate response and position to such matters. Sometimes the questions themselves are framed by the *mujtahid's* entourage to elicit a response, a fatwa or *hukm*, an edict, which is then publicised. The answers are usually given in short, curt statements that focus on the jurisprudential basis for the *mujtahid's* answers. On 5 November 1922, a group of the followers of the grand ayatollahs in Najaf and those of Ayatollah al-Khalisi addressed a letter to them requesting their confirmation that they had indeed categorically banned any participation in any elections to a constituent assembly. Each of the grand ayatollahs responded in his own way, but they were all united in affirming their utter ban on in such elections. They all deemed participation, or helping in such elections, one of the most egregious acts of defiance: 'Declaring War on God and His Prophet'.[2] Some ayatollahs went even further. Grand Ayatollah al-Isfahani declared that those who participated in the elections were apostates, whose wives must desert them forthwith. The fatwas were widely circulated and galvanised the street opposition to the upcoming elections.

Ayatollah al-Khalisi not only attacked the religious legality of the elections but launched an assault on the British and on what he considered to be their pliant agents in the Free Party led by the naqib's son.[3] In an unprecedented act of unison, nearly all the *mujtahids* of Kadhimain, some fierce enemies of al-Khalisi, issued similarly worded fatwas. Al-Khalisi now began to attack Faisal personally, accusing him of betraying the commitments he had made to him when Faisal had first arrived in Iraq. To a large group gathered at his seminary, al-Khalisi said, 'We gave allegiance to Faisal to become king of Iraq but with conditions. He has now nullified these conditions and as a consequence the allegiance that we and the Iraqi people gave him is no longer valid.'[4]

'Abd al-Muhsin al-Sa'adoun

Faisal was noticeably affronted by al-Khalisi's comments, but the naqib panicked over the gathering storm of opposition that often targeted him personally. In some pamphlets he was even accused of apostasy, a grave insult hurled at a pious man who headed a religious brotherhood. The naqib may have hidden his aspiration to stay in office – Bell wrote that 'the Naqib will only leave office if he [is] carried out with his feet pointing forward' – but his support was waning. Faisal was never particularly enamoured with the naqib and started a campaign to undermine him.[5] The British wanted a stronger and more energetic personality in office who would do their bidding, and it was to al-Sa'adoun that they now looked. The naqib sensibly resigned, and on 22 November 1922, al-Sa'adoun became prime minister. The Residency kept suspiciously silent about the naqib's travails, signalling that in effect it had abandoned him. Faisal had wanted his close acolyte Ja'far al-'Askari to form the new cabinet, but the Residency blocked his nomination, thinking him a weak personality and too much the king's instrument.

'Abd al-Muhsin al-Sa'adoun was a scion of the powerful Sa'adoun family, lords of the Muntafiq tribes of southern Iraq.[6] The Sa'adouns were hereditary princes, unusually ruling as Sunni Arabs over predominantly Shi'a tribes. Their power and ambitions had often clashed with the Ottoman authorities, and their authority waxed and waned depending on the strength of the Ottoman state at particular historical periods. 'Abd al-Muhsin al-Sa'adoun, born in 1879 in Nasiriya in southern Iraq, was a beneficiary of the Ottoman policy of educating the sons of important tribal shaikhs in the modern schools of Istanbul. He later attended the military college in Istanbul and left with the rank of lieutenant, but did not serve long in the army, resigning after the CUP revolution. He was elected twice to the Ottoman parliament as representative of the 'Amara and Muntafiq areas of Iraq, but like many Arab parliamentarians from tribal areas, chose to remain silent in parliamentary debates. They generally supported the standing state authority and hardly veered from its policies or instructions as to how to vote when parliament divided. Al-Sa'adoun stayed in Istanbul throughout the war years and was not known for any anti-Ottoman positions. In fact he had been totally indifferent to the nascent Arab nationalist movements of the period. Turkish in mannerisms and speech and with a Turkish wife, he left Istanbul for Iraq in November 1921, only after the situation in the Ottoman capital had deteriorated into warring factions and the parliament itself dissolved in 1919. Many Turkified Iraqi families who had remained in Istanbul throughout the war also returned home after conditions in Iraq had stabilised.[7]

Al-Sa'adoun was quiet, melancholic and self-effacing, tolerant and accommodating to Iraq's varied population and to his political enemies. His forgiving nature even extended to those who sought him physical harm. When an assailant attacked him with a knife in 1926 and nearly killed him, his response was to pardon his would-be assassin and be considerate to his beleaguered family.[8] But he also had a steely and determined side. He was dubious about the patriotism of Iraqis, believing that it would take time before they could be melded into one people. When added to Iraq's external enemies, who were legion, and the lack of domestic resources, al-Sa'adoun believed that there was no choice for the country but to cooperate fully with the British. Unlike his political colleagues and adversaries, al-Sa'adoun did not hide his true assessments behind a facade of nationalist bravado. He openly declared his commitment to the British alliance. He was also immune to Faisal's charm, and did not feel intimidated by either his status or his presence.

Al-Sa'adoun now set to work to organise the elections for the constituent assembly, but the process itself was running into serious trouble. Ostensibly, the elections were supposed to be free and fair, but instructions had gone out to the governors of the provinces to engineer the selection of candidates who would support the treaty's ratification. Faisal was aware of these secret instructions and no doubt supported them.[9] However, the fatwas of the Shi'a *mujta-hids*, now backed by a number of Sunni religious figures,[10] was having its effect on the willingness of the people to participate in the elections. The process itself, a cumbersome two-stage affair, with the first stage involving the election of supervisory committees, was grinding to a halt. The supervisory committees in the shrine towns all resigned after the fatwas became public. In other *liwas* (provinces), governors reported that the process was abandoned as the electors stayed away from nominating themselves to the supervisory committees. The simple matter was that overwhelming numbers of Shi'a were abstaining from involvement in the elections. Even in Baghdad, which had a predominate population of Sunnis, Jews and Christians, the process collapsed, with no quorum achieved for electing the supervisory committee. Christian religious leaders of Mosul also urged their flock to boycott the elections.[11]

The halting of the election process posed a serious dilemma for Faisal. On the one hand, he was committed to the election of a constituent assembly. It

22 Faisal with his son Ghazi, 1924. Faisal's relationship with Ghazi was troubled. He had his doubts about Ghazi's ability to rule Iraq.

23 Faisal with Harry Sinderson in 1928.

24 'Abd al-Muhsin al-Sa'adoun, many times prime minister of Iraq under Faisal. Sa'adoun, a close ally of the British, beset by personal and political problems, was ultimately driven to take his own life.

25 Sir Henry Dobbs, longest serving high commissioner in Iraq. His relations with Faisal were often acrimonious.

26 Faisal reviewing detachment of Iraqi cavalry, 1929. Faisal believed an effective army was essential to securing the nascent Iraqi state and his own power.

27 Faisal in London, 1930. Faisal enjoyed his European forays away from the serial crises in Iraq.

28 Faisal and Nuri, 1930.

29 Faisal with Askari at SOAS, London University, 1930. Faisal was keen to expand the number of Iraqis receiving higher education in Europe and the US.

30 Faisal in 1930.

31 Yasin al-Hashimi, an ambitious but enigmatic figure who served as minister and prime minister under Faisal.

32 Faisal with 'Abd al-Aziz of Saudi Arabia on board HMS *Lupin*, 1930. The two kings agreed to patch up the differences between their two rival dynasties of Arabia.

33 Faisal and brothers, 'Abdullah (c) and Ali (l), Baghdad, 1932. Faisal respected Ali and often sought his counsel. But his relations with Abdullah were more guarded and sometimes testy.

34 Official photo, 1932.

35 Nuri al-Sa'id, a brilliant soldier,
politician and statesman was a close
collaborator with Faisal.

36 Faisal at celebrations of Iraq's independence and acceptance into League of Nations, 6 October 1932. This was the culmination of Faisal's struggle to achieve Iraqi independence.

37 Unveiling in Baghdad of an equestrian statue of Faisal by Italian sculptor Canonica, 1932. It pointed towards Damascus and to Faisal's lost Syrian kingdom and the hopes for Arab unity.

38 Faisal (in white suit and sedara) in Jerusalem, 1933. Huge crowds of well-wishers greeted him throughout his trip to Palestine.

39 (above) Faisal with 'Abdullah in Jerusalem, 1933. Faisal was received by ecstatic crowds.

40 Faisal at Gleneagles, Scotland, 1933, conversing with Ja'far al-Askari.

41 Faisal in Switzerland, 1933, with his ubiquitous cigarettes. His chain smoking contributed to his premature death.

42 Faisal in Bulle, Switzerland, 1933. Lady Paget, on the left.

43 Faisal at the racecourse in Berne, 1933. Faisal was an authority on Arabian horses.

44 Faisal at lunch in Interlaken, Switzerland, a few hours before his death. His earlier convalescence in Switzerland was cut short by the Assyrian crisis.

45 The funeral of Faisal in Baghdad, September 1933. At the time, it was the largest funeral in the history of the modern Middle East.

was the necessary platform to provide the stamp of legitimacy and popular sanction for both the treaty and the constitutional framework for his reign. On the other hand, Faisal was unprepared at this stage to confront the Shi'a religious authorities directly, both because of his concern regarding alienating the Shi'a as well as his fear that such a move might trigger violence and a new insurrection. He tried to placate the *mujtahids* by appointing the moderate and conciliatory figure of Ali Jawdat as governor of Karbala, but with little effect. Faisal was also working to undermine the power of the ayatollahs by trying to peel away the tribal shaikhs from the embrace of the *mujtahids*. In a letter to Cox of 30 November 1922, Faisal said as much: 'I am fully confident that if we succeeded in winning over these shaikhs and separating them from the *Ulama*, who think they are blindly obedient to them, we shall obtain our desire to make success in the elections and to ratify the treaty without trouble.'[12] In a private letter to Faisal, Cox seemed to go along with this approach and indicated his willingness to meet with Shaikh 'Abd al-Wahid Sikkar, one of the key figures of the 1920 rebellion.[13] There were other factors behind the widespread lack of enthusiasm towards the elections, not least the popular belief that the electoral registers would be used to establish conscription. Furthermore, the Turkish threat to Iraq was gathering in intensity by the end of 1922, raising in many the suspicion that the partly formed state of Iraq might be an ephemeral entity to be swept away by a returning Turkish army.[14]

With the widespread boycott of the elections and the need to keep the domestic front united against possible Turkish attacks, Faisal now saw it prudent not to press for holding early elections. Conditions in Britain towards the end of 1922 also changed in ways that called for caution. Lloyd George's government fell in October 1922, and with it Churchill as the colonial secretary. The new government under Bonar Law delayed ratifying the Anglo-Iraqi Treaty, its decision to delay ratification no doubt being affected by a loud press campaign that questioned Britain's large expenditure in maintaining its presence in Iraq and in demanding an immediate withdrawal from the country. In mid-January 1923, Cox was recalled to London for consultations with the new secretary of state for the colonies, the Duke of Devonshire. In his stead remained Acting High Commissioner Sir Henry Dobbs.

The threat from Turkey

Mustafa Kemal had won a series of crushing victories against the invading Greeks, and reoccupied Smyrna (Izmir) in September 1922. His armies marched on to the Dardanelles Straits, then occupied by Anglo-French troops. A new war beckoned, but the British public was emphatically against the opening of hostilities with Mustafa Kemal, as were Britain's dominions. An armistice was declared between the Turkish and the British forces in the area, which effectively paved the way for a new treaty with Turkey, replacing the unsigned and now defunct Treaty of Sèvres. This episode, known as the Chanak Affair, played a direct part in bringing down Lloyd George's government. It immensely strengthened Mustafa Kemal's authority and gave him the means to press for Turkey's claims on northern Iraq. The Turks started to amass their forces on the borders of the former wilayat of Mosul, poised to attack the province and perhaps even march on to Baghdad where alarm bells rang. The victories of the Turks were immensely popular with Iraqis, and there was real fear amongst the unsteady general staff of the Iraqi army that Mustafa Kemal would now turn his attentions to recapturing not only the wilayat of Mosul but the whole of Iraq. The Iraqi army was in no position to repulse any invader from the north. Faisal shared in these apprehensions and sought confirmation from the high commissioner that Britain would defend Iraq against any Turkish invasion.[15] He also passed on a list of known sympathisers with the Turkish cause to the Residency for their possible deportation. At the same time, he used the crisis as an opportunity for the country to rally round him in the face of foreign pressures. He despatched his brother Zaid to Mosul in January 1923 to act as a focus for the Arab nationalist sentiment in a province that had a large population of Kurds and Turcomen.

By January 1923 a Turkish invasion of northern Iraq appeared imminent. The Turkish army had instituted conscription in the steppes of northern Syria and southern Turkey. The Turks were also stockpiling large quantities of foodstuffs and had ordered over two thousand river rafts. Turkish forces attacked British garrisons in the borderlands between Iraq and Syria and the air strip at the Kurdish frontier town of Zakho. Gertrude Bell, wrote fearfully in her diary on 30 January 1923 of the coming of the Turks. She met with Faisal on the afternoon of that day. Faisal's conversation dwelt on the need to avert a war, but if it came to it, he would lay down his life in defence of the country. 'Today H.M. summoned me to tea; he was very gallant and courageous, but naturally anxious to know whether at the last resort we were prepared to defend the country, or whether we meant to leave it to him. He told me that if necessary he would accept a plebiscite, on condition that it should extend also to predominantly Arab districts now held by the Turks, such as Nisibin and Mardin, and that on both sides armed forces should be withdrawn while a neutral Power presided over the plebiscite. But he would ask us also to strengthen his hand by renouncing the mandate, and basing our position on the treaty alone. If this proposal was not accepted, if British troops were in danger in Mosul . . . and or if we withdrew and left the Arabs to defend themselves, he would go himself to the frontier and spend his life in the last stand.'[16] Bell's influence on the formation of Iraq policy had dwindled, and with the departure of Cox was destined to reduce even further. Acting High Commissioner Sir Henry Dobbs was less considerate of her advice than Cox had been, even though Bell thought highly of Dobbs's qualities. Faisal grew less in need of her guidance as he became more acquainted with his environment, but continued to receive her as a friend and as an informed observer of the Iraqi political scene. She was still responsible for compiling the weekly intelligence reports for the Colonial Office as well as writing the annual reports for the British government that summarised events in Iraq. But she was gradually excluded from political affairs, both by the Residency and the Palace, a situation that upset her deeply.

Turkish propaganda in Iraq was based on religious principles that Iraq as a Muslim country had to support their Turkish co-religionists rather than the 'infidel' British. This was ironic, given Mustafa Kemal's totally secular bent and his subsequent attempts to root out Turkey's Islamic legacy. Nevertheless, Turkish propaganda found a powerful echo in Iraq and appealed to the religious classes who did not think in national categories or fully accept the idea of a nation state. The *mujtahids* issued a fatwa, posted on the gates of the shrine in Kadhimain, forbidding the defence of the country in the event of a Turkish invasion, a direct challenge to the government, Palace and Residency. Cornwallis, as adviser to the Ministry of Interior, had wanted to arrest and deport the offending *mujtahids* on the grounds that they were Persian subjects. Faisal, however, counselled caution. He was still hoping to keep his lines open with the *mujtahids*, especially Ayatollah Mahdi al-Khalisi, the most vocal and vehement of the *mujtahids* in his opposition to the mandate.[17] Bell wrote to her father with a note of exasperation regarding Faisal's accommodating attitude to the ayatollahs in the face of the Turkish threat:

Meantime the King (this is very secret) has been trying to get hold of the Shi'a divines – very mistakenly and against the advice of all his best friends, including his Prime Minister. They have played a deeper game than he knows how to do and this morning a fatwah forbidding the defence of the 'Iraq against the Turks was posted up in the Kadhimain mosque . . . The question is now what should the 'Iraq Govt do? I've just been talking to Mr Cornwallis about it. He thinks they ought to deport the *Mujtahids* who are signatory to the fatwah to Persia – they are all Persian subjects. On the whole I'm inclined to believe that they will have to take this step or go under, but it's a very serious decision. If only the King would have left things alone and ignored the *mujtahids*! Even now I wonder if he'll acknowledge himself defeated. With Ramadhan close upon us, and the religious excitement it induces – well, we have a difficult road to travel. The next few days may be rather momentous.[18]

Faisal's policy of accommodating the opposition at this difficult time also extended to the deportees to Henjam Island. He had discussed the issue of the deportees with Cox before the latter's departure for Bahrain, from where he was to meet with ibn Saud. It was agreed that the deportees would be allowed to return to Iraq if they gave written undertakings that they supported the king's policies regarding the Anglo-Iraqi Treaty. After his return from his meetings with ibn Saud, Cox visited Henjam Island and finalised the arrangements for their return. It was a barren island where the British had installed a telegraph relay station and a coal depot. The only houses were huts for the workers at the coal depot. These dwellings, surrounded by barbed wire, were used to house the Iraqi deportees during their time in exile. They whiled away their time by walking on the beach during the early morning and evening hours, when the heat was more bearable, guarded by Indian soldiers. They were not allowed to correspond with anyone or to have any reading material.[19] By the time Cox had arrived, the deportees had had their fill of the island. With the exception of Ja'far Abu al-Timmen, all agreed to provide the signed undertakings and so returned to Iraq In February 1923. Abu al-Timmen remained as the sole occupant of Henjam Island until he, too, was allowed to return on May 1923, in spite of the fact that he had refused to give any undertaking. Faisal was concerned that Abu al-Timmen would become the focus of nationalist opposition and a symbol of resistance, akin to Sa'ad Zaghloul in Egypt.[20]

By April 1923, the fear of a Turkish invasion had greatly receded. The British had managed to expel the Turkish forces from the areas around Rawanduz in northern Iraq, with the RAF's systematic bombing campaigns against Turkish positions playing a large part in pushing the Turkish forces back. The Turkish advances into Iraq had to be seen in the larger context of the negotiations then underway in Lausanne between the Allies and the Turkish national government regarding the final frontiers of Turkey. The Turks were insisting that the entire wilayat of Mosul should be part of the new Republic of Turkey. However, the degree of Britain's involvement in Iraq was still a matter of great public concern and there was no let-up of the newspaper campaign, led by the British *Daily Mail* and *Daily Express*, demanding the evacuation of Iraq, 'bag and baggage'.[21] The former prime minister Herbert Asquith declared in parliament on 20 February 1923 that Britain had no vital interests in Iraq and should withdraw immediately. The outcry became louder when the costs of maintaining Britain's presence in Iraq were revealed to parliament. Bonar Law ordered the formation of a special committee to evaluate Britain's commitments in the country. The committee came out against immediate British withdrawal because the 'Arab kingdom in Baghdad' would then fall and the whole country would be absorbed into Turkey. It would be very dangerous to have Turkey threatening Britain's lines of communication with India and acting as a magnet for the Muslims of India.

Cox was attending the cabinet deliberations that dealt with Iraq throughout the spring of 1923. Britain could not 'evacuate' Iraq as the press was demanding, and certainly not before the Turco–Iraqi frontiers have been demarcated. But what could be done to placate the hostile press somewhat was to reduce the period of the Anglo-Iraqi Treaty from twenty to four years. Accordingly, Cox returned to Baghdad on 31 March 1923, bringing with him a 'protocol' amendment to the treaty reducing its duration to four years. This development proved a great boon to Faisal, who hailed it as a major victory on the road to reducing British influence and achieving complete independence. The protocol called for Iraq's admission into the League of Nations after the end of the four years and after a definitive settlement had been reached with Turkey. The treaty would then be completely terminated. On 4 May 1923, Faisal issued an enthusiastic proclamation to the Iraqi people. 'By the Grace of God and the Spirit of His Prophet . . . our government has managed to take a huge step in fulfilling the hopes of the nation,' the statement began. Faisal went on to praise Britain as a loyal and essential ally. He called on the people to support him and the government, and stressed that the road was now clear for Iraq's entry to the League as an independent country.[22] What mattered most was to proceed with the elections for the assembly and promulgate the Organic Law, the constitution for the country.

Restarting the elections

Faisal now fervently pushed to restart the stalled elections. He began a long and arduous journey to all of Iraq's main regions, including Mosul, Suleimaniya, Kut, 'Amara, Basra and the towns of the mid-Euphrates valley. He started his journey to the south by sailing down the Tigris River from Baghdad in a river boat belonging to the flotilla of a business grandee, 'Abd al-Qadir al-Khudhairi. Faisal was accompanied by the justice minister Naji al-Suwaidi, Rustum Haidar and others. But there was another purpose to his trip, especially to the southern regions. Ayatollah al-Khalisi was preparing to reissue the fatwa that prohibited all participation in the elections, an eventuality that could scupper the entire election process and with it Faisal's claims that Iraq was now embarking on a clear path to independence. Faisal had wanted to gain the confidence of the leading tribal figures of the 1920 rebellion for the elections, and to convince them that the protocol was a major achievement for the country. Their support would not only expand the base of participation in the elections but also enhance their legitimacy. The tribal leaders could also play a part in bridging the gap between the government and the religious leaders, who were adamant in their opposition of the elections. Nearly all the tribal chieftains he met accepted Faisal's representations that the best way forward was to hold the elections and enact the Organic Law.[23] The only person who held out, Shaikh al-Muhsin Abu-Tabikh, stated that he could not veer from the fatwa prohibiting participation in the elections, but that he would help to find a common ground between the terms of the fatwa and the policies of the government.[24]

The king then prevailed on 'Alwan al-Yasiri and Gat' al-'Awadi to call on Ayatollah Mahdi al-Khalisi to try to convince him to withdraw the fatwa. The ayatollah, however, accused them of blasphemy. Later, after the tribal chiefs had left the ayatollah to visit the shrine of the Imam Musa al-Kadhim, al-Yasiri was accosted and attacked by a crowd incited by al-Khalisi. Al-Yasiri had to flee the scene ignominiously. On 17 May notices were affixed on the main doors of the Kadhimain shrine, reminding the people of the earlier fatwa that prohibited participation in the elections. The notices carried the signature of an unknown party called al-Hizb ul-Mukhalas (the Salvation Party), a front for dissenting *mujtahids*. The notices began, 'the Government is trying to deceive the people with the Protocol to the treaty, and is exerting all its efforts to hold elections thereby trampling over the fatwa of the *mujtahids*. So beware O People and do not be deceived.'[25] On 30 May 1923, the grand ayatollahs reaffirmed their earlier fatwa banning participation in the elections. In a response to a query from 'a believer' regarding the permissibility of the elections, the *mujtahids* all responded by confirming their earlier prohibition. Ayatollah al-Khalisi, as was his wont, went one step further by stating that participation in the elections was tantamount to 'apostasy' and 'on the level of *shirk* [associating other deities with the one God, the greatest transgression in Islam].'

The Residency and al-Sa'adoun had become exasperated with the position of the ayatollahs. Al-Sa'adoun in particular pushed for a showdown, and the pro-government press launched a campaign to discredit the *mujtahids*. Its stance was that ayatollahs were Persian subjects and as foreigners should not interfere in domestic Iraqi politics.[26] Although a number of the ayatollahs were indeed Persian in origin, many of them, such as the Khalisis, were in fact Arabs who held Persian nationality. They had acquired this status mainly to avoid conscription in Ottoman times. However, the Persian nationality of the ayatollahs was their Achilles heel and was used by al-Sa'adoun and his cabinet to prepare for their arrest and deportation. On 17 June, as Faisal was still on his tour of the south of the country, the cabinet decided to go ahead and hold the elections following Faisal's return to Baghdad. They also decided to punish the opposition by deporting recalcitrant *mujtahids* of Persian nationality and putting on trial those of Iraqi nationality. A few days earlier, amendments to the criminal code had given the government the power to deport foreign criminals. Whether Faisal would have approved of such draconian measures is subject to conjecture. He undoubtedly was prepared to increase the pressure on the *mujtahids* if they were totally uncompromising and, while on tour in

Basra, he condemned those *mujtahids* who stood against the elections and were enemies of the Arab cause. In a speech given on his behalf by Naji al-Suwaidi, Faisal said, 'The government will block by legal measures all actions leading to preventing the nation from achieving its parliamentary sovereignty.' In a speech in Hilla, Faisal referred to measures against those who conspired against the interests of the country, 'and the Arab cause'.[27] But, as his later actions would confirm, he would have much preferred a less confrontational approach to Shi'a religious leadership.

On 21 June the government began to implement its policy in earnest. One of Ayatollah al-Khalisi's nephews was arrested by plainclothes policemen while he was posting up notices at the main door of the Kadhimain shrine denouncing the elections. After interrogation, the culprit, Shaikh Ali Taqi, confessed that the notices were all being printed at the Khalisi seminary. While this was happening, one of al-Khalisi's sons, Shaikh Hassan al-Khalisi, was also arrested by a uniformed policeman for posting unauthorised notices. Shaikh Hassan started shouting out at passers-by that he was being assaulted. The crowd dragged the policeman into the shrine's courtyard. Shaikh Hassan took out a knife and threatened to kill him, but in the scuffle the policeman managed to escape.[28] This was a sufficient cue for the police to arrest two of al-Khalisi's sons, his nephew and a fourth person, an associate of al-Khalisi, Suleiman al-Qutayfi. Strengthened by the muted response to these arrests, the government now set its sights on the ayatollah himself. A decision was taken to arrest him on 26 June.

The ayatollahs depart

Faisal had no great love for Ayatollah al-Khalisi. He had incited the public against the elections, and had now turned his guns on Faisal. The ayatollah was notorious for his sanctimony and stubbornness. Faisal would have gone along with al-Khalisi's exile, but he was fearful of its possible consequences. Dobbs, who had become the high commissioner in May 1923, was equally concerned about the effects of al-Khalisi's deportation. However, al-Sa'adoun was convinced that the deportation of the ayatollah could be managed by the government, and any negative reaction contained by the police. Before leaving on his southern journey, with his absence timed to coincide fortuitously with the arrests in Baghdad, Faisal had agreed with al-Sa'adoun on a coded phrase to indicate his acceptance of the measure against al-Khalisi. The word was 'chicken' when referring to the ayatollah. After reaching Basra, Faisal appeared to have settled on not exiling him. He sent al-Sa'adoun a coded cable, which read, 'Leave the chicken alone', indicating that the government should not arrest al-Khalisi. However, al-Sa'adoun was determined to push ahead with his plans, as were the British advisers who wanted the ayatollah out of the way.[29]

Al-Sa'adoun cabled Faisal stressing that the activities of al-Khalisi and his supporters threatened the credibility of the state and that there was no alternative but to banish him.[30] Faisal gave his assent. He cabled back: 'If such action towards the shaikh [Ayatollah al-Khalisi] is necessary, then I wish it be done with the utmost courtesy and in a way that would not affect his personal dignity or cause distress and fear to his family.' In a follow-up telegram Faisal anticipated the adverse reaction this move might generate amongst the grand ayatollahs of Najaf: 'You have full authority to undertake the appropriate measures in Baghdad and Kadhimain to preserve security and the dignity of the government. You must have a firm plan of action. After [the arrests of] Kadhimain, inform the *mujtahids* of Najaf through the governor of all that has happened with al-Khalisi . . . and ask them to stay tranquil and to continue in their religious duties. Let them know about the government's sorrow at undertaking these actions in light of the peaceful measures it has taken to date. Publicise these decisions in the press at the right time.'[31] A few days later, on 25 June 1923, the government issued a communiqué that accused the offending *mujtahids* – 'those meddling strangers' – of deceiving their public and of irreligious conduct that defiled the sanctity of the holy shrines.

On the night of 26 June, Ayatollah al-Khalisi was arrested at his home. He offered no resistance. He was put in the first-class carriage of a special train that conveyed him, and four members of his family who had been arrested earlier, to Basra. There he stayed, at the mansion of a local shipping magnate, Agha Ja'far, where he was installed, inadvertently, in a hot and airless room. His discomfort was soon alleviated, however, and on 30 June he was put on a steamer bound for Bombay. On board the ship was a police chief, Ahmad al-Rawi, with two of Faisal's bondsmen, Salim and Birjis. Their instructions were to look after the shaikh and his entourage until the ship reached Bombay. In Bombay, al-Khalisi boarded another ship bound for London via Aden. He and his entourage were all given first-class tickets and provided with ample funds to meet the expenses of their journey. The party arrived in Aden, and as the Haj season had arrived al-Khalisi and his group decided to go on the pilgrimage. They made their way to Jeddah on the last of the pilgrim vessels leaving Aden. The ayatollah was given a grand reception at Jeddah, where King Hussein had sent an emissary to receive him. He was to be the king's guest throughout the Haj. At the end of the pilgrimage al-Khalisi accepted the government of Iran's invitation to go to Iran, and arrived there in late July 1923. Now an implacable enemy of Faisal, he was treated with the utmost courtesy and respect throughout his early exile period, clearly on account of Faisal's instructions not only to Iraqi officials but also conveyed through the British to all their officials at the ayatollah's ports of call.

A meeting was arranged for al-Khalisi with King Hussein, who treated the guest with exaggerated consideration, calling him 'Your Eminence the Shaikh'.

During his meeting with Hussein, al-Khalisi noticed an eleven-year-old lad, whom Hussein called 'Awn, hiding behind the screens. When told the lad was Faisal's son Ghazi, al-Khalisi naturally asked why his grandfather addressed him thus. Hussein's reply was that he had had dreamt of the martyred Imam Hussein, who in his dream had instructed him that, if Faisal had a son, he should be called 'Awn. But Faisal's family wanted to call the boy Ghazi, whose name meant conqueror, in honour of Faisal's victories over the Idrisi in 'Asir. A compromise was found so that the baby boy was called Ghazi in recognition of his father's victories, while Hussein always addressed the boy as 'Awn![32]

When the news of Ayatollah al-Khalisi's expulsion from Iraq reached the people of Kadhimain, protesters began to gather at the courtyard of the shrine. In Baghdad, the coppersmith bazaar shut down in protest. But firm measures by government officials against striking shopkeepers and tradesmen quickly put an end to the nascent protest movement. An attempt to galvanise the key religious figures of Kadhimain against al-Khalisi's deportation backfired. The ayatollah had many enemies, including a leading *mujtahid* of the town who declared that he had received his comeuppance because of his incessant meddling in politics. However, in Najaf the situation was totally different. There, protesters closed the town and the grand ayatollahs declared their solidarity with al-Khalisi. They saw his deportation as an intolerable insult and assault on the *mujtahids'* dignity and authority. They dramatically stated that they, too, would leave Iraq in protest against the government's move. The apex of the religious hierarchy of the Shi'a was now preparing to evacuate the country. The intent was obviously to mobilise their followers in an irresistible wave of protest against the government's measures.

The ayatollahs, led by the supreme *mujtahids* al-Isfahani and al-Na'ini, made their way to Karbala in preparation for their departure from Iraq. Added to their entourage were large numbers of seminary students and junior clerics. The governor of Karbala tried to reason with them and to convince them to return to Najaf, but to no avail. Having failed to dissuade them from this drastic course, he received strict instructions to facilitate the departure of all those who held Persian nationality, but to prevent the departure of Iraqi religious leaders. On 1 July 1923 a cavalcade of nearly twenty-five of the Shi'a world's highest religious authorities, under police guard, made their way to a railhead near Baghdad where they boarded a special train to Iran.[33] In spite of protests from the Persian consul in Baghdad that the *mujtahids* had been treated shabbily, the truth was that they were extended all the courtesies due their position. In response, the government stated that it had not ordered their deportation but had simply acceded to their demands that they leave the country and had facilitated their decision. Their case was in no way comparable to the deportation of Ayatollah al-Khalisi.

As these momentous events were taking place, Faisal was nearing the end of his southern journey. In a remarkable coincidence, his train was just leaving Basra for the Euphrates towns when the train carrying al-Khalisi was entering Basra station. An eyewitness to the event later claimed that the passengers on the al-Khalisi train could clearly see the king's carriage, which was well lit.[34] Faisal arrived in Diwaniya on 28 June 1923, with al-Khalisi an unwilling guest at the Agha Ja'far mansion in Basra, and the grand ayatollahs preparing to leave the country. The public response to these events in the towns of the lower and mid-Euphrates valley, the heartland of tribal support for the grand ayatollahs, had been astonishingly muted. No demonstrations of any sort broke out except in the town of Hilla. There, a local representative of one of the grand ayatollahs tried to organise a demonstration, but his efforts were thwarted. The governor simply banished him to Baghdad.[35] Matters began to swing to the other extreme. With the government and the king the apparent victors in the confrontation with the ayatollahs, the tribal leaders in Diwaniya were effusive in their support for Faisal. The newspaper al-Iraq reported on Faisal's reception by the tribes of the Euphrates valley and the leaders of the 1920 rebellion. 'The shaikhs and leaders of the tribes met in the afternoon with His Majesty the King and swore their absolute fealty to the policies of His Majesty and their obedience to his commands. They are prepared to crush any idea or plot that threatens the main national interests and Arab nationalism . . . and they will not tolerate any further delays to the elections, even by a single day.'[36]

A disturbing side-effect of the ayatollahs' exile was the deluge of newspaper articles and commentaries that condemned the ayatollahs and their challenge to the government. The government's propaganda focus on the Persian nationality of the ayatollahs and the link between Iraqi interests and those of the 'Arab nation' carried in it the whiff of sectarianism and ethnic nationalism. The press took this several steps further by denouncing the character, motives and competence of the leading Shi'a mujtahids. In several articles in the pro-government paper al-Iraq, the idea of pan-Islam, supposedly the ayatollahs' political aim, was unfavourably contrasted with the principles of nationalism. 'These meddlers [the offending ayatollahs] had lived for years under Iraq's Arab sky . . . but they never failed in undermining it behind the cover of religion and religious unity.' The writer continued, 'I am certain that these people had no purpose but to damage the blessed Arab movement, and in this manner were traitors to the country under whose canopy they had found abundance . . . Their intent was to serve a foreign power which was the main cause behind the destruction of the Arab state [the Abbasid Empire] and its glittering capital [Baghdad].'[37] These themes of the presence of a 'fifth column' conspiring against the interests of Iraq and Arab nationalism, of evil clerics linked by blood to a malevolent Iran, of the forces of darkness represented by religious elements fighting to destroy the bases of civilisation, progress and modernity recurs throughout the modern history of Iraq, and its genesis was in this crisis. Faisal recognised the inherent long-term danger of this perspective, because it strayed too close to driving the entire religious leadership of the Shi'a, the majority of his country, into a category of obscurantist outsiders. He wanted to counter the ayatollahs' powers to block or subvert his plans, but not to the point where the Shi'a might become fatally alienated from his rule.

The grand ayatollahs entered Iran on 7 July 1923 and began a campaign against the Iraqi government, and specifically against Faisal. They publicly stated that they would not return to Iraq unless Faisal 'Abdicated'. Their anti-Faisal position appeared to be strengthened by a petition signed by four hundred Iraqi personages appealing to the now-impotent Ottoman caliph for 'the deliverance of Iraq from the foreigners . . . and from Faisal and his father who came to dominate over the Muslims by fighting in the ranks of the Allies and by disuniting the Muslims under the cloak of Arab nationalism in disobedience of the orders of God.'[38] In Iran, the presence of the self-exiled ayatollahs had created a great deal of disturbance. The public believed that they had been expelled under British instructions, and this increased the agitation in Iran against British influence on their own government. The British ambassador in Iran, Sir Percy Lorraine, travelled to Baghdad in August to convince the Iraqi government to take them back, but al-Sa'adoun would hear none of it. He believed the government had won a famous victory and was not prepared to allow them back. Lorraine also met with Faisal, in the presence of Dobbs, Cornwallis and al-Sa'adoun. The king, however, was amenable to the return of the ayatollahs. He felt that after their unceremonious exit, they would be more than likely to accept the government's conditions that they did not involve themselves in politics. Faisal knew that the ayatollahs' bluster would wane with time as they felt the loss of their influence by their prolonged absence from their physical and financial base of support in Iraq. The grand ayatollahs of Iran would also, in time, tire of these powerful rivals from Iraq who might appeal to their own base of supporters.[39] Moreover, Faisal recognised the need to rebuild his standing with the Shi'a community, and the return of the ayatollahs, shorn of their political interference, would be an important element in this strategy. It was therefore agreed between Faisal, Dobbs and al-Sa'adoun that the matter of the ayatollahs' return to Iraq would be reopened after the elections to the constituent assembly.

Faisal, however, began secret contacts with the self-exiled ayatollahs in Iran without the knowledge of either al-Sa'adoun or the Residency. The ayatollahs had come into conflict with the Iranian government under Reza Khan, whose modernising policies greatly disturbed them. In their absence from Iraq, another grand ayatollah who had remained in Iraq, Sayyid Muhammad al-Firozbadi, was taking charge and belittled the significance of the ayatollahs' absence from the religious and educational duties of the Najaf seminaries. Letters were exchanged between Faisal and the ayatollahs in Iran, whose contents were hinted at when the RAF intelligence department in Iraq captured a batch of documents. Bell wrote in a letter of 29 November 1923:

> The R.A.F. intercepted in the post a packet of most important letters from the *Mujtahids* in Persia to their agents here, saying that H.M. [Faisal] had promised to overturn Muhsin Sa'dun's Cabinet, put in a Shi'a ministry with a Shi'a premier, recall the *Mujtahids* and reject the treaty. They did not trust his promises but they enclosed a signed and sealed fatwa withdrawing the ban on the elections on the ground that H.M. had carried out the above pledges. This was to be shown to him but not published till he had done his part. We can't think how they came to entrust all this to the post; they have till now sent all their letters by the hand of messengers. We have known about them, after their arrival, from police agents, but never actually had them in our possession. After long consultations we decided that Sir Henry should take them to H.M. and observe that though H.M. had told H.E. [Sa'adoun] that he was keeping the *mujtahids* in play, he had gone dangerously far and given them a weapon against him. H.M. took it quite cheerfully, saying that they had exaggerated his offers, but that they could now safely be left to stew in their own juice and he would cease negotiations with them. So that's that.[40]

This episode greatly raised tensions between Faisal and al-Sa'adoun, but there would need to be more exchanges before the way could be paved for the return of the ayatollahs.

Final hurdles

The last serious domestic hurdle to the restart of the elections was the situation in north-eastern Iraq: the regions of southern Kurdistan under British administration. This matter was also intertwined with the entire British policy towards a resurgent Turkey. The 1920 Treaty of Sèvres, and with it the promise of an independent Kurdistan, was a dead letter after the military successes of Mustafa Kemal. Peace with Turkey was now of the 'utmost importance', as Churchill had earlier said to parliament. In the Lausanne conference with Turkey, which commenced in November 1922 during Lloyd George's government, the negotiators confronted the intractable problem of the wilayat of Mosul. Turkey was claiming nearly the entire province, while Britain sought to set the border between Iraq and Turkey at the northern frontiers of the former wilayat. As a gesture to Turkey, though, the British were prepared to drop the articles in the defunct Treaty of Sèvres that called for an independent Kurdistan. On the ground, however, in southern Kurdistan, both Turkey and Britain were manoeuvring to advantage.

Turkish propaganda affected the population of the region, leaving the pro-British notables and tribal chiefs 'pallid with terror'.[41] The nationalist leader Shaikh Mahmud, from his base in Suleimaniya, saw his opportunity and in March 1923 rose against the British.[42] The RAF bombed the town, forcing his retreat into the mountain redoubts of the region, but the town itself remained under the control of his followers. Shaikh Mahmud was conspiring with the Turkish general Ozd Amir, whose forces had occupied the town of Rawanduz, and both prepared for a general uprising with an attack on the major towns of Irbil and Kirkuk.[43] The RAF responded with an extensive bombing campaign against the tribes supporting the uprising and Ozd Amir's units. The incipient rebellion then collapsed, and on 9 May 1923 British and Iraqi forces occupied the town of Suleimaniya.

By the summer of 1923, the region of southern Kurdistan was a hotchpotch of administrative units and conflicting claims, with its final status still undefined. The cabinet had carved a new *liwa* out of the area of Irbil, and the British had asked the Suleimaniya town council to rule the city as a separate *liwa*. The councillors agreed, on condition that the British maintained a military presence in the area. But the hard-pressed British could not give such a guarantee and withdrew their forces, whereupon the town council resigned and Shaikh Mahmud re-entered the city. His presence was tolerated there as long as he did not seek to extend his authority beyond the narrow confines of Suleimaniya and its surrounding region.

The British policy had been to keep the Kurdish districts loosely connected to the Baghdad government. Faisal and his cabinet, on the other hand, wanted to bind the northern provinces to the central government and create a unitary and centralised state. In December 1922, Cox had prevailed upon Faisal to accept a joint Anglo-Iraqi declaration that gave the Kurds rights tantamount to independence. Faisal had demurred before agreeing to the declaration, but Cox had privately assured him that this in no way implied a political or economic separation from Iraq. In any case, Iraq could not enforce its writ in the Kurdish districts without British support, and the British still maintained the prospects of an independent Kurdistan, both as a bargaining ploy at Lausanne and to pressure the Iraqi government. Faisal was worried that another nationalist insurrection might break out in Suleimaniya, thus jeopardising the entire future status of the wilayat of Mosul and encouraging the League of Nations to hand it over to Turkey. A policy of conciliation towards Kurdish demands for cultural and political autonomy was therefore an essential prerequisite for the involvement of the Kurdish districts in the elections to the constituent assembly. Accordingly, the cabinet passed a resolution on 11 July confirming that the central government would not appoint Arab officials to Kurdish districts except for technical positions. The government also promised not to force the inhabitants of the Kurdish region to use Arabic in their official correspondence, and maintained that it would preserve the rights of the inhabitants and the religious and civil communities of these districts. These measures mollified most of southern Kurdistan and, with the exception of Suleimaniya, paved the way for the inhabitants of the area to participate in the elections to the constituent assembly.

With the path now clear for restarting the elections, the cabinet met on 3 July 1923 at the Royal Palace, under Faisal's presidency, to agree to move ahead with the elections. But behind this superficial unanimity on holding the elections lurked a power struggle between Faisal and his prime minister, al-Sa'adoun, with the latter strongly backed by the Residency. The composition of the assembly would be a determining factor in Iraq's power equation, and Faisal was intent on having his allies and supporters in a prominent position in the chamber. Also at stake was the fate of the Anglo-Iraqi Treaty, which had to be ratified by the new assembly. Faisal began to plan his moves to ensure that the assembly elections went his way. The main opposition parties were split in their attitude towards the elections. Al-Nahdha decided to boycott the elections completely, while al-Watani mainly stayed away as some of its leaders participated in their individual capacities. The pro-British party of the naqib, Hizb al-Hur, went along with the elections initially, but then pulled out and dissolved itself on the issue of the registration of tribesmen as electors. The boycott movement that had been spearheaded by the *mujtahids* had essentially fizzled out and the elections proceeded relatively smoothly, even in the Shi'a strongholds of the shrine towns. In Najaf a budding protest movement led by the religious classes failed to take off after the new governor, Mawlud Mukhlis, managed to quieten the dissenters, allowing the elections to continue normally.

The election was a two-stage process, with primary voters, basically all male adults above the age of twenty-one, electing a group of secondary voters who would then select the members of the constituent assembly. Faisal had installed his allies as governors (*mutassarif*) and as district administrators, and they threw their weight behind individual candidates whom the king supported. These included not only people who were beholden to Faisal but also anti-treaty candidates whom Faisal wanted to see in the assembly. Faisal also wanted to regain some credibility with the Shi'a community after the deportation of al-Khalisi and the self-exile of the grand ayatollahs. His strategy was not simply to thwart the passage of the Anglo-Iraqi treaty but rather to give himself a solid base inside the parliament to counter the British and pressure them into accepting amendments to the treaty. The British, of course, steered the elections towards candidates who would ensure a pro-treaty majority in the assembly. Matters came to a head when Dobbs, in a letter to Cornwallis of 31 August, accused Faisal of conspiring with the opposition to obtain a majority in the new assembly. Faisal denied these imputations and asserted that he had exerted all efforts to ensure an orderly election in all parts of the country.[44] But the Residency was not content with Faisal's representations. An article in the Residency's mouthpiece, the *Baghdad Times*, declared that if the treaty was not ratified, the British would have to withdraw, a disastrous consequence for Iraq. The pro-government newspaper *al-Iraq* followed with an article in a similar vein, and on 25 September in an interview with the same newspaper, al-Sa'adoun warned that Iraq would be in a critical position if the treaty were to be rejected. Faisal was obliged to demonstrate his open support for pro-treaty candidates. In early October 1923, he journeyed to Mosul in the company of the adviser to the Ministry of Interior, Kinahan Cornwallis, and a number of his ministers, where his intervention tipped the scales in favour of pro-treaty candidates.[45]

There was another reason, though, for Faisal's trip to Mosul. Tensions were rising between Assyrians who had been resettled in northern Iraq by the British and the inhabitants of the northern districts. There were already long-established Assyrian villages in the Mosul district, but the influx of large numbers of newly resettled Assyrians affected the balance of this multi-ethnic region. In Mosul, an altercation between members of the Assyrian Levees, auxiliary forces attached to the British army, and locals nearly led to an explosion in the town. Faisal wrote to al-Sa'adoun's cabinet regarding the growing resentments of the local population to the Assyrian Levees' presence in the town, and presciently warned of a coming disaster if nothing were done to alleviate the concerns of the inhabitants: 'the hearts of the Mosul people are full of rancour and resentment. The Assyrian matter is very serious. It is a smouldering fire. That is why I have postponed my return until I resolve the matter finally, by forcing the departure of the Levees from Mosul. I am determined to have their headquarters relocated, because I can see the coming disaster with my own eyes. And the greatest predicament is that these armed groups are under British officers' command. If something were to happen can Britain accept fatalities and especially amongst its officers?' Al-Sa'adoun took this matter seriously and agreed with the Residency to stop the further resettlement of Assyrians in northern Iraq except with specific government approval.

The firm measures that al-Sa'adoun had taken with the *mujtahids* and his open advocacy of the British alliance made him a favourite of the Residency. Dobbs in particular was very partial to al-Sa'adoun and saw in him all the virtues of the Bedouin Arab. Faisal, however, viewed al-Sa'adoun as an alternative node of power, a rival to his own growing stature in the country, and one who could conceivably displace Faisal's paramount standing with the British. He was also alarmed about al-Sa'adoun's policies, especially regarding the Shi'a *mujtahids*. Al-Sa'adoun was adamant about blocking their return to Iraq while Faisal was actively negotiating the conditions of their return. It is possible that in these secret negotiations Faisal had promised the *mujtahids* that he would replace al-Sa'adoun's government.[46] Faisal sought to appear fair and impartial between the sects, and to remove any hint that he had acted out of sectarian considerations in approving the exile of the *mujtahids*. In fact, he had asked al-Sa'adoun to deport a number of Sunni figures who appeared to be too pro-Turkish, but al-Sa'adoun firmly rejected this obvious attempt by Faisal to appear impartial.[47]

By the autumn of 1923, Faisal had made up his mind to remove al-Sa'adoun as premier. He addressed a letter to the cabinet complaining of the government's ineffectuality in improving the economic conditions of the country and of their raising of taxes to burdensome levels.[48] Al-Sa'adoun was deeply offended by the accusatory tone of the letter, and asked for it to be withdrawn. The king feigned an apology, but his pressures on al-Sa'adoun continued regardless. Al-Sa'adoun tried to retaliate by refusing to have Faisal's name read out at the Friday congregational prayers at Baghdad's mosques. Faisal was indignant about this, not only because it gave the Ottoman caliph a residual stature in Iraq that was not commensurate with his real significance in Istanbul. (Mustafa Kemal had rendered the sultan-caliph all but impotent by this time.)[49] He was also indignant because it implicitly denied that Faisal's sharifian lineage had any spiritual authority. On 15 November 1923, the king got his way. Al-Sa'adoun resigned and was replaced by Ja'far al-'Askari, the king's man.

By the end of 1923, Faisal had reigned for over a year. His early hesitancy had given way to confidence and even brashness in his handling of the countless and complex problems that descended on him. He could still make blunders and overplay his hand, but these faults were being replaced by a sureness of touch and a deeper understanding of the maze of Iraqi politics and society. For an outsider with no previous experience in the country, his progress was nothing short of remarkable. He had immersed himself in the minutiae of Iraq's internal affairs and was developing the palace as a formidable and essential focus of power. Britain's influence in Iraq was still there for all to see, but Faisal had struggled free from its suffocating and dependent embrace. He lived in the same house afforded him by the government when he had first arrived in Iraq. His private palace was still in the early stages of construction. The palace secretariat was now housed in its own building in the Waziriya district of north Baghdad. It was such a modest affair that a visiting Syrian delegation asked Faisal why he had not built a palace that was fitting to his position. Faisal replied, 'I have come here to build a kingdom and not a palace.'[50] He had asked the Ministry of Finance to allocate a supplement of 50,000 rupees[51] to the palace's budget to furnish the palace secretariat and to illuminate the streets in its environs, but the ministry had declined to meet his request. They suggested that the palace secretariat should instead use the worn furniture of the old secretariat.[52]

For nearly a year, Faisal tried not to move from Iraq. He made only one journey outside Iraq during this period, to visit his brother 'Abdullah in Transjordan in July 1923. His immediate family remained in the Hijaz, but he was paving the way for them to join him in Iraq, and Ahmed al-Rawi, the police director who accompanied Ayatollah al-Khalisi on the first leg of his exile, had been charged with arranging the travel of Faisal's wife Huzaima to Iraq, together with his son Ghazi and his daughters. Faisal had brought a number of Hijazis with him to Iraq, but they were more retainers than advisers or confidants. Rustum Haidar, who became the royal chamberlain, was his closest adviser and friend from the Syrian days, and he was still dependent on the support of those Iraqi officers who could broadly be called sharifian. But they were developing their own power bases and were driven by personal ambitions now that they were back in their own country. Their support for Faisal was also checked by the demands made on them by the Residency. They had to tread a fine line between the palace, the Residency and the opposition.

Faisal enjoyed the company of women, and rumours often abounded regarding his supposed liaisons with western women in Baghdad. Bell hinted at one such affair, where a Madame Safwat was rumoured to be the king's mistress. Bell went on to suggest that the king should marry the mistress's daughter. 'Mme Safwat [is] generally reputed to be the King's mistress! She brought a daughter grown perfectly charming, speaking excellent French and playing the piano remarkably well, while she sang queer little Turkish tunes. I really don't see why H.M. should not marry the daughter. It's not their custom to have two wives at once, but 'Abdullah has, and after all you can't say that Faisal has any wife at all, since King Husain won't let her leave Mecca. It would be much better for him to have a wife and family here.'[53] Nothing has ever been substantiated but rumours regarding Faisal's private life continued to circulate. The Residency parties and functions allowed Faisal the opportunity to mix with foreign residents or travellers, but it was at private gatherings, often at the palace or at Gertrude Bell's residence, that Faisal was able to have his moments of relaxation. Bell was besotted by Faisal in those early days, but there was no hint of any inappropriate relationship in Bell's correspondence beyond an infatuation that wore off with time. Faisal liked and respected Bell's views, but she hardly deserved the king-maker label that later attached to her. It was Cox and then Dobbs who firmly implemented policy and made decisions. At Bell's parties and at his own home, Faisal would turn to card-playing for relaxation. He had picked up these habits after the war and he had become an accomplished bridge and chemin-de-fer player. In her letters, Bell frequently mentions the king's playing bridge for small wagers. Faisal's bridge partners would often be English ladies resident in Baghdad, wives of senior officials and officers posted to Iraq.

Faisal went out to regular hunting parties, often with British officers, for partridge and other wild fowl. Iraq was a halting point for vast flocks of migratory birds. In later years, he would go after larger prey such as wild boar and gazelles. He was an excellent shot and often held shooting matches against the two of his companions with whom he hunted most, Tahsin Qadri and Kinahan Cornwallis. But it was Faisal's love of horses that dominated his leisure hours. He regularly attended the Baghdad races and watched polo matches, which had been introduced to the Iraqi army by the British. He was no amateur when it came to equestrians, and on Arabian horses he was a veritable authority. His knowledge and expertise was plainly revealed during a visit by Shaikh al-Muhsin Abu-Tabikh, who had returned from his temporary exile in Syria in the autumn of 1923. The shaikh had made a courtesy call on Faisal and brought along his eleven-year-old son. Recalling this episode decades later, the shaikh's son, Mashkour, recorded:

I accompanied my father on a visit to King Faisal I . . . My father had brought with him as a gift a famous breed of horse known as Saglawiyat. The horse had a strange grey colour but was pure bred . . . The King was residing at the Sha'shou' mansion [the house that was rented for him when he first came to Baghdad as his private residence] . . . The King received us in his Arab dress . . . He shook hands with my father and I kissed his hand, and he kissed me twice in return. He asked me about my age and what I was studying . . . He told me that I was the same age as his son Ghazi and encouraged me in my studies. My father told him that he had brought him a gift of a pure bred and rare horse . . . We left for the garden to see the horse and when the King saw it he admired the horse greatly and was very pleased as the King was an authority on pure bred horses and turning to my father asked about the horse's pedigree. The King then said as I recall, 'I have never seen a more beautiful horse, either in colour or shape'. He then started to examine the horse with an eye of an expert, inspecting its body, its feet and its hooves, and opened the horse's mouth to ascertain its age from its teeth. He then said: 'I will always ride only on this horse and I consider this the best gift I have ever been given.'

The writer goes on to detail Faisal's generosity. He gave the horse's groom a large cash gratuity and an *abaya* [Arab cloak]. Later, Faisal put his hand in his pocket and gave the shaikh's son a gold watch, a gift that made the young lad ecstatic.[54]

CHAPTER 21

✦✦✦✦✦◆⋅⋅❖◆✦✦✦✦✦

ASSEMBLIES, TREATIES, CONSTITUTIONS

T HE RESIGNATION of the al-Sa'adoun's cabinet gave Faisal the opportunity to frame the new government in directions that were more to his liking. The fact that he had brought down al-Sa'adoun and had installed his own candidate to power was a reflection of his growing self-confidence and the strengthening of his power base in Iraq. Dobbs wrote to London regarding the rise in Faisal's stature. 'In spite of his disconcerting mutability of temper [Faisal] is easily predominant and the people are growing used to his rule, and his personal charm has gained an increasing number of adherents. He has to guard above all against the allegation that he is a puppet King propped up by our bayonets. He can hope to strike roots in the soil by an attitude of independence.'[1] The Residency went along with Faisal's moves as they did not threaten the main objective of ensuring the election of an assembly that would ratify the Anglo-Iraqi Treaty. For all of Ja'far al-'Askari's shortcomings, he was not part of the opposition. He was the king's man and well-disposed to the British alliance. Faisal had complete trust in him. 'Ja'far will always walk with me; he won't cut me off; and he won't leave me until the day I die', Faisal wrote of him.[2] In his letter of instructions, Faisal advised al-'Askari 'not to show too much irritation or be overconfident. Always chose the middle way; because the one who knows does not always reveal his knowledge to others.'[3]

The choice of Ja'far al-'Askari, one of Faisal's principal lieutenants in the Arab Revolt, also offered the leading sharifian officers access to power in the new government. Both Nuri al-Sa'id and Ali Jawdat were included in the cabinet. Faisal also wanted to expand the representation of the Shi'a in the new government, and under his urging two Shi'a ministers, for finance and education, were included in al-'Askari's cabinet. The impact on the Shi'a community was immediate. A deputation of Shi'a personnel called on the palace soon thereafter. Although they would have preferred a Shi'a prime minister, they commended Faisal for his actions and expressed their loyalty to the king.[4] Two weeks later,

Faisal made a visit to the shrine towns, where he was enthusiastically received. His relationship with the Shi'a was well on the mend. He even intervened on their behalf on matters that were not technically within his ambit or competence. Gertrude Bell describes an episode where Faisal overturned a court order that was not in favour of a Shi'a litigant. 'But how to prevent the King from interfering in administration – that's the problem. There has been a terrific affair today. (This is all secret.) It arose out of an order given by H.M. which quashed a decision of the Court of First Instance, confirmed by the Court of Appeal. It's a complicated case, a Shi'ah suit against the Bahais for the possession of a house; religious fanaticism lies at the bottom of it and H.M., who is playing up to the Shi'ahs, backed them. The Council [of Ministers] backed H.M., Ja'far [al-'Askari] not being one who would ever go against him. It was a clear case of the executive overruling the judicial and Sir Henry took an absolutely firm stand. He pointed out that if such things occurred the Courts would lose all credit and the abrogation of capitulations would become impossible. He insisted on the King's withdrawing his order and the King has undertaken to do so.'[5]

Ja'far al-'Askari was an amiable and well-liked, jocular figure. He was popular with all classes of people, and frequently used common expressions and terms expressed in the most colloquial Iraqi Arabic, even while addressing parliament. It was a disarming way of getting people to adhere to his points of view. Since the days of the Arab Revolt, he had gained considerable weight and tended towards corpulence. He loved Iraqi food, and while serving as ambassador in London was often seen by friends hard at work in the legation's kitchen preparing with his own hands his favourite dish of okra stew (bamiya).[6] His mind was agile and his humour infectious. He was good at languages snd spoke English and passable French and German. He had a great love of learning and self-improvement. Upon his return to Iraq he enrolled at the Law College, sitting in class with students who were half his age. While ambassador in London, he joined the inns of court and became a fully fledged barrister.[7] He was a moderniser in his own jocular way. He was a great advocate of Faisal's campaign to replace the wearing of the Ottoman-era fez with the Faisalian sedara, and used to have handy supplies of sedaras to pass out to anyone who wanted to replace his fez with the more befitting headgear of the new order.

Completing the elections

The first order of business for the new cabinet was to complete the elections for the constituent assembly. The Ministry of Interior had instructed all the administrative inspectors in the liwas to send a list of candidates who would be supportive of the government line. These were then pruned, compiled by Cornwallis, the adviser to the ministry, and distributed to the inspectors of the provinces as a list of safe names to be supported.[8] The Residency now accepted the king's idea that it was better to have a number of open opposition figures inside the assembly, as long as they did not form a majority. A number of anti-treaty shaikhs, such as 'Abd al-Wahid Sikkar and Sha'lan Abul Jawn, were thus included on Faisal's insistence, but in all likelihood they would have been elected in any case. The final list of candidates that the administrative inspectors were asked to promote was thus a joint effort on the part of the Residency, the king and the prime minister.[9]

Further afield, however, the course of Faisal's relationships with the British was vitally affected by the election of the first Labour government in Britain in January 1924 under Ramsay MacDonald. A trade unionist, James ('Jimmy') Thomas, had become colonial secretary and thus responsible for Iraq policy and the mandate. Rumours were rife in Baghdad that the British were about to withdraw from the country. Faisal was well aware of the disastrous impact a precipitous British withdrawal would have on Iraq's claims to the Mosul wilayat. Without the on-the-ground and in-the-air presence of the British forces, Turkey would likely impose its writ on Mosul. Faisal wrote to Dobbs asking for clarification of the Labour government's position on this vital matter. These disturbing developments gave Faisal an added impetus to call for holding the final round of elections for the constituent assembly as soon as possible. The passage of the Anglo-Iraqi Treaty by a legitimate Iraqi authority would help to secure Britain's support for Iraq's northern frontiers.[10]

On 25 February 1924, the elections for the secondary electors commenced. With the exception of the troubled Mosul area, they progressed smoothly. In Mosul, the opposition planned a boycott because one of its leading lights had been removed to Baghdad. The final tally for the elections was that out of the ninety-eight government candidates, seventy-four had been elected to the hundred-man assembly, but many of those elected within the governmental list were oppositionists. Dobbs wrote a brusque estimate of the outcome. 'Practically all the advanced Nationalists (opposition) were on the list of candidates favoured by the Government, which was thus given another proof of its foolish desire to hedge and be popular with everyone.'[11] The rigging of the elections was clear, but nevertheless limited. A completely fair and free vote would not have returned a significantly different outcome. Most of those elected were established landowners, merchants and members of notable families. Six members were lawyers; another six were officers who had served Faisal in Syria or had joined the Arab Revolt. These included the rising star Yasin al-Hashimi, from whom a great deal was expected. Four had been members of the Ottoman Majlis. About a third of the assembly were tribal chieftains. It was estimated that the government could secure a majority of at least sixty members for the passage of the Anglo-Iraqi Treaty.

The constituent assembly was convened on 27 March 1924 in a festive atmosphere. Flags were draped on buildings and prisoners were released or had their sentences reduced. The route leading to the assembly building was crowded with onlookers and schoolchildren. Faisal had invited all the elected members to a banquet at his palace a day earlier, where they had given their oath of allegiance. On the appointed day, Faisal rode in an open convertible car, wearing his traditional Arab dress and carrying a magnificent golden sword. The crowds broke out in loud cheers at this spectacle. His opening speech to the assembly was well received. Bell wrote of the historic moment: 'The King in Arab dress made an admirable speech. He was very nervous . . . [but] he was received with enthusiasm.' Faisal's speech focused on the three outstanding matters in front of the assembly: the ratification of the Anglo-Iraqi Treaty; the passing of the Organic Law; and the enactment of an electoral law. Faisal also referred to the role of the assembly in helping to consolidate the country's borders. 'We want to direct your attention towards the Anglo-Iraqi Treaty, the result of our political labours in turbulent times over the past two years . . . Our government will present [the Treaty] to you with a view to its ratification. The resolution of many vital issues affecting the country will be dependent on it and on the help of the British government and the League of Nations. This [the passing of the treaty] will allow our national entity to avoid catastrophes and troubles . . . The most important matters remain the entry of our country into the ranks of nations and governments of high standing, and the establishment of its frontiers.' Faisal continued by paying allegiance to the principle of consultation and dialogue: 'The ordinances of Islam are based on consultation . . . and the greatest error committed by Islamic sects is to ignore God's command "to enjoin consultation amongst them [the Muslims]". All Muslims must act according to the rulings of their religion and support this godly order [consultative government]. Any deviation from this is to disobey God's order.'[12] Faisal's commitment to consultation and democratic processes at that time was certainly genuine, but it also allowed him considerable freedom to play off the assembly's contrary positions against the Residency's demands.

Following the king's speech, the assembly had to elect its speaker. The Residency's candidate was al-Muhsin al-Sa'adoun. Faisal had gone along with that as a quid pro quo for al-Sa'adoun's resignation as prime minister. The British had already lined up the tribal shaikhs to vote for al-Sa'adoun. The shaikhs were more than eager to demonstrate their loyalty by publicly declaring their vote in al-Sa'adoun's favour.[13] But the Residency would soon learn of the vagaries of tribal declarations of loyalty. The assembly also elected Dawood al-Haideri, a Kurd from Irbil and former aide-de-camp to Sultan 'Abd al-Hamid, and Yasin al-Hashimi as vice presidents. The election of Yasin was an unwelcome surprise to the Residency. Yasin had run against al-Sa'adoun for the speakership but had been outvoted. Bell, whose views on al-Hashimi had completely changed, wrote of him as the 'villain of the piece'.

The grand ayatollahs return

The Shi'a members had expected that the assembly would vote for one of their own, Sayyid 'Alwan al-Yasiri, as vice president. Faisal himself would have welcomed such an outcome, especially as his policy of conciliation with the Shi'a was bearing fruit. He had reopened the channels of communication with the exiled grand ayatollahs and had instigated a number of nationalist figures to raise the issue publicly of the exiled religious leaders so that a head of steam could be built to pressure Dobbs into reconsidering the matter. Letters began to appear in the nationalist press thanking the new government for its supposed intention to allow the return of the ayatollahs. By February 1924, Faisal had reached an agreement with Dobbs to pave the way for the return of the grand ayatollahs. Dobbs, however, remained adamant regarding Ayatollah Mahdi al-Khalisi, and would not entertain his return. The conditions imposed on the grand ayatollahs required that they confirm to Faisal in writing that they would desist in interfering in the political affairs of the country. The desirability of the ayatollahs' return was also prompted by other factors. The crisis between Iran and Iraq as a result of the mass exile of the leading religious figures had created serious financial problems for the Iraqi government. The flow of Iranian pilgrims had dwindled to a trickle and the economic conditions in the shrine towns were now dire. There was also a major loss of revenue for the Iraqi railroads as a result of conveying the pilgrims. Faisal did not, however, want to see the ayatollahs back in Iraq before the opening of the constituent assembly. Their premature return might cause disturbances and would detract from the significance of the opening ceremonies of the assembly. Fortuitously, Faisal and Dobbs had calculated that it would take at least six weeks before the exchanges with the grand ayatollahs would lead to any final outcome, well after the opening date for the constituent assembly.[14] If the grand ayatollahs appeared on the Iran–Iraq frontiers before they had given their undertaking they would simply be refused entry.

Faisal now began serious negotiations with the grand ayatollahs for their return to Iraq, but these soon ran into trouble. The latter would only return to Iraq if they were accompanied by Ayatollah al-Khalisi. It would be dishonourable to abandon their colleague, or so they said. But Faisal remained firm. He would not allow the return of al-Khalisi. The grand ayatollahs then relented and agreed to meet with Faisal's representative on the negotiations, an 'alim called Sayyid Baqir Wahid-al-'Ayn. Accompanied by two senior religious figures, he travelled to Iran on 1 March 1924, to convince the grand ayatollahs to sign their commitment letters and return to Iraq. Negotiations with the grand ayatollahs were helped by the Iranian prime minister, Reza Khan, who was eager to see the grand ayatollahs return to Iraq.[15]

The letters that the grand ayatollahs wrote to Faisal categorically affirmed that they would no longer be involved in political affairs. Grand Ayatollah al-Isfahani said, 'we have taken it upon us not to interfere in political affairs and to refrain from involvement [in political matters] if asked to do so by Iraqis and we have no hand in this . . . The person responsible for meeting the needs of the people and its direction is Your Majesty . . . Supporting the Hashemite King according to our Islamic religion is one of our Islamic principles, and to strengthen the bonds between Iran and Iraq is also part of our religious duties.'[16] It was a remarkable statement that should not be seen merely as a capitulation by the highest religious authorities of Shi'a Islam to Faisal's rule. Rather, it was a firm declaration that the realm of politics was not a fit place for grand ayatollahs. It could bring disrepute and ruin to their office and undermine their ability to guide and influence their followers. On 21 April 1924, the grand ayatollahs and their entourage arrived at the border town of Khanaqin, where they were officially met by government ministers and other high officials. A special train carried them to Baghdad, where they were met by other government ministers and Faisal's representative, Safwat al-'Awa. Faisal, in true conciliatory fashion, wanted to honour them in their return and not publicise any loss of face that they might have suffered by agreeing to his conditions.[17]

Faisal also had the chance to burnish his Islamic credentials after the caliphate was abolished in early March 1924 by Mustafa Kemal. Hussein, increasingly disillusioned by the results of his revolt against the Ottomans, and with his Hijaz kingdom tottering, offered himself as the new caliph. He was visiting his son 'Abdullah in Transjordan when the announcement of the abolition of the caliphate was made. A group of Palestinian and Syrian religious figures gave Hussein the formal baya'a as caliph in the village of Shunah in Transjordan. But Hussein's would-be caliphate was hardly a universal demand of Muslims, and Hussein's stature as caliph was short-lived and ultimately inconsequential.[18] Nevertheless, it was an event of some importance at the time. In Iraq, Faisal was deluged with cables of congratulations and support for his father, including, surprisingly, messages from the ulema of the Shi'a holy shrine towns.[19] He replied with thanks and appreciation, but he was hardly convinced of the longevity of his father's new status. He was well aware of his father's isolation and mounting difficulties – with the British, with ibn Saud and with his own crumbling state in the Hijaz.

Bell wrote to her father on 12 March 1924, detailing Faisal's reaction to this news. 'On Saturday morning they telephoned to me from the Palace saying that the King [Faisal] had had telegrams from his brothers and from two leading Palestinians announcing that his Father had been proclaimed Khalif . . . Just as I was leaving for home, the Reuters came in, announcing that the Turks had scrapped the lot, so I telephoned the news at once to the Palace.' Faisal asked Bell to drive over to the Palace. 'The King was very calm, deeply moved but behaving very sensibly. He said that it was the duty of every good Moslem to find a new Khalif. He didn't mean to force his father or anyone else on the people of the 'Iraq, but he intended to summon the divines and notables and ask them their opinion.'[20]

Mounting opposition to the Anglo-Iraqi Treaty

The Residency erred in believing that the elections had produced a pliant assembly with a reliable majority that would quickly pass the treaty. Opposition to the passage of the treaty emerged almost immediately after the assembly had convened. Voices were raised that the treaty could only be ratified through a referendum. Surprisingly, these were led by the supposedly moderate politician Naji al-Suwaidi. Outside the assembly, a group of lawyers canvassed to hold a public meeting, where legal minds would be allowed their say and their advice taken into consideration by the constituent assembly. Bell scathingly described them as 'scoundrely lawyers without a practice'.[21] This meeting quickly turned into a nationalist gathering, with patriotic songs and anti-treaty sloganeering. Bell was driven to remark that this episode had been secretly instigated by a scheming Yasin al-Hashimi to create a conflagration that only he could stifle. Yasin had just been elected as the chairman of a special committee formed by the assembly to scrutinise the treaty and report on its findings. He had promised Faisal that he would produce a favourable report, but Yasin was a different man to different people. His true position on the treaty was known only to himself and he used the platform of the committee to push for his own agenda. He was determined to undermine al-'Askari's cabinet and show it up as a feeble and incompetent government, unable to shepherd the country through trying times.

Agitation against the treaty continued outside the assembly. Two institutions whose formation Faisal had supported, the Reform Club and the Scientific Institute, were spearheading the anti-treaty campaign amongst the intelligentsia. Children and women were mobilised. Strong-willed women confronted tribal shaikhs in the assembly and accused them of dishonouring their kinfolk by selling the country to foreigners. Children stood outside the homes of assembly-men, and when they emerged pleaded with them to vote against its ratification.[22] But anti-treaty agitation was sometimes more violent. On 20 April 1924, two prominent pro-treaty shaikhs were nearly killed by volleys fired at them by would-be assassins. Another sought refuge in Faisal's palace against the possibility of his assassination. The anti-treaty tribal shaikh, Salem al-Khayyun, brought his armed retainers into the assembly chamber to intimidate the pro-treaty shaikhs. Not to be outdone, the pro-treaty Nuri al-Sa'id marched into the chamber carrying a hand grenade to threaten the anti-treaty assembly-men.

The tribal shaikhs who were supposedly the bedrock of British support in the assembly wavered as soon as they had been elected. They had given their pledges to Faisal and the Residency that they would support the treaty. However, soon after the assembly convened, a majority faction split, demanding from Faisal that the Organic Law specifically confer a number of tribal privileges.[23] These included the continuation of the British-instituted special tribal laws, introduced in 1918, that allowed the resolution of tribal disputes in a separate legal framework. Although designed to take into account the peculiar nature of tribal customs and rights, they were also meant to draw the tribes closer to the British authorities. Defining Iraqi society in urban-tribal terms was a constant in British official thinking, contrasting the unsympathetic figure of the half-modernised and volatile effendi with that or the noble tribesman with his traditional virtues. Obviously British officialdom favoured the tribesmen over the urbanites. Faisal, however, though immersed in tribal ways and lore, was a determined moderniser, and his instincts ran counter to the strengthening of tribal powers. Following the Ottoman pattern of creating special schools for the sons of tribal leaders, Faisal had sought to found a similar school in Iraq to introduce them to modern ways. But he abandoned this particular scheme when it was opposed by Sati' al-Husri, the director of the Ministry of Education, who favoured a completely uniform and centralised education policy for the country.[24]

Disturbances outside the assembly were matched with rising turmoil inside. The government was forced to bring a detachment of police to secure the area around the assembly, and stopped a number of opposition publications.[25] Yasin al-Hashimi's actions were opaque, apparently egging on the opposition while at the same time insisting in his private discussions, statesman-like, that Iraq had no choice but to ratify the treaty. Ali Jawdat, an assembly-man, put a different perspective on Yasin's opacity during this period and its relationship with Faisal's real position. Writing in his memoirs, Ali Jawdat said: 'I used to speak to the leaders of the opposition in the Assembly, at whose head stood Yasin al-Hashimi, and organise their contacts with the King, and bring nearer their points of view in the interests of the country and what would achieve our national goals . . . We had agreed with the King and the leaders of the opposition to take advantage in whatever way we could from the opposition's position to whittle down certain points in the Treaty. [We did this] during our internal discussions on these points before they were brought up to the full Assembly and even after they had been put in front of it.'[26] Faisal's hand in these complex gyrations of policy was not lost on Dobbs. He wrote to the Colonial Office that 'the King is directly responsible for the present difficulties as in most instances I'm assured that if the electors had been left to themselves these extremists would not have been elected at all'.[27] Dobbs was obviously referring to Faisal's insistence that a number of opposition leaders be supported in the elections to give credibility to the assembly. The king's own party, represented by the sharifian officers and the palace officials, was still far too weak and widely disliked to act as an independent force between the tribal shaikhs, the urban effendis and the smattering of notables in the assembly. The British drew on the distaste that some tribal chiefs in particular had for the king's entourage, to claim that these shaikhs' change of heart regarding the treaty was motivated more by resentment against Faisal's rule than by a rejection of Britain's control.[28]

Privately, Dobbs was dismissive of the whole process – with epithets of 'ignorant Arabs' to describe the Iraqi representatives – and was even preparing himself to abandon the country if bad came to worse. In a letter to his mother of 1 May 1924, he uncharacteristically discussed political matters.

> We have had a prolonged political crisis, the Assembly elected to ratify our Treaty with the Iraq Govt shirking the responsibility of ratification and I don't know at the moment whether it will end in the British Govt deciding to evacuate or not. The idea of calling together an assembly of ignorant Arabs and throwing a complicated treaty at their heads was of course absurd; but that was the original fiat of the Lloyd George Govt and of the League of Nations which has had to be carried out. After giving full explanations regarding the Treaty, I have maintained an attitude of complete indifference, as if I showed myself over anxious for its acceptance, they would think that the British Govt was longing to remain here at all costs. It is very difficult to get the Cabinet to give any decision, with so many other things for them to attend to, although I had written beforehand a long despatch prophesying exactly what has happened and discussing all the alternative courses which we could adopt in the event of the Assembly not ratifying the Treaty. If things continue to go wrong, I suppose I shall have to wait here until we evacuate the country. If things go right, I have been granted leave for two months from July 20 or thereabouts.[29]

In early May 1924, faced with these mounting problems, al-'Askari offered to tender his resignation. He firmly believed that the troubles were all instigated by the hidden hand of Yasin to discredit the government and to offer himself as the only plausible alternative. Faisal consulted Dobbs and invited Yasin al-Hashimi to form a new government. Yasin sought a twenty-four hour grace period during which he asked Dobbs to amend a number of offending articles in the Anglo-Iraqi Treaty. When Dobbs refused point blank, Yasin withdrew from contention, but assured Faisal that the committee that he headed to review the treaty would decide in its favour. On this basis, al-'Askari agreed to continue to head the government. Bell, who had once again fallen for Yasin's charisma, predicted that the treaty would be passed because of Yasin's determination. But this did not happen.

On 20 May 1924, the committee set up to review the treaty recommended in a lengthy report that it be rejected because it did not ensure Iraq's complete independence. Specifically, it rejected the clauses that called for continuous British scrutiny over Iraq's budget, and demanded a drastic curtailing of the employment of British advisers. It also demanded that Iraq should have the freedom to deploy its military and to use its wireless and telegraph installations freely.[30] On 29 May, the opposition mounted large demonstrations coinciding with the assembly's final debate on the treaty. The assembly building itself was surrounded by an angry mob, and live ammunition was used to disperse the crowds. The session was postponed until 31 May and again to 2 June. On that day, Dobbs, accompanied by Cornwallis, appeared at the assembly in a futile attempt to change the minds of the recalcitrant deputies. Dobbs pointed to the negotiations between Britain and Turkey on the Mosul issue and cautioned the deputies that the Turks were taking umbrage because of the reluctance of the assembly to ratify the treaty. The Turks' position on Mosul had become far more entrenched as a consequence, and Iraq was liable to lose Mosul province.[31] With the mounting tensions in the assembly and on the streets in Baghdad, the prospects for passing the treaty looked bleak. The pressures on Faisal increased, not least from Dobbs and the Colonial Office. Faisal sought to extract some concessions from Dobbs regarding the possibility of amending the treaty after its ratification. Dobbs informed the king that the British government would not accept any alterations to the treaty after its ratification. If the impasse was not broken, Faisal would face a reprise of the 1922 debacle.

The Residency was now facing the possibility of the collapse of their Iraq policy. Dobbs suggested to the Colonial Office that he should be empowered to pressure Faisal to dissolve the assembly if it refused to endorse the treaty. Faisal would then bring in a new cabinet that would conform to British policy. If Faisal refused or was unable to meet these demands, then he would be forced to 'Abdicate and Britain would rule the country directly.[32] In effect it was an ultimatum to Faisal. The assembly would be given until 10 June to ratify the treaty. If not, Dobbs's contingency plan would be put into effect.

Faisal's position had become critical. On the one hand, he knew that a treaty was necessary because it regularised Anglo-Iraqi relations and set the parameters for the mandate, but at the same time many of the terms of the treaty were harsh and would slow Iraq's path towards full independence. He was conscious that if he forced an unpopular treaty on his people at the beginning of his reign, he would find it difficult to rally popular support to his rule. The treaty had to be seen as a way station on the path towards greater freedom, and as a politically necessary measure that Iraqis would have to stomach, but only for an interim period. On 9 June 1924, with a few hours left to Dobbs's ultimatum, Faisal asked for the assembly to adjourn its debates and send three representatives from each *liwa* at the assembly to meet him in the Palace that afternoon. When the representatives assembled, Faisal addressed them in stark terms:

> When I first read the Treaty and its annexes I felt what the Assembly and the nation felt. I do not hide anything from you nor do I want to hold back what I feel in my breast. I see the country in great danger. We must not be driven by emotions but by reason. You are now responsible and I hold you responsible … I am not telling you to accept or reject the Treaty. Do what you think is right for the country's interest. If you want to reject the Treaty do so but don't leave Faisal high and dry. You must find another way apart from the Treaty. You can see for yourselves that we are in need of funds and men to fight the Turks, to resist the British Mandate, to stop the Persians and others. I am with you in the fields of battle and politics, and my past is well known to you so don't lose what is already in your hands … in the vain hope of finding something more than what you have … If you want to reject it you have to find another way to [do so].[33]

It was a clear sign that Faisal saw the treaty as a necessary evil, but one whose baneful effects could be overcome with time.

The assembly met on 10 June to take a final position on the treaty. The representatives were all told that the time for grandstanding was over. The vociferous naysayers were noticeably subdued, but there was still some hope that a third way could be found between ratification and rejection.[34] A move to adjourn the assembly was mooted and Faisal asked Dobbs for another day's grace. Dobbs exploded in anger and refused to offer an extension. Bell wrote: 'I never saw anyone angrier [than Dobbs] and as we talked [there] came a telephone from the Palace asking if he would give them a day's grace. No he wouldn't, he would call on the King to dissolve the Assembly at midnight if it couldn't be got together in the afternoon and anyway he would come up at 4 and tell the King what he thought.'[35] The day before, instructions had gone out to all the British advisers to the ministries that direct rule was now a serious possibility, and the British government had already told the League of Nations that it might be forced to propose an alternative form of government for Iraq. Faisal tried to reconvene the assembly for the afternoon of the 10th, but no quorum could be achieved. Dobbs arrived at the Palace with an unsigned note in Arabic demanding that the king dissolve the assembly. Faisal ordered the prime minister and speaker of the assembly, al-Sa'adoun, to summon the assembly well before midnight. Bell described the hectic last minute rush to collect the deputies. 'Up till 8.30 p.m. Ja'far [al-'Askari] didn't think he could get a quorum. Most of the antis were purposely keeping away in order to secure this end. Rustum Haidar, head of the King's *diwan*, went to the 'Iraq Club a little after 8 and found a lot of them, Rauf Chadirji, Naji Suwaidi and others, hanging about and gossiping. He asked them why they weren't at the Assembly. Naji tried to laugh it off by saying that was all nonsense – of course there wouldn't be a meeting. Rustum replied "All I can tell you is that if you don't come to a decision before midnight the Assembly will be dissolved." Again Naji and Rauf attempted a bluff of disbelief but in 5 minutes they had all slunk off – to the Assembly, to vote against the treaty. Ja'far gave orders to the police – his brother is Commandant of Police here – to take taxis, drive round and fetch the deputies from their houses. At 10.30 he had a quorum – 69, the quorum is 51'[36] One member 'had been dragged out of bed by the police, thrust into a car, not knowing whether he was being taken to the scaffold or where, and when he got to the Assembly was too bewildered and alarmed to cast his vote!'

Dobbs told the assembly that any further adjournments would be considered a vote against the treaty. All adjournment motions were defeated, as was the opposition motion calling for incorporating the recommended changes of the treaty committee into the final treaty before ratification. The government motion was then tabled. It recommended that Faisal ratify the treaty and that immediately after ratification Faisal should open discussions with the British government to secure the amendments suggested by the treaty committee. The resolution passed with thirty-seven votes in favour, twenty-four against, and eight abstentions. A caveat was inserted which invalidated the treaty if Britain failed to secure Mosul province for Iraq.

The crisis over the treaty had been averted. But the response in Iraq to a treaty that was seen as iniquitous and harsh was surprisingly inert. Newspapers reported on the indifference of the general public to the passage of the treaty, and the disappearance from the streets of the knife-wielding thugs and ruffians who figured prominently in the demonstrations against it.[37] Equally surprising was the lack of response of the Colonial Office when told of the passage of the treaty. The fact was simply acknowledged a week after the event. There were no thanks or words of appreciation for Dobbs, which greatly upset him.

Sir Henry Dobbs

The relentless pressures of Dobbs and his willingness to go to the limit had convinced Faisal and many of the representatives that there was no point in further delay. Sir Henry Dobbs was well trained for the job of high commissioner. He was born in 1871 to an Anglo-Irish family, educated as a scholar at Winchester and then Brasenose College, Oxford. He joined the Indian Civil Service in 1892 and was subsequently posted to the United Provinces as private secretary to the lieutenant governor.[38] He held several positions in India before joining the British mission to Kabul in 1904. There Dobbs advised the Afghan ruler, Amir Habibullah, in his negotiation with the Russians. Dobbs returned to India in 1906 where he held several administrative posts, mainly in the Baluchistan province. His experience there in handling the tribes of the region would be of great significance when he later came to Iraq. At the outbreak of war, Dobbs was seconded to Chief Political Officer Percy Cox of the Indian Expeditionary Force in Mesopotamia. In January 1915 Dobbs arrived in Mesopotamia as Cox's senior officer. His main task was to act as the revenue commissioner with headquarters in Basra. This was not Dobbs's first exposure to what was then called 'Turkish Arabia'. He had visited Baghdad in 1902 and had investigated the oil fields straddling the Persian–Ottoman border at Qisr Shirin. In fact he had been scheduled to be the consul-general in Baghdad when war broke out.

Dobbs was predisposed to Arabs and was enthusiastic about his task. Writing in February 1915 to his mother from his quarters in Basra, Dobbs commented,

I don't know much Arabic yet and have to deal with Arabs largely through interpreters, though I retain something of what I learnt in my expedition down the Euphrates in 1903. The Arabs are vastly superior to the Indians in type and civilisation, fine independent men with great ideas of hospitality and a kind of chivalry of their own; and they live in excellent brick houses. . . . One hears great tales of Turkish corruptness and incompetence. But I have a sad suspicion that, even so, the Arabs are happier under them than they eventually will be under us when we have irrigated the Mesopotamian deserts and regularized everything and screwed everyone up to concert pitch and allow no dirt or slackness and rule with the vast and crushing minuteness of our records. So I look upon it as an act of providence that I have been sent here to help in laying the foundations and to have an opportunity of countering from the very beginning the methods of excessive red tape. If I have my way, everything will be done to revive a true Arab civilisation, and the lines of administration will be so set that an increase in prosperity shall not mean spiritual decay and the dying out of all local custom and native force of character.[39]

Dobbs's duties as revenue commissioner soon expanded to include other financially sensitive departments that came under the control of the British as their forces advanced into Iraq. These included the pious foundations, state lands, customs and excise, and the management of the financing of local authorities and educational institutions. It was a mammoth undertaking that Dobbs undertook effectively but at the expense of his health. In August 1916, exhausted by the strenuous labours of his job and the trying climate, he had to be invalided to India. He continued in senior postings in India, and was knighted for his services. In December 1922 Dobbs returned to Iraq to the newly created post of counsellor to the high commissioner, with the prospect of succeeding Sir Percy Cox. Cox had made it clear to his superiors that he only wanted the posting for three years, or until a national government was formed in Iraq, and Dobbs was his own preferred successor. Cox had prepared to leave Iraq after the protocol to the Anglo-Iraqi Treaty was signed on 30 April 1923, and the following month Dobbs succeeded Cox as the high commissioner. In honouring the suitability of Dobbs for the posting, Cox later said, 'It was not often that a retiring official had the profound pleasure of being followed, as in this case, by the comrade whom he had most wished might succeed him.'[40]

Dobbs was a tall, heavily built man. He was quick to temper and hid his true character behind a dour exterior. Examples of his bouts of irritability abound. He was reputed to have thrown inkpots at members of staff who displeased him. Bell recalls an episode of Dobbs's temper in the spring of 1924 in a letter to her father of 1 April 1924. 'Oh I must tell you a heavenly story of the Dobbs pair. It is said that Sir Henry gave some seeds to his gardener who sowed them in pots, but when they came up, he let the birds eat them and Sir Henry was so angry that he threw the pots down the steps and broke them on the gravel below. Then Lady Dobbs, coming up behind, said, "That's right, Henry. If the High Commissioner mayn't do what he likes, who may?" It was so true to life that, remembering your adage, I asked her if it had indeed happened. "No," she replied gravely. "Henry broke the pots before I came. But what I always do say is that Henry is perfectly in his rights to beat the gardener every Sunday morning. It's the only sport he has." '[41] Most who knew him, though, thought him to be a thoroughly decent man with a kindly disposition. Gertrude Bell also thought well of him, even though Dobbs had brought along his own oriental secretary, Captain Vyvyan Holt, rather than keep her on. Holt acted as a combination of his translator, secretary and public relations officer.

The Organic Law and the royal prerogatives

With the passage of the Anglo-Iraqi Treaty, the next item on Faisal's agenda was the country's constitution or Organic Law. The constitution would define the nature of the country as well as the powers of the king. It was of vital importance to Faisal, and he had been working on the drafting process since 1922.

Faisal's main objective was to ensure his powers would be dominant in the country, and that he would have the authority to override the decisions of the legislative branch of government as well as appoint his own cabinet ministers. Faisal was not a proponent of a constitutional monarchy whose powers are symbolic and subservient to elected officials. In fact, the idea of kingship of this type was alien even to the radical nationalists, who expected the king to have considerable powers. Faisal understood the significance of electoral politics and the imperative of having elected legislative chambers to reflect the political currents in the country, but he would not rule as second fiddle to politicians, most of whom he saw as self-serving and driven by mean interests. He might have to deal with them, and in certain instances defer to them, but modernising Iraq could best be achieved by a strong-willed and determined king, and not by a rabble of argumentative politicians. He had seen what had happened in Syria, where he laid the collapse of his regime partly on the squabbling and opportunist politicians with their irresponsible radicalism. Throughout the east, rulers were emerging who were driven by dictatorial tendencies. They had not yet fully seized power in countries such as Turkey, Iran and Afghanistan, but they all shared the belief, common in that period, that bringing their countries out of backwardness could only be achieved by iron rule. Faisal was not cast in the same mould. His autocratic tendencies were not a result of a military background, but were more to do with his sharifian heritage and his own natural authority; his sense that his lineage, exploits and political instincts gave him precedence over the politicians. At the same time, Faisal was acutely conscious of the diversity of Iraq, which moderated, but not voided, his plans to centralise the country and bind it together in a new purpose.

Given the struggles that accompanied the passage of the Anglo-Iraqi Treaty, the Organic Law was passed with remarkable speed. Dobbs had made it clear that it could not have in it articles or stipulations that contravened the Anglo-Iraqi Treaty.[42] The opposition in the assembly went along with these limited restrictions, relating mainly to the employment of foreign advisers in the Iraqi government. A feeble attempt was made by two assembly-men to prohibit the right of the king to nominate senators to Iraq's proposed upper house of parliament. They proposed that they should be elected, but their motion was soundly defeated. Faisal was not squeamish about employing his own methods of persuasion on wavering parliamentarians, including promises of future posts in the government or the senate, to get his way.[43]

Faisal's desire to establish wide-ranging royal prerogatives in the country's constitution meshed with those of Britain. The power that Britain had reserved for itself in the Anglo-Iraqi Treaty was expressed through the high commissioner as the king's adviser. In that role, the high commissioner's influence could only be exercised if the king had the constitutional power to act broadly. It was therefore in Britain's manifest interest to give as much constitutionally sanctioned power to Faisal. In fact the treaty relationship with Iraq was expressed formally, with the person of the king as the signatory counterparty. The official communications between London and the Residency reflected this policy position. In Cox's letter to Churchill of 4 December 1921, Cox had written, 'The more nominal power the King has, the easier it will be for the High Commissioner to influence the course of events.' Minutes of the Middle East Department of 31 March 1923 also recorded this position. 'It was necessary for the Organic Law to be so framed as to enable us to control the Iraqi parliament through the King in order to secure the fulfilment of Treaty relations.'[44]

The Organic Law established Iraq as a hereditary constitutional monarchy, with the king as head of state. The king was empowered to oversee the whole process of law-making, confirming and promulgating laws, and supervising their implementation. The king could convene, open, adjourn, prorogue or dissolve the Majlis or parliament. He could select the prime minister and his ministers and accept their resignation. He was empowered to appoint and dismiss any official. The king was the commander-in-chief of the armed forces, and could declare war and proclaim martial law. Faisal could now build his power and his base of support on these sweeping royal prerogatives. But he also had to manage the powers held in reserve by the high commissioner. This tension would be a prominent feature of Faisal's reign from now on: not the wresting of power, because it was now his constitutional right to have these prerogatives, but rather its management in the face of resistance by the high commissioner. Faisal also had to plan for the conditions where the high commissioner's advice was unpalatable or unacceptable.

With its work on the Anglo-Iraqi Treaty, the Organic Law and the passing of an electoral law done, the constituent assembly was dissolved on 2 August 1924. On the same day that al-'Askari's government resigned, the king, in consultation with Dobbs, appointed Yasin al-Hashimi as prime minister. Yasin's conduct during the tortuous passage of the Anglo-Iraqi Treaty was contradictory. He voted against the treaty while advising his supporters to vote in its favour, and several newspapers took him to task for his studied ambiguity. But he was a formidable presence and there was an inevitability about his nomination to the post of prime minister. Faisal wanted him inside the 'tent' of the governing party, and Dobbs, who questioned Yasin's ultimate loyalties, eventually acceded to Faisal's decision. Yasin appointed himself as minister of foreign affairs as well as minister of defence. However Faisal wanted to maintain effective control over the army, and, using his position as commander-in-chief, created the position of deputy commander. He entrusted this new post to his close ally Nuri al-Sa'id. Faisal would not allow this key institution to become a plaything of the politicians.

Faisal was now in his third year on the throne. He was growing into his role as king and, equally important, his subjects had become accustomed to his regal presence.[45] His pull was also felt outside of Iraq. Tribal chiefs from the Hijaz or southern Syria seeking to counter the Wahhabi menace to their traditional domains; nationalist politicians escaping French tyranny in the Levant; leaders of the Indian Khilafat movement, all beat a path to Faisal. Baghdad was becoming a magnet for footloose Arabs and Muslims who sought Faisal's material and financial support for their causes. Coming across Faisal at polo matches, Bell saw him surrounded by tribal leaders from Nejd. 'I saw the King this afternoon at the Arab polo. He was all smiles, I'm bound to say; he was dressed in his most beautiful Arab clothes and he was playing the part of King of the Arabs in his finest manner. He was surrounded by shaikhs of the tribes of Nejd who had fled from Ibn Sa'ud and come up to Faisal, much to the gratification of the latter!'[46] In another episode, Bell described an afternoon when, visiting Faisal for tea, she came across the old fox Nuri al-Sha'lan of the Ruwala tribe.

I was having tea with H.M. that afternoon; it was the loveliest oriental scene. He was sitting in his garden near a fountain in full Arab dress, the white and gold of the Mecca princes. And by him, sitting on the stone lip of the fountain, were three of the great chiefs of the desert. Nuri al Sha'lan, grim and scowling, with his red *kaffiyah* drawn up over his mouth and chin as he wears it; 'Ajil al Yawar, 6 ft 4 of huge body, long fine hands holding a chain of amber and his face illumined with his slow, sweet smile; 'Ali Sulaiman, the sturdy peasant shaikh whose word runs from Fallujah along all Euphrates to the frontier. Everywhere round them, tossed over the fountain edge, lying in swathes in the garden beds, gold and orange marigolds – waves and waves of them, with the white and yellow of chrysanthemums above them, echoing the King's white and gold. And the low sun sending long soft beams between the willow bushes and the palms, brushing the gold and the orange, the white and yellow into a brighter glow. – Such a talk we had too, of the desert and its secular strife. Nuri was trying to persuade the King to recapture Jof for him, held now by Ibn Sa'ud. The King who has no reason to love Nuri, for he follows any hand that pays him, was delicately mocking him: 'Whose subject are you Nuri? When you want a passport do you go to the French or to Sidi 'Abdullah or to whom? Or is your camel your passport or your sword and lance?' Nuri couldn't meet him; his face grew blacker and he drew the red kerchief closer round his mouth.[47]

Faisal had not lost his deft authority with the tribesmen.

✦✦✦✦✦❖❖❖✦✦✦✦✦

CHAPTER 22

OIL AND THE MOSUL QUESTION

T HE PASSING of the Anglo-Iraqi Treaty, and the organic and election laws set the institutional framework for Faisal's kingdom, at least as long as the mandate continued in force. But another critical factor now loomed, for it raised the question of the literal form of the Iraqi state. The status of nearly one-third of Faisal's putative realm was still in dispute. Sovereignty of the entire former Ottoman province of Mosul was contested by the new Turkish state. The area was militarily controlled by British forces, and Iraq had de facto authority over the territory, but Faisal still needed the official sanction of the League of Nations to incorporate this huge territory into Iraq proper. The Mosul 'question', however, was not just a matter of annexing a large swath of land into Iraq, even though it was a well-populated and well-endowed land. The prospects for the discovery and exploitation of large oil resources were very real, which would give the new Iraqi state a vital boost for its precarious public finances. It also had immense significance for the balance of power inside the country and the type of nation that Faisal was to rule over. The great majority of the population of the province was Sunni Muslim, and if the wilayat of Mosul were to be incorporated into Iraq, the overwhelming preponderance of the Shi'a in the rest of Iraq would be diluted. The reality of a majority Shi'a Iraq, presided over by a foreign-born king and dependent on a Sunni Arab ruling elite, would not have been so anomalous and ultimately unsupportable. Conversely, however, the wilayat would bring into Iraq a mixed population of Arabs, Kurds, Chaldeans, Assyrians and Turcomen, introducing a large non-Arab element into Faisal's kingdom. The task of forging a cohesive national unit out of this diverse population would certainly be more problematic. The Kurds especially would be hesitant into being drawn into an explicitly Arab nationalist state.

Faisal's intent was to fashion a nation out of this mixed population, but he was trapped in a contradictory set of policies. On the one hand, he was naturally conciliatory and treated the diverse communities of the country with respect and a measure of equality. Faisal's project was to transcend community loyalties and identities by forging a national consciousness that emphasised the bonds of common nationhood. Dwellers in the land of Iraq should above all be loyal to the territorial nation state of Iraq. He constantly emphasised the need to accept and acknowledge the country's diversity, and sought to be impartial between the claims of sect, religion and ethnicity. This had always been his predisposition. But he was also tied to a small coterie of Sunni Arab officers and functionaries who formed the base of his power in Iraq. They did not always see matters with the same benign perspective as he did. Acutely aware of their statistical disadrantage, their plan was to consolidate their power as a class using hard-knuckle politics, intimidation and the propagation of a strident Arab nationalist rhetoric. Faisal was aware of this conundrum. He himself had been an advocate of the nationalist idea, and never relinquished his hope for a broad Arab confederation, under his, or at least his family's, leadership. This jumble of conflicting objectives and schemes could be reconciled by the force of his leadership, but as the Mosul issue became ever more pressing, these finer subtleties were left aside. What mattered most to him was the incorporation of the Mosul province to provide the final definition of Iraq's frontiers and to cement his power over this state.

The Mosul question

The vital importance of Mosul to his rule was not lost on Faisal, even in his earliest days in Iraq. The first trip that he made outside Baghdad after his coronation was to Mosul. Addressing a delegation from Mosul, Faisal reminded them that their unity and perseverance were essential if the province were to be joined to Iraq.[1] He sent his brother Zaid to stiffen the locals' resolve in the face of continuous Turkish incursions into the province. In his second visit to the city in May 1923, Faisal openly confronted the Turkish claims on the province, stating that the province 'had separated from them [the Turkish Republic] in a final way and there is no return to the past'.[2] He also reminded the Turks that their claims could be met with Iraqi counter-claims on the Turkish provinces of Diyarbakir, Orfa and Mardin with their substantial Kurdish and Arab populations.[3]

The Mosul dispute involved territory of some 35,000 square miles with a population of nearly 900,000 people. Iraq's claim to the territory had been substantially upheld by the unratified Treaty of Sèvres. The replacement Treaty of Lausanne between the Allies and the Turks could not reach agreement on the disposition of the territory. However, it was agreed that the military status quo would continue, and that the matter would be referred to the League of Nations if Britain and Turkey could not reach agreement on Mosul within nine months of the treaty's ratification. On 6 August 1924, Britain referred the matter formally to the League of Nations for its resolution.[4] This was none too soon. The Turkish army had crossed into Iraq and, although repulsed by RAF action, it left a trail of destruction, especially on villages inhabited by Assyrians. In September 1924 the League authorised the establishment of a technical Commission of Inquiry to investigate the facts on the ground. The three-man commission was presided over by a Swedish diplomat, Carl Einer de Wirsen, and included Count Pal de Teleki, a former Hungarian prime minister and noted geographer, and a retired Belgian officer, Colonel Albert Paulis. The League also set a provisional border slightly south of the northern boundary of the Ottoman province (the so-called 'Brussels Line'), until the matter was definitively resolved. The commission now made its preparations to visit Iraq, arriving in Baghdad in mid-January 1925. There, it was joined by its secretariat and by assessors from both sides. To the outrage of Iraqis, the Turkish assessors included two former Iraqis – labelled renegades by the Baghdad press – on their team, a Turcoman from the Naftchi family and a Kurd, a brother-in-law of the insurgent Shaikh Mahmud.[5]

In anticipation of the Commission of Inquiry's expected visit, in December 1924 Faisal toured all the major urban centres of the north of Iraq: Mosul, Kirkuk, Irbil and Suleimaniya. He was accompanied by a senior Kurd, Ibrahim al-Haidari, a religious dignitary and now minister of endowments (*awqaf*), and a Turcoman, Sabih Nashat, a notable from Kirkuk and an ex-minister.[6] The results of this trip were generally good. The Turcomen notables of Kirkuk were generally supportive of the area's inclusion into Iraq. Faisal had judiciously offered a number of them key posts in the provincial government and in the senate. The Kurds were more equivocal, but Faisal had managed to garner the support of the traditional rivals to Shaikh Mahmud. However, it was in Mosul city, where the greatest concentration of Arabic-speakers was to be found, that Faisal found his most fervent supporters. There was a genuine desire on the part of most of the Arab inhabitants to be included in the new Iraqi state and Faisal's visit galvanised their resolve. The governor of the province, 'Abd al-Aziz al-Qassab, wrote in his memoirs that Faisal's visit 'left an excellent impression on the inhabitants of the province and on its leaders and notables. It encouraged the waverers and the anxious ones. Many offered to fight for the Arab nature of Mosul, and that they would organise petitions and memoranda for the Commission [of Inquiry] that would demand that the Turks cease their plans to 'turkify' the province; and that would call for keeping the province within a united Iraq.'[7]

The commission arrived in Baghdad on 16 January 1925. They were entertained at Faisal's palace with other leading political and social figures of the country and with officials from from the Residency. Later, Faisal presented the commission with his own memorandum on the importance of the Mosul province to the future of Iraq. After reviewing Iraq's progress since the end of the war, and his own plans for the country's development, Faisal wrote, 'Bringing into existence and consolidating a permanent government of Iraq is dependent on the preservation of the status quo . . . It is impossible for a government in Baghdad to live if Mosul is detached from it and held by another government . . . I consider that Mosul is to Iraq as the head is to the body.'[8] The commission stayed in Baghdad for only a few days. In those days Baghdad had many street demonstrations, some involving schoolchildren mobilised by the government for this purpose, demanding that Mosul be joined with Iraq.[9]

The commission then departed for Mosul, where it stayed for nearly two months, undertaking painstaking investigations into the true conditions in the province and assessing the sentiments of its people. Given the excited state of public opinion in Mosul and the fear of disturbances, the commission's work was undertaken mainly in secret sessions where depositions were taken and interviews conducted. Nuri al-Sa'id, the deputy commander of the Iraqi army, organised a large military procession in the town, which was attended by large crowds cheering for Faisal and for an Iraqi Mosul.[10] But the attitudes of the people of the province, in contrast to those in the town of Mosul, were as varied as their population mix. Some Arab merchants sought to reconnect with Turkey because of the obvious commercial advantages; religiously minded people, on the other hand, were aghast at Mustafa Kemal's secular policies and much preferred Iraq. Minorities, especially the Assyrians, preferred Iraq on the understanding that it would remain under British influence. Kurds, on the other hand, were divided between supporters of independence, those who expected continuing British control over Iraq, and those who had adjusted and benefited from Faisal's rule. There was a probable majority in favour of union with Iraq, but with the qualification of an ongoing role for Britain in the running of the country. Dobbs in fact had written to the Colonial Office in February 1925 saying that he expected that the commission would rule in favour of union with Iraq if the rights of minorities could be protected. These would be assured if the British mandate were extended for another lengthy period.[11] Faisal had also kept himself independently well informed of the progress of the investigations of the commission through his aides and the governor of the province, al-Qassab. The latter wrote him regularly of all important developments. Sabih Nashat, who had stayed behind in Mosul after Faisal's December trip, wrote to the government on 16 February 1925 that 'the head of the Commission gave him the good news that the province would stay in Iraqi hands'.[12]

The commission left Iraq on 19 March 1925 for Geneva where it was to prepare and then present its findings. Faisal sent them a farewell telegram expressing his view that they would affirm Iraq's just demands 'upon which rests the safety of our young kingdom and the future happiness of our people'.[13] Faisal was confident that the commission would find in favour of Iraq. In a speech to the National Assembly on 16 July 1925, Faisal spoke of his 'joy and gratitude at what the people [of Iraq] generally and the people of the northern provinces in particular, had shown of their national pride and their commitment to a unified Iraq in all their positions, and not least when the international commission was doing its work with them.[14]

Oil politics

The possibility that the northern provinces of Iraq might contain large oil deposits was known to the British and other European powers even before the outbreak of war. However, at the onset of the mandate, the Turkish Petroleum Company (TPC), holder of the Ottoman-era concessions on oil exploration and development, had not yet begun any serious exploration work on these deposits. In a speech to the Lausanne conference in 1923, Curzon emphatically denied that the attitude of the British government towards the Mosul question was in any way connected to the oil issue. This was at best disingenuous. The Admiralty and Foreign Office had known about these oil deposits for a long time, and even though the world was awash with oil in 1925, the deposits in Iraq were potentially of immense strategic importance to Britain. Oil may not have loomed large in the protracted negotiations over Mosul, but it was certainly there in the background.

During the San Remo negotiations at which the mandates for Iraq, Syria and Palestine were awarded, Iraq was offered an option to acquire 20 per cent of the capital of the TPC. Britain had wanted this option to be employed as a lever in negotiations with the Turks. Iraq would offer to surrender this option in exchange for Turkey dropping its claims on Mosul. In the event, this sleight was not employed as the Lausanne conference could not reach an agreement on the Mosul question. However, the Iraqi government resurrected the issue with the TPC, which fiercely resisted granting Iraq a stake in the company, much preferring to pay a royalty on any future oil revenues, rather than have Iraq as a significant equity partner and thus entitled to review the company's operations and management. Moreover, Iraq had demanded that royalties should be paid in gold rather than in sterling or any other currency. Iraq also made other claims that the oil company refused to consider, such as imposing import duties on the equipment needed by the TPC, and claiming exploratory rights for itself for all the land outside the narrow scope of the fields actually developed by the TPC. Negotiations between Iraq and the TPC were suspended between May 1924 and February 1925 as both sides held adamantly to their positions.

Apart from contending with the oil concession issues, the Yasin cabinet was confronted with a major economic crisis in the country. The harvest in 1924 was very poor and the government suffered from a sizable drop in its fiscal revenues. Near-famine conditions prevailed in parts of the country, including the northern provinces. There was also the matter of the Ottoman public debt, for which Iraq had to bear part of the cost. The details of Iraq's share of the debt were being worked out in Istanbul in the autumn of 1924, but whatever the final figure, Iraq would be responsible for its servicing.[15] The government's commitment to building a strong army, one of Faisal's main preoccupations, was also sapping public finances.[16] By the end of 1924, the country was facing the prospect of bankruptcy. Faisal pleaded with the Residency to absolve Iraq from any obligations regarding the Ottoman debt. In as much as the French were the main Ottoman bondholders they, Faisal argued, should also be prepared to bear part of the burden by taking a discount on their bonds. In a sign of solidarity with the country's financial predicament, Faisal asked Yasin al-Hashimi to cut the budget of the royal household, which then stood at 780,000 Indian rupees or about £55,000. Yasin flatly refused, and the royal household's budget stayed fixed at this level for a number of years.

It was under such dire financial and economic circumstances that the Residency forced a reluctant Iraqi government to reopen talks with the TPC. Faisal, probably more than his cabinet, was acutely aware of the need to reach a resolution on the matter. The overhang of the concession issue might affect the final decisions of the Commission of Inquiry regarding the Mosul boundary question. At the same time, the need to have Britain as a firm advocate of the Iraqi case was essential for influencing the disposition of the commission. In fact, Count Teleki had warned that the oil concession issue had to be resolved as soon as possible and that Iraq should drop its insistence on a 20 per cent share in TPC. The combined pressures from Faisal and the Residency finally succeeded, and the cabinet approved the oil agreement with the TPC on 14 March 1925, but not before two of its members had resigned in protest.[17] The cabinet dropped its demands for a 20 per cent stake in TPC, but did manage to extract some important concessions from TPC, including the payment of the royalties in gold. The concession was not ratified, however, until the following year, after the Mosul dispute had been settled. But the cabinet decision cleared the outstanding issues that had delayed the final enactment of the Organic Law. On 21 March 1925 Faisal signed the Organic Law, Iraq's first constitution, using a specially commissioned gold pen, amidst scenes of widespread celebrations and festivities. This also paved the way for the holding of the second round of elections for a new parliament.

The new parliament was heavily skewed towards government nominees who were selected by Faisal and Prime Minister al-Hashimi, and approved, with minor adjustments, by Cornwallis, adviser to the Ministry of Interior. There were widespread accusations of rigging in favour of government candidates, especially in Shi'a districts. On 8 June 1925 elections were held without disturbance. Out of the eighty-eight deputies in the Majlis, seventy-six were government candidates. The two main organised parties, the reconstituted al-Nahdha, which was overwhelmingly Shi'a, and al-'Umma, failed to secure any seats.[18] Faisal used his royal prerogative on 7 July to select the seventeen-man senate, only five of whom were Shi'a. Two weeks earlier al-Hashimi's cabinet had resigned, riven by internal disputes and further weakened by the resignation of the two ministers over the TPC concession. Nevertheless, Yasin's year-long cabinet had a number of notable achievements. An important dredging scheme in the Shatt-al-Arab estuary was launched and a trade agreement had been signed with French-controlled Syria. But the cabinet crumbled after the wrangling over the TPC concession. Faisal charged 'Abd al-Muhsin al-Sa'adoun to form a new cabinet. There were precious few other politicians of the stature and authority needed to manage the country's day-to-day affairs. Al-Sa'adoun's cabinet included the usual coterie of Sunni Arab politicians, many of whom were not too friendly to Faisal.

A debilitating illness

Faisal's indifferent state of health had taken a turn for the worse in the spring of 1925. His appendix operation had been successful and he appeared to be in fine form, but in early 1925 he began to lose weight very fast. His appetite was poor and he was plagued with indigestion and physical and mental fatigue. By the time he gave his speech from the throne at the opening of parliament in mid-July, his weight had dropped to forty-four kilograms, an almost skeletal level. A battery of tests and medical examinations failed to reveal anything of significance, and his doctors, led by Harry Sinderson, saw no alternative but to recommend that he seek treatment in Europe. Faisal resisted the advice, as it would mean leaving Iraq at a critical moment. A new parliament was in session and the Mosul question was still awaiting resolution in Geneva. The cabinet was also loath to see him go. Yasin, who was still prime minister when the matter had been raised, argued that Faisal could be treated in Iraq. Dobbs, on the other hand, thought that Faisal had to leave for treatment. His own diagnosis was cancer and he in fact cabled the Colonial Office with his suspicions.[19] Eventually Faisal accepted that his condition was serious and that he had to leave for Europe for treatment. The new prime minister al-Sa'adoun raised no objections, and preparations were made for Faisal's departure in early August 1925. Amir Zaid, then an undergraduate at Oxford, was recalled to Baghdad to act as regent in Faisal's absence.

On the night of his departure, 4 August 1925, Faisal invited the entire Majlis, senate and cabinet to dinner at his palace. He expressed his great regret at having to leave the country at this juncture, but his health was deteriorating and he needed treatment. He also reminded them that the findings of the Commission of Inquiry on Mosul would be released soon. 'The report [of the Commission] will be long and detailed and for this reason I am concerned that some will misread it. But you should have full confidence that Iraq's rights will be protected.' Nevertheless, he went on, there was the matter of extending the term of the Anglo-Iraqi Treaty as one of the requirements of the Commission of Inquiry. Faisal attempted to deflect the anxiety and panic that this might induce in his listeners, but he himself was aware that this would cause no end of trouble when it was announced in public. The prospect for another show-down between the Residency, palace, parliament and cabinet was all too real.[20]

Faisal's motorcade crossed the desert to Syria and then to Beirut. From Beirut, he was to board the ship SS *Cordillere* that would carry him to Europe. There was, of course, the alternative air route to Egypt via Palestine, but Faisal felt that he was not well enough to take this shorter route to Egypt and then Europe. The desert route was not in itself short of problems. The motorcade had to follow the tracks of the coaches of the Eastern Transport Company – popularly known as 'Nairn', after its founders, two intrepid Scottish brothers – which wound their way through the desert from Baghdad to Damascus. The security conditions were also far from good in Syria, which was then in the throes of a major uprising by the country's Druze population. The motorcade had to avoid passing through Damascus. British armoured convoys accompanied Faisal to Palmyra in Syria, after which the French, no great friends of Faisal, were to escort him to Beirut via Homs. Arriving in Beirut, Faisal's entourage discovered that the staterooms, which were supposedly reserved for him on board the ship, were not available. Faisal had to make do with ordinary rooms on the main deck. These were cordoned off from the rest of the cabins by a considerate ship's captain.

The ship's first port of call was Jaffa, where the civil governor of Jerusalem Sir Ronald Storrs and a host of Palestinian notables boarded the vessel to welcome the king. The visiting party included the famous chronicler of the 'Arab Awakening', George Antonius, who had effusively praised Faisal in his writings. Storrs had last seen Faisal in less than auspicious circumstances when Faisal had been forced to leave Syria in the summer of 1920. Faisal, however, was too weak to spend much time with the delegation, a situation that was not helped by the heavy swells that induced chronic sea-sickness. On the ship's next stop, Alexandria, Faisal was rapturously met by a throng of excited well-wishers. 'Long before the ship, was berthed, cheers and shouts of greeting filled the air,' wrote Dr Sinderson, who was accompanying Faisal to Europe. 'As soon as the ship was berthed countless admirers swarmed up the gangways and it was with the greatest difficulty that any semblance of order could be sustained.'[21]

Faisal's crossing to Marseilles left him exhausted and he was in no condition to stay the few days in Paris that he had earlier planned. As the press release said of his sudden departure to London, 'Owing to 'Abdominal trouble, his medical adviser ordered him to proceed direct to London.' No sooner had Faisal arrived and was ensconced at the Hyde Park Hotel, than reporters, visitors, well-wishers and curious crowds descended on the hotel. News had already spread of Faisal's deteriorating health, encouraging all sorts of people to recommend their own remedies. A delegation from the Woking Mosque expressed their scepticism at the efficacy of the treatment that he was receiving, and suggested that he should submit himself to the administration of practitioners of traditional medicine.[22] Lord Headley, the first Muslim peer in parliament, chimed in with his own recommendations for treatment. Mail poured in: from well-wishers, favour-seekers and charlatans, including occultists who claimed they could cure him by the 'laying of hands'. However, Sinderson took Faisal's treatment firmly in hand. After a series of complex tests, the diagnosis of an unusual form of amoebic dysentery was made, but not before Faisal had had a number of teeth extracted because of a misdiagnosis of oral sepsis. Sinderson was greatly relieved as amoebic dysentery was a treatable disease. 'It was great news to me,' Sinderson wrote, 'and by a strange coincidence, the King sent for me an hour or two later and asked: "As a friend, tell me if I shall recover." After I had answered very definitely in the affirmative, His Majesty replied, "I have no fear of death, but I have so much to do for my country before I die. If you think I am not likely to get better, let me know now so that I can speed up my life's programme".'[23]

Faisal's treatment continued over a few weeks. In late September 1925 he moved out of the Hyde Park Hotel to a house in Princes Gate in London's Kensington district. The house was owned by a wealthy Iraqi Jewish businessman, Eliezer Saleh Kedouri. His convalescence progressed well, but he was still fatigued by evening engagements. He did not relent from his chain-smoking habit, which caused his doctors to take away his beloved cigarettes whenever they could. He accepted an invitation from Gertrude Bell, who was then in England on vacation, and as his recovery progressed he went out and about more often. He also called on the new colonial secretary, Leo Amery, on 29 September 1925. Amery recorded the meeting in his diary: 'Feisal looking ever so much better for having his teeth pulled out, and deeply grateful for the help that I have been able to give over the Mosul. I told him he could go back and give his people good courage.'[24] Faisal also raised the subject of the tottering realm of his brother King Ali in the Hijaz, who was now bottled up in Jeddah and in dire financial straits. Ali was expecting an immediate injection of funds as a result of his plan to hand out the concessions for the Jeddah port and Hijaz rail to a British concern.

Faisal had met Amery previously when the latter had been on a fact-finding mission to Iraq in March and April of 1925, reviewing Britain's military prepar-edness and the situation in Mosul. Amery was very taken by Faisal and later recalled his meetings with him,

My first respects, of course, were paid to His majesty King Feysal[25] at his palace some little distance from Baghdad, and I had a number of talks with him subsequently. One of the most interesting arose out of a full account he wished to have from me of the exact rights of a constitutional monarch in relation to his Ministers, and of the extent to which he was entitled to be informed and consulted on policy in process of formation, and not merely presented with cut-and-dried decisions. Whatever the precise constitutional position as adapted to Iraq conditions, Feysal was every inch a king. His lineage, dating back to the time of the Prophet himself, showed itself in his handsome features, in his every gesture, and in his exquisite courtesy. The story of his gallantry in war has been told by his devoted friend and adviser, Lawrence. He had little to learn as a master of statecraft in the narrower sense, and had not spent his time at the Ottoman Court, or amid factions of the Arab world, for nothing. But he also had real statesmanship.[26]

Lawrentian interludes and the return home

The under secretary of state for India Lord Winterton invited Faisal for a weekend at his country retreat in Surrey, Shillinglee Park 'so old, so carelessly cared for,' as Lawrence uncharitably called it.[27] Just before Faisal's party were to leave for the weekend, Lawrence showed up at Faisal's Kensington residence. He was dressed as an ordinary aircraftsman of the RAF and the doorman would not let him in. Lawrence proceeded to sit on the doorsteps, whereupon the worried doorman sought out Tahsin Qadri, Faisal's aide, who recognised Lawrence and ushered him in. Lawrence had abandoned any interest or involvement in Middle Eastern affairs and revelled in his unreal anonymity in the lower ranks of the RAF. Sinderson, who was present, later recorded how Faisal had received Lawrence. 'The King greeted Lawrence cordially. They had not met since His Majesty's last visit to Europe and jestingly, he asked his late Chief of Staff why he had been reduced to the ranks!' Lawrence had leave only for the evening but was persuaded to accompany the party to Surrey after Faisal arranged a return journey to London in his own car. Sinderson's diagnosis of Lawrence was that he suffered from a psychopathic personality common to genius, and quoted approvingly from A. T. Wilson's scathing condemnation of Lawrence for his 'beardlessness, his love of dressing and being photographed in long clothes'. But also importantly, Sinderson noted that Faisal hardly ever spoke of Lawrence. 'It was rare for Faisal to make any reference to Lawrence, and when he did the epithet *meskin* (a poor soul) was almost invariably employed.'[28] Clearly Faisal also believed that Lawrence's eccentricities masked a far more tortured and complex personality.

Faisal continued to see Lawrence whenever he visited England. Lawrence could never shake off the conceit that he was solely responsible for Faisal's rise to glory. This condescension, masked as quiet pride in the rise of a star pupil, is gratingly obvious in Lawrence's correspondence with Charlotte Shaw. In the summer of 1927 Faisal visited London and met with the Shaws. Charlotte sent Lawence her impressions on Faisal, to which he replied: 'I'm awfully glad you liked him. For so long he was only my duckling; and I crow secretely with delight when he gets another inch forward on his road.' In the same letter Lawrence responded to the rumour that he might be coaxed out of the RAF to become Faisal's adviser in Iraq. 'I don't think he wants me, really. Not even the nicest man on earth can feel wholly unembarrassed before a fellow to whom he owes too much. Feisal owed me Damascus first of all, and Bagdad second; and between those stages most of his education in kingcraft and affairs. When with him I am an ominpotent adviser [but] it is derogatory to a monarch: especially a monarch who is not entirely constitutional. Feisal often has to lead his people . . . and since 1921, under Feisal's guidance [Iraq] has done much good trying and no falling. But I don't think it yet walks very well.'[29]

Lawrence might have pondered on why King Faisal would go out of his way to see a person with whom he might not have been too comfortable. He genuinely loved Faisal but his love was always tinged with the pride of the nanny in the blossoming of her favourite ward. 'He is one of the best people I have met,' Lawrence wrote to Charlotte Shaw.

> Your remark about his tenacity interested me. He is both tenacious and weak; perhaps these qualities go together. It is easy to swing him off his point: and when released he tends to swing back to it. Therefore the French called him treacherous . . . Very gentle you know and very kind, and very considerate, and outrageously generous to friends, and mild to his enemies, and cleanly honest and intelligent: and full of wild freakish humour: though I suppose that is a little overlaid with kingliness, now . . . I wish you could have known him, as I did, when he was Feisal, just. One of the most attractive human beings I have ever met . . . You know, without my telling you, how much I liked him . . . Meanwhile Feisal is serving his race as no Arab has served it for many hundred years. He is my very great pride: and it's been my privilege to have helped him to his supremacy, out there, and to have made him a person, for the English-reading races.[30]

Lawrence preferred his Faisal to be unsullied by the corrupting ways of the world. The image that he preserved in his mind was the Faisal of the desert war, not the Faisal who presided over the unpleasant and possibly futile task of modernising the Arabs. Soon after Faisal's death Lawrence wrote, 'I think of his death almost with relief – as one would see enter the harbour a good-looking but not sea-worthy ship, with the barometer falling. He is out of it, intact.'[31]

Faisal's last weeks in London had their share of unpleasantness. In a rather ill-conceived notion that he should placate the mighty Beaverbrook press, especially the *Daily Express*, Faisal agreed to be interviewed at length by one of their reporters. The newspaper had carried an unremitting assault on the British government's Iraq policy, and in the past had often called for Britain's withdrawal from the country. The Beaverbrook press also carried on a campaign that supported the transfer of the Mosul province to Turkey. The ploy to appease the Beaverbrook press failed miserably. The reporter, who spent nearly an hour with the king, filed a story that was carried under lurid headlines about the mysterious whereabouts of Faisal and his disappearance from public view. Faisal was described as an 'unhappy monarch of a puppet throne, stranger in the country where he reigns, created by a political blunder and looking for another blunder to save him from the fate of failure. King Faisal smiles, for he is not without courage, but I shall always think of him in his quiet London retreat as a tragic figure in the grip of events too momentous for him to control.' Faisal was incensed but tried to take it in his stride as part of the ongoing political struggles over Britain's commitments in Iraq.[32] It was only at a farewell dinner at his residence for leading political figures that Faisal's despondency lifted when the Colonial Secretary Leo Amery assured him that there was no possibility that Mosul would be handed over to Turkey.

On 9 October 1925, Faisal left England for France. In Paris, where he remained for nearly two weeks, he met French Foreign Minister Briand. France's attitude to Faisal had dramatically shifted from open hostility to one where the Quai d'Orsay was actively soliciting his views on the crisis in Syria. In mid-1922, the French mandate authorities in Syria had instigated a vicious newspaper campaign against Faisal, and were actively supplying arms to Iran with a view to creating border problems with Iraq.[33] But conditions had now changed. France's mandate in Syria had been strewn with problems from the start, and its aggressive policies there were unfavourably contrasted with Britain's less high-handed and arrogant exercise of power in Iraq.

There was also remorse in Damascus, especially held by formerly anti-Faisal elements, about the lost kingdom of Syria. Nuri al-Sa'id had visited Damascus in February 1924, on his way to Amman to greet King Hussein. In Damascus, Nuri met a number of political leaders who had opposed Faisal in 1920. As Gertrude Bell later wrote of these meetings, 'The people that Nuri called on were all men who in 1920 had been anti-Faisal. One and all said in front of the French Officer [who was attached to Nuri]: "We are eating our own flesh; if this goes, next year we shall be dead." . . . Nuri said [to the French officer]: "I can't help thinking that it was mistake on your part to turn out Faisal." "Of course it was," he replied. "But what can we do now?" '[34] On the return leg of his journey Nuri stopped in Beirut, where he met the French high commissioner in the Levant at the time, General Maxime Weygand. Weygand bitterly complained to Nuri about the problems of governing Syria. ' "What's to be done? There's no trade. There's nothing. We are spending millions without return." . . . Nuri replied: "It's a pity that you turned out Faisal." Weygand retorted, "Do you think that I don't know that? It was a cardinal error. But I am not responsible for it; it was before my time . . ."[35] It was a remarkable admission.

By the summer of 1925, a budding revolt in the Druze heartlands had spread to Damascus. While Faisal was in Paris, the rebels had infiltrated Damascus and the new French high commissioner in the Levant, General Maurice Sarrail, ordered a full-scale bombardment of the city that went on for twenty-four hours. When the smoke had lifted, much of the city was left in ruins. There was an immense loss of life and property, and France's actions were universally condemned as indiscriminately brutal. The League of Nations in fact refused to accept France's 1925 report on its Syrian mandate because it did not cover the period of the revolt.[36] Faisal, however, remained diplomatically aloof from proffering any solution to the Syrian crisis. He knew the French were re-examining their Syrian policy and rumours abounded that they might even be considering a return to monarchy as a solution to their predicament.[37] But a precipitous move on his part might backfire. Instead, he repeatedly offered Briand assurances of friendship, knowing that France was now most anxious to secure his good will. While in Paris, Faisal attended a session of the Chamber of Deputies and was much amused to see the scenes of pandemonium and table-thumping that accompanied the debates on the Syrian crisis. 'How peaceful Iraq's *Majlis* is compared to this!', he commented.[38] News also reached him in Paris of the 'Abdication of the last Qajar shah of Iran. 'It was inevitable,' the king said, presciently adding, 'I prophesy that Reza Khan will be on the throne before the year is out.'[39]

Faisal spent a few days on the Riviera, where he stayed at the mansion of his Egyptian friends, Prince and Princess Ibrahim Hilmi, in Cimiez, near Nice. Faisal also wanted to meet the last Ottoman caliph, 'Abd al-Majid, who was living in straitened circumstances also in Cimiez. 'Abd al-Majid would have been totally destitute were it not for the financial support he was receiving from the nizam of Hyderabad and other Indian Muslim well-wishers. He was now an old man whose frailty was accentuated by his slight build. He called on Faisal wearing his morning dress and a fez, and accompanied by his son and heir, Prince Farouq. The meeting was strained and painful for the old caliph. Comparing his present impecunious and forlorn state with what he had left behind, he broke into tears and continued to weep even as he was leaving. Faisal also visited the last Ottoman sultan, Wahid al-Din who was staying at San Remo. Unlike his relative 'Abd al-Majid, the ex-sultan was living in lavish style in an imposing villa and was altogether more successful in resigning himself to a life of exile.

Faisal's recovery was now complete and preparations were made for his return journey to Iraq. Leaving the Riviera by the Orient Express to Venice, Faisal embarked on the ship that took him to Alexandria, which he reached on

9 November 1925. An enormous crowd had assembled at the quayside to greet the king. His immense popularity in Egypt and the Levant had not diminished. Proceeding on to Cairo, Faisal stayed there for two days before embarking on a plane journey to Iraq. The Vickers Vernon plane flew over the Sinai desert to Palestine, and near the Dead Sea the weather turned bad. The small craft was tossed around in heavy turbulence and landed near Amman after a harrowing experience for all on board. Faisal spent a day with his brother 'Abdullah before continuing on to Baghdad. A large welcome party, including al-Sa'adoun and Dobbs, met him at the Hinaidi air base south of Baghdad and Faisal, in a two-hundred-car procession, entered Baghdad to the cheers of large crowds. Sinderson had accompanied Faisal throughout the period of his treatment and convalescence. On seeing the crowds and the burdens imposed on Faisal, he was moved to recite Shelley's lines on the travails of kings: 'Kings are like stars – they rise and they set, they have / The worship of the world, but no repose'. [40]

A new Anglo-Iraqi treaty

Throughout Faisal's period in Europe, the League of Nations had been considering the report and recommendations of the Commission of Inquiry on Mosul. The commission's findings rejected the idea of dividing the territory of the wilayat and generally accepted the facts and figures offered by the British on the province's population and ethnic mix. Apart from a small piece of territory in the northern part of the province, which the Assyrians had hoped would be the basis of their autonomous region, the commission recommended that the entire province stay united with Iraq, but with two important provisos. Referring to Iraq's 'still unstable conditions', the commission recommended that Iraq should remain under the mandate for another twenty-five years. Faisal was aware of this precondition well before its public airing, and may even have supported it as the price to pay for Mosul province. [41] The second condition was that the Kurdish people of the province should have a measure of autonomy, with the employment of local Kurds in Kurdish areas and the official recognition of their language in education, culture, administration and the courts. The commission's findings, which were greatly supportive of the Iraqi case, were no doubt influenced in part by Britain's power in the League of Nations' councils, and it was to Britain's manifest advantage to have the territory controlled by a country over which Britain had such influence and power. But it also broadly reflected the wishes of the population of the province. The Kurds much preferred to take their chances inside a weak state under a British mandate than under a stridently nationalist Turkish regime that was already exhibiting great intolerance to its ethnic minorities, especially the Kurds. The other non-Arab groups were also mainly in favour of living under a government supervised by the British. In the end, pan-Islamic sentiments and the commercial interests of the Arab mercantile classes were insufficient to tip the balance of the Arab population in favour of continued association with Turkey.

Faisal now set himself to the task of ensuring the speedy passage of a new Anglo-Iraqi treaty, the precondition for absorbing the Mosul province into Iraq. However, the twenty-five year extension of the mandate required by the commission had also to be militated against. Faisal had made it clear to the Residency that an extension of the treaty period would only be accepted if there were specific provisions in it that would allow for periodic reviews of Iraq's progress. In these four-year reviews, it would be determined whether Iraq qualified for admission to the League of Nations. It would be difficult otherwise, Faisal argued, to have a new Anglo-Iraqi treaty passed without a nationalist uproar and possible disturbances.[42]

The League of Nations formally endorsed the findings of the Commission of Inquiry on 16 December 1925. Two days later the acting high commissioner in Baghdad, Bernard Bourdillon, presented Faisal with a letter stating that Iraq should endorse the draft Anglo-Iraqi treaty as soon as possible, as the treaty was the only means by which Iraq could secure its northern province.[43] Faisal wrote to Leo Amery on 26 December, restating his position that the draft treaty with its contemplated twenty-five-year period would only be acceptable if there were amendments to it that allowed for the periodic reviews he was calling for. In addition, Faisal asked for changes in the financial and military supplements to the draft treaty. Al-Sa'adoun's cabinet was uncertain of the position to adopt regarding the twenty-five-year extension of the mandate that the League was expecting. Al-Sa'adoun offered his resignation and it took all of Faisal's persuasive powers to stop the cabinet collapsing.[44] The Colonial Office rejected Faisal's calls to amend the financial and military supplements to the treaty – the heart of Britain's administrative control over the Iraq state machinery – but it did accept the demand for four-yearly reviews of Iraq's progress with a view to the country being eligible for admission to the League of Nations. It was the best that could be obtained under the circumstances.

The amended draft treaty was tabled at the cabinet meeting of 13 January 1926 and passed. It was now up to the Majlis to approve the final package. The Colonial Office applied further pressure on Faisal and his cabinet to see that the treaty was speedily approved by the Majlis. The British parliament was due to reassemble on 2 February 1926 and the Colonial Office expected the treaty to be ratified by that date. Once again the fate of Mosul and its joining with Iraq was held up as the price that Iraq might have to pay if the new Anglo-Iraqi treaty were not approved in good time.[45] But the Majlis approved the treaty on 18 January. Of the eighty-eight deputies, fifty-eight voted in favour and nineteen, mainly those associated with Yasin al-Hashimi, abstained. The expected parliamentary opposition was defused by al-Sa'adoun's pleas that the fate of the province of Mosul hung in the balance, and by the government's control over a large number of deputies.[46] The Iraqi press was outraged at the speed with which the treaty was passed and laid the blame squarely on al-Sa'adoun. Leo Amery and the Colonial Office, however, were delighted at the outcome, and al-Sa'adoun was later granted a knighthood for his efforts.

The League of Nations resolution to grant Mosul to Iraq was met with savage outbursts in the Turkish press, even to the point where war over Mosul was held up as a real possibility. But wiser councils prevailed, and the Turks finally agreed to demarcate the frontiers with Iraq in line with the League's decision. An added inducement for the Turks was that they were granted 10 per cent of the net revenues that Iraq garnered from the TPC for the next twenty-five years. On 5 June 1926, a tripartite Anglo–Turkish–Iraqi Treaty was signed, which adopted the decisions of the League of Nations as the basis for demarcating the frontiers between Iraq and Turkey. Faisal deputised Nuri al-Sa'id to sign the treaty on his behalf, and on 18 July it was ratified by the Majlis. The threat posed by the new Kemalist Republic of Turkey to the still wobbly state of Iraq had passed. The frontiers of Faisal's kingdom were now finally settled, and the critical province of Mosul was now securely within its boundaries. Faisal could now focus his energies on widening his authority inside the country and loosening British control over its administration. The way to do this was by ensuring the swift entry of Iraq into the League of Nations, using the thin end of the wedge inside the Anglo-Iraqi Treaty of 1926: the obligatory provision to review Iraq's progress at four-yearly intervals as a gauge of its eligibility.

Faisal and the collapse of the Hijaz kingdom

Faisal's difficult relationships with his father were overshadowed by the growing Wahhabi threat to Hussein's Hijazi kingdom. The consolidation of Wahhabi control over the Arabian Peninsula would strengthen the hand of ibn Saud and might have serious repercussions on the stability of his own rule in Iraq. Faisal lobbied hard with the British to gain their support for the Hijaz, in spite of 'the mad obstinacy of his father which has alienated his subjects and "hostilised" his neighbours'.[47] By the middle of 1924, Hussein's rule was tottering. The merchants and notables of the Hijaz had turned against him, prompted by his erratic and capricious policies. Lawlessness reigned throughout the land. The financial condition of the state was appalling and its military capabilities had drastically deteriorated. Most of the tribes, the military backbone of the Hijazi forces, were either neutral, or wavering, in the mortal struggle with the Wahhabis. Faisal did what he could to help his father. The Yasin cabinet authorised the sum of R15,000 for the relief of Hijazi refugees, which was subsequently diverted for military use by Hussein. This prompted a strong censure from the Residency, which in turn led Faisal to defend his cabinet's action spiritedly. But it was too little to have any effect on the fatal struggle going on in the Hijaz.[48] Faisal could only watch helplessly as the gathering storms threatened to bring down the sharifian household in its historic home.

Britain tried to organise a conference in Kuwait to carve out definitive borders for the Hijaz, Nejd and Transjordan but the effort collapsed. There was too much distrust between the protagonists, further exacerbated by Hussein's assumption of the caliphate that was very badly received by ibn Saud. A large Wahhhabi army advanced from Riyadh towards Ta'if, which fell in early September 1924 amidst scenes of horrible massacres. Mecca itself was threatened and the failure of a counter-attack by Amir Ali to retake Ta'if signalled the beginning of the end. On 4 October 1924, Hussein, under pressure from the notables of the Hijaz, 'Abdicated in favour of his son, Ali. Ten days later, Ali and his battered army abandoned Mecca for Jeddah. On the same day, Hussein left Jeddah for Aqaba. This was the end of the Hijaz kingdom. Ali held out in Jeddah for nearly a year, with practically no money and a disintegrating army. On 5 December 1925 Medina capitulated to ibn Saud, and on 19 December, Ali 'Abdicated. He left Jeddah on board HMS *Clematis* for Aden. A millennium of nearly continuous sharifian rule over the Hijaz and the holiest two cities of Islam had come to an end.

The aftershocks of the Hijaz disaster were now lapping at Faisal's doors. The exile of the sharifian family of Mecca and their relatives and retinue was set to begin. The two ports of refuge for these unfortunates were Amir 'Abdullah's Transjordan, and, more significantly, Faisal's Iraq, a much larger and better-endowed country. The first to arrive was Faisal's only son Ghazi. He had been kept at his grandfather's side until Hussein agreed that he should join his father in Baghdad. A delegation led by al-Sa'adoun went to Amman to fetch the young prince in September 1924. Faisal was delighted by the arrival of his son. Bell wrote to her father about Ghazi's arrival in Baghdad: 'The great event of Sunday was the arrival of the Amir Ghazi, the King's only son. He is very little for his age. He has the long sensitive face of his father and charming manners, a shy dignity which is most engaging.'[49] Bell, who took a personal interest in Ghazi's upbringing, wrote to her father about his sad condition and about the imminent arrival of the rest of Faisal's immediate family. 'He has been very much neglected in a household of slaves and ignorant women. I expect the womenfolk will come out now, after the break-up at Mecca. There are two daughters – one of them must be nearly eighteen. [There was of course a third daughter but she was incapacitated and no one talked of her.] Anyhow, having Ghazi will make a great difference to Faisal. It was pretty to see them the other day when I was sitting in H.M.'s garden, going off to pray hand in hand when the sunset prayers were called.'[50]

Faisal loved Ghazi, but with time he became deeply concerned that Ghazi might not be up to the task of running the country. In fact, Faisal harboured suscpicions that Ghazi might be mentally deficient. Sati' al-Husri recalled an episode when the king asked him to the palace on an emergency. Arriving there al-Husri saw Faisal slumped on a chair at the far end of the room. He gestured to al-Husri to take a seat by him and for a while kept silent. Then he started the conversation by repeatedly muttering the word 'Ghazi'. Al-Husri guessed what was on Faisal's mind. Faisal had been told by those who supervised Ghazi's education in the Hijaz that he was a slow learner. He started the conversation with al-Husri by saying, 'You know Sati' that I love my family and I love my son Ghazi and I would like to start a dynasty. But I love my country more than my family and Ghazi . . . If the situation [regarding Ghazi's learning disabilities] is as they say, and if Ghazi does not have the necessary intelligence to become crown prince and then king . . . then I will not hesitate to do what is my patriotic duty. I will call the *Majlis* and tell them: "I relieve the nation of the obligation to support the crown pince, and leave the matter entirely to you [the Majlis] to decide . . ." He said that in a low but determined voice and repeated himself, "I love my son, but I love my country more than my son . . . I have to carry out my duty towards it, before anything else."' Al-Husri was moved by Faisal's comments and gave him some comforting advice about Ghazi's condition, although he had met Ghazi only once before. As al-Husri was taking his leave, Faisal repeated his forebodings: 'I know Sati', that you are direct and say what you believe without ambiguity . . . But I ask you not to allow yourself to swerve in this matter. Don't think of me; don't think of Ghazi; think of the country, of the nation.'[51] Ghazi might have been a slow learner, but although headstrong and prone to outbursts, he was more disturbed than deficient. He was also a charmer, and when he reached maturity indulged his taste for fast cars and the fast life. He abandoned the hated rigours and isolation of his British public school and returned to Iraq to mingle with officers and the military. He was immensely popular with them and developed a reputation for being a nationalist and anti-British. He died, inebriated, in 1939, in a terrible car crash.

The possible arrival of the exiled Hussein in Baghdad was another matter. Neither Faisal nor the British wanted to see the old man in Iraq. 'I do pray that Hussein won't take refuge here; he would be the centre for every kind of mischief, anti-Faisal, anti-British,' wrote Bell.[52] There were rumours that Hussein would be brought to Basra on condition that he did not take part in politics. Faisal even toyed with the idea that he could galvanise the Shi'a *mujtahids* to declare a jihad against the Wahhabi occupation of Mecca, on behalf of Hussein. In the end, however, Hussein went to Aqaba until he was removed by the British to the safer confines of Cyprus. By 1931 Hussein's health was deteriorating and he sought permission from the British to be allowed to leave Cyprus. Approval was received from the Colonial Office to move him to 'Abdullah's place in Amman. Faisal and 'Abdullah travelled to Cyprus to arrange for the removal of the ex-king to Amman. A few months later Hussein died and was interred at the cemetery of al-Aqsa Mosque in Jerusalem.[53]

Faisal was not enthused by the arrival of the womenfolk from Mecca. His relations with his wife Huzaima were at best correct but lacked any passion. He had been away from his family for inordinate lengths of time and had no domestic family life worth remembering. Nevertheless, their arrival in Baghdad was inevitable after the surrender of Mecca and they duly turned up in Baghdad on 16 December. 'The Queen [Huzaima] and family – not King Hussein – arrived yesterday. I haven't seen any of them but I dutifully telephoned this morning to ask after them . . . I think the King is fearfully bored at their coming, but as he is away for another week yet, the evil moment is still to come,' wrote Bell.[54] She took over the task of arranging the queen's receptions and other ceremonies, and was at first taken by Huzaima. But Huzaima's apparent shyness and sensitivity masked a more insidious, jealous and vindictive side and she quickly became Bell's implacable foe. Bell kept her views on Huzaima out of her letters, for she considered that her true opinions about the queen might reflect badly on Faisal. However, the hostility between the two clearly emerges in the private letters of Sir Henry Dobbs to his wife. Huzaima believed that Gertrude Bell was behind the plans to marry Faisal to the Safwat girl. 'Gertrude is in a great twitter because the Queen has forbidden Madam Safwat ever to enter the Palace again. There was a plan to bring their eldest daughter from Syria and place her before Faisal which has thus been nipped in the bud,' wrote Dobbs.[55] But she was equally jealous of Bell and her easy access to and familiarity with the king. Dobbs wrote in a letter to his wife of 4 June 1925: 'Faisal is having a nervous breakdown and . . . had to go home. It comes from domestic squabbles. The Queen having rudely forbidden Mrs. Safwat the house, the Safwats have accused some of the Queen's handmaidens of carrying on with the military guard and the Queen has had furious scenes with Faisal which have quite broken down his nerves. Little Ghazi also has had scenes about some black page boy who has been removed from him. And altogether Faisal is very unhappy. Gertrude is negotiating but I fear the Queen will be jealous of her as Faisal kissed Gertrude on both cheeks yesterday.'[56] In a later letter to his wife, Dobbs wrote, 'The King has been on his estate for a while, eluding the jealousy and complaints of the Queen. Gertrude now hates and condemns the Queen and thinks her intolerable.'[57] Faisal himself seems to have been exasperated by his wife's behaviour.

Ex-King Ali of the Hijaz also found his way to Baghdad. Ali was closer to Faisal than to 'Abdullah, and it was therefore natural that he would choose Baghdad over Amman for his exile. Faisal also confided in him and sought his advice on matters of state.[58] Whether he acted on them was another matter, but Faisal was very respectful of his elder brother. He needed his brother's presence in Iraq to act as regent when he travelled abroad. On 26 January 1926 Bell went to see Ali and Faisal. She wrote her father: 'Yesterday, I went to see the King and ex-King Ali, a very attractive and pathetic figure ... He is meant for a life of contemplation I should say, not for war and politics.'[59] A few months later, the rest of the extended sharifian family arrived in Baghdad. On 16 June 1926, Bell, in one of her last letters before her death, wrote, 'I foresee that I shall have to devote some afternoons to visiting the King's female relations who have arrived with troops of servants from Amman – namely his grandmother, an unknown quantity of aunts, Ali's wife and three children. I don't know where or how they are all to be lodged and kept – at least, all I know is that it's out of H.M.'s pocket that they are kept. He appears to support the whole family except his father and his brother 'Abdullah.'[60] A few days later Bell accompanied Faisal to visit the recently arrived group. 'I found Faisal with 'Ali and we all went together to see the old grandmother who being 90 or so is moribund from the effects of her motor journey from 'Amman. She was lying on a mattress on the floor, almost incapable of speech, poor thing. 'Ali's wife is a nice woman but as she was brought up in Constantinople she scarcely talks any Arabic. There are two girls of about 17 and 18, quite pretty, and a pleasant looking boy of 16, and two other little girls of 4 or 5. 'Ali seems to be very fond of them all and delighted to have them. He had not seen them for nearly two years. I could wish that they had anything to live on but Faisal's civil list.'[61]

There were other non-Hijazis, a few who found their way to Iraq after the collapse of Hussein's rule and had somehow to be supported by Faisal. Some were political exiles from Syria, who had left after the French occupation of their country. Faisal took them all in, but none had a more poignant and tragic end than the nationalist figure Ahmad al-Maraywid. Bell describes what then happened.

There was a man called Ahmad Muraiwid, a very wealthy landowner and an ardent nationalist. He was concerned in an attack on Gouraud (in 1922 I think) after which he fled first to Amman, then to Mecca. After Husain was ejected he came here and the King established him on his farm at Khanaqin – as far as possible from the Syrian frontier. The French asked no questions and the High Commissioner let sleeping dogs lie. I saw the man often at Khanaqin and I liked and respected him, as one would have liked and respected Garibaldi. He was a genuine patriot. Finally, to make a long story short, he slipped off and went back to Syria where he began to lead Druze bands. The French caught him and his brother and shot them, as they had every right to do. But then they took their bodies to Damascus, stripped them and paraded them for hours through the streets on the backs of donkeys. It is an act which would turn the mildest people into rabid nationalists – don't you agree? I know many other stories of the same sort only I don't happen to have known the victims personally. How can the Syrians ever forgive?[62]

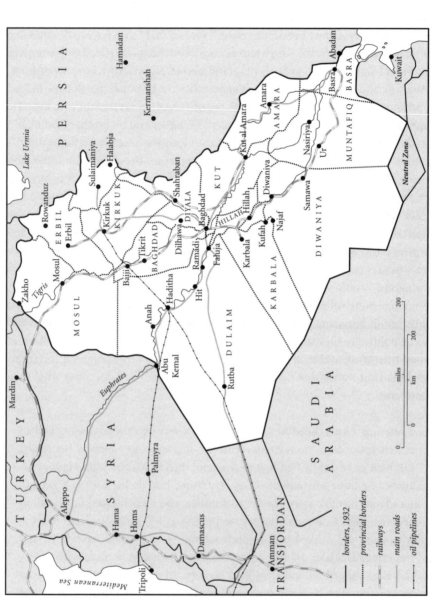

7. The Kingdom of Iraq

borders, 1932
provincial borders
railways
main roads
oil pipelines

••••••◆❖◆••••••

CHAPTER 23

STRUGGLING TO BREAK FREE

S ECURING THE northern frontiers of Iraq and absorbing the province of
Mosul was a great boon for Faisal and his rule of Iraq. He was elated over
the Turkish treaty and it showed. Bell wrote: 'Tonight the King comes to dine
and play bridge, Ken [Cornwallis] and Rustum Haidar, the head of H.M.'s
diwan, to meet him. The King is radiant over the Turkish treaty. Has it not been
a wonderful volte face on their part.'¹ Faisal now turned his attentions to
removing the mandate and securing unfettered independence for Iraq. The
ratification of the 1926 Anglo-Iraqi Treaty was the tool by which Faisal hoped
to prise loose British control over Iraq. Article 3 of the treaty opened up the
possibility of reviewing Iraq's progress in four-yearly intervals. It negated the
baneful effects of the extension of the mandate period for another twenty-five
years. The Colonial Office had agreed to the four-year review requirement
mainly to give Faisal some concessions and allow him to deflect domestic criticism over the treaty. But Faisal was determined to use it to open negotiations
immediately for securing complete independence, as early as 1927 if possible.

On 30 June 1926, Faisal left for Europe, partly for a holiday to be spent
mainly in recuperation at the thermal baths at Vichy in France. He also sought
to sound out the Colonial Office in person regarding the reopening of negotiations on Iraq's independence. Bell wrote of Faisal's departure: 'H.M. is off next
week to make a cure at "Wichy" – Arabs can't pronounce a V. He may come
over to England but I think it's more likely that he will have his boy [Ghazi] out
to Vichy. He looks very well and is much elated at the solution of the Turkish
difficulties, but there is little for him to do in the summer and his Ministers are
just as glad that he should be away.'² Bell called on Faisal a few days before his
departure. 'I went to tea with him on Monday to say goodbye . . . 'Ali is Regent
while he is away. Faisal has given me a bronze bust of himself by Feo Gleichen³
to put in the Museum. I shall set it up in the big Arab room. It's not bad, dignified, but not very like him.'⁴ It was the last time that Faisal saw Gertrude Bell.
Less than two weeks later she was dead.

The death of Gertrude Bell

In her last year in Iraq, Gertrude Bell had become less involved in the political and administrative affairs of the country and more in the establishment and running of Iraq's first museum. She continued to be consulted on political matters, but her influence had receded. Faisal had drifted away from using her undoubted political knowledge; nevertheless, he trusted her for advice and guidance on his family. Faisal had confided in her that he would not bring his family over until he felt himself established in Iraq. He was too conscious of the debacle in Syria and the doleful effects it had had on his family. A large number of the Hashemite family had joined him in Syria in early 1920, including the family of his brother Ali. But no sooner had they settled down than Faisal ordered them to leave for Medina to escape the effects of the impending crisis with France.[5] But with the crumbling domain of the Hijaz, where most of his family still resided, and the more stable conditions in Iraq, Faisal agreed to bring his family over to Iraq. Apart from his main palace in Baghdad, Faisal now had a large villa set aside for his family's use in Harthiya, then a semi-rural district several miles outside Baghdad. It is there that Huzaima and the rest of his family were ensconced. At the end of a working day spent at his official palace, Faisal would drive to Harthiya where he would spend the night with his family.

Faisal was aware that he could not stray too far from convention when it came to the treatment of his womenfolk. Huzaima kept a form of purdah and would not appear in mixed company. The operation of a western-style court would therefore have been quite impossible. Gertrude Bell was charged by Faisal to look after his family and prepare them for their courtly roles. Bell wrote, 'The King sent for me on Monday to discuss what arrangements should be made about the Queen's household. I was very glad that he consulted me for there were some terrible pitfalls ahead.'[6] Bell took charge of the Queen's wardrobe, as well as those for Faisal's daughters and son Ghazi. Faisal was conscious that his son Ghazi should be brought up knowing European ways and dress. Faisal himself was now mainly dressed in European attire, and it was Bell's task to ease Ghazi into the same pattern. Ghazi was a frequent visitor to Bell's house, where she lavished attention on him and gave him presents of toys brought from London department stores. It was also Bell who suggested that Ghazi should be educated as a boarder at Harrow public school, another factor behind the Queen's growing estrangement from, and dislike of, Bell. She was intensely attached to her son and deeply resented his departure for England.

In spite of her reduced political role, Bell had remained confident of the soundness of her decision to back Faisal as king. Returning from a trip to Transjordan, Bell was struck by 'Abdullah's scant qualities when compared to his brother Faisal: 'Nor does 'Abdullah strike one as a good ally if it came to fighting . . . He combines with indolence a narrow and almost fanatical outlook . . . He cannot keep his jealousy of his brother Faisal out of his conversations. Every topic reverts to his chagrin at finding himself Amir in Amman while Faisal is King in Baghdad.' After one of her tea parties with Faisal, Bell wrote: 'I had come back with conviction that we were the only Arab province which was set in the right path, and that if we failed here it would be the end of Arab aspirations. [Faisal] was most affectionate and charming. I'm glad that it's he and not 'Abdullah! There may be difficulties in dealing with a creature so sensitive and highly strung but his fine vital qualities and his wonderful breadth of outlook make up for everything.'[7]

As her duties at the Residency had diminished, Bell was devoting more of her time to the development of the Iraq Museum and the preservation of Iraq's rich archaeological heritage. In fact, the idea that she should head the newly founded Department of Antiquities was Faisal's, after she had convinced him of the need for a special law to preserve Iraq's archaeological treasures and to regulate excavations. Faisal himself had taken a great interest in the excavations underway in Iraq during his reign. He visited the sites in Babylon and Nineveh, and made a special flying visit to the south of the country to see at first hand the excavations at Ur and the unearthing of the famous Ziggurat.[8] One of Bell's last functions was to invite Faisal formally to open the Museum's Babylonian Stone Room, a few weeks before his planned departure for Europe in the summer of 1926.

In spite of her army of admirers and acquaintances, Bell was essentially a private figure. She had become increasingly dejected by her loneliness and by her complex feelings for Kinahan Cornwallis, Faisal's old friend and adviser. In spite of their age difference, Bell had become ever more attached to Cornwallis after his estrangement from his wife. Whether it was unrequited love or just an infatuation, Cornwallis did not reciprocate Bell's feelings. Returning home on 11 July 1926, after her habitual swim and exhausted by the heat, Bell took to her bed. The following morning, she was discovered dead in her bed with a bottle of 'Dial' pills, a powerful sedative, beside her. The death certificate read that she had died from Dial poisoning. Whether she had killed herself or had accidently overdosed cannot be determined. Her letters in the last few weeks of her life were not necessarily morbid, but she had intimated that she no longer feared death or dying.

Her death took place while Faisal was in Europe. Faisal instructed his brother Ali, who was acting as regent, to manage the formalities for her burial, and Ali ordered a military funeral. Large crowds assembled as her coffin passed through the streets of Baghdad to her last resting place in the British cemetery outside Baghdad. The cortege was led by Ali, Prime Minister al-Sa'adoun and the high commissioner. Tributes came from near and far. Even the nationalist press of Iraq mourned her death.[9] Faisal instructed that a wing of the Iraq Museum be dedicated to her. Her death marked the passing of a person who had played an instrumental role in the formation of Britain's Middle Eastern policy and the founding of the kingdom of Iraq. She remained loyal to Faisal to the end.

Concentrating power

Faisal returned to Iraq in October 1926, determined to remove al-Sa'adoun from office and to set his mark on a new cabinet. The presence of al-Sa'adoun at the helm, with his close connections to the Residency, made Faisal's bid for independence more difficult. The opportunity to instigate al-Sa'adoun's resignation came when the position of speaker of the Majlis came up for election. Faisal sided with the opposition candidate Rashid 'Ali against al-Sa'adoun's candidate, and when the former won, al-Sa'adoun interpreted his defeat as tantamount to a vote of no confidence; he therefore tendered his resignation. Without further ado, and without consulting the Residency, Faisal accepted al-Sa'adoun's resignation. The Residency, now under Acting High Commissioner Bernard Bourdillon, pressured London to have Faisal rescind his acceptance of al-Sa'adoun's resignation. The Residency had supported al-Sa'adoun's demands that elections be held for a new parliament, which he expected would return his faction with a new majority. The Colonial Office, however, advised Bourdillon not to become entangled in what they thought was a purely domestic matter and to leave Faisal to deal with this task.[10] Faisal nominated his trusted aide Ja'far al-'Askari to form his second cabinet. Al-'Askari, who had returned to London as head of the Iraqi Legation, now headed back to Baghdad to form his cabinet. The cabinet was formed on 22 November 1926, with several holdovers from al-Sa'adoun's cabinet. It also included Nuri al-Sa'id in the important post of defence minister. With al-'Askari as prime minister, Faisal was firmly in control behind the scenes and could launch his complex manoeuvres to achieve the independence that he so impatiently sought from the British. But he still had to contend with the formidable presence of the Residency – and behind it the might of the British Empire – and its unwillingness to concede a large measure of power without a fight.

Faisal, by habit, was a restless man and not content to remain in his palace for any length of time. Whenever the opportunity arose, he would up stakes with a few of his closest advisers and head for the provinces for on-hand investigations of the conditions in these areas. This, of course, gave him direct exposure to the people of the outlying provinces as well as an intimate understanding of the patterns of administration there. Throughout the first half of 1927, Faisal was constantly on the move. In January of that year he journeyed to the mid-Euphrates area and the shrine towns. In April he went to Kirkuk to inaugurate the opening of the first oil fields; he then visited the Mosul countryside to inspect the efforts to combat a plague of locusts that afflicted the province. During the month of May he went to Basra for a general inspection of the province. He was developing a formidable understanding of the issues and workings of government at both national and provincial levels, and this gave him added confidence to embark on his plan to extend his powers. He now proceeded to impress his authority on the government of the country. He engineered the removal of two provincial governors, Naji Shawkat and Jamil al-'Azzawi, replacing them with candidates who were more beholden to him. The justifications Faisal gave for these measures were not altogether convincing, as the two governors were generally considered honest and efficient. Naji Shawkat, however, was a declared republican and harboured pro-Kemalist and Turkish sympathies.

However, it was Faisal's intervention in the administration of the Qadiri religious endowment that created the greatest fuss locally. The venerable naqib, who had always been less than enthusiastic about Faisal's kingship, died in June 1927. The Qadiri order over which he had singly presided, had extensive properties and disposed of large revenues. Faisal wanted to dilute the power of the office of the naqib, which had held him in check in the early days of his rule and which stood aloof from his authority. Another powerful presence at the head of the order would be in a position to challenge Faisal, if not directly at least for the loyalties of an important section of the Sunni Arab notables class. Faisal nominated a three-person committee of the wider Gailani family, the hereditary leaders of the order, to head the endowments office, rather than have a single person in charge. But the naqib's eldest son was violently opposed to this measure, which would have stripped his family of control over the endowments of the order. He sought the Residency's support in a bid to ensure that the office stayed under the control of a single member of his immediate family, namely himself.

Faisal himself was not in the business of amassing extravagant personal wealth, but he did overlook flagrant violations on the part of his associates and close confidants when it came to personal enrichment. This came mainly in the form of illicit transfer of the title of state agricultural lands to individual politicians or their families. Agricultural land was the basis of Iraq's economy, and control over choice estates conferred power, prestige and wealth on its owners. Nearly all the sharifian officers and ex-Ottoman officials were involved in these schemes. Some of these officers and officials, who could count on nothing but their government salaries, became important landowners in their own right, challenging the power of the established landed classes. Faisal countenanced these moves, partly to develop a new landed class that would be supportive of his rule, but their land grab reflected badly on him and aggravated a sense of restlessness that was becoming widespread in the country.

The Residency responded vigorously to Faisal's moves and saw them as attempts to veer from the role of pliant constitutional monarch that they had imagined for him. A flood of cables from the Residency to the Colonial Office resulted, complaining of Faisal's power grabs. 'King Faisal in pursuit of autocratic and personal influence has alienated important sections of the population of Iraq, and inspired them with the desire to return to British administration,' wrote Dobbs in June 1927.[11] Privately, Dobbs was even more incensed about Faisal's actions, and raised the issue of forcing Faisal to 'Abdicate.

> Faisal has been very tiresome again, arbitrarily dismissing the biggest officials in the state (*mutasarrifs*) for no fault in order to put in his own nominees, devoted to his person, and he has undermined the confidence of the whole official hierarchy and thrown the administration into confusion. I have telegraphed to Amery that I must put my foot down and insist on reinstatement, even at the cost of Faisal's 'Abdication; and have said that F. has slipped back into the bad old attitude which he had taken up with Sir Percy Cox just before his attack of appendicitis in April 1922 laid him low and saved the situation; but we cannot expect a second providential attack of appendicitis. I am awaiting Amery's reply. I suppose he will be rather disturbed. But nothing else can be done. It is all because Faisal is in a fit of temper over the British Govt's delay in saying whether they will get him into the League of Nations or not and tear up all the present treaties and agreements. Exactly the same as in 1922 when Winston Churchill was delaying his reply as to whether he would insist on a 'mandate' for Iraq or not. I am going to see Faisal tomorrow morning and give him a good talking to; but I feel that he is eluding my grasp.'[12]

Dobbs was not only referring to Faisal's meddling in the administration of the country, but also in a matter that was of much greater significance to the Colonial Office – the issue of conscription.

The crisis over conscription

The key to consolidating Faisal's rule over the country and developing its national identity had been the development of the machinery of a central state and the establishment of a strong army. A large army was necessary to defend the unstable frontiers of the country, to introduce a measure of stability in a fragmented and often divided country, and to meet any domestic challenges to the state's authority. The props of the state and the army were also necessary for the consolidation of power by Faisal's allies amongst the former Ottoman officers and officials classes. Their governing base was even narrower. They could not count on any other independent source of support. They were not part of the historic notable families, nor did they have any roots in the tribal, religious or mercantile families. Their tenuous hold on power in Iraq, which was drawn from either their proximity to the Residency or the Palace, could only be strengthened by their dominance over the machinery of the government and the military. From Faisal's perspective, the enlargement of the army was also important in defusing Britain's argument that its mandate was justified by the reality that Iraq's defences were dependent on the British. The British, so the argument went, had to ensure that the country was run in a way that would not put their military at risk. On 7 June 1927, al-'Askari sent the draft of a compulsory conscription bill to the speaker of the Majlis, emphasising that it could be undertaken with a minimum of incremental costs.[13] Given Iraq's strapped finances, this was an important consideration.

Faisal's plan was to increase the size of the army to 20,000, up from its current size of just 7,000. Surprisingly, the newly appointed British inspector general for the Iraqi army, Major General Arthur Crawford Daly, also concurred with the plan. But the Residency and the Colonial Office were firmly against the proposal. Dobbs saw this as a naked attempt on the part of Faisal and his supporters, especially Nuri al-Sa'id, to create the wherewithal to install an autocracy in Iraq. 'There is little doubt that Nuri Pasha really wanted an army of this size for the purpose of enabling him at some future date to make a coup d'état in favour of Faisal and declare him an absolute monarch, as both Faisal and Nuri chafe constantly against constitutional restraints,' wrote Dobbs to the Colonial Office in his report on conditions in Iraq.[14] Bourdillon went further and talked about Faisal's dreams to build a new Arab empire on the back of an enlarged army.

Other factors lay behind the British's resistance to conscription. The fact of the matter was that conscripts would have to be found amongst tribesmen and rural dwellers. They might strongly resist being pressed into the army. Armed tribesmen would certainly resist such measures, probably by force, and would jeopardise Britain's careful cultivation of the tribes as a pillar of their system of indirect and low-cost control. The inhabitants of Kurdistan would also be loath to be subjected to conscription. In addition, the Shi'a population of the south of the country, which had resisted innumerable Ottoman conscription drives, would certainly resist this one by a state that many saw as indifferent and even hostile to their community. In fact when the conscription bill was introduced in June 1927, the minister of education Sayyid 'Abd al-Mahdi, a notable Shi'a personality, resigned in protest. Anti-conscription feelings grew in intensity in the Shi'a areas throughout the summer of 1927, which well suited the Residency in its test of wills with Faisal.

Faisal now sought to defuse the fierce reaction to conscription in the Shi'a heartlands. In September 1927, he toured the Shi'a areas and met numerous tribal leaders and *mujtahids*. The latter had generally stayed within the terms of their commitment to Faisal not to engage in politics and were cautious in response to Faisal's approaches. They remained non-committal, but privately warned against conscription. Faisal's efforts were mainly in vain. He gave the army units names resonant with the Shi'a, but to little effect. Even though the Shi'a formed the bulk of the soldiery, the officer corps was entirely composed of Sunni Arab officers. To the mind of the average Shi'a the army was little more than an instrument of the ruling clique in Baghdad. The commotion over conscription increased even further and other groups were drawn in. Entire tribes along the Tigris and in Basra threatened to leave Iraq or take on Persian or Nedji nationality to avoid being conscripted. A group of Shi'a tribal leaders warned in a statement that conscription was just another mechanism to oppress their community.[15] The furore was too much for Faisal to override, and in November 1927 the government postponed the conscription bill until further notice. The issue had died and was not brought up again until late in Faisal's reign, after independence had been achieved. It was a salutary lesson for Faisal not to overreach and a signal to him that his regime was fast losing its popularity with the people.

The Nsouli affair and sectarian disturbances

The sectarian fissures that emerged in the anti-conscription campaign were emblematic of the deep sense of grievance that underlay Shi'a attitudes to the state. The fruits of office in the new state had gone overwhelmingly to the Sunni Arab officer and notables classes, and Shi'a resentment of the basic unfairness of the new order was never far below the surface. Faisal was aware of the grievance and conscious of the need to ameliorate this condition. His championing of the Aal al-Bait higher education college, established in 1924, was specifically designed to foster inter-sectarian reconciliation. The college was to teach both secular and religious subjects, and was named after the venerated Household of the Prophet to emphasise its ecumenical nature. The college was headed by Faisal's former chamberlain Fahmi al-Muddaris, but never garnered the expected support from either the Shi'a *mujtahids* or the government. It had a shadowy existence, was poorly funded and staffed, and closed down in 1930.[16]

Faisal regularly visited the Shi'a areas, especially the shrine towns, and kept his channels open to the leaders of the community. He personally promoted the establishment of water management and irrigation schemes in the shrine towns and mid-Euphrates valley, and presided at their inauguration. Faisal was certainly not swept up by the prevailing sectarian tensions in Iraq, and he never consciously took sides in the sectarian divide. He knew that his plans for building a coherent national identity could not ever be realised if the majority of the population felt alienated from his government. He championed the employment of Shi'as in the government, often against the wishes of his ministers. However there was no doubt that there were very few qualified Shi'a available to fill key government posts. The influence of the religious establishment on the education of the Shi'a was still noticeable in the 1920s, and the *mujtahids* generally cautioned the pious from sending their children to government schools. But these factors do not belie the deep discrimination that existed in the state apparatus against the Shi'a, amplified by the hostility that many Sunni Arab leaders had for their traditions and doctrines. By the beginning of 1927, the growing resentments of the Shi'a were primed for an explosion. The occasion was offered by the so-called Nsouli affair that broke out in January 1927.

Anis Zakaria Nsouli was a Sunni Arab from Lebanon emanating from a merchant family of Beirut. A graduate of the American University of Beirut in 1924, he was a writer on Arab and Islamic history in the literary magazines of the period. Nsouli was recruited by the director general of education, Sati' al-Husri, to serve as an instructor in the Baghdad Central Secondary School. Al-Husri had also brought three other recent graduates from Syria and Palestine to serve in the secondary schools of Baghdad, who were all cast in the mould of al-Husri's Arab nationalist ideology. Nsouli became a history instructor at the Central Secondary School and wrote a polemical book entitled *The Umayyad State in Syria [Sham]*. It was printed in 1926 by a local publishing house for a general readership, but was also intended for distribution to schoolchildren by the government. The book glorified the Caliph Muawiya, a detested ruler in the Shi'a litany, and belittled Imam Ali, the venerated figure in Shi'a Islam; it came close to calling the martyred Imam Hussein a rebel against legitimately constituted authority. The book was dedicated to the modern-day heirs of the Umayyad dynasty.[17] Nsouli passed out his book to his pupils, whereupon uproar ensued in the Shi'a community and demands were raised for Nsouli's expulsion.

Sayyid 'Abd al-Mahdi, the Minister of Education, ordered the dismissal of Nsouli and banned the teaching of his book. Nsouli's colleagues, whom al-Husri had recruited from the Levant, then wrote a scathing letter to the minister of education. They accused him of presiding over an inquisition and protested Nsouli's dismissal. This was quickly followed by a general strike of secondary school students and students at the teacher training college, demanding the reinstatement of Nsouli. A large student demonstration then marched towards the Ministry of Education, led by students at the Central Secondary School. (One of the leaders was a student who had earlier performed in front of the king as Shakespeare's Othello.) The demonstrators clashed briefly with the police and then dispersed. Counter-demonstrations denouncing Nsouli were organised in mid-Euphrates towns and in the south of the country. A dangerous polarisation of opinion had taken place. A Commission of Inquiry set up by the minister of education recommended the suspension of a number of the secondary school student demonstrators and the termination of the services of the teachers recruited by al-Husri. Faisal reinstated the suspended students after an interval, and after Faisal's death the other teachers were also brought back to Iraq and reinstated in their positions.

The Nsouli affair exposed the deep sectarian fissures that existed in Iraq. That a book which was so damaging to sectarian relations could be published and distributed to schoolchildren was testimony to the indifference of the new elite to the sensibilities of the Shi'a community. At the same time, the response of those who supported Nsouli, and not least his own students, was couched in terms of free speech and the right to publish controversial views. Faisal was not directly involved in managing the crisis, but the affair affected his opinion of the wisdom of Sati' al-Husri's Arab nationalist pedagogical plan. Muhammad Mahdi al-Jawahiri, the famous Iraqi poet who was an employee in the palace protocol office at the time, wrote of Faisal's reduced relationship with al-Husri. 'There were no strong bonds between King Faisal and Sati' [at the time], for the King was quite displeased with him. He did not receive him regularly as he did with his close associates. During my stay at the Palace for over three years, I never saw him [Sati' al-Husri] enter to see the King except on one occasion, and then only for five minutes. Faisal was angry with him, for as the King was trying to save Iraq from the poison of sectarianism, Sati' was busy in fanning its flames.'[18]

Faisal was an advocate of a mild and inclusive form of Arab nationalism, around which a consensus could be built, and as a shared platform that could span the differences between the sects. However, what al-Husri was offering was a more ideological strain of secular nationalism, heavily drawn from nineteenth-century European models and bordering on racism that rode roughshod over traditional loyalties. It would also provide a convenient camouflage for the perpetuation of rule by a military-bureaucratic elite, whose ambitions were kept in check partly by Faisal's personality and moderation. After his death, their dominance over the state was markedly accentuated and al-Husri's educational programme was put into effect.

By the summer of 1927, tensions in the Shi'a community were at a high. Apart from the Nsouli incident, a number of incidents had further inflamed the Shi'a. The leading Shi'a party al-Nahdha was denied a newspaper licence, while the government applied a mechanism for revenue assessment that disproportionally affected minor Shi'a shaikhs and the mass of rural cultivators in the south. Shi'a resentments boiled over in the Muharram commemorations which fell at the beginning of July 1927. In Kadhimain, a large crowd had assembled on the tenth day of the month, 'Ashoura, when passions reach their highest pitch. Apart from the usual religious slogans and chants, the crowd was also shouting out slogans against the government and the person of the king. A detachment of nearly a thousand troops commanded by an officer known to be loyal to Nuri al-Sa'id, and ostensibly there to ensure that order was maintained, fired off shots to ward off the marchers. The presence of the troops was unwelcome as the commemoration marches had been going on for several days without incident.[19] In the ensuing clash, three civilians were killed and a large number of mourners wounded.[20] Opinion quickly divided as to who was responsible. Shi'a leaders accused the government of deliberately provoking the incident so as to justify a crackdown on the opposition. The government, on the other hand, blamed the Shi'a opposition for the disturbances in order to undermine the government.

Faisal responded to this deepening sectarian crisis by acting quickly to defuse the tensions. He forestalled the government's attempts to deflect blame from the officer commanding the troop detachment in Kadhimain. He supported the formation of an independent Commission of Inquiry of three persons to include a prominent Shi'a figure, Ja'far Hamandi, who was the mayor of Kadhimain, and a judge and a British official. Faisal also demanded that the culprits amongst the detachment should be punished, and that the marchers, who had been provoked by the troops' firing, should be forgiven. He offered to pay compensation to the victims of the disturbances from his own private purse. When the Commission of Inquiry found that the officer in command was not directly responsible for the disturbances but was nevertheless negligent in his duties, Faisal ordered his court martial. The officer corps was indignant that one of their own should be subjected to this ordeal, but Faisal insisted on it. It was a small price to pay for preventing the further alienation of the Shi'a community from his rule. However, the anger of the Shi'a at the army's actions was still smouldering and the compensation that Faisal offered the victims was at first refused. It was only through the intervention of Sayyid Muhammad al-Sadr, now a firm Faisal supporter and his main conduit to the Shi'a community, that the victims' families finally agreed to the offer.

Faisal's conciliatory approach to the Shi'a had another side. He was concerned that the Shi'a would now seek redress by drawing closer to the Residency. This would give the Residency a powerful new ally in their tussle with Faisal over independence and his own personal powers. There was already common ground between the Residency and the Shi'a community regarding opposition to conscription. The Residency was also reporting to London the steady stream of Shi'a visitors who were demanding that the British intervene more directly in the affairs of the country to stop what they saw as the excesses of the government against their community.[21] To mollify Shi'a opinion further, Faisal quickly arranged for two Shi'a ministers to be brought into the government, and convinced the cabinet of the need to allocate funds for draining the marshes around the shrine town of Karbala. On the eve of his planned departure for Europe and the mooted possibility of opening talks on the modification of the Anglo-Iraqi Treaty, Faisal could ill afford to have the Shi'a in a state of unrest that might weaken his negotiating position and even scupper it. At a palace meeting with Shi'a deputies and notables, Faisal extracted a pledge from them not to engage in political agitation during his absence. Faisal's measures were motivated by genuine concern that the Shi'a grievances had to be addressed. But his moderating instincts and common sense were counterbalanced by the depths of sectarian divisions and by the evolving power structures in Baghdad. These firmly favoured the Sunni Arab elites upon whom his rule was partly based, at least for a while.

The treaty once again

Faisal's relationships with Dobbs had never been easy. Dobbs believed that Faisal should stick to the role of a constitutional monarch and greatly resented Faisal's efforts to wriggle free from his treaty obligations to consult with the high commissioner. Dobbs understood the treaty obligations to imply a regular process of consultation where Faisal would defer to the Residency's recommendations, rather than Faisal's interpretation that he had wide latitude for decision-making and should consult the high commissioner only in matters of the highest significance. Dobbs was also annoyed at Faisal's constant probing of the limits of his personal powers and his efforts to shore up his domestic power base. Dobbs's disquietude was reflected in the tone of the despatches that he sent to his superiors, which often portrayed Faisal as a schemer and an ingrate.

Dobbs also scoffed in private at Faisal's attempts to lift the burden of the mandate from the country, and ridiculed Faisal's conviction that he could dent the British government's position by his personal representations. In a letter of 27 May 1927, Dobbs wrote to his wife:

> Faisal is really being very naughty and foolish and I am going to give him as stern a talking to as I can manage tomorrow and warn him of the pitfalls towards which he is setting his feet. Ja'far's Ministry has resigned at his orders as a demonstration of resentment at the British Government's delay in promising to get Iraq into the League of Nations next year, the whole point being it now appears that Faisal has set his heart on going to London almost at once with me and two of his ministers to negotiate a new agreement direct with

King George and the British Govt. in record time and return to Baghdad as the saviour of his people. He fumes at the delay in the British Govt agreeing to get him into the League and make a new Treaty, because he sees the days slipping by and knows that the British Ministers will soon disperse for their summer holidays and then his chance of making a splash this year will have gone. He is quite impervious to argument, puerile and petulant. I have managed to restrain him from having a public protest made against the delay of the British Govt and have told him that it would prevent them even trying to get him into the League. I have restrained him only for a few days and have telegraphed reporting the facts to Amery and giving the draft of a rude message which I recommend that I should deliver to him. I don't know whether I shall be able to hold him until the answer arrives.[22]

The Colonial Office was aware of the deteriorating relationship between the two, and tried to calm the situation by engineering an extensive leave for Dobbs that continued through the summer of 1927. Faisal in turn was invited to London to discuss the possible revision of the treaty. Both protagonists would thus be outside of Iraq for a lengthy period, which, it was believed, would facilitate an improvement of the working relationship between the Residency and the government.

Faisal left for Europe on 6 August 1927 for his regular thermal cures and with the expectation that he would be invited to London to negotiate modest modifications to the Anglo-Iraqi Treaty. En route to Europe, Faisal stopped in Cyprus to visit his father. Hussein would have much preferred to have gone to either Palestine or Transjordan after his departure from the Hijaz, but the British would have none of it. Hussein refused to be exiled anywhere in Europe, however, and only agreed to Cyprus after he was shown a map that convinced him that Cyprus was geographically a part of Asia! On 18 June 1925 Hussein boarded the warship *Delhi* from Aqaba bound for Cyprus. Ronald Storrs had become the governor general of Cyprus and found a small villa for the ex-king. There Hussein spent his time in reading the Quran and raising a few Arabian horses. In a supreme irony, Storrs was delegated by Britain to present Hussein, belatedly, with the Order of the Bath, well after Hussein had been shorn of all his power and authority and had lost his kingdom. The ceremony was held in, of all places, the Cyprus public library.[23] Malicious tongues had spread the rumour that Hussein had left the Hijaz with millions of pounds pilfered from the British subsidies to the Arab Revolt. Hussein, though not needy, never disposed of a large fortune. Faisal spent the time with Hussein at a resort hotel in the Troodos Mountains where Faisal indulged in rounds of golf and croquet. He also met Storrs and told him that if the British procrastinated on the revisions to the treaty that Faisal was seeking, he would 'Abdicate the throne.[24]

From Cyprus, Faisal departed for France and the thermal springs at Aix-les-Bains. The Colonial Office sent him Sir John Shuckburgh of the Middle East Department in early September 1927, to hold preliminary conversations before Faisal was formally invited to London. In attendance was Muzahim al-Pachachi, the head of Iraq's legation in London. Faisal had to wait nearly two months in Aix, however, before the invitation to London arrived. On 30 October 1927, Faisal left Aix for London.

The Colonial Office had no intention of meeting Faisal's expectations that Britain would allow Iraq to enter the League of Nations in 1928. Faisal had received enough warning prior to his arrival in London to know that this was not on the cards. What the British might agree to, however, was the possibility of independence and membership of the League of Nations by 1932. To the British, Iraq was a prize that they were not prepared to relinquish quickly, but neither could they determine its immediate interest to them. Their expenditure of blood and money on the country gave their presence some degree of legitimating sanction. The issue of maintaining the security of imperial supply routes and communications by their control over the country was obviously an important one, but it could have been managed without the need for a near-colonial relationship. Now that they were there, the British were driven by the logic of their presence. According to the British, they were there to protect minority rights, to meet international obligations as a mandatory power, to stop the country being invaded by aggressive neighbours, to keep the peace with the tribes, to stop an insurrection by 'Persian-led Divines', to block the seizure of power by a small oligarchy, to ensure that any future oil riches did not fall into unfriendly hands, and so on. They could bring a whole list of apparently valid reasons to justify their continued presence in the country. Faisal had to address each one of them, and convince his interlocutors that independence would not materially affect their interests.

Faisal's most powerful argument was ultimately a moral one: that Iraq could not remain indefinitely in a position of even partial dependency on a foreign power, and that the country was ready to assume responsibility for its own affairs. But moral arguments do not necessarily sway big powers. They could only go so far. He had to make a case based on his ability to diminish or demolish the thicket of counter-arguments that would be proposed. It was a tedious but necessary task, made more difficult by the hostility shown towards him by the Residency, and especially by the high commissioner. In a telling letter, which says a great deal about Dobbs's real attitudes to Faisal and his own blinkered view of power, Dobbs wrote to his wife:

> For now I am in another *pleine crise*, Faisal having promised me that he would not cancel the orders expelling students who took part in a riot and assault on the police in the course of a political demonstration and now having done it

without consulting me; so that we shall probably now have a 'practice' of schoolboy demonstrations growing up as in Egypt. I am very angry and have written to the Colonial Office to say Faisal is incapable and shifty and am going to tell him that I have done so. He will be much discomposed, as it will probably prevent his getting into the League of Nations, just after I had drawn so beautiful a picture of his regime. But I think I must work on Arthur Ramsay's mottos of *nemo me impune lacessit* and *oderint dum metuant*' (No one injures me without getting hurt and Let them hate me so long as they fear me.)[25] In another letter to his wife, Dobbs made no bones about his growing opposition to Faisal, and threatened to leave if the confrontation continued. 'I seem to be drifting into opposition to Faisal and the Iraqis who are being extraordinarily obstructive and dilatory over everything. I feel that I shall really shortly be outstaying my period of usefulness.[26]

The Residency's qualms about Faisal and his tactics made their way to the Colonial Office. Negotiations between Faisal and the Colonial Office started in London's Hyde Park Hotel. In the first meeting Faisal was handed an aide-memoire that was very critical of his interference in domestic affairs and his role in encouraging anti-British sentiment in the country. The note urged Faisal to act as a constitutional monarch – one of Dobbs's refrains – and to leave the running of the country to his government (advised, of course, by a bevy of seconded British officials). The note went on tactlessly to suggest that if Faisal did not mend his ways, he would lose British support and his entire rule would be jeopardised.[27] Faisal's immediate response was a theatrical offer to 'Abdicate in favour of his son, which was soon forgotten as serious discussions on the aide-memoire continued in the Colonial Office. Faisal stoutly defended his actions and reiterated his strong commitment to the British alliance. The aide-memoire was set aside and negotiations on the revision of the treaty began in November. The plan was for Dobbs to negotiate the matter directly with Prime Minister Ja'far al-'Askari, with Faisal consulted but remaining in the background. Faisal, however, took over the negotiations directly. He valued al-'Askari's loyalty and friendship, but had doubts about his competence and felt he was not up to this task.[28] Faisal's objectives had changed. He knew that the British would not concede independence for Iraq in 1928. Instead, he now sought to remove the right of the high commissioner to advise the king. Faisal was conscious that Britain had already recognised ibn Saud's full independence in the treaty that they negotiated with him prior to Faisal's arrival in London. However, the high commissioner's residual powers were a key prop of British control over the administration of Iraq. The British view had also been fortified by the biased reports from the Residency in Baghdad that alleged that the public would be alarmed at Britain's withdrawal and that the country would become unstable. Dobbs was present and wrote to his wife on 20 November 1927, about the negotiations: 'It is distressing. Faisal insists on an article to say that Iraq is "completely independent" and Austen Chamberlain won't allow the "completely" and it has broken down on that. Silly, I call it, as the rest of the proposed Treaty showed that independence was not complete and it didn't matter whether Iraq called herself completely independent or not ... I am afraid we are in for a bad time in Iraq, demonstrations and agitations and all the rest of it, and of course now I shall not have any help from Faisal. I should not be surprised if I had eventually to fall back upon martial law because I expect that having failed to get a new treaty, no Iraqi will take office as a minister. I have told the British Cabinet in a note that they must keep in Iraq all the British forces which they now have and that they must not expect to reduce them as they had hoped to do. Possibly they will say that then they must get another High Commissioner. If they want to, I shall be glad to go and live at home by my pen.'[29]

It soon became clear to Faisal that the British would only countenance cosmetic changes to the treaty and he backtracked on his demands. The changes that the British finally agreed to admittedly accepted that Iraq was 'an independent sovereign state', but that meant little without removing the high commissioner's veto powers or supporting Iraq's application for full membership of the League of Nations. In spite of his obvious disappointment, Faisal put the best light on the outcome. He left London on 5 December 1927, having been away for over four months, in itself a prolonged absence that raised hackles from the opposition in Baghdad and in the Majlis.[30] Before he left, he wrote to Ja'far al-'Askari, who had been recalled to London to sign the new treaty, a private letter in which he expressed the reasons why he had agreed to drop his demands for immediate and complete independence.[31] He related his discussions with the foreign secretary, Austen Chamberlain, and with Churchill, now the chancellor of the exchequer. They had felt that he should not return to Iraq empty-handed, and convinced him to continue with the discussions after he had threatened to break them off. Faisal then wrote, 'There is no doubt Ja'far, that this agreement is not what we sought. It is true that we had wanted more than what we got, but what more could we have done? We struggled to the end and there was nothing left for us except to continue in the fight. We have managed to change the Treaty in a way that no one had expected in April; but the nation unfortunately is ignorant of what we have achieved and instead of supporting us, they fight us ... Even if we had not returned with the total independence [that we wanted], we did achieve important amendments within our powers. No one can accuse us of not exerting all our efforts to this end.'[32]

The signing of the new treaty elicited precious little interest in Baghdad. The gains that Faisal spoke of were insufficient to placate the opposition, and even members of the cabinet were disappointed at the meagre achievements. The al-'Askari cabinet itself was shaken by the resignation in late December

1927 of Yasin al-Hashimi and Rashid ʿAli. The cabinet had already discredited itself with the Shiʾa community with the serial crises over Nsouli, conscription and the Kadhimain disturbances. It was no longer a useful vehicle for Faisal, and when Jaʾfar al-ʿAskari tendered his resignation on 8 January 1928, Faisal quickly accepted it.

The year had ended badly for Faisal. He was palpably disappointed at not achieving the breakthrough that he had striven for, and his reputation in the country had suffered accordingly. The Shiʾa were seething at their treatment by an indifferent government, and the nationalist opposition grew more vocal in its campaigns against the British alliance. The Residency, and Dobbs in partic-ular, had become distrustful of Faisal and his manoeuvres. Dobbs had also become increasingly exhausted and weary of his work in Iraq, and expressed this in no uncertain terms in his private letters. His tetchiness towards Faisal extended to the numerous British advisers employed in Iraq.

> I don't think I am a really difficult person to get on with. But the truth is that the peculiar circumstances of service here go to the heads of a lot of people when they get out here. They are all 'Advisers' and everything is vague without any procedure or traditions and each person thinks he has a wonderful field of raw material for untrammelled experimenting and trying his own theories. They can't bear to be criticised and checked and they each think they have an unlimited right to my support against the Iraq Government when the Iraqis don't agree with them, but that I have no right to oppose them when I don't agree with them. Sir Percy Cox suffered from this sort of thing much more than I have because he really knew nothing about administration and was reduced to looking on open mouthed at the squabbles and differences between the British Advisers; until there was some crash or other and people like Philby . . . had to be cleared out in a hurry. All the same I am not sure that I have not outstayed my usefulness in this country. I have been here 4 ½ years and my methods are growing stale. Faisal and his ministers are beginning to look on me as an Old Man of the Sea whom they can't get rid of and I believe that a man like Sir Gilbert Clayton would suit them much better. I don't think I should like to see Bernard [Bourdillon, the Acting High Commissioner] succeed me. He is so *Daily Mail* in his methods.[33]

By the beginning of 1928, Faisal and Dobbs could barely tolerate being together.

CHAPTER 24

TOWARDS INDEPENDENCE

FAISAL RETURNED to Baghdad carrying a pointless new treaty and facing a crumbling government and widespread disaffection with his rule. When the treaty was first presented to Iraq's parliament, the response was at best tepid. One of the opposition deputies, Muhammad Baqir al-Shibibi, stood up and accused the government of fooling the country and Faisal of going on an extended pleasure trip.[1] A new cabinet had to be formed and Faisal had little option but to acquiesce to the return of the Residency's favourite, 'Abd al-Muhsin al-Sa'adoun. In some ways Faisal could also turn the appointment of al-Sa'adoun, his most prominent rival, to his advantage. If necessary he could always distance himself from any of al-Sa'adoun's unpopular policies by claiming that al-Sa'adoun had been foisted upon him by the British. Al-Sa'adoun was deeply disliked by the Shi'a, who laid the blame for the exile of the *mujtahids* in 1923 squarely on his shoulders, and his unpopularity with them was not dented when he formed his cabinet, which included only two Shi'a ministers out of eight, another gross under-representation of this community in the highest executive offices of the land. Shi'a leaders had been expecting at least four ministers. Al-Sa'adoun himself was derisive of the 1927 treaty. It was much ado about nothing, and negotiated only to meet Faisal's insistence that something tangible be produced to establish that Iraq was moving towards independence.

But no sooner had al-Sa'adoun been selected as prime minister than Faisal, in league with political opponents of al-Sa'adoun, began to scheme to bring him down. The first test was al-Sa'adoun's demands that the Majlis be dissolved and new elections called for a new parliament. With al-Sa'adoun in charge of the machinery of government, and with Residency backing, Faisal's not unreasonable fear was that the elections would be manipulated to return a chamber that would be packed with al-Sa'adoun's followers. The Residency, however, stood firm in support of al-Sa'adoun and insisted that elections for a new chamber of deputies should go ahead. Faced with the inevitable, Faisal reverted to his pragmatic and functional self. He formed a tacit alliance with the nationalist opposition and disgruntled Shi'a leaders to prevent a clean sweep of the new chamber by al-Sa'adoun and his supporters. The nearly five-month-long electoral process, still based on the system of primary and secondary electors, gave Faisal sufficient time to try to affect the outcome and leave his imprint on the new parliament.

Faisal was not motivated only by tactical considerations to prevent a rival political leader from amassing too much power. Al-Sa'adoun's premise hitherto had been that the alliance with the British was not only necessary but was supported by a public wary of the consequence of precipitous independence. This was an argument that the Residency had constantly used with London in order to scuttle Faisal's claims that the country at large demanded immediate independence.[2] The British had the self-serving *idée fixe* that the agitation for independence was the work of a small clique of urban-based extremists and nationalists and had no resonance in the rest of the country.

The elections all went al-Sa'adoun's way. Eighty-eight deputies in the new chamber were al-Sa'adoun supporters and joined his revived governing party as the majority. However, the election results were only a temporary setback for Faisal. In the intervening years since his accession, he had developed the skills of a formidable player in domestic politics, and had brought into being a distinct 'palace party' – a group of prominent and influential figures whose composition often shifted but who were beholden to him alone and to his drive to strengthen his base in the country. Nuri al-Sa'id had become the king's undisputed right-hand man in domestic political affairs. Al-Sa'adoun had appointed himself the minister of defence, but Nuri had remained the deputy commander of the Iraqi army. The post gave him an important perch from which he used to advance his and, through him, Faisal's control over the army. Nuri was also not averse to using trusted acolytes amongst the army's officers to undertake unsavoury tasks of intimidation and violence against his and the king's opponents.

The founding of the *bilat*

The heart of Faisal's office, the palace secretariat or *bilat*, had grown in size and importance from those early days when Faisal had arrived as a lone figure, uncertain of his moorings and overly dependent on British advisers and a small band of associates. In the spring of 1926, the Tigris flooded disastrously and Faisal had to abandon the modest premises of the *bilat*, which were inundated. The entire *bilat* secretariat, together with the king, moved to a mansion belonging to a wealthy Jewish merchant and Baghdadi notable, Menachem Daniel. The effects of the flood were made worse by the inopportune opening of flood gates by the manager of the king's farm in the neighbourhood of

Baghdad. After the flood, the *bilat* returned to its former quarters, but Faisal
remained in the Daniel mansion until suitable private premises were found
for him in the former Ottoman college of arts and crafts, the Sanayi'. For the
rest of his reign Faisal's private residence was in the Sanayi', while the palace
secretariat was in a different location. After Iraq's independence in 1932,
Faisal finally received the approval of the cabinet for sufficient funds to
construct a new building for the *bilat*. However, disputes over land purchases
and the inadequacy of the budgetary allocations for the project delayed
the matter of the *bilat's* premises until Faisal's death. His entire reign was
spent in either inadequate premises or in the rented houses and mansions of
wealthy Baghdadis.[3]

The early officials of the *bilat* were drawn mainly from Faisal's coterie of
friends and allies from his days in Syria. Rustum Haidar was the first head of the
royal secretariat (*rais al-diwan al-malaki*). His principal task was to act as the
official intermediary between the king and the institutions of state. Tahsin
Qadri was Faisal's personal aide-de-camp. His former tutor, Safwat al-'Awa, was
charged with managing the private estate of the king. Haidar was by far the
most influential of his advisers. He was an exceptionally gifted and intelligent
man, worldly and with wide-ranging experience in, and knowledge of, the
western world. He was not driven by the prospects of amassing riches; he lived
in a modest house provided by the Ministry of Endowments, and had no income
apart from his salary. His loyalty to Faisal was total, and Faisal reciprocated the
trust. He wrote Faisal's speeches and Faisal consulted him on all matters of state.
Faisal's reliance on Haidar was such that whenever he had finished delivering a
speech, he would turn to him and determine from his expression whether he
had presented it appropriately.[4] Faisal did not hide his reliance on this key
adviser. 'The duty of a sovereign is to look after his trust, [who are] the people.
If I had missed anything, then I have Haidar. I never felt that he ignored any
important political matter, and I did not spend even a second in supervising
him,' Faisal said of his relationship with his most trusted adviser.[5]

Haidar's seven years as head of the *diwan* were not without problems,
however. His access to the king and the alacrity with which government departments and ministers responded to his inquiries and requests made him a focus
of envy. Even so, his Lebanese origins were not held against him by his opponents. Rather, it was his Shi'a identity that his enemies latched on to, even
though Haidar was thoroughly secularised and westernised in his outlook.
He was often accused of providing Faisal with biased advice that served to
promote the cause of the Shi'a, but this hardly stands up to scrutiny. Haider was
conscious – as was Faisal – of the disadvantage of the Shi'a in the evolving state
of Iraq, and both recognised that the situation had to be ameliorated in the
national interest. He could hardly proffer advice that contradicted with Faisal's

own inclinations and understanding of the sectarian situation.[6] The public campaign against him, however, spearheaded by a number of Sunni Arab politicians, had little effect on Faisal. In a private message that Faisal wrote to the shah of Iran in April 1929, carried by Haidar as his legatee, Faisal wrote that the bearer of the letter enjoyed his 'utmost confidence and trust'.[7] Haider continued in his post until October 1930 when he was appointed minister of finance, essentially to serve as Faisal's eyes and ears in the cabinet. The nine years that he spent as Faisal's adviser and confidant gave him an unparalleled knowledge of, and influence over, crucial matters of state.

Faisal replaced Haider with another Lebanese, 'Abdullah al-Haj, as head of the *diwan*. However al-Haj's tenure was a stopgap measure and Faisal replaced him, in June 1932, with the veteran politician and opposition leader, Rashid 'Ali. It was an unexpected and controversial move. Faisal became wary of Nuri al-Sa'id's increasing power in the latter years of his reign and he wanted to balance Nuri's authority by drawing closer to politicians who were opposed to him. Rashid 'Ali's appointment as head of the *diwan* may also have owed a bit to Faisal's former tutor and now head of the royal estates, Safwat al-'Awa. Safwat was a close friend of Rashid 'Ali and played an important part in drawing the king closer to him. His appointment elevated a mischievous politician to a high post. There, he could impede the palace's relationship with the British, as well as with the prime minister. Rashid 'Ali's tenure, however, was also cut short when the king appointed him prime minister. The post of head of the *diwan* then fell to Ali Jawdat during the last six months of Faisal's rule.

The palace secretariat was a small affair. It was housed in a building which was no more than a series of hut-like rooms, linked together by covered walkways. Its grounds and palm trees were lit by coloured light bulbs whenever an evening party was held there. At these parties, Faisal could be seen desultorily playing bridge, mainly to avoid tedious conversation with the British and Iraqi officials. He often 'won' a small sum, left the table, made his farewells and drifted away.[8] The secretariat started with no more than three permanent staff and grew in fits and starts to not more than ten by the end of Faisal's rule. The king also had a protocol office, headed at first by Fahmi al-Muddaris, and then by the Mosul notable Khayr al-Din al-'Umari. Five scions of notable families of Iraq were employed in the protocol department of the palace. The office was started in March 1922, mainly to regulate the chaotic throngs that descended on Faisal requesting, sometimes demanding, to see him. Faisal allocated two days of the week, Sundays and Wednesdays, generally in the mornings and evenings, to meet people and review their concerns on an individual basis. He looked forward to these audiences which drew him closer to ordinary citizens.[9] He did not stand on ceremony, and by all reckonings was courteous, moderate and considerate with visitors.[10] The minimal rules were that people should remain standing in his presence, that they did not prolong the audience beyond five minutes, and that they should motion to kiss his hands on departure, a common Arab practice at that time.

However, these rules were often breached. The diplomat Talib Mushtaq, a nationalist firebrand in his youth, was returning to Baghdad on holiday from his posting in Ankara. He was charged by Amir Zaid, then the Iraqi ambassador to Turkey, to hand-carry a letter from the amir to Faisal. Mushtaq received an audience with the king and was instructed by the protocol officer on the three points of court etiquette. The protocol officer then accompanied Mushtaq into the presence of the king and retreated out of the room. 'I greeted the king by bowing my head', wrote Mushtaq.

> The King extended his hand to greet me and I shook it with respect and courtesy. This was the first breach of the rule that Sarkasht [the protocol officer] had given me. I then gave the King the letter from the Amir [Zaid]. After taking the letter Faisal sat down on a couch and pointed to me to sit next to him. This was the second breach of the instructions. He then asked me about Zaid's wellbeing . . . and then rained on me all kinds of questions relating to Turkey: its progress in modernisation and educational reform; its social development; its political circumstances; military dispositions; and so on. It was a very tough examination. I answered him the way a pupil would who had been preparing days for an exam by reading all the books available to him. I felt that the king was satisfied by my answers because he persisted in the discussion and did not leave a matter that he did not ask me about. He nodded his head whenever he agreed with my answer. This interrogation went on for 45 minutes. This was the third breach of the instructions I received from the protocol officer. His Majesty then stood to indicate that the audience had come to an end. I stood up in turn, bowed my head and proceeded to leave the room.[11]

Faisal was a true workaholic. He was at his desk at 7 a.m. during the summer and at 8 a.m. during the winter, often arriving before the department heads. Even his meal or leisure hours were mixed with work. He hardly ever ate alone, mixing his meals with discussions of the topics of the hour.[12] Rihani recalls an episode when he was invited for dinner at Faisal's house. Arriving in the evening he saw the king wearing a grey *dishdasha* and reading documents that covered the table in front of him. ' "It sees there is no end to your work, Your Majesty," said Rihani. "Every day we have enough work for two days," said Faisal. "Does that mean you have to work at night?" replied Rihani. "If necessary, but the average is ten hours and sometimes twelve hours per day," said Faisal. "This is against any work norms," exclaime Rihani. "Then blame time for not respecting work norms," said Faisal, and quickly changing the subject, asked Rihani, "And what do you make of the Bolshevik government?" '[13]

Poets and the king

Another person who had the opportunity to examine Faisal's conduct in private was a young member of his protocol office, Muhammad Mahdi al-Jawahiri. Later, he went on to an illustrious career as not only one of Iraq's but the Arab world's most significant poets of the twentieth century. Al-Jawahiri, from a notable Arab family of Najaf, had ended up in the palace protocol office by the most extraordinary route imaginable. The young poet prodigy, who was also a schoolteacher in his native town, had written some lines admiring Iran and the Iranian landscape during a vacation there. These lines were then used against him by Director General Sati' al-Husri at the Ministry of Education to dismiss him from his post. Ostensibly, by waxing lyrical about Iran, al-Jawahiri had impugned Iraq and Arabism, and had showed his obvious preference for Iran and its culture. Al-Jawahiri, of course, protested this ridiculous charge and his unfair dismissal, and the issue became a cause célèbre in Iraq in 1927. It divided opinion and pitted people against each other along strictly sectarian lines, with al-Husri and his cronies at the Education Ministry accused of rampant sectarianism and hostility to the Shi'a, and al-Jawahiri charged with having an indeterminate nationality and accused of the dreaded crime of *Shu'ubiya*, or partiality to Iran. When the tide in this tussle seemed to be turning against al-Husri, with al-Jawahiri agreeing to resign rather than being humiliatingly fired, al-Husri sulked in his home for a month.[14]

Faisal was kept abreast of developments in the al-Jawahiri case, given its potential as a trigger for sectarian conflict. The then minister of finance, 'Abd al-Muhsin Shlash, a friend of the al-Jawahiri family, recalled to the young poet his representations on his behalf with the king. 'I was with King Faisal and the discussion revolved around your case, which has become the case of all of Iraq. I told His Majesty: "Your Majesty, the al-Jawahiri family is known to you, as is its patriotic stance, and the family's roots in Iraq that extend for over 400 years."'[15] Faisal was in fact preparing to defuse the case by recruiting al-Jawahiri for the palace protocol office.

While visiting Sayyid Muhammad al-Sadr, Faisal's main link with the Shi'a leadership, al-Jawahiri was astonished by al-Sadr's suggestion that the two should call on Faisal there and then. The two proceeded to the king's offices where they were immediately received by Faisal. Al-Sadr was one of the few people who could enter the king's presence without prior notice. 'The King received al-Sadr, as was his custom, with the utmost courtesy and respect,' wrote al-Jawhiri in his memoirs. 'There was no doubt that the King was aware of my case and the kerfuffle it was creating.' Faisal in fact was sizing up the poet and establishing whether he was suitable for the palace staff. A week later al-Jawahiri once more met with al-Sadr, who asked him whether he had been up to see the King again. Al-Jawahiri rushed to the palace in his best traditional robes, and there met the King who congratulated him on his new appointment to the staff of the protocol office. 'This position, Muhammad, is a bridge which you can use to cross over [to a more lasting career].'[16]

Al-Jawahiri was not the usual sycophant who clings to those in power. He had composed verses that were critical of Faisal but now, working in his proximity in the palace, he drastically revised his opinion of the king. There was no pomp or ceremony or the grandeur of potentates in Faisal's palace. 'The word *Bilat* resonates with power, but the private office of King Faisal, the most significant King in the Arab lands at the time, carried nothing but its name. It was only a simple room with a large rectangular table, a carpet and three or four chairs. It had no other furnishing. Visitors never exceeded the number of chairs,' wrote al-Jawahiri. Its sole wall decoration was an oil painting of Faisal and the French writer Anatole France.[17] The *bilat* proper comprised the king's private office, with six adjacent rooms for the staff of the palace secretariat. 'There was no superfluity in the *bilat*. I am a witness to that. I saw King Faisal holding a feather duster and with great modesty personally cleaning his desk.'[18] Faisal was certainly not above manual labour. On another occasion, he was seen to be moving furniture about himself, the workmen in the palace having left early because of the Ramadhan fast.[19]

Faisal took a liking to the poet and after a while suggested to him that he should move from the protocol office and take responsibility for preparing a digest of the daily newspapers for the king. He also took him along on his visits to the shrine towns and the south of the country, where al-Jawahiri witnessed a procession of tribal shaikhs pleading with the king for support for the agriculture of the region. Faisal had taken a personal interest in reviving the irrigation systems of the area, repeating his famous slogan, 'No project will take precedence over the Gharraf [a major irrigation scheme in the south].'

The poet's verses, however, also gave Faisal no end of trouble. The opening of the first girls' school in Najaf in 1929 had been greatly resisted by the religious and traditional groups in this conservative town. On the occasion of the school's opening, al-Jawahiri penned scathing lines attacking these groups in a poem entitled 'The Reactionaries'. The poem was published under an assumed name in the newspapers, and an uproar ensued which reached the king's ears. Faisal confronted the poet with the damage he had caused him. 'Are you aware of the calls and cables I have received who all say that this is the work of your "son, Muhammad", who works under your auspices and protection? And do you know how much grief this has caused me?' Al-Jawahiri responded to the effect that he would not give up his poetry for his job but that he did not want to cause any problems for the king. In effect he offered the king his resignation. 'No, No. Muhammad, return to your desk. I wanted to point this out to you so that in the future you are aware [of your actions],' said Faisal.[20] Faisal's indulgence as regards the wayward poet was partly due to his own liking of poetry and his sense that al-Jawahiri was an exceptionally gifted poet, even though he had an acerbic and difficult personality.

On another occasion, al-Jawhiri wrote a poem entitled 'Jarriibni' [Try me], which was published under an assumed name on the front page of *al-Iraq* newspaper. The poem had anti-religious overtones, and this time it was not Faisal but his brother Ali who was offended. Faisal was very aware of his brother's religious sensibilities and that al-Jawahiri's poem would only cause him pain. It was also indicative of how Faisal was conscious of the need to preserve his brother's dignity and reputation for piety. 'I received a call from my brother, King Ali,' Faisal told al-Jawahiri, 'and I respect him as you know for he is older than I and he is a religiously devoted man. He was very angry. He told me to read the newspaper to see what your "son, Muhammad [al-Jawahiri]" had wrought. That is why I called you. All I ask you to do is to visit my brother and apologise to him.' Al-Jawahiri did as he was bid, but had no intention of changing course in writing provocative poetry.

Al-Jawahiri left Faisal's service after three years. Although he was seeking a journalistic career, Faisal nearly convinced him to take up a government scholarship in France to pursue his higher education. The king also asked al-Jawahiri to help the government in recruiting suitable candidates for scholarships from the youth of the mid-Euphrates valley and the shrine towns.[21] Writing sixty years later in his memoirs, al-Jawahiri's judgement on the king was that he 'was the first true Arab ruler of Iraq, but he was more than what Iraqis deserve or what Iraqi society could tolerate at the time . . . The King bore the burdens of Iraq more than he should have, for Iraq is a country that has exhausted both its governors and the governed over its history. I believe that Faisal was fit to be king over Syria, a country that was crying out for him, but not over Iraq.'[22]

Faisal recognised the importance of Iraq's leading poets in setting the cultural agenda and propagating images of his person and rule that would carry great weight with the public. A few choice lines of praise or obloquy could go a long way in a society that was still mainly illiterate and put great stock on the power and imagery of a well-constructed poem. Iraq's two great contemporary poets during Faisal's reign were Jamil Sidqi al-Zahawi and Ma'arouf al-Rusafi, and there was great rivalry between the two. Al-Zahawi had already made his mark by praising not only the King and his rule but also Sir Percy Cox. Faisal had wanted him as the poet laureate for the country but al-Zahawi declined. Al-Rusafi's fortunes, on the other hand, had declined sharply, and he would compose biting lines against the king that were widely circulated. In one egregious poem, al-Rusafi broke all bounds of courtesy and portrayed Faisal as marking time while collecting a fat salary. However, the grudge that al-Rusafi bore the king was finally patched up. Through the intercession of the exiled Tunisian leader 'Abd e-Aziz al-Tha'alabi who was then in Iraq, Faisal agreed to receive al-Rusafi. Al-Tha'alabi had known Faisal during the Paris Peace Conference, where he had made representations on behalf of Tunisian independence from France. Receiving the embittered poet and the Tunisian leader, Faisal asked al-Rusafi directly: 'Am I then the person who counts the days and draws a salary? And here I am burdened with all kinds of problems and challenges and with the concerns of an entire nation.'[23] Faisal was magnanimous with al-Rusafi and forgave his slights and more. He allocated him a stipend of 500 rupees, a princely sum at the time. Doors opened for al-Rusafi and he became a deputy in Iraq's parliament.

Faisal's interest in poetry and literature extended beyond the Arabic-speaking world. Informed that the great Indian Bengali poet and Noble Prize laureate Rabindranath Tagore was touring Iran in the spring of 1932, Faisal sent Tagore a personal emissary to invite him to Iraq. Faisal wanted not only to meet the poet but also to put Baghdad on the map of world cultural figures. On 21 May 1932 an official reception committee, headed by the poet al-Zahawi, met Tagore at the frontier with Iran and escorted him to Baghdad. Faisal then invited Tagore to the palace, where he introduced him to the leading figures in Iraq's polititcal and cultural life. Tagore described Faisal as an extremely modest person and simple in his living tastes. He also found him knowledgeable and keenly interested in poetry. In the evening Faisal hosted a banquet in honour of the poet, at which Tagore saluted 'one of the world's great leaders who have fashioned history'. He then recited a poem that he had written especially for the occasion:

> Night has fallen / Extinguish the lamps / In your narrow dark corners / Full of smoke / For the light of dawn has appeared in the East / Let its light whisper to us all / All who are travellers on the same path / Towards the Haj

Before he left Iraq ten days later, Tagore gave Faisal a gift of one of his oil paintings with the poem inscribed on it.[24]

The finances of a king

Faisal's reduced circumstances during his years in Syria and in the political wilderness improved to some extent when he reached Iraq. The assets of the crown, which were managed by Safwat al-'Awa, at first held a paltry 8,500 rupees, but Faisal augmented them by the purchase of four main agricultural estates, most of them barren land in need of investment and upgrade. Faisal was greatly concerned with matters of Iraq's agricultural development and expended a great deal of effort on his own farms. Whenever the opportunity arose he expressed his commitment to agricultural regeneration by planting trees during public ceremonies. His speeches were peppered with remarks about the need to revitalise and develop Iraq's agricultural sector. He strongly supported the founding of the first agricultural college in 1926 and the establishment of a ministry of agriculture in 1927. He directly sponsored the founding of the Royal Agricultural Society, which grouped government officials, landowners and representatives of the rural community. He was an avid reader of books and manuals on the subject and his own rose garden at his palace in Harthiya was considered the finest in the Middle East.[25]

Faisal's first foray in agricultural development was his acquisition of land near Baghdad on the Tigris known as the 'Dairy Farm'. It was state property and it was unclear where Faisal found the purchase money. In all likelihood he had borrowed it. A further property was added to his estates in 1923, but this piece of land was severely affected by the flooding of the Tigris in that year. A great deal of the investment that Faisal had made in the property was lost because of the total inundation of this estate. The second permanent estate that Faisal acquired was in the Khanaqin area. Faisal then added other farms to his estate during his reign, most of them on leased land. The ex-king Ali was also awarded a large estate in the Kut area of eastern Iraq by the government, which was managed on his behalf by Faisal's farm managers.

The management and development of Faisal's farms occupied a considerable amount of the time that he did not devote to matters of state. Faisal was particularly interested in growing crops for export, and most of his farms' acreage was given over to grains and cotton. He was one of the first to introduce the growing of cotton that yielded export-quality fibres. His farm in Khanaqin in particular was given over mainly to cotton growing. The quality of the cotton was superior and found ready markets in England.[26] He employed a specialist cotton-growing expert from Britain at his Khanaqin estate. He also employed agricultural experts from Egypt to improve the productivity of his farms.[27] Faisal was enamoured with the most up-to-date technology and engineering, and he readily adopted new agricultural processes and technologies. Very often the implements used were the first of their kind introduced into Iraq, as was the case when he bought American harvesters. He proudly rattled off the names of the pulsating pumps in his farm to a reporter from the London *Daily Herald*, who was interviewing him at his estate in Harthiya. 'What you hear is a Gas Bendi machine. Hundred of these pumps can now be found all over Iraq,' he enthusiastically told the reporter.[28] What Faisal's estates might have lacked in size they made up in productivity and innovation. Nevertheless, Faisal's agricultural income was erratic and dependent on world commodity prices. With the collapse in agricultural prices at the start of the Great Depression, his income was greatly reduced.

The expansion of his estates was often effected haphazardly, and not all the innovations employed were economically justifiable. At his death, the king's estates were in debt to the tune of about £30,000, a considerable sum in the period (Iraqi currency was equivalent to pounds sterling). The debt was held mainly by the Ottoman Bank branch in Baghdad and collateralised by mortgages on the estates. Faisal himself was indebted to the bank. He was not personally extravagant in his habits and his impecunious years in Syria and exile had taught him the value of money, but his obligations as king were many and to many types of people. Ali Jawdat, who was Faisal's last head of the *diwan*, wrote in his memoirs: 'King Faisal I suffered from a heavy debt burden, most of it owed to the Ottoman Bank. This was because of the assistance that he gave to those in need, and what he contributed to charities and foundations from his private purse. The government could offer him no help because of its own budgetary constraints. He used to spend as an Arab king and founder of a modern Arab state ought to. He had to abide by these norms and thus the incurrence of personal debt.'[29]

Faisal had personal obligations that crossed many boundaries. His privy purse had to cover his charitable donations to community and educational institutes. He supported the parochial schools of the Shi'a, Christian, Jewish and Armenian communities, as well as schools attached to the Sunni pious foundations. His payroll included stipends to widows of those who had served him in Syria, supporters in the Arab world who had fallen on hard times, as well as nomadic tribal chiefs along Iraq's frontiers with Syria and Nejd. He also had to support his extended family. Their number had increased with the arrival of the ex-king Ali and his family, as well as their households. A number of *ashraf* were also on Faisal's payroll as well as religious dignitaries and notables from the Hijaz who were now dispossessed. In the last year of his reign, the salaries, wages and stipends that were covered by Faisal's privy purse amounted to nearly 750,000 Iraqi dinars, a not inconsiderable sum.[30] By far the largest chunk went to supporting the *ashraf* and exiled Hijazis, as well as the tribal chiefs. Faisal's main sources of income were his own government salary of 52,000 Iraqi dinars as well as his farming revenues and rental income that still came to him from properties in the Hijaz.[31] The British government had undertaken, together with ibn Saud, that the properties of the *ashraf* of Mecca would be protected and not sequestered after the departure of ex-kings Hussein and Ali. Faisal received the income due him from these properties from his agent in the Hijaz, Muhhamad Nassif. In spite of these varied sources of income, however, and Faisal's and his family's own moderate and unaffected lifestyles, there was a persistent deficit in his personal budget. His squeezed finances reached a point where he could not afford the £1,000 price tag to buy the two portraits painted for him by the artists Augustus John and Philip de Laszlo.[32]

Faisal and the public

Faisal came to Iraq a stranger to the country's social and cultural life. He could have easily tried to rule by limiting his contacts to Iraq's political class and its social, religious and tribal elites. But rather than adopt a pose of royal hauteur and remaining aloof from Iraq's people, he immersed himself in trying to understand the ways of his new country. A few weeks after he first set foot in Iraq, he met with learned Iraqis to ascertain their perspectives on its conditions. He received the greatly respected religious scholar, Mahmud Shukri al-Alousi, a leader of the modernist pan-Islamic movement in Iraq. The views of poets and writers were actively solicited by the palace. Faisal put great store on their ability to frame public opinion and tried to draw them to his side, frequently through financial gifts and other inducements. He also acted as patron to the cultural clubs, such as the Irshad Club, that sprang up in Baghdad in the 1920s. In 1924, Faisal started a tradition of receiving artists and calligraphers at the palace. The noted calligrapher Abbas Hilmi al-Baghdadi received several commissions for his work from Faisal. Musicians and performers were also welcome at the palace. An Egyptian theatre troupe, the Fatima Rushdi Company, performed in the palace gardens in front of a large audience of dignitaries, as did a Circassian dance company. The great Egyptian composer and singer Muhammad 'Abd al-Wahhab gave a prominent recital in April 1932, on the occasion of the opening of Baghdad's first industrial and agricultural fair. 'Abd al-Wahhab had put to music and song a poem written in honour of Faisal by the great Egyptian poet Ahmad Shawki. The effect on the assembly was electric. The poem compared Faisal to the great rulers of Baghdad and praised his civilising work.[33]

Teachers were another group that Faisal felt it was important to encourage and cultivate. He regularly toured the schools of the capital, including Jewish and Christian parochial schools, and inspecting schools was often on his agenda during his provincial visits. He was usually accompanied by Rustum Haidar and often the king would order him to take immediate steps to ameliorate one condition or another at the schools that he visited. Meeting a large group of men and women teachers at the palace in a specially convened gathering in April 1932, Faisal addressed them 'Be sure that the work that you are doing is greater than that of the King's and greater than that of a minister. Any work that relates to the future of the country cannot be as significant as yours.'[34]

Faisal regularly attended Friday congregational prayers, which gave him an opportunity to meet with the public. Although not overtly pious, Faisal had an instinctive belief in Islam and in the veracity of the Quran. He was horrified when on one occasion a British official mentioned that the Quran had two hundred foreign words, implicitly suggesting that it might not have been a direct revelation from God. This was rank blasphemy to Faisal.[35] He was proud of his lineage but he did not carry it to the point of claiming any special access to, or drawing direct inspiration from, the Prophet Muhammad. Once, on leaving the mosque after prayers, Faisal mildly rebuked his brother Ali for claiming to have seen the Prophet. 'Keep your faith in God alone,' Faisal told him.[36] He was also noticeably unaffected by sectarian considerations, even in matters of doctrine or theology. 'His faith had many aspects to it that clearly reflected all the various Islamic sects,' wrote Rihani. 'I used to feel when talking to him that his religious faith had an unprejudiced base to it, that made him respect all the world's religions ... In his rationality and moderation were found the hallmarks of the highest wisdom; in his tolerance and broad-mindedness were the signs of love and sincerity.'[37] Apart from his open support for the religious foundations of the major sects, Faisal supported the reconstruction of derelict Sufi religious sites and shrines, such as the *tekke* of the Shadhili order in Mosul. This put him in good standing with the main Sufi orders that were active in the north of the country and in Kurdistan.[38] Faisal also allowed foreign missionaries to operate in Iraq without much hindrance, as long as they did not flout their proselytising. During his reign, Jesuits from Boston College in the US opened Iraq's first western-style academy, Baghdad College, which became the main high school, graduating generations of Iraq's new elite.

Being of the Hanafi sect of Sunni Islam, Faisal's Friday prayers were invariably held at one of Baghdad's main Sunni mosques. Although his contacts with people would be no more than fleeting, petitions would be thrust on to him or his aides, to which he always responded. An eye witness, the social historian Abbas Baghdadi who was then a youth described the scene of Faisal attending the Friday prayers on one such occasion. 'After two or three years [of Faisal's accession] I used to go with others of my young friends to the mosque that Faisal had chosen for the Friday prayers. There we watched him in his Arab clothes and his high black boots. Finally it was decided that Friday prayers would henceforth be held at the Serai mosque near the Qishla square. I used to go every Friday afternoon to this mosque to see the Royal Guards in their wonderful red outfits and their giant commander. Faisal drove in his red open Fiat saloon car, with a glass divider between himself and his driver. The driver I believe was an Indian who wore a red fez. After the Royal Guards saluted the king, we waited outside until Faisal left the mosque and rode away.'[39] Faisal usually made do with one adjutant who sat next to the driver or often drove the car himself.

But his main direct contacts with ordinary people were the two days in the week that he set aside for this purpose. The crush of people at the palace doorway trying to see the king once drove Prime Minister al-Sa'adoun, who was there on official business, to exclaim loudly: 'Throw these people out and let them go back to those people whom the government pays to act as intermediaries for them with the King. Give the King a break and throw them out!'[40] The ease of access to Faisal often went beyond the usual bounds. Letters of the most personal nature were received at the palace, requesting Faisal's intervention in some family matter or another: wives complaining of husbands, parents of their children, people asking for his help in returning runaway spouses, and so on. Faisal also received letters that exposed ministerial malfeasance or mismanagement, which gave him an important source of information on the conduct of his government.[41] Letters from job seekers were also aplenty, many of them coming from Lebanese, Palestinians, Syrians and Egyptians asking for any available position in Iraq. Some even asked Faisal to be granted Iraqi nationality. Most were driven to seek jobs in Iraq, or to relocate there, because of the widespread sense in the Arab lands that a promising new order under Faisal was being constructed in Iraq.[42]

His regular travels to the provinces were also an opportunity for Faisal to elicit the views and concerns of the population outside of the capital. Petitions came from towns and cities demanding Faisal's intervention in their municipal affairs – in making appointments or sacking incompetent or corrupt officials, or in providing support for buildings and roadworks. He regularly hosted visiting provincial delegations who would often be met formally by the palace representatives at Baghdad's railroad station, adding to their sense of dignity and importance. Faisal also played a major role in resolving tribal disputes and rivalries, especially in the mid-Euphrates valley. He had a special protocol officer specifically charged with liaising with the tribes. Many tribal leaders saw Faisal as above tribal affinities, and welcomed his good offices to settle inter-tribal disputes. A case in point is when Faisal successfully overcame the antipathy that had grown between some of the tribal leaders of the 1920 rebellion. The British in their despatches looked askance at these attempts as they were often conducted in secret, and saw them as signs of Faisal's meddling and plotting.

Faisal always redoubled his energies whenever a serious natural or manmade disaster occurred. He visited the affected areas of Baghdad in the great flood of 1926, and in one instance personally supervised efforts to combat a plague of locusts. In another case, the village of Karamlis, lying in a rich agricultural area and inhabited mainly by Christians, had burnt down and lost its entire storehouse of grains. Responding to a plea by the Chaldean archbishop, Faisal led a major fundraising drive that helped to compensate the victims. Religious leaders from other, smaller communities were also in regular contact with Faisal, including the chief rabbis of Baghdad and Mosul. Sunni clerics, who were mostly paid employees of the Ministry of Endowments, complained to him of the paucity of their salaries; some complained of their superiors, who were accused of behaviour unbecoming of a religious figure, such as consuming liquor, and requested that Faisal replace them. Senior Shi'a clerics also sought Faisal's intervention to commute capital sentences. In one significant case, where the culprit was convicted, by a split decision of the court, of killing a policeman and two others during the 1920 rebellion, Faisal did accede to the request. The death sentence was commuted to life imprisonment.

The press

Faisal was an avid reader of newspapers. Copies of the Cairo newspaper *al-Ahram*, the most authoritative Arabic-language daily, had been sent to him regularly ever since his days in Aqaba in 1917. They continued to be sent to him in Syria and then Iraq.[43] Faisal's daily routine was to examine the newspapers after rising, and only then to deal with official correspondence and papers. Cuttings from newspapers and magazines were also prepared for his perusal on a regular basis. The press corps was the first to be received by him after his coronation. He was very conscious of the power of the press in moulding the public's impressions of his positions and policies. His experiences with the press since the Paris Peace Conference were not altogether happy ones. In Iraq, Faisal and his palace staff set themselves the task of managing press coverage, by directing the press if necessary. The process was far from easy. The number of newspapers and magazines in Iraq had exploded, covering all shades of opinion. Many of them were not much better than scandal sheets and rags, whose proprietors' main interest was not in boosting circulation or advertisements but in cornering people of influence into various forms of blackmail. A few newspapers, though, were run up to reasonable journalistic standards. Many newspapers had been founded to reflect the views of specific politicians or political parties. The political opposition, therefore, could rely on a number of newspapers to carry its messages and positions. The British were naturally very aware of the damage that newspapers could do in questioning or attacking their policies and decisions, and the cabinet was often put under pressure by the Residency to close or fine newspapers who spoke out against Britain's policies in Iraq and elsewhere in the Middle East.

The palace's relationship with the press was fraught from the beginning. A few months after his accession to the throne, Faisal was forced to call in editors of newspapers who had strongly attacked French policies in the area. He cautioned them that intemperate attacks on the French might jeopardise Iraq's relations with this important power. In July 1922, Faisal asked the minister of interior to prevent newspapers from publishing any articles on the palace, or interviews and statements from the king, before they had been cleared by his secretariat.[44] Faisal also pressured the government to act against newspapers that he perceived had abused their freedoms. The satirical magazines and literary journals were a particular bugbear for the palace, on account of their irreverent and often insulting reportage on individual politicians and social figures. In such cases, Faisal was not so much driven by personal attacks on himself – which were very rare and muted – but rather by the coarsening of public language and the hurt that it might cause to the targets of the satirical magazines. On one occasion Faisal asked the cabinet to take action against a journal, *al-Istiqlal*, that had used defamatory language against religious leaders.[45] In another instance he demanded that a newspaper be fined for using inappropriate language when writing about former ministers. On the other hand, newspaper proprietors often resorted to pleading with Faisal whenever their newspaper was closed down for infringing the press laws and their coverage of either the Residency's or the government's policies.

Faisal was undeniably over-sensitive to what the press wrote, and often overreacted. He was certainly no champion of the idea of unhindered free speech or the right of the press to cover issues and personalities in any way they saw fit. Iraqi press laws, dating from the Ottoman press code of 1909, were also restrictive on the freedom of the press. In spite of these restrictions, however, the press in Iraq was outspoken and incessantly skirted the risks of being fined or even closed down. The only exception was *al-Iraq* newspaper. It took a generally pro-government and pro-British line. Its proprietor, Razoouq Ghannam, had easy access to Faisal and often carried long interviews with him that reflected his thinking and presaged some important changes in policy or direction. In one interview, Faisal revealed what he thought of the press generally: 'I recognise the great effect that the press can have in the development of nations . . . and in strengthening national consciousness. But the press, because of its widespread distribution and its great impact, must also move with awareness and wisdom. And even as I acknowledge the welcome efforts of the press in serving the nation, many times it rushes to judgement.'[46] Later in his reign he was even harsher on the abuse of the freedom of the press, as newspapers had by then become more persistent in their attacks on the palace and some of its staff, especially on Rustum Haidar. 'I would like to include the journalists as opinion leaders of the country. I ask them to fear God in their sacred duty, and not to trade with the country's patrimony simply to publicise their newspapers.'[47] By the end of his reign, Faisal was an advocate of controlling the press and supported the passage of restrictive press laws that made it cumbersome to receive a newspaper licence. Nevertheless, in spite of repeated closures and fines and even imprisonment of journalists, Iraq's newspaper industry thrived in the period of Faisal's rule.

Undermining prime ministers

Faisal knew very well the detailed workings of his governments, and the interventions of the *bilat* in the operations of the cabinet were unrelenting. It was not unusual for Faisal to make surprise visits to senior government officials, or to appear, unannounced, at military parades or official functions. These unheralded inspections had an excellent effect on ordinary people.[48] The constitution gave Faisal extraordinary powers, most notably in the selection of the prime minister, who could not be appointed without Faisal's agreement. Faisal, of course, had to take the views of the Residency into account, and these were often forcefully expressed especially during Dobbs's tenure. Faisal would consult a range of politicians before he made his choice and would consider the candidates' stature in parliament and whether he could achieve a majority vote in his favour. Faisal approved the selection of the ministers, refusing some nominees while imposing others on the prime minister. The position of parliamentarians hardly featured in Faisal's calculations. He was confident that the government party would mostly fall into line, partly to ingratiate themselves with him and the prospective prime minister. Even though the Majlis held ultimate power over the cabinet and could theoretically require the dissolution of the government, often in fact it was the other way round, with the government dissolving the Majlis to suit the needs of political leaders. The threat of dissolution was an additional power that Faisal never hesitated to use in bringing the Majlis to heel.

Another power the constitution afforded Faisal was the ratification of cabinet decisions. This obliged the prime minster of the period to bring all prospective decisions or plans to Faisal prior to their submission to the cabinet. The success or failure of Faisal's cabinets was thus dependent to a large degree on whether he was satisfied with their behaviour. Later in his rule Faisal used the *bilat* as a focal point for discussing issues of national significance. These were not designed to thwart the work of the cabinet; rather, they reflected the Palace's ability to initiate and fashion policies independently. During his reign, several large conferences were organised around important themes to which the political leaders of the country and the high commissioner were invited. The first such national conference was in January 1928, where the issue of Wahhabi raids on Iraq were discussed. Another conference, a month later, dealt with Iraq's military preparedness and the size and equipping of the army. The third conference was held in April 1931, which dealt with conditions in

Kurdistan and the renewed rebellion of Shaikh Mahmud. Other conferences followed on the levels and fairness of agricultural taxes, and one on defence and national security. These conferences gave Faisal the opportunity to press for his own solutions and recommendations on the government and the Residency.

Of all of Faisal's prime ministers, the one who could best resist the pressures and blandishments of the palace was 'Abd al-Muhsin al-Sa'adoun, partly because of his character and partly because of the strength that he drew from the support of the Residency. Soon after al-Sa'adoun became prime minister for the third time, Baghdad was convulsed with demonstrations denouncing the visit to Iraq of the prominent British industrialist, politician and Zionist sympathiser Sir Alfred Mond, later Baron Melchett.[49] Mond was instrumental in founding the giant Imperial Chemical Industries. He had been in regular contact with the leaders of the Iraqi Jewish community, trying to elicit their support for the Zionist project in Palestine. In 1923, he had written to Menachem Daniel, possibly the wealthiest member of the Jewish community in Baghdad and a member of the Senate, to help in a forthcoming visit by an official of the Jewish National fund. The fund was an offshoot of the Fifth Zionist Congress of 1901 and was organised to acquire and develop land in Palestine.[50] The Jews of Iraq in the 1920s were at best indifferent to the Zionist project, at least in so far as it related to them.

Word had spread of Mond's visit to Iraq, and he was scheduled to arrive in Baghdad in early February 1928 by the Nairn desert coach transport from Damascus. A large protest demonstration by students from the Central Secondary School, the Law College and Teacher Training Institute, and augmented by ordinary civilians and passersby, assembled in central Baghdad. The intention of the protesters was to block Mond's arrival and stop him from entering Baghdad. Mond's coach, however, had been met by police earlier and escorted into Baghdad by another route. The demonstrators clashed with mounted police sent to prevent the march from getting out of hand. There were several injuries but no fatalities. An intelligence report prepared by the Residency's oriental secretary directly blamed Faisal for the demonstrations. The hand of Faisal might have been behind the organisers of the demonstration, but it was mainly the work of Arab nationalist clubs angered by British policies in Palestine and the increasingly serious confrontations between Arabs and Jewish settlers in Palestine. The intelligence reports attributed Faisal's supposed backing for the demonstrators as part of his plan to weaken the government of al-Sa'adoun.[51] Faisal uncharacteristically approved the flogging punishment recommended by the Ministry of Interior for the secondary school students who had been arrested in the disturbances.

Following the failure of the 1927 treaty to provide any meaningful British concessions to Faisal's demands for independence, his priorities now revolved around amending the financial and military protocols that provided the substance of British power in Iraq. These were due to expire in mid-1928. Al-Sa'adoun had stayed away from these contentious matters and left the negotiating to Faisal and his chosen lieutenant Nuri. Faisal presented far-reaching demands for changes in the military agreement that were tantamount to breaking the dependency on the British. The Iraqi army would no longer be subject to inspection and control by the British, and Iraq would assume full control over its internal and external defences. However, Leo Amery and the Colonial Office categorically rejected Faisal's demands for control over Iraq's defences. To the usual arguments about securing the imperial lines of communication were now added the matter of Britain's commercial interests in Iraq, greatly expanded with the development of the Kirkuk oil fields. Amery cabled the Residency to say that the 'New proposals show so complete a disregard of the realities of the situation, that HM Government cannot resist the conclusion that King Faisal and his minsters are suffering from self-deception on the question of Iraq's ability to dispense with British support.'[52] The Colonial Office could not bring itself to admit that most Iraqis were now chafing at the prospect of indefinite British tutelage.

Dobbs, ever the correct and loyal administrator in his official despatches, revealed his true opinions on the impasse in his private letters to his wife. He admitted that the crisis was partly Britain's fault 'because the British Govt in 1926 pledged themselves to withdraw all their forces in 1928 and now find that they can't do so'.[53] In another letter, Dobbs was leery of using a near ultimatum that Amery had sent him to be delivered to the government.

> I shall be very busy packing and finishing up and probably trying to get my new agreements though the Iraq parliament. For there is a crisis on again. I received a portentous telegram from Mr. Amery yesterday, in cypher, extending over 9 foolscap pages dictating the ultimatum which I am to issue to any objection to king Faisal and his Ministers, if they won't accept *our* military agreement. A declaration such as we made in Egypt and I don't know what all, practically the tearing down of our Treaty façade and a reversion to the naked mandate. Of course in fact I shall merely make a gesture towards my pocket and never produce the ultimatum and I suppose they will yield at the gesture. If they don't, Gilbert Clayton [the incoming high commissioner] is in for a rule of force, though I don't think he will find such a difficult situation as Percy Cox left for me. But it is depressing that my last three months should be tumultuous.[54]

The stand-off between Faisal and the British on the one hand, and Faisal and al-Sa'adoun on the other was amplified by the latter's growing qualms regarding his pro-British positions. He was constantly on edge from Faisal's manoeuvres and the nationalist agitation against him in the streets and in the press. British intransigence on the renegotiations of the financial and military accords was another source of disquietude for him. The paralysis that affected the country in 1928 as a result of these unresolved conflicts became widely known as the *Wadh' al-Shadh* or anomalous situation. Iraq had evolved a system of administration where ministers and Iraqi government officials were constantly watched over, and second-guessed by their British advisers. The tensions that arose as a result of this dual responsibility grew as Iraqis became more accustomed to power and administration. Contradictions and anomalies abounded. The Iraqi government ran the ports and railroads and had to cover their deficits, but did not own them; they were owned by the British. Under the military protocols, Iraq could declare martial law but could not administer it. It had an army, but could not deploy it without the high commissioner's say-so. Foreign nationals had extraterritorial rights in Iraq, but these were not reciprocated for Iraqis. Half the costs of the Residency were borne by the Iraqi budget, but there was no Iraqi control over how it was expended. Ministers and officials, supposedly responsible and accountable to parliament, might have their decisions countermanded by their advisers.[55] And at the apex of this dual responsibility structure stood Faisal and the Residency. It was an unacceptable condition in Iraqi eyes, and was primed to erupt.

Dobbs awoke to this situation late in the day and he tried to soften the intransigence of the Colonial Office, but to little avail. The Colonial Office's position on this matter was best reflected in their dismissive comment in the Report on Iraq in 1928, written for the League of Nations. According to the Colonial Office, grievances over the dual responsibility structure was imaginary and existed 'only in the minds of fervid patriots'.[56] By the end of 1928, al-Sa'adoun had exhausted his options. Despondent and unable to break the impasse, he offered his resignation on 21 December 1928. In a meeting with Dobbs, al-Sa'adoun blamed Faisal directly for his travails. 'It was really King Faisal who had made his position impossible,' reported Dobbs on this conversation, and quoting from al-Sa'adoun. 'His Majesty has, for the last six months at least, been telling that anyone who accepted the principle of agreements, (as presented by the British), would be a traitor to the country, and now such a feeling had been produced that he [al-Sa'adoun] could not stand it.'[57] This was not far from the truth, for Faisal had been working against the government ever since it was formed. His favourite tactics to improve his bargaining position with the British had usually been to escalate matters and create a crisis; and this case was no different. Faisal had few other tools with which to convince or force the British to make concessions. Commenting on the unfolding deadlock, Dobbs wrote to his wife: 'Well, the great crisis has I fear arrived at last. The Iraq Government has finally refused to accept the British terms in the two

new agreements and I shall have to present a kind of ultimatum to King Faisal
and the Prime Minister tomorrow saying here we are and here we stay, and on
such and such conditions. I suppose 'Abdul Muhsin [al-Sa'adoun] will resign
and I don't know who will take his place if anyone. It is a pity that my last five
weeks should be embittered and that Gilbert Clayton's beginnings should be
disturbed.'[58]

The impasse continued with no resolution in sight. No serious politician
came forward prepared to form a cabinet in the face of widespread public
opposition, a hostile press, and a king bent on using the crisis to push for
concessions. Al-Sa'adoun stayed on in a caretaker capacity until an opportunity
arose to break the deadlock with the arrival, in early March 1929, of the new
high commissioner Sir Gilbert Clayton, an old friend of Faisal's. It was none
too soon. Dobbs had become thoroughly exhausted and exasperated with Iraq.
'It is sickening that I should have to end my time in acute quarrels and I almost
wish I had decided to leave now, in spite of the financial loss,' he wrote to his
wife.[59] The American chargé d'affaires in Baghdad reported exaggeratedly that
relations between Faisal and Dobbs had deteriorated to the point where they
'could hardly bear the sight of each other'.[60] But as the date of Dobbs's departure
beckoned, the coolness bordering on antagonism between the two mellowed
into mutual respect. Faisal gave him a farewell dinner and awarded him the
highest possible Iraqi decoration, one that only the king held. In his last weeks
in Iraq, Dobbs was showered with gifts, but he was reluctant to accept them as
it contravened official policy. The Colonial Office, however, advised him to
accept them, because otherwise he would cause offence. 'People are being very
kind and flattering here; but I am glad to be going. I feel that I am growing
superannuated and that little more would make me sour and crabbed. So closes
my official career – not much of a thing after all,' he wrote to his wife in one of
his last letters from Baghdad.[61]

Gilbert Clayton, the new high commissioner, had unparalleled experience
with conditions in the Arab Middle East and with the key personalities, both
British and Arab, who had played their parts in the birth of the modern Arab
world. He had an intimate knowledge of Faisal, his character and his qualities,
garnered not only from the Arab Revolt but also from the ensuing post-war
developments that had led to Faisal's enthronement in Iraq. Clayton was a
product of the Royal Military Academy at Woolwich. He was commissioned
into the artillery in 1895, and immediately afterwards posted to Egypt. For the
next thirty years, with few interruptions, Clayton spent his working career in
the Middle East, either in Egypt, Sudan or in Palestine. During the war Clayton
was instrumental in organising the Arab Bureau in Cairo and headed its intelligence unit. The arrival of Clayton in Baghdad gave Faisal a new opportunity
to try to break the deadlock with London. In a prescient letter to his wife,

Dobbs expected that Clayton's arrival might improve the prospects of reaching an agreement between London and Baghdad: 'It may be easier for the British Govt to give way and make it up with the Iraqis when they have got a new man here,' he wrote. But continuing, Dobbs said, 'In the meanwhile, Clayton has behaved foolishly by giving an interview to "The Referee" in which he says "Trust the Arab and he will trust you: and my policy is going to be one of non-interference and never giving advice except when asked to do so." '62

Faisal offered Clayton a new set of proposals that were anchored on Britain making a binding commitment to support Iraq's membership to the League of Nations in 1932. The other aspects of his proposal included the abandonment of the 1927 treaty, Britain agreeing not to oppose conscription, and a pledge to encourage British investments in the Iraqi economy. Clayton backed Faisal's initiative and sent strongly supportive despatches to the Colonial Office. However, Amery continued to balk at making such a commitment. The disagreements with London and the sour political climate in Baghdad made it difficult for would-be prime ministers to accept their assignation. Al-Sa'adoun rejected Faisal's appeal to take up the reins of office again, and Nuri al-Sa'id was effectively vetoed by the Residency, motivated by al-Sa'adoun's personal hostility to him.

In the end Faisal reluctantly offered the job to Tawfiq al-Suwaidi, brother of Naji, and a friend and ally of al-Sa'adoun. Faisal was apprehensive of the Suwaidi family, an established Baghdadi family with a growing power base in the country. Tawfiq's father was head of the senate and his brother was now chairman of the financial committee of the Majlis.[63] Few believed that al-Suwaidi's cabinet would be anything but a stopgap. It was also deeply unpopular. Nationalists saw it as a betrayal of the united front needed to push the British to accept unconditional independence for Iraq. Faisal began to float the idea of a 'national government' that grouped all the major political figures in the country as a better alternative to al-Suwaidi's cabinet. True to predictions, al-Suwaidi's government, opposed by the palace at all levels, submitted its resignation at the end of August 1929.

However, events were moving in a direction that promised an easing of the stand-off between Faisal and London. The British general elections of May 1929 returned a hung parliament, but Labour was able to form a minority government with Liberal support. The new colonial secretary was Lord Passfield, formerly Sidney Webb, the noted socialist reformer and one of the founders of the London School of Economics. Clayton reiterated to the new colonial secretary his views that British interests would be best served if concessions were forthcoming from London regarding Iraq's entry to the League of Nations in exchange for a clear delineation of Britain's interests in Iraq. These might form the basis of a new treaty that would safeguard Britain's interests while granting what Faisal and the nationalists most wanted: complete independence and sovereignty. Clayton also urged London to act quickly. Faisal's representation was that the relatively calm situation then prevailing in Iraq masked a growing uneasiness with Britain's prevarications, and pressures were building up that might result in a blow-up. In a despatch of 1 September 1929, Clayton wrote to the colonial secretary that the situation in Iraq was 'gradually deteriorating as a result of doubt and uncertainty as to the HM Government real policy'.[64] He also brought up the spectre of another uprising, a reprise of 1920, which could only be controlled with the help of the Iraqi police and army.

Clayton's relentless pleadings on behalf of Iraqi independence and the changed situation in London finally had their effect. The British government was now prepared to drop the 1927 treaty and to recommend unconditionally Iraq's entry into the League of Nations in 1932. A detailed telegram to this end went out to Clayton on 11 September 1929. However, Clayton did not see his efforts rewarded. The day after the Colonial Office had sent out the welcome news, Clayton, after a game of polo, collapsed and suddenly died. He was barely fifty-four. His funeral on the following day was attended by a large number of Iraqi officials and dignitaries. He was interred in the British cemetery in Baghdad. It was up to the acting high commissioner, Air Officer Commanding Robert Brooke-Popham, to bring the cabinet decisions to Faisal on 14 September 1929. Faisal was elated. This was the culmination of a prolonged and unremitting effort on his part to bring the British government unconditionally to work for Iraq's independence and entry into the League of Nations.

Al-Sa'adoun's suicide

Faisal was well aware that Britain's promise to support Iraq's entry to the League did not imply the end of British influence in Iraq. He never sought Britain's complete disengagement from the country: this was neither desirable nor possible. Iraq's dependence on Britain for economic, military and diplomatic support could not be wished away, but what was possible was the end of the intervention of the high commissioner in Iraq's internal affairs and the sense that Iraq, under the mandate, was a country deficient in the qualities needed to manage its own affairs. Faisal did not share his minsters' aversion to the British advisers who were scattered throughout the government and military. Many of them, such as Cornwallis, had been his trusted advisers. Nevertheless, their veto powers and often lordly ways grated. It was yet another expression of Iraq's embarrassing status as a half-free country. The September declarations of the British government gave Faisal the first solid basis on which to build Iraq's pathway to independence, and he intended to exploit it to the full.

Al-Sa'adoun had taken a prolonged vacation in Lebanon during the summer of 1929. The burdens of office and the constant wrangling and backbiting within Iraq's political class had worn him down, and he was reluctant to return to political life. His status as the Residency's favourite Iraqi politician could not mask the reality that he himself had changed his views on the mandate and now sought an orderly transfer of unrestricted power to the Iraqi government. The shift in British policy manifested by the September declarations was certainly welcomed by al-Sa'adoun. When Faisal offered him the premier's job on 19 September 1929 he accepted it, but with reservations. He was acutely sceptical of the Iraqi political class and was weary of the mischief that they could cause his government.[65]

His relations with Faisal, however, had improved, and he formed his fourth cabinet with the knowledge that the palace would either be supportive or neutral in its disposition towards his cabinet and his policies. Al-Sa'adoun's cabinet was not quite the national coalition that Faisal had sought, but it did include a number of key politicians and strong personalities, such as Yasin al-Hashimi at the Ministry of Finance, Nuri al-Sa'id as minister of defence and Naji Shawkat as minister of justice. Al-Sa'adoun's bête noir Rashid 'Ali was kept outside the government. The cabinet had an ambitious agenda, for there had been no effective government for several months while the wrangling between Faisal and London had been going on. The most important item, of course, was preparing for negotiations with Britain on a treaty that would pave the way for Iraq's independence.

But al-Sa'adoun was slowly disintegrating inside. His domestic life was miserable, overshadowed by his evil-tempered and neurotic Turkish wife. She enforced a strictly Turkish lifestyle on the family, including the use of the Turkish language at home. He took to drink and playing cards, and would often talk morbidly of welcoming death to his close friends and hinting at suicide.[66] Al-Sa'adoun had a thin skin and could not stand the press onslaughts that cast him as a British tool and a traitor to his country. He saw himself as a conscientious patriot, whose moderate and accommodating policies were necessary in the light of Iraq's backwardness. After he had formed his fourth cabinet, the newspaper attacks were unprecedented in their harshness. His own majority party in the Majlis gave his governing programme only lukewarm support. When Faisal delivered the speech from the throne on the occasion of the formation of al-Sa'adoun's cabinet, there were only a few murmurs of assent from deputies of the governing majority. Matters came to a head on 11 November 1929. A tumultuous session of the Majlis saw the opposition tear into al-Sa'adoun and his policies, while his own party, al-Taqaddum, appeared to acquiesce on account of its muted defence of their leader. In the afternoon al-Sa'adoun sat down to write his resignation. When Faisal heard of it, he sent his aide Safwat al-'Awa to plead with him to withdraw his resignation. Al-Sa'adoun retorted to Safwat: 'Pasha! Go tell our Sire that if he insists, I will commit suicide.'[67]

On the following day, 12 November 1929, Faisal was giving a farewell party for Kinahan Cornwallis, who was heading for England on leave. Al-Sa'adoun attended the party and was greatly perturbed by Cornwallis's views that there had been no fundamental shift in British policy towards Iraq. It was unlikely that Cornwallis would deliberately downgrade the significance of the 14 September declaration, and in all likelihood his comments were distorted as they passed through the agitated and distressed mind of al-Sa'adoun. On leaving the party, al-Sa'adoun talked to Faisal about his conversation with Cornwallis and gloomily said: 'Whatever we have asked from the British is merely a mirage and has no substance in reality.'[68] Al-Sa'adoun had made up his mind to take his own life.

On 13 November, al-Sa'adoun attended an ordinary cabinet session, and in the afternoon visited an ailing cabinet colleague laid up at his home. He then went to his club for a game of poker, where he met with a number of his party stalwarts. His resigned and distant demeanour troubled his friends but none could suspect what was swirling in his mind. Al-Sa'adoun then returned home intent on doing the deed. He retired to his library, wrote his suicide note, and proceeded to his bedroom. His wife, sensing that something was untoward, rushed to the bedroom to see her husband loading his gun. 'I ran towards him shouting "What are you doing? If you want to kill someone, kill me!" He said, "Leave me alone, or otherwise I *will* kill you." I grabbed his arm but he tried to slip from my grasp. He moved to the balcony with me holding his left arm, thinking that I had prevented him from doing [any harm]. But alas, his gun was in his right pocket and he had a firm hand on it. I fainted and only recovered when I heard a loud sound of gunshot reverberating on the balcony. He had one leg inside the bedroom and one leg on the balcony. He immediately dropped down.'[69] He had shot himself in the heart.

Al-Sa'adoun's suicide note, written in Turkish for his son Ali, who was then a student at Birmingham, became one of the most controversial documents in modern Iraqi history. It was the work of a deeply depressed and troubled soul.

To my son Ali, [the apple of] my eye and the pillar that sustains me. Forgive me for the crime that I have committed. For I am disgusted with this life and I have despaired of it. I have not found in my life any joy, or pleasure or honour. The nation awaits those who serve her. The English do not agree. I have no supporter. The Iraqis who demand independence are weak, powerless and far from independence. They are incapable of accepting the advice of honourable people such as I. They think that I am a traitor to the country and a slave of the English. How great is this calamity! I am a martyr for my country and the most sincere to it. I have patiently borne all sorts of insults and humiliations, and only for the sake of this blessed land where my ancestors and forbears lived in prosperity. My son, my last words of advice to you are: Be kind to your small siblings who will be orphaned. Respect your mother. Be loyal to your country. Be utterly faithful to King Faisal and his heirs. Forgive me, my son Ali.[70]

The note was discovered by the first senior official to arrive at al-Sa'adoun's house after his suicide, Minister of Agriculture 'Abd al-Aziz al-Qassab. The press got hold of the note, and a garbled version of it was published that seemed to lay the blame for al-Sa'adoun's suicide on the British. The Residency indignantly complained to Faisal about the public impression that it was British policies that drove al-Sa'adoun to his suicide. Faisal rectified this situation by ensuring that the original note was published in full and providing copies of al-Sa'adoun's suicide note in Turkish and Arabic to the Residency. Nevertheless, the widespread public feeling remained that it was indeed British intransigence and double-dealing that had pushed al-Sa'adoun to take his own life. The lines from the suicide note, 'The nation awaits those who serve her. The English do not agree,' entered into Iraq's political lexicon, in both its Turkish and Arabic forms, a shorthand for imperious perfidy.[71]

Al-Sa'adoun's death came at a critical time for Faisal. Although not friendly to Faisal, al-Sa'adoun had grown closer to him politically. His departure from the political scene might have removed an obstacle in Faisal's rise to absolute political pre-eminence, but it also was a serious loss for him. Al-Sa'adoun had the necessary authority and credibility to navigate the doubtlessly fraught and tedious process towards a new treaty with Britain successfully. Naji al-Suwaidi, who was the minister of interior in al-Sa'adoun's cabinet, was now offered the premiership by Faisal. Naji kept most of the personnel from al-Sa'adoun's cabinet, but without al-Sa'adoun's moderating hand the new cabinet swung to a recklessly hostile attitude to the British and towards Britain's advisers in the government. Radicals in the government, such as Yasin al-Hashimi, misread the 14 September declaration as an indication of Britain's fading power in Iraq. They fanned anti-British agitation that had already been fired by a ferocious press campaign against the British, and by the distorted interpretation of the causes behind al-Sa'adoun's suicide, which laid the blame entirely on the duplicity of Britain.

In earlier times such agitation might have worked to Faisal's advantage by pointing out to the British the extent of the public's disquietude at their policies, and by his offering his own prescriptions as the appropriate alternative. However, the campaign spearheaded by the prime minister and Yasin was reaching dangerous levels in tone as well as in content. Faisal pressed for the closure of two newspapers because of their strident attacks on the British and the advisers.[72] British power was certainly not on the wane to the extent that the radicals thought, and maintaining the good will of the Residency in the forthcoming negotiations might be jeopardised by an imprudent policy of confrontation. At the same time, Faisal was welcoming the new high commissioner Sir Francis Humphrys, who was known to be in favour of ceding more power to Iraq. It became increasingly clear that the Naji al-Suwaidi cabinet would not be able to negotiate the decisive treaty that would pave Iraq's pathway to independence. Naji al-Suwaidi was also facing calls for his resignation from the Majlis, partly prompted by the unauthorised settlement of the Ottoman debt by Minister of Finance Yasin al-Hashimi. Naji saw the writing on the wall and offered his resignation on 9 March 1930, a scant four months after he formed his cabinet.

Faisal now had a free hand to appoint his own man and to put his stamp on the negotiations for a new Anglo-Iraqi treaty. He chose Nuri al-Sa'id as his new prime minister.

CHAPTER 25

VINDICATION AT LAST

THE 14 September declaration gave Faisal a clear pathway to independence and to securing his power in Iraq. He pushed ahead vigorously with a prime minister who had not only become his most important support but was also a formidable character in his own right. Nuri was equally determined to negotiate the all-important treaty with Britain as soon as possible and was prepared to ride roughshod if necessary over all domestic opposition. Both Faisal and Nuri were by now sceptical as to whether parliamentary democracy dominated by fractious political prima donnas could provide the scaffolding for Iraq's consolidation and development. They were prepared to work within the forms of the parliamentary system that the constitution called for, but the squabbles of politicians over the rewards of power turned every proposal, initiative or decision into a prolonged test of wills. The nationalist opposition, which claimed to stand for the virtuous political goals of constitutional democracy and unbridled independence, frequently lost its key leaders to Faisal after he had dangled the fruits of office in front of them. Faisal saw them for what they were, and always maintained a minimal working relationship with them for the time when he needed one of their leaders to form a new government. Pragmatism and flexibility were his watchwords, but Faisal also grabbed an opportunity when he saw it. A new treaty that would build on the 14 September declaration was just such an opportunity to allow him to escape from the straitjacket of the mandate system.

Faisal was a close observer of developments in nearby countries and in Europe. A new model of government was evolving around the region and in Europe. It did away with the trappings of constitutional rule and seemed at the time to be a superior way to organise and develop backward societies. He watched with fascination the evolution of nationalist and authoritarian systems in both Turkey and Iran. Mustafa Kemal had brutally imposed a radical

modernisation programme on his country in a very short while through draconian measures that were against all the vestiges of traditional society and
authority. In Iran, Reza Pahlavi, now the shah of Iran, was following a similar
course, but in an altogether different society than Turkey's and with different
dynamics. Further afield, Faisal was also intrigued by the experience of
Mussolini in fascist Italy. All these great experiments in social engineering had
their attractions when viewed from afar. They promised a quick and sure path
out of backwardness and dependency, and held the promise of effective and
efficient government unencumbered by a gaggle of self-serving politicians and
a strident and corrupt press.

In the summer of 1930, Faisal had visited Rome and was shown around the
major monuments and the housing estates, government buildings and engineering feats that were proud features of Mussolini's government. Faisal was
evidently impressed by what he saw. During the visit, Mussolini had hosted
Faisal at a state dinner. At the banquet Mussolini had invited the noted Italian
sculptor Pietro Canonica, a friend of the Italian foreign minister Dino Grandi,
and seated him near Faisal. Mussolini had launched a cultural push in the east
to highlight the achievements and promise of fascist Italy in contrast to the
moribund colonial powers of Britain and France. Canonica's imposing sculp-
tures were an important element of this strategy. Over dinner, Canonica
brought the conversation around to his sculptural works and announced, with
Mussolini's manifest approval, that he wanted Baghdad to be adorned with one
of his statues. Its subject would be King Faisal himself. Faisal agreed to
Canonica's proposal. The sculptor arrived in Baghdad later in the year from
Ankara, where he was working on a heroic marble statue of Mustafa Kemal, to
start on his famous equestrian statue of Faisal.[1]

The American chargé d'affaires in Baghdad, Alexander Sloan, a shrewd
observer of the Iraqi political scene, wrote about the changing perspectives of
Faisal. 'It has been evident for some time that King Faisal believes that he, with
the assistance of a small body of prominent men, can govern Iraq without
much necessity for considering public opinion, and signs are not waning that
he is preparing to do so. The recent increase in army and police forces is one
indication of his plans. . . . He is in favour of conscription and will probably
soon put it into force.'[2] In an earlier cable to Washington, the chargé d'affaires
openly stated that Faisal had become an admirer of Mussolini. 'Quite evident
that Faisal began to emulate Mussolini whom he had met on his trip and whose
policies he admired.'[3] The Residency, far better equipped to analyse and
comment on Faisal's views and policies, also talked about Faisal and Nuri's
desire to establish a 'palace autocracy'. 'There is Nuri Pasha looking perhaps to
such a model as Mussolini and Mustafa Kemal, and determined with King
Faisal to set up an autocratic government in Baghdad.'[4] But they also knew that

Faisal did not have the character or the desire to railroad his ideas by force, and their assessment of Faisal's autocratic tendencies were modified by knowledge of his essentially conciliatory nature.

Faisal's moderation was proverbial and his instincts were naturally towards the *via media*. Once, he was visited by his friend the Lebanese writer and historian Amin Rihani, as he was posing for the sculptor Canonica. Rihani drew Faisal into a conversation about identity and modernisation. 'Can we preserve our culture, Amin, and here we are immersed in the culture of Europeans? And is it right that we denounce our national culture and take on all the attributes and culture of the West?' Faisal asked rhetorically. Rihani answered him provocatively: the choice was between religious reaction and the shock policies of Mustafa Kemal. Faisal replied,

It is neither the *ulema* nor Mustafa Kemal in my opinion. Our religious schools are old and barren. They are schools of clerics and for clerics, and they keep going around in circles the way the turbans of the *ulema* do. But we still need them. If we abandon them today and teach our children only natural sciences then they will turn to atheism and materialism. The Jewish or Christian child is taught his faith at home by his mother, who impresses on the child faith in God. But Muslim children learn nothing at home. Their mothers are ignorant; their fathers are at work and mostly illiterate. So the child comes to the mosque school with an empty mind that is filled by the imam with superficial religious knowledge . . . But I promise you that we will reform our religious schools and we will form a cadre of knowledgeable clerics, God Willing. The students will learn the fundamentals of their religion but they will be immersed in the scientific spirit of the age. In this way we will have a modern-minded religious class . . . We can then dispense with the teaching of religion in government schools.[5]

Faisal rejected Mustafa Kemal's solution of simply closing the religious schools and force-feeding modernity to a mainly rural and traditional population.

Nevertheless, Faisal launched his experiment with a pseudo-autocratic government. He was not willing to allow bothersome domestic opposition to scuttle the negotiations for the vital new treaty with Britain.

The Anglo-Iraqi Treaty of 1930 and its aftermath

Nuri formed his cabinet on 23 March 1930. Apart from the Shi'a Minister 'Abd al-Hussein al-Chalabi, the entire cabinet, hand-picked by Faisal, comprised ex-sharifian officers who had served with Faisal in the Arab Revolt or in Syria. Yasin al-Hashimi was pointedly excluded. Nuri's political credentials were such that he could not be accused of falling under British influence or direction. At the same time, his credibility with the Residency was high enough to ensure that the Residency was also satisfied with the composition of his cabinet. There was also the new high commissioner Sir Francis Humphrys, who looked favourably on a Nuri government. Humphrys had been a noted cricketer in his youth, and was a product of the familiar route that led from public school to Oxford to the Indian army and then to political service in India and Afghanistan. He was intent on having a good working relationship with Faisal. Humphrys had a pleasant demeanour and possessed an analytical and insightful mind. In the changed world of the 1930s and the rise of nationalist movements, Humphrys was conscious of the need for Britain to modify its imperial policies. His experiences in Afghanistan, where he had witnessed the revolt against the reforming King Amanullah, also convinced him of the need for moderation in pursuing change. He reflected this in his accommodating and non-confrontational approach to the treaty negotiations.[6]

Faisal and Nuri quickly opened negotiations with the British. It was a tightly controlled process with little consultation with other political leaders. Within the spate of three months the new draft treaty was sent to London for its final legal gloss. It gave Faisal most of what he wanted: Britain's recognition of complete independence for Iraq; Iraq's responsibility for preserving internal order and external defence; and the withdrawal of British forces from Iraq with the exception of two remaining air bases, which would be given extraterritorial status. Iraq, however, would be bound by a twenty-five year treaty of alliance with Britain, and the British ambassador in Baghdad would be given a higher status than the ambassadors of other countries. Iraq would also employ British advisers in preference to those from other countries. The British agreed to provide the Iraqi army with equipment and training. The text of the treaty was published in London on 18 July and the following day was carried in the Baghdad press.

The treaty was another example of Faisal's strategy of taking the most of what could be taken that was on offer and postponing disputatious matters to later times. There was no doubt that Britain's residual power in Iraq and its preferential status would grate on the nationalists in Baghdad. But his policy of chipping away at the privileges of the imperial power had borne fruit. Iraq was in an immeasurably better condition in terms of the degree of its political independence than other Arab countries under French mandate rule or those that were outright colonies. Faisal genuinely believed that the Anglo-Iraqi Treaty of 1930 and Iraq's subsequent independence would be a great boon to other Arab countries trying to break out of the mandate system and colonial dependency, and in fact he was proved right. The overwhelming tenor of opinion in other Arab countries, especially in the Levant, was to contrast Iraq's political progress

favourably with the travails of those countries still under French rule. At the
back of Faisal's mind loomed the opportunity that would arise for Iraq to take
the lead in drawing these countries into the grand Arab confederation that was
the promise of the Arab Revolt. At the same time, Faisal was conscious of the
need for Britain's commitment to Iraq's economic development and to its military preparedness. He certainly was not averse to maintaining the alliance with
Britain as a cornerstone of Iraq's foreign policy. The temptation to switch alliances, for example towards fascist Italy, was a fleeting one, and Faisal did not
seriously contemplate ditching the British connection in favour of an untried
power such as Italy.

However, radical nationalists in Baghdad rejected this sanguine view of the
treaty and stepped up their agitation against it.[7] The Kurds, alarmed at the
absence of any mention of Kurdistan's special circumstances in the treaty,
joined in the anti-treaty alliance. Furthermore, the loyalty of the deputies in the
Majlis, some beholden to Nuri's political enemies, could not be assured for a
majority in favour of the new treaty. Elections for a new parliament, with an
unassailable pro-treaty majority, were therefore essential if Faisal's programme
were to be ratified. Before leaving for Europe in June 1930, Faisal instructed
Ali, the regent during his absence, to dissolve the Majlis and call for new
elections. Nuri set to work to ensure that the government would have
an unquestionable majority. Returning to Baghdad on 1 October 1930, after
visiting Britain, France, Italy and Germany, Faisal approved Nuri's list of
pro-government candidates for the elections.

The elections of 1930 were tightly managed by Nuri, who left nothing to
chance. He became the acting minister of interior to supervise the elections
directly. The opposition were harassed, newspaper editors were threatened and
potential dissidents were kept in check. The land laws were used liberally to
bribe compliant shaikhs with tracts of state land, or alternatively threaten the
withdrawal of land grants for recalcitrants. An attempt to boycott the elections,
spearheaded by the Shi'a leader and head of the opposition al-Watani party,
Ja'far Abu al-Timmen, failed. His own collaborators in the party were determined to participate, mainly for their own selfish interest. It was better for
many to be a sitting deputy in the chamber, though sullied by compromise,
than to sit impotently outside. The Najaf *mujtahids* rejected an attempt on Abu
al-Timmen's part to marshal their support for a boycott. They had no interest
in the political squabbles of nationalist politicians. The only state that mattered
to them and that could exercise their interest was an Islamic state, and Iraq was
hardly headed in that direction.[8] In desperation, Abu al-Timmen wrote to
Faisal to complain of the government's interference in the elections and to
demand that Faisal protect the constitution by stopping Nuri's blatant intervention in the electoral process. Faisal's reply was categorical. The elections

were legal and the troubles were all caused by those who were seeking to disrupt them. He wanted and needed a pliant parliament. The elections were held on 20 October, and returned a chamber that had an overwhelming government majority. Only a few of the opposition leaders, such as Yasin al-Hashimi and Rashid 'Ali, were elected, and then only with a bare majority. On 16 November 1930, the new Majlis with its rock-hard government majority duly voted in favour of the treaty with a lop sided margin.

The opposition to the treaty, however, was widespread. It is possible that without the brazen interference of the government in the electoral process, Faisal and Nuri would not have been able to manage the new chamber, and ratification of the treaty would have been difficult. At the same time, the choices open to Faisal were limited. The termination of the mandate could not be done unilaterally. It required the active involvement and agreement of Britain. There was no 'international opinion' to which Faisal could appeal in the event that Britain did not acquiesce to negotiations. The League of Nations was already dominated by the European colonial powers, and, if anything, it was leaning towards maintaining the mandate. It was greatly concerned about the future of minorities in an independent Iraq. Ja'far Abu al-Timmen sent a long letter to the League of Nations protesting the terms of the 1930 treaty and the conduct of the elections, but was met with stony indifference. Faisal also knew that few of the opposition leaders were in fact motivated primarily by nationalist considerations. Many of them had switched their loyalties between opposition and the government whenever an official government position beckoned. There were precious few like Ja'far Abu al-Timmen, who was committed to a course that would accept nothing less than complete severance of the 'special relationship' with Britain. He had acted consistently throughout in his opposition to British influence, and was genuinely desirous in seeing a nationalist Arab/Islamic government for Iraq. His patriotic credentials were often abused by his erstwhile allies, who would often dump him when their interest suited them.[9] A great deal of the opposition of the ordinary Shi'a in Iraq to the 1930 treaty was driven by a fear that it was a prelude to mass conscription, while the Kurds were worried that independence would mean their subservience to a blatantly centralised and Arab nationalist state. In October 1930, a large anti-treaty demonstration in Suleimaniya led to the death of a score of protestors.[10]

Faisal's leaning to autocracy, which many noticed after his return from his European trip, was not a personal proclivity. It was more a desire to control a negotiating process whose outcome was of fundamental importance to Iraq's future. If the opposition had its way, the treaty negotiations would have foundered with the certain British refusal to surrender their position and privileges in the country completely. The stage would be set for a prolonged and bitter confrontation with Britain, probably accompanied by considerable violence. The alternative was more palatable but also fraught with dangers. Riding roughshod over a fractious opposition carried its own risks. It could drive the disparate groups that formed the opposition into a common front that would then challenge the government in parliament, the press and the streets. The risks of polarisation of opinion were great and might poison the political life of the country for years to come. At the same time, Faisal could not offer the customary largesse that could cajole or bribe the opposition's leaders into acquiescence with his policies. Iraq and the world were going through a serious economic crisis that had gravely affected Iraq's public finances.

Faisal, while firmly in control over the details of the negotiations, left Nuri as the public face of the Iraqi negotiators. This gave him continuing credibility, and some room for manoeuvre, with the opposition when the inevitable reaction set in. But Faisal left no doubt that the treaty was a good deal for Iraq. In a speech to representatives from the provinces in October 1931, Faisal said: 'I would like to reiterate to you that Iraq is a free and independent country, with no master on it except its own will. Our ally Britain has no claim on us except for an air route. Yes indeed, Britain has no other claim on us, and apart from that we are free and independent, and I ask the journalists amongst you to proclaim this in bold letters . . . Go to your friends and broadcast what I have said and don't mislead yourselves or the people. I and my country are free. We have no partners in our venture, and no one to can act as ward over us when we enter the League of Nations except God.'[11]

However, what Faisal saw as his great vindication came at a most difficult time, as the country's economy was in dire straits. Iraq's grain production had slumped and world commodity prices had collapsed. Unrest had spread to the rural areas and tribesmen were busy arming themselves. For the first time, not only his government but Faisal himself was being personally attacked. Swallowing his deep dislike for Yasin al-Hashimi, Ja'far Abu al-Timmen worked to have the two main opposition parties, his own al-Watani and al-'Ikha of al-Hashimi, join forces in a new grouping. In March 1931 the two parties formed a joint coalition party, al-'Ikha al-Watani, to oppose the government. They were determined to bring the government down. Yasin al-Hashimi and Rashid 'Ali both resigned from the Majlis, thereby putting greater pressure on the government.

Unrest also built up in the mid-Euphrates valley. Unable to address the deeper causes behind Shi'a grievances, Faisal sought to calm the agitation by personally touring the main towns of the area. On 13 April 1931 Faisal visited the towns of Hilla, Najaf and Karbala, accompanied by two Shi'a figures: Sayyid Muhammad al-Sadr, now the head of the Senate, and 'Abd al-Hussein al-Chalabi, one of the two Shi'a ministers in the cabinet. The trip was not successful. There were demonstrations in all the towns they visited, denouncing the policies of the Nuri government and its restrictions on political activity and the freedom of the press. In Hilla, Faisal was presented with a petition by the demonstrators demanding redress for the clampdowns and asking Faisal to withdraw his support for the treaty. In Najaf, a leading *mujtahid*, Sayyid Baqir al-Hilli, barged into Faisal's presence, made a statement regarding the demands of the Shi'a, and abruptly left without hearing Faisal's reply.[12] Faisal's authority and prestige in the south had sunk. His palliative solution was to appoint the first ever Shi'a governor of a province, but it was too little to have any serious effect on the dangerous alienation of the Shi'a. Reporting on the abortive trip, the American chargé d'affaires was moved to comment on the dissatisfaction amongst the Shi'a: 'Signs of unrest among the Shi'ah communities along the lower Euphrates have been evident for some time. In fact these Shi'ahs have never become wholly reconciled to the fact that for the last ten years there has been a Government in the country which exercises a certain amount of super-vision over them, nor are they pleased by the fact that the Arab members of the Government are Sunni Muslims.'[13]

The general strike of 1931

The trigger for social instability came with the passage of a municipality tax that appeared to affect small traders and craftsmen inordinately. Although the tax had been discussed for some time as a means to boost the chronically underfunded Iraqi budget, its passage into law on 2 June 1931 provided the opportunity for the opposition to capitalise on the discontent amongst merchants. On 4 July Faisal, accompanied by Nuri al-Sa'id, left for a state visit to Turkey, to be followed by his regular vacation for rest and recuperation in Europe. He was also planning to canvass the League of Nations for a definite date for Iraq's entry into the League of Nations. On the following day a general strike was called in Baghdad. It was organised by the Tradesmen's Guild of Baghdad and was widely observed. Baghdad was a ghost town. All the shops and markets were closed. People in the city had to fend for themselves for food and other necessities. All facilities such as hotels, restaurants, cinemas, clubs and even underground bars observed the strike. It lasted for twelve days and spread to nearly all the major towns of Iraq, including Basra, which had always been noted for its easy-going ways and tranquillity.[14]

Nuri's cabinet had taken some precautions against the worst effects of the strike, but the government was taken aback by its scale and widespread observ-ance. Faisal cabled his brother, Ali, who was acting as regent in Faisal's absence, to inform the cabinet to act firmly with the strikers but to avoid the use of force. In Nuri's absence, the strike was handled by the deputy prime minister

Muzahim al-Pachachi, a figure reviled by the opposition after he had bolted from its ranks to join the government. Striking shopkeepers and tradesmen took to the streets in rowdy parades and clashed with the police. The demonstrators soon picked up the political opposition's slogans and demands, and the general strike took on ugly overtones. Muzahim reacted with excessive force, arresting scores of demonstrators and ordering police to beat the crowds and fire live rounds to disperse them. He also floated the idea with the regent of imprisoning the leaders of the opposition and even stripping Yasin al-Hashimi of his Iraqi nationality, a most draconian measure.[15] The regent panicked and sent Faisal in Ankara an alarming cable that the situation in Baghdad had become perilous and was slipping outside the government's control. He pleaded with Faisal to return and if he couldn't then the prime minister should do so. Faisal ordered Nuri to return to Baghdad immediately. Within a few days after Nuri's arrival, the situation had quietened down. Nuri, through a judicious mix of conciliatory moves and firm measures, soon brought the matter under control, but it had been a near-run thing. The RAF had to make sorties over the Euphrates valley to dissuade tribesmen from rising and turning the general strike into a full-scale insurrection. Faisal's popularity had plummeted and there were cries in the striking crowds calling for a republic with Yasin al-Hashimi as president.

Although Nuri had backed Muzahim al-Pachachi's fierce measures against the strikers, Muzahim was left to carry the opprobrium for the violence and mayhem that ensued. He was deeply unpopular with the public and pressure built up for him to resign from the cabinet. He left in October 1931, and Nuri reshuffled his cabinet, bringing in Naji Shawkat, then the legatee in Turkey, as the new interior minister. Faisal sought to mollify Muzahim by offering him the Iraqi legation in London, but a scandal broke out in May 1932 that threatened to sully Faisal's personal standing. During the general strike, four unsigned letters had circulated that implicated Faisal in a liaison with the wife of the mayor of Baghdad, the popular Mahmud Subhi al-Daftari. She was alleged to have made frequent visits to Faisal's palace at Harthiya. There was a great deal of bad blood between al-Daftari himself and Muzahim. The entire Baghdad Municipal Council had resigned in protest against the anti-strike measures of Muzahim.[16] In retaliation, Muzahim fired al-Daftari for not stopping his councillors from resigning. The defamatory letters talked about Faisal's liaisons with other women from prominent Iraqi families. They also directly accused Faisal of favouritism in government appointments and the misappropriation of public funds. The letters demanded the abolition of the monarchy and its replacement by a republic.[17] An official investigation was conducted into the affair, which was led by a Major Wilkins, the deputy inspector general of the police, egged on by Muzahim's many political enemies. The police report directly implicated Muzahim in the scandal as the originator of the scurrilous letters, and demanded that his parliamentary immunity be removed, prior to his indictment. Muzahim resigned his seat before the Majlis could strip him of his immunity.

Faisal, in spite of Nuri's entreaties on behalf of Muzahim, his political ally, now insisted that he be put on trial. It was a streak of unbecoming and unwonted vindictiveness, but driven by Faisal's certainty that Muzahim was behind these letters. At his subsequent trial, the witness statements conflicted with each other and Muzahim was declared innocent of the charges, but the damage to Faisal's reputation and character was extensive. The public was engrossed in the scandal and the trial, and the stain on Faisal from the charges of his womanising, even though unsubstantiated, remained. Writing on the decline of the king's popularity, the American chargé d'affaires wrote to Washington, 'King Faisal has never been very popular with the Iraqi people as a whole. . . . Consequently many of the people feel that he has been foisted upon them . . . When King Faisal appears in his automobile on the street in Baghdad there is never the least indication that his presence is noted. I have seen him pass along the street time after time, but the only people who seemed to pay any attention to his passing were foreigners, who as a rule paused and lifted their hats. However, although the King has never been popular, he has not been very unpopular until recent months. As far as I can learn this is for the most part due to the fact that the opposition leaders have been conducting an unceasing campaign against him.'[18]

The poison letters were certainly the work of one or more of Iraq's scheming politicians, intent on sabotaging the king's standing on a morality issue. In a conservative and traditional society, accusations of moral lassitude and indecent conduct carried a great deal of weight. But Faisal himself did not openly philander. There were rumours of his womanising in Europe; if true, his affairs were certainly carried out with the greatest discretion. He enjoyed his visits to Europe, which afforded him the time and leisure to enjoy the company of people whom he would not normally meet in Baghdad. There have even been been claims that Faisal disported himself under the name 'Prince Usama' in such European jaunts, but this has not been corroborated.[19] It was not that Faisal was above these matters, but he was also acutely aware of the need to always maintain a profile of high moral standing. Open liaisons held inside Iraq of the kind implied in the slanderous letters would have been unthinkable.

The clash between Faisal and Nuri on the handling of the Muzahim affair masked Faisal's growing apprehension about Nuri's power. The government was deeply unpopular in the country at large, but Faisal and Nuri had successfully split the opposition and Nuri's firm measures had cowed them into ineffectual action. Nuri's international stature had grown with his frequent forays to Arab and European countries and to London. Nuri's position with the

Residency had markedly improved and though not quite a favourite the way al-Sa'adoun was, Nuri nevertheless held the Residency's ear. Faisal looked askance at the growing power of his assertive prime minister, and was undoubtedly concerned with the threat that Nuri might have posed to his own primacy in the country. Tensions mounted between the two, with Nuri complaining to the Residency of Faisal's constant encroachments and interference with the business of government. The acting high commissioner Hubert Young reported to London on Nuri's claims that Faisal was making his life difficult: 'The root of the difference with King Faisal [claimed Nuri] was that the latter was continually abusing his position to secure petty personal advantages for himself and his entourage, and regaled me with a number of instances of evasion of taxes and custom duties, illegal granting of pensions and the like, the continuation of which no self-respecting Prime Minister would be expected to tolerate.'[20] Faisal also had his grievances regarding Nuri. He told Humphrys that 'Nuri Pasha contrary to HM [Faisal's] advice persistently appointed and promoted to the posts of administration men without either ability or integrity, men of his supporters. This was known to the man in the street and Nuri had fallen into a disrepute and his administration suffered. And in spite of Nuri's exhortation, Nuri refused to change his tactics.'[21]

However, Nuri's claims of Faisal's interference and ingratitude smacked too much of a spurned favourite. Faisal was already taking measures to bring the opposition back into the political mainstream; he did not have the instinct for the jugular. He pulled away from the destruction of his political opponents, even when the opportunity afforded itself after he had emerged victorious from one test of wills or another. On the eve of Iraq's formal independence, Faisal was not too keen to have an alienated opposition facing an over-confident prime minister. His instincts were to redress a condition of gross imbalance that might arise between the various figures in Iraq's thin political class. This would afford him the opportunity to alter his course if necessary, and to keep the palace as the final arbiter in the incessant power struggles between the leading politicians.

In the struggles between king and premier, the Residency mostly sided with the premier as a matter of course. The Residency believed it was easier for it to pursue British interests with a pliant or sympathetic prime minister than with Faisal. Whenever Faisal appeared to the Residency as intransigent or unwilling to bend to British demands or policy prescriptions, the adjectives used to describe Faisal in official despatches take on a disparaging, and even threatening tone. Dobbs and Cox before him often resorted to raising the spectre of forcing Faisal's abdication, which was well within Britain's theoretical power. Humphrys, in the changed circumstances of the early 1930s, was more circumspect. Whenever his advice was spurned, he would raise the prospects of an aroused public demanding Faisal's resignation or forcing his departure. Once the Residency got wind of Faisal's intentions to replace Nuri, Humphrys tried to dissuade him from this 'rash' act by the prospects of Faisal losing his throne in consequence. 'I propose to tell the King that if he alienates his best friends by underhand Palace intrigues, it will be a question of time before his wings are clipped by some future cabinet, and indeed before he is pushed from the throne altogether. There are signs that he has become jealous of Nuri and wants to force his resignation. If he [Nuri] is jockeyed out by Palace intrigues, Faisal will lose his staunchest friend in the country and he has very few left.'[22] But Nuri remained in Faisal's estimate the most competent and worthy politician and the spat over his powers and actions did not seriously alter Faisal's opinion of him. He was the longest-serving premier in Faisal's reign and his cabinet had a number of achievements, not least the negotiation of the 1930 treaty that brought about the end of the mandate.

Securing frontiers: Nejd

Wahhabi raids on southern Iraq were a continuous feature of Faisal's reign. The onslaught of 1922 gave way to smaller raids, but they picked up in scale and tempo in the autumn of 1927. Ibn Saud, who had restyled himself as sultan of Nejd and the Hijaz after the fall of the Hashemite kingdom of the Hijaz, had been tacitly instigating these raids even though he was bound to Britain in an alliance. Ibn Saud had even signed two border accords with Iraq, which were ignored. Faisal's response was to try to assemble a Bedouin border force under his relative Sharif Shakir to repel the aggressors and to carry out counter-raids in the Nejd. This was rejected by the high commissioner as it would have drawn the RAF into the conflict as the ultimate defender of Iraq's frontiers. Britain's reluctance to sanction the expansion of the Iraqi army to counter the Wahhabi raids naturally fed rumours in Baghdad. Britain was deliberately holding back the development of the Iraqi army the longer to perpetuate Iraq's dependence on the RAF.

As Faisal's powers grew with the approach of the end of the mandate, he now sought to put an end to the struggle with ibn Saud. It must have been a bitter pill for him to swallow, for the Hashemite quarrel with ibn Saud had stretched back to the eighteenth century, ever since the rise of the Wahhabi movement. In addition, the presence in Baghdad of Faisal's much-respected elder brother the ex-king Ali of the Hijaz was a poignant reminder of the loss of the sharifian domains in the Hijaz at the hands of ibn Saud. As the veteran Iraqi politician and many times premier Tawfiq al-Suwaidi wrote in his memoirs, 'It was difficult for King Faisal to reconcile his feelings as a member of a family that had lost its domains in the Hijaz, and his feelings as king. [He was now] responsible for an altogether different policy than that of his father or his brother King Ali, who was forced to abandon the throne. But it is clear that the wisdom of King Faisal the First and his strong nerves prevailed over what he had to constantly hear in complaints [about ibn Saud] from his brother ... [Faisal] though, as King of Iraq overrode all these problems and was determined to face Ibn Saud as it was in the interests of Iraq to establish good working relations with him.'[23] The opportunity presented itself towards the end of 1929, with ibn Saud's campaign against the Ikhwan, renegade Wahhabis under Faisal al-Duwaish. The latter, facing defeat, took refuge in Iraq. Faisal relayed an invitation to meet ibn Saud through High Commissioner Humphrys. Ibn Saud was unwilling to meet on Iraqi soil, but neither was he prepared to meet in neutral desert territory between the two countries. Humphrys came to the rescue with a proposal to meet on board a British warship, the *Lupin*, then in the waters of the Gulf. The kings agreed and on 21 February 1930, both monarchs made their way to the ship that was moored near the mouth of the Shatt-al-Arab waterway.

Apart from the inevitable one-upmanship – who would arrive first, the size of their entourage, the length of their speeches – the two kings were easy in each other's company. Faisal's doctor Harry Sinderson, who was present, wrote: 'They embraced each other in Arab fashion and grasping hands for a full minute, exchanged warm-hearted greetings with mutual assurance of a happy outcome of the deliberations to follow ... Immediately afterward the two protagonists, still hand in hand, were conducted to a spacious state-room which had been made ready for the conference.'[24] Both Faisal and ibn Saud wanted to put their bitter quarrels behind them in the interests of the security and stability of their realms. The negotiations went ahead speedily and by the end of the day, to the obvious discomfit of ibn Saud's more cautious advisers, agreement had been reached on a huge array of issues. It was a remarkable example of Faisal's pragmatism as well as a sense of duty that went beyond personal and family considerations. As Faisal explained to Rihani why he was willing to let bygones be bygones, 'If the quarrel was personal between me and Ibn Saud, and we met on the field of battle and fought, and one of us died, and that was the end of the matter, then so be it. But dragging Arabs to kill Arabs for our own narrow interest then that would be not only a disgrace but a great transgression against God. We Kings and *Ashraf* are trustees over the interests of the Arab lands, and it is a disgrace and a transgression if we pursue a course that only favours our personal interest ... And if the King's personal interest prevails over his patriotism then the nation has the right to hold him accountable, in fact it must do so.'[25]

Ibn Saud thought highly of Faisal and made an obvious exception of him when he compared to him to other Hashemites. 'I swear to God that I don't have a scintilla of hatred or contempt for Faisal. I only have love and great respect for him. I followed my heart when I came to this conference [on board the *Lupin*], and I ask God to give success to all in what is of interest to the Arab people.'[26] He told the writer Rihani that he considered Faisal 'a great and sincere friend, an honourable Arab of the noblest qualities, and a wise and accomplished leader.'[27] The good will between the two kings continued until the end of Faisal's life. When ibn Saud's son, Faisal, visited Baghdad in the summer of 1932, he was feted by the government and the king, and stayed as a guest at Faisal's Harthiya palace.[28] Deep in Faisal's heart must have been the feeling that in the final analysis his family, led by his father and 'Abdullah, had made irretrievable errors in their dealings with ibn Saud. They had lost their kingdom and indeed their birthright to a more capable, charismatic and forceful leader.

Securing frontiers: Turkey

The resolution of the Mosul issue in favour of Iraq should have removed a powerful impediment to the normalisation of relations between the two countries. Nevertheless they remained stiffly formal, and there was an undercurrent of unease in Iraq about the permanence of Turkey's renunciation of its claims on Mosul. Faisal made the first move to try to improve the tenor of the relations between the two countries. While in London during the abortive negotiations over the 1927 treaty, Faisal invited the Turkish ambassador in London, Ahmad Farid Bey, for tea at the Hyde Park Hotel on 5 November 1927. At this meeting, Faisal talked about the importance of transcending old conflicts and building good relations between the countries. He expressed his admiration for Turkey and Mustafa Kemal. 'I and all Iraqis are following the development and revolution in Turkey with great admiration,' said Faisal. 'It is impossible not to admire the accomplishment of His Excellency Mustafa Kemal Pasha and wish its continuation. I should confess that I did not think you would reach such brilliant results in your national struggle. Your advancement in every field is beyond all expectations. We are observing your development with amazement and pleasure. Without a doubt you are an example for all the nations of Asia. Unfortunately, since the people of Iraq are not as developed, we have not been able to do much [of modernizing reforms] yet. Our eventual goal, however, is to match you in your great work.'[29]

Mustafa Kemal initially resisted any personal approach from Faisal, aware of the painful memories that the Arab Revolt against the Ottomans could still provoke in Turkey. He was certainly worried that domestic opinion, still reeling from the effects of the First World War, would take umbrage at Faisal being invited to Turkey, what with Faisal's reputation as the field commander of the Arab Revolt. Feelings on the Mosul issue, whose resolution in favour of Iraq was seen by Turkish public opinion as a 'loss' for Turkey, might also be inflamed by a state visit of the king of Iraq. Lastly, Mustafa Kemal was concerned that the abolition of the caliphate, which had been received with great misgivings in the

Arab lands, might be raised by Faisal during a state visit. However, Kemal now saw an opportunity to turn around these issues to his advantage. First, Faisal could now be portrayed as a fellow warrior who was resisting foreign tutelage, fired by the example of Mustafa Kemal himself. The abolition of the caliphate could be re-read as a boon to Arab–Turkish relations in the modern era, as it removed the moral authority that the Ottoman caliphs had over the Arabs. Arabs and Turks could now meet each other as equals, bearers of their own separate nationalist identities.[30]

Following his second election to the Turkish presidency in 1927, Mustafa Kemal sent a good-will message to Faisal, alongside other world leaders. He expressed his best wishes for Faisal's rule and for the people of Iraq, and spoke of his desire that the two countries should have the most cordial relations. The two countries soon set up legations in their respective capitals. Faisal first appointed Sabih Nashat, who had been an officer in the Ottoman army and was known for his close relationship with Mustafa Kemal, as Iraq's first consul general and then as ambassador to Turkey. He met the Turkish ambassador in Baghdad on a number of occasions where he effusively expressed his respect and admiration for Mustafa Kemal. The improved climate in relations between the two countries led to Mustafa Kemal extending a formal invitation to Faisal to visit Turkey.[31] Faisal had planned to schedule his visit on his way back from Europe, but then changed his itinerary so that his state visit was now fixed for early July 1931, at the start of his European tour.

Flying by plane to Aleppo and then to Ankara by train, Faisal and his entourage arrived at Ankara station on 2 July 1931. He was greeted by Mustafa Kemal and the entire top civil and military leadership of Turkey. The two leaders left the station in an open car, to the enthusiastic cheers of large crowds. In the state dinner that was hosted for him at Ankara's Palace Hotel by Mustafa Kemal that evening, Faisal sat next to the Turkish leader and chatted in fluent Turkish. During the dinner, Mustafa Kemal asked Faisal for his first impressions of the city. Faisal stated that he was amazed at Ankara's development and that he wished to invite Mustafa Kemal to Baghdad once the conditions in the city were appropriate. Faisal then said, 'Well, it appears that we will spend the winter in Baghdad and summer in Ankara from now on.' Mustafa Kemal added, 'Ankara and Istanbul.'

Skirting over Mustafa Kemal's comments that Turkey had conceded Mosul to Iraq, Faisal replied 'But in return, you have won the whole of Iraq. Today the streets of Baghdad are filled with admirers of Mustafa Kemal.' Faisal was greatly pleased by his visit to Ankara and the hospitality and cordiality shown him. He was particularly moved by Mustafa Kemal's exhortatory speeches that were collected in a book. Faisal was quoted by the Turkish press as saying of these speeches: 'A masterpiece . . . You cannot get enough of it, you want to keep reading more and a melancholy sets in as the book ends. You just wish that it would never end. You wish he would just keep talking. In the words, writings and deeds of great men, there is an endless sense of security and greatness.'[32]

Faisal's state visit to Ankara culminated in a series of significant agreements on trade, migration and the exchange of prisoners. He then went on to Istanbul where he was met with equally large and enthusiastic crowds. He visited the Dolmabahce Palace of Sultan 'Abd al-Hamid, a visit which brought back painful memories. He recalled the episode later to the writer Amin Rihani,

> When we were at the Istana we used to go with our father to visit the Sultan. We entered the throne room with our head bowed, and we presented ourselves to the king and then kissed his hands. We then retreated a few steps while still facing the throne, and stood silently at attention. After that we left as we came in, with our hearts beating in fear, and by God, with awe. These days have gone! The Sultan has gone! We fought the Turks and we were victorious over them. I have now returned to the Istana as King of Iraq. And when we entered the Haider Pasha [railroad station on Istanbul's Asian side], coming from Ankara, a motor boat was awaiting us at the pier. It was the same launch boat of the Sultan, and it carried us to Galata [a district of Istanbul]. We alighted at the European side of Istanbul and we visited the palace, the Dolmabahce Palace, the same palace that we used to enter so scared, between rows of guards, so as to stand like slaves in front of the king. This time we entered it with serenity. The corridors and halls were eerily empty and quiet. As for the throne room, I felt its emptiness as I stood at its doorway. But the throne itself, the unoccupied and abandoned throne, was still there. This time I took firm steps forward, stepped up to the throne and sat on it! I was, by God, greatly pleased. I thank God the Master of all thrones, their Originator and Destroyer, and said to myself: You have received your recompense today.[33]

Securing frontiers: Iran

Another troublesome frontier, also the longest, was with Iran. The deportation of Shaikh Mahdi al-Khalisi and the self-exile of the ayatollahs early in Faisal's rule had cast a pall over an already troubled relationship. Apart from border wrangles, especially the demarcation of the frontier along the Shatt-al-Arab waterway, it was the sectarian issue that hovered over most of Iraq's disputes with Iran. The Residency, together with a number of Sunni Arab politicians, never ceased to believe in the malevolency of 'Persian divines', their power over the masses and tribal lords of the south of Iraq and their troublesome meddling in Iraq's internal politics. Faisal never shared in the overt racism of the new breed of Arab nationalists and did not define Iraqi patriotism in terms of its hostility to

Iran. Nevertheless, the trade between the two countries and the movement of pilgrims, families, merchants and even corpses – of pious Iranians destined for burial in the shrine towns of Iraq – was an important factor in their relations. All these elements called for good neighbourliness between the two countries, but Iran did not recognise the sovereignty of Iraq until well into Faisal's eighth year as king. By the spring of 1932, efforts to bridge the gap between the two countries had finally born fruit. Faisal had deputised Rustum Haidar to Teheran to help in the negotiations and pave the way for Faisal's state visit to Iran.[34]

The royal motorcade left Baghdad for Faisal's farm near Khanaqin along the Iranian frontier, where the party rested for the night before entering Iran. Faisal was accompanied by both Nuri al-Sa'id and his predecessor as prime Minister, Naji al-Suwaidi. The entourage also included Naji's brother Tawfiq, now Iraq's ambassador in Teheran, and Harry Sinderson, the king's private doctor. The following day, after entering Iran the party stopped at the ruins of the Sassanian Queen Shirin's palace. 'Naturally, I knew of Faisal's great interest in the archaeology of Iraq,' wrote Sinderson, 'But I had no idea that he had a profound knowledge of Persian antiquities. I am sure that all of us were surprised when, standing before some ruined columns on our way to Hamadan [in Iran], he delivered impromptu, an erudite discourse in Persian on the Sassanian dynasty, its rise and fall ... Faisal spoke with admiration of the conquests and achievements of Ardashir I and II, Shapur I and Chosroes I and II. He referred briefly to the hundred years of almost ceaseless conflict with Rome[35] and, very tactfully, as a descendant of the Prophet, of the Moslem invasion immediately following the death of Mohammed.'[36]

Arriving in Teheran, which had been bedecked with flowers, with its rutted streets paved for the occasion, Faisal was met by the shah, inaugurating three days of meetings, banquets and balls. At one such function, the Soviet ambassadress, an accomplished opera singer, regaled the party with her arias. She then asked Faisal to dance, which he politely refused. The two kings had contrasting personalities: Faisal, a descendant of the Prophet and a scion of one of the noblest families of Arabia; and the taciturn and fierce former Persian cossack brigade officer who had clawed his way up to power. Faisal was a king hemmed in by constitutional niceties and a fractious political class, while the shah was an absolute monarch who inspired dread and awe in his subjects and retainers. The contrast was not lost on Faisal, who was dubious of the type of kingship that the shah represented. Faisal was too courteous to show it, but he did reveal his thoughts in private. The British ambassador in Teheran, Reginald Hoare, wrote to the Foreign Office regarding Faisal's impressions of the pomp and grandeur of the Pahlavi court. 'King Feisal was not in the least impressed by the splendours of the Persian Court. Having been privileged to dine with His Majesty on the way here, I can state confidently that the contrast between the manner of life of the two Sovereigns is very marked. At Baghdad I was impressed by the sensible simplicity of the Sovereign of a poor country. Here, King Feisal seems to have been unfavourably impressed by the money wasted in a country as poor as his own; for instance, speaking at the Shah's palace at Saadabad, he expressed surprise at the heavy expenditures on a large house and garden which apparently nobody ever saw.'[37]

Faisal's visit continued apace when he returned to Iraq via an overland route that took him for the next ten days down the western spine of Iran to the southern port of Muhammara in Iran on the Shatt-al-Arab waterway. Commenting on the scale of the BP refinery in nearby Abadan, Faisal remarked that 'it was a gigantic and lasting monument to British expertise and enterprise'.[38] From Muhammarah, Faisal boarded a vessel to cross the river to Basra. The launch carrying the Basran official welcoming party sprang a hole and filled with water, and the unfortunate dignitaries were tipped into the harbour waters. This comic episode did not dampen the spirits of the official celebrations in Basra and the tumultuous welcome he was given by the citizenry of the city. Faisal's visit to Iran cemented the bonds between the shah and the king, and the terrifying Reza Shah had developed a soft spot for Faisal. '[Faisal's visit] was akin to a spark of light in the dark, and people's vision were directed to it to ascertain the truth,' wrote Tawfiq al-Suwaidi in his memoirs. 'For Iranians of all hues, whether simple, educated or powerful, found in the person of Faisal and his entourage representatives of a people on their western frontiers that they should get to know. The personal bonds between King Faisal and the Shah were very strong ... The haughty Pahlavi monarch became kind, courteous and gentle, and very considerate of Iraq and Iraqis and what concerned them!'[39]

Admission to the League of Nations

The Anglo-Iraqi Treaty of 1930, and with it the end of the mandate, would only become effective after Iraq's admission to the League of Nations. Britain had committed itself to recommending Iraq's admission, and informed the League of its decision to do so. The League in turn asked Britain for a report on the progress of the mandate during the 1921–31 period, and Iraq's admissibility under the mandate criteria. The report on the ten-year mandate was presented to League members in June 1931, and with it Britain's positive recommendation that Iraq was fit for independence. The French were naturally concerned lest Iraq's independence would be a test case for Syria's own call for independence, given that the French mandate in Syria had started a year earlier than Iraq's and that Syria was by most measures a more advanced country than Iraq. The report was extensively deliberated. Numerous objections were raised and clarifications were called for regarding Iraq's suitability, the role of foreign advisers, the competence of the Iraqi government, and above all the question of the rights and protection of minorities. However, by December 1931 Sir Francis Humphrys, who had taken the lead in addressing the issues raised, had through his spirited support for Iraq's case overcome all the hesitations and delaying tactics of the French. The committee charged with recommending on Britain's ten-year report favourably recommended Iraq's entry to the League of Nations, but with conditions. The committee required a formal and binding declaration from Iraq regarding a whole range of constitutional, political, judicial, human, civil and community rights and freedoms. No part of the statement contravened in any significant way the articles of Iraq's constitution. On 3 October 1932 Iraq was informed that it had been accepted as a member state in the League of Nations.

There was great rejoicing and celebration when the decision reached Baghdad and other parts of the country. The opposition press was unimpressed by Iraq's entry into the League, but its sour note could not hide the jubilatory mood in the country. Official celebrations marking Independence Day were scheduled for 6 October 1932, with Faisal to feature in all the main proceedings. He met with government ministers and provincial officials, and attended military parades and marches by young people and scouts. In the late afternoon, Faisal appeared at Baghdad's Majidiye Gardens to deliver his valedictory speech. It was heartfelt and poignant in turns. Faisal spoke of the long and arduous struggle to reach this day, and the need to redouble efforts to build the country into the image of what it had been in times gone by. He also profusely thanked the efforts of Britain in assisting and sponsoring Iraq in its application to the League.[40] The Majidiye Gardens were then turned over to the public in the evening with entertainers, songs and festivities lasting through the night.

Three weeks later Nuri submitted his resignation. His policies had been mostly in harmony with Faisal's and his success owed a great deal to Faisal's active support. Faisal recognised Nuri's invaluable service and offered him Iraq's highest medal of honour, even though Nuri had also alienated the opposition by his harsh tactics and his unwillingness to brook serious criticism. He had evolved into Iraq's foremost statesman-politician, but his enemies were legion, with none more lethal than Yasin, another strong personality chafing at his lack of power. It was up to Faisal to see that Nuri's success did not diminish the king's power and prerogatives, but Faisal was also aware that he could not afford to lose Nuri's support. The latter left, forswearing any further dealings with Faisal, although he soon overcame his resentment. Faisal, on the other hand, saw his differences with Nuri as a spat that would be quickly forgotten.

They 'were like husband and wife; they had their occasional differences and must from time to time see less of one another,' Faisal told Hubert Young.[41]

✦✦✦✦✦◆❖◆✦✦✦✦✦

CHAPTER 26

A CALAMITOUS END

THE INDEPENDENCE that Faisal had sought for so long was seen by the opposition as, at best, flawed and incomplete. True, it had delivered Iraq from the obvious and humiliating tutelage of Britain. But the residual authority and preferences given to the British were still significant, enough, in fact, to give credence to the opposition's claim that Iraq was still in thrall to the great power. There was some justification to that view. The independence of Iraq was conditional to the extent that Iraq's strategic direction did not clash with Britain's vital interests. There was no way of overlooking this reality. But Faisal did not claim, like Voltaire's Dr Pangloss, that all was well in the best possible of worlds. He was acutely aware of the conditions that Britain imposed on Iraq when agreeing to the 1930 Anglo-Iraqi Treaty. However, he followed in his usual pragmatic prescription of accepting what could be maximally extracted from his adversary rather than hanging on to impossible demands. He could see for himself that neighbouring Turkey and Iran had rid themselves to varying degrees of control by foreign powers, but Iraq was unlike these countries. Mustafa Kemal's war for independence gave him the authority and the power to make over his country in ways that were free from foreign influence. Reza Shah in his own way also worked to free his country from foreign interference. But he was unencumbered by a burdensome and internationally sanctioned regime of foreign protection and tutelage. Freeing Iraq from British oversight in domestic affairs benefited the king, but, more importantly, also benefited the narrow Sunni Arab political class. That is why opposition leaders such as Yasin al-Hashimi joined in the celebrations marking independence. Iraq's new status gave them a free hand to pursue their power struggles and grabs without the need to look over their shoulders. But as Faisal saw it, the greatest beneficiary of Iraq's independence would prove to be the Iraqi people themselves. It would provide a still fragmented and insecure country with the wherewithal to chart out its own political future, without severing its ties to an imperial power whose continuing support was essential for Iraq's own stability and prosperity.

Ever since his arrival in Iraq in 1921, Faisal had to fight three determining battles on three different fronts. The first involved the British, and the battle there involved the widening of the latitude given to Iraqis generally, and the king in particular, to govern the country. Power had to flow, seep or be extracted from Britain to Iraq, and this proved an exhausting process of negotiating, cajoling, confronting and intriguing against Britain. It required patience, perseverance and wisdom. But there was also frustration, anger and even despair evident in Faisal's conduct with the British. The British despatches sometimes talked of his irregular outbursts, temper tantrums and histrionics. The contradictory impressions given of his character by self-serving official reports gave ample ammunition to those who sought to question or disparage his qualities or his goals. But there was no doubt about Faisal's determination to upend the relationship with Britain, and he succeeded to a large extent. Iraq of 1932 bore no relationship to the half-formed and prostrate country of 1921. The second front was his struggle to achieve dominance over the emergent Sunni Arab political class, which in turn was riven with disputes and rivalries. Faisal shifted alliances within this class, but he always maintained links to even the most alienated. The ambitions of these leaders had to be kept in check, and his strategy was to maintain the palace as their main point of reference rather than the Residency, and block them from moving, or staying in outright opposition. He nurtured and took maximum advantage of the royal prerogatives to ensure his pre-eminence, if not his outright dominance, over the country's political life. By 1932, he was undoubtedly the country's premier political figure, more than a *primus inter pares* but less than an outright autocrat. It was no mean feat for an outsider with no roots in the country's social or political life.

The last and possibly the most problematic of his more than decade-long presence in Iraq was how to evolve a common identity and purpose for the country that would preserve for himself and his successors legitimacy, respect and honour with the country's myriad groups. This was an issue that Faisal wrestled with for all his life in Iraq. At certain periods, he was resented by important religious and civil leaders of the Shi'a community, for example, during the bitter struggles over the constituent assembly elections and the expulsion or self-exile of the *mujtahids*. The Kurds were also mainly sceptical, if not in outright opposition, to the unitary state that Faisal proposed, even though Faisal had sprinkled his administration with a proportionate number of Kurds. Tribal leaders were erratic in their support for his rule, and Baghdadi politicians competed with Faisal for their loyalties. The nascent intelligentsia and professional classes owed their existence to the king's strong advocacy of modernisation and higher education, but this did not stop them from extreme nationalism and a drift towards irreverence to the monarchy and even republicanism. In bald terms, what kept the country physically and politically united was the power and reach of the RAF, and beyond it the might of |an imperial power. But the British could not be expected to articulate a national vision for the country. It fell to Faisal to elaborate on the dilemmas of ruling Iraq.

Al-Mudhakara – Faisal's memorandum of 1932

Sometime between the autumn of 1931 and the winter of 1932, Faisal wrote a remarkable eight-page memorandum that he sent to the leading politicians of the country to read and comment on.[1] In it Faisal pondered on the nature of the country that he ruled and the difficulties and prospects of forging a common national purpose. The memorandum is remarkable in a number of ways, not only for its methodical treatment of Iraq's problems but also as a window into his thinking on matters of deep importance. There is no other similar document in modern Arab history – and precious few anywhere else like it, for that matter – in which a ruler lays out his innermost thoughts about the conditions and issues of his country. These matters are best left to private exchanges. Political leaders might discuss their views later in memoirs or reminiscences, when the effects of airing these opinions are limited. But Faisal's document is a systematic attempt to come to terms with the fundamental problems that face a ruler embarking on a course of national development. One can only speculate as to why Faisal sought formally to express his opinions in written form rather than in quiet one-to-one sessions with his advisers and ministers. The best explanation is that he wanted to leave his ideas for posterity and to dispel any speculation as to his true motives. The timing of the memorandum is also significant. It came at a time when the mandate was ending and Faisal could look forward to a period where his vision for the country could be put into effect without constantly looking over his shoulder at Britain. He genuinely sought to draw the country's varied and fractious political class into the dialogue for articulating a national vision for the country. He sent the memorandum to a broad spectrum of leaders, irrespective of whether they were supportive of the government or in opposition to it.[2]

Faisal wrote as follows: 'For a long time I had felt that there were views and opinions on how to manage the affairs of state expressed by my minsters and those whom I trust, that differed from my own views and opinions. I pondered on the reasons behind this . . . and finally concluded it was because they were uncertain as to my own views, thoughts and visions for the country, and how these could be organised and implemented . . . There are the factors and influences that affect the country's progress; some are positive and could be built upon while others are ruinous and destructive, such as ignorance and divided ethnicities, religions, sects, beliefs and natural environments. That is why I found it necessary to detail my thoughts and elaborate on my plan to combat these maladies and to establish the Kingdom on a firm foundation.'

Faisal characterises Iraq as a country that lacks the essentials of a cohesive social unit, namely a people 'united by a common ethnicity, set of beliefs, and religion. In this situation, [Iraq's] potential is scattered and its people divided against themselves.' Iraq's politicians must therefore hold the highest qualities of wisdom and competence, and be immune to personal, sectarian and extreme views. 'They must pursue a policy of justice, balance, alongside firmness, as well as greatly respect the traditions of the people, and not be pulled either towards reactionary or to extremist, counterproductive policies.' Faisal then goes on to define Iraq's conflicting political categories: modernising groups, including youth and government officials; traditionalists and reactionaries; Sunnis; Shi'a; Kurds; non-Muslim minorities; tribes; tribal leaders; and the 'great mass of ignorant people who are prepared to accept any evil idea without discussion or discernment'. Faisal warns against the single-minded pursuit of the goals of the modernisers in government, who are prepared to ride rough-shod over traditionalists on the spurious grounds that the views of traditional-ists were useless in the modern era. 'Ignoring the views of others, no matter how backward, is an error that cannot be forgiven,' he writes. The government does not have the force to impose its will on the mass of people and it 'has to proceed in a manner with which people are comfortable, without trampling over their traditions'. Faisal was also gravely concerned with the imbalance of force between the government and the people. The government disposed of 15,000 rifles while there were 100,000 rifles in private hands. 'This discrepancy has made me ponder and think, and to counsel wisdom on the government ministers and not to indulge in adventures.'

Faisal then goes on to describe Iraq in what has since become a classic, if controversial, characterisation.

> Iraq is a kingdom that is ruled by a Sunni Arab government established on the ruins of the Ottoman state. This government rules over a region of Kurds whose majority are uninformed, and which harbours individuals whose personal ambitions drive them to renouncing [allegiance to] Iraq on the grounds that it is governed by another ethnicity. [Iraq] has an uninformed Shi'a majority that shares the same ethnicity as the governing class, but whose oppression under the Turkish years blocked them from sharing in the fruits of government . . . This [has] opened a huge divide between the Arabs [of Iraq] divided as they are between these two sects. All of this has made this majority [the Shi'a], or at least certain individuals amongst them with personal ambitions, including religious

leaders, and those who unworthily seek positions in government, or have not
benefited materially from the new order, to appear as if they are still oppressed
simply because they are Shi'a. They entice this majority to abandon the new
state on the grounds that it is an unmitigated evil, and we must not ignore the
effects that such people have on the simple but ignorant people.

Faisal then details the position of the non-Muslim minorities who are encouraged by foreign powers to stay aloof from the state so as to pressure it for
more autonomy. The cohesion of the state is also threatened by the tribes,
whether Sunni, Shi'a or Kurd, who want to stay as independent from the state
as possible.

Confronted with these myriad problems and issues, the governing political
class is accused of being, in turn, Sunni-dominated, irreligious and exclusively
Arab. The governing class ignores the implications of these epithets at its peril.
It pushes for modernisation and believes it is stronger than its detractors. Faisal
then raises the spectre of Shi'a alienation and the threats this could pose for the
new state. 'I do not want to justify the claims of the unaware mass of the Shi'a,
but I will repeat what I have heard thousands of times . . . Taxes are borne by
the Shi'a. Death is ordained for the Shi'a while official positions are all for the
Sunnis. What is left for the Shi'a then? Even their religious days are given no
consideration . . . I say this only to illustrate my case, because of the huge differences between the sects that is exploited by evil-doers.' The litany of troubles
that Faisal enumerates extends to the other minorities, as well as to the tribal
leaders and the Bedouin mentality that dominated tribal thinking. 'All these
conflicts and grievances combine or clash and disturb the peace and tranquillity of the country. If they are not appropriately treated by timely, judicious and
material means, and these differences are displaced and a genuine patriotism
evolves to supplant religious and sectarian partisanship, a patriotism that can
only evolve out of continuous efforts and government direction, then our situation is truly dangerous.'

Faisal then provides a devastating critique of the condition of Iraq. 'In this
regard and with sadness, I have to say that it is my belief there is no Iraqi people
inside Iraq. There are only diverse groups with no patriotic sentiments. They
are filled with superstitious and false religious traditions. There are no common
grounds between them. They easily accept rumours and are prone to chaos,
prepared always to revolt against any government. It is our responsibility to
form out of this mass one people that we would then guide, train and educate.
Any person who is aware of the difficult circumstances of this country would
appreciate the efforts that have to be exerted to achieve these objectives. This is
the people for whom I have taken personal responsibility to form and mould,
and this is my view of them.'

The second part of Faisal's memorandum deals with the solutions that he proposed for dealing with this unacceptable condition. They were a complex blend of building the powers of the centralised state, especially its military capabilities, placing the state above sectarian biases while respecting the religious and ethnic diversity of the country, and putting a limit to the executive powers of the central government. The army, Faisal believed, should have the capability of facing two simultaneous insurgencies in the country. 'What I will ask of the army now is that it should be prepared to put down two uprisings that could fall, God forbid, in two different parts of the country that are far from each other at the same time.' Once the army possessed this capability, Faisal then proposed to introduce general conscription to build the army's strength to meet any foreign challenges. Faisal also recognised that the overwhelmingly Sunni component of the officer class of the Iraqi army had to change. He had earlier pushed for a special preparatory school for sons of tribal leaders from the overwhelmingly Shi'a south to prepare them for entry into the military academy, and had always taken a personal interest in seeing that the cohort of officer cadets had at least some Shi'a representation.[3]

Regarding the sectarian issue, Faisal proposes a series of measures that would draw the Shi'a closer to the state while increasing their opportunities to participate in the government. The government should exhibit no sectarian preference and should aim for the unification of the religious calendar of the two sects of Islam. He also called for a government-led effort to develop the shrine towns. '[The government] must develop the shrine towns so that they [the Shi'a] do not feel that the government is ignoring these sites which are sacred to all groups, and which are of historic importance that adorn the country.' Lastly, Faisal proposes to create special endowments for the Shi'a, so that their religious leaders did not feel that they were discriminated against in the apportionment of state resources and jobs. Faisal had earlier proposed the establishment of a special college of administration to improve the quality of the civil service as well as to attract a better sectarian and ethnic representation in the upper reaches of the bureaucracy. Once again, Faisal's proposals were met with resistance by senior political figures.[4]

In education policy, Faisal called for a system that would take into account the needs of each community while building up loyalty to the nation. This was in marked contrast to the education policies advocated by extreme Arab nationalists, especially the director of education, Sati' al-Husri, who wished to impose a uniform educational system with a strong Arab nationalist bias. 'It is necessary that our education policy reassures all the inhabitants of Iraq,' Faisal wrote, 'and that they [the Shi'a and the Kurds] will participate equally in the national effort with the people of Baghdad and Mosul. This will dispel the accusation that the government is exclusively Sunni and Arab as some malicious types from the Shi'a and the Kurds claim.' Aligned to this accommodating educational policy, Faisal calls for a large measure of administrative decentralisation. This was unexpected at a time when the modernising currents of opinion all demanded a powerful central state. 'I say, but with caution, that if we can grant the *liwas* [provinces] powers akin to the provincial councils of the Ottoman period, then this would be one of the ways that we could draw the inhabitants of the provinces to participate in the government.' Faisal also pushed to reduce the executive powers of the central state by a constitutional amendment that would separate the executive from the judicial authorities.

Faisal's attitude towards political freedoms and rights and democracy also found their expression in the memorandum. He was a temperate and accommodating man, but he was not accustomed to the modern notions of democracy. Faisal believed that Iraq's political fragmentation made it difficult to enforce the whole gamut of democratic rights without ensuing factionalism and chaos. A strong executive was essential to guide the country and propose and implement reforms, but Faisal was willing to accept an active press and opposition if it did not veer into destructive practices. 'We must not allow an opportunity for artificial parties, the press and individuals to unreasonably condemn the government by fabricating facts and misinforming the public. We must give them room to constructively and honestly criticise, within the bounds of courtesy, but those who do so unreasonably must be firmly censured.' He was insistent that civil servants must be completely apolitical in the conduct of their official business. 'A civil servant must know that he is an official above all else and a servant to any government in power.'

The memorandum also deals with important economic and fiscal issues. Faisal pushed for the passage of a land tenure law whose intent was to safeguard the rights and functions of landowners, agents and farmers. Faisal's concern was that the mildly redistributive aspects of the law would frighten large landowners, especially the tribal chiefs, into believing that the state was arrayed against them. The issue of land tenure and agricultural taxes was central to Iraq's economy and public finances. It was also a means by which tribal leaders and city merchants and politicians could get hold of large tracts of former state lands and turn them into personal fiefdoms. The iniquitous system that subsequently evolved, with its huge discrepancies in large ownership and the land hunger of the peasantry, were issues that had not come to the fore at the end of Faisal's reign.[5] Faisal's memorandum envisaged a role for the state in launching key industries that would help in the development of the country. Though not a believer in untrammelled state control over the economy, Faisal recognised that in a country with a weak modern sector and inadequate capital in private hands, the state had to involve itself in economic development projects. Faisal had supported large infrastructure projects, particularly in irrigation and flood control, but the conditions of the Great Depression had greatly affected Iraq. 'I say with all regret that agriculture in our country has collapsed, given our kingdom's distance from the main markets,' he wrote. 'We have invested millions in irrigation projects, but what are we going to do with the agricultural output? At the present time we cannot dispose of the output of our lands, and what will be our situation after the completion of these immense works? Is it only to build mountains of crops and look at them? What use is it if we are unable to reach foreign markets or at least domestic markets? Why spend all these millions before we are able to develop markets for our crops and are forced to rely on imports for the majority of our need?' Looking at the experience in Turkey and Iran, which obviously impressed him, Faisal called for an import substitution policy that would establish Iraq's economic independence. 'We [the government] must support, in meaningful ways, those of our people who are inclined towards business and entrepreneurship . . . And if no person comes forward to establish a profitable industrial venture, then the state must do so relying on its own resources in association and with private domestic capital if possible, and if not with foreign capital, or with both.' He also called for an early form of state-backed industrial policy. 'The government must establish a special department to study various types of industrial projects, and . . . start building the most important ones of them. The government must advise businessmen on how to establish smaller ventures and focus itself on the larger projects if the public is not prepared to establish such enterprises.'

'It is a cause of sadness and mockery together that we are putting up large edifices at huge expense, and building roads that cost millions of rupees; we forget the corruption and theft of the resources of this poor people that has seen not a single factory established to meet its needs,' Faisal wrote in conclusion. 'I would rather see a cotton ginning mill instead of a government building; or a glass factory than a royal palace.'

Faisal died a year and a half after writing the memorandum, so it had the features of a last will and testament to posterity about his vision for the country. However, it slipped into an undeserved obscurity. Although it has appeared from time to time in the texts of certain historical works on Iraq, only in a few instances has it been afforded its true significance. Only a very few of the political leaders to whom Faisal addressed the memorandum felt obliged to respond to it. 'Abd al-Karim al-Uzri was an assistant to the head of the royal *diwan* in 1933. (Later, he became an important political figure in monarchical Iraq and often minister of finance.) After Faisal's death, he tried to compile the responses of the political leaders to whom Faisal had addressed the note, but found only two detailed ones. They were from Naji al-Suwaidi and Naji Shawkat.[6] Some of the recipients of the note mentioned it in their memoirs but did not refer to their responses. Other leaders, such as Yasin al-Hashimi, Rashid 'Ali and Nuri al-Sa'id left no memoirs and therefore their responses are unknown. Ja'far Abu al-Timmen's reply was a meaningless three or four-line response.[7] It was a curious, even sinister, conspiracy of silence regarding one of the most important political documents in modern Iraqi history. It was not out of laziness or forgetfulness that the majority did not respond to Faisal, but rather because, coming from such an authoritative source, the memorandum raised uncomfortable issues and questions about the country. By responding, it would have obliged the respondents to take a position on the matters raised by Faisal. If they disagreed with the memorandum, they would have been negating what was a factual and objective assessment of the realities of the country and would have been forced to come up with a plausible alternative exposition of the issues facing Iraq.

Faisal and Arab unity

The 1930 Treaty and Iraq's admission to the League of Nations greatly strengthened Faisal's hand in foreign affairs and in the Arab region. Faisal's concern with Arab affairs, stretching from the Levant, Palestine and the Hijaz, remained vital and constant throughout the 1920s, but he was constrained in his ability to influence events and formulate policies by the overbearing presence of Britain's mandatory powers. It effectively relegated the conduct of Iraq's foreign affairs to Britain, and made any of Faisal's initiatives in dealing with Arab issues ultimately contingent on Britain's acquiescence. This undoubtedly upset Faisal. As soon as the mandate ended, Faisal quickly seized the opportunity provided by Iraq's release from the conditions of the mandate to put his imprint on the region. But he still had to contend with the realities of power in the Near East and the fact that Britain and France were by far the predominant forces in the area. Britain still had its troubled mandate in Palestine, and the French remained entrenched in Syria and Lebanon. In addition, Faisal's pan-Arab policies were now constrained by another factor: the realities of Iraq's complex ethnic and sectarian make-up and the unstable domestic equilibrium that could be easily threatened by misguided regional policies and adventures. In particular, the idea of Arab unity had to be carefully calibrated to appeal to the ethnicity of the Shi'a Arabs of Iraq without raising in them the parallel fear that unity with the majority Sunni Arab countries of the 'Fertile Crescent'[8] would further undermine their precarious role and position.

Faisal's pan-Arab views, which were sincerely held, would only make sense if they transcended the historical cleavages between the sects. *In extremis*, as, for instance, during the Ottoman period, the Shi'a of Iraq had been forced to look towards Persia for succour and guidance. Faisal had seen the deleterious effects of an inconsiderate form of Arab nationalism in the Nsouli affair and the sectarian passions that this could arouse. He had woken up late to the threats that the extreme forms of Arab nationalism being propagated in Iraq's schools by the theories of Sati' al-Husri and his acolytes might pose for the unity of the country. He more than hinted at this in his 1932 memorandum when he called for an educational policy that would respect the particularities of each community. The issue, however, would not go away. The large numbers of Syrians and Palestinians who were employed in Iraq's educational system were often resented, not only because of their foreign origin but also because they promoted a version of Arab history that was offensive to the Shi'a.[9] In one egregious incident in 1933, a certain 'Abd al-Razzaq al-Hassan distributed a pamphlet that questioned the racial origins of the Shi'a of Iraq and considered them to be heretics and subservient to Iran. Faisal's response was to jail the writer and to deplore the pamphlet in a letter that he wrote to the *mujtahid* Shaikh Muhammad Hussein Kashif al-Ghita'. Faisal's Arab nationalism was conditioned by his sensitivity to both the Shi'a and the Kurds, who formed the overwhelming majority of his country. The sense that his pan-Arab ambitions were somehow connected with his desire to dilute the Shi'a/Kurdish majority in Iraq does not really stand up to scrutiny. There is no doubt that he saw the inclusion of the Mosul province into Iraq as strengthening the viability of his state, but Mosul brought with it not only a substantial Sunni Arab population but also a large Kurdish and Turcomen population.

Faisal's pan-Arabism comprised a mixture of complex motives, including dynastic and personal ambitions, economic and strategic considerations – as well as a belief in the idea itself. Faisal did not abandon his schemes for Arab unity, or more accurately Arab confederation, because of the problematic effects it would have on the ethno-sectarian balance in Iraq. The idea that Iraq might act as the engine for an Arab renaissance, akin to the role that Prussia played in the unification of Germany, or Piedmont in that of Italy, had grown in the early 1930s.[10] Throughout the negotiations for the 1930 treaty, the British were impressed with the Iraqi team's concern regarding the effects of the treaty on other Arab countries, particularly Syria. Sir Francis Humphrys noted that the Iraqi government saw an independent Iraqi state as 'the first step towards the distant goal of Arab unity'.[11] And, *pace* the Iraqi opposition, so did Arab nationalist opinion outside of Iraq. Arab nationalists rejoiced in the independence that Iraq had achieved and compared it favourably with the increasing instability in mandate Palestine and the difficulties of the French in Syria. As the pan-Islamist and supporter of Arab unity, Shakib Arslan wrote in 1931, 'Iraq cannot be expected, at the present time, to achieve more than it already has in securing its rights ... and cannot safeguard its rights until the Arab unity that we call for is established.'[12] Greater unity amongst the Arab states carved out of the Ottoman Empire also made economic sense. The division of the Near East had severely disrupted traditional trade routes, especially along the axis that ran from Aleppo through Mosul to Iran. Increasing trade flows could only have a positive effect on Iraq's meagre public finances. Faisal took a personal interest in the development of the desert motor routes that linked Baghdad with Damascus and with Amman, and was a strong advocate of building a pipeline from Iraq's northern oil fields to the Mediterranean port of Haifa in Palestine.[13] He also pressured the Iraq Petroleum Company, the successor to the TPC, to construct a railroad alongside the pipeline.

The Syrian revolt of 1925 had pushed the French to entertain, at least for a while, the possibility of installing Faisal, or one of his brothers, as king over Syria. But these approaches, which had reached a climax of sorts during Faisal's visit to France in the autumn of 1925, retreated as the French reasserted their control over Syria. At best, the French had thought of Faisal as a mediating force with the Syrian nationalists, but these tentative approaches did not stop the Residency in Baghdad from filing alarmist reports about Faisal's revanchist intrigues and his ambitions to remount the Syrian throne. 'His excitable brain will again be filled with dreams of immediate restoration of glories of early Arab empire, and encouraged by him there will be a recrudescence here and in Syria of the extremist forms of Arab nationalism, deep calling to deep and each crying with other,' wrote Dobbs in feverish panic.[14] In reality, Faisal and al-Sa'adoun's government exhibited remarkable restraint in the face of the massive French force used against the Syrian rebels. Besides a committee formed under Yasin al-Hashimi's patronage to provide relief for the victims of the Syrian uprising, there was precious little that either Faisal or the government did to advance the idea of a Faisalian restoration in Damascus. Even the visit by the Syrian nationalist and pro-Faisal figure 'Abd al-Rahman al-Shabandar to Iraq in 1925 to drum up support for the cause of the Syrian rebels was met with official indifference. Faisal was too aware of the roadblocks that the British could throw against any scheme to advance his interests in Syria, and he was equally dubious that the Syrian rebels could overcome French supremacy in Syria, at least in the short term.

The Syrian issue remained dormant until Iraq had gained a measure of control over its affairs after the signing of the Anglo-Iraqi Treaty of 1930. Sensing that the climate had changed and that France was seeking a plausible way out of its Syrian quagmire, Faisal began to strengthen his support base in Damascus. In the summer of 1931, he sent Yasin al-Hashimi to Damascus to recruit a leading Syrian nationalist, Faris al-Khuri, to the cause of a Faisalian restoration in Damascus. Al-Khuri was a leader of the National Bloc, the main Syrian opposition group, and his support for Faisal was a major boon to Faisal's still-hesitant campaign to promote Iraqi–Syrian unity under his banner. In

September 1931 Faisal visited France, ostensibly to tour the Colonial Exhibition, and was feted by the government, which included a meeting with the president and lunch with Minister of the Colonies Paul Reynaud. The latter toasted Faisal as 'King of the Arabs'. Faisal's meeting with the French foreign minister, however, was no less encouraging. Berthelot, whom Faisal had known for years, suggested that the Syrians would be free to choose between a republic and a monarchy when France ceded power to an independent Syrian national government. In Paris Faisal also met with his Syrian supporters, including Faris al-Khuri and Ihsan al-Jabiri. Shakib Arslan, the exiled pan-Islamist advocate and Druze prince, was also in attendance. Arslan, who was based in Geneva, had been an indefatigable supporter of the Ottoman Empire, but he now viewed Faisal as the champion of the unity that he sought for the Arab lands. He even pushed Faisal's case as the right choice to be king of Syria with ibn Saud.[15] Arslan became a regular visitor of Faisal's during his summer retreats in Europe, first in Antibes in 1930 and then during Faisal's stays in Switzerland, usually in Berne. He also entertained Faisal privately at his flat in Geneva.[16] At these meetings, Faisal coordinated strategy with these Syrian leaders, encouraging them to push the National Bloc into supporting him as king of an independent Syria, united with Iraq.

Returning to Baghdad, Faisal despatched Rustum Haidar to Damascus to drum up support and to ensure the presence of a pro-monarchical group in Syria's parliament following the country's December 1931 elections. In the event, Faisal failed to create the basis of a strong revivalist monarchical movement in Syria, partly because the Syrian opposition was mainly in favour of a republican system, and partly because of factionalism inside the National Bloc. Neither did Faisal enjoy the whole hearted commitment of his own family to regaining the Syrian throne. His brother 'Abdullah also had his eyes on the throne, and he regarded Faisal's activities in Paris with alarm.[17] Also, now that the Syrian throne, no matter how fancifully, appeared to be up for grabs, other Arab kings jumped into the fray. The ex-khedive of Egypt, Abbas Hilmi, pushed for his own candidature, as did King Fuad of Egypt, and for a while Amir Faisal, ibn Saud's son, was mentioned as a possible king for Syria.

The British would have nothing to do with Faisal's unity schemes. After a period of prevarication, the Foreign Office came out firmly in opposition to Iraqi–Syrian unity, or indeed any unity that would overturn or modify the division of the Arab Near East. It feigned indifference to the Syrian throne being offered to the ex-king Ali, knowing full well the extreme improbability of France doing so, but it was dead set against any scheme that would bring Palestine into the unity formula, which would put an end to Britain's policy commitment to a Jewish National Home in Palestine. Drawing smaller states that were under British protection, such as Kuwait, into unity schemes was also an outcome that Britain was determined to avert.[18] On 20 October 1931 the Standing Official Sub-Committee on Middle East Affairs of the British cabinet concluded that Britain should prevent the union of Iraq and Syria and baldly stated that any attempt by Faisal to take the crown of Syria would be contrary to British interests.[19] In a most bizarre analysis of the prospects of Arab unity, the Foreign Office concluded that if Iraq and Syria were to merge, Iraqis would gravitate towards living in Damascus or Lebanon, which were more salubrious environments. Damascus was, after all, 'an infinitely pleasanter town than Baghdad'. French influence would then seep eastwards into Iraq, jeopardising the relationship between Iraq and Britain![20] It was therefore best to keep the Arab Near East divided into the zones of influence that had emerged out of the First World War.

Faisal, however, pushed ahead with his unity projects. They were remarkably similar to what later became known as the plans to unite the 'Fertile Crescent': Iraq, Syria, Lebanon, Transjordan and Palestine. Faisal's plans were best outlined by Nuri al-Sa'id in a discussion with a staff member of the Colonial Office in September 1932. In these talks, Nuri said that Faisal's aim was to create a confederation of Arab states that would include the countries of the Fertile Crescent, to which the Hijaz might be added after the death of ibn Saud. Faisal was confident that ibn Saud's realm would disintegrate after his demise, and that the Hijaz would then return to the Hashemite fold. Faisal was silent about the type of government that Syria would have, but he had no doubt that it would be drawn into Iraq's orbit. Transjordan would be absorbed into Iraq. The way for a confederated Arab state, under his leadership, appeared clear. 'His [Faisal's] objective is fixed,' wrote Humphrys, 'but the means whereby it is to be obtained are likely to be adapted to the tendencies of current events.'[21]

The Islamic Congress was held in Jerusalem in December 1931, to discuss the deteriorating situation of the Arabs of Palestine. Iraq actively participated in it, and in its wake, Arab nationalists, led by al-Istiqlal Party of Syria, called for holding a Pan-Arab Congress. Faisal seized on the idea and pushed for holding the congress in Baghdad. During his visit to Amman and Jerusalem in September 1932, he met with the organising committee of the congress and appeared to have impressed them with his ideas for Iraq–Syrian unity.[22] In November 1932 he despatched Yasin al-Hashimi to various Arab cities to enlist support for his plan for an Arab congress in Baghdad. Humphrys reported to Foreign Secretary Sir John Simon in detail on Faisal's plans: 'There can be no doubt that he [Faisal] still hopes and works for the close federation under the rule of his House of all the Arab territories in Asia . . . He has never ceased to nurse his Syrian supporters carefully nor to maintain close touch with the Nationalist elements in Syria . . . His plan is that the [Arab] congress should bring both unity among the Arabs by substituting the pursuit of a clearly-defined common aim for the present chaos of conflicting views . . . His Majesty also professes to believe that by gathering together a number of representative Arab leaders in Bagdad he will be able by demonstration to convince them of the reality of independence which Iraq has achieved.'[23] Britain quickly took a stand against holding the congress and Humphrys applied unrelenting pressure on Faisal to abandon the idea.

On 25 February 1933, Humphrys cabled London that Faisal had dropped the idea of holding a congress at least until the autumn of that year. Humphrys had raised the likelihood that France would feel threatened by such a meeting. Faisal wanted some confirmation as to Britain's true attitude towards Arab unity. 'He asked me,' Humphrys wrote, 'to acquaint him with the general attitude of His Majesty's Government towards the ideal of Arab unity, which he had so much at heart. Was it the same attitude as that which had been explained to him in 1921, or had we changed our views since then?' Whether it was asked disingenuously, as a *cri de coeur*, or even sarcastically, Faisal knew that uniting even a small part of the fragmented Arab lands would be an uphill struggle. He continued to enlist British support for his unity schemes by appealing to British interests, and how they could best be safeguarded by Iraq pulling the disparate states of the Near East into a coherent pro-British alliance. During his state visit to Britain in July 1933, Faisal held talks with Simon over the prospects for Arab unity under Iraq's leadership. He proposed to raise the issue of France's mandate in Syria in front of the League of Nations and demand that Syria be freed from French control. When the British once again raised their objection to the proposed Arab congress, Faisal's reply was that 'he attached far more importance to working out with His Majesty's Government a policy which would offer a reasonable hope of bringing about Arab aspirations than the congress, and provided such a policy could be agreed upon, he would exercise all his influence to prevent the congress from being held in Baghdad or elsewhere.'[24] Faisal received no reply for the Foreign Office as to Britain's 'true' policies in the Arab region, and within two months of Faisal's last visit to Britain, he was dead.

Palestine and the Zionist movement

Throughout the early part of his reign, Faisal was guarded in expressing his views on the situation in Palestine and the risks of increased tensions between the Palestinian Arab population and Jewish immigrants. He maintained friendly relations with the large Jewish community of Iraq and had open channels with their political, commercial and religious leaders. It was his confirmed view that Zionism would have little interest to the Jews of Iraq; they were as indigenous to the country as its Arab population. By the late 1920s, however, the mood in Iraq following events in Palestine had greatly soured. The demonstrations following Sir Alfred Mond's visit were just such an expression, and the risks to the Arab identity of Palestine began to exercise the nationalist clubs and political leaders. Attempts were made by some ministers to purge some of their Jewish staff, but these were resisted by Faisal. Rustum Haidar addressed a note to the concerned ministers, informing them of Faisal's displeasure at these measures and demanding their reinstatement.[25] However, it was the outbreak of large-scale inter-communal violence in Palestine in August 1929 that radically altered the landscape in Iraq. The genesis of large-scale organised anti-Zionist activities in Iraq could be traced to these developments. In Baghdad, leading politicians such as Yasin al-Hashimi and Ja'far Abu al-Timmen headed a committee to support the Palestinian Arabs. A large rally was organised at the Hyderkhana Mosque, evocative of the 1920 rebellion, in which speeches were made denouncing the Balfour Declaration and British policy in Palestine. The situation in Palestine and fervent anti-Zionism were quickly becoming the chief rallying issues for nationalist opinion throughout the Arab lands, and Iraq was no exception to this. Faisal encouraged the growing concern with Palestinian issues, partly as a matter of nationalist conviction, but also as part of his complicated political manoeuvrings with the British. The Residency in turn was loath to see anti-British sentiment grow in Iraq as a result of the conditions in Palestine. Under pressure from the Residency, Faisal and the then prime minister Tawfiq al-Suwaidi ordered the closure of two newspapers that carried incendiary reporting on the situation in Palestine. On 3 November 1929, during a meeting with the acting high commissioner Hubert Young, Faisal suggested that the British government might wish to have his views on the crisis in Palestine. He had obviously been preparing his thoughts on this matter. When the British government expressed its interest in Faisal's views, Faisal had his memorandum ready. It was his most detailed and considered view on the Zionist question and the appropriate policies for managing the growing confrontation between the Arab and Jewish population of Palestine.

Faisal's memorandum in the form of an eight-page letter to Young was dated 8 December 1929.[26] It opened with the two options open for Britian to handle the crisis: either rely on the use of force and ignore the views of the inhabitants; or 'endeavour to satisfy the inhabitants and the interested parties and as far as possible reconcile their demands. This would be the ideal course.' He quickly dismissed the first course, which would entail huge expenditure and involve the permanent stationing of a large military garrison in Palestine. The second course was the only viable option, but it would require a review of the pledges given to the Arabs and Jews regarding their conflicting claims to Palestine. He defined the two pledges given to the Arabs as those given to Hussein before and during the Arab Revolt, and those embodied in the Allied declaration of November 1918 following the Armistice. The pledge given to the Jews is embedded in the Balfour Declaration, but it is this pledge that is the source of the conflict. 'I believe that, but for the pledge made to the Zionists, there would have been no need for a discussion of the pledges given to the Arabs, because the latter are natives of the land and the Declaration of 1918 can bear no misconstruction or argument.' Faisal continues with an implied denunciation of the demands of radical Zionists. 'As regards the Zionists, they claim that the Balfour Pledge makes Palestine a national home for them. While claiming this the Zionists declare, notwithstanding their being a minority, that the object of that pledge is the establishment of a purely Jewish government in which nobody else shall participate. We find that they take no account of any other race even a race which possesses a crushing majority, and has been settled in the country for hundreds of years and holds the same sacred promises, and promises as they themselves claim to hold.' The only way out of this impasse was by reverting 'to the pledge responsible for the creation of this troubled situation and by interpreting it in such manner as will enable the determination of its scope and of the manner of giving effect to it'. Faisal then states his understanding of the meaning of a 'Jewish National Home'. The British government's oft-stated policy was that 'they did not intend to expel the Arabs, at once or gradually, from their home and replace them with Jews, with the object of establishing a purely Jewish government in Palestine, but that they only intended to find a place of refuge for the Jews . . . in order that if any Jew wished to emigrate he might find a place in which he could take shelter and reside'. Faisal's solution for the crisis in Palestine was based on this fundamental understanding of the meaning of the Balfour Declaration. The Arabs should then stop demanding its repeal, and the Jews must accept this final restrictive definition of the meaning of their national home.

The solutions that Faisal offered fell mainly inside his own schemes for Arab unity. The ideal outcome would be to push for a state that would combine Iraq, Syria and Palestine to form a 'national home for the Semitic race, both Arab and Jew'. He admitted that this outcome was 'far-reaching and complicated (or difficult) but is based on lofty principles', and therefore merited consideration. The second outcome was to unite Palestine with Transjordan, also a difficult possibility. The third, and the most realistic, was to form an elected national government in Palestine in which all parties remained silent about the Balfour Declaration, with a fixed quota for Jewish immigration limited by the country's absorptive capacity. The British response was at first tepid, and then turned negative. The British were not prepared to abandon the Palestine mandate. Faisal, on the other hand, doggedly pursued his proposals for Palestine and raised them once again with the British government during his state visit to Britain in July 1933. Sir Francis Humphrys, now the British ambassador in Baghdad, recorded the conversation that he had with Faisal at the Hyde Park Hotel, London on 13 July 1933. Faisal referred 'to the rising tide of Jewish immigration and to the steady deterioration of the political, social and economic situation of the Arabs'. He also expressed his confidence that the Arabs of Palestine would join in a representative government 'provided they were given an adequate representation and that a final limit was set to the flood of Jewish Immigration'. Controlling immigration was absolutely essential according to Faisal, 'otherwise in the near future the Arab would either be squeezed out of Palestine or reduced to economic and social servitude'. It was a prophetic warning of what was actually to transpire. Faisal also appeared to be sensitive to the accusation that his views on Palestine simply masked his ambitions to extend his rule and influence. He recognised that his friendly relations with Britain would be rendered difficult if a serious struggle were to break out between the Arabs and the Jews. Faisal also had some harsh words regarding the lease and sale of Arab land in Transjordan to Jews. His brother 'Abdullah had entangled himself in a scheme to sell land to Jewish settlers and to use the proceeds to develop his own properties. Faisal was indignant and launched an invective against his brother. In a meeting of 7 March 1933 with Humphrys, Faisal, 'gave vent to his feelings about 'Abdullah with quite unusual vehemence,' wrote Humphrys, 'declaring that he ['Abdullah] had brought disgrace and humiliation on his family and all but ruin on himself. His position, he said, was becoming impossible and the respect he enjoyed in his own coutry was rapidly dwindling.'[27] Faisal offered 'Abdullah to lease the land himself. 'Abdullah's reply moved Faisal to tears for his brother's sorry state. 'Abdullah complained of his powerlessness in his own country, and being forced to accept the ultimate humiliation of recognising ibn Saud as ruler in his own homeland of the Hijaz. 'Abdullah had reproved Faisal 'for his treachery to the Hashemite family [by settling with ibn Saud],' wrote Humphrys. 'Ever since then, Faisal had been personally anxious to prove that he was right and that 'Abdullah was wrong, and has been urging him to recognise Ibn Saud and face the inevitable.'[28]

A disastrous cabinet

Faisal's choice of Naji Shawkat to replace Nuri as prime minister was at best a stopgap measure. Naji had little independent political support and had spent most of his time as a senior functionary in one government post or another. He was born in 1893 in Kut in Iraq. His father, Shawkat Pasha, of Caucasian extraction, had been a deputy in the Ottoman Majlis. Naji himself was taken into the Ottoman army as a reserve officer and saw action in the Battles of Salman Pak and Kut in 1915. He was taken prisoner by the British army on its march on Baghdad and interred in an Indian prisoner-of-war camp, from which he joined the Arab Revolt. He returned to Iraq in 1919 and served as governor of several provinces in an administrative career that spanned the 1920s. He was a principled and decent man who suffered from chronic deafness, which made it difficult to communicate with him.[29] His government was composed of similarly bland functionaries. No one, including the high commissioner, thought it would last. Its prime task appeared to be to supervise the holding of general elections for a new Majlis that would replace the one that was packed with Nuri al-Sa'id's cronies. A new Majlis would also give Faisal the opportunity to woo back the opposition, especially Yasin al-Hashimi, to power. The opposition parties, led by al-'Ikha, participated in the elections with the sure knowledge that the palace would look favourably on their candidates this time. Naji's government delivered the type of parliament that Faisal sought. On 18 March 1933, Naji submitted his resignation as prime minister, the first and last time he would preside over a cabinet. Its achievements were meagre, one of the most notable being the introduction of driving on the right-hand side of the road after the British had previously obliged Iraqis to drive on the left!

Faisal's next prime minister was Rashid 'Ali. He had been appointed head of the royal *diwan* in June 1932 in a move that was partly aimed at coopting an opposition figure into the palace party, and as a means to apply pressure on Nuri's cabinet. Rashid 'Ali was an inveterate intriguer and an ambitious politician. His loyalty to Faisal, sometimes manifested in the most cloying expressions of fealty, never got in the way of his ambition. Though Rashid 'Ali's father was a member of the illustrious Gailani family, his mother came from humbler stock, a fact which coloured his personality and behaviour. His cabinet was dominated by Yasin al-Hashimi, who returned to office as minister of finance. Faisal had wanted the latter to be the next premier, but Yasin had declined. Rashid 'Ali, under Faisal's prodding, also brought in Nuri al-Sa'id as the foreign minister. Faisal believed that the cabinet, a modified version of the 'National Coalition' that he had long sought, should focus on urgent matters of economic and social development. Faisal also reckoned that the terms of the Anglo-Iraqi Treaty of 1930 would not be subject to further debate. He thought that he had secured, if not the support, at least the grudging neutrality of the main opposition leaders to its terms.

Behind the scenes, however, the former opposition leaders, now in office, were playing a double-game. They orchestrated a campaign to undermine the treaty and demand a revision of its terms, while in public insisting that they remained committed to it. The opposition to the treaty was also bolstered by the formation of the Ahali Group, a radical political grouping of mainly young professionals from prominent families. They issued a widely read newspaper, *al-Ahali*, which took a strident line against the treaty.[30] The cabinet also began to assert its powers in opposition to Faisal's wishes, as when it procrastinated in agreeing to allocate a plot of land for building a new British embassy. Bringing together all the 'big men' of Iraqi politics into one cabinet was not a recipe for constructive action, as Faisal had thought. It was turning into a vehicle for drawing power away from the palace. On the eve of his much-anticipated state visit to Britain in June 1933 as the monarch of an independent kingdom, Faisal was having second thoughts about the wisdom of his cabinet choices.

Faisal was keen to establish his international status as a king of an independent country, and a state visit to Britain was to be the most important step in this direction. The invitation from Britain was tardy in coming, though. It may have been expedited when the British heard that Mussolini had suggested that Faisal visit Rome in the summer of 1933. On 5 June 1933, Faisal left for Britain by way of Amman on the first leg of his journey. He was accompanied by a large entourage that included Foreign Minister Nuri al-Sa'id, Minister of Economy Rustum Haidar, Ali Jawdat, Tahsin Qadri and Faisal's personal physician Harry Sinderson. Faisal had a crowded agenda set out for his state visit, mainly focusing on economic and technical matters. At issue was the status of the Iraqi rail system, and the conditions under which Britain was to transfer ownership to Iraq. Faisal was to discuss the possibility of constructing a rail link between Baghdad and Haifa and was to seek loans to expand Iraq's railroad network and build its irrigation network.[31] The flight to Amman started uneventfully, but soon hit terrible weather. The entire party was violently air sick. A three-and-a-half hour flight instead took five hours. Faisal spent four days in Amman, and during that period Sinderson observed the interaction between the three brothers, Faisal, Ali and 'Abdullah. Sinderson did not think that 'Abdullah was much concerned with statecraft. He surrounded himself with retainers of no particular significance. His conversations were like harangues, in which he expostulated on one subject or another, frequently topics of a literary nature. One argument with Faisal involved the literary merits of Persia's greatest poets. They both agreed that the mantle of the greatest poet of Persia belonged to Firdausi, but Faisal much preferred the lyrical poetry of Hafez to the moralising intonations of Sa'adi, 'Abdullah's favourite. Another topic was the role of women in Islamic societies. Faisal was much in favour of women's emancipation, while 'Abdullah, true to his conservative instincts, thought that women should stay in seclusion.[32]

During his stay in Amman, Faisal arranged to travel to Jerusalem to meet the high commissioner in Palestine and to visit his father's grave. As Faisal's motorcade approached the outskirts of Jerusalem, it was stopped by an immense throng 'composed not only of Palestinians but also numerous Syrians,' wrote Sinderson. 'His Majesty [Faisal] was given a tumultuous reception and from the throats of thousands in unison was roared the catch-phrase, "Faisal,

King of the Arabs!" . . . Banners were raised and flags waved as the excitement mounted, and it was a full half an hour before anything like order was restored and the train of cars was able to move forward. Notice of the royal visit to Jerusalem must have been extremely short, and yet thousands of Palestinians and Syrians had got wind of it.'[33] Huge crowds also met Faisal as he approached the sanctuary of al-Aqsa Mosque. 'The procession was compelled to stop because of an ever larger concourse of wildly excited Arabs blocking the way,' continued Sinderson. 'I was of course well aware that His Majesty was held in very high esteem throughout the Middle East, but a demonstration of such magnitude as this both surprised and delighted me. The King was so affected by the size of the throng and the warmth of his reception that as he acknowledged the clamorous cries of salutations, tears were mingled with his smiles.'[34]

After his stay in Amman, Faisal travelled to Cairo by plane, where he made a courtesy call on King Fuad. Faisal was favourably impressed by the modernisation of the city and the relative emancipation of Egyptian women. The entourage then took the ship from Alexandria to Naples in Italy. In Naples, Faisal indulged his interest in archaeology by visiting the sights of Pompeii. En route to England he stopped in Brussels, where he visited King Albert of the Belgians, returning a private visit that Albert had made to Iraq in the spring of 1930. Arriving at London's Victoria Station on 20 June 1933 off the boat train from Ostend to Dover, Faisal was struck by the full panoply of British pomp and grandeur. He was met by King George V, the prince of Wales and the duke of Gloucester. The duke of York had met Faisal at Dover and travelled with him to London. Faisal emerged from the train in splendid ceremonial attire, wearing a plumed helmet. He then proceeded in an open carriage with King George through London's crowded streets to Buckingham Palace. It was the most impressive welcome that London had given to any state visitor for years. The official state visit went on for the customary three days and included endless rounds of official meetings, state dinners and banquets.

Faisal had planned to spend a further month in Britain in a private capacity, but these days were also filled with visits, displays and celebrations. He visited military installations, attended aerial acrobatics at RAF Hendon, a pageant at Greenwich, the Wimbledon tennis finals in the company of King George V, and made a trip to Torquay and Torbay to witness manoeuvres on board HMS *Renown*. (His host at Torquay had been Admiral Sir William James, and Faisal was delighted to learn that he had been the child model known as 'Bubbles', whose visage was on the famous brand of Pears soap, widely available in Iraq.) Faisal gave a short speech on board the ship in halting English. In Baghdad, he had wanted to improve his language skills and hired a Lebanese teacher, a Monsieur Debbas, to help him with his enunciation and delivery. On this trip, he felt confident enough to deliver a number of speeches in English. Faisal later spent ten days in Scotland, visiting Edinburgh, and then a few days of rest and recreation at the Gleneagles Hotel in the Highlands. He was in dire need of this break, His doctor, Harry Sinderson, was concerned about his physical well-being. As Sinderson wrote of this time, 'His appetite was now poor; he was sleeping badly and smoking far too much, and I begged him to reduce his consumption of cigarettes. He attributed recent excess to continuing bad news from Iraq and promised to halve their number as soon as existing Moslem-Assyrian tension in the north of the country came to an end.'[35]

While Faisal was being feted in Britain and idolised by the press, Iraq was about to be convulsed by the gravest crisis since its independence – one which surely hastened Faisal's premature death.

The Assyrian Crisis

Most of the Assyrians in Iraq had originally come from the Hakkari mountainous borderlands between Iraq and Turkey. In 1915 they rose against the Ottoman state and were driven en masse to Iran and then southwards to Hamadan, where they established contacts with British forces. The British resettled them in camps in Baqubah in Iraq and then in 1920 moved them to the Mosul area. By the mid-1920s, the Assyrian population in Iraq numbered about 40,000, a quarter of whom were indigenous Iraqi Assyrians and the rest transplanted refugees from Turkey. The vast majority of these refugees had found work in the major towns of Iraq, or had settled in predominantly Assyrian villages inside Iraq. Only a few hundred remained unsettled. Several hundred of the Assyrian men were also recruited into the Iraq Levies, a British-trained and officered force, established in 1922, which remained distinct from the Iraq army. The Assyrians were known for their martial qualities and the British inculcated in them a sense of distinct separateness and haughty superiority to Arabs.[36] Bell noted in her diaries that British officers 'constantly reminded the Levies that they're good British soldiers and not dirty little Arabs'.[37] The resentments of ordinary Iraqis against the Levies, with their distinct headgear and swaggering attitude, were intense. The Levies were the face of British dominance, guarding British-owned companies and the railroad, posted in front of the RAF bases, and employed as mess boys and batmen. Few of the Assyrians took out Iraqi nationality and were little interested in being integrated into Iraq as one of its many minorities.

When the Anglo-Iraqi Treaty was signed, the Assyrians, working through their religious and temporal leader, Patriarch Mar Shimun and his formidable aunt Surma Khatun, petitioned the League of Nations for protection from the new Iraqi state. The League had demanded assurances from Iraq regarding the treatment of minorities before the country was granted admittance. The Iraqi government had been forthcoming, and religious and ethnic rights had been expressly confirmed in legislation and in government statements and declarations. But Faisal was also aware that the pretext of protecting minority rights was a tool often used to perpetuate foreign control and interference. Faisal had met Mar Shimun in August 1932 in 'Amadiyya in the north of the country, to dissuade him from travelling to Geneva and pressing with his petition. However, Mar Shimun had insisted and also had the audacity to ask that Faisal arrange to provide him with a special passport to travel to Geneva to present the Assyrian case, which was tantamount to seceding from the country.[38] But Mar Shimun returned to Iraq in January 1933 empty-handed. The Assyrians were advised to work for their rights within a unitary Iraqi state.[39]

On the eve of Faisal's departure to Europe, however, the Assyrian situation was still unsettled, and tensions had been mounting in the north of the country between Assyrians and the local inhabitants. Mar Shimun had been invited to Baghdad towards the end of the May 1933 to discuss the resolution of the outstanding issues. The government had been particularly sensitive to the status of the patriarch, offering him a seat in the senate and a handsome stipend. They were also prepared to recognise his religious authority over his people, but not his temporal power. The government needed his active cooperation for a policy of resettling the Assyrians, but in fact Mar Shimun had threatened those of his people who cooperated with the government, and had rejected the limitations of his powers to the religious realm.[40] Meanwhile, one of his followers, former Levies officer Yaqu Ismail, had taken to the mountains with two hundred men, calling for resistance to the Iraqi government. The commander of the Iraqi forces in the north, Colonel Bakr Sidqi, responded by calling a state of emergency without prior clearance from the government. Sidqi, a forty-three-year-old Kurdish ex-Ottoman officer, was a hard-living, hard-drinking and belligerent man, prone to taking matters in his own hands. 'In a country where every kind of vice is rampant, he is a byword for debauchery,' said a British report on Sidqi. He was also ambitious, incorruptible and a strong leader who seized an opportunity when he saw it. Faisal recognised the dangers in having a person of this profile in charge of operations in the north. Before his departure to Europe, Faisal told the British chargé d'affaires, George Ogilvie-Forbes, that he intended to remove Bakr Sidqi from his command, and offered to despatch the chief of staff, Taha al-Hashimi and the minister of interior, Hikmat Suleiman, to Mosul to help in defusing the tensions.[41] But Bakr Sidqi was popular with his officers, as was the anti-Assyrian line that he espoused.

The crisis escalated when the Iraqi government, with the support of the British adviser to the Ministry of Interior, decided to detain Mar Shimun in Baghdad at the YMCA hostel until he agreed to give the desired assurances to the government. He was allowed to travel freely inside Baghdad, but could not leave for Mosul. There was an international uproar after the news of the arrest of Mar Shimun, and the British press launched an attack on Iraq's disregard for its minorities. Faisal, who was then a guest at Buckingham Palace, immediately cabled the cabinet to release Mar Shimun.[42] Rashid 'Ali replied by stating that the return of Mar Shimun to the north without giving the necessary undertakings to the government would simply embolden the Assyrian rebels. Faisal was incensed that the government did not follow his advice, and reaffirmed his position that releasing Mar Shimun would earn international good will, while leaving the government the option of confronting the mutineers if the situation deteriorated further.[43] The cabinet, however, supported the prime minister in his position to keep the patriarch under detention in Baghdad. At this juncture, the cabinet's unwillingness to accede to Faisal's recommendations must have raised serious alarm bells with him, but he was not willing to push his case any further. He left for Switzerland for medical treatment in mid-July 1933, with a simmering crisis going on in Iraq. It took a turn for the worse on 21 July when two Levies officers crossed the Iraqi border into French-controlled Syria with several hundred armed men. All Assyrians of military age had disappeared from their villages, and there was an ominous concentration of armed Assyrians on the Syrian side of the Iraq border. This movement had likely been planned and instigated by Mar Shimun. The threat of these armed Assyrians returning to Iraq prompted Bakr Sidqi to move forces to the frontier to block the return of any armed Assyrians. The government also asked the French authorities to disarm the Assyrians, and the French initially complied with the request. However, within a few days the French had returned their arms to the Assyrians, who then crossed back into Iraq in force on 4 August and attacked Iraqi army positions at Dayrbaun, near the border. A subsequent report by the British acting inspector general of the Iraqi army, Brigadier General E. H. Headlam, puts the blame squarely on the Assyrians, who acted premeditatedly in attacking the Iraqi army garrison.[44]

Faisal in Berne was watching the escalation of events with evident alarm. He cabled his son Ghazi, who for the first time was acting as regent, to inform the cabinet that any Assyrians returning to Iraq who showed remorse should not be forcibly disarmed. The cabinet rejected Faisal's recommendation and a confrontation loomed between the government and the king. Faisal had no choice but to interrupt his medical treatment and return to Iraq. The messages cautioning moderation that he had sent to Baghdad were partly prompted by the British, but now the British were piling on the pressure for him to return to Baghdad to involve himself directly in the management of the crisis. Faisal was quite confident that he could diffuse the crisis within a few days, and wanted to return to Baghdad with the least official fuss. He arrived in Baghdad on 2 August 1933 accompanied by Nuri al-Sa'id. He was met by Ghazi and the cabinet at the aerodrome, but there was no official announcement of his arrival.

The Assyrians overran the Dayrbaun base but it was later recaptured. There were credible stories of Assyrian atrocities committed on Iraqi army officers and men. Not to be outdone, Bakr Sidqi executed fifteen Assyrian prisoners whom Kurdish tribesmen had captured and disarmed.[45] But the attack on the army post at Dayrbaun shocked Faisal and panicked the government. There was genuine fear that the armed Assyrians, secretly backed by the French, would ignite the entire north of Iraq in an insurrection that the nascent Iraqi army would be unable to put down. A defeat for the army under such circumstances would destroy the integrity of the Iraqi state. Faisal's attitude towards the Assyrians hardened. For two days Faisal did not eat and chain-smoked. He even spoke of moving north, rallying the Shammar, Jubur and other tribes, and personally leading the counter-attack against the Assyrians. He was not particularly concerned about the ensuing deaths of mutinous Assyrian men, but villages, women and children had to be protected.[46] By mobilising ill-disciplined and irregular Kurdish forces and Arab tribes against the Assyrians, Faisal might have set the stage for the excesses that ensued. And these were quick in coming.

Bakr Sidqi had in fact rapidly regained the initiative after the Dayrbaun incident and had succeeded in bringing most of the rebellion under control. A mixture of ruthlessness and determination, as well as the use of Iraqi planes for bombing and strafing had reduced the rebellion. However, he purposefully misinformed the government and Faisal of the true position in order to harvest the subsequent glory that was to come to him for suppressing a dangerous rising. In the subsequent reprisals after the rebellion had died down, a detachment of Iraqi troops under Ismail 'Abbawi Tohalla, by all reports a brutal man, attacked the Assyrian village of Summayl. The village had been swollen by Assyrian refugees fleeing from the looting and mayhem that accompanied the collapse of law and order in the area. On 10 August 1933 the outskirts of the village had come under attack by looters from Arab and Kurdish tribes. On the following morning, Tohalla's men came into the village and rushed to join the generalised looting. In the process the army detachment, either independently or alongside the tribesmen, began the systematic killing of unarmed villagers, mostly men. Three hundred and five men, four women and six children were slaughtered.[47] It was a terrible episode that brought the condemnation of the world, not only on Iraq but also, by inference, on Faisal.

Last weeks in Iraq

Faisal was in no way responsible for this atrocity. The Summayl massacre could only cast his rule in the worst light, notwithstanding the inhumanity of the outrage. There is no episode in Faisal's life where he exhibited any trace of acquiescence in gratuitous violence in a military situation, let alone against unarmed civilians. It was completely out of character; but there is also no doubt that he wished to smother the Assyrian rebellion lest it destroy his own kingdom in Iraq. After the Dayrbaun debacle, Faisal faced what he thought was the possibility of defeat of the Iraqi army by the well-trained former members of the Levies. He undoubtedly overreacted by drawing tribesmen into the conflict on the side of the government forces. Nuri al-Sa'id himself confided to the British ambassador in Baghdad much later in 1936 that 'In the matter of the killings of the Assyrians, King Faisal had been the chief culprit. What had been done had been the result of his directions'. At the time Nuri was taking refuge in the British embassy on account of the after-effects of a coup engineered by Bakr Sidqi. What Nuri implied was that Faisal did not want to hold back in the use of force against the Assyrians, the stakes were simply too high. But that is a leap from accusing him of direct responsibility for the Summayl massacre. Faisal had no knowledge that most of the Assyrian rebels had surrendered by 9 August 1933.[48]

When news of the atrocities reached Baghdad, the British embassy demanded an immediate end to the operations of the Iraqi army, and set up an inquiry to investigate the details of the events at Summayl and the punishment of the officers responsible. Faisal went along with these demands. An impartial inquiry would be necessary to assuage international opinion and avoid an intrusive investigation by the League of Nations. British public opinion was also greatly aroused. Archbishop of Canterbury Cosmo Gordon Lang took a special interest in the fate of the Assyrians. (In fact, an earlier archbishop had sent an Anglican mission to the Assyrians in 1886, and it was thanks to this mission that the Assyrians became known in Europe.) So did King George V, who showed great interest in the evolving crisis. Underlying the British position was the barely concealed belief that it was Faisal who had been behind the calamities in the north. The British had set their minds on Faisal putting things aright, and deemed his presence in Baghdad essential to regaining the government's credibility and deflecting public opinion in Iraq from ascribing responsibility for the Assyrian crisis on the British themselves.

Popular indignation about the Assyrian rebels after their attack on the army had reached fever pitch. There was little doubt as to the party that the public held responsible for these events: it was the British. For how else could the Assyrians, the pampered protégés of the British, deign to launch an attack on the army without British connivance? Was it not in Britain's interest to show the impotence of the Iraqi army and state in the face of the Assyrians' rebellion? Rumours fed the public's anger: that the Assyrians forced wounded Iraqi troops to eat the flesh of their dead comrades; that T. E. Lawrence was in the north personally organising and leading the rebellion against the Iraqi state; that British intelligence officers were guiding the Assyrians every step of the way. The mob was braying for the lives of Mar Shimun and his aunt. Both were served with deportation orders on 17 August and left Iraq for good. They were ferried to Cyprus on separate RAF flights. Faisal secretly agreed to provide Mar Shimun with a stipend of £65 sterling from his private purse. The hero of the hour was not Faisal, but the Iraqi army and its commander in the north, Bakr Sidqi. Crown Prince Ghazi, who had openly stood by the Iraqi army and Bakr Sidqi, had also won the adulation of the crowds.

Faisal was caught in these swirling eddies. The British did not believe that he was seriously ill. When Nuri informed George Ogilvie-Forbes on 14 August that Faisal was unwell and wanted to return to Switzerland to continue his treatment, he was quickly rebuffed. Faisal had wanted air transport from the British to take him to Egypt, after which he would take a normal commercial flight, but the Foreign Office wanted him to remain in Iraq at least until Humphrys returned from leave. Earlier, Ogilvie-Forbes had met with Faisal to discuss the removal of Bakr Sidqi from his command, but Faisal curtailed the meeting, complaining of fatigue. Ogilvie-Forbes, obviously dubious of Faisal's illness, wrote insensitively to the Foreign Office, 'I shall continue to haunt him with this.' The tone of Ogilvie-Forbes messages to London became scathing, even insulting to Faisal. Ogilvie-Forbes was a staunch Catholic and the massacre of Summayl had affected him greatly. He believed that Faisal was feigning illness to escape responsibility for taking remedial and unpopular measures. He accused Faisal of 'taking refuge in his harem and is not to be seen', when in actual fact he had only retired to rest at his Harthiya palace. On another occasion, he visited Faisal who was in bed and scoffed at his effete application of cologne, a common eastern custom to ward off germs. Faisal's medical advisers all prescribed immediate rest in an agreeable climate, but Ogilvie-Forbes did not believe a word of it. In fact, Faisal was dangerously ill and exhausted. It was only after Humphrys had returned to Baghdad on 23 August that the tone of the cables from the Baghdad embassy changed. 'I have consulted leading British officials here about King Faisal's continued stay in Baghdad and they are of the opinion that his health would probably break down completely and he would be unfit for the heavy burden of reconstruction and legislation which awaits him in Autumn. I must therefore acquiesce in his disappearance on September 1st,' wrote Humphrys.[49] Other Iraqis, including Ja'far al-'Askari, the Iraqi minister in London, were also of the opinion that Faisal had exaggerated his illness to avoid staying in Iraq. 'The King's departure at this moment would amount to 'Abdication . . . If the King disappeared, the last hope for establishing the country of Iraq as a nation might be lost,' he wrote.[50]

Public opinion had also veered sharply against Faisal. The widespread notion was that Faisal had counselled a moderate course regarding the Assyrians. Few knew that he had sharply swung course after the Dayrbaun attack on the Iraqi army. There was also a sense that Faisal was not quite committed to the actions of the Iraqi army, and that he would buckle under British pressure and remove Bakr Sidqi from his command. It was ironic that the army on which Faisal had pinned so many hopes would now be seen as the heroic protector of the state with no reference to the efforts that Faisal had put into its build-up. On 26 August the whole of Baghdad turned up to welcome the army units that had participated in crushing the Assyrian rebellion. The delirious crowds cheered the troops and shouted out the names of Bakr Sidqi and Crown Prince Ghazi. There were few cheers for Faisal, even as the crowds assembled in front of the Royal Palace and Faisal greeted them from the balcony.[51] A few days later, Bakr Sidqi himself arrived in Baghdad. It was said that 50,000 turned up to welcome him at the aerodrome. His triumphant procession marched through the streets of Baghdad and paraded in front of the Royal Palace. Faisal stood at his balcony to salute the victorious officer. It was a watershed moment for Faisal.

Faisal prepared to leave Iraq on 2 September 1933. There were barely fifty people to see him off at Baghdad's aerodrome. He was a very sick man, buffeted by baseless chatter about his 'Abdication, with an army that had grown danger-ously and arrogantly powerful. His last message to the Iraqi people on the eve of his departure held a premonition of his impending fate. 'I will not stint in the service of my people and country no matter how much it will cost me,' he said.

Faisal's plane took him to Cairo, where he spent a day before taking a flight to Switzerland. One of the last people to see him in Egypt was the Lebanese writer and Arab nationalist figure As'ad Daghir. They met on the hotel's terrace overlooking the famed Azbakiya Gardens. Daghir had been involved with the preparations for the Arab Congress and was concerned that Iraq might not sponsor the congress after all. Faisal looked tired and haggard, but perked up when Daghir gave him some encouragement on his handling of the Assyrian crisis. Daghir was moved by what Faisal said to him in reply. 'We can never accept the kind of life that our British allies have planned for us. We have only remained patient until now because of our weakness and our needfulness. This situation can continue until the volcano of resentment and anger inside us erupts. Or we unite our positions and close ranks. In that way, our will becomes manifested and both our friends and enemies will take note of us.' Daghir saw Faisal off at Cairo railway station where he was to take the train to Alexandria, and thence a plane to Europe. '[Faisal] continued to talk to us from his carriage's open window until the train began to move. I then experienced a feeling that I could not explain. My eyes welled up with tears and I gazed at that great and beloved king with a look of love and hope . . . I did not know that this would be my last farewell.'[52]

Six days later, Faisal lay dead in the Bellevue Palace Hotel, in Berne, Switzerland. He was as ill as he had said he was.

EPILOGUE: FAISAL THE GREAT

Faisal's life ended just when he had approached his full political maturity and at a time when independent Iraq, and indeed the broader Arab world, was in dire need of his leadership. The epithet 'great' can be fittingly applied to Faisal. His contemporaries instinctively felt the absence of a great leader when news of his demise reached them, and the sense of severe loss permeated their reflections on Faisal in their memoirs and reminiscences. Sati' al-Husri, neither a sentimentalist nor a man to mince his words, said flat out that Faisal deserved to be called Faisal the Great.[1] He had all the qualities of a great political leader: acute intelligence, flexibility and pragmatism, and a desire to learn and willingness to adapt. Faisal was comfortable with all kinds of people, from tribal chiefs and ordinary Bedouins to European diplomats and courtiers, from generals and proconsuls of empire, to Arab nationalists and *mujtahids*. Moderation, realism and a single-minded focus on the final goal were the hallmarks of Faisal's dealings with individuals, tribes, nations and empires. Faisal also had the drive and motivation to tackle the huge obstacles that were strewn in his path and to recover from setbacks that would have felled another person. He was undoubtedly ambitious but not so much for his glory or for that of his family or dynasty. Rather, it was for the Arab states that emerged from the wreckage of the Ottoman Empire. The Arabs deserved their place in the comity of civilised nations. If that could not be achieved inside the broad Arab confederation that he envisaged, then it had to be done through the territorial states with which the Allies pockmarked the Near East in place of the grand empire of the Ottomans. The core of his personal and political perspectives was a profound devotion to the cause of Arab renascence, expressed by an equal dedication to the betterment of the kingdom over which he finally ruled: Iraq.

Nearing the centenary of the outbreak of the First World War, that cataclysmic event without which it would be inconceivable to imagine the modern Near East, one is reminded of another great figure, whose life criss-crossed the fall of empires, a global conflagration and the birth of new states. Faisal's life bears a remarkable similarity to that of the Liberator Simón Bolívar. Both were born into the elites of outlying provinces of empires, the Ottoman and the Spanish, respectively. Both took up arms against the metropolitan power in the middle of a global conflict, the First World War and the Napoleonic Wars. Both presided over the creation of new states. Both died, away from their countries at a relatively young age: fifty in the case of Faisal and forty-seven in the case of Bolívar. Bolívar and Faisal also shared common ideals and goals, notably the unity of their liberated lands in one grand political entity or confederation. Both had to deal with leading countries that were deeply divided: by race and class in the case of Bolívar; by ethnicity and sect in the case of Faisal. They also shared many personal characteristics: generosity; courage under fire; a charming disposition. In their campaigns, both led their forces by example and out in front.

But here the narrative diverges. Faisal's reputation was at its height immediately after his death and then slowly percolated away; Bolívar's, on the other hand, was swiftly eclipsed after his death, but then rehabilitated. He was then elevated to an almost mythical heroic figure and a veritable cult has been built around him. A country was named after him (Bolivia), and another attached the Bolívarian prefix to its formal title (Venezuela). But why these differing outcomes in what are, after all, remarkably similar stories?

Greatness in a leader can only be uncontested if there is no plausible and sustainable counter-narrative. It was to Faisal's enormous detriment as a historical figure of the first rank that his time was marked by his continuous struggle to break free from the suffocating embrace of Britain. The division of the Near East, the imposition of mandates and the establishment of Israel are all potent factors that have been used to undermine the achievements of Faisal, if only by inference. What does greatness mean if your lands are divided and handed over to foreign powers? If your key ally is also the one who has sown the seeds of instability and conflict in your region? But in fact these undeniable realities, when contextualised, add to, rather than diminish, Faisal's greatness. It requires superhuman strength to be able to swim towards your goal while there is a ball and chain tied to one of your legs. Faisal had to exert enormous effort to struggle even partly free from the constraints imposed on him, and he finally succeeded in doing so, even though his victory was tentative and short-lived. Bolívar, on the other hand, had few of Faisal's constraints, and his reputation as *el Libertador* is now unchallenged. Even so, Faisal's constraints did not paralyse him into dependency, despondency or inaction. They spurred him onwards, even at the end, at the cost of his health. No country will be named after him, and the title 'Liberator' will not be applied to him. Nevertheless, in the modern history of the Arabs it would be hard to find an equivalent figure who combined the qualities of leadership and statesmanship with the virtues of moderation, wisdom and essential decency.

◆◆◆◆◆❖❖◆◆◆◆◆

NOTES

Prologue – September, 1933: Death of a King

1. Musa al-Shabandar, *Dhikriyatt Baghdadiya: al-Iraq bayn al-'Ihtilal wal Istiqlal*, Riad El-Rayess Books, London and Cyprus, 1993, p. 132.
2. Letter from Heath Riggs, chargé d'affaires, US Embassy, Berne to Secretary of State, State Department, Washington D.C., No. 3071, 6 September, 1933.
3. Muhammad 'Abdin Hammadeh and Muhammad Tayseer Dhibyan, *Faisal Ibn al-Hussein: Min al-Mahad illa al-Lahd*, Part I, Al-Matba'a al-'Asriya, Damascus, 1933, p. 49; Muhhamad Yunus al-'Abadi, ed., *Mudhakarat al-Malik Faisal al-'Awal, Malik al-Iraq*, Amman, 2002, pp. 83–89.
4. Muhammad 'Abdin Hammadeh and Mohammad Tayseer Dhibyan, op. cit., pp. 49–50.
5. Musa al-Shabandar, op. cit., p. 132.
6. Ibid.
7. Muhhamad Yunus al-'Abadi, op. cit., pp. 86–87.
8. *Daily Express*, London, 12 September 1933.
9. Foreign Office (FO) FO 371, E5519/16924, letter no. 211/7/23, Howard Kennard, Berne, to George Rendel, Foreign Office, 14 September 1933.
10. *Daily Express*, London, 12 September 1933.
11. FO 371, E6202/16924, F. Humphrys, Baghdad to George Rendel, Foreign Office, letter, Personal and Secret, 5 October 1933.
12. Musa al-Shabandar, op. cit., pp. 132–34.
13. Ibid., p. 134.
14. Message and letter from Captain Drummond, No. 3009/68, HMS *Despatch*, 12 September 1933 and 14 September 1933.
15. Muhammad 'Abdin Hammadeh and Muhammad Tayseer Dhibyan, op. cit., pp. 56–59.
16. Ibid., E. Keith Roach, District Commissioner, Palestine to The Chief Secretary, Palestine High Commission, *The Passing of King Feisal*, 17 September 1933.
17. 'Abd al-Razzaq al-Hasani, *Tareekh al-Wizarat al-Iraqiya*, Vol. 3, 7th edn, Dar ash-Shu'oun al-Thaqafiya, Baghdad, 1988, pp. 313–15.
18. Ibid.
19. P. Knabenshue, Baghdad to State Department, Washington, D.C., No. 194, Diplomatic, 19 September 1933.
20. 'Abd al-Razzaq al-Hasani, op. cit., pp. 56–59.
21. Muhammad 'Abdin Hammadeh and Muhammad Tayseer Dhibyan, op. cit., pp. 61–67.
22. Ibid.
23. BBC Broadcast by Field Marshal Viscount Allenby, on Friday, 8 September 1933, quoted in Mrs Steuart Erskine, *King Faisal of Iraq*, Hutchinson, London, 1934, pp. 3–4.
24. Muhhamad Yunus al-'Abadi, op. cit., pp. 106–07.
25. Khalil Ibrahim al-Nabout, *Ruwayat Wathbat al'Arab, Aw al-Amir Faisal ibn al-Hussein*, Imprimerie Rustum Hnos, Buenos Aires, 1933.
26. Grace Dickinson Sperling, *Feisal, The Arabian*, Ralph Fletcher Seymour Publishers, Chicago, 1933. The last lines read: 'Abu Ben Adam [Father of the Sons of Adam – or God] write on a white paper / And write with a golden pen / The name of Feisal of Iraq / Who loved his fellow men.'

27. See, for example, the influential work of Anis Sayegh, *Al-Hashimiyun wal Thawra al-'Arabiya al-Kubra*, Dar al-Tai'a, Beirut, 1966.

28. For example, 'Ala Jassim Muhammad, *Al-Malik Faisal al-'Awal, Hayatahu wa Dawrahu as-Siyasi*, Maktabat al-Yaqdha al-'Arabiya, Baghdad, 1989; 'Abd al-Majid Kamil al-Takriti, *Al-Malik Faisal al'Awal wa Ta'sis al'Dawlat al-Iraqiya al-Haditha*, Dar al-Shu'oon al-Thaqafiya al-'Amma, Baghdad, 1990; Muhammad Mudhaffar al-Adhami, *Al-Malik Faisal al-'Awal: Dirasat Wathaqi'iya fi Hayatihi wa Dhuroof Mamatihi al-Ghamidha*, Dar al-Shu'oon al-Thaga fiyoe, Baghdad, 1919; Kadhim Ni'ima, *Al-Malik Faisal al-'Awal wal Ingiliz wal Istiqlal*, Dar al-Shu'oon al-Thaga fiyoe al-'Amma Baghdad, 1988.

29. See, for example, the now classic work of C. Ernest Dawn, *From Ottomanism to Arabism: Essays on the Origins of Arab Nationalism*, University of Illinois Press, Urbana, 1973, and the excellent 'revisionist' work of Hasan Kayali, *Arabs and Young Turks: Ottomanism, Arabism and Islamism in the Ottoman Empire, 1908–1918*, University of California Press, Berkeley, 1997.

30. David Fromkin, *A Peace to End All Peace*, Avon Books, New York, 1990.

1. From the Desert to the Metropolis

1. This section draws a great deal from the work of Serif Mardin, *The Genesis of Young Ottoman Thought*, Princeton University Press, Princeton, 1962, and Niyazi Berkes, *The Development of Secularism in Turkey*, Routledge, London, 1998.

2. Hafiz Wahba, *Jazirat al-'Arab fi al-Qarn al-'Ishrin*, Matba'at Lajnat al-Tal'lif wa'l-Tarjamah wa'/-Nashr, Cairo, 1970.

3. Saleh Muhammad al-Amr, *The Hijaz Under Ottoman Rule 1869–1914*, Riyadh University Publications, Riyadh, March 1978.

4. Ibid., pp. 460–68.

5. Ibid., pp. 45–50.

6. Ibid., pp. 50–53.

7. See Jacob Landau's excellent history of pan-Islam, *The Politics of Pan-Islam: Ideology and Organization*, Oxford University Press, New York, 1994.

8. Hasan Kayali, op. cit., especially chapter 1.

9. Muhammad 'Abd al-Hussein, *Dhikra Faisal al-'Awwal*, Matba'at al-Sha'b, Baghdad, 1933, gives the date of his birth as Ta'if, 1933; Amin al-Rihani, *Faisal al-'Awal: Rihlat wa Tarikh*, Dar al-Jeel, Beirut, 1988, gives the date as Rabi' al-Awal 1301 AH in Mecca; Kingdom of Iraq, Directorate of Public Information, *Faisal ibn al-Hussein fi Khutabihi wa Aqwalihi*, Matba'at al-Hukuma (Government Printing Press), Baghdad, 1945, gives the date as 20 May 1885; Mrs Steuart Erskine, op. cit., gives the date as 20 May 1885, in Ta'if.

10. Randall Baker, *King Hussein and the Kingdon of the Hejaz*, Oleander Press, Cambridge, 1979, p. 6.

11. Ibid., p. 6.

12. Ibid., p. 6, and T. E. Lawrence, *Seven Pillars of Wisdom*, Penguin Books, London, 1977, p. 100.

13. Randall Baker, op. cit., p. 7.

14. Saleh Muhammad al-Amr, op. cit., pp. 125–35.

15. Amin Rihani, op. cit., pp. 11–14; Mrs Steuart Erskine, op. cit., pp. 25–26.

16. Private correspondence with Walid and Basil 'Abd al-Qadir Sa'id, authorities on Bedouin customs.

17. Mrs Steuart Erskine, op. cit., pp. 20–21.

18. Amin Rihani, op. cit., pp. 12–14.

19. T. E. Lawrence, op. cit., pp. 125–26; Mrs Steuart Erskine, op. cit., pp. 20–21.

20. 'Abdullah ibn al-Hussein, *Mudhakkirati*, Al-Ahliya lil-Nashr wal Tawzi', Amman, 1989, pp. 10–12.

21. Ibid., pp. 11–12.

22. George Antonius, *The Arab Awakening*, Khayat's College Book Cooperative, Beirut, 1955, p. 72; Hasan Kayali, op. cit., p. 101.

23. Saleh Muhammad al-Amr, op. cit., pp. 128–29.

24. 'Abdullah ibn al-Hussein, op. cit., pp. 17–19.

25. Mrs Steuart Erskine, op. cit., p. 25.

26. 'Abdullah ibn al-Hussein, op. cit., pp.18–19.

27. Amin Rihani, op. cit., p. 12.

28. 'Abdullah ibn al-Hussein, op. cit., pp. 26–29.

29. Randall Baker, op. cit., p. 10.

30. Carter V. Findley, *Bureaucratic Reform in the Ottoman Empire: The Sublime Porte, 1789–1922*, Princeton University Press, Princeton, 1980, p. 228.

31. Ibid., pp. 228–30.

32. Ercumend Kuran, 'Küçük Said Pasa (1840–1914) as a Turkish Modernist', *International Journal of Middle East Studies*, Vol. 1, No. 2, April 1970, pp. 124–32.

33. Corinne Lee Blake, 'Training Arab-Ottoman Bureaucrats: Syrian graduates of the Mülkiye Mektebi, 1890–1920', unpublished PhD thesis, Princeton University, 1991.
34. She had a scandalous affair a few years after Faisal's death, which led to her being disowned by her family. She ran away with a Greek waiter who soon abandoned her, robbing her of her money and jewellery. She was left to roam for years in Europe, disgraced, alone and penniless, practically a beggar, until one of her cousins, 'Abd al-Illah, the son of Ali, took pity on her and arranged a small allowance on condition that she left Europe and moved to Jerusalem, then a part of Mandate Palestine. Izzat's tragedy was somewhat softened later when her uncle, King 'Abdullah of Jordan, consented to receive her in Amman and tacitly forgave her on behalf of the family. She died in London in 1960, barely acknowledged by her family.
35. Rajiha died in Geneva in 1959, escaping the massacre of the Iraqi royal family in the 1958 revolution that overthrew the monarchy. Faisal's grandson, King Faisal II of Iraq, was killed in that revolution.

2. Return to Mecca

1. The opposition to the rule of Sultan 'Abd al-Hamid is covered in detail in M. Sukru Hanioglu, *The Young Turks in Opposition (Studies in Middle Eastern History)*, Oxford University Press, Oxford, 1995. See also Serif Mardin, op. cit., which covers the early period of Hamidian rule, as well as Niyazi Berkes, op. cit. There are good biographies (some translated into English and Arabic) of some of the leading opposition figures to 'Abd al-Hamid, especially Midhat Pasha. See, for example, Ali Haider Midhat, *The Life of Midhat Pasha*, Murray, London, 1903.
2. M. Sukru Hanioglu, op. cit., p. 3.
3. The name was coined by the Paris press to describe Ottoman oppositionists based in Paris.
4. 'Abd al-Hamid's pan-Islamic policies are well described in Jacob Landau, op. cit. By the turn of the century, many advocates of pan-Islam from outside the Ottoman Empire had gravitated to Istanbul, especially the famous agitator, Sayyid Jamal ad-Din Asadabadi (al-Afghani). See Nikki Keddie, *Sayyid Jamal ad-Din 'al-Afghani*, University of California Press, Berkeley, 1972.
5. See in particular Hasan Kayali, op. cit. This is destined to become a classic work. Through meticulous use of the Ottoman archives, Kayali has deconstructed a number of myths about the rise of Arabism in the Ottoman Empire.
6. See M. Sukru Hanioglu, op. cit.
7. The character of Prince Sabah al-Din is especially interesting. A short, dapper man, he went on to become the leader of the liberal opposition to the CUP. After the fall of the Ottoman Empire he remained in Istanbul for a while and became associated with the circles around the strange mystic figure of G. I. Gurdjieff. See J. G. Bennett, *Witness: The Story of a Search*, Hodder & Stoughton, London, 1962. Bennett, later a well-known industrial chemist and follower of G. I. Gurdjieff, was stationed in Istanbul after the First World War as an intelligence officer, and got to know Prince Sabah al-Din very well.
8. See Andrew Mango's description of the conspiratorial cells in Macedonia in his masterful work, *Atatürk: The Biography of the Founder of Modern Turkey*, Overlook Press, New York, 2002, pp. 57–79.
9. Hasan Kayali, op. cit., p. 42
10. Ibid., pp. 44–51.
11. Saleh Muhammad al-Amr, op. cit., pp. 132–33. Joshua Teitelbaum, *The Rise and Fall of the Hashimite Kingdom of Arabia*, Hurst, London, 2001, pp. 40–41; Hasan Kayali, op. cit., chapter 5.
12. Hasan Kayali, op. cit., p. 101.
13. William Ochsenwald, *The Hijaz Railroad*, University Press of Virginia, Charlottesville, 1980. This is the standard work on the construction of the Hijaz railroad.
14. See George Stitt, *A Prince of Arabia: The Amir Shereef Ali Haider*, Allen & Unwin, London, 1948, p. 103. His biography of Sharif Ali Haider is not very reliable on the details, and repeats the allegations of Ali Haider without qualification.
15. Saleh Muhammad Al-Amr, op. cit., pp. 134–35.
16. Andrew Mango, op. cit., pp. 85–89.
17. C. Ernest Dawn, op. cit., p. 6; 'Abdullah ibn al-Hussein, op. cit., pp. 42–44; Joshua Teitelbaum, op. cit., p. 56.
18. Kingdom of Iraq, Directorate of Public Information, op. cit., p. 33.
19. Amin al-Rihani, op. cit., p. 12.
20. R. S. O'Fahey, *Enigmatic Saint: Ahmad Ibn Idris and the Idrisi Tradition*, Northwestern University Press, Evanston, 1990.
21. Ibid., p. 122.
22. Hasan Kayali, op. cit., p. 110.

23. 'Abdullah ibn al-Hussein, op.cit., p. 62.
24. 'Abdullah ibn al-Hussein, op. cit., pp. 63–69. However, the Ottoman governor in 'Asir, Suleiman Pasha, gave a dramatically different account of the first battle of Quz. He blamed the defeat of the relief column on military incompetence on the part of 'Abdullah. 'Abdullah had no knowledge of the terrain, and was unable to secure water for the regular Ottoman troops, some of whom died of thirst on the retreat. During the battle itself, Suleiman Pasha claimed that the troops under 'Abdullah's command panicked and fled the battlefield. See al-Arab magazine, Year 5, issue no. 10, (June 1971) and Year 6, issue no. 2 (October 1971), 'Fi Mudhakkirat Suleiman Shafiq Kamali Pasha'.
25. 'Abdullah ibn al-Hussein, op. cit., p. 66.
26. Amin al-Rihani, op. cit., p. 13.
27. Ibid., pp. 13–14.
28. Stanford J. Shaw and Ezel Kural Shaw, The History of the Ottoman Empire and Modern Turkey, Vol. II, Cambridge University Press, Cambridge, 1995, pp. 281–90. Also Hasan Kayali, op. cit., pp. 73–74 and Andrew Mango, op. cit., pp. 101–11.
29. Saleh Muhammad Al-Amr, op. cit., p. 157.
30. Ibid., p. 157. Also, Sharaf al-Barakati, Al-Rihlah al-Yamaniyah, Dar al-Nafa'is, Beirut, 2005. Al-Barakati witnessed most of the events of 'Asir and gives a full account of the expeditions against the Idrisi.
31. Letter from Faisal to Sharif Hussein, dated 21 Rabi'i al-Awal, 1331 (28 February 1913), from Bariq in the 'Asir. The letter is reproduced in Suleiman Musa, ed., Al-Murasalat al-Tarikhiya 1914–1918, Vol. 1, self-published, Amman, 1973.

3. Prelude to War

1. The CUP's unorthodox leadership, in terms of ethnic and religious background, gave rise to a number of conspiracy theories.
2. This was the thesis of the classic, but now dated, work by George Antonius, op. cit.
3. The rise of Arab nationalism is covered in detail in Rashid Khalidi, Lisa Anderson, Muhammad Muslih and Reeva S. Simon, eds, The Origins of Arab Nationalism, Columbia University Press, New York, 1991. The pioneering work of C. Ernest Dawn, op. cit., greatly affected the study of modern Arab nationalism and moved it away from the Antonius thesis.
4. See Hasan Kayali, op. cit., pp. 86–87.
5. Quoted in Zeine N. Zeine, Nashou' al-Qawmiya al-'Arabiya, 4th edition, Dar al-Nahar, Beirut, 1986, pp. 92–93.
6. The story of the Arab secret societies is exhaustively covered by Eliezer Tauber, The Emergence of the Arab Movements, Routledge, London, 1993.
7. A profile of 'Aziz Ali al-Misri is given by Majid Khadduri, Arab Contemporaries: The Role of Personalities in Politics, Johns Hopkins University Press, Baltimore and London, 1973. See also As'ad Daghir, Mudhakkarati 'ala hamish al-Qadhiya al-Arabiya, Dar al-Qahira lil Tab', Cairo, Egypt, n.d. pp. 37–39.
8. See James Jankowski, 'Egypt and Early Arab Nationalism, 1908–1922', in Khalidi et al., op. cit, chapter 12, especially pp. 247–49.
9. See Lord Birdwood, Nuri As-Said: A Study in Arab Leadership, Cassell, London, 1959, pp. 12–19.
10. See Amin Sa'id, Al-Thawra al-'Arabiya al-Kubra, Vol. 1, Matba'at Isa al-Babi, Beirut, n.d. pp. 18–25, and Hasan Kayali, op. cit., pp. 86–88.
11. A profile of al-Zahrawi is given by Ahmad Tarabein in Rashid Khalidi et al., op. cit., pp. 97–120.
12. The Arab Congress was opposed by many conservative notables and supporters of the traditional forces in the empire. In the Hijaz, Sharif Hussein sent a cable to the grand vizier denouncing the congress, and accusing it of serving foreign interests and bordering on treason. The text of the cable was published in the Turkish-language newspaper Iqdam. See Tawfiq al-Suwaidi, Mudhakarati: Nusf Qarn min Tarikh al-Iraq wal Qadhiya al-'Arabiya, al-Mou'assasa al-'Arabiya lil Tiba'a â wal Nashr, Amman, 2010, p. 35.
13. See Khalid M. al-Barazi, 'The Majlis Mabusan', unpublished PhD thesis, University of London (SOAS), 2002, on the mechanics of the Ottoman electoral system.
14. 'Abdullah ibn al-Hussein, op. cit., pp. 54–55.
15. See Mim Kemal Oke, 'The Ottoman Empire, Zionism, and the Question of Palestine (1888–1908)', International Journal of Middle East Studies, Vol. 14, No. 3. (August 1982), pp. 329–41.
16. The Ottoman millet system divided non-Muslim Ottoman subjects into religious rather than national or ethnic groups. Each millet, or community, was essentially self-governing according to its own religious laws and had its own officially sanctioned leadership structures. These would act as the interlocutors between the community and the sultan.

17. See Hasan Kayali, op. cit., pp. 81–84, and Rashid Khalidi, 'The 1912 Election Campaign in the Cities of Bilad al-Sham', *International Journal of Middle East Studies*, Vol. 16, No. 4 (November 1984), pp. 461–74.
18. Quoted in Khalid M. al-Barazi, op. cit., pp. 32–33.
19. See Stanford J. Shaw and Ezel Kural Shaw, op. cit., pp. 273–301.
20. Kingdom of Iraq, Directorate of Public Information, op. cit., p. 34.
21. Ibid., p. 39.
22. As'ad Daghir, op. cit., pp. 48–49.

4. The Road to the Rising

1. See, for example, Amin al-Rihani, op. cit., p. 14, in referring to Faisal's parliamentary activities between 1913 and 1914.
2. See, for example, Eliezer Tauber, op. cit., p. 115. This is also quoted in Hasan Kayali, op. cit., p. 124.
3. Hasan Kayali, op. cit., p. 125.
4. Suleiman Musa, op. cit., p. 77.
5. *British Documents on the Origins of the War*, eds G. P. Gooch and Harold Temperley, Vol. X, Part 2, HMSO, London, 1938, p. 827.
6. 'Abdullah ibn al-Hussein, op. cit., pp. 87–94.
7. T. E. Lawrence, op. cit., p. 74.
8. Mrs Steuart Erskine, op. cit., p. 41.
9. 'Abdullah ibn al-Hussein, op. cit., pp. 100–02.
10. See Hafiz Wahba, op. cit., pp. 57–58, and quoted in C. Ernest Dawn, op. cit., p. 14.
11. The friendship between the two families stretched to 1909, when 'Abdullah was hosted by the family in Damascus following the Haj. Hussein used his influence with the sultan to issue a decree that allowed the youth of the Bakri family to serve their military conscription periods in Mecca. Fawzi was the eldest of the children of 'Atta al-Bakri, and would later join Faisal in the Arab Revolt. Suleiman Musa, op. cit., n. 127.
12. See Ulrich Trumpener, 'Turkey's Entry into World War I: An Assessment of Responsibilities', *The Journal of Modern History*, Vol. 34, No. 4 (December 1962), pp. 369–80.
13. Liman von Sanders, *Five Years in Turkey*, US Naval Institute, Annapolis, 1927, p. 206. Von Sanders's description of Faisal's anti-Turkish sentiments may have been coloured by subsequent events and the circumstances of the Arab Revolt.
14. 'Abdullah ibn al-Hussein, op. cit., pp. 103–04.
15. The declaration of jihad itself was widely circulated in the empire, but the Entente powers blocked its distribution in their territories. Nevertheless, there was great fear on the part of all the Entente powers that their Muslim populations would heed the call for jihad. In fact there were few desertions from the Entente armies to the Ottomans.
16. Jamal Pasha in his memoirs stated that the campaign needed eleven thousand camels as pack animals to carry water supplies through the Sinai desert. Jamal Pasha, *Mudhakarrat Jamal Pasha (Al-Saffah)*, translated by Ali Ahmad Shukri, al-Dar al-'Arabiya lil Mowsou'aat, Beirut, 2004, pp. 182–83.
17. Ibid., p. 185.
18. Ibid., pp. 186–87.
19. The authenticity of the reported find of these documents has been questioned by some historians (for example, Joshua Teitelbaum, op. cit., p. 71, who calls the episode a 'story'), and even those who do accept them have been tentative about their use (see Hasan Kayali, op. cit., pp. 127–28). However, the details given by Amin Sa'id in his memoirs and the credence given to them by Faisal in his interviews with Mrs Steuart Erskine are clear enough evidence of their authenticity. C. Ernest Dawn also accepts their validity (see C. Ernest Dawn, op. cit., pp. 27–28). The actual documents may have been destroyed or lost after the fall of Mecca to ibn Saud in 1925.
20. Amin Sa'id, op. cit., pp. 105–06. Sa'id speaks of Faisal as 'being known for his pro-Turkish leanings and his desire to keep their goodwill'.
21. Mrs Steuart Erskine, op. cit., p. 40.
22. Amin Sa'id, op. cit., p. 106.
23. Ronald Storrs, *Orientations*, Potnam, New York, 1937, pp. 165–66.
24. Elie Kedourie, *In the Anglo-Arab Labyrinth: The McMahon–Hussein Correspondence and its Interpretations 1914–1939*, Cambridge University Press, Cambridge, pp. 21–22.
25. Mrs Steuart Erskine, op. cit., pp. 40–42.
26. See Ahmad Qadri, *Mudhakarati 'an al-Thawra al-'Arabiya al-Kubra*, Vol. 1, second ed., Ministry of Culture Publications, Damascus, 1993, pp. 45–46.
27. George Antonius, op. cit., p. 152.

28. Fa'iz al-Ghusain, *Mudhakarati 'an al-Thawra al-'Arabiya*, Matba'at al-Taraqi, Amman, 1956, pp. 202–03.
29. Yasin's role in the unfolding drama is perplexing. He stayed loyal to the Ottoman war effort until almost the end of hostilities, but nevertheless joined al-Fatat. See Sami 'Abd al-Hafidh al-Qaisi, *Yasin al-Hashimi wa dawrahu fi al-Siyassa al-'Iraqiya*, Part 1, Haddad Press, Basra, 1975, pp. 43–45. Phebe Ann Marr makes 'Yasin a supporter of the Ottoman Empire and very pro-German in his leanings. See Phebe Ann Marr, 'Yasin al-Hashimi: The Rise and Fall of a Nationalist (A Study of the Nationalist Leadership of Iraq, 1920–1936)', unpublished PhD thesis, Harvard University, Massachusetts, 1966, p 70.
30. George Antonius, op. cit., pp. 152–53; Suleiman Musa, op. cit., pp. 129–29; Ahmad Qadri, op. cit. pp. 40–41. Amin Sa'id in his memoirs appears to overlook Faisal's first visit to Damascus in 1915.
31. It was actually 26 March 1915.
32. Mrs Steuart Erskine, op. cit., p. 42.
33. Jamal Pasha, op. cit., p. 250.
34. Mrs Steuart Erskine, op. cit., p. 42.
35. Wahib was in fact promoted to head the Ottoman Second Army based in Istanbul.
36. According to a despatch by Lawrence in January 1917, Faisal was still predisposed to the Turks after his visit to Istanbul, believing in the assessment of the Turkish officers of an imminent German victory on the Western Front. Faisal, according to Lawrence, also believed that public opinion in Syria was not yet willing to accept a decisive break with the Ottoman Empire. This made him counsel caution to his father. See F.O. 686/6, Part II, 8 January, 1917. Quoted in Suleiman Musa, op. cit., p. 134. This would seem to be an argument made in hindsight, after the Ottoman victory in Gallipoli. Things looked quite different in April 1915, and it is unlikely that Turkish officers would make such a prediction given the presence of an Allied expeditionary force a hundred miles from the capital.
37. See Amin Sa'id, op. cit., Vol. 1, p. 107.
38. Jamal Pasha, op. cit., p. 250. Jamal mixes up the dates of Faisal's speech to the officers and staff of the Fourth Army, making it contemporaneous with Hussein's first communications with the British high commissioner in Egypt in September 1915. This could not possibly be the case. This incorrect dating became received wisdom amongst detractors of the Arab Revolt, and has been used to infer a dubious and duplicitous character for Faisal. A number of historians such as Elie Kedourie have built their arguments on this incorrect dating. For example, Faisal's second visit to Damascus *preceded* the execution of the Arab nationalist 'conspirators' and the arrests that decimated the secret societies. As such, his meetings with them were with groups that still had their basic strengths intact and could launch an uprising without much foreign support. The claim, therefore, that Faisal was dealing with a few unrepresentative elements of Arab opinion is fundamentally wrong, if we place Faisal's visit in May/June 1915, rather than, incorrectly, September 1915. The situation drastically changed after the first batch of executions of the so-called conspirators in August 1915.
39. 'Capitulations' was the term given to the legal and commercial concessions given to Europeans who were resident in the Ottoman Empire. In essence, they were not subject to the Ottoman judicial system, and could only be tried in special court, supervised by their native country's consular representatives.
40. The protocol has been dismissed by some historians as being non-representative of general Arab opinion, and as being the work of a small cabal of ambitious Arab officers and politicians. For example, David Fromkin calls the protocol the work of a handful of conspirators whose plot had been discovered by the Turks, and misquotes Dawn's work to make his case (David Fromkin, *A Peace to End All Peace*, Avon Books, New York, 1990, p. 175). Again, the issue of dating of the meetings between Faisal and the nationalists in Syria is essential for a proper understanding of the events of the time.
41. Mrs Steuart Erskine, op. cit., p. 43.
42. Amin Sa'id, op. cit., Vol. 1, pp. 108–09; Qadri, op. cit., Vol. 1, pp. 46–47; Suleiman Musa, op. cit., pp. 131–33.
43. Ibid., p. 109.
44. Mrs Steuart Erskine, op. cit., p. 43.
45. Jamal Pasha, op. cit., pp. 250–51.
46. Mrs Steuart Erskine, op. cit., p. 44.
47. Jamal Pasha, op. cit., p. 178.
48. Ibid., pp. 232–33.
49. Hasan Kayali, op. cit., pp. 130–31.
50. Halidé Edib Adivar, *Memoirs of Halidé Edib* (first edition 1926), reprinted by Gorgias Press, New Jersey, 2004, pp. 403–04. Another eyewitness, Dr Ra'if Abi Al-Lam', also spoke of these harrowing

scenes. See Nicholas Z. Ajay Jr, 'Political Intrigue and Suppression in Lebanon during World War I', *International Journal of Middle East Studies*, Vol. 5, No. 2 (April 1974), p. 155.

51. Ali Fouad Ardin, *Kayfa Ghazouna Masr*, quoted in the appendix, written by the editor, Ali Ahmad Shukri, to Jamal Pasha's memoirs, op. cit., pp. 286–88. Ali Fouad was one of the commanding officers on the abortive Suez front.

52. Jamal had conceived of the first Suez Canal campaign as an example of pan-Islamic unity. The attacking forces had contingents composed of Kurdish, Circassian, Libyan and Bulgarian Muslims, as well as Druze volunteers. These forces were united as the so-called 'Islamic Army to Save Egypt'. See Hasan Kayali, op. cit., p. 128.

53. Jamal Pasha, op. cit., pp. 249–50.

54. Liman von Sanders complained to his superiors about Jamal's policies: 'The harshness of Djamal Pasha prevents the Arabs in Syria from being for the Turkish cause'. Liman von Sanders, op. cit., p. 140.

55. Mrs Steuart Erskine, op. cit., pp. 44–45.

56. C. Ernest Dawn, op. cit., pp. 30–31; Amin Sa'id, op. cit., Vol. 1, p. 110.

57. Ronald Storrs, op. cit., pp. 166–69.

58. This was probably composed by Storrs. See Elie Kedourie, op. cit., p. 70.

59. It is clear that Hussein's demands regarding the frontiers of the Arab state were not simply tactical. He genuinely believed that the demands that he expressed were shared by all right-thinking Arabs, and he repeated them in a separate letter that he wrote to the Governor-General of the Sudan Sir Reginald Wingate. FO 882/12. See also Suleiman Musa, op. cit., pp. 210–11.

60. Elie Kedourie, *Anglo-Arab Labyrinth*, op. cit., p. 75.

61. This is a highly condensed account of the background to the Faruqi affair, and the feverish exchanges of notes between the various actors in this drama in London, Cairo, Delhi and Khartoum. The protagonists included, to name a few: in Cairo, Gilbert Clayton, Henry McMahon and John Maxwell; in London, Herbert Kitchener, Edward Grey, Austen Chamberlain (head of the India Office) and Arthur Hirtzel; in Delhi, Charles Hardinge (the Viceroy); in Khartoum, Reginald Wingate and Cyril Wilson. Even General John Nixon, head of the British force in Mesopotamia, chimed in with his views about its implications on future British interests in southern Iraq.

62. FO 371/6237, p. 18 and FO 141/461, quoted in Suleiman Musa, op. cit., p. 220; and Elie Kedoure, op. cit., p. 94.

63. Elie Kedourie, op. cit., p. 95.

64. The entire correspondence between Sharif Hussein and McMahon was published by the British government in 1939: *HMSO Correspondence between Sir Henry McMahon and the Sherif Hussein of Mecca*, Cmd. 5957, 1939.

65. Mrs Steuart Erskine, op. cit., p. 45.

66. US 867.4016/283. Philip to Secretary of State (Istanbul [via Copenhagen], 21 May 1916). Quoted in Hasan Kayali, op. cit., p. 131. The scale of these deportations was dwarfed by those of Armenians from eastern Anatolia at the same time, some of whom eventually made it to Syria. That the fate of the Armenians could befall the Syrians if a general uprising against the Turks materialised must have left a deeply sobering effect on the Syrians.

67. The famine in Syria and Lebanon caused the death of nearly a tenth of the population because of starvation and disease. See Hasan Kayali, op. cit., p. 134; Meir Zamir, *The Formation of Modern Lebanon*, Cornell University Press, Ithaca, 1988, p. 36.

68. Mrs Steuart Erskine, op. cit., p. 45.

69. The letter was written on lightweight paper that could be folded into a tiny packet. Its dating is based on the fall of Erzerum in February 1916 and Bitlis in early March 1916. See Suleiman Musa, op. cit., pp. 191–92.

70. Amin Sa'id, op. cit., Vol. 1, p. 110.

71. Mrs Steuart Erskine, op. cit., pp. 36–37; Suleiman Musa, op. cit., p. 191.

72. Amin Sa'id, op. cit., Vol. 1, pp. 110–11.

73. Amin Sa'id, op. cit., Vol. 1, p. 111; 'Abdullah ibn al-Hussein, op. cit., p. 112.

74. Suleiman Musa, op. cit., p. 195.

75. Ibid., p. 196.

76. Jamal Pasha has Sharif Hussein threatening, 'If you really want me to stay quiet, then you have to admit to my independence in all of Hijaz'. Jamal Pasha, op. cit., p. 252.

77. Ibid., pp. 253–54.

78. Ibid., p. 254.

79. Ibid., p. 255.

80. George Antonius, op. cit., pp. 190–91. Jamal Pasha offers another version in which Faisal visits him a few hours after the hangings and applauds the execution of traitors. This is false, as Faisal's presence at the Bakri farm was witnessed by dozens of people. Jamal, op. cit., p. 258.

81. Jamal Pasha, op. cit., p. 259.
82. Jamal Pasha, op. cit., p. 260. Jamal had asked General Ali Fouad to be present at this meeting, which should corroborate Jamals' recollections of the events. Jamal also claims that Faisal then went to General Fouad's house where he wept bitterly, and feared that Jamal intended to hang his brother Ali.
83. Amin Sa'id, op. cit., Vol. 1, p. 115.
84. Ibid., p. 114.
85. Ibid., p. 115; George Antonius, op. cit., p. 194.
86. Amin Sa'id, op. cit., Vol. 1, pp. 116–17; C. Ernest Dawn, op. cit., p. 37.
87. Ibid., p. 116.
88. See Elie Kedourie, 'The Surrender of Medina, January 1919', Middle Eastern Studies, Vol. 13, No. 1 (January, 1977), p. 133.
89. This is the site of the famous Battle of Uhud, 625 CE, where the Prophet's uncle, Hamza, was killed. Sayidunna Hamza means 'Our Lord, Hamza'.
90. Jamal Pasha, op. cit., p. 263.
91. Amin Sa'id, op. cit., Vol. 1, pp. 116–17. Jamal Pasha asserts in his memoirs that the letter to Fakhri Pasha was from Ali and not Faisal, and that its contents were different (Jamal, op. cit., p. 263). The Sa'id version rings truer as it is supported by three different accounts of the incident.
92. Jamal Pasha, op. cit., pp. 263–64.
93. Ibid., p. 265.

5. The Arab Revolt I: Consolidating the Revolt

1. Two of Faisal's relatives, Sharif Shahat Ibn Ali, who was Hussein's agent in Medina, and his brother, Sharif Nasir, played a major part in mobilising the tribes in the Medinan area in support of the revolt. Sharif Nasir went on to become a senior commander in Faisal's Northern Arab Army. See Suleiman Musa, op. cit., p. 273.
2. T. E. Lawrence, op. cit., pp. 94–95.
3. Ibid., p. 95.
4. The Arab Bureau was founded in the spring of 1916. Its primary activity was to harmonise British policy in the Middle East by gathering, analysing and disseminating intelligence on the Arab world, and to track the activities and analyse the plans of the Central Powers and the Ottoman Empire in the Middle East. It was directly responsible to Gilbert Clayton, head of British military and political intelligence in Cairo, and through him to the British Residency in Egypt. Ultimate authority over the bureau rested with the Foreign Office in London. Hogarth had been an archaeologist in Oxford and keeper of the Ashmolean Museum before joining the Admiralty intelligence services. Most of the bureau's staff came from an intelligence or military background. See Bruce Westrate, The Arab Bureau: British Policy in the Middle East: 1916–1920, Penn State University, Pennsylvania, 1992.
5. See Sheila Ann Scoville, 'British Logistical Support to the Hashemites of the Hijaz: Ta'if to Ma'an, 1916–1918', unpublished PhD thesis, University of California, Berkeley, 1982, p. 55.
6. Sharif Hussein relied a great deal on the support of some of his ashraf relatives, two of whom, Sharif Sharaf and Sharif Shakur, would play an important part both in the revolt and in the subsequent states established in the Arab provinces of the empire. Sharif Sharaf in particular was a close companion-in-arms to Faisal and acted as one of his main advisers. In 1926, he joined Faisal in Iraq.
7. Sharif Hussein was a music aficionado and his court orchestra continued to perform in his palace courtyard during the bombardment. When a shell landed near the orchestra and the musicians scrambled for cover, Hussein ordered them back to perform in spite of the bombardment.
8. Faruqi had been despatched to the Hijaz by the British, together with other Syrian and Iraqi officers, to assist in the rising. See Storrs, op. cit., p. 175. Faruqi was appointed in early July 1916 as Sharif Hussein's emissary in Cairo. He occupied this position until September 1917.
9. 'Abdullah ibn al-Hussein, op. cit., p. 116. See also George Antonius, op. cit., pp. 195–99.
10. See Arab Bulletin, no. 23, 26 September 1916 p. 303.
11. In their first meeting after the Ottoman surrender of Ta'if, Ghalib Pasha, the former Ottoman governor, bemoaned to 'Abdullah the breach between the Arabs and the Turks. 'What a catastrophe! Once we were friends and now we have become enemies!' After reaching Jeddah, where he was to be transported to a prisoner-of-war camp by the British, Ghalib sent his personal sword to 'Abdullah to avoid surrendering it to a foreign officer. See 'Abdullah ibn al-Hussein, op. cit., pp. 127–128.
12. Most of the coastal Hijazi villages, such as Yanbu', al-Laith, Qunfudha and Amlaj, also fell to Arab forces, but not always to those aligned to the Sharif Hussein. The British authorities in Aden had

asked the Idrisi, who was now tied to them by a formal agreement, to occupy Qunfudha. It took a great deal of pressure to dislodge the Idrisi from Qunfudha after Sharif Hussein strenuously objected to this move.

13. See Sheila Ann Scoville, op. cit., p. 87.
14. T. E. Lawrence, op. cit., p. 96.
15. The character and exploits of T. E. Lawrence are the subject of numerous biographies. His brilliant literary masterpiece, *Seven Pillars of Wisdom*, describes the progress of the Arab Revolt as seen through his peculiar perspective.
16. The *Arab Bulletin* had some very perspicacious contributors, including a number of the Arab Bureau's leading lights, such as David George Hogarth, Lawrence, Gertrude Bell and Philip Graves. Although its circulation was restricted to those on a need-to-know basis within the British government, its secrecy was breached and its contents were known to Britain's allies, Italy and France. See Bruce Westrate, op. cit., pp. 103–06.
17. T. E. Lawrence, op. cit., p. 92.
18. Ibid., pp. 98–100.
19. Al-Ghusain was a member of al-Fatat party and served as an Ottoman parliamentarian. It was in Istanbul as a member of the Majlis al-Mab'uthan that he had first became acquainted with Faisal. He was picked up in Jamal Pasha's 1916 dragnet and, though acquitted, was sent off to exile in the Diyarbekir region. There he witnessed at first hand the deprivations and massacres suffered by the Armenians, which he later recounted in his famous memoir (Fa'iz al-Ghusain, *Martyred Armenia*, C.A. Pearson, London, 1917). Al-Ghusain also wrote a two-volume memoir on his days with the Arab Revolt.
20. T. E. Lawrence, op. cit., pp. 127–28.
21. Ibid., p. 102.
22. Ibid., p. 99.
23. See, for example, Wingate's cable to the War Office, in which he complained about Faisal's prolonged discussions with tribal chiefs and their effect on the war effort against the Turks. (From the private papers of Sir Reginald Wingate at Durham University, Sudan Archives 145/4, 15 April 1917, quoted in Ronald colman, 'Revolt in Arabia, 1916–1919: Conflict and Coalition in a Tribal Political System', unpublished PhD thesis, Columbia University, New York, 1976.)
24. Suleiman Musa, op. cit., p. 292.
25. Subhi al-'Umari, *Awraq al-Thawra al-Arabiyya: Al-Ma'arek al-Uwla*, Vol. 1, Riad El-Rayess Books, London and Cyprus, 1991, pp. 125–26.
26. "'And why did you retire to the camp-ground behind us during the battle?" asked Faisal. "Only to make ourselves a cup of coffee," said 'Abd el Karim [the chief of the Juhayna]. "We had fought them from sunrise and it was dusk: we were very tired and thirsty." T. E. Lawrence, op. cit., p. 132.
27. Ibid., p. 134.
28. Colman, op. cit., p. 228.
29. Sheila Ann Scoville, op. cit., p. 90.
30. According to an account by Subhi al-'Umari, op. cit., Vol. 1, pp. 124–25, who was a serving officer in Faisal's army, another group of Iraqi prisoners of war who had been held in India were landed in Jeddah after they had mutinied on learning that they were to form part of an Arab contingent to fight the Turks on the Gaza front. They insisted that they had volunteered to fight the Turks as part of an Arab army and not as a unit of a British force.
31. Recruits for the regular fighting forces of the revolt came instead from Yemenis, Bedouins and the underclass of the towns. Some, however, were pressed into service.
32. Subhi al-'Umari, op. cit., Vol. 1, gives the names of about 130 Iraqi officers who served with the Arab Revolt, and about 60 Syrians.
33. Misri was sidelined by Hussein when he appointed him as his 'Minister of Defence', a toothless position.
34. See 'Ali Jawdat (al-Ayubi): *Dhikrayat, 1900–1958*, Matabi' al-Wafa's, Beirut, 1967, pp. 40–47.
35. See John Fisher, 'The Rabegh Crisis' 1916–1917, *Middle East Studies*, Vol. 38, No. 3 (July 2002), pp. 73–92.
36. See Joshua Teitelbaum, op. cit., pp. 82–83.
37. See *Arab Bulletin*, No. 28, 28 November 1916.
38. T. E. Lawrence, op. cit., p. 137.
39. See *Arab Bulletin*, No. 36, 26 December 1916.
40. *Arab Bulletin*, no. 57, 24 July 1917.
41. Malcolm Brown, ed., *The Letters of T. E. Lawrence*, Dent and Sons, London, 1988, p. 101.
42. *Arab Bulletin*, no. 36, 26 December 1916.
43. FO 686/6, Intelligence Report, 12 December 1916, cited in Joshua Teitelbaum, op. cit., p. 87.

44. T. E. Lawrence, op. cit., p. 138.
45. Ibid., pp. 144–49.
46. *Arab Bulletin*, No. 31, 18 November 1916.
47. 'Abdullah's march on Wadi 'Ais, where arrived on 15 January 1917, had an unexpected side benefit. On his way, 'Abdullah had captured a Turkish emissary travelling to Medina with over £20,000 in gold coins.
48. Letter from Faisal to Sharif Hussein, dated Bir Sa'id, 10th Muharram, 1333 AH (6 November 1916), quoted in Suleiman Musa, op. cit., pp. 91–92.

6. The Arab Revolt II: Breaking Out

1. T. E. Lawrence, op. cit., pp. 168–69.
2. Ja'far al-'Askari, *Mudhakkarat Ja'far al-Askari*, ed. Nejdat Fathi Safwat, Dar al-Lamm, London, 1988, pp. 79–88.
3. Ibid., pp. 99–107.
4. T. E. Lawrence, op. cit., p. 172.
5. Ja'far al-'Askari, op. cit., pp. 106–07.
6. Ibid., p. 108.
7. FO 882, 6 December 1916, quoted in John E. Mack, *A Prince of Our Disorder: The Life of T. E. Lawrence*, Harvard University Press, Cambridge, MA, 1998, p. 148.
8. Sheila Ann Scoville, op. cit., p. 165.
9. Fisher, op. cit., pp. 78–79; T. E. Lawrence, op. cit., pp. 113–14.
10. T. E. Lawrence, op. cit., pp. 172–73.
11. By March 1917, there were nearly forty British serving officers with the Arab Revolt, mostly with Faisal's Northern Army. In addition, the British fielded a detachment of about a thousand Egyptians, including about forty Egyptian officers, most of whom were with the Northern Army. The French had a detachment of mainly Algerian and Moroccan troops, led by a mixture of Algerian and French officers. They numbered about a hundred. They were all with the Northern Army.
12. T. E. Lawrence, op. cit., p. 182.
13. Ja'far al-'Askari, op. cit., pp. 110–13.
14. Lawrence devotes considerable space in the *Seven Pillars of Wisdom* to his own journey to Wadi 'Ais, where he met with 'Abdullah. He creates a telling portrait of 'Abdullah, and more than hints at 'Abdullah's growing jealousy of Faisal. But Lawrence never mentions Faisal's far more significant mission to Wadi 'Ais with his principal military advisers.
15. Ja'far al-'Askari, op. cit., p. 113.
16. See Suleiman Musa, op. cit., pp. 300–01; T. E. Lawrence, op. cit., pp. 178–81.
17. Auda had already established contact with Faisal. According to Lawrence's despatch to Cairo of 14 February 1917, Auda had requested permission from Faisal to attack Ma'an. Suleiman Musa, op. cit., p. 301, footnote 2.
18. T. E. Lawrence, op. cit., p. 181.
19. Suleiman Musa, op. cit., pp. 300–01; FO 882/6, 15 April 1917, note from Clayton to the War Office describing the arrival of the tribal delegation at Faisal's camp.
20. T. E. Lawrence, op. cit., pp. 228–29.
21. Sheila Ann Scoville, op. cit., p. 164, citing Sudan Archives, Box 145/1, Faisal's Report, 15 January 1917. In true bureaucratic fashion, the War Office suggested that the funds advanced to the tribes should be debited later to a future 'Arab Kingdom'.
22. Subhi al-'Umari, op. cit., Vol. 1, p. 132.
23. FO 882/19; also quoted in Suleiman Musa, op. cit., p. 300.
24. FO 882/4, quoted in Suleiman Musa, op. cit., p. 300, footnote 1.
25. Lawrence merely hints at such an indiscretion on his part in *Seven Pillars*, but his official biographer, Jeremy Wilson, gives the issue more emphasis. Jeremy Wilson, *Lawrence of Arabia: The Authorized Biography of T. E. Lawrence*, Atheneum, New York, 1989, pp. 361–62.
26. FO 686/6, 24 March 1917; also quoted in Teitelbaum, op. cit., p. 116, footnote 126.
27. Sheila Ann Scoville, op. cit., p. 184.
28. Letter from Faisal to King Hussein, dated Wejh, 25 Jamadi Thani, 1325 AH (equivalent to 17 April 1917), from the papers of Amir Zaid, reproduced in Suleiman Musa, op. cit., p. 103.
29. Sharif Nasir (1890–1934), known as Abu Saif ('Father of Saif', or the sword) was a sharif of Medina and one of Faisal's most skilled commanders. He was a decent man, much loved by his followers. Lawrence describes him as a person of 'lucent goodness'.
30. Subhi al-'Umari, *al-Ma'arik*, op. cit., p. 133.
31. Ibid., pp. 132–35; Suleiman Musa, op. cit., pp. 300–03.

32. Suleiman Musa, op. cit., pp. 125–27.
33. Ja'far al-'Askari, op. cit., pp. 113–17.
34. Allenby to William Robertson, Chief of Imperial General Staff, WO 158/634, quoted in Jeremy Wilson, op. cit., pp. 426–27.
35. However, in the Arabic version of their correspondence with the king, the Allies addressed him using the Arabic equivalent of 'Your Majesty'.
36. Joshua Teitelbaum, op. cit., p. 93.
37. Ja'far al-'Askari, op. cit., p. 120.
38. Suleiman Musa, op. cit., pp. 135–36.
39. Joyce to Clayton, 25 September 1917, Akaba Archive H72–73, Kings College Library, London, quoted in Jeremy Wilson, op. cit., p. 448.
40. FO 882/7, 2 November 1917, quoted in Suleiman Musa, op. cit., p. 307, footnote 1.
41. Suleiman Musa, op. cit., p. 308–09.
42. In the Arab mind, 'Sykes–Picot' has become shorthand for all that is duplicitous, self-serving, dishonest and unjust in the policies and actions of imperial and post-imperial powers in the Middle East. Otherwise, it is mostly glided over in embarrassed silence as a relic of a bygone era with few defenders except for the odd historian.
43. See the excellent essay on Sir Mark Sykes, in Elie Kedoune, *England and the Middle East: the Destruction of the Ottoman Empire, 1914–1921*, Mansell, London, 1988, pp. 67–87. See also the biography of Sykes: Roger D. Adelson, *Mark Sykes: Portrait of an Amateur*, Jonathan Cape, London, 1975.
44. According to George Antonius, op. cit., p. 248; T. E. Lawrence, op. cit., p. 282.
45. FO 882/16 10 March 1917; Suleiman Musa, op. cit., p. 250, footnote 2.
46. Elie Kedoure, *Anglo-Arab Labyrinth*, p. 163.
47. FO 882/12, dated April 28 1917, in the form of a letter from Clayton to Wilson outlining Sykes's terms of reference for his visit to Jeddah. See Suleiman Musa, op. cit., p. 354, footnote 2.
48. FO 882/16, note by Lieutenant Colonel Newcombe, 20 May 1917, 'Conversation between Sharif and Sykes', quoted in Suleiman Musa, op. cit., p. 358, footnote 1.
49. FO 882/16, Wilson to Clayton, letter dated 24 May 1917; also quoted in Suleiman Musa, op. cit., p. 359, footnote 1.
50. From Leonard Stein, *The Balfour Declaration*, The Magnes Press, The Hebrew University, Jerusalem and London, 1983.
51. *Al-Qibla* newspaper, Mecca, no. 183, 23 March 1918. The article was actually written by Hussein.
52. T. E. Lawrence to Sir T. M. B. Sykes, 9 September 1917, Clayton Papers 693/11, Durham University, quoted in Jeremy Wilson, op. cit., pp. 442–43.
53. George Antonius, op. cit., p. 268. This is a verbatim quote from Antonius, translated from Hussein's handwritten notes in Arabic on his meeting with Hogarth. Hogarth's report to Wingate on his meetings with King Hussein, dated 15 January 1918, can be found in FO 882/7 and Command 5974.

7. The Arab Revolt III: Railroad War

1. Subhi al-'Umari, op. cit., Vol. 1, pp. 142–43.
2. Ibid., p. 143. Al-'Umari, a teetotaller with traditional sensibilities, describes a scene in the Aqaba camp where he, a lieutenant aged only nineteen, endured snide bantering at his expense by senior officers enjoying their drink.
3. Zeine N. Zeine, *Al-Sira'a al-Dawli fi al-Sharq al-Awsat wa wiladat Dawlati Sooria wa Lubnan*, Dar al-Nahar, Beirut, 1977, pp. 74–75.
4. George Antonius, op. cit., pp. 255–56.
5. Jamal also sent a third letter, two weeks later, to 'Abdullah. This letter was very brief and reminded 'Abdullah of their common loyalty to the Muslim homeland.
6. Suleiman Musa, op. cit., pp. 152–53.
7. George Antonius, op. cit., p. 254.
8. It is extraordinary that Ja'far Pasha does not refer at all in his memoirs to Jamal's letter, in spite of its significance.
9. Suleiman Musa, op. cit., p. 156.
10. Suleiman Musa, op. cit., pp. 378–79. This source asserts that Hussein's exchanges with the Allies did not situate them in the context of the revelations of the Sykes–Picot Agreement. This is improbable, as the Turks distributed the agreement assiduously and widely, and details of it would have probably reached Hussein by the time of these exchanges with the British.
11. Suleiman Musa, op. cit., pp. 156–59.

12. George Antonius, op. cit., p. 258.
13. Ibid., pp. 431–32.
14. Ibid., p. 257.
15. FO 686/37; Suleiman Musa, op. cit., p. 384, footnote 1.
16. There were three different people carrying the name 'Jamal' on the Syrian front. The first was Jamal Pasha, the governor of Syria and commander of the Syrian–Palestine theatre of war. He was also known as Jamal Pasha the Elder. The second was Jamal Pasha the Younger, who commanded the Ottoman Fourth Army until September 1918. The third was Jamal Pasha the Third, commander of Ottoman troops on the Ma'an sector.
17. Suleiman Musa, op. cit., pp. 284–85.
18. T. E. Lawrence, 'Sidelights on the Arab War', unsigned article in the London *Times*, 4 September 1919.
19. Jeremy Wilson, op. cit., p. 470.
20. Ibid., p. 511.
21. FO 688/38 and Suleiman Musa, op. cit., pp. 384–85, footnote 1. The British themselves were also conducting their own secret talks with the Turks in Switzerland in December 1917.
22. Suleiman Musa, op. cit., p. 162.
23. The list included a few, such as Dr 'Abd al-Rahman al-Shabandar, who became allies of Faisal in his Arab government in Syria.
24. Osmond Walrond's partiality to the Syrians ran counter to the feelings of Lawrence, who had nothing but contempt for the urban Arab effendi.
25. Bruce Westrate, op. cit., pp. 162–64.
26. George Antonius, op. cit., pp. 433–34.
27. At Mount Vernon on the occasion of the Fourth of July, 1918.
28. Jeremy Wilson, op. cit., pp. 468–69, from the Sykes Papers, St Antony's College, Oxford.
29. CAB 27/23 of 9 January 1918; also carried in Jeremy Wilson, op. cit., p. 512.
30. Ibid.
31. FO 887/7 fo. 268; Jeremy Wilson, op. cit., pp. 512–13.
32. Ibid., p. 513.
33. Weizmann had already met with leading Palestinian Arab figures in Jerusalem, where he strongly iterated the pacific nature of the Zionist project in Palestine.
34. FO 882/14; Jeremy Wilson, op. cit., p. 513.
35. Ibid., p. 514.
36. Ibid., pp. 465–66. Guweira stood fifty miles to the north-east of Aqaba, and lay between Aqaba and the Hjiaz railroad.
37. 'Subhi al-'Umari, op. cit., Vol. 1, p. 176.
38. Ibid., pp. 163–85.
39. T. E. Lawrence, Seven Pillars, pp. 478–92. Lawrence was awarded the DSO for his part in the battle.
40. Subhi al-'Umari, op. cit., Vol.1, pp. 203–05.
41. Lord Birdwood, op. cit., pp. 60–66; Subhi al-'Umari, op. cit., Vol. 1, pp. 207–32.
42. Lord Birdwood, op. cit., p. 65.
43. According to Ja'far, the Turks were preparing to destroy their documents as they were certain that the assault would succeed. Lord Birdwood, op. cit., p. 43.
44. Ibid., p. 66.
45. Jeremy Wilson, op. cit., pp. 505–06.
46. Ibid., p. 385.

8. To Damascus!

1. Lowell Thomas was an experienced journalist and skilled public speaker who met Lawrence, in the company of Ronald Storrs, in Jerusalem in early 1918. See Jeremy Wilson, op. cit., p. 489–94.
2. See Jeremy Wilson, op. cit., p. 1,061, footnote 7. Lawrence made unsubstantiated comments to Liddell Hart about Faisal losing heart at the first encounter with the Turks at Medina in 1916. However, the evidence runs counter to this, so it is unclear what Lawrence sought to make out of this claim. In fact, Lawrence, throughout the *Seven Pillars of Wisdom* as well as in his despatches to Cairo, talks about Faisal having a surfeit of courage. Later, some commentators, relying solely on Liddell Hart's fragmentary record of his conversations with Lawrence, would make the claim that Lawrence deliberately exaggerated Faisal's qualities in his despatches so as to appeal to British respect for courageous leaders. This hardly makes sense.
3. The French produced a few war memoirs of the campaigns in the east, the most significant of which for the purposes of this biography are those of Edouard Brémond, *Le Hedjaz dans La Guerre Mondiale*, Payot, Paris, 1931.

4. Lawrence seemed to be in need of a hero himself. His affections switched from Faisal at the beginning of the Arab Revolt to Allenby by its end. Perhaps Lawrence was resentful that his 'pupil' did not always dance to his tune. T. E. Lawrence, *Seven Pillars*, p. 582.

5. Lord Birdwood, op. cit., pp. 62–63.

6. For example, Lawrence was asked by the Arab Bureau to influence Faisal to react positively to the Weizmann mission. Lawrence wrote offhandedly to Clayton that 'As for the Jews, when I see Feisul next I'll talk to him, and the Arab attitude *shall* be sympathetic', absurdly implying that he could sway Faisal on this critical issue simply by elucidating his position. Jeremy Wilson, op. cit., pp. 512–13.

7. T. E. Lawrence, *Seven Pillars*, p. 45.

8. Lord Birdwood, op. cit., p. 70.

9. 'This gross insult to all of us had been published by King Hussein . . . out of pique at his son's too-great success and to spite the northern town Arabs whom the King despised and feared,' wrote Lawrence. Jeremy Wilson, op. cit., p. 539.

10. Joyce to Bassett (Jeddah), 3 September 1918, FO 686/52, quoted in Jeremy Wilson, op. cit., p. 540.

11. T. E. Lawrence, *Seven Pillars*, pp. 595–99.

12. Ibid., pp. 598–99.

13. Suleiman Musa, op. cit., p. 394.

14. This is an intriguing comment as it implied that Faisal still sought an outcome that would leave the Arabs and Turks in some form of confederal arrangement. Faisal may not have known of the nuances of the administrative arrangements in imperial Germany, but his comments made it clear that he was aware that the German state was built on a high level of decentralisation. The inferences are obvious.

15. Suleiman Musa, op. cit., p. 394.

16. The majority of Faisal's Syrian and Iraqi followers during the war years were Sunni Muslims. The reasons are quite plain: there were no Iraqi officers of Shi'a Muslim background in the Ottoman military, and the Shi'a populations in greater Syria were concentrated in the Jabal 'Amil area of South Lebanon and the Beqa'a Valley. Both were overwhelmingly rural areas. Sectarian tensions between Shi'a and Sunni Muslims in the Arab nationalist movement were rare until the 1920s.

17. Rustum Haidar, *Mudhakarrat Rustum Haidar*, ed. Nejdat Fathi Safwat, Al Dar al-Arabiya lil Mawsou'at, Beirut, 1988, pp. 8–17.

18. Ahmad Qadri received his medical education in France. He served also as Faisal's personal physician while in Damascus. He was a frequent presence in Faisal's private moments. In later years he wrote an influential memoir of the period, chronicling the early Arab nationalist movement, the Arab Revolt, and the short-lived Arab government in Syria.

19. Ahmad Qadri, op. cit., Vol. 1, pp. 63–64.

20. Lord Birdwood, op. cit., p. 71.

21. Jeremy Wilson, op. cit., p. 545.

22. Papers of Major Sir Hubert Young, No. 19, Liddell Hart Centre for Military Archives, King's College, London. 'Message from General Allenby to Amir Feisal', 20 September 1918, quoted in Jeremy Wilson, op. cit., pp. 548–49.

23. Dawnay to Joyce, Akaba Archive M11, Kings College London, quoted in Jeremy Wilson, op. cit., p. 549.

24. T. E. Lawrence, *Seven Pillars*, p. 649.

25. Rustum Haidar, op. cit., pp. 164–65.

26. Ibid., p. 180.

27. Jeremy Wilson, op. cit., pp. 557–58.

28. T. E. Lawrence, *Seven Pillars*, p. 573.

29. Rustum Haidar, op. cit., p. 184.

30. War Office Despatch, WO95/4510, 1 October 1918, quoted in Jeremy Wilson, op. cit., p. 560.

31. See especially Elie Kedourie, 'The Capture of Damascus, 1918', *Middle Eastern Studies*, Vol. 1, No. 1, October, 1964, pp. 66–83.

32. WO 157/738, 21 September 1918, quoted in Jeremy Wilson, op. cit., pp. 540–41, and footnote 27, p. 1,102.

33. FO 371/3381, quoted in Suleiman Musa, op. cit., p. 395.

34. Ali Ridha Pasha al-Rikabi (1866–1942) was born in Damascus and attended the military academy in Istanbul. He joined the Ottoman army and rose to become a general in 1912. He was appointed governor of Jerusalem and later governor and military commander in Medina. He was retired in 1914 after he criticised the Ottoman government for entering the war. During the war, he joined al-Fatat society, concealing his sympathies with the Arab Revolt by appearing deferential to Jamal Pasha, who appointed him head of the Damascus municipal council. Before the fall of Damascus,

in coordination with al-Fatat, he intensified his contacts with Faisal in preparation for assuming a role in the new order.

35. General Shukri Pasha al-Ayubi was an early nationalist figure and was arrested in the round-up of leading Syrian figures by Jamal Pasha in May 1916. He was sentenced to death, but subsequently the sentence was reduced. He was badly tortured in jail and remained incarcerated until Jamal's departure from Syria.

36. Khairiya Qasimiya, *Al Hukuma al-Arabiya fi Dimashq, 1918–1920*, Al-Mu'assassa al-Arabiya lil Dirasat wal Nashr, Beirut, 1982, pp. 47–48.

37. The Arab flag comprised four colours: red, symbolising the revolt; green symbolising the standard of the Prophet's household; black symbolising the Abbasid standard; and white, symbolising the Umayyad standard. Sykes claimed that it was he who drew the flag of the revolt and chose its colours. However, Muhyi al-Din al-Khatib, a Syrian intellectual and early nationalist, claimed that the colours were suggested to Sharif Hussein by a group of Arab nationalists. See Khairiya Qasimiya, op. cit., p. 48, footnote 1.

38. Hadi Hassan Alaywi, *Faisal Ibn al-Hussein: Mu'assis al-Hukm al-'Arabi fi Suria wal 'Iraq, 1883–1933*, Riad El-Rayess Books, Beirut, 1993, pp. 64–65.

39. Subhi al-'Umari, *Awraq al-Thawra al-'Arabiya*, Vol. 2, 'Lawrence- al-Haqiqa wal Ukdhouba,' Riad El-Rayess Books, London and Cyprus, 1991, pp. 188–90.

40. Ibid., p. 10.

41. Malcolm B. Russell, *The First Modern Arab State: Syria under Faysal 1918–1920*, Bibliotheca Islamica, Minneapolis, 1985, pp. 9–10.

42. Malcolm B. Russell, op. cit., p. 12. Russell is dismissive of Kedourie's thesis that Chauvel deliberately held back from taking the city because of a prior agreement to let the Arab army enter the city first.

43. Jeremy Wilson, op. cit., p. 561.

44. This was the plaza in the city centre where the nationalists had been executed in 1916.

45. Subhi al-'Umari, *Awraq al-Thawra al-'Arabiya*, Vol. 3, 'Maysaloun', Riad El-Rayess Books, London and Cyprus, 1991, pp. 289–90.

46. Rustum Haidar, op. cit., p. 186.

47. Jeremy Wilson, op. cit., p. 562. In fact, Lawrence had nothing of note to say about Islam and considered any pan-Islamic sentiment as a mortal enemy of his version of Arab independence.

48. Subhi al-'Umari, *Awraq al-Thawra*, Vol. 3, pp. 299–300.

49. A different version of these events has been given by the Syrian officer of the Arab army, Subhi al-'Umari. It was Sharif Nasir who always acted as Faisal's representative, and it was clear that Nasir was deputising for Faisal in Damascus and not Lawrence. Subhi al-'Umari, *Awraq al-Thawra*, Vol. 2, pp. 190–91.

50. Lawrence's confrontation with the Jaza'iris was also prompted by his sense that they would not be acceptable to nationalist opinion. This is corroborated by the account given of this incident in Ahmad Qadri's memoirs, (op. cit., pp. 73–74). Sa'id al-Jaza'iri, on the other hand, wrote in his memoirs that this was part of a plan to ensure that the Arab government came under British influence, and the Jaza'iri brothers were seen to be an impediment to this plan. See Khairiya Qasimiya, op. cit., p. 49. This is not a credible statement if intended to show that the Jazai'iris were nationalists and were not beholden to any foreign interests. The Jaza'iris were in fact positioning themselves to receive support from the French. See Malcolm B. Russell, op. cit., p. 212, footnote 17.

51. Subhi al-'Umari, *Awraq al-Thawra*, Vol. 3, pp. 293–94.

52. Malcolm B. Russell, op. cit., pp. 13–14.

53. Jeremy Wilson, op. cit., p. 565.

54. Rustum Haidar describes the scene at Faisal's camp in considerable detail, as does Dr Ahmad Qadri.

55. Jeremy Wilson, op. cit., p. 565.

56. Drawn from Rustum Haidar's diary, op. cit., pp. 186–89.

57. Subhi al-'Umari, *Awraq al-Thawra*, Vol. 3, pp. 295–96.

58. Lord Birdwood, op. cit., p. 89.

59. War Office to General Headquarters, Egypt, telegram 67558, 1 October 1918. WO 37/960, quoted in Jeremy Wilson, op. cit., p. 360.

60. T. E. Lawrence, *Seven Pillars*, p. 683.

61. Sir H. G. Chauvel, statement given to the Australian War Memorial, 1936. Quoted in Jeremy Wilson, op. cit., pp. 567–88.

62. Jeremy Wilson, op. cit., p. 568.

63. Rustum Haidar, op. cit., p. 187.

64. Ibid.

65. Lord Birdwood, op. cit., p. 90.

9. The Rudiments of a State

1. War Office to General Headquarters Egypt, telegram 67558, 1 October 1918, WO 37/960, quoted in Jeremy Wilson, op. cit., footnote 74, p. 1,108.
2. Ibid., p. 566.
3. Sir Archibald Wavell, *Allenby: A Study in Greatness*, George G. Harrap, London, 1941.
4. Allenby to WO, EA 1808, 23 October 1918, FO 371/3384, quoted in Malcolm B. Russell, op. cit., p. 214, footnote 46.
5. Mrs Steuart Erskine, op. cit., p. 96.
6. Drawn from Abu Khaldun Sati' al-Husri, *The Day of Maysalun: A Page from the Modern History of the Arabs*, trans. Sidney Glazer, The Middle East Institute, Washington, DC, 2004, pp. 101–02.
7. Malcolm B. Russell, op. cit., p. 18.
8. Suleiman Musa, op. cit., p. 397. The colours of the flag were cabled to Beirut from Damascus, and it was hoisted by Fatima al-Mahmasani, the sister of two of those hanged by Jamal Pasha. See Khairiya Qasimiya, op. cit., p. 57.
9. It is still unclear whether Shukri was dispatched by Faisal of his own volition or as a result of pleas from Faisal's supporters in Beirut. See Zeine N. Zeine, *Al-Sira'a al-Dawli*, pp. 78–79.
10. Rustum Haidar, op. cit., pp. 191–93.
11. Zeine N. Zeine, *Al-Sira'a al-Dawli*, pp. 83–85.
12. Ibid., p. 220, footnote 3, and p. 83.
13. Quoted in Meir Zamir, op. cit., p. 51.
14. Jeremy Wilson, op. cit., pp. 569–70, quoting Lawrence's letter to Yale of 22 October 1929.
15. Haidar's diaries include a facsimile of the original instructions given to Haidar and Shukri al-Ayubi by al-Rikabi. However, Haidar would not have moved without the explicit authorisation of Faisal.
16. The French had already designated François Georges-Picot as their high commissioner for Palestine and Syria, but he had not yet arrived on the scene.
17. Meir Zamir, 'Faisal and the Lebanese Question, 1918–20', *Middle Eastern Studies*, Vol. 27, No. 3 (July 1991), pp. 404–06.
18. Known as Le Detachement Français de Palestine et de Syrie.
19. Meir Zamir, 'Faisal and the Lebanese Question', p. 406; Khairiya Qasimiya, op. cit., p. 58.
20. Clayton to FO: FO 371/3384, 171564/747, No. 115, 12 October 1918, quoted in Meir Zamir, 'Faisal and the Lebanese Question', footnote 8, p. 423.
21. FO 371/3384 fo. 221, quoted in Jeremy Wilson, op. cit., p. 571.
22. Suleiman Musa, op. cit., pp. 221–22, quoted from the papers of Amir Zaid.
23. FO 371/3384, Clayton to Foreign Office, 30 October 1918, quoted in Meir Zamir, 'Faisal and the Lebanese Question', p. 407.
24. Lord Birdwood, op. cit., p. 91.
25. Subhi al-'Umari, who was in the last campaigns of the Syrian front, relates how, upon entry into Aleppo, he moved with his detachment towards Le Baron Hotel, headquarters of the Turkish army. While setting up his machine gun post in front of the hotel he saw a car speeding away. The car carried Mustafa Kemal, the commander of the Turkish forces in Aleppo, and his staff. If they had arrived at the hotel a few minutes before, 'Umari would have captured the entire Turkish command in Aleppo. Subhi al-'Umari, *Al Mar'arek*, Vol. 3, pp. 311–12.
26. Ibid., p. 93.
27. FO 371/3364, Clayton to FO, 24 October 1918, quoted in Malcolm B. Russell, op. cit., p. 214, footnote 54.
28. Yusuf Hakim, *Dhikrayat: Sooria wal 'Ahd al-Faysali*, Vol. 3, Dar al-Nahas, Beirut, 1986, pp. 35–45.
29. Abu Khaldun Sati' al-Husri, op. cit., p. 120.
30. Yusuf Hakim, op. cit., pp. 36–37.
31. For example, the deputy military governor 'Adil Arslan was from Lebanon; Nuri al-Sa'id, Ja'far al-'Askari and Yasin al-Hashimi, all Iraqis, were political adviser, military adviser and head of the army, respectively; Sa'id Shuqair, a Christian from Beirut, was head of finance; Iskandar 'Ammun, also a Christian from Mount Lebanon, was director of justice.
32. For example, travellers to Syria had to receive prior permission from the British, in effect banning those whose actions or statements were hostile to the Allies' line. See Khairiya Qasimiya, op. cit., p. 62.
33. See C. Ernest Dawn, op. cit., pp. 69–86.
34. In fact the Victorian poet and writer Wilfred Blunt, writing in 1882, had earlier advocated such a course. See Wilfred S. Blunt, *The Future of Islam*, Nonsuch Publishers, Dublin, 2007.
35. As'ad Daghir, op. cit., p. 106.

36. Muhammad Izzat Darwaza, *Hawl al-Haraka al-'Arabiya al-Haditha*, al-Matba'a al-'Asriya, Sidon, 1950, pp. 86–87.
37. Ibid., pp. 80–86.
38. Khairiya Qasimiya, op. cit., pp. 66–68.
39. Mohammad Izzat Darwaza, op. cit., pp. 88–89.
40. As'ad Daghir, op. cit., p. 107.
41. Suleiman Musa, op. cit., pp. 220–21 The letter is undated, but probably written in mid-October 1918.
42. Ahmad Qadri, op. cit., Vol. 1, pp. 84–85.
43. Ibid., p. 85.
44. This was the first time that the idea of a constitutional congress was mooted for the entire Arab lands of the Ottoman Empire.
45. The full text of Faisal's speech is from Amin Sa'id, op. cit., Vol. 2, pp. 3–8; Ahmad Qadri, op. cit., Vol. 1, pp. 86–87.
46. Jeremy Wilson, op. cit., pp. 581 and 1,111, footnote 36.
47. Arnold Wilson, *Mesopotamia, 1917–1920*, Oxford University Press, Oxford, 1931, pp. 102–103.
48. Jeremy Wilson op. cit., p. 1,110, footnote 18.
49. Ibid., p. 1,111, footnote 41.
50. Muhammad Izzat Darwaza, op. cit., pp. 415–16.
51. Elie Kedourie, 'Surrender of Medina', pp. 124–43. Fakhri's' scathing reply to Hussein when asked to surrender was: 'I beg you not to trouble me with useless requests.'
52. Ahmad Qadri, op. cit., Vol. 1, p. 90.
53. Lord Bridwood, op. cit. p. 103.
54. Faisal to Allenby, letter 19 October 1918, FO 141/438, quoted in Malcolm B. Russell, op. cit., p. 217, footnote 29.
55. Suleiman Musa, op. cit., pp. 244–45.

10. First Footsteps in Europe

1. Kingdom of Iraq Directorate of Public Information, op cit., p. 55.
2. Edouard Brémond, op. cit. pp. 310–11.
3. FO 371/3418, E. Vicars (British Consul General, Lyons) to Foreign Secretary, London, quoted in Jeremy Wilson, op. cit., p. 1,111, footnote 49.
4. Mrs Steuart Erskine, op. cit., p. 97.
5. Ahmad Qadri, op. cit., Vol. 1, p. 92.
6. Ibn Ghabrit headed an Islamic charitable organisation and was the director of the Islamic Institute of Paris. Faisal's entourage thought his translation abilities rather poor, probably because of the divergence between North African and Near Eastern dialects of Arabic.
7. Edouard Brémond, op. cit., pp. 315–16.
8. Ahmad Qadri, op. cit., Vol. 1, p. 93.
9. Ibid., pp. 316–17.
10. 'Awni 'Abd al-Hadi, *Mudhakarrat 'Awni 'Abd al-Hadi*, ed. Khairiya Qasimiya, Markaz Dirasat al-Wahda al-'Arabiya, Beirut, 2002, p. 49–50.
11. Ibid., p. 51.
12. Ibid., pp. 51–52.
13. Ibid., p. 317.
14. Ibid., p. 318.
15. Suleiman Musa, op. cit., pp. 251–52.
16. Ibid., p. 250.
17. Ibid., p. 52.
18. Ibid, pp. 50–51.
19. Jeremy Wilson, op. cit., pp. 589–90.
20. Ibid., p. 1,111, footnote 50.
21. Ibid., p. 1,111, footnotes 55 and 56.
22. Ibid., p. 1,111, footnote 59.
23. Suleiman Musa, op. cit., p. 252.
24. *The Times*, Wednesday, 11 December 1918, p. 8. A few days later Lawrence wrote an article for *The Times*, partly to rectify the press's neglect of Faisal's visit, in which he stressed the Arab contribution to the war effort.
25. Suleiman Musa, op. cit., pp. 252–53.
26. Ibid., p. 252.

27. Ibid., p. 256.
28. Ibid., p. 252.
29. In the same letter to his father of 25 December 1918, Faisal also discussed the deteriorating situation in Yemen and 'Asir, where the Idrisi was making another bid for total independence. Faisal also thought these areas could be subject to discussions during the Paris Peace Conference. In the absence of any representations from these states at the conference, Faisal told his father that he would seek to push for the Yemen's independence, but with a loose association under Hussein's Hijaz. As for 'Asir, he would insist on its inclusion as part of the territory of the Hijaz kingdom.
30. H. W. V. Temperley, ed., *A History of the Peace Conference of Paris*, Oxford University Press, London and New York, 1920, reprinted 1969, Vol. 1, p. 142.
31. Muhammad Izzat Darwaza, op. cit., pp. 437–38; FO 371/4162, 27 December 1918.
32. Rustum Haidar, op. cit., pp. 208–10.
33. The United States position was outlined by President Wilson in his addresses in 1917 and 1918, and in the Fourteen Points of January 1918.
34. H. W. V. Temperley, op. cit., p. 144.
35. FO 608/80; FO 680/92; Suleiman Musa, op. cit., pp. 45–48.
36. H. W. V. Temperley, op. cit., p. 143.
37. Even George Antonius, whose views on Faisal were very favourable, was obliged to admit, 'In Feisal's mind this view had gradually developed into a positive belief in the possibility of Arab-Jewish cooperation in Palestine.' George Antonius, op. cit., p. 285.
38. Chaim Weizmann, *Trial and Error*, Harper, New York, 1949, pp. 235–42. Weizmann also stated that Faisal's grasp of French was enough to sometimes break the tedium of talking through interpreters, but that his knowledge of English was nil, a point that seems to contradict the impression of von Sanders.
39. Suleiman Musa, op. cit., pp. 436–37.
40. *Jewish Chronicle*, 3 January 1919, p. 20.
41. George Antonius, op. cit., p. 439. The confusion in dates stems from the fact that the memorandum that Faisal referred to was in fact signed on 1 January 1919. Faisal appended his signature to the codicil and then Weizmann signed under his name.
42. 'Awni 'Abd al-Hadi, op. cit., pp. 56–57. 'Awni had a negative perception of Lawrence and saw him as primarily motivated by British interests. 'Awni saw Lawrence's attitude to Zionism as very supportive, a view that was also shared by Weizmann in his memoirs.
43. The other being the purported letter written by Faisal to Felix Frankfurter, a member of the American Zionist mission to the peace conference.
44. Joseph Jeffries, *Palestine, the Reality: The Rise of Jewish Nationalism and the Middle East*, Hyperion Press, New York, 1939.
45. P. Knightly and C. Simpson, *The Secret Lives of Lawrence of Arabia*, Nelson, London, 1969, pp. 119–20.
46. 'Awni 'Abd al-Hadi, op. cit., pp. 54–55.
47. Suleiman Musa, op. cit., p. 260.

11. At the Paris Peace Conference I

1. As late as 16 January no mention of an Arab or Hijazi delegation to the Paris Peace Conference was made in the French official listing of the countries represented at the conference and their delegations. Rustum Haidar, op. cit., p. 216.
2. 'Awni 'Abd al-Hadi, op. cit., p. 58.
3. Jeremy Wilson, op. cit., p. 598.
4. Awni 'Abd al-Hadi, who was antipathetic to Lawrence, relates that Faisal had not informed Lawrence of the meeting with Clemenceau. Upon leaving the hall of the War Ministry where they had been meeting, Faisal and Clemenceau saw Lawrence sitting on one of the benches in full uniform. Faisal was then obliged to introduce Lawrence to Clemenceau. 'Awni 'Abd al-Hadi attributes this unusual event to Lawrence's desire always to impress on the French his closeness to Faisal, and that Faisal was ultimately dependent on Lawrence and the British. 'Awni 'Abd al-Hadi, op. cit., p. 61.
5. 'Awni 'Abd al-Hadi, op. cit., p. 60. A somewhat different version was given by Lawrence, probably relying on the information given him by one of the attendees at the meeting. Improbably, Gout is presented as talking to Faisal in a very harsh and intimidating, even insulting tone. It is highly unlikely that a trained diplomat, even while bearing bad news, would indulge in insulting behaviour. Jeremy Wilson, op. cit., p. 599. The most complete description

of the meeting between Gout and Faisal is given in Faisal's letter to his father of 19 January 1919.

6. 'Awni 'Abd al-Hadi, op. cit., p. 60.
7. Zeine N. Zeine, Al-Sira'a al-Dawli, p. 66, footnote 1. Faisal's letter to his father of 19 January 1919, states that he himself set in motion the events that led to two seats at the conference being allocated to the Hijaz. As soon as Gout had left his presence, Faisal 'hurried to send someone [Lawrence?] to the British Foreign Secretary and informed him of all that transpired between myself and Gout. The Foreign Secretary became very agitated when he heard this news, and pushed the powers to accept two delegates from the Hijaz government' Suleiman Musa, al-Murasalat, Vol. 2, p. 39.
8. Ibid., p. 36.
9. Mrs Steuart Erskine, op. cit., p. 97.
10. Suleiman Musa, al-Murasalat, Vol. 2, pp. 36–37.
11. 'Awni 'Abd al-Hadi, op. cit., p. 61.
12. Ibid., p. 37.
13. Gertrude Bell was then the political adviser to the British administration of Mesopotamia, and attended the Paris Peace Conference specifically on behalf of the Baghdad-based government.
14. Lawrence, of course, expected that such a state would be ruled by Hussein and his sons, preferably Faisal.
15. Dated 11 March 1919; Jeremy Wilson, op. cit., pp. 601–02.
16. Suleiman Musa, al-Murasalat, Vol. 2, p. 41.
17. Rustum Haidar, op. cit., p. 220. According to Leonard Stein in his book, The Balfour Declaration, Faisal's meeting with Wilson was arranged by Rabbi Stephen Weiss, head of the American Committee for Zionism. See Leonard Stein, op. cit., p. 594. However, this appears improbable as the British delegation would more likely have arranged the meeting.
18. The Council of Ten comprised the heads of government and foreign ministers of the five major victors (Britain, France, the United States, Italy and Japan). Given its large size and unwieldy nature, the Council of Ten was pre-empted by decisions taken independently by the 'Big Four' (Britain, France, the US and Italy).
19. Rustum Haidar, op. cit., pp. 221–23.
20. Ibid., pp. 225–29.
21. Ibid., pp. 233–34.
22. Some of Lawrence's biographers have claimed that it was Lawrence who wrote the speech for Faisal in Arabic. This is absolutely false. Lawrence's written Arabic was poor, grammatically incorrect and almost childlike. The task of writing such an important speech was well beyond his linguistic capabilities. See Michael Korda, Hero, The Life and Legend of Lawrence of Arabia, HarperCollins, New York, 2010, p. 473.
23. Ibid., pp. 235–36. Sykes also offhandedly remarked to Haidar that if the Arab nationalist movement had been more apparent in 1916, he would have needed to have amended his agreement with Picot, presumably to take cognisance of Arab demands for independence. Haidar reminded him that the nationalist movement had been around well before the Arab Congress of Paris of 1913.
24. Ibid., p. 236.
25. Ibid., p. 237.
26. 'Awni 'Abd al-Hadi, op. cit., pp. 62–63.
27. Ibid., p. 63.
28. Ibid., p. 63.
29. Rustum Haidar, op. cit., pp. 237–38. Also, D. H. Miller, My Diary at the Conference at Paris, 1918–1919, vol. IV, G. B. Putnam's Sons, New York, 1928, p. 296. Pichon rather foolishly asked Faisal about the French contribution to the war effort in the Near East. Faisal enumerated the French contribution as being '4 60-calibre guns, 2 80-calibre guns, but in spite of this we thank France as long as we are alive because she helped us, and she is much greater than to be merely praised.' Rustum Haidar, op. cit., p. 239.
30. Suleiman Musa, al-Murasalat, p. 60.
31. 'Awni 'Abd al-Hadi, op. cit., pp. 64–66.
32. Interview with Faisal in Outlook magazine, 2 April 1919, quoted in Zeine N. Zeine, Al-Sira'a al Dawli, p. 70, footnote 3.
33. Zeine N. Zeine, Al-Sira'a al-Dawli, p. 69.
34. Rustum Haidar, op. cit., pp. 246–47.
35. Zeine N. Zeine, Al-Sira'a al Dawli, pp. 71–73.
36. James T. Shotwell, At the Paris Peace Conference, Macmillan, London, 1937, p. 178.

37. Suleiman Musa, op. cit. Vol. 2, pp. 53–54. In the same letter, Faisal informed Zaid that he intended to bring the Christian Syrian politician Faris al-Khoury, and the Druze Prince Amin Arslan, to Paris as members of his delegation.
38. Yusuf Hakim, op. cit., p. 58.
39. Rustum Haidar, op. cit., pp. 251–52. Al-Ghusain did have his supporters though. The writer Muhammad Kurd Ali was told by al-Ghusain that he had left Faisal because the latter was difficult to work with and temperamental. Another writer, the Iraqi journalist and editor Raphael Butti, said that Haidar was jealous of al-Ghusain and wanted to be the sole confidant of Faisal. But 'Awni 'Abd al-Hadi supported Haidar's observations on al-Ghusain and his claim that he misappropriated money from Faisal. Suleiman Musa, relying on a conversation that he had with al-Ghusain, considers his departure to have been routine as his assignment had come to an end.
40. David Lloyd George, *Memoirs of the Peace Conference*, Vol. II, Yale University Press, New Haven, 1939, pp. 673–74.
41. Robert Lansing, *The Big Four and Others of the Peace Conference*, Hutchinson, London, 1922, pp. 161–77.
42. Ibid., pp. 161–65.
43. On 21 January 1919, the 'Intelligence Section' of the American delegation to the peace conference recommended to Wilson that a Syrian state should be established, under the mandatory system but with no decision as to the mandatory power, and that such a state should be allowed to join a confederation of Arab states. Zeine N. Zeine, *Al-Sira'a al-Dawli*, p. 69.
44. 'Awni 'Abd al-Hadi, op. cit., p. 58.
45. Ibid., pp. 58–59.
46. Rustum Haidar, op. cit., pp. 265–66.
47. Or the 'Dagger Ode'. Faisal composed its twelve lines as a bantering refrain to 'Abdullah, because he had given Zaid a gold dagger which Faisal had not seen before.
48. Rustum Haidar, op. cit., pp. 273–74. Haidar was usually meticulous in the reporting of those who were with Faisal at any given time, but he makes no mention of Lawrence during these meetings with Anatole France. This is strange as Bernard Shaw acted as the editor of the *Seven Pillars of Wisdom* and his wife Charlotte had a voluminous later correspondence with Lawrence. But according to Michael Holroyd, Bernard Shaw's biographer, Shaw was only introduced to Lawrence in March 1922. Michael Holroyd, *Bernard Shaw*, Vintage, London, 1998, p. 525.
49. 'Awni 'Abd al-Hadi commented that 'it was customary at that time [for] leading politicians, even the President of the Republic, to consider visiting scientists such as M. Aular a great privilege'. 'Awni 'Abd al-Hadi, op. cit., p. 59.
50. Harry N. Howard, *The King–Crane Commission: An American Inquiry in the Middle East*, Khayats, Beirut, 1963, p. 43, note 1.
51. James T. Shotwell, op. cit., pp. 129–31.
52. Ibid., pp. 196–97.
53. Rustum Haidar, op. cit., p. 511.

12. At the Paris Peace Conference II

1. Not to be confused with Iskandar Ammun, a relative, who was a prominent Faisal supporter.
2. The pre-1860 frontiers referred to so-called Greater Lebanon and were a deliberate attempt to extend the understanding of the geographic limits of Lebanon beyond the Mutasarifiya period in the Ottoman era. This had basically confined Lebanon to the area of Mount Lebanon. Greater Lebanon included the Beqa'a Valley and the coastal plain from Tyre to Tripoli.
3. Harry N. Howard, op. cit., p. 25.
4. In Faisal's meeting with Wilson on 23 January, he repeated his wish for such a commission. See Jukka Nevakivi, *Britain, France, and the Arab Middle East, 1914–1920*, Athlone Press, London, 1969, p. 134.
5. Faisal had the highest regard for the Bliss family and the American University of Beirut. In an interview given to *Outlook* magazine on 7 March 1919, Faisal said: 'Without the education that this college had given, the struggle for freedom would never have been won. The Arabs owe everything to these men.' Zeine N. Zeine, *Al-Sira'a al-Dawli*, pp. 69–70, footnote 3.
6. Ibid., pp. 24–25.
7. Ibid., pp. 25–26.
8. David Lloyd George, op. cit., p. 677.
9. Zeine N. Zeine, *Al-Sira'a al-Dawli*, pp. 77–79.
10. Harry N. Howard, op. cit., pp. 31–35.
11. H. W. Steed, *Through Thirty Years, 1892–1922*, Vol. II, Heinemann, London, 1924, p. 298.

12. George Antonius writes: 'It is related that when news of the decision reached Faisal's ears he drank champagne for the first time, and drank it as though it were water. Then he went for a drive past the headquarters of the American and British delegations and threw cushions at the Crillon, the Majestic, and the Quai d'Orsay, saying that as he had no bombs, he could only express his feelings in that way.' George Antonius, op. cit., p. 288.

13. Woodrow Wilson Papers, IX-A, p. 33, quoted in Harry N. Howard, op. cit., p. 35.

14. Jukka Nevakivi, op. cit., pp. 108–09. This was typical of Lawrence's idiosyncratic style and led to grumblings in the British delegation that he was conducting his own private diplomacy.

15. David Garnett, *The Letters of T. E. Lawrence*, Doubleday, New York, 1939, pp. 273–75.

16. Harry N. Howard, op. cit., p. 39.

17. Ibid., pp. 44–45.

18. Ibid., p. 37.

19. Ibid., p. 73.

20. *Le Matin*, issue 12786, 1 March 1919, in Rustum Haidar, op. cit., pp. 281–83, footnote 2.

21. CO 733/414 (75928).

22. 'Awni 'Abd al-Hadi, op. cit., pp. 67–68.

23. Stephen Bonsal, *Suitors and Suppliants, the Little Nations at Versailles*, Prentice-Hall, New York, 1946, p. 56.

24. Rustum Haidar, op. cit., pp. 347–48.

25. Jukka Nevakivi, op. cit., p. 126.

26. Ibid., p. 127.

27. David Lloyd George, op. cit., p. 678.

28. Subhi al-'Umari, *Maysaloun-Nihayat 'Ahd*, Riad El-Rayess Books, London, 1991, pp. 77–79. 'Umari was then the adjutant to Sharif Nasir, responsible to Faisal for the Aleppo district.

29. Rustum Haidar, op. cit., pp. 277–92.

30. Malcolm B. Russell, op. cit., pp. 34–35.

31. Ibid., p. 35, and p. 217, footnote 53.

32. 'Awni 'Abd al-Hadi gives the date as 16 April 1919.

33. 'Awni 'Abd al-Hadi, op. cit., pp. 67–68. Malcolm B. Russell, op. cit., p. 36, quotes from the notes of ibn Ghabrit, where the latter reports that Clemenceau offered Faisal recognition of Syrian independence but insisted that a French flag fly alongside the Arab flag.

34. Rustum Haidar, op. cit., pp. 338–39.

35. Ibid., p. 341.

36. Ibid., pp. 345–47.

37. Ibn Ghabrit was often harshly viewed by Faisal's entourage. 'An employed servant of the French . . . what concerns does he have for Syria. He would sell it for a French medal worth two francs!' was Rustum Haidar's early view of him. Rustum Haidar, op. cit., p. 352. Later, Haidar seemed to change his personal views somewhat. Ibn Ghabrit was from Tlemcen, in Algeria, bordering Morocco. Haidar wrote: 'He had stayed in Paris [for the peace conference] in order to act as translator between Faisal and the French Government. When he understood the meaning of Faisal's language, he translated [the Arabic into French] with remarkable fluency and accuracy, but sometimes he would not be able to understand the meaning exactly. However, his translation from French into Arabic was very weak. That is why the Amir used to insist that one of us be present so that the translation was free of errors.' Rustum Haidar, op. cit., p. 366.

38. Suleiman Musa, op. cit., Vol. II, p. 63.

39. Rustum Haidar, op. cit., pp. 352–53.

40. Rustum Haidar, op. cit., pp. 342–43.

41. Jeremy Wilson, op. cit., p. 610, quoting Faisal's personal diary at the conference.

42. Rustum Haidar, op. cit., p. 343.

43. Rustum Haidar, op. cit, pp 355–356 and Malcolm B. Russell, op. cit., p. 37.

44. Ibid., p. 355.

45. Ibid., pp. 355–58.

46. Ibid., p. 350.

47. Ibid., pp. 357–62.

48. Ibid., p. 359.

49. Amin Sa'id, op. cit., Vol. II, p. 23. Both the Italian government and the papacy sought to compete with the French for the allegiance of the Levant's Christians, and especially the Catholic population. An alliance with Faisal could prove useful in this game. From Faisal's point of view, it would also undermine French claims that they were the only protectors of the area's Christians.

50. Malcolm B. Russell, op. cit., pp. 38–39.

51. Jeremy Wilson, op. cit., p. 611, and p. 1,114, footnote 32.

52. Malcolm B. Russell, op. cit., p. 38.

13. The Struggle for Syria

1. Yusuf Hakim, op. cit., pp. 70–71.
2. Kingdom of Iraq, Directorate of Public Information, op. cit., pp. 190–91.
3. Malcolm B. Russell, op. cit., pp. 39–40.
4. Meir Zamir, 'Faisal and the Lebanese Question', p. 410. The apparent tilt towards reaching an agreement with Faisal that would put him at the head of a French-influenced confederation of Lebanon and Syria seriously alarmed Maronite opinion. Shukri Ghanem asked Clemenceau if France had 'abandoned' the Christians of the Levant. Robert de Caix thought that Faisal was deliberately exploiting the discussions he had had with Clemenceau and de Caix to create the impression with the Christians of the Lebanon that France had deserted them. Malcolm B. Russell, op. cit., p. 218, footnote 67.
5. Yusuf Hakim, op. cit., p. 71.
6. Ibid., pp. 71–72.
7. Rustum Haidar, op. cit., p. 403. Haidar is clearly partial to Toulat, comparing him most favourably with Pisani, whom he dismisses as an ignoramus.
8. James L. Gelvin, *Divided Loyalties: Nationalism and Mass Politics in Syria at the Close of Empire*, University of California Press, Berkeley and London, 1998, p. 28.
9. A notable addition to Faisal's camp was Sati' al-Husri. He was made responsible for educational matters. Al-Husri was a prominent Ottoman-era functionary and pedagogue, but would later feature as the main ideologue of the Arab nationalist cause.
10. To make its financial situation worse, the Arab government, in a bid to boost its popularity, abolished a number of Ottoman-era special taxes and levies.
11. All the quotations from Faisal's speech are from: Abu Khaldun Sati' al-Husri, *Yawm Maysaloun: safha min tarikh al-'Arab al-Hadith*, Wizarat al-Thaqafa al-Soorya, Damascus, 2004, pp. 106–11. The speech was widely reported and variations of it have appeared in Amin Sa'id, op. cit., Vol. 2, pp. 24–34, and in Foreign Office, *Documents of British Foreign Policy*, First Series, Vol. IV, HMSO, London, pp. 267–72.
12. Clayton to Curzon, 5 June 1919, in Foreign Office, op. cit., p. 266.
13. Nasib al-Bakri, however, was gradually distanced from Faisal and later broke with him over the issue of the French mandate for Syria.
14. Foreign Office, op. cit., Vol. IV, p. 264.
15. These could only have been exacerbated by a private letter that Faisal received from Rustum Haidar dated 7 May 1919, in which Haidar wrote, 'Every day makes me believe more intensely my original views and confirms to me the evil intentions of the French government. We must not believe in France's scorpion-like promises.' Suleiman Musa, op. cit. Vol. II, pp. 71–73.
16. Rustum Haidar had already warned Faisal of the determination of the Allied powers to have a mandate system and pleaded that the calls for complete independence were not only impractical but might fatally alienate the powers. Foreign Office, op. cit., Vol. IV, p. 264.
17. Ibid., p. 265.
18. Ibid., pp. 287–89.
19. Ibid., p. 288.
20. Ibid., pp. 278–80; Memorandum by Colonel K. Cornwallis.
21. Jukka Nevakivi, op. cit., pp. 145–46; Amin Sa'id, op. cit., Vol. II, pp. 45–46.
22. See Mary Wilson, *King 'Abdullah, Britain and the Making of Jordan*, Cambridge University Press, Cambridge, 1960, pp. 36–38, on 'Abdullah and Turaba.
23. Yusuf Hakim, op. cit., p. 74; Abu Kaldun Sati' al-Husri, Mudhakarati Fil-'Iraq, Vol.1, Manshourat Dar al-Tali'ah, Beirut, 1967, pp. 112–13.
24. Khairiya Qasimiya, op. cit., pp. 108–09.
25. The Syrian Congress later moved to a building in Damascus's main square at al-Marja.
26. As'ad Daghir, op. cit., pp. 131–32.
27. See James L. Gelvin, op. cit., pp. 82–83. The Aleppan elite in particular were concerned about the economic effects of the separation of Syria from Iraq.
28. Rustum Haidar, op. cit., p. 414.
29. The sincerity of these anti-French sentiments was somewhat suspect; a number of the deputies would later open up channels to the French and some would become openly supportive of a French mandate over Syria.
30. The full text of the resolution can be found in George Antonius, op. cit., Appendix G, pp. 440–42.
31. Ibid., p. 441.
32. Yusuf Hakim, op. cit., p. 100.
33. James L. Gelvin, op. cit., pp. 150–52.
34. Harry N. Howard, op. cit., pp. 119–23.

35. Malcolm B. Russell, op. cit., p. 90.
36. France provided a supplementary funding of two million francs to sway wavering opinion in its favour. In one case, the head of the powerful 'Annaza tribal confederation in Northern Syria supported a French mandate in exchange for one million francs. See Malcolm B. Russell, op. cit., p. 88.
37. Ibid., p. 134.
38. Zeine N. Zeine, *The Struggle for Arab Independence: Western Diplomacy and the Rise and Fall of Faisal's Kingdom in Syria*, Caravan Books, London, 1977, pp. 88–91.
39. Foreign Office, op. cit., Vol. IV, pp. 318–20.
40. Muhammad Izzat Darwaza, op. cit., pp. 494–95.
41. Ibid., p. 366.
42. Foreign Office, op. cit., Vol. IV, pp. 388–90.
43. Ibid., pp. 385–88.
44. Neither did the British much care about the cable that Hussein sent to King George V on 9 September 1919 expressing his worries about the rumours of the partitioning of the Arab lands.
45. Fouad al-Khatib was a Lebanese who had graduated from the American University of Beirut and was a founder of the De-Centralisation Party. He fled Lebanon during the governorship of Jamal Pasha and later joined Sharif Hussein in Mecca. Hussein later appointed him the Hijaz's foreign minister. He was then appointed by Hussein as the Hijaz's representative to the Arab government in Damascus.
46. General Gabriel (Jibrail) Haddad was born in Tripoli and a graduate of the American University of Beirut. He joined the Egyptian gendarmerie under its British chief, Harvey Bey. Allenby then appointed him as the assistant to the governor of Jerusalem, with the rank of major, after its occupation by his forces. After the occupation of Damascus by Faisal's army, Allenby recommended to Faisal that Haddad be used to organise and lead the police and gendarmerie forces in Syria. Haddad was then promoted to the rank of brigadier general (in the British army).
47. Suleiman Musa, op. cit., Vol. II, p. 101.
48. Mrs Steuart Erskine, op. cit., pp. 100–01.
49. Rustum Haidar, who was then in Paris, set out twice to meet Faisal's train in Paris, but found to his chagrin that the train was not stopping in Paris. Haidar, op. cit., p. 466.
50. The full minutes of the meeting of 19 September 1919 are carried in Foreign Office, op. cit., Vol. IV, pp. 395–404.
51. Ibid., pp. 403–04.
52. Ibid., pp. 406–09.
53. Suleiman Musa, op. cit., Vol. II, p. 142.
54. Rustum Haidar, op. cit., p. 472.
55. Rustum Haidar, op. cit., pp. 472–74.
56. 'Awni 'Abd al-Hadi, op. cit., pp. 81–82; Joseph Jeffries, op. cit., pp. 306–08.
57. Suleiman Musa, op. cit., Vol. II, pp. 141–43.
58. Ibid., p. 144.
59. 'Awni 'Abd al-Hadi, op. cit., p. 81.
60. Foreign Office, op. cit., Vol. IV, pp. 443–44.
61. Ibid., pp. 444–49.
62. Clemenceau, however, torpedoed these arrangements and refused to countenance the establishment of such a commission, or to send General Gouraud to London to open discussions with Faisal.
63. *The Times*, 11 September 1919.
64. Foreign Office, op. cit., Vol. IV, pp. 422–24.
65. Ibid., p. 491.
66. Ibid., pp. 510–11.
67. Rustum Haidar, op. cit., pp. 482–83. 'Awni 'Abd al-Hadi also met Polk subsequently, who wrote to his government advocating support for Faisal's position, but nothing came of this effort.
68. Ibid., pp. 513–15; 'Awni 'Abd al-Hadi, op. cit., pp. 82–84.
69. Ibid., pp. 516–19.
70. Ibid., pp. 520–22.
71. Suleiman Musa, op. cit., Vol. II, p. 90.

14. The Collapse of the Kingdom of Syria

1. Foreign Office, op. cit., Vol. IV, pp. 565–66.
2. Rustum Haidar, op. cit., pp. 512–14.

3. Ibid., p. 566. Meinterzhagen was not the most reliable or dispassionate of observers (in fact many of his claims were later proven fraudulent), but his comments on the loss of standing of the sharifians can be corroborated by contemporary observers.

4. Phebe Ann Marr, op. cit., p. 80.

5. Ibid., pp. 409–11.

6. Khairiya Qasimiya, op. cit., pp. 143–44. Hakim gives the date as 10 November 1919. Yusuf Hakim, op. cit., p. 116.

7. Ibid., p. 116.

8. Al-Qassab had studied at al-Azhar in Cairo, and was an early member of al-Fatat society. He had left Syria for Egypt at the onset of war, and cooperated for a while with Sharif Hussein. He was one of the 'Seven' to whom the British government had addressed its famous declaration. He returned to Damascus after the formation of the Arab government.

9. Many people have taken credit for the formation of the Lajna, including Dr Ahmad Qadri, Faisal's physician. See Ahmad Qadri, op. cit., Vol. 1, pp. 149–50.

10. Amin Sa'id, op. cit., Vol. 2, pp. 101–03.

11. Khairiya Qasimiya, op. cit., p. 144, footnote 2, citing a personal interview with al-Khatib.

12. Ibid., pp. 144–45.

13. Ibid., p. 523; Amin Sa'id, op. cit., Vol. 2, p. 102.

14. Yusuf Hakim, op. cit., pp. 116–17.

15. Ibid., p. 122.

16. Malcom B. Russell, op. cit., p. 111.

17. Rustum Haidar, op. cit., p. 527.

18. Ibid., p. 112.

19. Ibid., p. 113.

20. Suleiman Musa, op. cit., Vol. II, p. 234.

21. Al-Rikabi was also unpopular with the moderates. He was accused of nepotism and corruption.

22. Yusuf Hakim, op. cit., pp. 123–24; Khairiya Qasimiya, op. cit., pp. 149–51.

23. Al-'Asima newspaper, issue 87, 25 December 1919.

24. The Arab government had nearly run out of money by November 1919, and in desperation Zaid had cabled his father for an immediate transfer of £E50,000. Nothing was forthcoming. Suleiman Musa, op. cit., Vol. II, p. 232.

25. Gertrude Bell, 'Syria in October 1919', India Office, IO L/PS/10/802, 15 November 1919.

26. Khairiya Qasimiya, op. cit., pp. 151–52.

27. Eliezer Tauber, 'The Struggle for Dayr al-Zur: The Determination of Borders between Syria and Iraq', International Journal of Middle East Studies, Vol. 23, No. 3 (August 1991), pp. 361–85.

28. Rustum Haidar, op. cit., pp. 514–15. Haider wrote in his diary that Faisal was incensed at this action and instructed Zaid to denounce it as a crime and to arrest the culprits.

29. Ibid., p. 154, footnote 1, and Zeine N. Zeine, The Struggle for Arab Independence, pp. 147–48.

30. Ahmad Qadri, op. cit., Vol. 2, p. 160.

31. Ibid., pp. 164–65.

32. Ibid., pp. 162–69.

33. Malcolm B. Russell, op. cit., pp. 123–24; Ahmad Qadri, op. cit., Vol. 2, pp. 169–71.

34. Malcolm B. Russell, op. cit., pp. 124–26. Both al-Qassab and Yusuf al-'Azma made speeches that affirmed their readiness to fight if necessary.

35. Foreign Office, op. cit., Vol. IV, pp. 629–30.

36. Ahmad Qadri, op. cit., Vol. 2, p. 175.

37. Al-Muqattaf, Cairo, Part 3, Vol. 83, 1933.

38. Khairiya Qasimiya, op. cit., pp. 160–61; Ahmad Qadri, op. cit., Vol. 2, p. 173.

39. Malcolm B. Russell, op. cit., p. 66 and p. 120, footnote 49.

40. Philip S. Khoury, Syria and the French Mandate: The Politics of Arab Nationalism, 1920–1945, Princeton University Press, Princeton, New Jersey, pp. 38–39.

41. Murasalat Faisal–Gouraud (Faisal–Gouraud Correspondence), ed. George Edib Karim, Qism al-Dirasat al-Tarikhiya, Manshourat al-Jami'a al-Lubnaniya (Publications of the Lebanese University, Historical Studies Division), No. 50, Beirut, 2009, pp. 51–78.

42. Rustum Haidar, op. cit., p. 649; Malcolm B. Russell, op. cit., p. 131 and p. 235, footnote 73. Madame Berthe-George Gaulis was a well-known French writer, noted for her knowledge and experience of Middle Eastern affairs. She met Faisal many times during his stay in Paris and after in Damascus.

43. 'Awni 'Abd al-Hadi, op. cit., p. 87.

44. Joseph Jeffries, op. cit., p. 321.

45. Ahmad Qadri, op. cit.,Vol. 2, pp. 176–77.

46. Khairiya Qasimiya, op. cit., p. 164.
47. Ahmad Qadri, op. cit.,Vol. 2, pp. 178–81, where the full text of Faisal's speech is given.
48. *Al-'Asima*, Damascus, No. 108. 11 March 1920, as quoted in Khairiya Qasimiya, op. cit., p. 165, footnote 1.
49. Abu Khaldun Sati' al-Husri, op. cit., p. 136.
50. At a much smaller conference of Iraqi political and military leaders in Damascus on the same day, the independence of Iraq was also announced by Tawfiq al-Suwaidi, with 'Abdullah as the putative king.
51. Malcolm B. Russell, op. cit., p. 236, footnote 12; Khairya Qasimiya, op. cit., pp. 165–66. Faisal was not crowned as such because no crown was available. That was left for a later date, 20 March, but then forgotten.
52. *Murasalat Faisal–Gouraud*, op. cit., pp. 98–99.
53. Rustum Haidar and 'Awni 'Abd al-Hadi, who were probably the closest of Faisal's confidants at this time, refer to this constantly. Indeed, Ja'far Pasha al-'Askari said that Faisal had no personal ambition. See Mrs Steuart Erskine, op. cit., p. 3.
54. Malcolm B. Russell, op. cit., pp. 137–38, quoting French despatches.
55. See Zeine N. Zeine, *Struggle for Arab Independence*, p. 147, footnote 2.
56. Foreign Office, op. cit., Vol. XIII, pp. 224–25.
57. Suleiman Musa, op. cit., Vol. III, pp. 82–83.
58. Foreign Office, op. cit., Vol. XIII, pp. 223.
59. Ibid., p. 225. Two days earlier the French ambassador in London had sent a note to Curzon, vigorously protesting the decisions of the Syrian Congress and demanding that the Powers declare them void.
60. Ibid., pp. 226–29.
61. Ibid., p. 232.
62. Foreign Office, op. cit., Vol. XIII, pp. 233–34. The use of the term 'Damascus Congress' in official documents to refer to the Syrian Congress was a deliberate attempt to diminish the latter's significance and legitimacy.
63. Suleiman Musa, op. cit., Vol. III, p. 85.
64. Malcolm B. Russell, op. cit., pp. 158–59.
65. Foreign Office, op. cit., Vol. XIII, pp. 237–39. In a record of his meeting with the French ambassador on 30 March 1920, Curzon wrote that the Anglo-French subsidy to Faisal of £100,000 per month had not been paid since the end of 1919, and that it should be withheld if Faisal pursues 'an unfriendly and independent policy'.
66. Rustum Haidar, op. cit., pp. 623–27.
67. David Lloyd George, op. cit., Vol. I, p. 622.
68. Abu Khaldun Sati' al-Husri, op. cit., p. 145.
69. Foreign Office, op. cit., Vol. XIII, pp. 257–58.
70. Yusuf Hakim, op. cit., pp. 156–58.
71. Ibid., p. 162.
72. Suleiman Musa, op. cit., Vol. III, p. 111.
73. Yusuf Hakim, op. cit., p. 162.
74. Foreign Office, op. cit., Vol. XIII, pp. 271–72.
75. *Murasalat Faisal–Gouraud*, pp. 238–39.
76. Ibid., p. 247.
77. Ibid., pp. 178–81.
78. Foreign Office, op. cit., Vol. XIII, pp. 282–83.
79. *Murasalat Faisal–Gouraud*, op. cit., pp. 192–93.
80. The issue of whether the delegates were planning to present their case of their own volition, or were induced to do so by bribes, was contentious. It was still not settled when, years later, 'Adil Arslan, Faisal's adviser, wrote in the Lebanese daily *al-Hayat* on 21 November 1952 that the delegation had coordinated their actions with Nuri al-Sa'id and the Lebanese Sunni politician Riyadh al-Solh. A wealthy Lebanese Muslim merchant, 'Arif al-Nu'mani, provided them with their travel funds. However, Amin Rihani, the traveller and historian, says that the funds came from Faisal but were routed through al-Nu'mani. However, al-Nu'mani, writing in 1953 and also in *al-Hayat* newspaper, claimed that the entire amount of £10,500 gold pounds came from him and was routed through Riyadh al-Solh.
81. Foreign Office, op. cit., Vol. XIII, p. 288.
82. Malcolm B. Russell, op. cit., pp. 89–90.
83. Khairiya Qasimiya, op. cit., pp. 195–96 and p. 196, footnote 1.
84. *Murasalat Faisal–Gouraud*, op. cit., pp. 268–75.

85. Ibid., 279–82.
86. Foreign Office, op. cit.,Vol. XIII, p. 313.
87. Kingdom of Iraq Directorate of Public Information, op. cit., pp. 213–17.
88. The French tried – and succeeded – in subverting some of the cabinet through generous cash handouts and promises of jobs in the new French order. In particular, Ala' al-Din al-Durubi, the minister of interior, was won over to the side of the French.
89. Khairiya Qasimiya, op. cit., pp. 200–01; Yusuf Hakim, op. cit., pp. 180–81; Malcolm B. Russell, op. cit., pp. 180–81.
90. Yusuf Hakim, op. cit., pp. 181–82.
91. Khairiya Qasimiya, op. cit., pp. 200–01; Yusuf Hakim, op. cit., p. 182.
92. Ibid., p. 202, footnote 1.
93. Ibid., pp. 202–03.
94. Taha al-Hashimi, *Mudhkarat Taha al-Hashimi*, ed. Khaldun S. al-Husry, Vol. I, Manshourat Dar al-Tali'a, Beirut, 1967, pp. 61–62.
95. Subhi al-'Umari, *Maysaloun*, Vol. 3, pp. 137–38.
96. The issue of why the telegraph lines were cut and by whom has been contentious. The best evidence is that the lines were cut – or allowed to be cut – as a deliberate ploy by the French to avoid receiving the acceptance of the ultimatum. See Malcolm B. Russell, op. cit., pp. 191–94.
97. Khairiya Qasimiya, op. cit., pp. 203–04, footnote 1.
98. Ahmad Qadri, op. cit., Vol. 2, p. 251.
99. Abu Khaldun Sati' al-Husri, op. cit., pp. 60–74; Ahmad Qadri, op. cit., Vol. 2, pp. 261–73.
100. Abu Khaldun Sati' al-Husri, op. cit., pp. 79–82.
101. *Murasalat Faisal–Gouraud*, op. cit., pp. 354–56.
102. Ahmad Qadri, op. cit., Vol. 2, pp. 272–73; Amin al-Rihani, op. cit., Vol. 2, p. 206.
103. As'ad Daghir, op. cit., pp. 148–49.
104. Ahmad Qadri, op. cit., Vol. 2, pp. 274–75.
105. Yusuf Hakim, op. cit., pp. 203–04.
106. Ibid., pp. 198–99. Those who left for the relative safety of Palestine, included al-Shabandar and Shaikh Kamil al-Qassab. Iraqi officers such as Yasin al-Hashimi and Jamil al-Madfa'i were in a quandary. The British were no friends to them so they took their chances and stayed in Syria. As'ad Daghir, op. cit., p. 146.

15. Adrift

1. Foreign Office, op. cit., Vol. IV, p. 323.
2. Ibid., pp. 320–22.
3. Ibid., p. 321.
4. Ibid., pp. 323–24.
5. Ahmad Qadri, op. cit., pp. 276–77; Amin Sa'id, op. cit., Vol. 2, p. 208.
6. Ronald Storrs, op. cit., p. 455. Storrs in a letter home reflected on Faisal's condition and noted, 'We are all exceedingly grieved for him, and are far from certain he has been quite fairly treated.' Ronald Storrs, op. cit., p. 455.
7. Foreign Office, op. cit., Vol. IV, pp. 325–26.
8. Ibid., p. 330.
9. Ibid.
10. Suleiman Musa, op. cit., pp. 141–43.
11. 'Awni 'Abd al-Hadi, op. cit., p. 101.
12. Abu Khaldun Sati' al-Husri, op. cit., p. 85.
13. Ahmad Qadri, op. cit., pp. 277–78.
14. This account contradicts the mischievous and erroneous comment made by Samuel in his memoirs that some person had told Samuel that Faisal was on the verge of collapse because he thought the guard of honour was an arresting party. See Herbert Samuel, *Memoirs*, Cresset Press, London, 1945, pp. 158–59.
15. Muhammad Izzat Darwaza, op. cit., pp. 570–71.
16. Ronald Storrs, op. cit., p. 456.
17. Abu Khaldun Sati' al-Husri, op. cit., pp. 85–86.
18. Foreign Office, op. cit., Volume IV, p. 334.
19. Abu Khaldun Sati' al-Husri, op. cit., pp. 87–90. Al-Husri's main contact with the Kemalists had been Ferid Bey, the minister of finance. Ferid Bey was almost dismissive of al-Husri's overtures. 'We do not know the present attitude of the Hijazi ruling group towards us [the Kemalists]. However, we think that this government is too responsive now to English influence.'

20. Ibid., pp. 90–92.
21. Suleiman Musa, op. cit., p. 151.
22. Foreign Office, op. cit., Vol. IV, pp. 344–45.
23. The Lutfallahs were prominent backers of the Hashemite cause. Their father, Habib Lutfallah, was a Syrian Orthodox Christian who had made a fortune in Egypt. He became a friend, financial adviser and confidant of Hussein, who gave him the title of amir (prince). His three sons, Michel, Habib Junior and George, were active supporters of the Hashemites. Michel was a key fundraiser for Hussein, Habib Jr became head of the Hijaz delegation in Paris and George was a key financial backer to the Syrian Unity Party that supported Faisal in Damascus. All three brothers inherited the title of prince.
24. Rustum Haidar, op. cit., pp. 704–08.
25. Abu Khaldun Sati' al-Husri, op. cit., pp. 88–93.
26. Rustum Haidar, op. cit., p. 716 and pp. 728–29.
27. FO to Kennard, Rome Telegram No. 429; FO 371 E11251/5040.
28. Rustum Haidar, op. cit., pp. 715–16.
29. Ibid., pp. 719–20.
30. The Khilafat (Caliphate) movement in India started as a call to safeguard this venerable institution from its possible abolition by the victorious Allies in the First World War. However, the movement was more to do with the political organisation of India's Muslims, and was an instrument supported by Ghandi for joint Muslim–Hindu action in the struggle against the British Raj. The Ali brothers, Muhammad and Shawkat, were important figures in the movement.
31. Mahmud al-Hassan was an important Indian Muslim religious figure, associated with the Dar ul-Uloom seminary at Deoband. He was known to his followers as Shaikh al-Hind. While in Mecca for the Haj in September 1915, he contacted Turkish officials to help a group of his followers to launch a revolt against the British in India. He was in Mecca when the Arab Revolt broke out. He refused to sign a fatwa in support of the uprising and Hussein had him arrested and handed over to the British, who had earlier got wind of the conspiracy.
32. The entire text of the letter is reproduced in Amin Sa'id, op. cit., Vol. 2, pp. 211–33. It is a very long letter, twenty pages in Arabic, and unlikely to have been read in its entirety by Lloyd George. Curiously, Lloyd George does not mention it at all in his memoirs. Faisal to Lloyd George, 11 September 1920, FO 371, E11500/5040.
33. Suleiman Musa, op. cit., pp. 148–57.
34. Fritz Groppa, *Manner und Macht im Orient*, Musterschmidt-Verlag, Gottingen, Zurich, Berlin, Frankfurt, 1967, pp. 173–75. Translated into Arabic by Nejdat Fathi Safwat and reproduced in his book, *Al-'Iraq fi Mudhakarat al-Diplomasiyin al-Ajanib*, Maktabat al-Tahrir, Beirut, 1969, pp. 130–33.
35. Timothy J. Paris, 'British Middle East Policy-Making after the First World War: The Lawrentian and Wilsonian Schools', *The Historical Journal*, Vol. 41, No. 3 (September 1998), p. 779.
36. Fahmi al-Muddaris was an Iraqi writer and journalist. He was the editor of the official *Zawra'* newspaper in Baghdad during the Ottoman era and taught Arabic literature and Islamic Sharia at Istanbul University. He was one of the founders of al-'Ahd Party. He briefly joined Faisal in Damascus but left for travels in Europe where he moved between London, Paris and Madrid. He returned to Baghdad and held a number of official positions, including chamberlain to Faisal and director general of the Ministry of Education.
37. Foreign Office, op. cit., Volume IV, p. 418.
38. Timothy J. Paris, op. cit., pp. 777–78. The India Office, of course, thought less of Lawrence's capabilities. '[Lawrence] had practically no first hand at all knowledge of Mesopotamia . . . [and his plans for Mesopotamia] had nothing to commend it,' wrote Arthur Hirtzel.
39. Young was awarded the DSO for gallantry during a battle with the Turks at Mezerib in September 1918.
40. Timothy J., Paris, op. cit., p. 786.
41. Foreign Office, op. cit., Volume IV, pp. 337–37.
42. Minute, 16 June 1920, FO 371/5227, quoted in Timothy J. Paris, op. cit., p. 789.
43. Minute, 29 September 1920, L/P&S/10/936, quoted in Timothy J. Paris, op. cit., p. 790.
44. Minute, 5 December 1920, ibid., quoted in Timothy J. Paris, op. cit., p. 791.
45. FO 371,E10953/5040, 'A report on a conversation between Faisal and 'Abd-ul-Malik al-Khatib', Despatch no. 970, quoted in Nur Masalha, 'King Faisal I of Iraq: A Study of his Political Leadership, 1921–1933'. PhD Thesis, London University, 1988.
46. Minute, R. Marrs, 178/10/1920 IO L/P&SW/10/927, 17 October 1920.
47. Note of a conversation between Colonel Frank Balfour and General Haddad, September 1920. Balfour Papers, Sudan Archive, Durham, Box 303. Quoted in Peter Sluglett, *Britain in Iraq 1914–1932*, Columbia University Press, New York, 2007, p. 63.

48. Rustum Haidar, op. cit., pp. 716–17.
49. Suleiman Musa, op. cit., pp. 158–59.

16. A King in Waiting

1. Elizabeth Burgoyne, *Gertrude Bell from her Personal Papers, 1914–1926*, Benn, London, 1961, p. 245.
2. 'Awni 'Abd al-Hadi, op. cit., pp. 126–27.
3. Jeremy Wilson, op. cit., pp. 641–42.
4. Rustum Haidar, op. cit., p. 750.
5. Ibid., pp. 751–52. Later, several British companies were organised to undertake large-scale agricultural schemes in Iraq, but operating within the constraints of Iraqi law.
6. Ibid., p. 752.
7. Rustum Haidar, op. cit., pp. 751–52.
8. Ibid., pp. 756–57.
9. Ibid., p. 755.
10. Ibid., p. 755.
11. Foreign Office, op. cit., Vol. IV, p. 411.
12. Suleiman Musa, op. cit., pp. 160–62.
13. Jeremy Wilson, op. cit., p. 646.
14. Foreign Office, op. cit., Vol. IV, pp. 422–23.
15. Rustum Haidar, op. cit., pp. 757–58. The night before, Faisal had invited Cornwallis for dinner, where he had been equally obstreperous.
16. Rustum Haidar, op. cit., p. 565.
17. FO 371/6349, Document E-583, dated 7 January 1921.
18. Ibid.
19. Rustum Haidar, op. cit., pp. 765–66.
20. Lord Winterton, *Orders of the Day*, Cassell, London, 1953, pp. 101–02.
21. Alan H. Brodrick, *Near to Greatness: A Life of the Sixth Earl Winterton*, Hutchinson, London, 1965, p. 19.
22. Rustum Haidar, op. cit., pp. 766–67.
23. Guinness became Lord Moyne, and was resident minister in Cairo during the latter part of the Second World War. He was assassinated in Cairo in November 1944 by operatives of the Zionist terrorist group, the Stern Gang.
24. Rustum Haidar, op. cit., pp. 765–66.
25. Ibid., pp. 768–69. Haidar believed that the India Office, together with the Zionists, supported the actions of ibn Saud mainly to weaken the drive towards Arab unity that might threaten their interests.
26. Suleiman Musa, op. cit., pp. 174–76; FO 371/6371.
27. Rustum Haidar, op. cit., pp. 769–70.
28. Ibid., pp. 770–71.
29. See, for example, Anis Sayegh, *Al-Hashimiyoun wal Thawra al-Arabiya al-Kubra*, Dar al-Tali'a, Beirut, 1966.
30. Even the War Office came on board. In a memo written on 17 February 1921, FO 371/6349, the general staff commented on Faisal's candidature for the 'Proposed Kingdom of Mesopotamia', by detailing the French objections and the alarm that this would be raised amongst the leaders of Arabia such as ibn Saud. 'In short, if Feisal is proclaimed King of Mesopotamia, there is a great possibility of a conflagration flaring up throughout the Arabian Peninsular.' But there were many other advantages on grounds of imperial prestige, his acceptability to all Iraqis on religious grounds, his steadying effect on the Middle East and his hostility to Bolshevism. The report concluded that 'yet it is the opinion of the General Staff that the advantages distinctly outweigh the disadvantages; and that the accession of Feisal as King of Mesopotamia would produce beneficial results.'
31. 'Awni 'Abd al-Hadi, op. cit., pp. 127–28.
32. They also had time to indulge Faisal in his literary interests. Lawrence and Faisal lunched with E. M. Forster, the novelist, at the Mayfair Hotel, and Faisal was introduced to the writer and poet of Iraqi Jewish extraction, Siegfried Sassoon. Malcolm Brown, editor, *The Letters of T. E. Lawrence*, Dent and Sons, London, 1988, p. 256.
33. Rustum Haidar, op. cit. pp. 773–75.
34. Jeremy Wilson, op. cit., p. 645.
35. Ibid., pp. 776–77.

36. Jeremy Wilson, op. cit., pp. 646–47.
37. 'Abd al-Rahman al-Gailani, known as *naqib al-ashraf* (Master of the Lords), was a direct descendant of 'Abd al-Qadir al-Gailani, the eleventh-century founder of the Qadiri Sufi order. The *naqib al-ashraf* was a formal Ottoman post denoting primacy amongst those who claim descendence from the Prophet Muhammad. (The equivalent Shi'a term is *Sayyid*.) The naqib was born in 1845 in the Bab al-Shaikh neighbourhood of Baghdad, close to the shrine of Shaikh 'Abd al-Qadir. He studied the traditional religious sciences but was also a man of high literary sensibilities, engrossed in chivalrous pursuits worthy of his lineage. He became *naqib al-ashraf* after the death of his brother in 1898. His first involvement in politics was when he, together with other *ashrafs*, founded a political party in 1909 in opposition to the policies of the CUP and in support of the Sultan 'Abd al-Hamid.
38. FO 371/6343, Minutes of the First Meeting of the Political Committee, 12 March 1921.
39. Ibid., p. 647 and p. 1,118, footnote 17, Winston Churchill to Lloyd George, WSC docs 4/2, p.1389.
40. Suleiman Musa, op cit., pp. 195–200.
41. Ibid.
42. Ibid., pp. 200–02.
43. Suleiman Musa, op. cit., pp. 191–93.
44. FO 686/85, Curzon to Lord Hardinge, 23 March 1921.
45. FO 686/85, Curzon to Lord Hardinge (Paris), 6 April 1921.
46. 'Awni 'Abd al-Hadi, op. cit., pp. 127–28.
47. Ibid., pp. 128–29.
48. Ibid., pp. 134–35.
49. Ibid., p. 101.
50. Jeremy Wilson, op. cit., p. 648.
51. FO 371/6343, Lloyd George to Churchill, 22 March 1921.
52. Jeremy Wilson, op. cit., p. 615.
53. 'Awni 'Abd al-Hadi, op. cit., p. 132.
54. Ibid., pp. 132–33.
55. Ibid., pp. 133–35.
56. Another attendee from Baghdad at the conference was the Jewish minister of finance in the interim Iraqi government, Sassoon Heskeil. Sassoon made an inopportune remark to Churchill that Iraq was used to being governed by people from the north, but that this time it would be getting a man from the south, Faisal. Churchill replied that the man from the south would be assisted by a man from the north, Cornwallis. Faisal was upset by Sassoon's indelicate remark and was never at ease with him.
57. FO 404 E5784/46, also Nur Masalha, op. cit., p. 50.
58. 'Abd al-Razzaq al-Hasani, *Tarikh al-Wizarat al-Iraqiya*, Vol. I, Afaq 'Arabiya, Baghdad, 1988, p. 40.
59. CO 730/2/23117; Nur Masalha, op. cit., p. 54.

17. From Mesopotamia to Iraq

1. The population of Iraq in 1920 was estimated at 2,849,000. A majority of the population (56 per cent) were Shi'a Arabs, while the Kurds and Sunni Arabs accounted for about 18 per cent of the population each. The remainder was Jews, Christians, Yazidis, Persians and Mandaeans. *Statistical Abstract for Several British Overseas Dominions and Protectorates from 1907–1921*, No. 56, HMSO, London, 1921.
2. Ali al-Wardi, *Lamhat Ijtima'iya min Tareekh al-Iraq al-Hadith*, Vol. 4, Baghdad, n.d., p. 83.
3. A. J. Barker, *The First Iraq War, 1914–1918: Britain's Mesopotamian Campaign*, Enigma Books, New York, 2009, pp. 39–55. A group of Anatolian soldiers tied their knees together to stop themselves from escaping and fought to the end.
4. Ghassan Atiyyah, *al-'Iraq: Nash'aat al Dawla*, Lam Publishers, London, 1988, pp. 252–53.
5. Ghassan Atiyyah, op. cit., pp. 132–34.
6. There were nearly 1,500 Iraqis studying in the Ottoman war colleges in 1914. Ghassan Atiyyah, op. cit., p. 134.
7. Ibid., p. 131.
8. Ibid., pp. 92–95, and pp. 124–28. Also, Suleyman Faydhi, *Mudhakarat Suleyman Faydhi: Fi Ghumrat al-Nidhal*, Dar al-Qalam, Beirut, 1974.
9. His favourite companion was a prostitute by the name of Film. He was reputed to have told her, 'I am the Commander over Iraq – but you command me!' Abbas al'Azzawi, *Tareekh al-Iraq bayn Ihtilalayn*, Vol. 8, al-Maktaba al-Hayderia, Qum, 2004, pp. 291–301.

10. A. J. Barker, op. cit., p. 261.

11. Ghassan Attiyah, op. cit., pp. 214–17.

12. FO 371/3387/142404. Enclosure – 'The Future of Mesopotamia' by Sir Percy Cox, London, 22 April 1918. See also Ghassan Attiyah, op. cit., p. 220, footnote 26.

13. John Marlowe, *Late Victorian: The Life of Sir Arnold Talbot Wilson*, Cresset, London, 1967.

14. Lawrence's earliest proposal, as it would be recalled, included the division of Iraq into two states: Baghdad and Lower Mesopotamia, with 'Abdullah as king; and Mosul, with Zaid as its amir.

15. Philip Ireland, *Iraq: A study in Political Development*, Jonathan Cape, London, 1937, p. 157.

16. These included: a Mosul notable, Hadi Pasha al-'Umari; a member of the family of the sultan of Egypt; a son of the sharif of Mecca; and the naqib of Baghdad, 'Abd al-Rahman al-Gailani.

17. Philip Ireland, op. cit., pp. 166–67.

18. Ali al-Wardi, op. cit., Vol. 5, p. 69.

19. Ibid., pp. 75–76. There were other princes that the dignitaries of Karbala had considered, including a scion of the Qajar dynasty and an Ottoman prince.

20. Ali al-Wardi, op. cit., Vol. 5, pp. 79–84; Philip Ireland, op. cit., pp. 170–71.

21. Ibid., pp. 88–90.

22. Curzon was instrumental in formulating Britain's 1919 treaty with Persia.

23. Philip Ireland, op. cit., pp. 180–81.

24. Ibid, p. 182.

25. Ali al-Wardi, op. cit., Vol. 5, pp. 92–94. In inimitable fashion, the two parties were soon at each other's throats.

26. Ibid., p. 102.

27. Ibid., pp. 104–05.

28. Ibid., pp. 106–08.

29. The tribes of the Euphrates contained a large contingent of *sayyids*, descendants of the Prophet Muhammad. The *sayyids* were important glue in tribal society and were in the front line in settling tribal disputes and stopping them from turning into full-scale war. They were also an important link between the tribes and the religious hierarchies in the shrine towns.

30. Ali al-Wardi, op. cit., Vol. 4, pp. 298–99.

31. Ali 'Abd Shnaw, *Muhammad Ridha al-Shibibi wa dawrahu al-fikri wal siyasi- hata 'am 1932*, Dar Kufan lil Nashr, London, 1995, pp. 126–28.

32. Ibid., p. 129.

33. Ali al-Wardi, op. cit., Vol. 5, p. 123.

34. Ghassan 'Attiyah, op. cit., pp. 378–79. The letter was signed by Naji al-Suwaidi, Mawlud Mukhlis, Thabit 'Abd al-Nour and Naji al-Aseel.

35. Ibid., p. 386.

36. Arab Bureau Papers, Series C, Document No. SY/19/10; memorandum by Gertrude Bell, 'Syria in 1919', November 1919.

37. Ghassan 'Attiyah, op. cit., p. 386.

38. Ali al-Wardi, op. cit., Vol. 5, p. 189.

39. Elizabeth Burgoyne, op. cit., Vol. 2, p. 137.

40. Ali al-Wardi, op. cit., Vol. 5, pp. 199–200. The letter remained undelivered as the courier chosen for the task, Shaikh Baqir al-Shibibi, could not travel to Damascus because of the outbreak of fighting in the mid-Euphrates area.

41. There is some dispute as to the exact timing of the fatwa, as it was undated. In all probability, it was issued after Wilson had refused to meet with the grand ayatollah's emissaries. Wilson also studiously ignored another appeal for calm by a leading ayatollah, Shaikh al-Shar'ia al-Isfahani.

42. Ali al-Wardi, op. cit., Vol. 5, p. 331.

43. The appeal was never delivered as the emissary who was to carry it to the various legations in Iran panicked and hid it; it was retrieved much later, too late to have any effect.

44. Ghassan 'Attiyah, op. cit., p. 443; Aylmer Haldane, *The Insurrection in Mesopotamia 1920*, Blackwood & Sons, London, 1922, p. 331.

45. Ibid, pp. 457–64.

46. Sassoon, born in Baghdad in 1860, was a scion of a prominent and long-established Jewish family of Baghdad. His father was the chief rabbi of Baghdad. He studied at the Alliance Jewish School in Baghdad, followed by legal studies in Istanbul, Berlin and London. He returned to Baghdad in 1885, where he was appointed translator to the Province of Baghdad, an important post that gave him access to foreign consulates. Sassoon was proficient in many languages, including Arabic,

Hebrew, Persian, Turkish, English, French and German. Later he was successively head of the Ottoman River Authority in Iraq and then member of the first Ottoman parliament after the 1908 revolution, representing Baghdad. He continued as an MP in Istanbul throughout the war, returning to Iraq at the beginning of 1920. He served five times as minister of finance during Faisal's reign, and later headed the parliamentary finance and economics committee. He died in Paris in August 1932. His eulogy was written by the poet Ma'arouf al-Rusafi. Its opening lines read:

> The telegraph line from Paris gave the woeful news [of Sassoon' death] / And Baghdad, the mother of Glory, broke out in tears and lamentations.

Its last lines are:

> If you meet any knowing man / Do not say that Sassoon has died but say / A planet has risen above the constellation of virtues.

18. King of Iraq

1. FO371/4179, Memorandum by Earl Curzon, 'A Note of Warning about the Middle East'. Also, 'Abd al-Majid Kamil al-Tikriti, *Al-Malik Faisal al-Awal wa Dawrahu fi Ta'sis al-Dawla al-Iraqiya al-Haditha*, Dar al-Shu'oon al-Thaqafiya, Baghdad, 1991, pp. 88–91.
2. Letters of Gertrude Bell, 23 June 1921, Gertrude Bell Archive, Newcastle University Library.
3. Ibid.
4. Muhammad Mudhaffar al-Adhami, op. cit.
5. Hussein Jamil, *Shahada Siyasiya 1908–1930*, Dar al-Lam, London, 1987, pp. 65–67.
6. Naji al-Suwaidi was born in Baghdad in 1882 into a well-established Sunni Arab family. He studied under the well-known Sunni cleric Muhammad Shukri al-Alousi before leaving to study law in Istanbul. He held several judiciary posts in the Ottoman Empire, before joining the administrative service and rising to the post of first inspector at the Ministry of Interior. He joined Faisal's government in Syria, serving as the deputy military governor of Aleppo. He returned to Baghdad in 1921, where he was appointed minister of justice in the second naqib cabinet. He held several ministerial posts under Faisal, finally becoming prime minister in 1929. He was involved in Rashid 'Ali's short-lived pro-Axis government as minister of finance. He was arrested by the British in 1941 and exiled to southern Africa, where he was held together with other Iraqis in an open prison. He died in Salisbury, Rhodesia (now Zimbabwe), in August 1942. Something of a dandy, he was known for his sharp legal mind and his eloquence. He was widely travelled, even visiting the nascent Soviet Union in 1923. Bell described him as 'slippery as an eel, but intelligent'.
7. *Al-Iraq* newspaper, 18 June 1921.
8. Ali al-Wardi, op. cit., Vol. 6, p. 86.
9. Al-Mandil had asked for a separate legislative assembly for Basra, a separate army and police service, and the power to levy its own taxes. However, he also indicated his willingness to accept Faisal as a common king for Basra and the remaining parts of Iraq. See Gertrude Bell, op. cit., letter of 23 June 1921.
10. Ali al-Wardi, op. cit., Vol. 6, pp. 86–87.
11. Elizabeth Monroe, *Britain's Moment in the Middle East 1914–1956*, Johns Hopkins Press, Baltimore, 1963, pp. 99–100.
12. Philip Ireland, op. cit., pp. 327–28.
13. Ali Jawdat, op. cit., pp. 144–46. Ali Jawdat had his revenge on Thomas. In 1924, while serving as minister of interior, Jawdat ensured that Thomas's employment contract would not be renewed.
14. Ibid., p. 144.
15. Ali 'Abd Shnaw, op. cit., pp. 166–67. Al-Shibibi also joined Faisal's train to Baghdad.
16. Ali al-Wardi, op. cit., Vol. 6, pp. 89–90.
17. Ibid., p. 90.
18. Nur Masalha, op. cit., p. 56.
19. Ali al-Wardi, op. cit., Vol. 6, p. 91.
20. Gertrude Bell, op. cit., letter of 30 June 1921.
21. Ibid.
22. Muhammad Mahdi al-Basir, *Tarikh al-Qadiyyah al-Iragiyyah*, Dar-al-Lam, London, 1988, p. 180.
23. Ali al-Wardi, op. cit., Vol. 6, p. 93.
24. Ghazi D'ham Fahad al-Marsoumy, *Al-Bilat al-Malaki fi al-Iraq wa Dawrahu fi Al-Hayat Al-Siyasiya 1921–1933*, Al-Dar al-Arabiya lil Mawsou'at, Beirut, 2002, pp. 19–20.
25. Ali 'Abd Shnaw, op. cit., pp. 165–166.

26. Khalid Abid Mushin, 'The Political Career of Ja'far Abu al-Timmen', Phd thesis, School of Oriental and African Studies, University of London, 1983, pp. 141–46.
27. CO 730/3/41687, Intelligence Report, 1 July 1921, No. 16, Secret. Also Nur Masalha, op. cit., p. 58.
28. The naqib later confided to Gertrude Bell that his change of heart regarding Faisal was mainly determined by the supportive attitude of the British to his candidature as king. He, the naqib, always took the advice of Sir Percy Cox and never acted against his wishes or those of the British government. But it is also true that the naqib saw Faisal as fit for kingship.
29. Al-Iraq newspaper, 9 July 1921; Ali al-Wardi, op. cit., Vol. 6, pp. 96–97.
30. Philip Ireland, op. cit., p. 331.
31. Ibid., p. 331.
32. Gertrude Bell, op. cit., letter of 16 July 1921.
33. Al-Iraq newspaper, 2 July 1921.
34. Gertrude Bell, op. cit., letter of 2 July 1921.
35. Ibid.
36. Al-Iraq newspaper, 11 July 1921. Two days later, the nationalist newspaper Dijla gave a different account of the event, reporting that the audience did not respond to Dawood's acclamation. This led to a protracted dispute as to what had happened, but the al-Iraq version is closer to the truth and was corroborated by intelligence reports. See Ali al-Wardi, op. cit., Vol. 6, pp. 101–02.
37. Gertrude Bell, op. cit., letter of 20 July 1921.
38. Al-Iraq newspaper, 16 July 1921. Dijla newspaper, in its usual provocative way, distorted Faisal's reply and made it appear that he was partial to the religious minorities. The paper was rapidly developing a reputation for malicious reporting against Faisal and his supporters. See Ali al-Wardi, op. cit., Vol. 6, pp. 101–02.
39. Al'aa Jasim Muhammad, Al-Malik Faisal al-Awal: Hayatahu wa Dawrahu al-Siyasi fi al-Thawra al-'Arabiya al-Kubra wa Suria wal 'Iraq, 1883–1933, Mustansiriya University, Baghdad, n.d., pp. 151–52.
40. Gertrude Bell, op. cit., letter of 31 July 1921.
41. Amin Rihani, op. cit., pp. 92–93.
42. Ali al-Wardi, op. cit., Vol. 6, pp. 109–10.
43. Ibid., p. 111.
44. Philby was replaced by Thomson, an adviser at the Iraqi Ministry of Finance. Philby then left for a three-month holiday in Iran, and after his return to Baghdad was offered the post of the British resident in Amman. There, he also got into altercations with the high commissioner, finally leaving British government service. He left for Jeddah, where he established an auto-importing firm, and became an adviser and friend to King 'Abd al-Aziz of Saudi Arabia. He converted to Islam in 1930 and became known as Haji 'Abdullah Philby. He left Saudi Arabia after he quarrelled with 'Abd al-Aziz's successor, Saud. He died in 1960. His son Kim was the notorious third man in the spy scandal that rocked Britain in the 1960s.
45. CO 730/3/41687, Intelligence Report, 1 July 1921, quoted in Nur Masalha, op. cit., p. 59. But there were also contrary reports. The American consul wrote that 'his candidacy is very unpopular', attributing it to a climate of apprehension and fear instilled by the British to anyone opposing Faisal's candidature. Nur Masalha, op. cit., p. 61.
46. Gertrude Bell, op. cit., letter of 7 July 1921.
47. 'Abd al-Razzaq al-Hasani, op. cit., Vol. 1, p. 51.
48. Ali al-Wardi, op. cit., Vol. 6, pp. 114–15.
49. The idea of madhbatas as a way of soliciting public opinion is not so outlandish. A similar process, the caucus system, was floated by the Coalition Provisional Authority in Iraq in November 2003, after the invasion and occupation of Iraq, to canvass opinion prior to the handover of power. It was shelved as a result of widespread opposition from the clerical leadership in Najaf and leading Iraqi politicians.
50. CO 730/4/40185, H. C. Baghdad to S/S for Colonies, 10 August 1921, Telegram 376.
51. CO 730/3/38478, Churchill, London, to Cox, Baghdad, 9 August 1921, Telegram 304.
52. CO 730/4/41449, Cox, Baghdad, to Churchill, London, 6 August 1921, Telegram 396.
53. Nur Masalha, op. cit., pp 65–67.
54. Gertrude Bell, op. cit., letter of 21 August 1921.
55. 'Abd al-Razzaq al-Hasani, op. cit., Vol. 1, pp. 66–68.
56. Ali al-Wardi, op. cit., Vol. 6, pp. 120–21. The poet then sought refuge at Sayyid Muhhamad al-Sadr's home, fearing arrest. Paradoxically, he gave the Baghdad newspaper Dijla another poem, which it published. It was in fulsome praise of Faisal. He had apparently written two poems, one for public recitation and one to be published.

19. Faisal, Cox and the Rise of the Opposition

1. Most of the information on Cox's life is drawn from his official biography: Philip Graves, *The Life of Sir Percy Cox*, Hutchinson, London and Melbourne, 1941.
2. *The Times*, 22 February 1937.
3. Documents of the Royal Palace, File K/11, Document Number 264, quoted in Ali al-Wardi, op. cit., Vol. 6, pp. 121–22.
4. FO371, E12643/6347, Cox, Baghdad to Churchill, London, 28 October 1921. Also Nur Masalha, op. cit., p. 74.
5. 'Abd al-Razzaq al-Hasani, op. cit. Vol. 1, p. 77.
6. See Tawfiq al-Suwaidi, *Mudhakaratti: Nusf Qarn min Tarikh al-Iraq wal Qadhiya al-Arabiya*, Al-Mua'assa al-Arabiyya lil Dirasat wal Nashr, Amman, 2011, pp. 76–77. Tawfiq al-Suwaidi hailed from a prominent Sunni Arab Baghdadi family that traces its origins to the Abbasid emperors. He was born in Baghdad in 1892 and completed his legal education in Istanbul before undertaking advanced studies at the Sorbonne. He was at the meetings of the Arab Congress in Paris in 1913. He also headed the Iraq Congress held in Damascus in 1920, at which 'Abdullah was nominated as king of Iraq. He occupied high positions in Faisal's administration, rising to be the speaker of Iraq's parliament in the latter years of Faisal's reign. Later, he held a variety of ministerial posts and first became prime minister in 1946. He was a staunch supporter of the monarchy and the western alliance until its overthrow in 1958. He died in Beirut in 1968.
7. When the flag was first flown at these processions, it was carried alongside the standards of the enemies of Imam Hussein. Sati' al-Husri, of all people, noticed it and ordered that the person carrying the new flag should march alongside the followers of Imam Hussein. Faisal was unaware of what was happening, but heartily approved when the matter was brought to his attention. Ali al-Wardi, op. cit., Vol. 6, pp. 128–30.
8. Ali Bazargan, *Al-Waqaiq al-Hakikiya fi Thawrat al-Iraq*, Assa'ad Printing Press, Baghdad, 1954, pp. 177–79. Baban turned out to be an excellent choice and became known for his concern for the welfare and safety of visiting pilgrims.
9. 'Abd al-Razzaq al-Hasani, op. cit., Vol. 1, pp. 80–82. The background to the raid was complex, involving the desire by ibn Saud to extract *zakat* tributes from the Iraqi tribes, and a dispute involving a tribal shaikh accused of embezzling who had taken refuge with his tribe with with ibn Saud. This shaikh was at the forefront of the Ikhwan raiding party.
10. Documents of the Royal Palace, File Number T/4/5A, Document 60.
11. They included Sassoon Effendi, the minister of finance, who was staunchly pro-British. His resignation was not accepted by Faisal, however.
12. He was particularly concerned with the loss of face of 'Abd al-Latif al-Mandil from Basra, who was known for his pro-Saud tendencies.
13. CO 730/21/16782 HC. Baghdad to S.S. for Colonies, 7 April 1922; also Nur Masalha, op. cit., p. 86.
14. Muhammad Mahdi al-Basir, op. cit., p. 202–03.
15. Al-Khalisi's original cables of invitation to the leaders and notables were blocked by the telegraph office, under orders from the Residency. Three days later, under public pressure, they relented and delivered the cables. Muhammad Mahdi al-Basir, op. cit., p. 203.
16. CO 730/21/21724, 15 April 1922.
17. Nur Masalha, op. cit., p. 87.
18. *Al-Istiqlal*, 6 April 1922; Ali al-Wardi, op. cit., Vol. 6, p. 144.
19. Khalid Abid Muhsin, op. cit., p. 161, footnote 63, quoting CO 730/35/25338, 28 April 1922.
20. *Dijla* newspaper, 16 April 1922.
21. Khalid Abid Muhsin, op. cit., pp. 152–55.
22. This petition was found in the papers of the Royal Palace, undated and unsigned. Ali al-Wardi, op. cit., Vol. 6, p. 151, footnote 73.
23. 'Abd al-'Aziz al-Qassab, *Min Dhikriyati*, Editions Oueidat, Beirut, 1962, p. 217.
24. FO 371/7770, 29 April 1922.
25. Philip Graves, *The Life of Sir Percy Cox*, Hutchinson, London, 1941, pp. 322–23.
26. Philip Ireland, op. cit., p. 340.
27. Gertrude Bell, op. cit., letter of 4 December 1921.
28. CO 730/23/37877, High Commissioner to S.S. for Colonies, 4 December 1921.
29. CO 730/20/10151, High Commissioner to S.S. for Colonies, 27 February 1922.
30. Amin Rihani, op. cit., p. 126.
31. Rihani adds that all these enemies subsequently became Iraq's friends, thanks to Faisal's diplomacy.
32. Amin Rihani, op. cit., pp. 126–27.

33. Amin Rihani, op. cit., pp. 127–28. The *sedara* was a type of headgear, introduced and popularised by Faisal, and was also known as the *faisaliya*. It was widely worn in 1920s Iraq, and up to the 1940s. It was meant to replace the Ottoman *tarboush* or fez, and to avoid going bareheaded. The hat was seen as too European while the *sedara* had the virtue of being both conservative and distinctive. It was a type of fore-and-aft cap worn by the military.

34. Amin Rihani, op. cit., p. 128.

35. Muhammad al-Sadr was born into the famous al-Sadr family, known for its religious learning, in Kadhimain on 30 October 1883. His father, Sayyid Hussein al-Sadr, was a known *mujtahid*. Muhammad al-Sadr studied at the seminaries of Najaf, and became one of the leaders of the nascent national movement, helping to form the Guardian of Independence party, and becoming its head. He was involved in the 1920 rebellion, escaping to Cairo and then Jeddah. He returned to Iraq with Faisal in June 1921. He was later exiled to Iran, but returned to become a member of the senate, which he headed for a long while. He became prime minister once, in 1948. He died in April 1956. Hamdi al-Pachachi was born in 1886, a scion of the well-known Baghdadi family. He attended the administrative college in Istanbul, from whence he graduated in 1905. He held several administrative posts in Ottoman Iraq, but was close to the Arab national movement, joining al-'Ahd society. He was exiled to Henjam Island in 1922 as a result of his nationalist agitations. Returning to Iraq in 1923, he became a member of parliament and held various ministerial posts in the 1920s and subsequently. In 1944 he formed his first cabinet as prime minister. He died in 1948.

36. Ali al-Wardi, op. cit., Vol. 6, p. 164.

37. CO 730/21/18047, Churchill to Cox, 20 April 1922.

38. CO 730/20/15491, Faisal to Cox, 9 May 1922. Also Nur Masalha, op. cit., p. 84.

39. Gertrude Bell, op. cit., letter of 4 June 1922.

40. Ibid., letter of 22 June 1922.

41. Amin Rihani, op. cit., p. 125.

42. Gertrude Bell, op. cit., letter of 8 June 1922.

43. Ali al-Wardi, op. cit., Vol. 6, pp. 173–74; CO 730/23/37397, HC to SS for Colonies, 28 July 1922.

44. Amin Rihani, op. cit., p. 138.

45. Abu al-Timmen had absented himself from the cabinet meeting, and subsequently resigned. The naqib, clearly angered at his breaking of rank, accepted his resignation. It is possible that Faisal had instigated his resignation.

46. CO 730/24/45283, Intelligence Report, 15 August 1922.

47. CO 730/23/37397, 29 July 1922. HC, Baghdad to SS for Colonies.

48. CO 730/24/41134, Cox, Baghdad to SS for Colonies, 29 July 1922.

49. CO 730/24/43046, Telegram No. 608, Private, Summary of Cornwallis's attitude in Despatch from Cox, Baghdad to SS for Colonies, 28 August 1922.

50. CO 730/23/37397, Churchill to Cox, 3 August 1922.

51. All the parties took advantage of a recently enacted law authorising the formation of political parties.

52. Hassoon ran a grocery and was known for his ardour during the Muharram rites.

53. Amin Rihani relates the incident in an entirely different fashion, with al-Muddaris climbing the platform to give a fiery speech and forgetting his official role as the king's chamberlain. This account, however, has not been corroborated by other Iraqi or British sources.

54. Al-Muddaris later blamed Rustum Haidar for his dismissal, accusing him of secretly working for the British. Khairy al-'Umari, *Shakhsiyat Iraqiya*, Afaq 'Arabiya, Baghdad, 1957, p. 55.

55. Sir Harry Sinderson Pasha, *Ten Thousand and One Nights*, Hodder & Stoughton, London, 1973, pp. 66–67. An Iraqi doctor, Sa'eb Shawkat, was also in attendance, and has suggested that it was he rather than Sinderson who made the correct diagnosis. Shawkat claimed that Sinderson's early diagnosis was of malaria. Ali al-Wardi, op. cit., Vol. 6, p. 190.

56. Harry Sinderson, op. cit., p. 67.

57. Amin Rihani, op. cit., pp. 118–19.

58. Philip Graves, op. cit., p. 317.

59. Harry Sinderson, op. cit., p. 68.

60. Ali al-Wardi, op. cit., Vol. 6, pp. 193–94.

61. Harry Sinderson, op. cit., p. 69.

62. Yasin's erstwhile supporter handed the document to the head of general security, a indication of where his true loyalties lay.

63. CO 730/24/43045, HC Baghdad to SS for Colonies, 27 August 1922, telegram 607.

64. CO 730/24/43045, SS for Colonies to HC Baghdad, 27 August 1922, telegram 492.

65. Amin Rihani, op. cit., pp. 122–23.

20. The Rebellion of the Ayatollahs

1. In Iran, the installation of Reza Khan as shah after the chaos of the constitutional revolution and the First World War was partly due to the support of the grand ayatollahs of monarchical rule. See Homa Katouzian, *State and Society in Iran*, I. B. Tauris, London, 2000.
2. Documents of the Royal Secretariat, File 3, No. 70. Also Ali al-Wardi, op. cit., Vol. 6, p. 202.
3. Ibid., File 115, Document 1.
4. Muhammad Mahdi Kubba, *Mudhakarati fi Sameem al-Ahdath*, Manshourat Dar al-Tali'a, Beirut, 1965, pp. 26–27.
5. CO 730/25/59936, Intelligence Report, 5 November 1922.
6. Lutfi Ja'far Faraj 'Abdullah, *'Abd al-Muhsin As-Sa'adoun, Dawrahu fi Tareekh al-'Iraq al-Siyasi al-Mu'assar*, Maktabat al-Yaqdha al-'Arabiya, Baghdad, 1998.
7. Ibid., pp. 46–47.
8. Mir Basri, *'Alam al-Siyasa fil 'Iraq al-Hadeeth*, Riad El-Rayess Books, Cyprus, 1985, pp. 71–72.
9. CO 730/25/57534, Intelligence Report, 1 November 1922.
10. CO 730/26/59936, Intelligence Report, 15 November 1922. Also Mohammed Modhafer Hashim al-Adhami, 'Political Aspects of the Iraqi Parliament and Election Processes 1920–1932', unpublished PhD thesis, SOAS, 1978, p. 54.
11. Mohammed Modhafer Hashim al-Adhami, op. cit., p. 56. Also, Mohammed Modhafer Hashim al-Adhami, *Al-Majlis al-Ta'ssisi al-'Iraqi, Dirasa Tarikhiya Siyasiya*, Baghdad University, Baghdad, 1972.
12. Nur Masalha, op. cit., p. 111, footnote 33.
13. Royal Palace Files, D/6/2, Letter from Cox to Faisal, 2 January 1923; quoted in Mohammed Modhafer Hashim al-Adhami, *Al-Majlis*, op. cit., pp. 342–43. Cox, ever the practical man, also asked Faisal to confirm that Sikkar had met all his tax obligations to the Ministry of Finance!
14. Philip Ireland, op. cit, p. 393.
15. CO 730/25/57534, Intelligence Report, No. 21, 1 November 1922.
16. Ibid.
17. Ali al-Wardi, op. cit., Vol. 6, pp. 214–15. Ayatollah al-Khalisi was also rumoured to be in touch with agents of the Kemalists in Iraq.
18. Gertrude Bell, op. cit., letter of 12 April 1923.
19. Muhammad Mahdi al-Basir, op. cit., pp. 224–25.
20. Zaghloul was the founder of the Wafd Party and led the opposition to British power in Egypt. He also had been arrested and deported by the British, but to the more salubrious island of Malta.
21. Philip Ireland, op. cit., p. 377.
22. Muhammad Mahdi al-Basir, op. cit., pp. 255–256.
23. The meetings with the tribal leaders were arranged by Ali Jawdat, and were held in Diwaniya. Present were 'Abd al-Wahid Sikkar, al-Muhsin Abu-Tabikh, Gat' al-'Awadi and Sha'lan Abul Jawn.
24. Ali al-Wardi, op. cit., Vol. 6, pp. 215–16.
25. Mohammed Modhafer Hashim al-Adhami, *Al-Majlis*, pp, 320–21.
26. For example, *al-'Asima* newspaper demanded that the government take stern measures against foreign intruders who had no connections with Iraq. *Al-'Asima*, 14 June 1923.
27. 'Abd al-Razzaq al-Hasani, op. cit., Vol.1, p. 169.
28. Mohammed Modhafer Hashim al-Adhami, *Al-Majlis*, pp. 321–23.
29. Philip Ireland, op. cit., p. 392.
30. Lutfi Ja'far Faraj 'Abdullah, op. cit., p. 90.
31. Ali al-Wardi, op. cit., Vol. 6, pp. 222–23.
32. Ibid., p. 245.
33. Ibid., pp. 228–29.
34. *Al-Hawadith* newspaper, 11 April 1930, 130.
35. Naji Shawkat, *Seera wa Dhikrayat*, Matba'at Salman al-'Adhami, Baghdad, 1974, pp. 68–73.
36. *Al-'Iraq* newspaper, 30 June 1923.
37. Ibid., 5 July 1923 and 10 July 1923.
38. Hanna Batatu, *The Old Social Classes and the Revolutionary Movements of Iraq*, Princeton University Press, Princeton, 1982, p. 323. The petition was organised by the Hizb al-Watani Party, but one of its key leaders, Ja'far Abu al-Timmen, did not sign it.
39. In fact something similar to this happened soon after the arrival of the ayatollahs in Iran. The first conflict was between Mahdi al-Khalisi and the grand ayatollahs of Iraq. Al-Khalisi refused to accept the return to Iraq of the grand ayatollahs. He left Qum where the ayatollahs were residing, for Mashhad in faraway Khorassan. There he was at first treated well, but came into conflict with the *mujtahids* over his support for Reza Khan and his modernising measures. Demonstrations against his presence in Khorassan were mounted by his rivals, which left Mahdi al-Khalisi greatly

embittered by the treatment he had received. He died in Khorassan on 5 April 1925. His funeral was attended by thousands of his followers. The news of his death was received in Iraq with great sorrow, and thousands of Shi'as and Sunnis marched in mourning. The lamentation of the crowd was: 'O Pillar of Islam, Guardian of the Sharia / You have orphaned us, Sunni and Shi'a.'

40. Gertrude Bell, op. cit., letter of 29 November 1923.
41. C. J. Edmonds, *Kurds, Turks and Arabs*, Oxford University Press, Oxford, p. 317.
42. Shaikh Mahmud had been interned by the British in Kuwait for nationalist activites, but returned to Suleimainya as governor in September 1922. The local town council had petitioned the British to bring him back as only he could secure law and order in the area. The British, short of resources to manage the region directly, agreed on the condition that Shaikh Mahmud gave a written undertaking not to engage in any subversive activities against either them or the Iraqi government.
43. Shaikh Mahmud in a captured letter sent to Ozd Amir was 'vowing that he would live and die in the service of the Turks'. Gertrude Bell, op. cit., letter of 12 March 1923.
44. Mohammed Modhafer Hashim al-Adhami, 'Political Aspects', p. 81.
45. Ibid., pp. 82–83.
46. The captured letters that Bell had spoken of seemed to imply that this was indeed the case.
47. Nur Masalha, op. cit., p. 119.
48. 'Abd al-Razzaq al-Hasani, op. cit., Vol. 1, p. 187. The letter, dated 27 October 1923, was actually signed by Rustum Haidar, now the royal chamberlain.
49. In February 1924, even this pretence was abandoned when Mustafa Kemal abolished the caliphate. After that date, both Hussein's and Faisal's name's were read out at the Friday congregational prayers.
50. Ghazi D'ham Fahad al-Marsoumi, op. cit., p. 21.
51. The Indian rupee was the legal tender in Iraq for most of the mandate period.
52. This would appear to be the response of a person trained in the shabby surroundings of a British government agency of the times.
53. Gertrude Bell, op. cit., letter of 22 December 1923.
54. Sayyid Ahmad Abu-Tabikh, *As-Sayyid Muhsin Abu Tabikh- Seera wa Tarikh*, self-published, Baghdad, 2005, pp. 172–74.

21. Assemblies, Treaties, Constitutions

1. CO 730/57/13271, 10 January 1924. High Commissioner, Baghdad to Secretary State for Colonies.
2. Khairy al-'Umari, op. cit, p. 105.
3. Ibid., p. 106.
4. CO 730/43/60035, Intelligence Report, 1 December 1923.
5. Gertrude Bell, op. cit., letter of 13 February 1924.
6. Khairy al-'Umari, op. cit., pp. 109–11.
7. Ibid.
8. From Adviser of the Ministry of the Interior, to all Administrative Inspectors, 8 February 1924 (Memo. Very Secret) no. S. O/41, File SB/28, Secret, The Ministry of the Interior, Baghdad. Also, Mohammed Modhafer Hashim al-Adhami, *Al-Majlis*, p. 87, footnote 229.
9. Modhafer Mohammed Hashim al-Adhami, 'Political Aspects', pp. 89–90.
10. CO 731/57/3931. A Note on Iraqi's internal affairs by G. Bell. Also Nur Masalha, op. cit., p. 124.
11. Ibid., p. 92, footnote 243.
12. 'Abd al-Razzaq al-Hasani, op. cit., Vol. 1, pp. 214–15.
13. Gertrude Bell, op. cit., letter of 1 April 1924.
14. Mohammed Modhafer Hashim al-Adhami, *Al-Majlis*, p. 561.
15. Ali al-Wardi, op. cit., Vol. 6, p. 260.
16. Documents of the Royal Archives, Baghdad, Sequence 3, Document 55; Ali al-Wardi, op. cit., Vol. 6, p. 263, footnote 16.
17. A few weeks earlier, Sayyid Muhammad al-Sadr, exiled for his agitations against the elections, had also returned to Iraq. Al-Sadr had apparently completely changed his political perspectives while in exile and now became a positive supporter of the government line. Shaikh Muhammad Mahdi al-Khalisi, son of the former Mahdi al-Khalisi, on the other hand, was not allowed to return formally until 1949. He remained in Iran except for a short abortive return to Iraq in April 1932, from which he was once more expelled. He suffered greatly at the hands of the Iranian government. Upon returning to Iraq in 1949, he was well received at first but was gradually abandoned by his erstwhile supporters.
18. The Muslims of India were generally against Hussein as caliph, as were ibn Saud, the Wahhabis and King Fuad of Egypt. The whole episode is well described in Joshua Teitelbaum, op. cit., pp. 241–48.

19. 'Abd al-Razzaq al-Hasani, op. cit., Vol.1, pp. 198-99; Joshua Teitelbaum, op. cit., p. 245, footnote 68.
20. Gertrude Bell, op. cit., letter of 12 March 1924.
21. Gertrude Bell, op. cit., letter of 24 April 1924.
22. Ali al-Wardi, op. cit., Vol. 6, pp. 277-78.
23. Ibid.
24. Abu Kaldun Sati' al-Husri, *Mudhakarati fil-'Iraq*, Vol. 1, Manshourat Dar al-Tali'ah, Beirut, 1967, p. 147.
25. Ali Jawdat, op. cit., p. 172.
26. Ibid., pp. 172-73.
27. CO 730/58/22744, High Commissioner Baghdad to Secretary of State for Colonies, 11 May 1924.
28. CO 730/59/18924, High Commissioner Baghdad to Secretary of State for Colonies, 17 April 1924.
29. Unpublished papers of Sir Henry Dobbs. Letter, 1 May 1924, courtesy of Anne and Henry Wilks.
30. CO 730/59/26329; Mohammed Modhafer Hashim al-Adhami, *Al-Majlis*, p. 112, footnote 64.
31. 'Abd al-Razzaq al-Hasani, op. cit., Vol. 1, pp. 226-27. Sir Percy Cox was leading the British delegation to Istanbul to negotiate with the Turks regarding the Mosul issue.
32. CO 730/59/24298, High Commissioner, Baghdad to Secretary of State for Colonies, 2 June 1924.
33. 'Abd al-Razzaq al-Hasani, op. cit., Vol. 1, pp. 220-22; Ali al-Wardi, op. cit., Vol. 6, pp. 291-92.
34. Mohammed Modhafer Hashim al-Adhami, 'Political Aspects', pp. 129-30.
35. Gertrude Bell, op. cit., letter of 11 June 1924.
36. Gertrude Bell, op. cit., letter of 18 June 1924.
37. The newspaper *Al-Awqat al-Baghdadiya*, 12 June 1924.
38. Obituary: Sir Henry Conway Dobbs, *Journal of the Royal Central Asian Society*, Vol. 21, No. 4, 1934, pp. 708-16. The obituary was signed by A.T.W. and P.Z.C., undoubtedly A.T. Wilson and Percy Cox.
39. Unpublished Papers of Sir Henry Dobbs. Letter, 14 February 1915, courtesy of Anne and Henry Wilks.
40. Obituary: Sir Henry Conway Dobbs, op. cit., p. 712.
41. Gertrude Bell, op. cit., letter of 1 April 1924.
42. Mohammed Modhafer Hashim al-Adhami, 'Political Aspects', p. 141, footnote 171.
43. FO 371, E7806/10/00 24 July 1924. Confidential letter from Acting High Commissioner, Baghdad, to Secreatry of State for Colonies. See also Nur Masalha, op. cit., pp. 134-35.
44. CO 730/23/10606, Minutes of the Middle East Department, 31 March 1923. See also Nur Masalha, op. cit., pp. 135-36, footnotes 152 and 153.
45. Gertrude Bell, op. cit., letter of 11 December 1923.
46. Gertrude Bell, op. cit., letter of 13 February 1924.
47. Gertrude Bell, op. cit., letter of 6 December 1923.

22. Oil and the Mosul Question

1. Kingdom of Iraq, Directorate of Public Information, *Faisal ibn al-Hussein fi Khutabihi wa Aqwalihi*, Matba'at al-Hukuma (Government Printing Press), Baghdad, 1945, p. 235.
2. 'Abd al-Razzaq al-Hasani, op. cit., Vol. 1, p. 168.
3. *Al-Iraq* newspaper, 30 May 1923.
4. Quincy Wright, 'The Mosul Dispute', *The American Journal of International Law*, Vol. 20, No. 3, July 1926, pp. 453-64.
5. Stephen Helmsley Longrigg, '*Iraq: 1900 to 1950, A Political, Social and Economic History*, Oxford University Press, London, 1953, pp. 152-54; 'Abd al-Razzaq al-Hassani, op. cit., p. 273.
6. CO 730/63/745, Intelligence Report, 25 December 1924.
7. 'Abd al-'Aziz al-Qassab, op. cit., p. 248. Al-Qassab also claimed that it was he who organised the demonstrations in Mosul in favour of union with Iraq and that these were done under Faisal's instructions.
8. 'Abd al-Majid Kamil al-Tikriti, op. cit., pp. 193-95; Nur Masalha, op. cit., p. 144.
9. 'Abd al-Amir Allawi, *Tajjarub wa Dhikrayat*, ed. Ali A. Allawi, Dar al-Makarim, London, 2000, p. 66, footnote 9. The slogans chanted included one that started with the line, 'O Mosul, You are the Abode of Pride and Dignity / He who does not defend You has met a fate of Ignominy'. Allawi, later a leading physician and government minister, was a schoolboy in 1925 and participated in these demonstrations. Longrigg, a noted historian of Iraq and then a district officer, called these demonstrations 'foolish and provocative'. They offer two wildly differing perspectives on the same events.

10. CO 730/73/12195, Intelligence Report, 5 March 1925, No. 5, Secret, para. 106. See also Nur Masalha, op. cit., p. 144.
11. Peter Sluglett, op. cit., pp. 84–85.
12. Documents of the Royal Archives, 'Mosul Dispute', No. 912-WA T/4/1Al-Tikriti. See also 'Abd al-'Aziz al-Tikriti, op. cit., p. 196, footnote 26.
13. *Al-Iraq* newspaper, 25 March 1925.
14. 'Abd al-'Aziz Al-Tikriti, op. cit., p. 196, footnote 39.
15. *Special Report on the Progress of Iraq 1920–1931*, Annual Reports by HM Government to the Council of the League of Nations, London, HMSO, 1931, p. 127.
16. CO 730/76/3206, Intelligence Report, 9 July 1925, No. 14, Secret; Stephen Helmsley Longrigg, op. cit., p. 205.
17. They were Rashid 'Ali al-Gailani and Muhammad Ridha al-Shibibi.
18. Mohammed Modhafer Hahim Al-Adhami, 'Political Aspects', pp. 174–80.
19. Sir Harry Sinderson, op. cit., pp. 78–79.
20. 'Abd al-Razzaq al-Hasani, op. cit., Vol. 2, pp. 12–13.
21. Sir Harry Sinderson, op. cit., pp. 79–80.
22. Ibid., p. 81.
23. Ibid., pp. 82–83.
24. Leo Amery, *Diaries, Volume 1: 1896–1929*, ed. John Barnes and David Nicholson, Hutchinson, London, 1980, p. 418.
25. Amery confusingly used different spellings for Faisal, calling him at times Feisul, Feisal and Feysal.
26. L. S. Amery, *My Political Life, Volume 2, War and Peace, 1914–1929*, Hutchinson, London, 1953, pp. 308–09.
27. Jeremy Wilson, op. cit., p. 765.
28. Sir Harry Sinderson, op. cit., pp. 84–85.
29. Jeremy Wilson, op. cit., p. 806.
30. Ibid., p. 807.
31. Ibid., p. 911. Faisal had met Lawrence several times during his last visit to London in June 1933, and had invited him to dinner at his quarters at the Hyde Park Hotel. See also Kathleen Scott, *Self-Portrait of an Artist*, John Murray, London, 1949, pp. 295–96.
32. Ibid., pp. 86–87.
33. 'Abd al-Majid Kamil al-Tikriti, op. cit., p. 222.
34. Elizabeth Burgoyne, op. cit., p. 332.
35. Ibid.
36. Joyce Laverty Miller, 'The Syrian Revolt of 1925', *International Journal of Middle East Studies*, Vol. 8, No. 4, October 1977, pp. 545–63.
37. Weygand had mooted to Nuri al-Sa'id the possibility of installing Ali as king in Syria; Elizabeth Burgoyne, op. cit., pp. 332–33.
38. Sir Harry Sinderson, op. cit., p. 90.
39. Ibid., pp. 89–90.
40. Ibid., p. 115.
41. In a letter to his wife of 6 August 1925, Dobbs wrote, 'You will have seen the Frontier Commission Report before this reaches you. I recommend though not very heartily 25 years Mandate under the League of Nations (which I suppose means the British) or a return of Mosul to Turkey. Faisal is quite pleased with the 25 years idea but I told him I doubted whether the British would take it.' Unpublished papers of Sir Henry Dobbs, letter, 6 August 1925, courtesy of Anne and Henry Wilks.
42. CO 730/78/46164, Intelligence Report, 1 October 1925, No. 20. See also Lutfi Ja'far Faraj 'Abdullah, op. cit., pp. 188–93.
43. Letter from the High Commisioner to Faisal, marked Secret, 18 December 1925, Royal Palace Archives G/09/1926, quoted in Lutfi Ja'far Faraj 'Abdullah, op. cit., p. 197.
44. Lutfi Ja'far Faraj 'Abdullah, op. cit., pp. 197–210.
45. Ibid.
46. 'Abd al-Razzaq al-Hasani, op. cit., Vol. 2, pp. 36–42. Al-Sa'adoun wrote a long and masterful letter to the speaker of the Majlis, setting out the case for accepting the treaty in its present form in spite of its obvious inadequacies.
47. Joshua Teitelbaum, op. cit., pp. 196–97; FO 371/7713/13/E 5412, High Commissioner for Iraq to the Secretary State for the Colonies, No. 364, 23 May 1922.
48. Hafidh al-Qaisi, op. cit., pp. 269–70, and footnotes 101 and 102.
49. Elizabeth Burgoyne, op. cit., p. 355.
50. Ibid., p. 356.

51. Abu Khaldun Sati' al-Husri, *Safhat min al-Madhi al-Qarib*, Dar al-'Ilm lil Malayin, Beirut, 1948, pp. 20–22.
52. Elizabeth Burgoyne, op. cit., p. 355.
53. According to the Palestinian leader Haj Amin al-Hassani, it was his suggestion that Hussein should be buried in the al-Aqsa Mosque, next to Maulana Muhammad Ali, one of the founders of the Indian Khilafat movement, and a strong proponent of the Jerusalem Islamic Congress of 1931. See Philip Matar, *The Mufti of Jerusalem: Al-Haj Amin al-Husayni and the Palestinian National Movement*, Columbia University Press, New York, 1988, p. 57.
54. Elizabeth Burgoyne, op. cit., p. 359.
55. Unpublished papers of Sir Henry Dobbs, letter, 14 May 1925, courtesy of Anne and Henry Wilks.
56. Unpublished papers of Sir Henry Dobbs, letter, 4 June 1925, courtesy of Anne and Henry Wilks.
57. Unpublished papers of Sir Henry Dobbs, letter, 18 June 1926, courtesy of Anne and Henry Wilks.
58. Ali's daughter Princess Badiy'a recalls the numerous occasions in her childhood when Faisal and Ali closeted themselves together for hours on end, when Faisal used to visit their house regularly on Thursdays in Baghdad. She and her siblings were in awe of their uncle and regarded him with great reverence. Badiy'a also recalled Faisal's traditional views regarding the women of the royal household. For example, he refused to countenance their wearing fashionable western clothes. Interviews conducted by the author with Princess Badiy'a in London, April/May 2012.
59. Elizabeth Burgoyne, op. cit., p. 383.
60. Ibid., p. 390.
61. Gertrude Bell, op. cit., letter of 23 June 1926.
62. Gertrude Bell, op. cit., letter of 16 June 1926.

23. Struggling to Break Free

1. Gertrude Bell, op. cit., letter of 6 June 1926.
2. Gertrude Bell, op. cit., letter of 23 June 1926.
3. Lady Feodora Gleichen was a British sculptress, and a relative of Queen Victoria. She had made a bust of Faisal during his sojourn in London in 1920.
4. Gertrude Bell, op. cit., letter of 30 June 1926.
5. 'Abd al-Hadi al-Khumasi, *Al-Amir 'Abd il-Illah, 1939–1958*, Al-Mou'assasa al-'Arabiya lil Dirasat wal Nashr, Beirut, 2001, pp. 33–34.
6. Gertrude Bell, op. cit., letter of 31 December 1924.
7. Letters of Gertrude Bell, quoted in Georgina Howell, *Daughter of the Desert: The Remarkable Life of Gertrude Bell*, Macmillan, London, 2006, pp. 430–31.
8. Mrs Steuart Erskine, op. cit., pp. 202–03.
9. *Al Alam al-'Arabi* wrote in tribute: 'The true sincerity of her patriotism, free from all desire for personal gain, and the zeal for the interests of her country which illuminated the service of this noble and incomparable woman makes her an example to all men of Iraq.'; see also H. V. F. Winstone, *Gertrude Bell*, Quartet Books, New York, 1978, p. 262.
10. CO 730/96/20549, 3 November 1926.
11. 'Note on the Internal Situation in Iraq,' by the High Commissioner, 27 June 1927. FO 371, E3220/12259.
12. Unpublished papers of Sir Henry Dobbs, letter, 24 June 1927, courtesy of Anne and Henry Wilks.
13. 'Abd al-Razzaq al-Hasani, op. cit., pp. 104–08.
14. 'Note on the Internal Situation in Iraq,' by the High Commissioner, 27 June 1927, pp. 233–50.
15. Quoted in Nur Masalha, op. cit., p. 175.
16. Fahmi al-Muddaris turned violently against Faisal after the closure of the college. He wrote a number of incendiary articles against him, prompting the king to demand that he be censured. He was arrested and sentenced for six months, but never served the sentence. He was the only person of note to refuse to attend Faisal's funeral. Nuri al-Sa'id in particular disliked Fahmi and had him banished for a while to Suleimaniya. Returning to Baghdad, Fahmi became a recluse with paranoid delusions, muttering about the perfidy of the British, who were behind all the ills of the world.
17. The Nsouli affair was a highly emotive issue in the Iraq of the period, and left formative impressions on a number of people who were students at the time. It is well covered in the memoirs of Abu Khaldun Sati' al-Husri, *Mudhakarati fil-'Iraq*, Vol. 1, pp. 557–75; those of Hussein Jamil (*Shahada Siyasiya 1908–1930*, Dar al-Lam, London 1987, pp. 183–203), and in 'Abd al-Razzaq al-Hasani, op. cit., Vol. 2, 88–90. It was also covered in the intelligence reports produced by the RAF and in Residency despatches.
18. Muhammad Mahdi al-Jawahiri, *Dhikrayati*, Part 1, Dar al-Rafidain, Damascus, 1988, p. 170.

19. 'Abd al-Razzaq al-Hasani, op. cit., Vol. 2, pp. 109–10. The commanding officer was Muhyi al-Dine as-Sahrawardy.
20. Intelligence Report, 21 July 1927, No. 15, Secret, FO 371, E3421/12264.
21. Ibid.
22. Unpublished papers of Sir Henry Dobbs, letter, 27 May 1927, courtesy of Anne and Henry Wilks.
23. Ronald Storrs, op. cit., pp. 526–27.
24. CO 730/120/40299, R. Storrs, Cyprus to Ormsby-Gore, London, 10 August 1927.
25. Unpublished papers of Sir Henry Dobbs, letter, 15 April 1927, courtesy of Anne and Henry Wilks.
26. Unpublished papers of Sir Henry Dobbs, letter, 13 May 1927, courtesy of Anne and Henry Wilks.
27. Note of 2 November 1927 by the Colonial Office; 'Abd al-Razzaq al-Hasani, op. cit., Vol. 2, pp. 134–35; Nur Masalha, op. cit., p. 192.
28. CO 730/120/40299A/135, Note on conversation with King Faisal on 2 November 1927, by H. Dobbs.
29. Unpublished papers of Sir Henry Dobbs, letter, 20 November 1927, courtesy of Anne and Henry Wilks. At this point, Dobbs was clearly tired and pined for retirement.
30. 'Abd al-Razzaq Al-Hasani, op. cit., Vol. 2, pp. 118–20.
31. Al-'Askari had reached Alexandria on his way back to Iraq when Faisal recalled him back to London. He reached London on 12 December 1927 and signed the new treaty on 14 December 1927.
32. 'Abd al-Razzaq al-Hasani, op. cit., Vol. 2, pp. 136–37.
33. Unpublished papers of Sir Henry Dobbs, letter, 20 May 1927, courtesy of Anne and Henry Wilks.

24. Towards Independence

1. FO 371, E93/13037, 21 December 1927.
2. FO 371, E2423/13027, 25 April 1928. Intelligence Report No. 9, Secret; Nur Masalha, op. cit., p. 202, and footnotes 16–18.
3. As'ad Daghir, op. cit., p. 19; Ghazi D'ham Fahad al-Marsoumi, op. cit., pp. 25–26.
4. Royal Archives Baghdad, File No.76, letter from Ja'far al-'Askari to Rustum Haidar, dated 7 March 1929.
5. Rufail Batti, 'Fi Dhikra Rustum Haidar', al-Bilad newspaper, Baghdad, 22 November 1956; Tawfiq al-Suwaidi, Wujooh Iraqiya 'abr al-Tarikh, Riad El-Rayes, London, 1987, pp. 135–37.
6. In a biographical note to Haidar's diaries, the diplomat and historian Nejdat Fathi Safwat interviewed a leading Sunni Arab notable, Mahmud Subhi al-Daftari, about Haidar's supposed sectarianism. Al-Daftari's reply was 'Rustum [Haider] was not sectarian in the narrow sense of the word that he differentiated between people on the basis of their sect and neither was he partial to his own sect . . . Rustum Haidar was conscious that it was necessary to rectify the situation [the disadvantage of the Shi'a] in a gradual way . . . But many people accused him of sectarianism simply because he employed or supported the Shi'a.' Rustum Haidar, op. cit, pp. 47–49.
7. Royal Archives, File 1112, Document 22, p. 34; Ghazi D'ham Fahad al-Marsoumi, op. cit., p. 35.
8. Gerald de Gaury, Three Kings in Baghdad, I. B. Taurus, London and New York 2008, p. 38. De Gaury, who was very impressed with the king, described him as 'very slim with small bones, narrow shoulders, thin fingers and hands, and a rather long face of great beauty in which large liquid eyes could appeal almost irresistibly'.
9. Amin al-Rihani, op. cit., p. 160.
10. Mrs Steuart Erskine, op. cit., p. 226.
11. Talib Mushtaq, Awraq Ayami, 1900–1958, Part I, Dar al-Tali'a lil Tiba'a'wal Nashr, Beirut, 1968, pp. 215–17.
12. Amin Rihani, op. cit., pp. 205–07.
13. Ibid., p. 226.
14. Both al-Jawahiri and al-Husri wrote about this episode. Al-Husri's memory, however, was selective, and al-Jawahiri's account, written well after al-Husri's memoirs had come out, is more explicit on the details. Muhammad Mahdi al-Jawahiri, Dhikrayati, Part 1, Dar al-Rafidain, Damascus, 1988, pp. 141–67; Abu Kaldun Sati' al-Husri, Mudhakarati fil 'Iraq, Vol.1, pp. 588–602. Al-Jawahiri in fact held Iranian nationality at the time, but this was not at all uncommon for many Shia Arab families who became Persian subjects to avoid Ottoman conscription.
15. Muhammad Mahdi al-Jawahiri, op. cit., p. 165.
16. Ibid., pp. 179–85.
17. Ibid., p. 197.
18. Ibid., p. 198.
19. Gerald de Gaury, op. cit., pp. 41–42.

20. Ibid., pp. 211–13.
21. Ibid., pp. 241–44.
22. Ibid., pp. 192 and 205.
23. Ibid., pp. 233–40.
24. Extracts from Tagore's book on his trip to Iraq and Iran, Arabised by Hussein 'Abd al-Zahra Majid Kitabat, 25 November 2010, "'Indama Zarunna Tagore al-'Adheen.
25. Ghazi D'ham Fahad al-Marsoumi, op. cit., pp. 99–112.
26. Faisal used Raphael al-Hakim, a London-based Iraqi trader, to market the cotton. The agent would deposit the proceeds of the sales into Faisal's account at the Ottoman Bank in London. In one case where the agent disputed the sale amounts, Faisal brought the dispute to arbitration which found in his favour. Royal Archives, File 271, Document 13, p. 22. See also Ghazi D'ham Fahad al-Marsoumi, op. cit., p. 133.
27. Ibid., pp. 118–27.
28. *Sawt al-Iraq* newspaper, 22 May 1930. Also Ghazi D'ham Fahad al-Marsoumi, op. cit., p. 127.
29. Ali Jawdat, op. cit., p. 209.
30. Royal Archives, File 74, Privy Purse, Documents 1–3.
31. Royal Archives, File 43, Palace Budget, Document 8, Budget Number 3, 1933, pp. 15–16. See also Ghazi D'ham Fahad al-Marsoumi, op. cit., p. 158.
32. Royal Archives, File 77, Document 68, pp. 89–90; Ghazi D'ham Fahad al-Marsoumi, op. cit., p. 98.
33. Ahmad Shawki, *Al'Amal Alshi'iriya al-Kamila*, Vol. 2, Dar al-'Awda, Beirut, 2008, p. 70.
34. Kingdom of Iraq, Directorate of Public Information, *Faisal fi Khutabihi*, pp. 318–19.
35. Gerald De Gaury, op. cit., pp. 62–63.
36. Amin Rihani, op. cit., p. 213.
37. Ibid., p. 214.
38. Royal Archives, File 1224, Document 13, 17 May 1924.
39. Abbas Baghdadi, *Li'ala Nansa: Baghdad fil 'Ishriniyat*, Al-Mowa'assasa al-'Arabiya lil Dirasat wal Nashr, Beirut, 1999, pp. 36–37. Faisal later replaced his Indian driver with an Iraqi from Samarra.
40. Ghazi D'ham Fahad Al-Marsoumi, op. cit. p. 169.
41. Ibid., p. 173, footnote 4.
42. Ibid., pp. 177–79.
43. Royal Archives, File 121, Document 16, 19 April 1921. Letter from the editors of the *al-Ahram* to Amir Faisal.
44. Ghazi D'ham Fahad Al-Marsoumi, op. cit. p. 190–94.
45. Ibid., p. 197.
46. *Al-Iraq*, 6 February 1924.
47. Kingdom of Iraq, Directorate of Public Information, *Faisal fi Khutabihi*, p. 296.
48. Gerald de Gaury, op. cit., p. 51.
49. Aldous Huxley used Alfred Mond as the basis of his composite character Mustapha Mond, the Resident World Controller of Western Europe, in his dystopian novel *Brave New World*.
50. Hussein Jamil, op. cit., p. 206.
51. Peter Sluglett, op. cit. pp. 110 and 268, footnote; Michael Eppel, 'The Elite, the Effendiya, and the Growth of Nationalism and Pan-Arabism in Hashemite Iraq, 1921–1958', *International Journal of Middle East Studies*, Vol. 30, No. 2, May 1998, p. 234.
52. FO 371, E5169/13035, 25 October 1928. Colonial Office to High Commissioner, Baghdad.
53. Unpublished papers of Sir Henry Dobbs, letter, 20 October 1928, courtesy of Anne and Henry Wilks.
54. Unpublished papers of Sir Henry Dobbs, letter, 27 October 1928, courtesy of Anne and Henry Wilks.
55. Philip Ireland, op. cit., pp. 368–69.
56. Peter Sluglett, op. cit., p. 112.
57. FO 371, E1131/13757, 29 January 1929. A note on conversation with al-Sa'adun by H. Dobbs.
58. Unpublished papers of Sir Henry Dobbs, letter, 29 December 1928, courtesy of Anne and Henry Wilks.
59. Unpublished papers of Sir Henry Dobbs, letter, 20 October 1928, courtesy of Anne and Henry Wilks.
60. Nur Masalha, op. cit., p. 216.
61. Unpublished papers of Sir Henry Dobbs, letter, 26 January 1929, courtesy of Anne and Henry Wilks.
62. Unpublished papers of Sir Henry Dobbs, letter, 29 December 1928, courtesy of Anne and Henry Wilks.
63. American chargé d'affaires, Baghdad, 1 April 1930, Despatch No. 50, 890g.00/128; Nur Masalha, op. cit., pp. 221–22.

64. CO 730/148/68403/4, pt. I; High Commissioner Baghdad to Secretary of State for the Colonies, 1 September 1929.
65. 'Abd al-Razzaq al-Hasani, op. cit., Vol. 2, pp. 233–65.
66. Lutfi Ja'far Faraj 'Abdullah, op. cit., pp. 346–48.
67. Ibid., pp. 348–51.
68. 'Abd al-'Aziz al-Qassab, op. cit., pp. 281–82. Al-Qassab, who was the minister of agriculture in al-Sa'adoun's final cabinet, could not attend the party because of 'flu. On the following day, al-Sa'adoun visited him in the evening to inquire about his state of health and relayed to him what had happened in the palace the night before with Cornwallis. Al-Sa'adoun left his house in great agitation, saying that he was going to his club.
69. Lutfi Ja'far Faraj 'Abdullah, op. cit., pp. 352–56. Al-Qassab, who was the first senior official to rush to al-Sa'adoun's house after his suicide, says that al-Sa'adoun's body was laid out on his bed. Al-Sa'adoun's wife probably embellished her story to show her wifely devotion.
70. Ibid., p. 375. Ali al-Sa'adoun was later to kill himself also.
71. Before giving the note to a trusted newspaper editor, al-Qassab made sure that other cabinet ministers who had congregated in al-Sa'adoun's house after his suicide would sign it to confirm its authenticity. The note was returned to al-Qassab by the editor, and al-Qassab gave it to al-Sa'adoun's wife. Somehow, the note ended in Tawfiq al-Suwaidi's possession, and was lost after his library and private offices were ransacked following the 14 July 1958 revolution in Iraq. Tawfiq al-Suwaidi's wife was al-Sa'adoun's niece.
72. FO 371, E6709/13760, Intelligence Report, 9 December 1929, No. 25. See also Nur Masalha, op. cit., pp. 231–32.

25. Vindication at Last

1. Amin Rihani, op. cit., pp. 230–31.
2. Alexander Sloan, Baghdad to Washington, 22 July 1932, Diplomatic 259, Confidential, 890g.00/211; Nur Masalha, op. cit., p. 235.
3. Alexander Sloan, Baghdad to Washington, 3 February 1932; Nur Masalha, op. cit., p. 240.
4. CO 730/170/88369, Young, Baghdad to Secretary of State for Colonies, 14 August 1931.
5. Amin Rihani, op. cit., pp. 233–34.
6. Ibid., pp. 184–85.
7. Stephen Helmsly Longrigg, op. cit., p. 183.
8. Khalid Abid Mushin, op. cit., p. 289.
9. A case in point is Muzahim al-Pachachi, who had been on the executive committee of Abu al-Timmen's al-Watani party, but resigned when offered a ministerial position by Nuri.
10. 'Abd al-Razzaq al-Hasani, op. cit., Vol. 3, pp. 70–72.
11. 'Abd al-Majid Kamil Takrit, op. cit., pp. 314–15.
12. Ibid., pp. 140–41.
13. American chargé d'affaires, Baghdad to Washington, 16 April 1931, Despatch No. 226, 890g.00/145; Nur Masalha, op. cit., p. 247.
14. 'Abd al-Razzaq al-Hasani, op. cit., Vol. 3, pp. 146–49.
15. Ibid., pp. 150–51.
16. Ibid., pp. 159–61.
17. Fahad Muslim al-Fajr, *Muzahim al-Pachachi wa Dawrahu fi al-Siyasa al-'Iraqiya, 1890–1933*, Al-Dar al-'Arabiya lil Mawsou'at, Beirut, 2004, pp. 187–203.
18. American chargé d'affaires, Baghdad to Washington, 3 June 1932, Despatch No. 119, ibid.
19. Gerald de Gaury, op. cit., p. 86.
20. FO 371, E5950/16049, H. Young, Baghdad to J. Simon, London, 3 November 1932.
21. FO 371, E6230/16032, F. Humphrys, Baghdad to J. Simon, London, 17 November 1932; Nur Masalha, op. cit., p. 259.
22. FO 371, E105/16903. J. Hall, Minutes of 9 June 1933.
23. Tawfiq al-Suwaidi, *Mudhakarati*, p. 200.
24. Sir Harry Sinderson, op. cit., p. 120.
25. Amin Rihani, op. cit., p. 220.
26. Ibid., p. 221.
27. Ibid., p. 222.
28. The visit of the Saudi amir was nearly called off because of rumours of an assassination plot to be carried out against him when he was in Iraq. Faisal, however, agreed for it to go ahead, as its cancellation would have sent the wrong signals to ibn Saud.

29. Omer Erden, *Foreign Leaders Who Have Visited Turkey During the Rule of Mustafa Kemal Ataturk,* redacted and translated by Alper Bahadir, Ataturk Research Center, Ataturk Culture, Language and History Institute, Ankara, 2006.
30. Ibid.
31. Ibid.
32. Ibid.
33. Amin Rihani, op. cit., pp. 243–44.
34. Tawfiq al-Suwaidi, *Mudhakarati,* pp. 200–02.
35. Faisal must have meant Byzantium. The Arabic word for Byzantium was 'Rum'.
36. Sir Harry Sinderson, op. cit., pp. 128–29.
37. FOE 2519/2154/34, No. 225, Secret, Hoare to Sir John Simon, Teheran, 9 May 1932.
38. Sir Harry Sinderson, op. cit., p. 141.
39. Tawfiq al-Suwaidi, op. cit., pp. 204–05.
40. 'Abd al-Razzaq al-Hasani, op. cit., Vol. 3, pp. 192–05; Alexander Sloan, Baghdad to Secretary of State, Washington, 10 October 1932, Diplomatic 294.
41. FO 371, E5950/16049, H. Young, Baghdad to J. Simon, London, 3 November 1932, Letter no. 1060.

26. A Calamitous End

1. The actual text of the memorandum is drawn from 'Abd al-Razzaq al-Hasanni, op. cit., Vol. 3, pp. 315–21.
2. The memorandum was sent to Nuri al-Sa'id, Naji Shawkat, Rustum Haidar, Yasin al-Hashimi, Naji al-Suwaidi, Tawfiq al-Suwaidi, Rashid 'Ali al-Gailani, Ali Jawdat, Jamil al-Midfa'i, Ja'far Abu al-Timmen, Muhammad al-Sadr, Hikmat Suleiman, and others in the cabinet. See 'Abd al-Karim al-Uzri, *Mushkilat al-Hukm fil Iraq,* self-published, London, 1991, p. 1.
3. 'Abd al-Karim al-Uzri, op. cit., pp. 10–15.
4. Ibid., pp. 16–24.
5. Ibid., pp. 24–26. The Land Tenure Law of 1932 was greatly abused by tribal leaders, city merchants and leading politicians so that they could accumulate large tracts of land. The land issue was one of the main causes of discontent and anger during the monarchical period, feeding the revolutionary opposition to what many considered to be a feudal system.
6. Al-Suwaidi's response was that of a liberal, slightly idealistic politician. One of his proposals was to form restricted franchises so that each community could vote in its own deputies. Naji Shawkat agreed with Faisal's assessment and most of his solutions. Both, however, studiously avoided mentioning the sectarian divide. See Naji Shawkat, *Awraq Naji Shawkat,* Matba'at Jami'at, Baghdad, 1977, pp. 76–87.
7. Ibid., pp. 361–63.
8. A common term for Iraq, Syria, Lebanon, Jordan and Palestine.
9. E. B. Main, 'Iraq: A Note', *Journal of the Royal Central Asiatic Society,* Vol. 20, No 3 (July 1933), p. 434.
10. The writer As'ad Daghir, who was a frequent visitor to Iraq in the early 1930s, notes in his memoirs that Iraq was known as the 'Piedmont of the Arabs' by nationalists. As'ad Daghir, op. cit., p. 186.
11. Nur Masalha, op. cit., p. 302.
12. Najib al-Bay'ini, *Min Amir al-Bayan Shakib Arslan,* Dar al-Manahil, Beirut, 1998, pp. 361–65. Arslan was responding to a newspaper article that was critical of the Anglo-Iraqi Treaty.
13. Faisal was against the idea that the pipeline should pass through French-controlled Syria, given the history of his troubled relationships with France. See Nur Masalha, 'Faisal's Pan-Arabism, 1921–33', *Middle Eastern Studies,* Vol. 27, No. 4 (October 1991), pp. 679–93.
14. Ibid., p. 682.
15. Khaldun S. Husry, 'King Faysal I and Arab Unity, 1930–33', *Journal of Contemporary History,* Vol. 10, No. 2, (April 1975), p. 328, footnote 15.
16. William L. Cleveland, *Islam against the West: Shakib Arslan and the Campaign for Islamic Nationalism,* University of Texas Press, Austin, 1985, p. 133.
17. Khaldun S. Husry, op. cit., pp. 323–40.
18. See Nur Masalha, op. cit., pp. 688–89.
19. Khaldun S. Husry, op. cit., pp. 329–30.
20. Ibid., pp. 330–31.
21. FO 371/16854, Humphrys, Baghdad to Foreign Office, London, 5 January 1933.
22. Khaldun S. Husry, op. cit., p. 333.
23. E 347/347/65, Humphrys, Baghdad to Sir John Simon, 17 January 1933.
24. Khaldun S. Husry, op. cit., pp. 337–38.

25. CO 730/138/68004/2 22 November 1928, memorandum No. 440/A.
26. CO 730/149/68478/49, King Faisal, Baghdad to H. Young, 8 December 1929.
27. FO 371/16854. Humphrys, Baghdad to Sir Arthur Wauchope, Jerusalem, 7 March 1933.
28. Ibid.
29. See Mir Basri, op. cit., pp. 141–45. In one instance a Kurdish tribal chief was seen arguing with him in Kurdish, a language that Naji did not understand. When an aide sought to interrupt the chief, Naji told him, 'Leave the man be! It is a case of the dumb speaking to the deaf!' Naji served in several cabinets in the 1930s and was minister of defence in Rashid 'Ali's ill-fated government of 1941, which declared war on Britain. Naji sought refuge in Italy for the remainder of the war. He was arrested by US forces in northern Italy in 1945 and handed over to the Iraqi government. He was imprisoned for two years and then pardoned in 1948. He retired from politics and died in Baghdad in 1980.
30. Kamil al-Chadirchi, *Mudhakarat Kamil al-Chadirchi*, Manshourat al-Jamal, Cologne, Germany, 2002, p. 75.
31. 'Abd al-Razzaq al-Hasani, op. cit., Vol. 3, pp. 246–47.
32. Sir Harry Sinderson, op. cit., p. 144.
33. Philip Matar, op. cit., pp. 146–47.
34. Ibid., pp. 147–48.
35. Ibid., pp. 151–52.
36. R. S. Stafford, *The Tragedy of the Assyrians*, Gorgias Press (Reprints), London, 2006, p. 70.
37. Elizabeth Burgoyne, op. cit., p. 318.
38. Khaldun S. Husry, 'The Assyrian Affair of 1933 (1)', *International Journal of Middle East Studies*, Vol. 5, No. 2 (April 1974), pp. 161–76. Mar Shimun was in fact issued with just such a special Iraqi *laissez-passer* document to allow him to travel to Switzerland.
39. Khaldun S. Husry, 'The Assyrian Affair of 1933(1)', p. 170, footnote 1.
40. 'Abd al-Razzaq al-Hasani, op. cit., Vol. 3, p. 265.
41. FO 371, E2952/16882, Ogilvie-Forbes, Baghdad to J. Simon, London, 24 May 1933.
42. 'Abd al-Razzaq al-Hasani, op. cit., Vol. 3, p. 273.
43. Ibid., p. 274.
44. FO 371/16891, Report by Brigadier-General Hugo Headlam, 6 September 1933.
45. Khaldun S. Husry, 'The Assyrian Affair of 1933(1)', op. cit., p. 176.
46. Ibid., p. 349.
47. There have been several inquiries into the Summayl massacre. The least convincing was the one produced by the Iraqi Ministry of Interior on 22 August 1933, which claimed that Summayl was a centre of sedition and that the killings were caused by a clash between armed villagers and marauding tribesmen. The army took no part in the massacre. Stafford in his near-authoritative work on the Assyrian crisis claims that the massacre was planned and premeditated by Bakr Sidqi and his men, behind the back of British officers attached to the Iraqi army, but he produces only circumstantial evidence (R. S. Stafford, op. cit., p. 162). A distillation of all the accounts is given in Khaldun S. Husry, 'The Assyrian Affair of 1933 (II)', pp. 344–60. Husry also interviewed Ismail 'Abbawi Tohalla before his death in 1968.
48. FO 371, E4440/16884, Ogilvie-Forbes, Baghdad to the Foreign Office, London, 9 August 1933.
49. FO 371 16889, E 5182.
50. FO 371, E4721/16881. A Note by Rendel, 16 August 1933.
51. Khaldun S. Husry, 'The Assyrian Affair of 1933 (II)', p. 352.
52. As'ad Daghir, op. cit., pp. 195–96.

Epilogue: Faisal the Great

1. Abu Khaldun Sati' al-Husri, *Safhat min al-Madhi al-Qarib*, pp. 9–22.